A Field Guide to the
Birds of Peru

Ibis Publishing Company

Cover: Golden-backed Mountain-Tanager *Buthraupis aureodorsalis* by Dana Gardner
Back cover: Marvelous Spatuletail *Loddigesia mirabilis* by Eustace Barnes

A Field Guide to the
Birds of Peru

James F. Clements
and Noam Shany

Illustrated by
Dana Gardner
and
Eustace Barnes

Other illustrations by Anderson Debarnardi, Shawneen Finnegan
Gamini Ratnavira, Noam Shany, Susan Smith and Fernando Zavala

Ibis Publishing Company

A Field Guide to the Birds of Peru
©2001 James F. Clements

Ibis Publishing Company
44970 Via Renaissance
Temecula, California 92590
ibispub@msn.com

All rights reserved. No part of this book may be reproduced in any form whatever without the express written consent of the publisher, except for brief extracts used in reviews or scholarly works.

ISBN Number 0-934797-18-8

Library of Congress Catalog Number 97-070300

Design and production by John Bass
Printed in Verona, Italy by Artegrafica

Contents

Map of Major Rivers and Life Zones	Inside front cover
Contents	v
Foreword	vii
Dedication	ix
Introduction	x-xii
Acknowledgments	xiii-xiv
Families	xv-xvi
Topography of a Bird	xvii
Species Accounts	1-237
Color Plates	127 plates
Appendix A: Wingtips and Tail Patterns of Nightjars	Plate 128
Appendix B: Endemic Birds of Peru	239-241
Appendix C: Gazetteer of Place Names	242-246
Bibliography	247-254
Index of Scientific Names	255-269
Index of English Names	271-281
List of Protected Areas in Peru	282
Map of Protected Areas in Peru	283
Map of Major Departments and Cities	Inside back cover

Foreword by
His Excellency Ambassador Javier Perez de Cuellar
President of the Council of Ministers and
Minister of Foreign Affairs
Republic of Peru

In our endeavors to develop the natural resources of Peru, it is vital to remember that one mark of civilization is the regard men bestow on wild things.

Peru is blessed with an abundance of natural resources, including one of the most prolific bird populations in the world. Not only does Peru boast a bird list of over 1800 species—almost one-fifth of the species known to science—it also harbors 118 endemic birds that are found nowhere else in the world.

To help preserve this priceless heritage, the Peruvian government has set aside over 13 million hectares (32.4 million acres) as protected areas, ranging in size from the 18-hectare Aledaño Bocatoma reserve in Lima to the two-million hectare Biabo Cordillera Azul and Pacaya Samiria reserves in Loreto, Ucayali and San Martín.

It is our hope that this guide will open the door to a new and exciting world where our youth and our visitors can help to discover yet more about the natural history of our land. This book should serve as a welcome work of international importance, filling as it does a long-felt need by ecotourists and ornithologists for an up-to-date guide to the myriad birds of Peru.

April 2001

In fond memory of
Ted Parker

Who set a new standard of field ornithology…
and whose talent was exceeded
only by his contribution to the
conservation and study of
Neotropical birds

Ash-throated Antwren
Herpsilochmus parkeri

Introduction

Species accounts: The basis for the species accounts in this field guide is the *Annotated Checklist of the Birds of Peru* by Parker, Parker and Plenge (1982). There has been an increase of nearly 200 species since this list was published, and we have used certain guidelines as outlined below in our addition of species to the Peru list. We have given citations for most species that have been added since the publication of Parker *et al*.

Taxonomy: We have followed the higher taxonomic sequence outlined in the fifth edition of *Birds of the World: A Check List* (Clements 2000), which in turn is based primarily on the family and genera in the *Handbook of Birds of the World* (del Hoyo *et al.*). Since only six volumes of this monumental work have been published, we give a reference to all species that do not appear in either Clements or del Hoyo.

English names: The basis for the original South American list of English names was *A Guide to the Birds of South America* by Meyer de Schauensee (1970), which has been closely followed by Clements (2000). While we are well aware that there are often "better" names that can be used to describe certain species, our goal has been the standardization of English names worldwide. Where names differ from other highly regarded works that deal with the region, including *The Birds of the High Andes* (Fjeldså and Krabbe 1990), *The Birds of South America* (Ridgely and Tudor 1989, 1994) and *A Guide to the Birds of Ecuador* (Ridgely and Greenfield 2001a), we have included alternate names in parentheses or in the species account.

Spanish names: We are indebted to Manuel Plenge for furnishing us with his unpublished list of Spanish names for the birds of Peru. The task of compiling Spanish names is extremely difficult, due to the great variation in names used by various countries, as well as within the country. We hope that by our including Spanish names in this field guide, we will bring the passion for birds closer to the Spanish-speaking Peruvian public.

Range and numerical status: These indications are only a *guide* to the relative abundance of individual species. While "common" indicates that it is common in the greater part of its range, it *may* be uncommon or even rare in different parts of the same life zone—especially with those species with a wide range in the country. There are often discrepancies in the literature, which we suspect is more a matter of exact location rather than the skill or judgment of the authors. The tremendous diversity in these humid tropics has led to the formation of numerous micro-habitats that might seem similar to us, but are vastly different to their avian occupants. Thus in small areas such as Pakitza we find specialists that do not occur in identical-looking (to us) bamboo patches. I have relied heavily on the distribution given by Parker *et al.* 1982, but realizing that much of this material is over 20 years old, have supplemented this with more recent information from Ridgely and Tudor (1989, 1994), Fjeldså and Krabbe (1990), and other observations as cited, including our own Peruvian field-trip notes dating back to 1972.

> **Abundant**: Almost impossible to miss on any given day, often in conspicuous numbers.
> **Common**: Frequently recorded in its preferred habitat, or encountered as individuals, in pairs, or in small groups.
> **Fairly common**: A few individuals or pairs may be seen daily.
> **Uncommon**: Present in an area, but may go unrecorded in one or two days of field observation.
> **Rare**: Present in an area but may not be recorded in a week or more.
> **Vagrant**: Out of its usual range, but could be expected once or twice a year.
> **Accidental**: Far from its normal range and not to be expected again.

Life Zones and elevations: As with indications of occurrence, our research revealed a considerable difference in altitudes cited by various authors. Thus elevations are given mainly as a reference, and are to be used primarily as a guide. In cases where our own field experience indicated a major discrepancy from published sources, we have noted it. All elevations are based on published sources or from our own field trips using a Magellan 5000 DX GPS. The following life zones and elevations are after Parker *et al.* 1982:

> **Arid tropical**: Coastal lowlands and lower slopes of Andes from Tumbes south to La Libertad, plus dry parts of the Marañón, Apurímac, Éne and Urubamba River valleys. Elevation: sea level-1500 m
> **Arid subtropical**: Coastal lowlands and west slope of Western Andes from Ancash to Tacna, and slopes of intermontane valleys. Elevation sea level-2500 m
> **Arid temperate**: West slope of Western Andes from Ancash to Tacna, and slopes of dry intermontane valleys. Elevation 2500-3400 m
> **Humid subtropical and temperate**: West slope of Western Andes from Piura to Lima. Elevation 1500-3000 m
> **Puna**: Upper Andean slopes and plateaus in highlands from Cajamarca south, includng the altiplano region between the two main Andean ranges. Elevation 3400-4500 m
> **Humid temperate**: East slope of Eastern Andes, including the *páramo*. Elevation 2500-3400 m
> **Humid subtropical**: East slope of Eastern Andes throughout Peru. Elevation 1500-2500 m
> **Humid upper tropical**: East slope of Eastern Andes throughout Peru, including upper slopes and crests of outlying mountains. Elevation 900-1500 m
> **Humid tropical**: All terrain east of the Andes, including lowlands, foothills and lower slopes of the main Andes. Elevation 150-900 m

Sight records: Where sight records of new species, or a significant extension of its known range, have been called to our attention by contributors, our decision to include them has been based on the available details, the known expertise of the observer(s), the relative difficulty in identifying the bird in the field, and the likelihood of the bird's occurrence in Peru.

Hypothetical species: Hypothetical species are included in the text in taxonomic order, but are placed in brackets. These species are those that have been reported with substantial documentation but are not supported by a specimen, a clearly diagnostic photograph, a tape-recorded vocalization, or extensive detailed information from multiple observers.

Threatened Species: The 98 birds marked with an asterisk (*) are those listed as threatened or vulnerable in the recently published *Threatened Birds of the World* by BirdLife International. Several species described since the publication of this volume have been listed as such because of the small population and/or limited range of the species (Zimmer's Woodcreeper, Vilcabamba Brush-Finch, Apurímac Brush-Finch, Black-spectacled Brush-Finch and Cusco Brush-Finch).

Subspecies: This work does not treat birds at the subspecies level unless obvious morphological diferences exist that are readily discernible in the field. We especially call to the reader's attention those subspecies that future study might prove to be valid species.

Illustrations: Almost 1800 species of birds have been illustrated, including every one of the 118 Peruvian endemics, plus those specialties with limited ranges in adjacent Ecuador, Colombia, Brazil, Bolivia and/or Chile (with the exception of the morphologically similar tapaculos). This is a greater number of birds than has ever been illustrated in a single field guide to date. Because of the evolution of this book from a bird-finding guide to a field guide, some of the plates do not reflect the taxonomic order as outlined in the text. We ask your kind indulgence for this departure.

Vocalizations: Many tropical species are much more easily identified by their calls than by morphological differences, especially such rarely seen birds as tinamous, tapaculos and some of the antbirds. Tape-recorded bird vocalizations are an excellent means of positive identification. Transcribing vocalizations is confusing, and one recording is worth a thousand words. The symbol ♪ followed by a number represents the American Birding Association (ABA Sales) catalog number of the cassette or CD-rom where the particular vocalization can be found. The vocalizations of over 1200 species of birds that occur in Peru are contained in these cassettes and CD-roms.

♪ 636T. Barlow, J. C. and J. W. Hardy. 1995. *Voices of the Vireos and Allies*
♪ JFC. Recordings by James F. Clements on deposit with Library of Natural Sounds
♪ 626T. Cornell Library of Natural Sounds. 1992. *A Field Guide to Western Bird Songs*
♪ 619T. English, P. H. and T. A. Parker. 1992. *Birds of Eastern Ecuador*
♪ 563T. Hardy, J. W. et al. 1994. *Voices of Neotropical Wood Warblers*
♪ 632T. Hardy, J. W. 1983. *Voices of Neotropical Birds*
♪ 553T. J. W. Hardy. 1996. *Voices of the Tinamous*
♪ 633T. Hardy, J. W. 1996. *Voices of the Wrens*
♪ 638T. Hardy, J. W. 1990. *Voices of New World Jays, Crows and Allies*
♪ 639T. Hardy, J. W. et al. 1987. *Voices of All Mockingbirds, Thrashers, and Their Allies*
♪ 646T. Hardy, J. W. and R. J. Raitt. 1995. *Voices of New World Quails*
♪ 652T. Moore, John V. 1996. *Ecuador, More Bird Vocalizations from Lowland Rain Forest* Vol. 2
♪ 654T. Hardy, J. W. et al. 1990. *Voices of New World Owls*
♪ 656T. Hardy, J. W. et al. 1989. *Voices of New World Pigeons and Doves*
♪ 658T. Hardy, J. W. et al. 1995. *Voices of the Woodcreepers*
♪ 624T. Hardy, J. W. et al. 1995. *Voices of New World Cuckoos and Trogons*
♪ 630T. Hardy, J. W. and T. A. Parker. 1992. *Voices of New World Thrushes*
♪ 797CD. Mayer, Sjoerd. 1998. *Birds of Bolivia 2.0 Sounds and Photographs*
♪ JM. Recordings by John Moore on deposit with Cornell Library of Natural Sounds
♪ 542T. Moore, John V. 1994. *Bird Sounds of La Selva (Ecuador)*
♪ 677T. Moore, John V. 1994. *Ecuador, More Bird Vocalizations from Lowland Rain Forest,* Vol. 1
♪ 631T. Parker, Theodore A. III. 1985. *Voices of the Peruvian Rainforest*
♪ 613T. Sanders, T. C. 1995. *Voices of Costa Rican Birds: Caribbean Slope*
♪ 627T. Peterson, R. T., ed. 1990. *Field Guide to Bird Songs of Eastern/Central North America*
♪ 1015CD. Ranft, Richard. 1998. *A Sound Guide to Nightjars and Related Nightbirds*
♪ 741CD. Schulenberg, Thomas S. *Voices of Andean Birds, Vol. 1: Birds of the Hill Forest of Southern Peru and Bolivia*
♪ 742CD. Schulenberg, Thomas S. *Voices of Andean Birds, Vol. 2: Birds of the Cloud Forest of Southern Peru and Bolivia*
♪ 816CD. Schulenberg, Thomas S., Curtis Marantz and Peter H. English. *Voices of Amazonian Birds, Vol. 1: Tinamous through Barbets*
♪ 817CD. Schulenberg, Thomas S., Curtis Marantz and Peter H. English. *Voices of Amazonian Birds, Vol. 2: Toucans through Antbirds*
♪ 818CD. Schulenberg, Thomas S., Curtis Marantz and Peter H. English. *Voices of Amazonian Birds, Vol. 3: Ground Antbirds (Formicariidae) through Jays (Corvidae)*

Abbreviations:
ca (near)
cf. (careful)
E; e (east)
LSUMZ (Louisiana State University Museum of Zoology)
m (meters)
mts. (mountains)
N; n (north)
NE; ne (northeast)
NW; nw (northwest)
S; s (south)
SE; se (southeast)
ssp. (subspecies)
subtrop. (subtropical)
SW; sw (southwest)
temp. (temperate)
trop. (tropical)
W; w (west)

Acknowledgments

This work would not have been possible without the help of many people. Many colleagues, birders and students have generously shared information on the distribution, habits and vocalizations of Peruvian birds. Without the constant help, support and encouragement of Ambassador Mikko Pyhälä, this field guide would have been almost impossible to complete.

Tom Schulenberg furnished us with an enormous amount of data, as well as important information on the taxonomy of the *Scytalopus* genus of tapaculos. In addition to allowing us to use his list of Spanish names, Manuel Plenge made important suggestions regarding the text. Barry Walker, Paul Coopmans, Peter Ginsburg and Richard Webster made numerous helpful comments on the manuscript, especially regarding range updates and the current distribution of Peru's 1800 species of birds. We have received constant cooperation from John P. O'Neill since the project first got underway over seven years ago, and we are particularly indebted to him.

Others to whom we are indebted are José Alvarez, the late Luis Baptista, Eustace Barnes, Paul Champlin, Tor Egil Høgsås, Gunnar Engblom, Jon Fjeldså, Jeremy Flanagan, Michael Force, Mort and Phyllis Isler, Oscar Gonzalez, Niels Krabbe, Dan Lane, Tom Love, Ernesto Malaga, Charles Munn, John Moore, Gary Rosenberg, Karl Schuchmann, Mark Sokol, Frank Todd, José Luis Venero, Bret Whitney and Kevin Zimmer.

Robert Pitman, Larry Spear and Lisa Ballace furnished us with years of data collected in Peruvian waters well offshore. Irma Franke at the Museo de Historia Natural, Lima, allowed us to consult the collection in her care.

We would like to thank the following artists for producing the magnificent illustrations: Dana Gardner, Eustace Barnes, Anderson Debarnardi, Shawneen Finnegan, Gamini Ratnavira, Susan Smith and Fernando Zavala.

JFC is greatful to his wife Karen, whose patience and support during the seven years of work on this field guide raised the expression "the patience of Job" to a new level. Through a fortuitous meeting four years ago, Noam Shany joined me as co-author, and there is no way I can thank him enough for the hard work, diligence, and expertise he has devoted to the field guide. For assistance and companionship to some of the most remote parts of Peru, JFC would especially like to thank Thomas Valqui. The first germs of the importance of a field guide to the birds of Peru were born during these trips.

NS would like to thank his parents, Geula and Asher Shany, for many years of coping gracefully with their absent son; to Peter Ginsburg, Hector Gomez de Silva and Akiva Boker, for companionship and assistance in field; and to Susan Smith for generous artistic and editorial advice. Many thanks to the people of Explorama Lodges, especially to Peter and Pamela; Hacienda Amazonia and the Yabar family; InkaNatura; and Rainforest Expeditions—especially to Maria Esther—for helping with the logistics in traveling to some remote places; to Peter Lonsdale and the RV Melville for allowing him on board. Special thanks to Jee Hi Park for constant encouragement and help in typing his hieroglyphics.

Contributors:

BPW (Barry P. Walker)
EB (Eustace Barnes)
EM (Ernesto Malaga)
GE (Gunnar Engblom)
JF (Jon Fjeldså)
JFC (James F. Clements)
JPO (John P. O'Neill)
MAP (Manuel A. Plenge)
ME (Mark Elwonger)
MP (Mikko Pyhälä)
MS (Mark Sokol)
NG (Nick Gardner)
NK (Niels Krabbe)

NS (Noam Shany)
NW (Nigel Wheatley)
OG (Oscar Gonzales)
PC (Paul Champlin)
RC (Robert Clements)
RH (Robert A. Hughes)
RAR (Roseann Rowlett)
RSR (Robert S. Ridgely)
RW (Richard Webster)
TAP (Theodore A. Parker III)
TSS (Thomas S. Schulenberg)
TV (Thomas Valqui)

Dana Gardner is grateful to Louisiana State University and the University of California, Berkeley, for the loan of specimens to make the plates. Valuable assistance was given by the late Luis Baptista at California Academy of Sciences; Carla Cicero at University of California, Berkeley; Mary LeCroy and Paul Sweet at the American Museum of Natural History, New York; and Barry Walker of Manu Expeditions, Cusco, Peru.

In undertaking the plates, Eustace Barnes has many people to thank who helped him. Not least, of course, was Jim Clements, for his enthusiasm and energy for getting this project up and running, and for his support and encouragement while work proceeded. Also to Jennifer Horne and Lester Short, whose work and help over the years fired his enthusiasm for Neotropical ornithology from being a resident naturalist at Explorers Inn, to pushing him in the direction of bird illustration. To John Forrest and Tambopata Reserve Society for first introducing him to the idea of working in Peru, and always providing assistance and advice during the painful emergence of Peru from the grip of terrorism. To Barry Walker for his generous help and thoughtful comments over the years. To all at the British Natural History Museum for their assistance, especially Mark Adams and Michael Walters. To Graham Green and Nigel Lauson for their enthusiasm for his painting over the years, and to John Cox for his friendship and support. Finally, to my wife Diana, for her tireless patience for putting up with months of absence over many years, and quite incredibly accompanied by good-natured support for such a self-evident, unlucrative activity.

Despite all the help we received from ornithologists, scientists, taxonomists and birders from around the world, this book is of necessity the product of our own research. Some errors in a work of this magnitude are almost inevitable. Any errors, omissions or commissions are solely our responsibility. Hopefully none of these will affect the usefulness of this field guide.

James F. Clements and Noam Shany
San Diego, California
August 2001

Families

Part I: Non-Passerines	Order	Family	Page
Rheas	Struthioniformes	Rheidae	1
Tinamous	Tinamiformes	Tinamidae	1-4
Penguins	Sphenisciformes	Spheniscidae	5
Grebes	Podicipediformes	Podicipedidae	5-6
Albatrosses	Procellariiformes	Diomedeidae	6-7
Shearwaters and Petrels	Procellariiformes	Procellariidae	7-10
Storm-Petrels	Procellariiformes	Hydrobatidae	11-12
Diving-Petrels	Procellariiformes	Pelecanoididae	12
Tropicbirds	Pelecaniformes	Phaethontidae	13
Pelicans	Pelecaniformes	Pelecanidae	13
Boobies and Gannets	Pelecaniformes	Sulidae	13-14
Cormorants	Pelecaniformes	Phalacrocoracidae	14
Anhingas	Pelecaniformes	Anhingidae	14
Frigatebirds	Pelecaniformes	Fregatidae	15
Herons, Egrets and Bitterns	Ciconiiformes	Ardeidae	15-17
Storks	Ciconiiformes	Ciconiidae	17-18
Ibises and Spoonbills	Ciconiiformes	Threskiornithidae	18-19
Flamingos	Phoenicopteriformes	Phoenicopteridae	19
Screamers	Anseriformes	Anhimidae	19
Ducks, Geese and Swans	Anseriformes	Anatidae	20-22
New World Vultures	Falconiformes	Cathartidae	22-23
Osprey	Falconiformes	Pandionidae	23
Hawks, Eagles and Kites	Falconiformes	Accipitridae	23-30
Caracaras and Falcons	Falconiformes	Falconidae	30-32
Guans, Chachalacas and Allies	Galliformes	Cracidae	32-34
New World Quail	Galliformes	Odontophoridae	34
Hoatzin	Opisthocomiformes	Opisthocomidae	35
Limpkin	Gruiformes	Aramidae	35
Trumpeters	Gruiformes	Psophiidae	35
Rails, Gallinules and Coots	Gruiformes	Rallidae	35-38
Sungrebes	Gruiformes	Heliornithidae	39
Sunbittern	Gruiformes	Eurypygidae	39
Jacanas	Charadriiformes	Jacanidae	39
Oystercatchers	Charadriiformes	Haematopodidae	39
Avocets and Stilts	Charadriiformes	Recurvirostridae	40
Thick-knees	Charadriiformes	Burhinidae	40
Plovers and Lapwings	Charadriiformes	Charadriidae	40-42
Sandpipers and Allies	Charadriiformes	Scolopacidae	42-46
Seedsnipes	Charadriiformes	Thinocoridae	47
Skuas and Jaegers	Charadriiformes	Stercoraiidae	47-48
Gulls	Charadriiformes	Laridae	48-50
Terns	Charadriiformes	Sternidae	50-52
Skimmers	Charadriiformes	Rynchopidae	52

Pigeons and Doves	Columbiformes	Columbidae	52-55
Parrots and Macaws	Psittaciformes	Psittacidae	55-61
Cuckoos	Cuculiformes	Cuculidae	61-63
Barn Owls	Strigiformes	Tytonidae	63
Typical Owls	Strigiformes	Strigidae	64-68
Oilbird	Caprimulgiformes	Steatornithidae	68
Potoos	Caprimulgiformes	Nyctibiidae	68-69
Nightjars and Allies	Caprimulgiformes	Caprimulgidae	69-71
Swifts	Apodiformes	Apodidae	72-73
Hummingbirds	Apodiformes	Trochilidae	74-89
Quetzals and Trogons	Trogoniformes	Trogonidae	89-91
Kingfishers	Coraciiformes	Alcedinidae	91
Motmots	Coraciiformes	Momotidae	91-92
Jacamars	Piciformes	Galbulidae	92-93
Puffbirds	Piciformes	Bucconidae	93-96
Barbets	Piciformes	Capitonidae	96-97
Toucans	Piciformes	Ramphastidae	97-99
Woodpeckers and Allies	Piciformes	Picidae	99-103

Part II: Passerines

Ovenbirds and Allies	Passeriformes	Furnariidae	104-119
Woodcreepers	Passeriformes	Dendrocolaptidae	119-123
Typical Antbirds	Passeriformes	Thamnophilidae	123-138
Antthrushes and Antpittas	Passeriformes	Formicariidae	139-143
Gnateaters	Passeriformes	Conopophagidae	143
Tapaculos	Passeriformes	Rhinocryptidae	144-146
Plantcutters	Passeriformes	Phytotomidae	146
Cotingas	Passeriformes	Cotingidae	147-150
Manakins	Passeriformes	Pipridae	150-153
Tyrant Flycatchers	Passeriformes	Tyrannidae	153-184
Sharpbill	Passeriformes	Oxyruncidae	185
Swallows	Passeriformes	Hirundinidae	185-188
Wagtails and Pipits	Passeriformes	Motacillidae	188
Dippers	Passeriformes	Cinclidae	188-189
Wrens	Passeriformes	Troglodytidae	189-192
Mockingbirds and Thrashers	Passeriformes	Mimidae	192
Thrushes and Allies	Passeriformes	Turdidae	192-195
Gnatcatchers and Gnatwrens	Passeriformes	Polioptilidae	196
Crows, Jays and Magpies	Passeriformes	Corvidae	196-197
Old World Sparrows	Passeriformes	Passeridae	197
Vireos and Allies	Passeriformes	Vireonidae	197-199
Siskins, Crossbills and Allies	Passeriformes	Fringillidae	199-200
New World Warblers	Passeriformes	Parulidae	200-203
Bananaquit	Passeriformes	Coerebidae	203-204
Tanagers and Allies	Passeriformes	Thraupidae	204-220
Buntings and Sparrows	Passeriformes	Emberizidae	220-231
Saltators, Grosbeaks and Allies	Passeriformes	Cardinalidae	231-233
Troupials and Allies	Passeriformes	Icteridae	233-237

Topography of a Bird

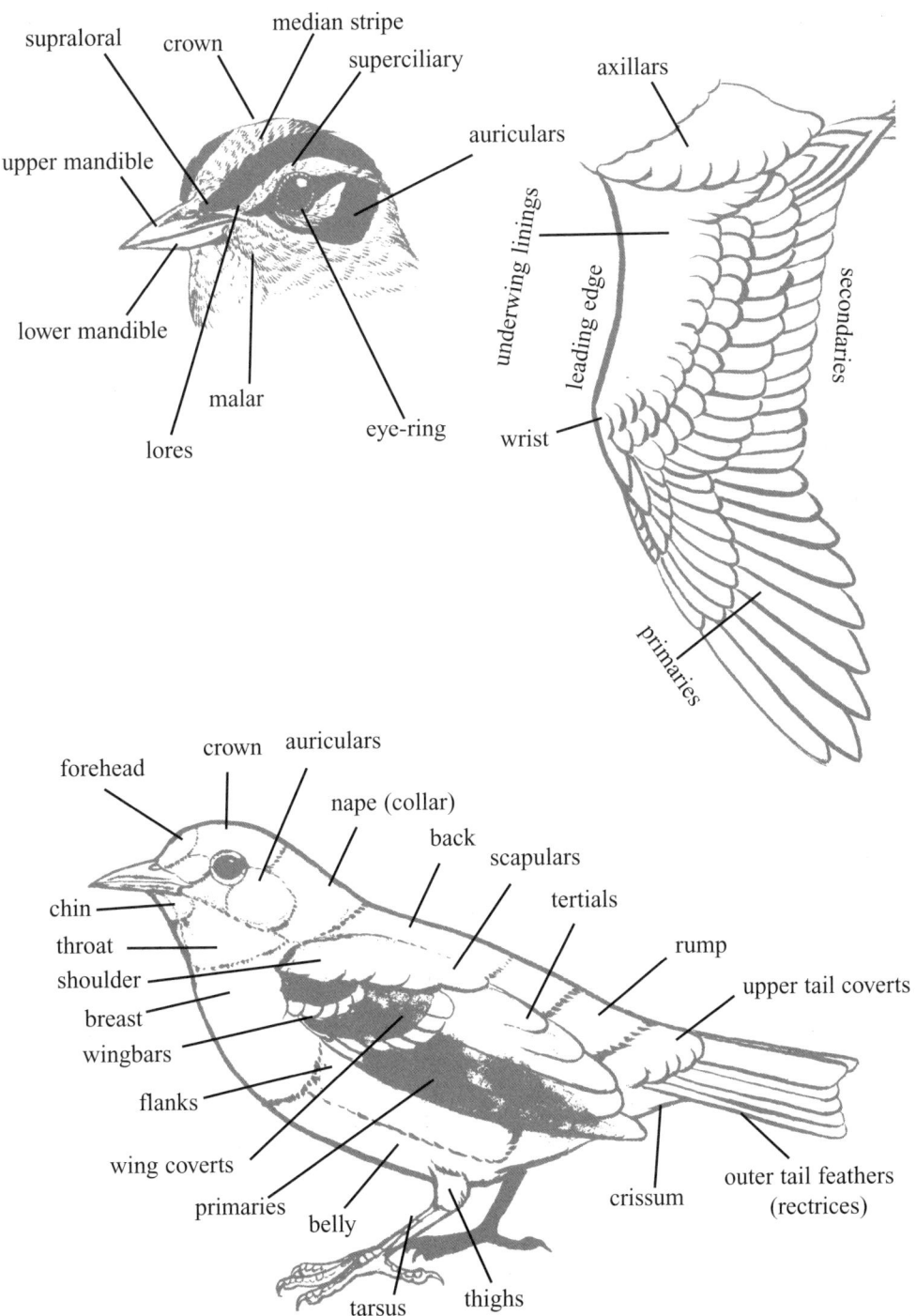

Rheidae (Rheas; Ñandúes). Species: World 2; Peru 1
Rheas are large flightless birds that are the ecological equivalent of African ostriches. They are capable of running long distances at high speeds in the open country they inhabit. The male is responsible for incubation, defends the nest, and cares for the young until they are four or five months old. Rheas are primarily vegetarians, but will eat insects, lizards and small mammals if the opportunity arises.

Lesser Rhea *Rhea pennata* Suri
96 cm (38"). Facing Plate 1. An unmistakable, huge ostrich-like bird. Peruvian race *garleppi* sometimes considered a distinct species (Puna Rhea). Rare and local (probably disjunct) in desert *puna* in Moquegua and w Puno at 3500-4500 m (rarely to 5000 m). *Disjunctly distributed in puna of Peru to steppes of Chile and Argentina.*

Tinamidae (Tinamous; Tinamúes). Species: World 47; Peru 26
Tinamous are an ancient family of shy, terrestrial birds that ranges from the dark rainforest floors to the barren, high-altitude *páramo* and *puna*. They are found only in Central and South America—from central Mexico to Patagonia. Tinamous are quite capable of flight, despite their reduced sternal keel, but usually escape detection by freezing and evaporating from view with the aid of their incredible protective coloration. Their food consists largely of seeds, berries and small fruits, which are supplemented with insects and other animal food. Lowland species are much more often heard than seen, and their flutelike calls are among the characteristic sounds of the tropical rainforest. Most Peruvians refer to tinamous as Perdiz, the Old World name for quails and partridge.

Identification of tinamous is very difficult at times. Due to their cryptic behavior and subdued colors, one should note especially the size and the color of legs, head and pattern on upperparts, wings and underparts. Calls are often the best key to the identification of lowland and subtropical species, as they call frequently.

Gray Tinamou *Tinamus tao* Perdiz Gris
45 cm (17.5"). ♪553. Plate 2. Very large, with gray legs, dark-gray above, lead-gray below and speckled with salt and pepper on side of face. Very similar to Great Tinamou, but latter is browner and lacks speckles on face. Uncommon in humid trop. and subtrop. forests on e slope of Andes to 1900 m. *Venezuela and Guyana to n Bolivia and Amazonian Brazil.*

*Black Tinamou *Tinamus osgoodi* Perdiz Negra
45 cm (17.5"). ♪553. Plate 1. The only large tinamou that is mostly black, somewhat paler on belly with gray legs. Cf. Smaller Berlepsch's Tinamou (dark belly and red legs). Rare in upper trop. and subtrop. forests in Cusco, Madre de Dios and Puno at 900-1400 m, with 3 records from Manu National Park. Recorded in Marcapata Valley 15 km e of Quincemil (Cusco) at 900 m, at Amazonia Lodge, on Cordillera de Pantiacolla at 900-1350 m, and on Cerros del Távara at 800 m. *Andes of s Colombia and se Peru.*

Great Tinamou *Tinamus major* Perdiz Grande
45 cm (17.5"). ♪553. Plate 2. A very large, grayish-brown tinamou with dusky vermiculations and gray legs. Very similar to grayer Gray Tinamou, but lacks latter's speckled face. Fairly common in lowland *terra firme* and *várzea* forests e of Andes to 1500 m. *Mexico to n Bolivia and Amazonian Brazil.*

White-throated Tinamou *Tinamus guttatus* Perdiz Gargantiblanca
33 cm (13"). ♪553. Plate 2. A large brownish tinamou (paler below) with greenish-gray legs. Wings and lower back spotted whitish. No other sympatric tinamou is brown with such spots. Uncommon in lowland *terra firme* forests e of Andes to 500 m. *Venezuela to Bolivia and Amazonian Brazil.*

Highland Tinamou *Nothocercus bonapartei* Perdiz de Monte
38 cm (15"). ♪553. Plate 2. A large tinamou (smaller than Great Tinamou) with cinnamon-rufous body, cinnamon throat, dark-gray crown and greenish-gray legs. Other similar montane forest tinamous have white throats. Cf. much smaller Brown Tinamou. Rare and local in humid montane forests south to Cajamarca, mainly at 1500-2500 m. *Costa Rica to Venezuela and n Peru.*

Tawny-breasted Tinamou *Nothocercus julius* Perdiz Pechileonado
38 cm (15"). ♪553. Plate 2. The only tinamou in its range with a rufous crown and sides of head, a contrasting white throat and rufous underparts (richest color on breast). Highland Tinamou lacks the white throat and has a slaty crown. Hooded Tinamou has browner underparts and blackish crown. Rare and local in montane forests on e slope of Andes from Piura to Cusco at 1700-3250 m. *Andes of w Venezuela to central Peru.*

Hooded Tinamou *Nothocercus nigrocapillus* Perdiz Cabecinegro
33 cm (13"). ♪797. Plate 1. A rather uniform brown tinamou with a conspicuous white throat. Similar to Tawny-breasted Tinamou (rufous on head) and Highland Tinamou (rufous throat). Also cf. Brown Tinamou (smaller and lacks white throat). Heard on several occasions on Manu road in October 2000 (MAP). Uncommon and local in humid montane forests along e slope of Andes at 2000-3000 m. *Andes of Peru and w Bolivia.*

***Crypturellus* Tinamous.** A genus of small to medium-sized forest tinamous. Some are found in the humid lowlands and others in montane forests. All bear a resemblance to a crake or quail-dove.

Cinereous Tinamou *Crypturellus cinereus* Perdiz Cinérea
27 cm (10.5"). ♪553. Plate 2. The only medium-sized, uniformly dark-gray tinamou in its range with reddish-pink legs. Berlepsch's Tinamou is blacker with deeper red legs. Some white speckling on neck is sometimes visible. Uncommon in lowland *várzea* forests e of Andes to 900 m. *S Venezuela and the Guianas to n Bolivia and Amazonian Brazil.*

Little Tinamou *Crypturellus soui* Perdiz Chica
23 cm (9"). ♪553. Plate 2. The only very small, rufous-brown tinamou with a gray head and whitish throat in its range. Replaced by Brown Tinamou at higher elevations. In contact zone note that slightly larger Brown Tinamou has richer, rufous-chestnut underparts, a darker hood and lacks whitish throat. Cf. also Undulated Tinamou. Fairly common in humid lowland forests e of Andes and w of Andes in Tumbes to 1500 m. *Mexico to n Bolivia and Amazonian Brazil.*

Brown Tinamou *Crypturellus obsoletus* Perdiz Parda
27 cm (10.5"). ♪553. Plate 2. The only medium-sized tinamou in its range with rufous-chestnut underparts, rufous (or blackish in Puno race *traylori*) upperparts with a dark gray hood. Compare Little Tinamou (limited overlap) and Hooded Tinamou (white throat). Race *traylori* of Marcapata Valley (Cusco) may be a separate species. Fairly common in humid montane forests on e slope of Andes in Huánuco and Cusco at 1500-2900 m. *Venezuela to ne Argentina, Paraguay and Amazonian Brazil.*

Undulated Tinamou *Crypturellus undulatus* Perdiz Ondulada
30 cm (11.7"). ♪553. Plate 2. Medium-sized. Over most of its range in Amazonia race *yapura* (illustrated) is a uniformly dull, olive-brown tinamou with a whitish throat. Easily confused with smaller Little Tinamou but latter is more rufous with a gray hood. In se Peru (Cusco and Puno) nominate *undulatus* is a richer rufous with dark vermiculations on upperparts. Its distinctive whistled call is one of the characteristic sounds of the lowland forests. Fairly common in humid lowland forests e of Andes to 900 m. *S Venezuela and the Guianas to ne Argentina and Amazonian Brazil.*

Pale-browed Tinamou *Crypturellus transfasciatus* Perdiz Cejipálida
27 cm (10.5"). ♪ 553. Plate 2. A medium-sized, sexually dimorphic tinamou. The only tinamou in its limited range with a pale superciliary. Female is a paler brownish-buff, heavily barred on wings and lower back. Fairly common along Pacific slope south to Lambayeque, mainly at 250-800 m, but locally higher. *Lowlands of w Ecuador and nw Peru.*

Brazilian Tinamou *Crypturellus strigulosus* Perdiz Brasilera
27 cm (10.5"). ♪ 553. Plate 2. A medium-sized, sexually dimorphic tinamou. Both sexes have gray legs, cinnamon-gray upperparts, brighter cinnamon on side of head and throat, a gray breast and whitish belly. Male has indistinct barring on rump and uppertail. Female is barred buff and black on wings and lower back. No other tinamou has such a bicolored look with rufous above and whitish below. Uncommon in dense humid lowland forests e of Andes south of the Amazon (especially along Río Tambopata) to 400 m. *Amazonian Brazil, adjacent Peru and Bolivia.*

Black-capped Tinamou *Crypturellus atrocapillus* Perdiz Gorrinegro
30 cm (11.7"). ♪ 553. Plate 2. A medium-sized tinamou with bright red legs, barred back, heavily spotted wings, dark-gray crown and neck and a contrasting cinnamon throat. Cf. Variegated Tinamou (rufous neck and greenish legs). Fairly common in foothill and second growth e of Andes in Cusco and Madre de Dios to 900 m. *Lowlands of se Peru and n Bolivia.*

Variegated Tinamou *Crypturellus variegatus* Perdiz Abigarrada
33 cm (13"). ♪ 553. Plate 2. A medium-sized tinamou, slightly larger than similar Black-capped Tinamou (both have heavy black barring on wings, back and upper tail). Dark-gray crown and sides of head of Variegated Tinamou contrast with white throat. Uncommon in humid lowland forests e of Andes to 1300 m. *S Venezuela and the Guianas to n Bolivia and Amazonian Brazil.*

Bartlett's Tinamou *Crypturellus bartletti* Perdiz de Bartlett
30 cm (11.7"). ♪ 553. Plate 2. A medium-sized, dark-brown tinamou with a dark throat, darker hood and inconspicuous dark barring on back, wings and uppertail. Variegated Tinamou has a white throat and bolder barring on back and wings. Cf. Cinereous Tinamou (reddish legs and lacks barring). Fairly common in humid lowland forests e of Andes to 900 m. Rusty Tinamou *C. brevirostris* included in Peru avifauna in error by Peters 1931 and Koepcke 1970 (Schulenberg *in litt.*) *W Amazonian Brazil, e Peru and n Bolivia.*

Small-billed Tinamou *Crypturellus parvirostris* Perdiz Piquicorto
20 cm (8"). ♪ 553. Plate 2. A very small tinamou, similar to Tataupa Tinamou (both have red bills, grayish head and neck and a scaly design on flanks), but Small-billed Tinamou is smaller, shorter-billed and duller-backed. Prefers more open forest, second growth and fields. Rare in humid lowland forests e of Andes in Cusco and Madre de Dios to 900 m. *Patchily distributed Amazon basin south to ne Argentina.*

Tataupa Tinamou *Crypturellus tataupa* Perdiz Tataupá
25 cm (9.8"). ♪ 553. Plate 2. A larger and brighter version (especially on upperparts) of Short-billed Tinamou. Prefers denser vegetation (forest and grassy areas). Rare in riparian thickets in Marañón Valley and in lowlands e of Andes to 1400 m. Fairly common near Jaén (Cajamarca). *Patchily distributed in Amazon basin south to n Argentina.*

Red-winged Tinamou *Rhynchotus rufescens* Perdiz Alirrojo
40 cm (15.5"). ♪ 553. Plate 2. A large tinamou of the low-lying grasslands. The only large tinamou in its habitat. Note red primaries. Fairly common in humid grasslands and savanna in Pampas del Heath. *Grasslands of Brazil to Argentina, Paraguay and se Peru.*

*Taczanowski's Tinamou *Nothoprocta taczanowskii* Perdiz de Taczanowski
33 cm (13"). Plate 1. A medium-sized, dark tinamou with contrasting pale streaks on blackish back, and conspicuous pale spots on gray breast. Primaries are barred cinnamon. Smaller Andean Tinamou is markedly paler, with less conspicuous streaks on back and smaller (nearly indistinct) spots on breast. Cf. also Ornate and Kalinowski's Tinamous. Rare in humid and semi-humid montane scrub from 2775 m to 3700 m in Junín, Apurímac, Cusco and Puno. Recorded 32 km e of Paucartambo, and recently recorded at Canchaillo at 3500 m; Abra La Raya at 4315 m; and Bosque de Ampay ca 3700 m. Two specimens collected at Valcón (Puno) on e slope of Andes at 3000 m and one at Bosque de Naupallagta (Apurímac) at 3650 m. Recorded between Abancay and Andahuaylas (MAP). Recently recorded in w Bolivia. *Endemic to Peru.*

*Kalinowski's Tinamou *Nothoprocta kalinowskii* Perdiz de Kalinowski
35 cm (14"). Plate 1. A medium-sized tinamou similar to Ornate Tinamou. Both share a "salt and pepper" speckled head but Kalinowski's Tinamou is more rufous, especially on underparts and secondaries. Black spots on back are more prominent than those of Ornate Tinamou. Tertials are barred rufous-brown. Known from two specimens taken over 900 km apart. Type specimen collected May 1894 at 4575 m in arid Cordillera de Licamachay (Cusco), and second at Hacienda Tulpo (w La Libertad) at 3000 m in May 1900. Recent possible sight record from extreme n Ancash 21 km from Hacienda Tulpo at 4250 m (pers. comm. GE). *Endemic to Peru.*

Ornate Tinamou *Nothoprocta ornata* Perdiz Cordillerana
35 cm (14"). ♪ 553. Plate 1. A medium-sized tinamou with a short crest and grayish underparts. The whitish head is speckled with black. Cf. rare Kalinowski's Tinamou. Uncommon in *puna* grasslands and *thola* heath north to Ancash at 3500-4800 m. *Andes of Peru to n Chile and nw Argentina.*

Andean Tinamou *Nothoprocta pentlandii* Perdiz Andina
27 cm (10.5"). ♪ 553. Plate 1. A medium-sized tinamou. Variable. Birds from w slopes of Andes are rufous brown and those of e slopes are gray brown. They all have grayish stripes on back and spotted breasts. Sympatric Ornate Tinamou lacks breast spots and stripes on back, but has speckles on the face. Cf. also Taczanowski's Tinamou. Fairly common but disjunct in thickets and scrub in semiarid zone in Andes at 1500 to 4000 m. On west slope rarely higher than 3600 m and replaced by Ornate Tinamou at higher elevations. Uncommon in coastal lomas. *Andes of s Ecuador to n Chile and nw Argentina.*

Curve-billed Tinamou *Nothoprocta curvirostris* Perdiz Piquicurvo
25 cm (9.8"). Plate 1. A medium-sized tinamou with deep rufous underparts, rufous flight feathers and orange legs. Uncommon in montane grasslands south to Huánuco at 2800-3700 m. *Andes of Ecuador to central Peru.*

Darwin's Nothura *Nothura darwinii* Perdiz de Darwin
25 cm (9.8"). ♪ 553. Plate 1. A small, buffy tinamou, heavily spotted and streaked. No other small tinamou occurs in its range and habitat. Uncommon in *puna* grasslands of e Andes in Cusco and Puno to 4300 m. *Highlands of s Peru to Patagonian steppes of central Argentina.*

Puna Tinamou *Tinamotis pentlandii* Perdiz de la Puna
45 cm (17.5"). ♪ 553. Plate 1. An unmistakable, large tinamou of *puna* grasslands. Neck stripes and chestnut lower belly are conspicuous. Often seen in small coveys. Uncommon in *puna* grasslands along w Andes north to Junín at 4000-5300 m. *Andes of Peru to n Chile and n Argentina.*

Spheniscidae (Penguins; Pingüinos). Species: World 17; Peru 1
A distinctive group of flightless birds highly adapted to an aquatic existence and restricted to the southern oceans. They are flightless, but are superb swimmers, and have been known to dive to 268 meters (880 feet). The larger species feed in deep water for squid and fish, but the smaller penguins feed in surface waters for shoaling crustaceans, small squid and fish. All penguins are residents of the cold southern oceans, except the three *Spheniscus* species, whose distribution ranges as far north as the equator.

[King Penguin] *Aptenodytes patagonicus* Pingüino Rey
95 cm (37"). Not illustrated. A large penguin that lacks a breast-band. The long black bill has an orange plate on the base of the lower mandible. Head is black with an orange patch behind the ear. Single specimen from Tacna (pers. comm. TV). This is probably from a ship-assisted bird, since it would be virtually impossible for a King Penguin to reach the west coast of South America unaided (Frank Todd *in litt.*). *Antarctic and subantarctic circumpolar.*

*Humboldt Penguin *Spheniscus humboldti* Pingüino de Humboldt
68 cm (27"). Plate 6. The only penguin in the region. Note that the immature lacks a breast-band, and has a brownish head and throat. Uncommon on offshore islands and along coast from Lambayeque south. Small and declining population; best seen on Islas Ballestas off Paracas Peninsula. *Coastal n Peru to s Chile.*

Podicipedidae (Grebes; Zambullidores). Species: World 19; Peru 7
Grebes are highly specialized aquatic birds distributed throughout the world, and are well adapted for diving from the surface and for underwater swimming. While most are poor fliers (including two flightless species resident in Peru), some make remarkable migrations. Their food consists primarily of fish and small aquatic animals caught underwater.

Least Grebe *Tachybaptus dominicus* Zambullidor Menor
23 cm (9"). Plate 5. ♪ 626. The only dark grebe with yellow eyes and a dark bill. Rare and local in lowlands in e Amazonian Peru, and in far northwest on coast in Lambayeque. *Extreme s US to n Argentina; West Indies.*

Pied-billed Grebe *Podilymbus podiceps* Zambullidor Picogrueso
33 cm (13"). Plate 5. ♪ 626. No other grebe in its range has a thick bill with a black band. In non-breeding plumage has a yellowish, unbanded bill. Uncommon along coast. Regular at Lagunas de Mejía and Pisco marshes. *Alaska to Chile and s Argentina; West Indies.*

White-tufted Grebe *Rollandia rolland* Zambullidor Pimpollo
30 cm (11.7"). Plate 5. In breeding plumage, the only grebe with a black head with white ear tufts and a black neck. Much browner non-breeding plumage has a whitish throat, lacks ear tufts, and neck is striped. Common in *puna* marshes and ponds at 3500-4500 m; southern breeders winter along coast. If gigantic Falkland Islands race *rolland* is elevated to species level, White-tufted Grebe would become *Rollandia chilensis*. *Peru and s Brazil to Tierra del Fuego; Falkland Is.*

Short-winged (Titicaca Flightless) Grebe *Rollandia microptera* Zambullidor del Titicaca
27 cm (10.5"). Plate 5. The largest grebe in its limited range. Note the yellow bill, white cheeks and throat, rufous foreneck (adult) or white (immature) and rufous nape. Cf. non-breeding White-tufted Grebe. A flightless, uncommon to rare grebe on Lake Titicaca and adjacent southern *puna* lakes. *Andes of s Peru and w Bolivia in Lake Titicaca basin.*

Great Grebe *Podiceps major* Zambullidor Grande
60 cm (23.5"). Plate 5. The largest grebe in the region, and the only one with a long, slender neck. Note the long, slightly upturned bill. Head is blackish (breeding), or with dark cap and whitish cheeks (non-breeding). Fairly common along coast. *Coastal Peru and s Brazil to s Argentina and central Chile.*

Silvery Grebe *Podiceps occipitalis* Zambullidor Plateado
27 cm (10.5"). Plate 5. The only silvery-white grebe over most of its Peruvian range. Note the red eyes and short, black bill. In Lake Junín cf. Junín Grebe. Fairly common in *puna* lagoons and ponds at 3000-5000 m, descending to coast in Arequipa. *Locally in Andes of Colombia to Tierra del Fuego.*

*Junín Grebe *Podiceps taczanowskii* Zambullidor de Junín
35 cm (14"). Plate 5. An endangered, flightless grebe confined to Lake Junín. Similar to Silvery Grebe, but has a longer, more slender neck and peaked crown. Compare to shorter neck and rounded crown of Silvery Grebe (at rest hard to judge). Also note that Junín Grebe has a longer bill and whitish flanks. It favors deeper waters of the lake. Population in 1998 ca 300 birds. *Endemic to Peru.*

Diomedeidae (Albatrosses; Albatros). Species: World 14; Peru 8
Large, long-winged seabirds with long, hooked bills and prolonged raised tubular nostrils. They are superb fliers ,and all species are highly pelagic, and rarely seen on land except on their remote breeding colonies. Their food consists mainly of large squid gathered from the surface of the sea, supplemented with fish and marine invertebrates. When identifying albatrosses note especially upperwing and underwing patterns and bill coloration.

*[Wandering Albatross] *Diomedea exulans* Albatros Errante
135 cm (53"). Facing Plate 3. The largest seabird in the world. Reaches adulthood through a complex molt pattern. In almost all plumages has a wide black terminal band to tail and dark leading edge to wing. Immature—most likely to be seen in Peru—has mostly chocolate-brown underparts with contrasting white underwing. Adult resembles Royal Albatross. Bill as in Royal Albatross but lacks dark cutting edge (seen at close range and in good light only). Probably occurs in Peruvian waters (recorded from Arica, Chile). Cited by Koepcke 1970 without definitive records. *Circumpolar southern oceans.*

*Royal Albatross *Diomedea epomophora* Albatros Real
122 cm (48"). Plate 3. The second-largest albatross. Normally the only albatross in Peruvian waters that has a white back. Tail is white, or white with a narrow black terminal band in immature. Bill is pale pinkish-yellow with a black cutting edge. Upperwing can be mostly dark (immature of both ssp. and adult *sanfordi*) or white with black trailing edge (adult *epomophora*). Usually leading edge is whitish. However cf. hypothetical Wandering Albatross. Rare pelagic migrant. *Circumpolar southern oceans.*

*Waved Albatross *Phoebastria irrorata* Albatros de las Galápagos
89 cm (35"). Plate 3. The only albatross with a dark belly and back and a whitish head. Cf. Antarctic Giant Petrel (bulkier, much shorter bill). Uncommon pelagic migrant south to Independence Bay, but during El Niño years wanders as far south as central Chile. *Breeds Galápagos Is.; ranges south to Peru.*

Black-browed Albatross *Thalassarche melanophris* Albatros Cejinegra
86 cm (34"). Plate 3. No other black-backed, white-bellied albatross has a combination of yellow bill, white head, and underwing with a thick black leading edge. Immature has a dusky bill with a dark tip, and nearly all dark underwing. Cf. immature Gray-headed Albatross (all dark bill) and immature Shy Albatross (diagnostic "thumbprint"). Fairly common pelagic migrant. *Breeds subantarctic islands; ranges southern oceans and North Atlantic.*

Buller's Albatross *Thalassarche bulleri* Albatros de Buller
78 cm (30.5"). Plate 3. In all ages, underwing mostly white but with a thick black margin on leading edge. Adult has a gray head but a white forecrown and a thick yellow frame to the bill. In all ages cf. Gray-headed Albatross, but note Buller's underwing is not nearly as dark, and adult Buller's has a thicker, yellow frame to the bill. Rare pelagic migrant. *Breeds New Zealand region; ranges to w South America.*

Shy (White-capped) Albatross *Thalassarche cauta* Albatros Frentiblanco
91 cm (36"). Plate 3. The three ssp. are often regarded as three distinct species, two of which have been confirmed in Peruvian waters. All have a narrow black frame to an otherwise white underwing, and a diagnostic black "thumbprint" at the base of leading edge of the wing. Most often recorded *T. c. salvini* (Salvin's Albatross) has a brownish-gray head, white forecrown, and gray bill with a yellow ridge. Infrequently recorded *T. c. eremita* (Chatham Island Albatross) has a dark-gray head and dark-tipped yellow bill. Nominate *cauta* (White-tipped Albatross) has not been confirmed yet in Peruvian waters. It has a white head, with a yellow-tipped, dusky bill. Gray-headed birds (adults of *D. c. salvini* and *D. c. eremita* as well as young birds of all races), may be confused with Buller's or Gray-headed Albatrosses, but both have a thicker, black underwing margin, and none has a similar "thumbprint" mark. Uncommon pelagic migrant north to Lima. *Islands off Tasmania and New Zealand; ranges cold southern oceans.*

*Gray-headed Albatross *Thalassarche chrysostoma* Albatros Cabecigris
81 cm (32"). Plate 3. In all ages, underwing has a thick black margin on leading edge, and dark margin on trailing edge. Adult has a dark bill with a yellow frame, and a gray head and gray forehead. Similar to Buller's Albatross (white forecrown). Immature has a dark bill (or dark with yellowish tip). Compare "Salvin's", "Chatham Island" and immature Black-browed Albatrosses. Rare pelagic migrant. *Breeds high southern latitudes; ranges north to 40° S.*

[Light-mantled Albatross] *Phoebetria palpebrata* Albatross Tiznado
79 cm. (31"). Not illustrated. An ashy-gray albatross with a dark head, dark wings and a fairly long wedge-shaped tail. Sight record from Mollendo, Arequipa (Hughes *in* Harrison 1983). *Circumpolar subantarctic islands; ranges north to 35° S.*

Procellariidae (Shearwaters and Petrels; Pardelas y Petreles). Species: World 75; Peru 26
A group of highly pelagic, tube-nosed seabirds. They breed in colonies in burrows on offshore islands, which are mainly visited only at night. Their food consists primarily of zooplankton, fish and cephalopods.

*Antarctic Giant Petrel *Macronectes giganteus* Petrel Gigante Antártico
89 cm (35"). Plate 3. A large seabird with a thick, heavy, yellow bill. Size of an albatross but bulkier bodied and shorter-winged, with a less graceful flight. Extremely variable plumage ranges from all white to all dark, or dark with a pale head. Not likely to be confused. Uncommon pelagic migrant. *Southern oceans south to the pack ice.*

Southern Fulmar *Fulmarus glacialoides* Petrel Plateado
50 cm (19.5"). Facing Plate 4. Gull-like plumage with stocky, bull-necked shape. Flight much like a shearwater. Rare pelagic migrant north to about Chiclayo. *Antarctic circumpolar; ranges widely in southern oceans.*

Cape Petrel *Daption capense* Petrel Damero
40 cm (15.5"). Facing Plate 4. Unmistakable. Upperwing pattern is diagnostic. Uncommon off coast year-round. *Breeds subantarctic islands; ranges southern oceans.*

Pterodroma **Petrels.** A large genus of small to medium-sized true pelagics, most likely to be encountered away from the continental shelf. They usually do not follow ships. They are very strong fliers, and glide and wheel in high arcs above the water. Identification is often extremely difficult. Head pattern and underwing pattern are often the most helpful keys for identification.

Murphy's Petrel *Pterodroma ultima* Petrel de Murphy
41 cm (16"). Plate 4. Accidental? A uniformly sooty gray-brown *Pterodroma* with variable whitish on throat and around the bill; dark underwings show paler primaries. Upperwings of dark morph Kermadec Petrel show white shafts at base of primaries. Sight record 120 km w of Lima (R. Pitman pers. comm.). *Breeds s Polynesia, disperses to ne Pacific Ocean.*

Kermadec Petrel *Pterodroma neglecta* Petrel de Kermadec
40 cm (15.5"). Plate 4. Multimorphic. All morphs have white at base of primaries, on underwing, and white shafts on upperwing. Underparts can be dark, light or light with dark head and dark undertail coverts. Herald Petrel *Pterodroma arminjoniana* seems likely to occur in Peru and is very similar (and also multimorphic), but upperwings lack white shafts; on underwing bases of secondaries are usually white. Uncommon to rare pelagic migrant. Sight records 50-70 km off coast of Peru north to Lima in May 1986 (pers. comm. Pitman and Spear). *Breeds Juan Fernández, San Ambrosio and San Félix islands off Chile, and South Pacific islands from New Zealand to Easter I.*

*Dark-rumped Petrel *Pterodroma phaeopygia* Petrel Lomioscuro
43 cm (17"). Plate 4. A large *Pterodroma* with a dark crown and nape contrasting with a white forehead. Upperparts dark (lacking "M"). White underwing has a dark margin close to leading edge and sometimes small but distinctive dark axillaries. Cf. Juan Fernández Petrel. Uncommon off coast south to Lima. *Breeds Galápagos and Hawaiian Islands; ranges Mexico to Peru and Polynesia.*

*Juan Fernández Petrel *Pterodroma externa* Petrel de Juan Fernández
43 cm (17"). Plate 4. Similar to Dark-rumped Petrel, but crown is pale gray. Back is gray and contrasts with the rest of upperparts. Note dark "M" marking on upperparts; underwing with much reduced margin. Cf. Buller's Shearwater (longer bill, different flight). Uncommon to rare pelagic migrant. As many as 91 individuals counted 70 km off coast of Lima on 7 May 1986 (pers. comm. R. Pitman). *Breeds Juan Fernández Is. off Chile; ranges to Hawaiian and Mexican waters.*

"Cookilaria" Petrels. A group of four small *Pterodroma* petrels, very similar to each other. Some have a black "M" marking on the silvery-gray back and upperwings. Watch for head pattern and amount of black on underwing margin. Prions' plumage is similar, but they usually have a grayish bill, and they fly close to the surface of the water.

*Cook's Petrel *Pterodroma cookii* Petrel de Cook
27 cm (10.5"). Plate 4. Similar to Defilippe's Petrel, but crown is paler gray and lacks the dark eye patch. Bill is thinner, and somewhat rounder tail has a dark terminal band. Rare pelagic migrant. *Breeds islands off New Zealand; ranges to e and n Pacific.*

*Defilippe's Petrel *Pterodroma defilippiana* Petrel Chileno
27 cm (10.5"). Plate 4. A "Cookilaria" petrel with a noticeable dark eye patch. A gray cap extends to a semicollar, and tail is wedge shaped—often without a darker terminal band. Note the strong "M" marking on upperparts, and fairly narrow margin on leading edge of underwing. Cook's Petrel is very similar. Cf. other "Cookilaria" petrels. Rare pelagic migrant. *Breeds Juan Fernández Is. (Chile) with northern dispersal to Humboldt Current region.*

Black-winged Petrel *Pterodroma nigripennis* Petrel Alinegro
30 cm (11.7"). Plate 4. Look for wide black margin on leading edge of underwing, silvery-gray head, back and semicollar, and dark upperwings. A single record 314 km off the coast of Mollendo (pers. comm. L. Spear). *Breeds islands in sw Pacific; ranges to s-central Pacific.*

*Stejneger's Petrel *Pterodroma longirostris*. Petrel de Más Afuera
27 cm (10.5"). Plate 4. Look for narrow black margin on leading edge of underwing, dark-gray crown and semicollar contrasting with silvery-gray mantle. Cf. other "Cookilaria" petrels. Rare (or overlooked) transequatorial migrant. Recent sight record 50 km off coast of Peru (Mackiernan *et al.* 2001). *Breeds Juan Fernández Is. off Chile; ranges e and n Pacific.*

[Blue Petrel] *Halobaena caerulea* Petrel Azulado
30 cm (11.7"). Plate 4. Recalls Defilippe's Petrel, but has a diagnostic white terminal band to tail (none of the prions or "Cookilaria" petrels have such a tail). A sight record outside Peruvian territorial waters (Meeth *et al.* 1977) and likely to occur in Peruvian waters. *Islands in subantarctic oceans and islands off Cape Horn.*

Pachyptila **Prions.** Small seabirds with light grayish upperparts and white underparts. All have a black "M" on the back and a black terminal band on uppertail. Identification of species is very difficult. Watch for bill size and structure, and facial pattern.

Broad-billed Prion *Pachyptila vittata* Petrel Azul Piquiancho
30 cm (11.7"). Plate 4. Bill is very wide (seen from above) and black, crown is dark, contrasting with short white superciliary. Relatively narrow black terminal band to tail. Collected off Mollendo (Hughes 1982). *Breeds islands off New Zealand and Tristan da Cunha group.*

Antarctic Prion *Pachyptila desolata* Petrel Azul Antártico
30 cm (11.7"). Plate 4. Very similar to Broad-billed Prion, but bill is narrower and grayer; gray mottling on sides of breast forms a dark semicollar. Rare pelagic migrant north to 12°S off coast (Plenge 1974). *Breeds scattered subantarctic islands.*

Slender-billed Prion *Pachyptila belcheri* Petrel Azul Picofino
30 cm (11.7"). Plate 4. A prion with a thin bill, distinct broad superciliary, faint "M" marking above, and a black tip only to central rectrices. Uncommon pelagic migrant north to Piura (pers. comm. L. Spear). *Breeds Crozet, Kerguelen and Falkland Is.*

[Fairy Prion] *Pachyptila turtur* Petrel Azul Piquicorto
30 cm (11.7"). Plate 4. Lacks blackish line behind eye. Bill relatively narrow with bulbous tip. Note thick black terminal tail band. Accidental (?) pelagic visitor to extreme southern waters. *Breeds scattered subantarctic islands.*

Procellaria **Petrels.** Four species of fairly large to large, heavy-bodied petrels that often follow ships. They fly with powerful flaps, followed by a glide, sometimes soaring in high arcs. Three of the species are dark to black, and can be very difficult to identify. Note size and bill color.

Gray Petrel *Procellaria cinerea* Petrel Gris
45 cm (17.5"). Plate 4. A fairly large, bulky petrel with a yellow bill, ashy-gray upperparts, white underparts and dark underwings. Cf. Pink-footed and Buller's Shearwaters (skinnier, whitish underwing, longer bill). Rare pelagic migrant. *Breeds and ranges circumpolar subantarctic seas.*

*White-chinned Petrel *Procellaria aequinoctialis* Petrel de Mentón Blanco
56 cm (22"). Plate 4. A large and bulky dark petrel with an ivory-colored bill. Diagnostic white chin may be seen at close range on some individuals. Westland and Parkinson's Petrels have a dark tip to bill. Sooty Shearwater has a longer black bill and silvery underwing. Common pelagic migrant. *Islands in southern oceans, normally from 55° S to 15° S.*

Parkinson's Petrel *Procellaria parkinsoni* Petrel de Parkinson
45 cm (17.5"). Plate 4. Very similar to larger White-chinned Petrel, but pale bill has a dark tip, and plumage is blacker (both are visible only at close range). Nearly identical to Westland Petrel. Uncommon pelagic migrant. *Islands off New Zealand; ranges to central and n South America.*

*Westland Petrel *Procellaria westlandica* Petrel de Westland
55 cm (21.5"). Plate 4. Accidental. Nearly identical to Parkinson's Petrel, but larger (almost the size of White-chinned Petrel). A sight record in fall 2000 50 km off coast of Tumbes (pers. comm. M. Force). *Breeds South I. (New Zealand); disperses to Australia and sw South America.*

Shearwaters. Medium to small-sized seabirds with long, thin bills. They usually fly very close to the water surface with strong wingbeats, followed by a glide, often banking from side to side.

*Pink-footed Shearwater *Puffinus creatopus* Pardela Patirrosada
50 cm (19.5"). Plate 4. The only shearwater that has light underparts with smudgy underwings, and brownish-gray upperparts. Feet and bill are pinkish. Cf. Buller's Shearwater. Fairly common pelagic migrant. *Breeds Juan Fernández Is. off Chile; ranges to north Pacific Ocean.*

Flesh-footed Shearwater *Puffinus carneipes* Pardela Patipálida
50 cm (19.5"). Plate 4. A large, all dark shearwater. Feet and base of bill are flesh-pink. Underwings are dark, but flight feathers are slightly paler. Sooty Shearwater has silvery underwings. Sight records from offshore Tumbes and Piura (Brown 1981) and off Ancash in May 1986 (pers. comm. R. Pitman). *Breeds s Pacific and Indian oceans, disperses northward.*

*Buller's Shearwater *Puffinus bulleri* Pardela de Buller
50 cm (19.5"). Plate 4. Underparts almost entirely glowing white, crown dark, upperparts silvery-gray with black "M" marking. Recalls some *Pterodroma* petrels, but flight is very different (none has a slender bill, etc.). Cf. also Pink-footed Shearwater. Rare pelagic migrant. *Breeds islands off New Zealand; wide transpacific dispersal.*

Sooty Shearwater *Puffinus griseus* Pardela Oscura
50 cm (19.5"). Plate 4. The only dark shearwater in Peruvian waters with silvery underwings. Cf. White-chinned Petrel. Note: Wedge-tailed Shearwater *Puffinus pacificus* is likely to occur in extreme northern waters. The wedge-shaped tail gives a distinctive long-tailed look. It has two morphs. An all-dark morph with dark underwings (not silvery as in Sooty), and a light morph (white underparts and underwing) that recalls Pink-footed Shearwater (latter's underwings are smudged dusky). Common pelagic migrant with peak numbers October-November. ±50,000 birds recorded off Paracas in Aug. 1998. *Transequatorial migrant in Pacific and Atlantic Oceans.*

Audubon's Shearwater *Puffinus lherminieri* Pardela de Audubon
33 cm (13"). Plate 4. Similar to Little Shearwater, but undertail coverts are dark; thicker black borders to underwing are thicker, and black on crown extends just below the eye. Favors warmer waters than Little Shearwater. Rare pelagic migrant south to Ancash. Sight records off coast of Peru (Jahncke 1998; Pitman and Spear data). *Ranges widely in pantropical oceans.*

Little Shearwater *Puffinus assimilis* Pardela Chica
25 cm (9.8"). Plate 4. A small shearwater that is black above and white below. Underwings are white with narrow black borders, undertail coverts white. Black crown is sharply defined from white face above the eye. Favors cold waters. Flies with fast, shallow wingbeats, followed by short glides. Cf. Peruvian Diving-Petrel. Rare pelagic migrant. Sight records from Mollendo (Hughes *in litt.*) and Pisco (pers. comm. Scott). *Ranges widely in Atlantic, Pacific and Indian Oceans.*

Hydrobatidae (Storm-Petrels; Paíños). Species: World 20; Peru 12
A family of small, highly pelagic seabirds that are occasionally encountered in large concentrations feeding on plankton and small fish on the surface of the water. Their webbed feet allow them to appear to be walking on the water, and in some harbors they flit among the fishing boats for any discarded offal. All fly fairly close to surface of the water. Identification in some cases is very difficult. Pay special attention to tail shape, presence and amount of white on rump, projection of feet beyond tail, and wing pattern. Known as Golondrina del Mar or Petrel de las Tormentas in Peru, but these long, compound names become awkward when used in the field.

Wilson's Storm-Petrel *Oceanites oceanicus* Paíño de Wilson
18 cm (7"). Plate 3, 6. All dark except for a white band on the rump that extends to outer undertail coverts. Similar to smaller White-vented Storm-Petrel, but latter has variable amounts of white on vent and belly, and paler wing lining. In both species, the yellow-webbed feet project behind the tail (White-vented's feet project farther). Both follow ships, patter on water surface, and have a straight flight with fluttery wingbeats. Cf. Band-rumped Storm-Petrel (feet do not project beyond tail, shearwater-like flight). Common transequatorial pelagic migrant. Often seen feeding in harbor at Pisco among fishing boats. *Breeds Antarctic and subantarctic; ranges oceans except n Pacific.*

White-vented (Elliot's) Storm-Petrel *Oceanites gracilis* Paíño Chico
15 cm (6"). Plate 3. A dark storm-petrel with a white rump band and variable amounts of white on vent and belly. Cf. similar Wilson's Storm-Petrel. Common Humboldt Current pelagic species. *Ranges Galápagos Islands and w South America; breeding grounds unknown.*

White-faced Storm-Petrel *Pelagodroma marina* Paíño Cariblanco
20 cm (8"). Plate 3. Mostly dark above, almost no wingbar, gray rump, conspicuous white superciliary, mostly white below. Recalls Ringed Storm-Petrel, but lacks pectoral band (Ringed lacks a white superciliary). Rare off coast during austral winter, with most records in July. *Breeds southern oceans; ranges north to tropical oceans.*

Black-bellied Storm-Petrel *Fregetta tropica* Paíño Ventrinegro
20 cm (8"). Plate 3. A diagnostic black median line divides a white belly, black chest and throat; white underwing lining. Dark above except a white rump (no wingbar). See White-bellied Storm-Petrel. Uncommon pelagic migrant. *Subantarctic circumpolar islands; ranges north to tropics.*

[White-bellied Storm-Petrel] *Fregetta grallaria* Paíño Ventriblanco.
20 cm (8"). Plate 3. Like Black-bellied Storm-Petrel, but white belly lacks a black median line. Sight records off coast of Peru (Jahncke 1998). *Breeds circumpolar islands in southern oceans.*

Least Storm-Petrel *Oceanodroma microsoma* Paíño Menudo
15 cm (6"). Plate 3. Tiny—the smallest storm-petrel. All dark like a mini Markham's Storm-Petrel, but tail appears short and is not forked. Flight is direct with deep wingbeats. Rare (accidental?) migrant south to extreme n Peru. *Breeds islands off Baja California; ranges south to extreme n Peru.*

Wedge-rumped (Galápagos) Storm-Petrel *Oceanodroma tethys* Paíño Danzarín
19 cm (7.5"). Facing Plate 3. The only storm-petrel whose entire uppertail coverts and rump are white, and the rest of body is dark. Fairly common breeding species on Islas Pescadores and Isla San Gallán. *Breeds Galápagos Is. and islands off w coast of Peru; ranges to Chile and Costa Rica.*

Band-rumped (Madeiran/Harcourt's) Storm-Petrel *Oceanodroma castro* Paíño de Madeira
21 cm (8.5"). Plate 3. Larger and proportionately longer-winged than very similar Wilson's Storm-Petrel, but feet do not extend past the tail. Shearwater-like flight, with a few quick wingbeats followed by a glide with stiff wings. Rare pelagic migrant south to Lambayeque. Individuals recorded year round (Pitman and Spear). *Breeds and ranges tropical Atlantic and Pacific Oceans.*

Leach's Storm-Petrel *Oceanodroma leucorhoa* Paíño Boreal
20 cm (8"). Plate 3. An all dark storm-petrel with long pointed wings and slightly forked tail. Normally has a white rump divided by a narrow dusky line, but dark-rumped birds also occur. Has a bold carpal bar. Feet do not project behind tail. In flight wings are swept back at carpal joint. Flight is erratic, with banking from side to side. Rare pelagic migrant. *Breeds Atlantic and Pacific Oceans; disperses to tropics.*

Markham's Storm-Petrel *Oceanodroma markhami* Paíño de Markham
24 cm (9.4"). Plate 3. A large, dark storm-petrel with a fairly long, forked tail. Flies with deep, slow wing strokes. Nearly identical to Black Storm-Petrel. Cf. Leach's Storm-Petrel (very different flight, smaller, with a shorter tail). Uncommon pelagic species; only known breeding grounds at Paracas (Jahncke 1993). *Breeds off coastal s Peru and probably adjacent n Chile; disperses to s Mexico and central Chile.*

Black Storm-Petrel *Oceanodroma melania* Paíño Negro
23 cm (9"). Plate 3. Nearly indistinguishable in the field from Markham's Storm-Petrel. Black Storm-Petrel is blacker, and its upper wingbar does not reach the carpal joint. Tail is slightly less forked, and wingbeats are slightly deeper. Cf. Leach's Storm-Petrel (very different flight, smaller, shorter tail). Rare pelagic migrant in n Peruvian waters (few records to central Peru). *Breeds islands off California and Baja; ranges south to Peru.*

Ringed (Hornby's) Storm-Petrel *Oceanodroma hornbyi* Paíño Acollarado
21 cm (8.5"). Facing Plate 3. The only storm-petrel with a gray back, dark cap, white forehead, pectoral band across white underparts ,and dark underwings. Cf. White-faced Storm-Petrel. Uncommon pelagic species; probably breeds in southern coastal deserts. *Ranges coastal Ecuador to central Chile.*

Pelecanoididae (Diving-Petrels; Potoyuncos). Species: World 4; Peru 1
Small aquatic petrels that are the southern hemisphere ecological replacement for the northern auks and puffins. They are superbly adapted for swimming and "flying" underwater. Their food consists mainly of planktonic invertebrates, which they gather off the coast and headlands.

*Peruvian Diving-Petrel *Pelecanoides garnotii* Potoyunco Peruano
23 cm (9"). Plate 6. A chunky, alcid-like seabird. Flies with very fast wingbeats. Note stripes on back. Rare pelagic species. Breeds from coastal Lobos de Tierra south, with largest remaining Peruvian population on Isla San Gallán 5 km off Paracas Peninsula. Population suffered major decline during the last few decades. *Arid coasts of Peru and Chile.*

Phaethontidae (Tropicbirds; Aves del Trópico). Species: World 3; Peru 2
Seabirds that resemble heavy-bodied terns, with short wings. They are generally seen plunge-diving for squid and fish, often seen flying high overhead far from the nearest land.

Red-billed Tropicbird *Phaethon aethereus* Ave del Trópico Piquirrojo
60 cm (23.5"). Plate 10. Like a large tern, with long white central tail feathers (streamers). Note the red bill. White except for black barring on back, and black outer primaries. Juvenile is similar, but lacks streamers, and the bill is yellower. A black line from the eye through the nape creates a nuchal collar. Cf. Red-tailed Tropicbird. Rare pelagic visitor. *Breeds and disperses widely in tropical oceans.*

Red-tailed Tropicbird *Phaethon rubricauda* Ave del Trópico Colirrojo
45 cm (17.5"). Plate 10. Accidental. Almost wholly white with red bill and red tail streamers. Slimmer than Red-billed Tropicbird. Juvenile is similar to that of Red-billed, but lacks black primaries and black collar. Recorded off extreme southern coast at Tacna 10 June 1996 (Høgsås 1999), and 56 km west of San Juan (Ica) in March 1992 (L. Spear). *Tropical Pacific and Indian oceans.*

Pelecanidae (Pelicans; Pelícanos). Species: World 8; Peru 2
Pelicans are large aquatic birds highly adapted for swimming and flying, but are most awkward on land. They are among the largest of flying birds, with some species having a wingspan approaching 2.7 meters (9 feet). Their most obvious feature is the enormous bill, with its large elastic pouch suspended beneath the lower mandible. Their diet consists primarily of fish, and like boobies and cormorants, their numbers are highly susceptible to fluctuations in the food supply, caused by such phenomena as the regularly occurring El Niños.

Brown Pelican *Pelecanus occidentalis* Pelícano Pardo
127 cm (50"). Plate 5. Limited overlap with Peruvian Pelican. Similar to latter but smaller, belly is darker, and has fewer white streaks. Fairly common along extreme north coast south to Piura. *Coastal US to n South America; Galápagos Is.*

Peruvian Pelican *Pelecanus thagus* Pelícano Peruano
152 cm (60"). Plate 5, 6. The only pelican over much of its range. Larger than similar (and sometimes considered conspecific with) Brown Pelican. Peruvian's secondary coverts are pale silver, in marked contrast to rest of upperwing. Adult breeding Peruvian has more extensive reddish tones to bill. In both species non-breeding adults have white necks. Juveniles of both are browner. Common breeder from central Peru south; disperses along coast north to s Ecuador. *Pacific coast of Ecuador to s Chile.*

Sulidae (Boobies and Gannets; Piqueros). Species: World: 10; Peru 6
Large plunge-divers that possess waterproof plumage, and frequently range far from land. Boobies often exploit shoaling fish, diving from large flocks with spectacular effect. They are entirely piscivorous, and during El Niño years often suffer disastrous population declines.

Blue-footed Booby *Sula nebouxii* Piquero Patiazul
86 cm (34"). Plate 10. Adult is similar to adult Peruvian Booby, but head is darker, and feet are bright blue. Note unspotted dark upperwing. Immature has a brown hood, whitish belly, dark upperwing and spotted back. Cf. Brown, Peruvian and Masked Boobies. Common along north coast; breeds on islands off n Peru. Immatures often seen off coast of Lima and Paracas. *Pacific coast of Mexico to Peru; Galápagos Is.*

Peruvian Booby *Sula variegata* Piquero Peruano
73 cm (29"). Plate 6. Adult is the only booby with a white head, dark upperwing, and mantle spotted with white. Immature like adult, but has mottled brownish head and underparts. Common along Humboldt Current; breeds on islands from Punta Parinas south. *Coastal sw Colombia to s Chile.*

Masked Booby *Sula dactylatra* Piquero Enmascarado
78 cm (30.5"). Plate 10. Adult is all white, except for black flight feathers and a black mask surrounding a yellow bill. Immature has a dark hood and dark unspotted upperwings separated by a white collar. Cf. immature Blue-footed Booby (paler hood, no white collar, spotted back), Brown Booby (no white collar). See Nazca Booby. Rare along coast. *Pantropical and subtropical oceans.*

Nazca Booby *Sula granti* Piquero de Nazca
73 cm (29"). Plate 10. Recently recognized as a full species (Pitman and Jehl 1998). Like Masked Booby, but bill is orange (instead of yellow). Immature usually lacks white nuchal collar. Rare along coast. *Nests almost exclusively on Galápagos Is. and Malpelo I. (Colombia).*

Red-footed Booby *Sula sula* Piquero Patirrojo
71 cm (28"). Plate 10. Accidental. Multimorphic. In all morphs adults have diagnostic red feet/legs and bluish-gray bill. White-morph adult (tail is either white or black) recalls Masked/Nazca Booby, but former has a black carpal patch on underwing. Dark morph is uniform pale brown. Intermediate morph occurs. Sight record and photograph 150 km off coast at 10° S in Ancash (Jahncke 1998). *Pantropical oceans.*

Brown Booby *Sula leucogaster* Piquero Pardo
76 cm (30"). Plate 10. Adult: yellow bill, dark brown upperwings and hood, with sharply contrasting white belly. Male has whitish crown, nape and a dusky-gray bill. Recalls immature Blue-footed Booby (spotted back) and immature Masked and Nazca Boobies (white collar). Immature is similar but duller, with a gray bill. Sight records from n Peru (Brown 1981; R. Pitman). *Pantropical, subtropical oceans.*

Phalacrocoracidae (Cormorants; Cormoranes). Species: World 39; Peru 3
Mainly black long-necked, long-billed diving birds with large and fully webbed feet. Cormorants are primarily piscivorous, with crustaceans and amphibians forming part of their diet. They are adept at diving for their prey, using their wings to aid in locomotion and steering. The Flightless Cormorant (*Spheniscus mendiculus*) of the Galápagos Islands has lost its ability to fly, while the Great Cormorant (*Phalacrocorax carbo*) is almost cosmopolitan in distribution. They are of great economic importance, trained cormorants being used in the Orient to catch fish. On a much larger scale, the collection of guano along the coast of South America has supported a vast fertilizer industry, that for years was one of the main sources of revenue for Peru. Generally called Cuervo in Peru, but this is misleading on a world scale, because of the confusion with the corvids.

Neotropic Cormorant *Phalacrocorax brasilianus* Cormorán Neotropical
71 cm (28"). Plate 5. The only all-dark cormorant. Immature is browner, with pale dusky underparts but never has a pattern like that of immature Guanay Cormorant (dark neck and pale belly). The only cormorant found away from the coast. Anhinga has a longer bill, longer tail, and snake-like neck. Fairly common from lowlands to *puna* zone throughout. *Extreme s US to Tierra del Fuego.*

Guanay Cormorant *Phalacrocorax bougainvillii* Cormorán Guanay
76 cm (30"). Plate 6. Unmistakable. Immature is similar, but has a duller brown hood and upperparts, and a whitish belly. Common along coast; breeds on offshore islands and coastal promontories. *Seacoasts and islands of Peru, Chile and s Argentina.*

Red-legged Cormorant *Phalacrocorax gaimardi* Cormorán Patirrojo (Chuita)
71 cm (28"). Plate 6. Colorful and unmistakable. Immature similar but duller. Common along coast; breeds from about Punta Negra south. *Coastal Peru and Chile; isolated population in s Argentina.*

Anhingidae (Anhingas; Aningas). Species: World 2; Peru 1
Anhingas are often referred to as "snakebirds" because of their snakelike appearance in the water. They are highly adapted to stalking fish underwater, much like herons and egrets stalk aquatic prey from above the surface. They are often seen soaring in thermals high above their swampy haunts, and are easily identified by their cross-shaped appearance.

Anhinga *Anhinga anhinga* Aninga
86 cm (34"). Plate 9. The long dagger-like bill, long tail, and long, slender, snake-like neck readily separate it from Neotropic Cormorant. Uncommon in humid lowland forests; rare in temp. zone. *Tropical s US to n Argentina and Brazil.*

Fregatidae (Frigatebirds; Tijeretas). Species: World 5; Peru 2
Large seabirds superbly adapted for aerial piracy. When not harassing gulls, terns or boobies by making them drop their catch, they feed on squid and fish, and are adept at catching flying fish. They are often seen high in the air over coastal thermals, and even well at sea will descend rapidly from great heights when other seabirds have located a school of fish.

Magnificent Frigatebird *Fregata magnificens* Avefragata Magnífica
106 cm (42"). Plate 10. A large predatory seabird with very long wings, a long, deeply forked tail, and a long, hooked bill. Male is all black with a red gular pouch. Female has a white chest and dark hood. Immature has variable amounts of white—from a complete white hood and most of the underparts to almost all black. Cf. very similar Great Frigatebird. Common along north coast from Tumbes to Cabo Blanco. *Tropical w Atlantic and e Pacific Oceans.*

Great Frigatebird *Fregata minor* Avefragata Grande
95 cm (37"). Plate 10. Very similar to more common Magnificent Frigatebird, and in some plumages cannot be safely separated in the field. Male is nearly identical to male Magnificent, but feet are red (instead of black in Magnificent), and upperwing coverts have a pale area (instead of all dark). Female similar but throat is ash-gray (instead of a complete black hood). One of the plumages of immature Great Frigatebird has a distinctive cinnamon hood. Rare vagrant offshore south to Ancash (Brown 1981; R. Pitman). *Widespread in tropical Pacific, Atlantic and Indian Oceans.*

Ardeidae (Herons, Egrets and Bitterns; Garzas y Mirasoles). Species: World 63; Peru 20
A family of mainly large wading birds. Herons and egrets are long-billed and long-legged, while the bitterns tend to be more compact than herons, and are distinguished by their booming calls. They are found throughout the world in suitable habitats, and feed mainly on fishes and other animal life caught in or near the water. The Cattle Egret has filled a niche created by the introduction of cattle into the New World, and has expanded its range dramatically throughout North and South America since World War II.

Capped Heron *Pilherodius pileatus* Garza Pileada
55 cm (21.5"). Plate 8. ♪ 797. The only heron that is all white with a black cap, blue bill and blue facial skin. Fairly common in aquatic lowlands e of Andes to 900 m. *Lowlands of e Panama to the Guianas, Brazil and n Paraguay.*

Cocoi Heron *Ardea cocoi* Garza Cuca
127 cm (50"). Plate 8. ♪ 797. The largest heron in Peru. Note the white neck and black cap. Fairly common in aquatic lowlands e of Andes to 900 m. Rare along coast and in highlands to 3000 m. Recent sighting on coast at Panatanos de Puerto Viejo (MAP). *E Panama to the Guianas, Brazil, s Chile and Argentina.*

[Great Blue Heron] *Ardea herodias* Garza Azulada
117 cm (46"). Not illustrated. Similar to Cocoi Heron, but neck is gray. Sight record from Río Llullapichis, Huánuco (pers. comm. P. Donahue). *Alaska to nw South America; Galapagos Is.; West Indies*

Great Egret *Ardea alba* Garza Grande
96 cm (38"). Plate 7. ♪ 797. A large white heron with a long, yellow bill, black legs and feet. Much larger than other white herons. Fairly common in aquatic lowlands e of Andes to 900 m; regular in *puna* zone to 4100 m; common along coast. *Cosmopolitan; wide distribution worldwide.*

Tricolored Heron *Egretta tricolor* Garcita Tricolor
60 cm (23.5"). Plate 7. ♪483. The only heron that is mostly dark gray, except for a white belly and white foreneck. Immature has a rufous hindneck, rufous shoulders and rufous edges to wing coverts. Rare along coast, but regular at Lagunas de Mejía and Pisco marshes. Common at Manglares de Tumbes. Recently recorded at Boca de Manu (Madre de Dios). *Tropical e US to s Peru, ne Brazil; Greater Antilles.*

Little Blue Heron *Egretta caerulea* Garcita Azul
58 cm (22.5"). Plate 7. Adult is the only dark, slate-blue heron. Dark maroon neck becomes brighter during breeding season. Adult and immature bill is gray with a blackish tip. Immature is all white, except for black tips to primaries. Fairly common in coastal marshes, mudflats and mangroves, especially at Lagunas de Mejía and Pisco marshes; accidental in Cusco at 3750 m. *US to s Brazil and Uruguay; West Indies.*

Snowy Egret *Egretta thula* Garcita Blanca
58 cm (22.5"). Plate 7. ♪626. The only white heron with black legs, yellow feet and a long, black bill. Cf. Great and Cattle Egrets. Common along coast and in humid aquatic lowlands; uncommon in Junín, Cusco and Puno to 4000 m. *Locally from US to central Argentina; West Indies.*

Cattle Egret *Bubulcus ibis* Garcita Bueyera
43 cm (17"). Plate 8. ♪626. Unmistakable in breeding plumage. In non-breeding, note fairly short yellow bill and greenish-yellow legs. Seasonally common to uncommon throughout. *Cosmopolitan; wide distribution worldwide.*

Striated Heron *Butorides striatus* Garcita Estriada
40 cm (15.5"). Plate 7. ♪797. A small, bittern-like heron, mostly grayish below, with a black crown and yellow legs. Both bitterns are buffy-rufous (not gray). Uncommon along coast and in humid lowlands e of Andes to 900 m; regular in September in Junín and Cusco to 4000 m. *Cosmopolitan (except North and Central America).*

Agami Heron *Agamia agami* Garza Pechicastaña
71 cm (28"). Plate 8. A dark heron with a very long bill, chestnut belly and rufous hind-neck. Immature is browner above, with dark stripes on a whitish belly. Cf. Tricolored Heron. Rare in humid lowlands e of Andes to 900 m. Largest-known nesting colony in world of ±150 birds at Lago Sándoval. *Mexico to n Bolivia and w Amazonian Brazil.*

Black-crowned Night-Heron *Nycticorax nycticorax* Huaco Común
63 cm (25"). Plate 7. ♪797. Adult has a black crown and back; underparts are white to smoky gray. Color pattern recalls that of Boat-billed Heron, but latter's bill is much wider and heavier. Streaked immature recalls smaller Striated Heron or immature Yellow-crowned Night-Heron. Uncommon along coast; fairly common in *puna* zone; rare in humid lowlands e of Andes. *Cosmopolitan (except Australasia).*

Yellow-crowned Night-Heron *Nyctanassa violacea* Huaco Coroniamarilla
71 cm (28"). Plate 7. ♪627. Adult's head pattern is unique (but cf. Black-crowned Night-Heron). Streaked immature resembles that of Black-crowned Night-Heron, but is ginger-rufous. Fairly common in mangroves along n coast. *Lowlands of s North America to Peru and Brazil; Galápagos Is.*

Boat-billed Heron *Cochlearius cochlearius* Garza Cucharón
60 cm (23.5"). Plate 8. ♪542. Nocturnal; small groups roost in trees. Recalls Black-crowned Night-Heron, but very wide bill is distinctive. Immature has buffy underparts and reddish-brown upperparts. Rare in humid lowlands e of Andes to 900 m. Large population at Lago Sándoval, possibly a predator in Agami Heron rookery. *Mexico to n Argentina and Brazil.*

[Bare-throated Tiger-Heron] *Tigrisoma mexicanum* Garza-Tigre Mexicana
71-81 cm (28-32"). Plate 7. Note limited range. Similar to Fasciated Tiger-Heron (no overlap), but adult has yellow bare skin on the throat ,and bill is longer and narrower. Rare and local in mangroves near El Algarroble in Manglares de Tumbes National Park (pers. comm. BPW). *Wet lowlands of Mexico to nw Colombia.*

Fasciated Tiger-Heron *Tigrisoma fasciatum* Garza-Tigre Oscura
66 cm (26"). Plate 8. Note habitat. Adult's gray neck readily separates it from adult Rufescent Tiger-Heron. Immature is very similar to that of Rufescent Tiger-Heron, but latter's bill is slightly longer (hard to discern unless compared directly). Uncommon in premontane fast-flowing streams and rivers e of Andes at 600-1800 m, and in semiarid valleys in Cusco, Ayacucho and Apurímac to 3300 m. *Costa Rica to nw Argentina and se Brazil.*

Rufescent Tiger-Heron *Tigrisoma lineatum* Garza-Tigre Colorada
71 cm (28"). Plate 8. ♪ 797. Adult's rufous neck is obvious; however, immature is very similar to that of Fasciated Tiger-Heron. Cf. possible occurrence of Pinnated Bittern. Common in humid lowlands e of Andes to 900 m. *Honduras to n Argentina and Amazonian Brazil.*

Zigzag Heron *Zebrilus undulatus* Garza Zebra
32 cm (12.5"). Plate 8. ♪ 542. A very small, heavily vermiculated, dark heron. Immature has a rufous head and neck and vermiculated back. Cf. small bitterns and Striated Heron. Rare in humid lowlands e of Andes to 900 m. *Locally along ponds and streams of Amazon basin.*

Stripe-backed Bittern *Ixobrychus involucris* Mirasol Listado
33 cm (13"). Plate 7. A very small, buffy bittern, with black stripes on the back. Least Bittern has a solid-colored back. Rare austral-winter migrant in humid lowlands e of Andes to 900 m. Recent records from Manu National Park. *S Venezuela and the Guianas to central Argentina and Chile.*

Least Bittern *Ixobrychus exilis* Mirasol Leonado
26 cm (10.1"). Plate 7. ♪ 797. Very small, similar to Stripe-backed Bittern, but only two white stripes on a solid back (black in male and chestnut in female). Hind-neck is rufous. Fairly common along coastal lagoons with extensive reed beds; uncommon in humid lowlands e of Andes to 300 m. *S Canada to Argentina; West Indies.*

Pinnated Bittern *Botaurus pinnatus* Mirasol Grande
76 cm (30"). Plate 7. Similar to immature tiger-herons, but breast is striped, and wings and back are streaked (not barred). Numerous sight records and photographs from Zona Reservada de Tambopata; also recorded near Iquitos. *Lowlands of se Mexico to n Argentina and Brazil.*

Ciconiidae (Storks; Cigüeñas). Species: World 19; Peru 3
A family of long-legged wading birds closely related to the New World vultures. The majority of species are found in the Old World tropics, with three species restricted to the New World. Northern species are migratory, and even the sedentary species exhibit considerable seasonal movements for food. They feed primarily on a wide variety of animals associated with their grassland and marshy habitats, including frogs, fish, snails and small reptiles. Several members of the family feed on carrion.

Wood Stork *Mycteria americana* Cigüeña Gabán
102 cm (40"). Plate 11. ♪ 626. No other large wading bird has a bare black neck and head, and a slightly decurved bill. In flight shows black flight feathers and white underwing coverts (somewhat like a King Vulture or Maguari Stork). Immature bill is yellowish. Uncommon in aquatic lowlands e of Andes; rare along n coast and in *puna* zone in Junín and Cusco. *Southern US to n Argentina and Brazil; Cuba and Hispaniola.*

Maguari Stork *Ciconia maguari* Cigüeña Maguari
96 cm (38"). Plate 11. A typical stork with a white body, black flight feathers, and a long, straight, grayish bill. In flight the white neck distinguishes it from Wood Stork. Rare but increasingly recorded visitor to lowland savanna e of Andes along Río Tambopata and Pampas del Heath. *Tropical plains and marshes of South America.*

Jabiru *Jabiru mycteria* Jabirú
132 cm (52"). Plate 11. ♪ 797. The huge, upturned black bill makes this large stork unmistakable. In flight shows all white underparts. Immature's body is spotted brown with a dark head. Rare to uncommon and local throughout, mostly in lowland aquatic habitats e of Andes. *Locally from s Mexico to n Argentina and Brazil.*

Threskiornithidae (Ibises and Spoonbills; Bandurrias y Espátulas). Species: World 33; Peru 8
Ibises are long-legged, aquatic birds, adapted for obtaining food by probing their long, decurved bills in shallow water, while spoonbills are adapted for catching floating prey in shallow water. Both find their food more by touch than by sight, and feed on a wide variety of vertebrates and invertebrates.

[Plumbeous Ibis] *Theristicus caerulescens* Bandurria Mora
73 cm (29"). Not illustrated. A uniformly gray ibis, with a white forehead and bushy crest. Records of Tschudi (1844-1846) are probably erroneous. *Lowlands of Brazil and Bolivia to n Argentina.*

Andean Ibis *Theristicus branickii* Bandurria Andina
71 cm (28"). Plate 11. Unmistakable in its range. Cf. its coastal counterpart Black-faced Ibis. Uncommon and local in *puna* zone north to Ancash and Huánuco at 3000-5000 m. Regularly recorded at Laguna Huacarpay at 3060 m. *Andes of Ecuador to extreme n Chile.*

Black-faced Ibis *Theristicus melanopis* Bandurria Carinegra
71 cm (28"). ♪ 797. Plate 11. Very similar to Andean Ibis (no overlap) but has a larger black wattle on throat. Rare in coastal hills from sea level to 2500 m. Recently recorded in Bosque Pomac near Chiclayo. *Coastal Peru, n Chile and Argentina to Tierra del Fuego.*

Green Ibis *Mesembrinibis cayennensis* Ibis Verde
58 cm (22.5"). Plate 11. ♪ 797. The only dark ibis in its range with dark-greenish bare parts and a dark-green body. Note relatively short legs. Uncommon in humid lowlands e of Andes to 600 m. *Lowlands of Costa Rica to ne Argentina and Brazil.*

White Ibis *Eudocimus albus* Ibis Blanco
60 cm (23.5"). Plate 11. ♪ 483. The attractive all-white adult with its decurved red bill and legs is distinctive. Brownish immature has a white belly and pinkish bill. Fairly common in mangroves along n coast. *S US to coastal n Peru; Bahamas and Greater Antilles.*

White-faced Ibis *Plegadis chihi* Ibis Cariblanco
50 cm (19.5"). ♪ 626. Plate 11. Non-breeding: like Puna Ibis, but bill is dusky-yellowish (not reddish), and legs are pale dusky-greenish. In breeding plumage has a white border to bare skin on face, a yellowish bill, maroon neck and red legs. Rare (accidental?) along southern coast. *Western US to central Argentina and s Brazil.*

Puna Ibis *Plegadis ridgwayi* Ibis de la Puna (Yanavico)
58 cm (22.5"). Plate 11. The only dark ibis in its range with a reddish bill. Cf. White-faced Ibis. Recently small populations have been established on the coast year round, and have bred at Pantanos de Villa (González et al. 1999). Common in *puna* zone north to Ancash at 3500-4800 m; rare along coast. *High Andes of central Peru to nw Argentina and n Chile.*

Roseate Spoonbill *Ajaia ajaja* Espátula Rosada
81 cm (32"). Plate 11. Easily identified by its unique bill shape and baby-pink plumage. Immature is much paler. Rare in coastal Tumbes and Piura; fairly common in humid lowlands e of Andes. Recent sight records at Pantanos de Villa. *Southern US to n Argentina and Brazil; West Indies.*

Phoenicopteridae (Flamingos (Flamencos). Species: World 5; Peru 3
A small family of large, brilliantly colored aquatic birds, distinguished from other waders by their long legs and necks and bent, thick, black-tipped bills. In flight they carry their necks extended like storks. Fossil evidence suggests they were once widespread in Europe, North America and South America, but they are now a relict group that occurs mainly in isolated pockets in the tropics. Flamingos are confined to shallow soda lakes and salt lagoons, often barren of vegetation and surrounded by desert-like wastes. They live in colonies and feed on minute mollusks, algae and diatoms, which they sift with their bill.

Chilean Flamingo *Phoenicopterus chilensis* Flamingo Chileno
119 cm (47"). Plate 6, 8. ♪797. In all plumages, bill is mostly black and pinkish-gray. Adults have gray legs with red "knees" (joints) and feet. Common on freshwater saline lakes on altiplano south of Ayacucho and Junín, and common austral-winter visitor along coast, especially at Paracas and Lagunas de Mejía. *Andes of s South America; pampas of s Brazil to s Argentina.*

***Andean Flamingo** *Phoenicopterus andinus* Parina Grande
127 cm (50"). Plate 8. In all plumages, the basal half of bill is yellow, and other half is black. Adults have yellow legs. Common on saline lakes at 2300-4300 m from Arequipa south, rarely north to Ayacucho. Accidental on coast at Lagunas de Mejía. *High Andes of s Peru to nw Argentina and n Chile.*

Puna (James') Flamingo *Phoenicopterus jamesi* Parina Chica
109 cm (43"). Plate 8. ♪797. Smaller that its two congeners, and in all plumages most of the bill is yellow with only the tip black. Adult legs are a dark pink. Uncommon on saline lakes above 4000 m in s Peru, especially at Lake Salinas (Arequipa) and Lake Parinacochas (Ayacucho). *High Andes of s Peru to nw Argentina and n Chile.*

Anhimidae (Screamers; Gritadores). Species: World 3; Peru 2
The screamers are large relatives of the waterfowl, usually encountered in marshes and aquatic habitats. They typically feed on marsh plants, but supplement their vegetarian diet with insects. The three species are restricted to South America.

Horned Screamer *Anhima cornuta* Gritador Unicorno (Camungo)
89 cm (35"). Plate 9. ♪797. Unmistakable. At close view note the horn-like plume. In flight shows white shoulders, and occasionally soars high like a raptor. Fairly common in lowlands e of Andes to 900 m. *Wet lowlands of Venezuela to n Bolivia and Amazonian Brazil.*

Southern Screamer *Chauna torquata* Gritador Austral (Chajá)
86 cm (34"). ♪797. Facing Plate 9. Note limited range. Built like Horned Screamer, but grayer overall, with a conspicuous crest to gray head. Legs and bare facial skin are red. Note the prominent black ring on neck (a second thinner white ring is sometimes visible). Recorded along lower Río Tambopata (Parker 1982) and recently recorded 52 km nw of Puerto Maldonado on Río Madre de Dios (Servat and Pearson 1991). *Wet lowlands of se Peru to n Argentina and s Brazil.*

Anatidae (Ducks, Geese and Swans; Patos y Gansos). Species: World 157; Peru 22
The ducks, geese and swans are usually associated with aquatic or marine habitats, and range in size from the 40-pound Whooper Swan (possibly the heaviest flying bird) to the minuscule 35-cm Ringed Teal. They breed on every major continent and island, and though usually associated with fresh water, many are well adapted to saltwater habitats. The dabbling ducks are primarily vegetarian, while the mergansers are entirely piscivorous. Many waterfowl are noted for their long-distance migrations, while others are year-round sedentary residents.

Fulvous Whistling-Duck *Dendrocygna bicolor* Pato-Silbón Canelo
48 cm (19"). Plate 10. ♪797. A tawny duck, best identified by the combination of brown back, dark line on hind neck and white crissum. In flight uppertail coverts form a bold "U". Rare throughout; one December nesting record from Lake Junín. *Southern US to Argentina; e Africa, Madagascar and s Asia.*

White-faced Whistling-Duck *Dendrocygna viduata* Pato-Silbón Cariblanco
43 cm (17"). Plate 10. ♪797. A distinctive duck with a white face and rufous neck. Uncommon in tropical lowlands e of Andes, occasionally in highlands. *Costa Rica to Brazil; Africa, Madagascar and Comoro Is.*

Black-bellied Whistling-Duck *Dendrocygna autumnalis* Pato-Silbón Ventrinegro
48 cm (19"). Plate 10. ♪797. No other duck has the combination of black belly, grayish face and reddish bill. In flight shows a conspicuous white wingbar. Uncommon in tropical lowlands e of Andes; occasional along coast. *Aquatic habitats of Texas to n Argentina.*

Andean Goose *Chloephaga melanoptera* Ganso Andino (Huallata)
76 cm (30"). Plate 9. ♪797. A large, unmistakable, black and white goose. Common in *puna* zone from Ancash south, breeding mainly at 4000-5000 m, and moves lower in winter, rarely to coast. *Andes of s Peru to nw Argentina and central Chile.*

Orinoco Goose *Neochen jubata* Ganso del Orinoco
58 cm (22.5"). Plate 9. Unmistakable. In flight shows white wing coverts and dark-green secondaries. Uncommon along waterways in lowlands e of Andes. Greatly reduced in numbers or extirpated in much of e Peru. *Orinoco and Amazon River basins to nw Argentina.*

Muscovy Duck *Cairina moschata* Pato Criollo
Male 83 cm (33"); female 66 cm (26"). Plate 9. A large, dark duck (appears black in the field) with a white wing-patch. Often perches in trees. Uncommon along lowland waterways e of Andes; casual along coast. *Lowlands of s Mexico to Argentina and Brazil.*

Comb Duck *Sarkidiornis melanotos* Pato Crestudo
Male 76 cm (30"); female 55 cm (21.5"). Plate 10. No other duck has a mostly white head (with some dark speckles), dark upperparts, dark sides of the body, and white on remainder of the underparts. New World race *sylvicola* sometimes considered a separate species from nominate race of tropical Africa and Asia. Rare and local on Pacific slope south to Lambayeque. Accidental at Lake Junín (Fjeldså and Krabbe 1990). *Africa, Madagascar to SE Asia; locally in South America.*

Torrent Duck *Merganetta armata* Pato de los Torrentes
38 cm (15"). Plate 9. Unmistakable. Two ssp. usually recognized in Peru. Race *leucogenis* (central Peru northward) and *turneri* (s Peru) differ by color of underparts. Females of both ssp. have rufous underparts and gray upperparts. Locally uncommon in clear montane streams with rapids at 900-4300 m. Commonly seen from train between Ollantaytambo and Machu Picchu. *Andes of nw Venezuela to Argentina and Chile.*

[Chiloe Wigeon] *Anas sibilatrix* Pato Overo
48 cm (19"). Plate 10. Accidental? The only duck with a dark green head, white face and rufous flanks. In flight shows a white rump and a large white panel on the upperwing. Reported as shot at Lake Junín by a local hunter. *Southern South America and Falkland Is.; winters to se Brazil.*

[Mallard] *Anas platyrhynchos* Pato Cabeziverde
58 cm (22.5"). Not illustrated. Both sexes have a violet-blue speculum bordered with white. Male has a narrow white collar that separates a chestnut breast from a green head. Pair observed at Pantanos de Villa (Wust 1994). Probably released captive birds. *Palearctic and North America; winters to India and Borneo.*

Speckled Teal *Anas flavirostris* Pato Barcino
43 cm (17"). Plate 10. The only duck with a dark-gray head, yellow bill and pale unmarked underparts. Chest is speckled. In flight shows a green patch to base of upperwing, and whitish trailing edge. Cf. Yellow-billed Pintail. Common on highland lakes at 2500-4500 m; descends to lower elevations July-October. *Andes of Venezuela to Tierra del Fuego.*

Crested Duck *Anas specularioides* Pato Crestón
60 cm (23.5"). Plate 9. ♪ 797. A large, brownish duck with a crested head, dark bill, and a dark patch around the eye. In flight shows a black tail, purple-coppery speculum, and white trailing edge. Common in temp. zone at 2500-4500 m, usually breeding above 4000 m. *Andes of Peru to Tierra del Fuego and Falkland Is.*

Yellow-billed Pintail *Anas georgica* Pato Jergón
55 cm (21.5"). Plate 10. ♪ LNS. A uniformly buffy-brown duck with a paler head, yellow bill and a rather long, pointed tail. Underparts are scaled, much darker than in Speckled Teal. In flight shows a dark-green speculum bordered with buffy above and below. Cf. Speckled Teal. Common in *puna* zone at 3400-4500 m; descends to coast where locally common. *Southern Colombia to Tierra del Fuego; South Georgia I.*

White-cheeked Pintail *Anas bahamensis* Pato Gargantillo
43 cm (17"). Plate 6. The white cheeks and red base to bill are diagnostic. Common along coast. Accidental at Lake Junín. *Locally in South America, West Indies and Galápagos Is.*

Puna Teal *Anas puna* Pato de la Puna
48 cm (19"). Plate 9. ♪ 797. No other Peruvian duck has the combination of a blue bill and a black crown sharply bordered with white cheeks and throat. In flight shows a green speculum bordered with white above and below. Common in *puna* zone at 3000-4600 m; rare on coast. *Andes of Peru to nw Argentina and n Chile.*

Blue-winged Teal *Anas discors* Pato Aliazul
38 cm (15"). Plate 10. ♪ 626. Male's dark blue head with a white crescent on the face and speckled body is distinctive. Brownish female is very similar to that of Cinnamon Teal (sometimes indistinguishable), but latter has a larger bill, and more rufous-brown tones to body. Both sexes have black bills. In flight the wing pattern is like that of Cinnamon Teal. Rare migrant September-May throughout. Of annual occurrence in small numbers in coastal lagoons. Recorded at Laguna Huacarpay and at Lake Junín. *Breeds North America; winters s US to central Argentina.*

Cinnamon Teal *Anas cyanoptera* Pato Colorado
40 cm (15.5"). Plate 6. ♪ 626. Male is uniform chestnut and distinctive. Female has a rather uniform brown body (cf. female Blue-winged Teal). Both sexes in flight have a light-blue forewing and green speculum separated by a white bar. Common along coast and patchily distributed in *puna* zone at 2500-4300 m. *Southwest Canada to Tierra del Fuego and Falkland Is.*

Red Shoveler *Anas platalea* Pato Cuchara Rojizo
45 cm (17.5"). Plate 9. Both sexes have a wide, shovel-like bill that is often held down, almost touching the water. Male has pale head, ginger body and black crissum. Female is uniformly grayish-brown, but head is paler. Male in flight shows white outer tail feathers, blackish rump, blue forewing and a green speculum. Small population resident in highlands of Puno and Cusco; recorded at Lagunas de Mejía (Pyhälä and Fjeldså). *Southern Peru and s Brazil to Tierra del Fuego.*

Rosy-billed Pochard *Netta peposaca* Pato Picazo
50 cm (19.5"). Plate 10. Austral-winter vagrant. Both sexes have a white bar on flight feathers. Distinctive male has a black head, neck and upperparts, silvery flanks and a red bill, somewhat swollen on its base. Female is similar to female Southern Pochard, but has white undertail coverts (not tawny), and more blurry whitish face markings. Two records, one from Lagunas de Mejía and one from Río Manu. *Lowlands of se Brazil to s Argentina and Chile.*

Southern Pochard *Netta erythrophthalma* Pato Morado
43 cm (17"). Plate 10. ♪ 797. Male is dark brown, and has a gray bill and red eyes. Female has a uniform tawny-brown body, and bold white facial markings. In flight shows a wide white wingbar. Cf. Rosy-billed Pochard. Rare, with scattered records from San Martín, s Ayacucho, Cusco and along coast. *Patchily distributed Africa and South America.*

Masked Duck *Oxyura dominica* Pato Enmascarado
35 cm (14"). Plate 9. The only stiff-tailed duck in its range. Fairly small. Often elusive. In flight shows a white wing-patch. Male has a black face mask and a tawny body. Female is buffy with two dark lines through the face. Cf. Andean Duck. Rare in lowlands e of Andes to 800 m. Several records from coast, primarily in department of Lima. *S Texas to n Argentina and Brazil; West Indies.*

Andean Duck *Oxyura ferruginea* Pato Andino
43 cm (17"). Plate 10. ♪ LNS. The only stiff-tailed duck in its range. Larger than Masked Duck. Male has a chestnut body, black head and blue bill. Female is dark brown with an indistinct face pattern. Fairly common in temp. and *puna* zones at 2000-4400 m; regular along coast at Lagunas de Mejía. *Locally in Andes of Colombia to Argentina and Chile.*

Cathartidae (New World Vultures; Cóndores y Gallinazos). Species: World 7; Peru 6
Primarily large, carrion-feeding birds, closely related to the storks—and not the Old World Vultures—which they resemble in their feeding habits. They range from Canada to Tierra del Fuego. The Andean Condor was highly regarded in the pre-Hispanic cultures. The Turkey Vulture has one of the most highly developed olfactory systems of any bird, and King Vultures habitually soar high in the sky, watching the low-flying Turkey Vultures for any sign of a hidden meal.

Black Vulture *Coragyps atratus* Gallinazo Cabecinegra
63 cm (25"). Plate 11. Note the black head. In flight has shorter wings and tail than other vultures and shows whitish base to primaries. Common to fairly common in lowlands, especially around human habitations; occasionally to 2900 m in n Peru. *Southern US to central Argentina.*

Turkey Vulture *Cathartes aura* Gallinazo Cabecirrojo
73 cm (29"). Plate 11. Widespread. Head is red. Race *ruficollis* east of Andes has a whitish nape. Often seen soaring with raised wings in a typical "V". Flight feathers are paler than underwing coverts, creating a two-tone effect. Sympatric and similar to both yellow-headed vultures. Cf. "mimic" Zone-tailed Hawk. Common throughout lowlands; rare and local in Andes; accidental at 4300 m in *puna* zone. *Canada to Tierra del Fuego.*

Lesser Yellow-headed Vulture *Cathartes burrovianus* Gallinazo Cabeciamarilla Menor
76 cm (30"). Plate 11. Note habitat. Longer-winged than similar Turkey Vulture. Note white shafts at base of outer primaries. Often forages low in savanna and marshland. Greater Yellow-headed Vulture is larger, bulkier and blacker. Rare in grassy marshes along larger Amazonian rivers e of Andes (mainly a savanna species). *Savanna of s Mexico to n Argentina and Brazil.*

Greater Yellow-headed Vulture *Cathartes melambrotus* Gallinazo Cabeciamarilla Mayor
83 cm (33"). Plate 11. Broad wings have contrasting inner primaries. Soars over forested areas with wings held flat. Larger, darker and broader-winged than both Turkey and Lesser Yellow-headed Vultures. Fairly common in humid lowland forests e of Andes. *S Venezuela and the Guianas to n Bolivia and n Brazil.*

Andean Condor *Vultur gryphus* Cóndor Andino
106 cm (42"). Plate 11. A huge vulture with a wingspan approaching ten feet (3.3 m)! Note the silvery upper wings and white collar on neck. Immature is a uniform sooty brown, and takes six years to obtain full adult plumage. Widespread but local in Andes. Regularly descends to coast, but extirpated by guano workers at Paracas Peninsula for supposed harassment of chicks of nesting guano birds. Most intimate and reliable views at Cruz del Cóndor (Arequipa). *Colombia to Tierra del Fuego.*

King Vulture *Sarcoramphus papa* Gallinazo Real
76 cm (30"). Plate 11. Adult is distinctive. High-soaring individuals may resemble a soaring stork. Dark immature has a black head and irregular whitish patches on underparts. Uncommon in lowlands and premontane forests, occasionally to 2300 m. *Andes and coasts of Colombia to Tierra del Fuego.*

Pandionidae (Osprey; Aguila Pescadora). Species: World 1
This large, fish-eating bird of prey is the only member in its monotypic family. The feet are very strong, and the toes bear tiny tubercles on their undersurfaces to give a good grip on slippery fish. Ospreys have a wide distribution worldwide, but occur in South America only during the northern winter.

Osprey *Pandion haliaetus* Aguila Pescadora
55 cm (21.5"). Plate 13. ♪ 626. In all ages a diagnostic dark line goes through the eye. Adult has a white cap and mostly white underparts. Juvenile is similar, but back and upperwing edged whitish. Osprey's long and slightly angled wings give a distinctive flight profile. In flight underwing shows a dark patch around carpal joint. Uncommon migrant and northern-winter visitor along tropical rivers and oxbow lakes. Fairly common along coast, especially at Lagunas de Mejía; occasionally to 4100 m during migration. *Cosmopolitan; wide distribution worldwide.*

Accipitridae (Hawks, Eagles and Kites; Elanios, Gavilanes y Aguilas)
Species: World 236; Peru 48
This is the largest family of diurnal birds of prey, ranging from the tiniest sparrowhawks to enormous eagles with wingspans approaching 8 feet (2.5 meters). They breed from the Arctic to the tropics, in every habitat from tundra and desert to dense tropical forests. They feed on insects, mollusks, crabs, fish, reptiles, birds and mammals. Many are year-round residents, but others, such as Broad-winged and Swainson's Hawks, make incredible annual migrations of thousands of miles.

Gray-headed Kite *Leptodon cayanensis* Gavilán Cabecigris
48 cm (19"). Plate 12. ♪613. Adult readily recognized by the combination of gray head, whitish underparts, slate-gray back and long banded tail. In flight note rounded wings with dark underwing coverts. Immature is polymorphic. Light morph (illustrated) is similar to adult Black-and-white Hawk-Eagle (sympatric in Loreto) but latter's back is grayer and it has an orange cere with black lores, and white shoulders. Dark morph has a brown hood, and brown streaks on chest. Uncommon in humid lowland forests e of Andes, occasionally to 2000 m. *S Mexico to the Guianas, Brazil, e Bolivia, Paraguay and n Argentina.*

Hook-billed Kite *Chondrohierax uncinatus* Gavilán Piquiganchudo
43 cm (17"). Plate 12. ♪626. Multimorphic. In all morphs can be recognized by heavy hooked bill, and bare skin above the lores. In flight note characteristic oval-shaped wings and banded tail. Dark morph has 1-2 broad white bands on tail. Uncommon in lowland and subtrop. forests e of Andes, rarely to 2500 m. *S US and w Mexico to Brazil and n Argentina; e Cuba and Grenada.*

Swallow-tailed Kite *Elanoides forficatus* Gavilán Tijereta
60 cm (23.5"). Plate 12. ♪797. Unmistakable. Uncommon in lowland and subtrop. forests e of Andes; uncommon along Pacific slope; recorded at Lake Junín and crossing Milloc Pass at 5000 m. Migrating flock of 92 birds recorded at Amazonia Lodge 12 Oct. 2000. *Coastal se US to Brazil and n Argentina.*

Pearl Kite *Gampsonyx swainsonii* Gavilán Perla
23 cm (9"). Plate 12. A tiny kite, smaller even than an American Kestrel. Uncommon along n Pacific slope south to la Libertad, and in drier trop. lowland forests e of Andes to 900 m. *Savanna of Nicaragua to nw Argentina and Brazil.*

[White-tailed Kite] *Elanus leucurus* Gavilán Coliblanca
38 cm (15"). Not illustrated. Note falcon-like shape, long, pointed wings, and long white tail. Mostly white below and pale gray above, shoulders black. Hovers like a kestrel. A single unconfirmed record from Cusco at 4200 m (Fjeldså and Krabbe 1990). *Southern US to Argentina and Brazil.*

Snail Kite *Rostrhamus sociabilis* Gavilán Caracolero
40 cm (15.5"). Plate 12, 13. ♪797. Note the strongly hooked, thin bill. In all plumages shows white at base of tail and white crissum. Immature is similar to female, but has less streaking on buff underparts. Slender-billed Kite is similar, but lacks white at base of tail. Fairly common e of Andes in lowland forest marshes and swamps with Apple (*Pomacea*) snails. *Freshwater marshes of Florida to Argentina, Brazil; Cuba.*

Slender-billed Kite *Rostrhamus hamatus* Gavilán Piquigarfio
36 cm (14"). Plate 12. Sexes are alike. Built like Snail Kite, but shorter-tailed, and lacks the white at base of tail. Tail is solid dark in adult and banded buff in immature. Cf. Slate-colored Hawk (single white band in mid-tail and much shorter bill). Common in humid lowland *várzea* forests e of Andes. *E Panama to the Guianas, n Bolivia and Amazonian Brazil.*

Double-toothed Kite *Harpagus bidentatus* Gavilán Bidentado
33 cm (13"). Plate 12. ♪652. A black stripe in middle of throat, combined with white fluffy undertail coverts and banded tail, are diagnostic in all ages and plumages. In flight note tapered wings and fairly long accipiter-like tail. Immature is similar to adult but browner above (especially on head) and whitish below (streaked or unstreaked). Uncommon in humid lowland forests e of Andes, occasionally in subtrop. zone to 2500 m. *S Mexico to n Bolivia and Amazonian Brazil.*

Mississippi Kite *Ictinia mississippiensis* Gavilán del Mississipi
38 cm (15"). 35 cm (14"). Facing Plate 12. Accidental. Similar to Plumbeous Kite, but primaries are black (no rufous), tail is black (no pale bands), appears pale headed, secondaries are pale gray. Sight record from Cocha Cashu (Terborgh *et al.* 1984). *Breeds southern U.S.; winters in South America*

Plumbeous Kite *Ictinia plumbea* Gavilán Plomizo
35 cm (14"). Plate 13. ♪ 797. Falcon-like. Very long pointed wings and white band on tail. Dark-gray adult shows rufous on primaries. Immature has whitish underparts streaked with gray, and mostly dark wings. Common in humid lowland forests e of Andes, occasionally in subtrop. zone to 2300 m and w of Andes in Tumbes. *Eastern Mexico to ne Argentina and se Brazil.*

Long-winged Harrier *Circus buffoni* Gavilán Alilarga
46-61 cm (18-24"). Plate 15. Accidental. A harrier of lowland savanna (no overlap with Cinereous Harrier). Male is mostly black above, except for white rump, gray primaries and gray bands on tail. Below: black breast and white belly (sometimes all black below). Female and immature similar but chocolate-brown above and buffier below. Sight record from Pampas del Heath (Schulenberg *in litt.*). *Grasslands of tropical South America, Trinidad and Tobago.*

Cinereous Harrier *Circus cinereus* Gavilán Cenizo
48 cm (19"). Plate 13. ♪ 797. Lightly built with an owl-like face. In flight long wings are held raised. Note long tail with a white rump. Bluish-gray male in flight shows black tips to primaries, and black trailing edge to secondaries. Female and immature are chestnut-brown, heavily speckled with white, especially on underparts and underwing coverts. Uncommon along entire coast; fairly common in *puna* zone at 2500-4500 m. *Andes of Colombia to Tierra del Fuego; Falkland Is.*

Gray-bellied Goshawk *Accipiter poliogaster* Gavilán Ventrigris
48 cm (19"). Plate 15. A large accipiter that resembles Slaty-backed Forest-Falcon, but lores on Gray-bellied Goshawk are gray (extensive bare yellow skin in the forest-falcon), crown is blacker than back (concolor in latter), and tail is square at the end (forest-falcons have a longer, graduated tail). Cf. also smaller Bicolored Hawk that has rufous thighs. Immature color pattern resembles that of Ornate Hawk-Eagle, but latter is much larger and has a spiky crest. Rare in humid lowland forests e of Andes to 500 m. *Rare and local in humid forests of South America.*

Tiny Hawk *Accipiter superciliosus* Gavilán Enano
25 cm (9.8"). Plate 13. ♪ 797. Like a miniature version of Barred Forest-Falcon, but lacks extensive bare skin around the eye. Tail is square and not graduated. Has a faint superciliary. Larger female is browner above and buffier below. Cf. very similar Semicollared Hawk. Rare in humid lowland forests e of Andes to 1500 m. *Nicaragua to extreme ne Argentina and Brazil.*

Semicollared Hawk *Accipiter collaris* Gavilán Semiacollarado
33 cm (13"). Plate 13. Very similar to Tiny Hawk, but normally found at higher elevations (limited overlap), is larger than respective sexes of Tiny Hawk, and has white or rufous nuchal collar, and finely streaked cheeks. Cf. also forest-falcons and other accipiters. Rare (accidental?) in humid subtrop. forests on e slope of Andes in Cusco ca 1700 m. *Mountains of sw Venezuela to s Peru.*

Plain-breasted Hawk *Accipiter ventralis* Gavilán Pechillano
30 cm (11.7"). Plate 13. ♪ LNS. Small. Normally found at higher elevations than any other small accipiter. Typical adult has rufous thighs and dark to rufous barring on breast. A rare all-black morph also occurs. Immature is similar, but streakier below. Cf. Semicollared Hawk (lacks rufous thighs). Uncommon in humid montane forests at 1500-3600 m. Together with Rufous-thighed Hawk *A. erythronemius* of se South America forms part of the superspecies of Sharp-shinned Hawk *A. striatus. Andes of w Venezuela to w Bolivia.*

Bicolored Hawk *Accipiter bicolor* Gavilán Bicolor
43 cm (17"). Plate 13. ♪613. Similar to smaller Plain-breasted Hawk (no overlap), but Bicolored Hawk has gray (sometimes pale) unbarred underparts. Rare in Pacific slope forests south to Lambayeque; uncommon in humid lowland forests e of Andes. *Lowlands of s Mexico to Tierra del Fuego.*

Crane Hawk *Geranospiza caerulescens* Gavilán Zancón
53 cm (21"). Plate 10. ♪797. When perched recognized by long red legs, slim, slate-gray body, and two white bands on tail. In flight easily identified by white crescent at base of primaries and two tail bands. Cf. Plumbeous and Slate-colored Hawks (more robust, orange cere, single tail band). Uncommon along Pacific slope south to Lambayeque to 1500 m; rare in lowland forests e of Andes to 900 m. *Mexico to Argentina and Brazil.*

Plumbeous Hawk *Leucopternis plumbea* Gavilán Plomizo
38 cm (15"). Plate 15. Note limited range. Like Slate-colored Hawk (no overlap), but underwings are white. Cf. Crane Hawk (slimmer body with two tail bands). Rare along Pacific slope in Tumbes to 1500 m. *Tropical forests of e Panama to nw Peru.*

Slate-colored Hawk *Leucopternis schistacea* Gavilán Pizarroso
43 cm (17"). Plate 12. ♪797. A robust, uniformly slate-gray hawk with an orange cere and a single white tail band (sometimes there is an additional band close to base of tail). Cf. Plumbeous and Crane Hawks. Uncommon in lowland *várzea* forests e of Andes to 900 m. *Venezuela to e Bolivia and Amazonian Brazil.*

Barred Hawk *Leucopternis princeps* Gavilán Barreteado
55 cm (21.5"). Plate 15. Accidental? A dark-hooded hawk with finely barred underparts, and two to three tail bands (median band more prominent). Recalls Black-chested Buzzard-Eagle, but latter has a much shorter unbanded tail. Recent sight records near Río Afluente (TV and MS) and headwaters of Río Cenepa (TSS). *Humid montane forests of Costa Rica to n Ecuador.*

Black-faced Hawk *Leucopternis melanops* Gavilán Carinegro
38 cm (15"). Plate 15. Note limited range. A *Leucopternis* recognized by its mostly white head (with a dark eye patch and fine black streaks on the crown and nape), dark mantle spotted with white and a median white band on a black tail. Cf. sympatric White Hawk (black tail with white terminal band), and White-browed Hawk (darker head, white superciliary). Rare in humid lowland forests e of Andes in Loreto to 500 m. Recently recorded in Iquitos region, and north of Pucallpa. *S Venezuela to ne Ecuador and n Amazonian Brazil.*

White-browed Hawk *Leucopternis kuhli* Gavilán Cejiblanco
35 cm (14"). Plate 13. No other hawk has a dark head and white superciliary combined with a white median tail band. Cf. White and Black-faced Hawks. Rare in humid lowland forests e of Andes south to Madre de Dios to 900 m. *Lowlands of e Peru, n Bolivia and s Amazonian Brazil.*

White Hawk *Leucopternis albicollis* Gavilán Blanco
55 cm (21.5"). Plate 15. ♪797. The only *Leucopternis* with a broad white terminal band to the mostly black tail. Head is all white. Cf. Black-and-white Hawk-Eagle (tail is mostly white with a few black bands). Uncommon in humid lowland and subtrop. forests e of Andes to 2800 m. *Humid forests of s Mexico to n Bolivia and Amazonian Brazil.*

*Gray-backed Hawk *Leucopternis occidentalis* Gavilán Dorsigris
50 cm (19.5"). Plate 13. The only *Leucopternis* in its limited range. Note the white tail with a broad black subterminal band. Crown, nape and sides of face are gray with fine black streaks. Rare in lowland forests in nw Peru to 1300 m. Recorded in Zona Reservada de Tumbes and Cerros de Amotope (Whiffen and Sadgrove 2000). *Montane forests of w Ecuador and adjacent nw Peru.*

Mangrove Black-Hawk *Buteogallus subtilis* Gavilán Manglero
53 cm (21"). Plate 13. Note limited range. Can be distinguished from larger Great Black-Hawk by dark base to tail, and a fairly narrow median tail band. Note brownish cast to belly and flight feathers. Immature is dark above and buffy below, underparts are heavily streaked, and tail is banded gray and buff. Uncommon in coastal mangroves in Tumbes. *Pacific coasts and rivers of El Salvador to extreme nw Peru.*

Great Black-Hawk *Buteogallus urubitinga* Gavilán Negro
66 cm (26"). Plate 13. ♪ 797. The only black hawk with a white base to the tail and a broad black terminal tail band. The only black hawk over much of its range. Cf. Solitary Eagle and Mangrove Black-Hawk. Immature similar to immature Mangrove Black-Hawk, but appears longer-tailed and broader-winged. Cf. also immature Solitary Eagle. Uncommon along Pacific slope to 1500 m; fairly common in humid lowland forests e of Andes to 900 m. *Lowlands of Mexico to n Argentina.*

Savanna Hawk *Buteogallus meridionalis* Gavilán Sabanero
60 cm (23.5"). Plate 13. ♪ 797. A stocky, mostly rufous hawk of open areas. In flight note short, dark tail (one white median band) and broad wings. Superficially similar to Black-collared Hawk. Fairly common along Pacific slope south to La Libertad to 1500 m; uncommon in humid lowland forests e of Andes to 900 m. *Savanna and marshes of w Panama to n Argentina.*

Harris' (Bay-winged) Hawk *Parabuteo unicinctus* Gavilán Mixto
48 cm (19"). Plate 13. ♪ 797. Adult is chocolate-brown overall with conspicuous chestnut shoulder patches, leggings and wing linings. Shows white at base of tail and wing linings. Immature is similar, but underparts are gray and streaky, wing linings rufous and flight feathers pale. Uncommon along Pacific slope to 2500 m; accidental in temp. zone in Lima at 3200 m. *Arid sw US to n Argentina, Chile and Brazil.*

Black-collared Hawk *Busarellus nigricollis* Gavilán de Ciénega
48 cm (19"). Plate 14. ♪ 797. Adult is unmistakable with its rufous body, pale head and black chest band. Immature is browner with a pale head. Uncommon along rivers and oxbow lakes in humid lowland forests e of Andes to 900 m. *Wet lowlands of s Mexico to n Argentina and Brazil.*

Black-chested Buzzard-Eagle *Geranoaetus melanoleucus* Aguilucho Pechinegro
68 cm (27"). Plate 14. ♪ 797. A large raptor. The combination of very short tail, wide-based wings with rather pointed tips, give it its characteristic flight silhouette. Adult has a distinctive dark hood and chest contrasting with a whitish belly. White wing lining contrasts with dark flight feathers. Upperparts are slate-gray, but silvery-gray on shoulders. Immature's wing shape as in adult, but tail is longer, underparts are mottled dark brown, and has buff wing linings. Uncommon in montane *puna* and *páramo* at 2500-3700 m; uncommon in coastal lomas. *Andes of Venezuela to n Argentina and s Brazil.*

Solitary Eagle *Harpyhaliaetus solitarius* Aguila Solitaria
71 cm (28"). Plate 15. ♪ 797. Similar to Great Black-Hawk (limited overlap) but larger, broader-winged and shorter-tailed. Note dark base to tail and white median tail band. Immature is similar to that of more widespread Black-chested Buzzard-Eagle, but has more rounded wings, and often shows a "shadow" of a tail band. Rare on humid montane forest slopes and cloud forests at 1500-4500 m. *Locally in montane forests of s Mexico to nw Argentina.*

Gray Hawk *Asturina nitida* Aguilucho Gris
43 cm (17"). ♪ 797. Plate 15. Buteo-like, paler and grayer than similar Roadside Hawk; tail is more contrasting and head is paler. Lacks rufous on primaries. Immature brownish (somewhat mottled) above, buffy underparts with dark spots and blotches. Rare in humid lowland forests e of Andes to 900 m. The South American populations have been considered a separate species (Gray-lined Hawk). *Southwest US to n Argentina and Brazil.*

Roadside Hawk *Buteo magnirostris* Aguilucho Caminero
38 cm (15"). Plate 13. ♪ 797. The only buteo-like hawk with rufous at the base of primaries (often seen only in flight) and a gray head. Note the evenly spaced banded tail. Relatively short-winged. Immature has dark streaks on breast and a barred belly. Cf. Gray Hawk and migratory Broad-winged Hawk. Fairly common in humid lowland and subtrop. forests to 2500 m, occasionally to 3000 m on e Andean slopes. *Mexico to n Argentina and Brazil.*

Broad-winged Hawk *Buteo platypterus* Aguilucho Aliancha
43 cm (17"). ♪ 626. Plate 15. Like Roadside Hawk, but lacks rufous on wings. Variable, but averages browner on back and more rufous on underparts than Roadside and Gray Hawks. Immature has lightly streaked whitish underparts, and whitish underwing (especially on primaries). Rare northern-winter migrant in Andes (Oct.-March) at 500-3000 m, occasionally to 4000 m. Occasional along coast during migration. *Breeds e North America and West Indies; winters to s Brazil and Bolivia.*

White-rumped Hawk *Buteo leucorrhous* Aguilucho Lomiblanco
38 cm (15"). Plate 15. ♪ 797. The only small black *Buteo* with a white rump, white undertail coverts and rufous thighs. In flight shows tawny wing linings, dark flight feathers and two white narrow tail bands. Immature is similar with heavily mottled underparts. Uncommon and local in premontane forests on e slope of Andes at 1500-2500 m. *Montane and lowland forests of Venezuela to n Argentina and s Brazil.*

Short-tailed Hawk *Buteo brachyurus* Aguilucho Colicorto
43 cm (17"). Plate 15. A buteo with a medium-length tail and broad wings. Typical light morph has dark-brown upperparts, a black helmet (crown and cheeks), white underparts, white wing linings and mostly whitish tail, with a narrow dark terminal band. Cf. White-throated Hawk (limited overlap). In dark-morph birds, dark wing lining contrasts with paler gray flight feathers, and pale-gray tail has a narrow black terminal band. Cf. Swainson's and Zone-tailed Hawks. Immature light morph is similar to adult, but tail bands are more evenly spaced, and underparts are lightly streaked. Fairly common in humid lowland forests e of Andes to 900 m; on Pacific slope recorded at Campo Verde (Tumbes). *Florida to n Argentina and Brazil.*

White-throated Hawk *Buteo albigula* Aguilucho Gargantiblanco
49 cm (19"). Plate 15. ♪ LNS. Recalls typical Short-tailed Hawk (very little overlap), but tail lacks a terminal band and is darker toward the tip. White underparts are streaked on flanks and side of breast (creating a semicollar), thighs are barred with rufous, and wing lining is mostly white. Cf. similar plumaged Variable Hawk (longer tail). Immature similar to adult, but has ginger wing lining and heavier streaks on underparts, especially on chest. Uncommon in montane forests on e slope of Andes at 2100-3500 m. Second record from w slope of Andes at Chiguata (Arequipa) at 3000 m (Høgsås *et al.* in prep.). *Locally in Andes of Venezuela to nw Argentina.*

Swainson's Hawk *Buteo swainsoni* Aguilucho de Swainson
50 cm (19.5"). Plate 15. ♪ 626. A buteo with long, pointed wings. Typical adult underparts are the diagnostic brown chest, white throat and whitish belly (often barred rufous on the sides). In flight white wing lining contrasts with blackish flight feathers. Grayish tail has a narrow black terminal band. Dark morph is similar to that of Short-tailed Hawk, but has much longer wings and tail. Immature is similar to adult, but buff underparts are heavily streaked on chest and breast. Rare migrant in lowlands e of Andes from August to October and in March. *Arid w North America; winters to Argentina.*

White-tailed Hawk *Buteo albicaudatus* Aguilucho Coliblanca
55 cm (21.5"). Plate 15. ♪ 797. Note limited range. A large buteo with long, pointed wings. Variable. All morphs have a whitish tail with a black subterminal band. Typical adult has mostly white underparts, gray upperparts and head, and rufous shoulders. Short-tailed Hawk has a shorter tail and wings. Immature has variable amounts of dark on underparts, but tail as in adult. Uncommon in open grasslands in Pampas del Heath. *Arid Texas to Argentina and Brazil.*

Variable (Red-backed) Hawk *Buteo polyosoma* Aguilucho Variable
(including Puna Hawk *Buteo poecilochrous*)
55 cm (21.5"). Plate 13. ♪ 797. A medium-sized to large buteo (populations at the higher elevations —Puna Hawk) average larger, and have broader, more eagle-like wings. All adult plumages have white to grayish tails with a fairly wide black subterminal band, and a narrow white terminal band. The red-backed morph is common. Immature lacks the black subterminal band. Fairly common in montane scrub to *puna* at 1800-5000 m, occasionally lower on coastal slope. Recorded as low as 760 m (JFC). There is considerable controversy regarding the recent lumping of these two forms (for a detailed analysis of the reasons for this treatment see Farquhar 1998). *Andes of Colombia to Tierra del Fuego; Falkland Is.; Más Afuera I.*

Zone-tailed Hawk *Buteo albonotatus* Aguilucho Colifajeado
50 cm (19.5"). Plate 11. ♪ 626. Surprisingly similar to Turkey Vulture (often soar together), and like it holds its two-toned wings in a dihedral. Has two whitish bands on tail and finely barred flight feathers. Other black hawks have shorter wings and tails. Immature has white spots on underparts, and a grayish tail with narrow black bands. Uncommon in trop. and subtrop. forests to 2500 m. *Southwest US to n Bolivia and Brazil.*

Crested Eagle *Morphnus guianensis* Aguila Crestada
83 cm (33"). Plate 15. ♪ 542. Very large, similar to Harpy Eagle, but slimmer and smaller. Single pointed crest. Lacks the black chest band of adult Harpy Eagle. Weaker bill, smaller tarsi and proportionately longer-tailed than Harpy Eagle. Barred morph has a darker head and barred underparts. In all ages has white unmarked wing lining. Rare in humid lowland gallery forests e of Andes to 600 m. *Forests of e Guatemala to ne Argentina and Brazil.*

Harpy Eagle *Harpia harpyja* Aguila Harpía
94 cm (37"). Plate 14. Huge, with enormous beak and tarsi. Prominent double-pointed crest. Adult's black chest band is diagnostic. Immature is similar to smaller Crested Eagle, but wing lining always shows some dark lines. Rare in humid lowland forests e of Andes to 600 m. Recent nesting records from Lago Sándoval and Tambopata. *Central America to northeast Argentina and Brazil.*

Black-and-white Hawk-Eagle *Spizastur melanoleucus* Aquila Blanquinegra
60 cm (23.5"). Plate 15. Note limited range. White below including wing lining, black above, white leading edge to upperwing often striking in flight, white head with a short black crest (when pressed looks like a black cap), and fairly long tail banded with gray. Smaller immature Gray-headed Kite lacks black lores and crest. Cf. immature Ornate Hawk-Eagle (barred thighs and flanks). Rare in humid lowland forests e of Andes in Loreto to 500 m. *Southern Mexico to n Argentina and Brazil.*

Black Hawk-Eagle *Spizaetus tyrannus* Aquila Negra
71 cm (28"). Plate 15. ♪ 797. All black except for white barring on legs and vent, a short, pied crest, and multi-banded long tail. In flight, rather rounded wings pinched at base, whitish flight feathers banded with black, and dark wing lining. Immature underparts are heavily streaked, dark facial mask, white superciliary and banded flight feathers. Cf. dark morph Collared Forest-Falcon. Uncommon in humid lowland forests e of Andes to 1500 m; rare on w slope in Tumbes. *S Mexico to ne Argentina and Brazil.*

Ornate Hawk-Eagle *Spizaetus ornatus* Aquila Penachuda
63 cm (25"). Plate 15. ♪ 797. Attractive adult unlikely to be confused (long spiky crest, black border to white throat, rufous back and sides of head, remainder of underparts and legs barred). Plumage of immature Gray-bellied Goshawk similar but lacks crest and is smaller. Immature has white underparts and head, with some barring on flanks, thighs and wing lining. Cf. Black-and-white Hawk-Eagle. Uncommon in humid lowland forests east of Andes to 600 m, occasionally to 1200 m. *S Mexico to n Argentina and Brazil.*

Black-and-chestnut Eagle *Oroaetus isidori* Aguila Negricastaña
73 cm (29"). Plate 15. ♪ EC-007T. A large, dark eagle with a long crest. Head and upperparts black, underparts deep chestnut, gray tail with a wide black terminal band. In flight, chestnut underwing lining and a pale panel on base of primaries. Immature can be identified by its large size, broad wings, streaked buffy underparts, cinnamon wing lining, wide dark terminal band, and 2-3 narrower bands on tail. Rare along montane slopes on e slope of Andes at 1750-2500 m (occasionally to 3500 m). *Andes of Venezuela to nw Argentina.*

Falconidae (Caracaras and Falcons; Caracaras y Halcones). Species: World 63; Peru 19
Diurnal birds of prey that resemble hawks and eagles, but differ in defecating directly below the perch, and killing prey by breaking the neck with the beak. Some of the forest-falcons are crepuscular and hunt mainly at dusk. They occur worldwide in every type of terrain, but only the genus *Falco* is cosmopolitan.

Black Caracara *Ibycter ater* Caracara Negro
48 cm (19"). Plate 14. ♪ 797. The only black bird of prey with extensive red on the face. Often seen along riverbeds. Fairly common in humid lowland forests e of Andes to 900 m. *S Venezuela and the Guianas to n Bolivia and Amazonian Brazil.*

Red-throated Caracara *Daptrius americanus* Caracara Ventriblanco
55 cm (21.5"). Plate 14. ♪ 797. The only black bird of prey with a red throat-patch and white belly. Cf. larger curassows. Uncommon in humid lowland trop. and upper trop. forests e of Andes to 1500 m. *Extreme s Mexico to n Bolivia and Brazil.*

Mountain Caracara *Phalcoboenus megalopterus* Caracara Cordillerano
53 cm (21"). Plate 14. ♪ 797. Unmistakable. White wing lining is conspicuous in flight. Brownish immature has pale rump and whitish panel at base of primaries. Very common in *páramo* and *puna* grasslands at 3000-5000 m; regularly occurs down to Pacific coast in s Peru. *Páramo of Peru to nw Argentina and n Chile.*

Crested Caracara *Caracara cheriway* Caracara Crestada
60 cm (23.5"). Plate 16. Very similar to Southern Caracara (recently considered conspecific), but Crested's upper breast is white, and lower breast only coarsely barred (entire breast finely barred in Southern). Lower back is black in Crested, but entire back is barred in Southern. Fairly common along Pacific slope s to La Libertad and San Martín from sea level to 2500 m. *S US through Central America to n Peru and Amazon River.*

Southern Caracara *Caracara plancus* Caracara Carancho
60 cm (23.5"). Plate 14. ♪ 797. Recent split from Crested Caracara (American Ornitholigists' Union 2000). Adult is very distinctive, but cf. Crested Caracara. Immature is like adult but underparts are spotted buff and upperparts are spotted white. Rare along Pacific slope north to central Peru from sea level to 2500 m; uncommon in savanna and deforested areas in se Peru to 400 m. *Central Peru and c Bolivia s to Tierra del Fuego and Falkland Islands.*

Yellow-headed Caracara *Milvago chimachima* Caracara Chimachima (Shihuango)
45 cm (17.5"). Plate 14. ♪ 797. A small and slender caracara. Note the pale head and underparts, long wings with pale panel on base of primaries and longish tail with a wide dark subterminal band. Cf. Laughing Falcon. Immature is similar, but browner. Locally common in humid lowland forests e of Andes to 900 m. *Savanna of sw Costa Rica to n Argentina and Brazil.*

Laughing Falcon *Herpetotheres cachinnans* Halcón Reidor
55 cm (21.5"). Plate 14. ♪ 797. Distinctive. Often seen perched atop dead trees. Cf. Yellow-headed Caracara (only a narrow black eye line). Rare along Pacific slope south to Lambayeque to 1500 m; uncommon in humid lowland forests e of Andes to 900 m. *Mexico to n Argentina and Brazil.*

Micrastur **Forest-Falcons.** Raptors superbly adapted for forest hunting, with short wings and long, graduated tails. They have a large area of bare skin on the face (cere, lores and eye-ring). Some *Accipiters* are similar, but they have a squarish tail, and lack such facial skin. Identification is challenging: note color of cere, number of tail bands and presence (or lack) of barring on underparts.

Barred Forest-Falcon *Micrastur ruficollis* Halcón de Monte Barreteado
38 cm (15"). Plate 12. ♪ 797. Very similar and often sympatric with Lined Forest-Falcon, but note that cere is yellow (Lined's cere is orange), and eye color is amber (white in Lined). Tail is relatively longer than that of Lined, but wings are shorter, giving it a different look. Barring (especially on lower underparts) is stronger in Barred Forest-Falcon. Note that Lined usually has two white tail bands, but Barred can have one, two or three bands. Cf. Semicollared Hawk and Tiny Hawk. Uncommon in lowland trop. and subtrop. forests e of Andes to 1500; recorded at Zona Reservada de Tumbes (TAP). *Mexico to n Argentina and Brazil.*

Lined Forest-Falcon *Micrastur gilvicollis* Halcón de Monte Listado
38 cm (15"). Plate 12. ♪ 797. A forest-falcon with barred underparts and two white bands on tail. Very similar to Barred Forest Falcon. Uncommon in humid *terra firme* forests e of Andes to 900 m. *S Venezuela and the Guianas to n Bolivia and Amazonian Brazil.*

Slaty-backed Forest-Falcon *Micrastur mirandollei* Halcón de Monte Dorsigris
40 cm (15.5"). Plate 12. ♪ 797. The only forest-falcon with a dark-slate back that lacks barring on the underparts, and a white nuchal collar. Usually has three tail bands. Cf. Collared and Buckley's Forest-Falcons and immature Bicolored Hawk. See also Gray-bellied Goshawk. Uncommon in humid lowland forests e of Andes to 900 m. *Costa Rica to Bolivia and Amazonian Brazil.*

Collared Forest-Falcon *Micrastur semitorquatus* Halcón de Monte Acollarado
60 cm (23.5"). Plate 12. ♪ 797. The largest of the forest-falcons. Multimorphic. Typical pale morph (illustrated) can be separated from Slaty-backed Forest-Falcon by its white collar and darker eyes. Very similar to Buckley's Forest-Falcon. Tawny morph has a cinnamon wash to underparts and tawny to white collar. Rare black morph can be identified by its size, long, graduated, banded tail, and finely barred vent area. Immature is brownish, with scales and broken barring on underparts. Uncommon in humid lowland forests e of Andes, and w of Andes in Tumbes to 900 m. *Mexico to n Argentina and Brazil.*

Buckley's Forest-Falcon *Micrastur buckleyi* Halcón de Monte de Buckley
50 cm (19.5"). Plate 12. ♪ 652. A smaller version of Collared Forest-Falcon. Note that outer tail feathers have four bands (rather than 5 or 6 as in Collared Forest-Falcon). Female shows white spots on scapulars. Immature is similar to that of Collared, but has a buffy wash on unmarked breast. Rare and local in humid lowland forests e of Andes to 900 m. Recent records from Manu Wildlife Center and Amazonia Lodge. *Locally in e Ecuador and e Peru.*

American Kestrel *Falco sparverius* Cernícalo Americano
27 cm (10.5"). Plate 14. ♪ 797. A very small falcon. Both sexes can be identified by their facial markings, rufous back and tail. Hovers in kite-like fashion. Often bobs its tail. Fairly common to abundant along coast, in Andean valleys and highlands, from sea level to 4500 m. *Widespread open country and scrub of North and South America.*

Aplomado Falcon *Falco femoralis* Halcón Aplomado
45 cm (17.5"). Plate 14. ♪ 797. Diagnostic head markings distinguish it from any other falcon. Immature has buffier underparts. In flight note long, narrow wings, and long tail. Uncommon throughout, mainly in drier regions, especially in Andes at 2000-4600 m; seasonally descends to coast. *Northern Mexico to Tierra del Fuego.*

Merlin *Falco columbarius* Halcón Esmerejón
33 cm (13"). Facing Plate 14. ♪ 626. Slightly larger than American Kestrel, and lacks conspicuous face markings. Back is brown to gray (never rufous), and tail has 2-3 pale bands. Much larger Peregrine Falcon always shows noticeable sideburns. Rare northern-winter migrant along coast. *Holarctic; winters to northern South America, India and Mediterranean region.*

Bat Falcon *Falco rufigularis* Halcón Cazamurciélagos
25 cm (9.8"). Plate 14. ♪ 797. Note the "vest" of mostly black with fine white barring. Throat and collar are mostly buff. Often sits on dead snags. Cf. Orange-breasted Falcon. Rare along Pacific slope to 1500 m. Fairly common and conspicuous along oxbow lakes and rivers in lowlands e of Andes. *Central Mexico to n Argentina and Brazil.*

Orange-breasted Falcon *Falco deiroleucus* Halcón Pechinaranja
38 cm (15"). Plate 14. Larger than more common Bat Falcon. Vest is coarsely barred (fairly equal thickness buff and black). Bat Falcon's vest is mostly black, finely barred with white. Conspicuous white throat often is the best indicator. Orange-breasted Falcon has proportionately larger head, larger feet and a shorter tail. Rare in humid lowland forests e of Andes; rarely to lower temp. zone in Cusco at 3000 m. *Southern Mexico to n Argentina and Brazil.*

Peregrine Falcon *Falco peregrinus* Halcón Peregrino
50 cm (19.5"). Plate 14. ♪ 626. A large falcon with distinctive black sideburns. Often seen near cliffs and in cities. Underparts lack any rufous. Immature is brown with streaky underparts and dark sideburns. Uncommon migrant throughout. Recorded regularly from coast to 4300 m, with possible breeding records from Cusco, Junín, Lambayeque and Piura. *Nearly worldwide distribution.*

Cracidae (Chachalacas, Guans, and Curassows; Chachalacas, Paujiles y Pavas)
Species: World: 50; Peru 15
A family of large gallinaceous birds, mainly confined to the New World tropics from Mexico to northern Argentina. Their food consists primarily of fruits, seeds and other vegetable matter. Chachalacas and curassows spend a great deal of time scratching for their food on the ground, but guans rarely descend to the ground. The dawn chorus of a flock of chachalacas is one of the characteristic sounds of the tropical and subtropical forests.

*Rufous-headed Chachalaca *Ortalis erythroptera* Chachalaca Cabecirrufa
55 cm (21.5"). Plate 17. The only chachalaca in its range. Note the rufous head and chestnut on primaries. Cf. Sickle-winged Guan. Rare along Pacific slope and foothills in Tumbes to 1850 m. Recorded in Zona Reservada de Tumbes and Cerros de Amotape. *W Ecuador and extreme nw Peru.*

Speckled Chachalaca *Ortalis guttata* Chachalaca Jaspeada
53 cm (21"). Plate 17. ♪ 542. The only chachalaca in most of Peru. Note the gray head and neck are speckled with white, and outer tail feathers are rufous. Fairly common in humid lowland and subtrop. forests e of Andes to 2700 m. *Patchily distributed Colombia to n Bolivia and Brazil.*

*Bearded Guan *Penelope barbata* Pava Barbada
60 cm (23.5"). Plate 17. ♪ LNS. The only guan in its range with a rufous terminal tail band. Cf. Andean Guan (lacks tail band). Uncommon in montane forests in Piura, Cajamarca and Lambayeque at 1200-3000 m. *Locally in Western Andes of sw Ecuador to nw Peru.*

Andean Guan *Penelope montagnii* Pava Andina
60 cm (23.5"). Plate 17. ♪797. The only "red-wattled" guan over most of its range. Cf. Bearded Guan (local, terminal tail band) and Spix's Guan (larger, larger wattle, usually at lower elevations). Fairly common in humid montane forests at 1800-3500 m (to 3900 m in Pasco). *Andes of w Venezuela to nw Argentina.*

Crested Guan *Penelope purpurascens* Pava Crestada
72-91 cm (36"). Not illustrated. Similar to smaller Spix's Guan (unlikely to overlap), but crest is slightly more developed, white speckling on throat and breast are more pronounced. Cf. also smaller Andean Guan. Numerous sight records from extreme n Peru, including Pozo del Pato (Whiffen and Sadgrove 2000). *S Mexico to e Venezuela and se Ecuador*

*White-winged Guan *Penelope albipennis* Pava Aliblanca
60 cm (23.5"). Plate 17. Note limited range. The only guan with white primaries. Rare and local in dry wooded foothill valleys in Lambayeque. 1997 population estimated at ±100 birds. Recorded at Quebrada Caballito above El Tocto, Hacienda Boca Chica, Quebrada Limón and Hacienda Recalí. *Endemic to Peru.*

Spix's Guan *Penelope jacquacu* Pava de Spix (Pucacunga)
66 cm (26"). Plate 17. ♪797. The only "red-wattled" guan over most of its range. In contact zone Andean Guan is smaller, has much smaller wattle, bare skin on face, and browner back. Fairly common in humid lowland and lower subtrop. forests e of Andes to 1500 m. *S Venezuela and the Guianas to n Bolivia and Amazonian Brazil.*

Blue-throated Piping-Guan *Pipile cumanensis* Pava Gargantiazul
60 cm (23.5"). Plate 17. ♪797. Unmistakable. Note the white crown and white wing panel. Fairly common in humid lowland forests e of Andes to 900 m. *S Venezuela and the Guianas to n Bolivia and Brazil.*

Wattled Guan *Aburria aburri* Pava Carunculada
71 cm (28"). Plate 17. ♪816CD. A black guan with a long yellow wattle, blue bill and yellow legs. Uncommon in humid subtropical forests at 1000-1900 m, with extremes at 500 m and 2300 m. *Subtropical forests of w Venezuela to s Peru.*

Sickle-winged Guan *Chamaepetes goudotii* Pava Alihoz
63 cm (25"). Plate 17. ♪797. Note the bare blue skin on face, and chestnut underparts. The only guan that lacks a throat wattle. Uncommon in humid montane forests at 1500-2500 m, with records at 900 m in Amazonas and 3000 m in Puno. *Montane forests of n Colombia to Andes of w Bolivia.*

Nocturnal Curassow *Nothocrax urumutum* Paujil Nocturno
66 cm (26"). Plate 17. ♪619. Note limited range. Note the yellow crescent above the eye and blue-gray skin under the eye. The only brown cracid with a curly crest. Often heard calling during the night, but rarely seen during the day. Rare in humid *terra firme* forests near rivers in Loreto; uncommon at ACEER. *S Venezuela to ne Peru and w Amazonian Brazil.*

Salvin's Curassow *Mitu salvini* Paujil de Salvin
89 cm (35"). Plate 17. ♪619. Note limited range. Similar to Razor-billed Curassow, but has a white belly. Sexes similar. Uncommon in humid *terra firme* forests north of the Amazon in Loreto. *S Colombia, e Ecuador and ne Peru.*

Razor-billed Curassow *Mitu tuberosa* Paujil Común
89 cm (35"). Plate 17. ♪797. Identified by the large red casque on its bill, chestnut belly, and white tip to the tail. Rare in humid lowland forests e of Andes south of the Amazon. Recorded at Cocha Cashu, Tambopata Reserve and Lago Sándoval to 900 m; recorded in Cordillera Vilcabamba at 1340 m. Fairly common at Pacaya Samiria National Reserve (Begazo and Valqui 1998). *SE Colombia to n Bolivia and Amazonian Brazil.*

*Horned Curassow *Pauxi unicornis* Paujil Unicorno
91 cm (36"). Facing Plate 17. ♪797. Sexes similar. No other curassow has a blue casque. Very rare in humid upper trop. forests at 450-1200 m in Cerros del Sira (Huánuco) and Cerros de Távara (Puno). *Andes of central Peru and central Bolivia.*

*Wattled Curassow *Crax globulosa* Paujil Carunculado (Piuri)
89 cm (35"). Plate 17. Both sexes have a curly crest, red cere (bare skin on base of bill), and lack white tail tips. Female is similar to male, but lacks bill knobs, and has a chestnut belly. Rare in humid lowland forests e of Andes to 300 m, mainly in Iquitos region, lower Río Marañón, lower Río Ucayali and Madre de Dios. Two birds shot by a hunter near village of Nueva Esperanza (Loreto) in 1996 (Begazo and Valqui 1998). *SE Colombia to n Bolivia and w Amazonian Brazil.*

Odontophoridae (New World Quail; Codornices del Nuevo Mundo). Species: World 31; Peru 4
A small family of medium-sized, terrestrial gallinaceous birds adapted to feeding on vegetable material on the forest floor. Their incredibly loud vocalizations are one of the characteristic sounds of the tropical and subtropical forests of Central and South America.

Marbled Wood-Quail *Odontophorus gujanensis* Codorniz Carirroja
27 cm (10.5"). Plate 18. ♪797. A rather uniform, rufous-brown wood-quail. Note the red eye-ring. Female is similar, but has a scaly throat. Recalls a dull Stripe-faced Wood-Quail, but lacks white spots on underparts. Uncommon in humid lowland subtrop. forests e of Andes to 1800 m. *Costa Rica to Bolivia and Amazonian Brazil.*

Rufous-breasted Wood-Quail *Odontophorus speciosus* Codorniz Pechirrufo
27 cm (10.5"). Plate 18. ♪797. No other wood-quail has a black throat. Uncommon (or overlooked) in humid tropical forests along e base of Andes to 1700 m. *E Ecuador, e Peru and central Bolivia.*

Stripe-faced Wood-Quail *Odontophorus balliviani* Codorniz Enmascarado
27 cm (10.5"). Plate 18. ♪797. Note limited range. The only wood-quail in its elevation. Note the white spots on underparts, black stripe under the eye, and red eye-ring. Rare (or overlooked) in dry montane forests in e Andean slopes of Cusco and Puno at 2000-3400 m. *Andes of se Peru and w Bolivia.*

Starred Wood-Quail *Odontophorus stellatus* Codorniz Estrellado
25 cm (9.8"). Plate 18. ♪646. The only wood-quail in its range with a gray neck and small white spots on chest. Female's crown is dark brown. Fairly common in humid lowlands e of Andes to 900 m. *W Amazon basin.*

Opisthocomidae (Hoatzin; Shansho). Species: World 1
A large, ungainly looking, sedentary bird, most often encountered in small, noisy groups along the flooded banks of rivers, streams and swamps in tropical South America. The Hoatzin is one of the few birds that has a digestive system that enables it to live on the leaves, flowers, seeds and fruits of marsh plants, especially the white mangrove *Avicennia* and *Montrichardia*. A taxonomic puzzle, with some authors suggesting they are closely related to the cuckoos or African turacos.

Hoatzin *Opisthocomus hoazin* Hoazín (Shansho)
63 cm (25"). Plate 8. ♪797. Unmistakable. Common in lowland aquatic habitats e of Andes. *Amazon and Orinoco basins and the Guianas.*

Aramidae (Limpkin; Carrao). Species: World 1
Limpkins are slender, long-necked wading birds confined mainly to the Neotropics. They are residents of wooded swamps and shaded places with an abundant vegetation of herbs, bushes and trees. Their diet consists mainly of large water snails of the genus *Pomacea*, supplemented with other aquatic animal matter.

Limpkin *Aramus guarauna* Carrao (Tarahui)
66 cm (26"). Plate 9. ♪797. Distinctive. Immature ibises aren't as spotted and have more slender, decurved bills. Rare along lowland forest streams, oxbow lake margins and rivers e of Andes to 900 m. *SE US to n Argentina and Brazil; West Indies.*

Psophiidae (Trumpeters; Trompeteros). Species: World 3; Peru 2
Trumpeters are plump, chicken-like residents of the Neotropical rainforests. They are primarily terrestrial, and fly only infrequently with considerable effort. They can run with surprising agility through the dense foliage of the rainforests, easily eluding dogs and other potential predators. Their food consists of fallen fruit, berries and other vegetable matter, supplemented with insects and small vertebrates. Pet trumpeters are often kept by native villagers to keep the area clear of snakes.

Gray-winged Trumpeter *Psophia crepitans* Trompetero Aligris
55 cm (21.5"). Plate 18. ♪542. Note limited range. Similar to Pale-winged Trumpeter, but secondaries are ash-gray (not white). Rare in humid lowland forests e of Andes in Loreto north of the Amazon. *Amazon basin.*

Pale-winged Trumpeter *Psophia leucoptera* Trompetero Aliblanco
55 cm (21.5"). Plate 18. ♪797. Unlikely to be confused. In limited contact zone cf. Gray-winged Trumpeter. Rare in humid lowland forests e of Andes. Recorded at ACEER, Pacaya Samiria National Reserve, Manu Wildlife Center and Lago Sándoval. *Humid forests of Amazon basin.*

Rallidae (Rails, Gallinules and Coots; Rascones y Gallaretas)
Species: World 134; Peru 29
A large assemblage of superficially fowl-like birds distributed throughout the world. Despite their skulking habits and reluctance to fly—in fact, a number are flightless—many members make long-distance migrations, and there is hardly an oceanic island in the world that has not had a population of these ground-dwelling birds among the resident avifauna. The family as a whole exhibits a catholic diet, ranging from such animal life as insects, worms, snails, crustaceans, fish and amphibians to a variety of vegetable matter.

Ocellated Crake *Micropygia schomburgkii* Gallineta de Ocelos
13 cm (5.2"). Plate 19. ♪797. Note limited range. A very small rail, tawny above with distinctive white spots on the back. Has red legs and a fairly short bill. Cf. immature Sora (larger with barred underparts). Rare in humid grasslands in Pampas del Heath. *Locally from s Venezuela and the Guianas to n Bolivia, central and se Brazil.*

Chestnut-headed Crake *Anurolimnas castaneiceps* Gallineta Cabecicastaña
23 cm (9"). Plate 19. ♪542. A medium-sized rail with a rufous-chestnut head and dusky-greenish bill. Cf. Russet-crowned, Black-banded and Uniform Crakes. Uncommon in lowland *terra firme* forests at 200-1500 m. *Colombia to n Bolivia.*

Russet-crowned Crake *Anurolimnas viridis* Gallineta Coronirrufa
16 cm (6.5"). Plate 19. ♪ 797. Like Chestnut-headed Crake, but note uniform rufous underparts, dark bill and gray cheeks. Cf. also Uniform and Black-banded Crakes. Rare in humid lowland forests e of Andes to 1200 m. *S Venezuela and the Guianas to e Peru and Amazonian Brazil.*

Black-banded Crake *Anurolimnas fasciatus* Gallineta Negrilineada
18 cm (7"). Plate 19. Like Chestnut-headed Crake, but bill is dark, and belly and crissum have dark bands. Cf. Russet-crowned Crake. Rare in humid lowland forests e of Andes to 500 m. *SE Colombia to e Peru and w Amazonian Brazil.*

Rufous-sided Crake *Laterallus melanophaius* Gallineta Flanquirufa
18 cm (7"). Plate 19. ♪ 797. A fairly small rail with a greenish bill. No other crake has the throat and mid-belly rufous on the sides with a white center. Mid-belly to vent is white with black barring. Fairly common in lowland marshes and wet grasslands e of Andes to 1000 m. *Venezuela and the Guianas to n Argentina and Brazil.*

Gray-breasted Crake *Laterallus exilis* Gallineta Pechigris
15 cm (6"). Plate 19. ♪ 797. A small rail with a gray head, rufous nape, greenish bill and legs. Belly and crissum are barred black and white. Cf. larger Ash-throated Crake, Sora and similar-sized Paint-billed Crake. Rare in aquatic lowlands e of Andes to 600 m. *Belize to Bolivia, Amazonian and e Brazil.*

Black Rail *Laterallus jamaicensis* Gallinetita Negra
15 cm (6"). Plate 19. ♪ 626. A tiny rail. Like Junín Rail (no overlap) but lacks heavy barring on back and wings. Note red eyes and rufous nape. Cf. Gray-breasted Crake (gray head and breast). Other young crakes are black, but none have a rufous nape or barred vent. Rare in coastal marshes, but regular at Lagunas de Mejía. *Very local from US to central Argentina and Chile.*

*Junín Rail *Laterallus tuerosi* Gallinetita de Junín
15 cm (6"). Plate 19. The only small crake in its very limited range. Cf. Black Rail (no known overlap). Confined to Lake Junín. Described as a race of Black Rail by Fjeldså and Krabbe 1990, but treated as a species by Collar 1992. Known from two sites on southwest shore near Ondores and Pari. *Endemic to Peru.*

Clapper Rail *Rallus longirostris* Rascón Manglero
33 cm (13"). Plate 19. ♪ 626. The only buffy-brown rail over most of its range. Note the dusky-reddish bill and dusky legs. Virginia Rail is similar but smaller, and has a reddish bill. Fairly common along north coast in Tumbes. *Coastal marshes of US to extreme n Peru and se Brazil; West Indies.*

Virginia Rail *Rallus limicola* Rascón Menor
24 cm (9.4"). Plate 19. ♪ 626. Like Clapper Rail (no overlap), but smaller, and bill and legs are redder. Rare and local along coast from Trujillo to Pisco. Peruvian race *aequatorialis* sometimes considered a separate species (Ecuadorian Rail). *Locally in North America; sw Colombia to w Peru; s Chile and Argentina.*

*Bogotá Rail *Rallus semiplumbeus* Rascón de Bogotá
30 cm (11.7"). Plate 19. Like Clapper Rail, but throat and breast are slate-gray, and long bill is reddish. Recalls Plumbeous and Blackish Rails, but both have yellowish-green bills, and lack barring on vent and lower belly. Single specimen (immature Virginia Rail?) from n Peru from an unknown locality (del Hoyo *et al.* 1996). *Andes of Colombia; single record from Peru.*

Rufous-necked Wood-Rail *Aramides axillaris* Rascón-Montés Cuellirrufo
30 cm (11.7"). Plate 18. The only wood-rail in its limited range. Note the rufous neck and breast, black posterior of underparts, and greenish-yellow bill. Cf. accidental Brown Wood-Rail. Fairly common in coastal mangroves in Tumbes (Parker *et al.* 1995). *Mangroves of nw Mexico to extreme nw Peru; Suriname and Trinidad.*

Gray-necked Wood-Rail *Aramides cajanea* Rascón-Montés Cuelligris
38 cm (15"). Plate 19. ♪797. Entire head and neck are gray, and lower breast to mid-belly are rufous. Cf. Red-winged Wood-Rail. Fairly common in humid lowland forests e of Andes to 2000 m. *S Mexico to n Argentina, Brazil and the Guianas.*

*Brown Wood-Rail *Aramides wolfi* Rascón-Montés Moreno
35 cm (14"). Plate 19. Similar to Gray-necked Wood-Rail, but neck is rufous-brown (not gray), and only head is dusky-gray. Single record from Puerto Pizarro (Tumbes) in September 1977 (Graves 1982). *W Colombia to sw Ecuador.*

Red-winged Wood-Rail *Aramides calopterus* Rascón-Montés Alirrojizo
35 cm (14"). Plate 18. Note limited range. Like Gray-necked Wood-Rail, but lacks rufous on underparts, and has a brown hind neck. Uncommon in seasonally flooded *igapó* forests in Loreto to 400 m. Regularly recorded near Tahuayo Lodge. *E Ecuador, ne Peru and w Amazonian Brazil.*

Uniform Crake *Amaurolimnas concolor* Gallineta Unicolor
23 cm (9"). Plate 19. ♪797. Very similar to Chestnut-headed Crake, but browner. Crown and upperparts are olivaceous-brown, and underparts rufous-brown. Chestnut-headed Crake has head and breast a brighter rufous. Cf. Russet-crowned Crake. Rare in humid lowland oxbow lake margins e of Andes to 900 m. *Locally from s Mexico to e Bolivia and Amazonian Brazil.*

Sora *Porzana carolina* Gallineta Sora
22 cm (8.6"). Plate 19. ♪626. Black mask surrounds a yellow bill. Brownish upperparts have dark streaks. Undertail coverts are unbarred, and legs are greenish. Buffier juvenile lacks mask on face, and recalls smaller Ocellated Crake. Rare northern-winter visitor (Sept.-May) in humid lowland oxbow lake margins. Accidental at Lake Junín (Fjeldså and Krabbe 1990). *S Alaska to n Baja California and s US; winters to West Indies and n South America.*

Ash-throated Crake *Porzana albicollis* Gallineta Garganticeniza
25 cm (9.8"). Plate 19. ♪797. Similar to Sora, but lacks black mask, has a grayer throat and breast, and barred undertail coverts. Bill is greenish-yellow. Uncommon in lowland savanna and scrub in Madre de Dios and Cusco to 600 m; fairly common in Pampas del Heath. *Venezuela and the Guianas to n Argentina and Brazil.*

Paint-billed Crake *Neocrex erythrops* Gallineta Piquipinta
20 cm (8"). Plate 19. A small rail with a red base to the yellow-tipped bill, unstreaked brown upperparts and gray underparts. Cf. Sora. Rare in coastal marshes from Lambayeque to Lima. Recorded at 3600 m in Cusco. *Venezuela and the Guianas to nw Argentina and Brazil; Galápagos Is.*

Spotted Rail *Pardirallus maculatus* Rascón Moteado
25 cm (9.8"). Plate 19. A medium-sized rail with distinctive black and white stripes on the neck, and barred underparts. Rare in coastal marshes and aquatic habitats from Tumbes to La Libertad. Fairly common in rice fields. *Mexico to n Argentina, Brazil and Greater Antilles.*

Blackish Rail *Pardirallus nigricans* Rascón Negruzco
27 cm (10.5"). Plate 19. ♪797. Very similar to larger and more common Plumbeous Rail. Blackish Rail has a white (not gray) chin, black vent and undertail coverts (not olivaceous-brown). Bill is duskier, and lacks a red spot on base of lower mandible. Rare in lowland oxbow lake margins e of Andes to 600 m. Accidental at Lake Junín (Fjeldså and Krabbe 1990). Regularly recorded at Amazonia Lodge. *Locally from sw Colombia to ne Argentina and e Brazil.*

Plumbeous Rail *Pardirallus sanguinolentus* Rascón Plomizo
27 cm (10.5"). Plate 19. ♪ 797. The only rail with lead-gray underparts (no barring), unstreaked brown upperparts, greenish bill and red legs. Cf. Blackish Rail. Common and local from coastal marshes to *puna* zone to 4500 m. *N Peru, e Paraguay and se Brazil to Tierra del Fuego.*

Purple Gallinule *Porphyrula martinica* Polla Morada
33 cm (13"). Plate 19. A colorful gallinule. Frontal shield is light blue, and bill is red with a yellow tip. Immature is buffy brown with a bluish tinge on the wings. Cf. Common Moorhen and Azure Gallinule. Uncommon in lowland oxbow lake margins e of Andes to 600 m; regularly reported from Urubamba Valley (Cusco); reported from coast at Pantanos de Villa. *Locally from s US to n Argentina and West Indies.*

Azure Gallinule *Porphyrula flavirostris* Polla Azulada
25 cm (9.8"). Plate 19. A small gallinule with a bluish wash on the neck, sides of head and wings (especially on shoulder area). Immature Purple Gallinule is similar, but neck is buffy. Uncommon austral-winter migrant in lowland oxbow lake margins e of Andes to 600 m. *Locally from s Venezuela and the Guianas to n Argentina and Brazil.*

Common Moorhen *Gallinula chloropus* Polla de Agua
38 cm (15"). Plate 19. ♪ 626. Widespread. Bill is mostly red with a yellow tip, and has a conspicuous white line on side of body. Immature similar but bill is dusky. Common along coast, and locally common in temperate and *puna* zones at 2000-4200 m. *Cosmopolitan except for Australia and New Guinea region.*

Spot-flanked Gallinule *Gallinula melanops* Polla Pintada
27 cm (10.5"). Plate 19. Patterned more like a crake with a brown back, gray neck and gray breast. Posterior underparts are brown with light spots. Bill and legs greenish. Accidental in humid lowlands e of Andes. *Locally in E Andes of Colombia; s-central South America.*

Andean (Slate-colored) Coot *Fulica ardesiaca* Gallareta Andina
40 cm (15.5"). Plate 6. ♪ 797. Two morphs occur. Red-fronted morph has entire frontal shield red and bill yellow. Cf. Red-fronted Coot has a larger, less rounded frontal shield, and base of bill is red. White-fronted morph has a white bill, and white or yellow frontal shield. Fairly common in *puna* zone north to Ancash at 2100-4700 m and along coast. *Andes of Ecuador to n Argentina and n Chile.*

Red-fronted Coot *Fulica rufifrons* Gallareta Frentirroja
48 cm (19"). Plate 18. Note limited range. Frontal shield is flatter, which gives the head a distinct profile, with an even slope from head to tip of bill. Cf. Slate-colored Coot and Common Moorhen. Uncommon along south coast in Lagunas de Mejía. *Paraguay, Uruguay, se Brazil and extreme s Peru to Tierra del Fuego.*

Giant Coot *Fulica gigantea* Gallareta Gigante
66 cm (26"). Plate 18. ♪ 797. A very large coot with a yellow and red bill and "bumps" on the head. Locally common in *puna* zone north to Ancash at 3100-5000 m; accidental on coast. *Andes of s Peru to n Chile and nw Argentina.*

Heliornithidae (Sungrebes and Finfoots; Aves Sol). Species: World 3; Peru 1
A small family of three species, with a wide range in the tropics. They are residents of tropical lakes and rivers, and swim readily (partially submerged), but usually remain close to the cover of marginal vegetation. Their food includes frogs, worms, crustaceans, mollusks and insects.

Sungrebe *Heliornis fulica* Ave de Sol Americano (Yacupatito)
27 cm (10.5"). Plate 8. ♪ 797. Distinctive. Often swims partially submerged. Male has a yellowish bill, and white (not rusty) cheeks. Uncommon along lowland forest streams, oxbow lake margins and rivers e of Andes to 400 m. *Southern Mexico to ne Argentina and Brazil.*

Eurypygidae (Sunbittern; Tanrilla). Species: World 1
The monotypic Sunbittern is a familiar sight along many oxbow lake margins and streams. Its spectacular nuptial and threat display, with wings widespread, is one of the most beautiful Neotropical bird displays. Their diet consists primarily of insects, small crustaceans and tiny fish, which are caught with a pecking action in shallow water.

Sunbittern *Eurypyga helias* Tigana (Tanrilla)
50 cm (19.5"). Plate 8. ♪ 797. Unique and unmistakable. Spread wings have an unusual "sun" pattern. Two ssp. occur in Peru. Junín and Cusco race *meridionalis* is illustrated. Widespread nominate race has a browner back. Uncommon along lowland forest streams, oxbow lake margins and rivers e of Andes to 500 m, rarely to 1850 m. *S Mexico to n Bolivia and Amazonian Brazil.*

Jacanidae (Jacanas; Jaçanas). Species: World 8; Peru 1
Jacanas are often called lily-trotters because of their extremely long toes and toenails, which enable them to walk over floating vegetation without sinking. They are common inhabitants of tropical ponds, lakes and swamps.

Wattled Jacana *Jacana jacana* Gallito de Agua Frentirrojo (Tuqui-tuqui)
25 cm (9.8"). Plate 19. ♪ 797. Adult is distinctive. In flight shows yellow primaries. Immature has an olive-brown back, yellow flight feathers, and is white below. Note the dark line from the eye to neck, and the white superciliary. Rare along coast south to La Libertad; common in lowland aquatic habitats e of the Andes. *W Panama to the Guianas and n Argentina; Trinidad.*

Haematopodidae (Oystercatchers; Ostreros). Species: World: 11; Peru 2
Fairly large wading birds with long red bills and legs, that frequent rocky shores and coastlines. Most oystercatchers have allopatric distributions, but Peru has two sympatric species, with different feeding and breeding habits. Most species are specialist feeders on bivalve shellfish, a food source utilized by very few other birds.

Blackish Oystercatcher *Haematopus ater* Ostrero Negruzco
48 cm (19"). Plate 6. The only all-black oystercatcher. Immature is sooty black, and has a yellowish bill. Fairly common along coast north to Lambayeque. *Coastal n Peru to Tierra del Fuego.*

American Oystercatcher *Haematopus palliatus* Ostrero Americano
43 cm (17"). Plate 22. ♪ 627. A striking black-and-white bird of the coasts. In flight has a bold white wingbar and rump. Fairly common along entire coast. *Seacoasts and islands of US to s South America.*

Recurvirostridae (Avocets and Stilts; Avocetas y Cigüeñuelas). Species: World 10; Peru 3
Avocets and stilts are long-legged, long-billed waders found throughout the subtropical and temperate regions of the world. They are nomadic, haunting the shores of shallow lagoons and lakes, moving about as conditions change. They feed on small aquatic animals taken from the surface of the water, or from the surface of the submerged mud, at times immersing their entire head and neck.

Black-necked Stilt *Himantopus mexicanus* Cigüeñuela Cuellinegra
50 cm (19.5"). Plate 20. ♪ 797. An elegant wader with very long legs, and black and white plumage. Similar to White-backed Stilt, but has a black crown that circles the eye, leaving a white spot above the eye. Lacks a white collar. Common along coast; fairly common in *puna* zone at 3500-4200 m; breeds at Lake Junín and Lake Titicaca. *US to s Peru and Brazil; Hawaiian Is.*

White-backed Stilt *Himantopus melanurus* Cigüeñuela Dorsiblanco
50 cm (19.5"). Plate 20. Like Black-necked Stilt, but White-backed has a mostly white crown and a white hind collar. Fairly common along lowland watercourses east of the Andes north to Ucayali to 500 m. Recorded at Huacarpay (Cusco). *Aquatic habitats of s South America e of Andes.*

Andean Avocet *Recurvirostra andina* Avoceta Andina
45 cm (17.5"). Plate 20. ♪ 797. Unmistakable, with its slender black upturned bill and white head. Uncommon in *puna* zone north to Lake Junín at 3100-4600 m; casual on coast. *Andes of s Peru to nw Argentina and n Chile.*

Burhinidae (Thick-knees; Alcaravanes). Species: World 9; Peru 1
Thick-knees are fairly large, long-legged waders with yellow eyes, and primarily nocturnal or crepuscular habits. They are mainly birds of open savanna and arid coasts. They are quite catholic in their choice of food, and eat a surprising range of both vertebrates (lizards and small mammals) and invertebrates (arthropods, worms and mollusks).

Peruvian Thick-knee *Burhinus superciliaris* Alcaraván Huerequeque
40 cm (15.5"). Plate 20. A large, unmistakable, nocturnal bird. Individuals or groups often stand motionless for long periods of time. Fairly common along arid Pacific littoral and dry Andean foothills to 2500 m. *Arid lowlands of sw Ecuador to extreme nw Chile.*

Charadriidae (Plovers and Lapwings; Avefrías y Chorlos). Species: World 66; Peru 15
Plovers and lapwings form a large family of waders that is widely distributed along the coasts and waterways of the world. A number of species have adapted to deserts and arid grasslands. Northern-hemisphere species undertake long transequatorial migrations, but tropical species tend to be mostly sedentary. They feed almost entirely on animal food, including insects, crustaceans, arthropods and other invertebrates.

Pied Lapwing *Vanellus cayanus* Avefría Pinta
23 cm (9"). Plate 20. ♪ 797. Attractive and unmistakable. In flight shows a bold wingbar, and black and white lateral lines on back. Fairly common in humid lowland forests e of Andes to 400 m. *Sandbars of larger rivers of South America e of the Andes.*

Southern Lapwing *Vanellus chilensis* Avefría Tero
33 cm (13"). Plate 20. Resembles Andean Lapwing, but foreface and breast are black. Recent records from Iquitos region, with a specimen from Putumayo. Accidental (?) in humid lowlands e of Andes. *Open country, savanna and marshes of South America.*

Andean Lapwing *Vanellus resplendens* Avefría Andina (Lique-lique)
33 cm (13"). Plate 20. ♪ 797. Unmistakable. In flight shows a white wingbar, white rump and sides of tail, and a black terminal tail band. Common in *puna* and *páramo* zones, mainly at 3000-4500 m. Accidental along coast. Recorded at Río Limón (Pyhälä and Brightsmith 1999). *Andes of s Colombia to nw Argentina and n Chile.*

American Golden-Plover *Pluvialis dominica* Chorlo Dorado Americano
27 cm (10.5"). Plate 22. ♪ LNS. A medium-sized plover with a small black bill and black legs. Feathers on upperparts are edged buff to fulvous. Favors fields. In breeding plumage has black on face and most of underparts. In flight lacks wingbars or pale rump, and has whitish underwings. In all plumages similar to respective Black-bellied Plover, but latter is larger, has a longer and heavier bill, is grayer, has a pale wingbar and rump, and a conspicuous black "armpit". Rare northern-winter migrant along coast; fairly common on altiplano March-April; uncommon migrant in humid lowlands e of Andes. *Breeds Arctic North America; winters in s South America.*

Black-bellied (Gray) Plover *Pluvialis squatarola* Chorlo Gris
30 cm (11.7"). Plate 22. ♪ 626. Similar (in respective plumages) to American Golden Plover. In flight black axillars (armpits) are diagnostic. In breeding plumage has black underparts but lower belly and vent are white. Common northern-winter migrant along coast; rare migrant in lowlands e of Andes; rarely to 4100 m on altiplano. *Holarctic; almost cosmopolitan post-breeding dispersal.*

Semipalmated Plover *Charadrius semipalmatus* Chorlo Semipalmeado
17 cm (6.6"). Plate 20. ♪ 626. A small plover with a short black bill (non-breeding and juvenile), or orange with a black tip (breeding). Legs are orange (dark in juvenile). A white collar with a complete breast-band is diagnostic in all plumages. No other small *Charadrius* plover has a white collar. Common northern-winter migrant along coast; accidental on southern altiplano at 4000 m. *Breeds n North America; winters to s South America and Hawaiian Is.*

Wilson's Plover *Charadrius wilsonia* Chorlo Piquigrueso
20 cm (8"). Plate 20. ♪ 540. A medium-sized plover with a fairly long, heavy black bill, and flesh-colored legs. Female has a rusty breast-band. Cf. smaller Collared Plover. Uncommon northern-winter migrant and winter visitor to central coast, with occasional records from as far south as Pisco. *Coastal US to s Peru and Brazil; West Indies.*

Killdeer *Charadrius vociferus* Chorlo Gritón
25 cm (9.8"). Plate 20. ♪ 626. No other plover has a double breast-band or rufous rump. Call is diagnostic. Common along coast and in agricultural areas on Pacific slope to 2500 m. *North America and coastal w South America; West Indies.*

Snowy (Kentish) Plover *Charadrius alexandrinus* Chorlo Nevado
15 cm (6"). Plate 20. ♪ 626. The only small pale plover with a grayish-brown back and an incomplete breast-band (black patch is only on side of breast). Legs are dark. Fairly common along coast. *Cosmopolitan; wide distribution worldwide.*

Collared Plover *Charadrius collaris* Chorlo Acollarado
16 cm (6.5"). Plate 20. ♪ 677. Adult is the only plover with rufous on hind crown and nape, a black breast and flesh-colored legs. Juvenile is duller with a rufous tinge on nape, an incomplete breast-band and pale legs. Uncommon along coast, fairly common on sandbars and rivers in trop. lowlands e of Andes to 600 m. *Coasts and rivers of Mexico to Argentina and Chile.*

[Two-banded Plover] *Charadrius falklandicus* Chorlo Dobleacollarado
18 cm (7"). Accidental. Not illustrated. Adult recalls Puna Plover, but has a conspicuous black breast-band, and an incomplete black band above it (instead of a rufous breast-band and lateral black bars above it). Non-breeding and juvenile have two dusky breast-bands. Cf. Collared Plover. Possible sight record from Boca del Rio, Tacna (pers. comm. T. Høgsås). *Breeds Argentina and Chile; winters n to Uruguay and s Brazil.*

Puna Plover *Charadrius alticola* Chorlo de la Puna
18 cm (7"). Plate 20. Adult is only plover with a rufous breast-band, black bars on side of breast (above rufous breast-band), rufous nape, white face and black legs. Non-breeding adults and juveniles are duller, with an indistinct but complete breast-band and dark legs. Uncommon migrant along coast; fairly common in *puna* zone north to Junín. *Andes of Peru to nw Argentina and n Chile.*

Rufous-chested Dotterel *Charadrius modestus* Chorlo Chileno
20 cm (8"). Plate 20. Adult in breeding plumage has a black band dividing the rufous chest from white belly, and a prominent white superciliary. Juvenile and non-breeding have chest, breast and face a uniform olive-brown (as back). In flight outer tail feathers and sides of rump are white. Rare austral migrant to s coast (north to Lima). *Tierra del Fuego and Falkland Is.; winters to s Brazil.*

Diademed Sandpiper-Plover *Phegornis mitchellii* Chorlo Cordillerano
18 cm (7"). Plate 20. ♫ 797. A unique wader of very high elevations. Easily identified by its black face and conspicuous white superciliary (that join in the forecrown). Juvenile is much duller. Back feathers are edged rufous, head is grayish, and breast is finely streaked. Note that medium-length bill droops near the tip. Rare, mainly in high-altitude *Distichia* bogs north to Ancash at 4000-5000 m. Reported from Milloc Bog and Bosque Unchog. *High-elevation bogs of s Peru to w Argentina and Chile.*

Tawny-throated Dotterel *Oreopholus ruficollis* Chorlo de Campo
27 cm (10.5"). Plate 20. Cinnamon throat is diagnostic. In flight note the black spot on belly and white underwing. Fairly common austral-winter visitor along coast and in *puna* zone. *Coasts and mountains of sw Ecuador to Tierra del Fuego.*

Scolopacidae (Sandpipers and Allies; Playeros, Becasinas y Falaropos)
Species: World 81; Peru 36
Typically birds of the seashore, but the family also includes such members as snipe that inhabit the barren altiplano. Most are high-latitude Holarctic breeders that engage in annual long-distance transequatorial migrations. They feed primarily by probing into mud, sand, silt or earth for insects, worms and crustaceans.

[Common Snipe] *Gallinago gallinago* Becasina Común
27 cm (10.5'). Not illustrated. Accidental? Probably cannot be safely separated in the field from South American and Puna Snipes (both are unlikely to be found on coast). Unconfirmed records from Pantanos de Villa (Wust *et al.* 1994). *Cosmopolitan except for Australasian region.*

South American Snipe *Gallinago paraguaiae* Becasina Sudamericana
27 cm (10.5"). Not illustrated. ♫ 797. Very similar to Puna Snipe (no overlap). The only snipe in its range. Cannot safely be separated in the field. Rare in lowland wet grassy savannas e of Andes to 300 m. *Swamps and marshes of South America e of the Andes.*

Puna Snipe *Gallinago andina* Becasina de la Puna
23 cm (9"). Plate 18. ♫ 797. Over most of its range the only snipe with a whitish belly and a rufous tail (conspicuous in flight). Andean Snipe's belly is barred. In Piura cf. Noble Snipe. Fairly common along boggy rivers in temp. and *puna* zones at 2500-4500 m. *Andes of n Peru to nw Argentina and n Chile.*

Noble Snipe *Gallinago nobilis* Becasina Paramera
30 cm (11.7"). Plate 18. ♫ LNS. Note limited range. Recalls Puna Snipe but is larger and darker. Has a longer bill and broader wings than Puna Snipe; yellowish bill has a dark tip. Puna Snipe's bill is uniformly dusky. Andean Snipe has barring on belly and flanks. Very local in *páramo* of Piura at 2500-4000 m. *Andes of Colombia, sw Venezuela, Ecuador and extreme n Peru.*

Andean Snipe *Gallinago jamesoni* Becasina Andina
35 cm (14"). Plate 18 ♪797. A brown snipe with a barred belly and flanks. Cf. Puna Snipe and Noble Snipe (white belly, back is more striped, rufous tail) and the very localized Imperial Snipe (much darker, heavily barred white belly). In flight has very broad wings. Fairly common and local in humid temp. zone at 2100-4300 m. *Andes of w Venezuela to e Bolivia.*

Imperial Snipe *Gallinago imperialis* Becasina Imperial
30 cm (11.7"). Plate 18. ♪LNS. Note limited range. A very dark, chestnut-brown snipe. Belly is whitish and heavily barred. In flight has very broad wings. Cf. Andean Snipe. Rare and local in elfin forests along e slope of Andes in Piura, Amazonas, La Libertad and Cusco at 2745-3500 m. *Locally in Andes of e Peru and Colombia.*

Short-billed Dowitcher *Limnodromus griseus* Agujeta Piquicorto
30 cm (11.7"). Plate 22. ♪626. Note the long, straight, rather snipe-like bill and fairly long, dusky greenish legs. In flight center of the lower back is white. In breeding plumage has rusty-brown underparts. Common northern-winter migrant along coast; occasional near Cusco at 3700 m (BPW); recorded along Río Heath at 200 m (JFC and PC). *Breeds Alaska and Canada; winters s US to central South America.*

Hudsonian Godwit *Limosa haemastica* Aguja de Mar
38 cm (15"). Plate 22. ♪626. A large, long-legged wader with a long, slightly upturned bill. The very long, pale bill has a dark distal half. Non-breeding birds are much grayer than larger Marbled Godwit. In flight in all plumages shows a white band on uppertail, a short white wingbar, and a diagnostic dark underwing lining. Rare northern-winter migrant along coast. Accidental on altiplano of extreme s Peru (Fjeldså and Krabbe 1990). *Canadian Arctic; winters in s South America.*

Marbled Godwit *Limosa fedoa* Aguja Moteada
45 cm (17.5"). Plate 22. ♪626. A large long-legged wader with a long, slightly upturned bill. Note the ochre, buffy and black "marbled" back. In flight shows diagnostic cinnamon underwing and tawny tail. Vagrant along coast during northern winter. *Great Plains of North America; winters to Argentina and Chile.*

Whimbrel *Numenius phaeopus* Zarapito Trinador
43 cm (17"). Plate 22. ♪797. The only large wader with a distinctive, decurved bill and striped crown. Fairly common northern-winter migrant along coast; rarely to 4000 m in Junín and Cusco. *Breeds Arctic and subarctic circumpolar; disperses worldwide.*

Upland Sandpiper *Bartramia longicauda* Pradero Batitú
30 cm (11.7"). Plate 22. ♪626. A wader usually found in fields and grasslands. Best identified by its conspicuous large black eye, and long pointed tail. Has a fairly short, mostly yellow bill, and longish yellow legs. Cf. Buff-breasted Sandpiper. Northern-winter vagrant. *Breeds Alaska to s US; winters in pampas of s South America.*

Greater Yellowlegs *Tringa melanoleuca* Patiamarillo Mayor
35 cm (14"). Plate 22. ♪797. Very similar to Lesser Yellowlegs, but larger, and bill is longer, thicker at base, and slightly upturned. In flight, uppertail coverts are white. Calls of both yellowlegs are very different. Common northern-winter migrant along coast; fairly common in *puna* zone. *Breeds Alaska and Canada; winters to s South America.*

Lesser Yellowlegs *Tringa flavipes* Patiamarillo Menor
25 cm (9.8"). Plate 22. ♪797. Long yellow legs and a "salt-and-pepper" back identify it as a yellowlegs. Bill is straight. In flight, uppertail coverts are white. Cf. Greater Yellowlegs. Common northern-winter migrant along coast and in *puna* zone; some birds remain during austral winter. *Breeds Alaska and Canada; winters to Tierra del Fuego; Galápagos Is.*

Solitary Sandpiper *Tringa solitaria* Playero Solitario
22 cm (8.6"). Plate 22. ♪ 797. Has light speckles on dark back, fairly short, dusky-olive legs, a medium length dusky bill, and a bold eye-ring. Cf. Lesser Yellowlegs. In flight, central tail feathers are dark (from above), outer white. Rare northern-winter migrant along coast and trop. zone; rarely to 4000 m in Andes. *Breeds Alaska and Canada; winters to s South America.*

Spotted Sandpiper *Actites macularia* Playero Coleador
19 cm (7.5"). Plate 21. ♪ 626. A common sandpiper that is brown above and white below, with a distinctive white "inlet" in front of wing. Bobs constantly. In flight, note white wingbar and whitish outer tail feathers. Has a characteristic flight in which wings are held below the horizontal. In breeding plumage has spotted underparts. Fairly common northern-winter migrant throughout; rare in *puna* zone from August-May. *Breeds North America; winters to s South America.*

Wandering Tattler *Heteroscelus incanus* Playero Vagabundo
25 cm (9.8"). Plate 21. ♪ 626. Note the straight dusky bill and white supraloral. In breeding plumage has barred underparts. Uncommon northern-winter migrant along coast; single record from *puna* zone (Fjeldså and Krabbe 1990). *Breeds Siberia and Alaska; winters to n South America, Hawaii and sw Oceania.*

Willet *Catoptrophorus semipalmatus* Playero Aliblanco
40 cm (15.5"). Plate 22. ♪ 626. Like a large, gray version of yellowlegs, but more uniform and with gray legs. In flight conspicuous wing pattern—basal 2/3 of primaries are white, contrasting with black tip of primaries and primary coverts. Fairly common northern-winter migrant along coast; accidental in Junín and Cusco to 3400 m (Fjeldså and Krabbe 1990). *Canada and US; winters to n Chile and s Brazil.*

Ruddy Turnstone *Arenaria interpres* Vuelvepiedras Rojizo
23 cm (9"). Plate 21. ♪ 626. A stocky shorebird with short, orange legs and a short bill. Striking pattern in flight—a bold wingbar, vertical line on base of each wing, and center of back, white tail with a broad black terminal band. In breeding plumage has brighter upperparts and stronger markings. Common northern-winter migrant along coast and Amazon river systems; accidental at Lake Junín (Fjeldså and Krabbe 1990). *Breeds Holarctic; wide post-breeding dispersal.*

Surfbird *Aphriza virgata* Chorlo de Rompientes
25 cm (9.8"). Plate 21. ♪ 626. A stocky shorebird of the rocky coasts. The short bill has a yellow lower mandible tipped with black. Short legs are greenish, and bird has a dark-hooded appearance. In flight has a white tail with a broad black terminal band, and a wingbar. Cf. Red Knot. Fairly common northern-winter migrant along coast. *Breeds Alaska and Yukon; winters to s South America.*

Calidris **Sandpipers.** Small to medium waders, with short to medium-length bills. All breed in the northern hemisphere and arrive in Peru as northern-winter residents or vagrants. Especially note body size and shape, bill size and shape, leg color, and any facial markings.

Red Knot *Calidris canutus* Playero Pechirufo
26 cm (10.1"). Plate 21. ♪ 483. The largest of the Peruvian *Calidris*. The straight, black bill is thicker at the base. Note the black legs. In flight shows a weak wingbar and barred rump. In breeding plumage has rusty brown underparts and face. Fairly common northern-winter migrant along coast. *Breeds Holarctic tundra; worldwide coastal post-breeding dispersal.*

Sanderling *Calidris alba* Playero Arenero
20 cm (8"). Plate 21. ♪ 626. A very pale sandpiper, often seen running along the shoreline margin. Has grayish-silver upperparts (or pale edges to dark back feathers in juvenile) and white underparts. Note the straight black bill, black legs, pale gray rump and tail. In flight black tips to flight feathers

contrast with white wingbar. In breeding plumage has rufous-brown head, chest and back. Common northern-winter migrant along coast; uncommon migrant in *puna* zone at 3500-4500 m; rare along humid lowland rivers e of Andes. *Holarctic region; worldwide coastal post-breeding dispersal.*

Semipalmated Sandpiper *Calidris pusilla* Playerito Semipalmado
15 cm (6"). Plate 21. ♪ 626. A small, black-legged sandpiper with a short, straight "even-width" bill, that looks less pointed than bill of very similar Western Sandpiper. Cf. also Least Sandpiper (greenish-yellow legs and thinner, more pointed bill). Common northern-winter migrant along coast. *Breeds Arctic North America; winters to s South America.*

Western Sandpiper *Calidris mauri* Playerito Occidental
16 cm (6.5"). Plate 21. ♪ 626. A small black-legged "peep" with a medium-length bill that droops slightly toward the tip. However bill size and shape vary—males tend to have shorter and straighter bills (rather pointed). Certain individuals cannot be safely separated from very similar Semipalmated Sandpiper (always straight bill with a fairly blunt tip). In breeding plumage has chestnut shoulders and crown. Cf. also Least Sandpiper (smaller, yellowish legs, short bill). Common northern-winter migrant along coast. *Breeds Siberia and Alaska; winters to n South America.*

Red-necked Stint *Calidris ruficollis.* Playerito Cuellirrojo
15 cm (6"). Plate 21. An accidental from Siberia. In breeding plumage has a mostly rufous head and back. In non-breeding plumage is very similar to Western and Semipalmated Sandpipers and probably indistinguishable in the field. The single record of a bird in diagnostic summer plumage 23 August 1985 from Lagunas de Mejía (Hughes 1988) is the first South American record for this species. *Breeds Siberia and Alaska; disperses to s Asia and Australasia.*

Least Sandpiper *Calidris minutilla* Playerito Menudo
15 cm (6"). Plate 21. ♪ 626. The only small "peep" with greenish-yellow legs. Bill is thinner than that of Semipalmated and Western Sandpipers. Cf. larger Pectoral Sandpiper. Common northern-winter migrant along coast; rare at Lake Junín, and one record from Sumbay (Arequipa) at 4100 m. *Breeds North America; winters to s South America and Hawaiian Is.*

White-rumped Sandpiper *Calidris fuscicollis* Playerito Lomiblanco
18 cm (7"). Plate 21. ♪ 797. Similar to Baird's Sandpiper, but has a white rump (best seen in flight). Back and breast are grayer than in Baird's Sandpiper. Rare northern-winter migrant along coast; uncommon along lowland rivers e of Andes; rare in *puna* zone. *Breeds Arctic North America; winters in South America.*

Baird's Sandpiper *Calidris bairdii* Playerito de Baird
18 cm (7"). Plate 21. ♪ 797. A slender *Calidris* with a short, black, pointed bill and black legs. Very long wings (at rest reaching past the tail) and buffy breast. Cf. White-rumped (similar but grayer, obvious white rump in flight), Least (smaller with yellowish legs), Pectoral (yellowish legs and dark breast sharply border white belly), and Buff-breasted (yellow legs) Sandpipers. Uncommon northern-winter migrant along coast; common migrant in *puna* zone at 3500-4700 m. *Breeds Siberia and Alaska; winters in Andes to Tierra del Fuego.*

Pectoral Sandpiper *Calidris melanotos* Playero Pectoral
23 cm (9"). Plate 21. ♪ 797. A medium-sized *Calidris* with a medium-length dusky bill, and yellowish legs. Best identified by the dark breast, sharply bordered with a white belly. Cf. Least and Baird's Sandpipers. Common northern-winter migrant along lowland rivers; fairly common migrant in *puna* zone at 3500-4500 m. *Breeds Arctic North America and Siberia; winters in s South America.*

Curlew Sandpiper *Calidris ferruginea* Playero Zarapito
20 cm (8"). Plate 21. Note the long, slightly decurved bill and black legs. White rump is conspicuous in flight. In breeding plumage has rich rufous on head, underparts and back. Cf. Stilt Sandpiper (longer greenish legs and different bill). Northern-winter vagrant along coast. *Breeds Siberia; winters to South Africa, SE Asia and Australasia.*

Dunlin *Calidris alpina* Playero Ventrinegro
19 cm (7.5"). Plate 21. ♪626. Accidental. Note the long, slightly decurved bill, and black legs. A dark line divides the whitish rump. In breeding plumage has a diagnostic black patch on belly. Sight record from Ica (Petersen 1981) and two recent sight records from Paracas (pers. comm. BPW). *Breeds Holarctic tundra; worldwide post-breeding dispersal.*

Stilt Sandpiper *Calidris himantopus* Playero Patilargo
20 cm (8"). Plate 21. ♪626. The fairly long bill is thick at the base and droops at tip. Note the long greenish-yellow legs. In flight shows a whitish rump. In breeding plumage has a rufous ear patch and barred underparts. Fairly common northern-winter migrant along lowland rivers; uncommon migrant in *puna* zone. *Breeds n North America; winters sw US to s South America.*

Buff-breasted Sandpiper *Tryngites subruficollis* Playero Canelo
19 cm (7.5"). Plate 21. Note the fairly short black bill, longish yellow legs, and clean buff wash on breast. Favors fields. In flight shows a dark rump and white underwing, and has a diagnostic black bar on primary coverts. Cf. Upland (streaked breast, longer tail and longer neck) and Baird's (black legs) Sandpipers. Rare northern-winter migrant along coast; uncommon migrant along lowland rivers e of Andes. *Breeds Arctic North America; winters in s South America.*

Ruff (or Reeve) *Philomachus pugnax* Playero Combatiente
Male 31 cm (12"); female 25 cm (9.8"). Plate 21. Accidental. Note medium-length, dark greenish to orange bill, and longish yellow to orange legs. In all plumages has a diagnostic white "horseshoe" on rump. It is unlikely that breeding birds with extravagant ruffs will turn up in Peru. Northern-winter vagrant along coast. *Breeds n Palearctic; winters to s Africa, s Asia and Australia.*

Wilson's Phalarope *Phalaropus tricolor* Faláropo Tricolor
23 cm (9"). Plate 20. ♪626. Note the fairly long, thin, straight bill and yellow (non-breeding and juvenile) or black (breeding) legs. Non-breeding birds have a pale silvery-gray back, and juvenile's back is scaled buff. In breeding plumage has a conspicuous striped neck. In flight shows a white rump and uppertail coverts, but no wingbars. Less often seen swimming than other phalaropes. Common northern-winter visitor (Sept.-March) along coast and in *puna* zone; uncommon migrant in humid lowlands e of Andes. *Breeds Canada and US; winters in w and s South America.*

Red-necked Phalarope *Phalaropus lobatus* Faláropo Picofino
18 cm (7"). Plate 21. ♪626. Smaller and shorter-billed than Wilson's Phalarope. Non-breeding and juveniles have a black postocular stripe and striped back. In flight shows two white stripes on back and a wingbar. Red Phalarope has a shorter, thicker bill, uniform gray back, and a more prominent wingbar. In breeding plumage Red-necked Phalarope has rufous on sides of neck (female has rufous on foreneck). Often seen swimming at sea in large flocks. Fairly common northern-winter visitor (Oct.-March) along Humboldt Current. *Holarctic; winters at sea in southern hemisphere.*

Red Phalarope *Phalaropus fulicaria* Faláropo Piquigrueso
20 cm (8"). Plate 21. ♪626. The short bill is thick at base. Non-breeding and juveniles have a black postocular stripe and uniform pale-gray back. In flight shows a pure-gray back, without stripes, and a bold wingbar (more prominent than in Red-necked Phalarope). In breeding plumage has rufous underparts and back, white cheeks, and a mostly yellow bill. Common highly pelagic northern-winter visitor (Oct.-March) along Humboldt Current. *Holarctic; winters at sea in s hemisphere.*

Thinocoridae (Seedsnipes; Agachonas). Species: World 4; Peru 3
Seedsnipes are terrestrial birds that are cryptically colored to blend in with the sparse vegetation characteristic of their bleak environment. Three species are montane residents, while the Least Seedsnipe occurs down to sea level. They are entirely vegetarian, feeding mostly on seeds and leaves, and apparently obtain all the water they need from their dry-appearing food supply.

Rufous-bellied Seedsnipe *Attagis gayi* Agachona Ventrirrufo
30 cm (11.7"). Plate 20. ♪ 797. The largest seedsnipe, and the only one with a rufous belly. In flight, underwing lining is buff. Locally uncommon in *puna* zone at 3400-4500 m. *Andes of Ecuador to w Argentina and Chile.*

Gray-breasted Seedsnipe *Thinocorus orbignyianus* Agachona Pechigris
23 cm (9"). Plate 20. ♪ 797. Male has a white chin outlined with black, and a gray breast. It lacks "anchor-like" pattern found on breast of Least Seedsnipe. Female has a buff breast with heavy dark streaks (appears blackish). Fairly common in *puna* zone at 3400-5000 m north to La Libertad. *Andes of Peru to w Argentina and Chile.*

Least Seedsnipe *Thinocorus rumicivorus* Agachona Chica
19 cm (7.5"). Plate 20. The smallest of the seedsnipes, and the only one found at lower elevations. Male has a diagnostic "anchor-like" pattern on gray breast. Female has a dark "anchor-like" pattern on buffy breast. Juvenile has an unstreaked buffy breast. In all plumages shows a weak wingbar in flight. Fairly common along coast and Pacific slope to 2500 m. *Arid Pacific littoral of sw Ecuador to Tierra del Fuego.*

Stercoraiidae (Skuas and Jaegers; Salteadores). Species: World 7; Peru 5
A group of predatory, aerial seabirds that inhabit the high latitudes of both hemispheres. Some species have an extensive post-breeding dispersal. They are masters of flight, and gather most of their food by harassing gulls and terns on the wing, and forcing them to disgorge their food—which they then catch in mid-air. They are notorious predators around penguin, gull and cormorant colonies, and any unguarded chick is instantly snatched up. Northern breeders regularly capitalize on the lemming plagues on the Arctic tundra.

Stercorarius **Skuas.** Two stocky, gull-like, predatory seabirds. Both have fairly short tails. The broad wings have white at the base of primaries.

Chilean Skua *Stercorarius chilensis* Salteador Chileno
58 cm (22.5"). Plate 22. Adult has distinctive pale cinnamon tones, especially on the underparts and wing linings, and a contrasting dark cap. Juvenile has fairly bright rusty underparts and a gray cap. Cf. South Polar Skua. Fairly common austral-winter migrant in offshore waters from April-October. *Coasts of s Chile and s Argentina; ranges north to tropics.*

South Polar Skua *Stercorarius maccormicki* Salteador del Polo Sur
53 cm (21"). Plate 22. Variable plumage. Built similar to Chilean Skua, but underparts never have cinnamon or reddish tones. In all morphs underwing coverts are dark. Dark morph is dark brown and sometimes shows a paler nape. Light morph has pale grayish underparts and head. In intermediate morph underparts are buffy brown and nape is pale. Rare transequatorial austral-winter migrant offshore. *Breeds Antarctica; ranges to n Atlantic, n Pacific and Indian Oceans.*

Stercorarius **Jaegers.** A trio of gull-like, predatory sea-birds, all polymorphic. Powerful flyers, longer-winged and lighter-built than the skuas (however Pomarine Jaeger approaches the skuas in size). Adults have diagnostic tail projections. Identification, especially of immatures, can be very difficult, and general shape and flight manners often provide the best clues for identification.

Pomarine Jaeger *Stercorarius pomarinus* Salteador Pomarino
65-78 cm (25-30.5"). Plate 22. ♪ 483. The heaviest jaeger, barrel-chested and broader-winged than the others. Structure like a large gull. Adult has spoon-like tail projections. Often shows pale base of primary underwing coverts (in addition to white base of primaries). Light morph has white underparts and a dark chest band. Dark morph is all dark, but has white on primaries and base of primary coverts. Both best identified by tail shape and body structure. Juveniles of all morphs have very short tail projections and are heavily barred below. Cf. Parasitic Jaeger and South Polar Skua. Fairly common northern-winter visitor to northern offshore waters. *Circumpolar Arctic tundra; winters at sea in southern oceans.*

Parasitic Jaeger *Stercorarius parasiticus* Salteador Parásito
46-67 cm (18-26"). Plate 22. ♪ 626. Structured like a small gull, somewhat between the slimmer Long-tailed Jaeger and the heavier Pomarine Jaeger. Adult has short- to medium-length pointed tail projections. All plumages have white base to most of primaries (seen from below). Juveniles are variable and have a barred vent and whitish belly, or barred underparts. Cf. Pomarine and Long-tailed Jaegers. Uncommon northern-winter visitor to offshore waters. *Circumpolar Arctic tundra; winters at sea in southern oceans.*

Long-tailed Jaeger *Stercorarius longicaudus* Salteador Colilargo
48-58 cm (19-23"). Plate 22. ♪ 626. The smallest and slimmest of the jaegers, rather tern-like. In all plumages shows characteristic light shafts to outermost two primaries (seen from above). Adult's very long tail projections are diagnostic. Upperparts are often paler gray (contrasting dark secondaries) than congeners. Juvenile has short, rounded tail projections, and is best identified by its upperwing. Rare highly pelagic northern-winter visitor to offshore waters. *Circumpolar Arctic tundra; winters at sea in southern oceans.*

Laridae (Gulls; Gaviotas). Species: World 51; Peru 13
A heterogeneous collection of long-winged, heavy-bodied, web-footed aerial birds found along coastal and inland waters. They are among the most familiar of all sea birds, being common and conspicuous around harbors and beaches. In addition to a diet of fish and shellfish, many gulls have become scavengers, and haunt garbage dumps and plowed agricultural lands. Gulls swim well, but they cannot swim underwater, nor do they plunge-dive for their food as many terns do. They are cosmopolitan in their distribution, with some being sedentary, and others undertaking annual long-distance migrations.

Band-tailed (Belcher's) Gull *Larus belcheri* Gaviota Peruana
50 cm (19.5"). Plate 23. Fairly large and long-legged, with a black terminal tail band in all ages. Adult breeding is black backed like adult Kelp Gull, but latter lacks terminal tail band and dark tip to bill. Non-breeding adult and second-year birds have a distinctive dark hood. First-year bird has a dark head and scaly, light-brown back. Common resident along coast north to islands off Piura. *Pacific coast of Peru and n Chile.*

Gray Gull *Larus modestus* Gaviota Gris
44 cm (17.5"). Plate 6. A distinctive medium-sized gull with a slender black bill and a white trailing edge to wing. Adult in breeding plumage is the only gray gull with a whitish head. Non-breeding: gray body, dark-brown head. Juvenile similar to non-breeding birds but browner. Common austral-winter visitor along coast. *Inland nitrate deserts of Peru and Chile; ranges north to Ecuador.*

Kelp Gull *Larus dominicanus* Gaviota Dominicana
53 cm (21"). Plate 6. A large "four-year" gull. Adult is the only large black backed gull that has an all white tail and a yellow bill with a red dot. Third year: similar to adult but has a black terminal tail band, and bill is similar to that of adult (compare Band-tailed Gull). First and second year: mottled brown body often paler on head, a scaled blackish back and black bill. Common resident along coast north to islands off Piura. *Widespread and common circumpolar southern coasts.*

Herring Gull *Larus argentatus* Gaviota Argéntea
58 cm (22.5"). Plate 23. Accidental. Adult like Kelp Gull, but back is silvery-gray. Wing tips only are black. Young birds have diagnostic inner primaries lighter than dark outer primaries (creating a light panel on wing). Otherwise similar to first-year Kelp Gull. Bird photographed at Ventanilla Beach resort 30 km north of Lima 14 Sept. 1983 (Krabbe *et al.* 2001). *N Eurasia and n North America; southerly post-breeding dispersal.*

Gray-headed Gull *Larus cirrocephalus* Gaviota de Cabecigris
40 cm (15.5"). Plate 23. Medium size. Adults in flight have a diagnostic pattern: white primary coverts, black primaries, and white spot near the tip of two outermost primaries. Breeding adult is distinctive: gray hood, bright-red legs, dark-red bill and white iris. Non-breeding adult: similar but head is white and soft parts duller. Juvenile and sub-adult: gray mantle, reddish-orange bill and legs, dark half-hood on head and narrow terminal tail band. Wing pattern similar to that of adult, but outermost primaries lack white spots. Fairly common along coast. *Africa and Madagascar; s and w South America.*

[Brown-hooded Gull] *Larus maculipennis* Gaviota Capuchicafé
35 cm (14"). Not illustrated. Small. Adult: red bill and legs, dark hood (breeding) or white head with a dark spot behind ear (non-breeding). Like larger Andean Gull but upperwing primaries appear white (only inner webs of primaries are black). Juvenile like non breeding adult, but has black terminal tail band; wing pattern recalls that of Gray-headed Gull. Accidental (?) austral-winter visitor to s coast. Recorded at Pisco (pers. comm. BPW). *Lakes, rivers and coasts of s South America and Falkland Is.*

Andean Gull *Larus serranus* Gaviota Andina
45 cm (17.5"). Plate 23. ♪797. Medium size. Adult: very dark-red bill and legs, black hood (breeding) or white head with a dark spot behind ear (non-breeding). In flight (in all plumages) a diagnostic white panel on the three outermost primaries. Juvenile has a subterminal tail band (and often dark hood). The only gull likely to occur in the highlands. On the coast compare Gray-headed, Laughing and Franklin's Gulls. Common on *puna* lakes at 3000-5000 m and common along coast during austral winter. Accidental at Boca de Manu (pers. comm. BPW). *Andes of Ecuador to n Argentina and central Chile.*

Laughing Gull *Larus atricilla* Gaviota Reidora
40 cm (15.5"). Plate 23. ♪626. Medium size. In all plumages similar to respective plumages of Franklin's Gull, but larger, with a longer, slightly decurved bill. Laughing Gull in all plumages lacks any white on wing tips (adult Franklin's Gull has white tips to base and tip of primaries). Juvenile has dark terminal tail band and dusky head. Juvenile Franklin's has more prominent half-hood, and incomplete terminal tail band. Fairly common northern-winter visitor along coast. *Coasts of e Canada and nw Mexico to n South America; West Indies.*

Franklin's Gull *Larus pipixcan* Gaviota de Franklin
35 cm (14"). Plate 23. ♪797. Like a smaller version of Laughing Gull. Non-breeding and juvenile have a diagnostic "half hood" (dark ear coverts and rear crown). Juvenile's wing pattern is like that of juvenile Laughing Gull (dark gray with dark unmarked primaries). Cf. Gray-headed and Andean Gulls. Common northern-winter visitor (Sept.-May) along coast; uncommon in *puna* zone and rare in humid lowlands e of Andes. *W-central North America; winters Pacific coast of South America.*

Sabine's Gull *Xema sabini* Gaviota de Sabine
33 cm (13"). Plate 23. A small, pelagic gull. In all plumages note distinctive wing pattern: gray mantle (brown in juvenile), contrasting white secondaries, and black primaries and primary coverts. Adult has a black hood (reduced to half collar in non-breeding) and black bill tipped yellow. Compare to Swallow-tailed Gull. Uncommon highly pelagic northern-winter visitor in offshore waters. *Arctic circumpolar; winters tropical e Pacific and Atlantic Oceans.*

Swallow-tailed Gull *Creagrus furcatus* Gaviota Tijereta
50 cm (19.5"). Plate 23. A large, pelagic gull. The only gull that has a deeply forked tail (white in adult, with a black terminal band in juvenile). In flight gray mantle (brown in juvenile) like much smaller Sabine's Gull, but most of the primaries in Swallow-tailed Gull are white (except outermost). Breeding adult has a black head, a mostly black bill tipped with yellow, with a white spot at base of bill. Fairly common highly pelagic northern-winter visitor in offshore waters. *Breeds Galápagos Is.; winters coastal Colombia to Chile.*

Black-legged Kittiwake *Rissa tridactyla* Gaviota Tridáctila
43 cm (17"). Plate 23. Accidental. Juvenile has a black "M" pattern on upperwing, black wing tips, and a black nuchal collar. Adult is white with a pale-gray mantle, black wingtips and yellow bill. Photographed off Pucusana (Lima) on 10 July 1993 (Haase 1993). *Arctic circumpolar; winters to nw Mexico and Mediterranean Sea.*

Sternidae (Terns; Gaviotínes). Species: World 44; Peru 15
Terns are generally smaller and more streamlined than gulls, with narrower, more pointed wings and thin, sharp-pointed bills. Most of their food consists of live minnows or shrimp, which they capture by plunging under the surface from some distance above the water. Terns are cosmopolitan in their distribution, with most species having extensive annual migrations. The long-distance record for annual migration goes to the Arctic Tern, which breeds in the high Arctic tundra and winters in Antarctic and subantarctic waters—an annual round trip of some 40,000 kilometers (24,000 miles)!

Gull-billed Tern *Sterna nilotica* Gaviotín Piquigrueso
35 cm (14"). Plate 23. ♪ 626. A heavy tern with a gull-like black bill. In flight only the tips of primaries are dark. Black crown (breeding), or white head with a dark ear patch (non-breeding). Juvenile has buffy spots on upperparts; bill browner. Cf. Snowy-crowned Tern. Rare resident along coast south to Piura and northern-winter migrant to south coast. *Locally in North America, South America, Eurasia, Africa and Australia.*

Elegant Tern *Sterna elegans* Gaviotín Elegante
40 cm (15.5"). Plate 23. A fairly large tern. In breeding plumage has a black crown and a long, shaggy crest. Similar to Royal Tern, but bill is more slender (thus appears longer) and slightly decurved. Common northern-winter visitor along coast. *Breeds s California (San Diego Bay) to w Mexico (Nayarit); winters Guatemala to Chile.*

Sandwich Tern *Sterna sandvicensis* Gaviotín Patinegro
40 cm (15.5"). Plate 23. A fairly large tern. In all plumages has a long, slender black bill with a yellow tip (juveniles sometimes lack yellow tip). Breeding birds have a black crown. Cf. Snowy-crowned Tern. Uncommon northern-winter visitor along coast. Flock of 400 reported at Pucusana 7 April 2001 (GE). *Atlantic coast of North America, South America, Europe and Africa.*

Royal Tern *Sterna maxima* Gaviotín Real
48 cm (19"). Plate 23. ♪ 626. A large tern. In breeding plumage has a black crown and a shaggy crest. Larger and thicker-billed than similar Elegant Tern. Fairly common northern-winter visitor along coast. *Coastal US to Argentina, West Indies and West Africa.*

South American Tern *Sterna hirundinacea* Gaviotín Sudamericano
43 cm (17"). Plate 23. A pale, medium-sized tern with a long tail (at rest tail is longer than wings). In flight wings appear almost completely white; only outermost primaries have a dark web. Breeding: black crown. Non-breeding: white forecrown. Common Tern is smaller, shorter billed and has darker tips to primaries. Artic Tern is pelagic, smaller and grayer. Juvenile: bill black, back is scaled with dark markings. Fairly common along coast. *Coasts and islands of s South America.*

Common Tern *Sterna hirundo* Gaviotín Común
40 cm (15.5"). Plate 23. ♪ 626. Similar to South American Tern, but smaller, with a proportionately shorter tail (at rest tail is shorter than wings). In flight shows dark edges to primaries from below (dark wedge on inner primaries from above). Breeding adult (rare in Peru) is black-capped with a dark-red bill. Non-breeding and juvenile have a distinctive dark shoulder bar, blackish crown and white forehead. Juvenile has somewhat brownish upperparts. Compare Arctic Tern. Common migrant along coast; several records from Iquitos (TAP, TSS). *Breeds Nearctic and Palearctic regions; winters to s South America, Africa and Australia.*

Arctic Tern *Sterna paradisaea* Gaviotín del Artico
38 cm (15"). Plate 23. ♪ 626. A medium-sized, pelagic tern. Arctic Tern has a proportionately longer tail, smaller body, and shorter wings than similar Common Tern. Underwing is gray, with only very narrow dark tips to the primaries. Lacks dark wedge on upperwing. Breeding: black crown, gray underparts and white cheeks. Common Tern has more uniform pale-gray underparts. Juvenile is similar to that of Common Tern but grayer, shoulder bar is less pronounced, and Arctic Tern juvenile has secondaries that are paler than mantle (in Common Tern secondaries are even darker than mantle). Common pelagic migrant along coast, with several records from Amazon lowlands. *Breeds Arctic circumpolar; winters subantarctic and Antarctic seas.*

Snowy-crowned Tern *Sterna trudeaui* Gaviotín Cabeciblanca
35 cm (14"). Plate 23. A medium-sized, almost completely white tern. A conspicuous black eye-patch contrasts with a white crown. Bill is black with a yellow tip (non-breeding), or yellow with a black ring near the tip (breeding). Cf. Sandwich and Gull-billed Terns. Rare austral-winter migrant to coastal Arequipa and Paracas (Donahue *et al.* 1980). *Lagoons and marshes of s South America.*

Least Tern *Sterna antillarum* Gaviotín Chico
23 cm (9"). Plate 23. ♪ 626. Tiny. Similar to Peruvian Tern, but whiter on underparts and uppertail. Non-breeding and juvenile (most Peru records) have a dark shoulder bar, dark bill, and a dark line that goes from the eye to the nape, and are similar to respective plumage of Peruvian Tern, but the latter's uppertail and rump are gray. Accidental northern-winter migrant along north coast. *Locally along coasts and rivers of North America; winters to n South America.*

Yellow-billed Tern *Sterna superciliaris* Gaviotín Piquiamarillo
25 cm (9.8"). Plate 9. ♪ 797. The smallest tern in the Amazonian river system. Common along lowland rivers and oxbow lakes e of Andes. *Rivers and lakes of South America e of the Andes.*

Peruvian Tern *Sterna lorata* Gaviotín Peruano
23 cm (9"). Plate 6. The smallest tern over most of its range. A tiny tern with gray underparts and uppertail. Cf. Least Tern. Breeding: black crown, white forehead, yellow bill tipped black. Non-breeding: white forecrown and black rear crown; bill is darker. Juvenile is similar, but underparts much paler. Wanders out to sea where often perches atop driftwood. Uncommon to rare along coast. *Arid coasts of Ecuador to n Chile.*

Sooty Tern *Sterna fuscata* Gaviotín Oscuro
40 cm (15.5"). Plate 23. A medium-sized pelagic tern. Adult is the only tern that has mostly black upperparts and mostly white underparts. Juvenile has a sooty-black body, and whitish edging to back feathers. Cf. juvenile Inca Tern. Rare highly pelagic austral-winter migrant in offshore waters. *Islands in tropical and subtropical oceans.*

Black Tern *Chlidonias niger* Gaviotín Negro
25 cm (10"). Plate 23. ♪ 626. Small. In all plumages has uniform gray upperwings and tail and whitish underwings. Non-breeding: a dark cap and diagnostic dark spot on sides of breast, close to base of wing. Often in different stages of molt. Breeding adult (rarely seen in Peru) is mostly black except for a white vent. Rare northern-winter visitor along coast. *Breeds Eurasia and North America; winters tropical Africa and South America.*

Large-billed Tern *Phaetusa simplex* Gaviotín Picudo
38 cm (15"). Plate 9. ♪ 797. Distinctive. The largest tern in the Amazonian river system. Bill is large and heavy. Gray mantle contrasts with black primaries and white secondaries. Common along lowland rivers and oxbow lakes e of Andes; accidental on Lake Junín and along coast. *Lakes and rivers of South America e of Andes.*

Inca Tern *Larosterna inca* Gaviotín Zarcillo
40 cm (15.5"). Plate 6. Unmistakable. Has an odd curled feather on side of face, red bill and legs. Juvenile has blackish bill, sooty plumage, no "plumes". In flight shows white trailing edge to wing. Common along Humboldt Current coastal region north to Isla Lobos de Tierra (Piura). *Breeds islands off Peru and Chile; ranges rarely n to Ecuador.*

Rynchopidae (Skimmers; Rayadores). Species: World 3; Peru 1
Skimmers are elegant, tern-like birds of tropical lakes, rivers and coasts. Their most remarkable feature is the bill—the lower mandible is up to 25 mm (1.0 inch) longer than the upper. In flight the bill is held at a downward angle, and they feed with the beak wide open, with the lower mandible knifing the water. Their diet consists primarily of small fish, crustaceans and other plankton. They feed primarily during the crepuscular or night hours, since during daylight hours the plankton moves deeper and is less readily available.

Black Skimmer *Rynchops niger* Rayador Negro
45 cm (17.5"). Plate 6. ♪ 797. Peculiar, unique bill shape and boldly patterned plumage eliminate any possible confusion. Fairly common along lowland rivers e of Andes; common northern-winter visitor along coast. *Locally along coasts and rivers of s US to s South America.*

Columbidae (Pigeons and Doves; Palomas y Tórtolas). Species: World 308; Peru 27
There is no biological distinction between pigeons and doves, the term "pigeon" being used to denote the larger species, and the term "dove" the smaller members of this large family. They are cosmopolitan in distribution, with the exception of the polar and sub-polar regions. Most are extremely strong fliers and have reached even the most remote oceanic islands. They are found in almost every habitat from tropical rainforests to coral islands. As with any large family with such a large distribution, they take a variety of foods, including berries, nuts, acorns, fruits, buds and leaves. Some species also take animal food.

Columba **Pigeons.** A cosmopolitan genus of 51 fairly large arboreal pigeons, eight species of which occur in Peru. They often perch in the canopy on exposed branches. Some species flock, but most lowland forest pigeons are solitary or found in pairs.

Rock Dove *Columba livia* Paloma Doméstica
33 cm (13"). Plate 24. ♪ 626. Almost invariably near settlements, often in large flocks. Extremely variable in plumage. Common in agricultural areas and towns from sea level to 4000 m. *Cosmopolitan and commensal to man.*

Scaled Pigeon *Columba speciosa* Paloma Escamosa
30 cm (11.7"). Plate 24. ♪ 797. Note scalloped underparts and neck. Wings and crown are uniformly dark brown. Bill has a reddish base and yellow tip. Uncommon in humid lowlands and upper trop. zone e of Andes to 1400 m and w of Andes in Tumbes. *Tropical s Mexico to Brazil and ne Argentina.*

Spot-winged Pigeon *Columba maculosa* Paloma Alimoteada
33 cm (13"). Plate 24. ♪ 797. Note the dark tail and conspicuous white band on the wings. Cf. Band-tailed Pigeon. Uncommon in montane forests and arid scrub, mainly at 2000-4000 m. Vagrants recorded in Santa Eulalia Valley (Lima) and along coast at Puerto Viejo (GE). *Andes and lowlands of s Peru to central Argentina and s Brazil.*

Band-tailed Pigeon *Columba fasciata* Paloma Nuquiblanca
35 cm (14"). Plate 24. ♪ 797. Note the light-gray tail with a dark band at the base. Shows a green iridescent patch on nape and white semicollar above it. Cf. Spot-winged and Pale-vented Pigeons. Fairly common in temp. and subtrop. Andes generally at 2000-3400 m. *SW Canada to nw Argentina.*

Pale-vented Pigeon *Columba cayennensis* Paloma Colorada
30 cm (11.7"). Plate 24. ♪ 797. No other *Columba* has a light-gray tail, whitish vent, and reddish tone on the shoulders. Common in humid lowland forests e of Andes to 700 m. *Gulf lowlands of se Mexico to s Brazil and n Argentina.*

*Peruvian Pigeon *Columba oenops* Paloma Peruana
30 cm (11.7"). Plate 26. The only pigeon in its limited range with the combination of vinaceous head, breast, and most of the folded wing (scapulars and inner coverts); grayish belly, dark tail, red base of bill (cere) and dusky tip. Uncommon in dry and riparian forests in upper Marañón Valley in Piura, Cajamarca, Amazonas and La Libertad. Recorded regularly near Comboca 30-40 km east of Bagua Grande, along La Peca Nueva trail (Amazonas) at 700 m, at Balsas in riparian habitat along Río Marañón, and at Soquián (La Libertad) at 1050 m. *N Peru; recently recorded in adj. Ecuador.*

Plumbeous Pigeon *Columba plumbea* Paloma Plomiza
30 cm (11.7"). Plate 24. ♪ 797. Very similar to Ruddy Pigeon but the latter is browner on the wings and somewhat redder on underparts, with a slightly shorter bill. They are very difficult to distinguish in the field and are best told by voice. Plumbeous sometimes has whitish eyes. Plumbeous has a low-pitched slow call and a soft, four-note call. Ruddy's call is a more decisive higher-pitched, four-note call. Common in lowland and subtrop. forests e of Andes to 2500 m. *S Venezuela and the Guianas to n Bolivia, Paraguay and Amazonian Brazil.*

Ruddy Pigeon *Columba subvinacea* Paloma Rojiza
33 cm (13"). Plate 24. ♪ 797. Smaller and more uniform coloration than Plumbeous Pigeon, but can be safely separated in the field only by voice. Rare in humid lowland and subtrop. forests e of Andes south to central Peru; recorded at Bosque National de Tumbes at Cotrina and Campo Verde (TAP). *Costa Rica to n Bolivia and Amazonian Brazil.*

Eared Dove *Zenaida auriculata* Tórtola Orejuda (Rabiblanca)
25 cm (9.8"). Plate 24. ♪ 656. Note facial markings and wing spots. In flight shows white tips to outer tail feathers and a wedge-shaped tail. Lacks the prominent white on wings that Pacific Dove shows. White-tipped Dove has a fan-shaped tail, and lacks facial markings. Fairly common from arid trop. lowlands to *puna* zone. *Semiarid s Lesser Antille and South America.*

Pacific Dove *Zenaida meloda* Tórtola Melódica (Cuculí)
27 cm (10.5"). Plate 24. No other dove or pigeon has such a conspicuous white band on the wings. Common and familiar in towns along the coast. Common in arid trop. and subtrop. zones. Formerly considered conspecific with White-winged Dove (*Z. asiatica*). *Coastal sw Ecuador to n Chile.*

***Columbina* Ground-Doves.** Small doves of fields and borders, mostly in the lowlands. They walk with quick steps, and occasionally roost in trees.

Plain-breasted Ground-Dove *Columbina minuta* Tortolita Menuda
15 cm (6"). Plate 25. ♪ 656. A pale, tiny ground-dove with no obvious field marks. In flight shows rufous primaries. Cf. female Ruddy Ground-Dove. In Tumbes cf. very similar Ecuadorian Ground-Dove. Uncommon in arid trop. and subtrop. zones to 2100 m. *Open country from s Mexico to ne Argentina and s Brazil.*

Ecuadorian Ground-Dove *Columbina buckleyi* Tortolita Ecuatoriana
18 cm (7"). Plate 25. ♪ 656. Patterned like Plain-breasted Ground-Dove, but larger. In flight shows black underwing coverts. (Cf. female Blue Ground-Dove). Uncommon in arid trop. zone in Tumbes and Marañón Valley to 1000 m. *Arid w Ecuador and extreme nw Peru.*

Ruddy Ground-Dove *Columbina talpacoti* Tortolita Rojiza
18 cm (7"). Plate 25. ♪ 656. Male is easily identified by its rufous body and gray crown. Female is similar to Plain-breasted and Ecuadorian Ground-Doves but is browner and warmer above, especially on rump. Cf. female Blue Ground-Dove. Common in humid lowland forests e of Andes to 900 m (occasionally higher). *Open country of n Mexico to n Argentina and Brazil.*

Picui Ground-Dove *Columbina picui* Tortolita Picui
18 cm (7"). Plate 25. ♪ 797. The only ground-dove in its range with a black shoulder bar, white on the wing, and black wing lining. Female is duller. Fairly common austral-winter visitor to southern humid lowland forests e of Andes to 400 m. *E Peru to central Argentina, Chile and e Brazil.*

Croaking Ground-Dove *Columbina cruziana* Tortolita Peruana
18 cm (7"). Plate 25. ♪ 656. Both sexes readily identified by the yellow base of the bill and dark shoulder bar. Underwing lining is black. Female is duller and lacks gray head. Has a distinctive frog-like call. Common in arid trop. and subtrop. zones, rarely to 2900 m in Arequipa. *Arid w Ecuador, Peru and n Chile.*

Blue Ground-Dove *Claravis pretiosa* Tortolita Azul
21 cm (8.5"). Plate 25. ♪ 797. Larger than *Columbina* ground-doves, usually found in forest edge and under cover. The light blue-gray male is unique. Either sex readily told by the large size and yellow bill. Female is brownish (cf. female Ruddy Ground-Dove). Fairly common in arid trop. zone and in humid lowlands e of Andes. *S Mexico to n Argentina and s Brazil.*

Maroon-chested Ground-Dove *Claravis mondetoura* Tortolita Pechimarrón
23 cm (9"). Plate 25. ♪ 656. Associated with seeding *Chusquea* bamboo. Both sexes have white undertail coverts. The male is blue-gray above with a maroon chest and breast, and two dark purple wingbars. Female is uniformly brown with two to three dark wingbars. Rare nomad in humid montane forests at 1500-3400 m. *Locally from s Mexico to w Bolivia.*

Metriopelia **Ground-Doves.** A trio of forest and woodland understory doves. Often seen walking on trails; when flushed they usually fly a short distance and land on nearby low branches.

Bare-faced Ground-Dove *Metriopelia ceciliae* Tortolita Moteada
18 cm (7.5"). Plate 24. ♪ LNS. No other ground-dove has as much bare yellow (sometimes yellow-orange) skin around the eye. The bare skin has a dark border. Other ground-doves in its range all have less bare skin and do not appear as mottled. In flight note white corners on the tail. Fairly common in arid subtrop. and temp. zones to 3400 m. *Andes of Peru to n Chile and nw Argentina.*

Black-winged Ground-Dove *Metriopelia melanoptera* Tortolita Alinegra
23 cm (9"). Plate 24. ♪ 797. Note the white at the bend of wings, the blackish legs and black tail. Fairly common in arid temp. zone at 2000-4300 m; accidental near sea level. *Andes of sw Colombia to nw Argentina and central Chile.*

Golden-spotted Ground-Dove *Metriopelia aymara* Tortolita Doradipunteada
18 cm (7.5"). Plate 24. ♪ 797. An inconspicuous, short-tailed ground-dove. Similar to Black-winged Ground-Dove but paler, with dark spots on the tertials, black on the sides, and inconspicuous golden spots on the wing coverts. In flight shows a rufous patch at base of the secondaries. Uncommon in *puna* zone north to Ayacucho and Junín at 3500-5000 m. *Andes of s Peru to nw Argentina and central Chile.*

Leptotila **Doves.** A trio of forest and woodland understory doves, often seen walking on trails. When flushed they usually fly a short distance and land on nearby low branches.

White-tipped Dove *Leptotila verreauxi* Paloma Coliblanca
27 cm (10.5"). Plate 25. ♪797. The two ssp. that occur in Peru differ mainly in color of orbital skin; blue in *decipiens* (eastern lowlands), and red in *decolor* (south to Marañón Valley and on Pacific slope south to La Libertad). Gray-fronted Dove has a gray forecrown. Cf. Eared and Ochre-bellied Doves. Fairly common in trop. and subtrop. zones to 3000 m. *S Texas to n Argentina and Brazil.*

Gray-fronted Dove *Leptotila rufaxilla* Paloma Frentigris
27 cm (10.5"). Plate 25. ♪797. Often sympatric with White-tipped Dove, but the crown (or at least most of forecrown) is gray and orbital skin is red. Cf. Ochre-bellied Dove. Fairly common in arid trop. zone and lowlands e of Andes to 1500 m. *S Venezuela and Guianas to ne Argentina and Brazil.*

*Ochre-bellied Dove *Leptotila ochraceiventris* Paloma Ventriocrácea
23 cm (9"). Plate 26. ♪656. Shy. The only *Leptotila* in its limited range with rich buff underparts. Has red orbital skin (sympatric race of White-tipped Dove has blue orbital skin). Rare in evergreen and deciduous forests in Tumbes and Piura at 500-2625 m. Reported from Zona Reservada de Tumbes. *Andes and lowlands of sw Ecuador and extreme nw Peru.*

Geotrygon Quail-Doves. Four plump, short-tailed terrestrial, doves of forest interior. They are shy and retiring and easily flushed. Best observed on trails during early morning hours.

Sapphire Quail-Dove *Geotrygon saphirina* Paloma-Perdiz Zafiro
26 cm (10.1"). Plate 25. ♪656. If seen well, note dark-blue tail and rump, white cheeks and forecrown, and whitish belly which distinguish this quail-dove. Uncommon in humid montane forests south to Cusco at 900-1500 m. *Humid forests of nw Colombia to e Peru and extreme w Brazil.*

White-throated Quail-Dove *Geotrygon frenata* Paloma-Perdiz Gargantiblanca
33 cm (13"). Plate 25. ♪797. A large quail-dove, and the only one with buffy cheeks and a black malar stripe. Also note the grayish on the nape and back of crown. Uncommon in humid montane forests at 900-3000 m. *Andes of Colombia to nw Argentina.*

Violaceous Quail-Dove *Geotrygon violacea* Paloma-Perdiz Violácea
23 cm (9"). Plate 25. ♪656. A quail-dove with a plain head (lacks malar stripe or cheek stripe). Recalls White-tipped Dove, but shorter tail lacks white tips, and mantle is violet. Rare and local in *terra firme* forest in extreme e Peru. Regularly seen visiting a clay lick near where Río Madre de Dios joins Río Blanco. A specimen was collected close to Brazilian border in Ucayali. *Nicaragua to Colombia, Venezuela, Suriname, e Brazil, Paraguay, Uruguay and ne Argentina.*

Ruddy Quail-Dove *Geotrygon montana* Paloma-Perdiz Rojiza
23 cm (9"). Plate 25. ♪797. A dark quail-dove with a distinctive rufous-brown cheek stripe. Upperparts are ruddy in male and brown in female. The rufous malar stripe and rufous upperparts are distinctive. Fairly common in humid lowland forests e of Andes, occasionally to 1500 m. *Tropical s Mexico to n Argentina and se Brazil; Greater Antilles.*

Psittacidae (Parrots and Macaws; Cotorras y Guacamayos). Species: World 354; Peru 49
A large family of birds, primarily restricted to the tropics, that extends into the high latitudes in the southern hemisphere. They range from the lowland rainforests to above treeline in the Andes. The larger members of the family, particularly the macaws and Amazon parrots, have loud, raucous calls, which can be heard over great distances—even with the muffled effect caused by the dense foliage of the rainforest. Although most members of the family have superb powers of flight, one species—the New Zealand Kakapo (*Strigops habroptilus*)—is flightless. The diet of most parrots consists primarily of vegetable foods, especially fruits, seeds and buds. Many Neotropical parrots visit "clay" licks (*ccolpas*) along streams and banks, but the nutritious value of this supplement is still in doubt.

Blue-and-yellow Macaw *Ara ararauna* Guacamayo Azul y Amarillo
83 cm (33"). Plate 27. ♪797. Unmistakable and beautiful. Underparts and underwings are almost all yellow. Fairly common and local in humid lowland forests e of Andes to 500 m. *Tropical e Panama to n Bolivia and e Brazil.*

*Military Macaw *Ara militaris* Guacamayo Militar
71 cm (28"). Plate 27. ♪797. Larger than the other green macaws, and the only one with a red forecrown and no red on underwing or belly. Rare in e Andes south to Huánuco at 500-1500 m, and occasionally to 2400 m in Marañón Valley. Rare visitor on Pacific slope south to Chiclayo (Sept.-Oct.) to exploit seasonally available fruit. *Dry forests of Mexico to nw Argentina.*

Scarlet Macaw *Ara macao* Guacamayo Escarlata
89 cm (35"). Plate 27. ♪797. The yellow bar on the upperwing distinguishes this stunning macaw from the equally beautiful Red-and-green Macaw. Facial skin lacks bold dark lines. Fairly common in humid lowland forests to 500 m. *Tropical s Mexico to n Bolivia and Amazonian Brazil.*

Red-and-green Macaw *Ara chloroptera* Guacamayo Rojo y Verde
96 cm (38"). Plate 27. ♪797. Similar to Scarlet Macaw, but upperwing has a green (not yellow) bar, and bare facial skin has dark lines. Fairly common in humid lowland forests e of Andes to 500 m. *Humid e Panama to n Argentina and Brazil.*

Chestnut-fronted Macaw *Ara severa* Guacamayo Frenticastaño
48 cm (19"). Plate 27. ♪797. Best told by its chestnut frontlet, "lined" facial skin, and red at bend of the wing. Underwings are red. Common in humid lowlands e of Andes, especially in *várzea* and *Mauritia* palm forests to 1000 m. *E Panama to n Bolivia and Amazonian Brazil.*

Red-bellied Macaw *Orthopsittaca manilata* Guacamayo Ventrirrojo
51 cm (20"). Plate 27. ♪797. The only green macaw with bare facial skin that extends to the frontlet. Lacks red on wing, wrist or tail. The red on belly is not always conspicuous. Common in humid lowland forests e of Andes to 500 m, especially in *Mauritia* palm forests. *S Venezuela and the Guianas to n Bolivia and Amazonian Brazil.*

Blue-headed Macaw *Propyrrhura couloni* Guacamayo Cabeciazul
40 cm (15.5"). Plate 26. ♪816CD. The only macaw with a blue head and dark facial skin. Fairly common and local in humid lowland forests e of Andes to 1500 m. *Forests of e Peru, n Bolivia and w Amazonian Brazil.*

Red-shouldered Macaw *Diopsittaca nobilis* Guacamayo Enano
35 cm (14"). Plate 27. ♪797. Note limited range. The smallest macaw (smaller than some *Aratingas*). Note the small bare facial skin patch, bicolored bill, and red underwing and shoulder. Fairly common in savanna and *Mauritia* palm forests in Pampas del Heath. Recent dramatic range expansion into Tambopata area. *E Venezuela and the Guianas to n Bolivia, n and e Brazil.*

Scarlet-fronted Parakeet *Aratinga wagleri* Cotorra Frentiescarlata
38 cm (15"). Plate 27. The only parakeet with red on the front part of crown (but does not extend below the eye) and on the shoulder. Cf. Mitred Parakeet. Common in montane forests on Pacific slope of Andes south to Tacna, and in central Andes from Marañón Valley south to Ayacucho and Apurímac, usually at 500-2000 m but occasionally 350-3000 m. *Mountains of n Venezuela and Colombia; w Ecuador to central Peru.*

Mitred Parakeet *Aratinga mitrata* Cotorra Mitrada
38 cm (15"). Plate 27. ♪797. A mostly green *Aratinga* that lacks red on the shoulders. Has variable amounts of red on the face (rather random pattern), especially extensive in nominate ssp., much

reduced in *alticola*. Scarlet- fronted Parakeet has a cleaner face than nominate and has (usually) red shoulders. Race *alticola* from Andes of Cusco is found at higher elevations than Scarlet-fronted Parakeet, has red on face reduced to forecrown, and may possibly represent a separate species. Common and local in intermontane Andean valleys from Huánuco south at 1000-3400 m (rarely to 4000 m), especially in *Prosopis* and *Ochroma* (*Shinus molle*) woodlands. *Andes of central Peru to nw Argentina.*

Red-masked Parakeet *Aratinga erythrogenys* Cotorra Cabecirroja
33 cm (13"). Plate 26. The only *Aratinga* with a red hood and red shoulders. Note leading edge of underwing is red. Common in semiarid scrub in Pacific lowlands south to Lambayeque and Cajamarca to 1400 m. *Arid w Ecuador and nw Peru.*

White-eyed Parakeet *Aratinga leucophthalmus* Cotorra Ojiblanco (Shamiro)
35 cm (14"). Plate 27. ♪797. Note the large orbital skin patch, red shoulders, and green head with few or no red spots. In flight underwing coverts have red and yellow bars. Common in humid lowland forests e of Andes to 1700 m. Recently recorded in Cordillera de Colán in humid elfin forests at 1950 m (Barnes 1997). *Venezuela and the Guianas to n Argentina and Brazil.*

Dusky-headed Parakeet *Aratinga weddellii* Cotorra Cabecioscura
27 cm (10.5"). Plate 27. ♪797. The only *Aratinga* with a combination of grayish hood and conspicuous orbital skin. Lacks red shoulders. Common in humid lowland forests e of Andes to 500 m, rarely to 750 m. *Lowlands of n South America e of Andes.*

Peach-fronted Parakeet *Aratinga aurea* Cotorra Frentidorada
29 cm (11.3"). Plate 27. ♪797. Note limited range. An *Aratinga* with mostly yellow underparts, an olive throat and orange forecrown. Fairly common in savanna and *Mauritia* palm forests in Pampas del Heath to 600 m. *Brazil south of the Amazon and se Peru to n Argentina.*

Golden-plumed Parakeet *Leptosittaca branickii* Loro Cachetidorado
35 cm (14"). Plate 26. ♪LNS. No other parakeet has a yellow tuft behind the eye. Note also the reddish-orange mid-belly band, and the maroon tail. Uncommon and local in stunted timberline forests south to Cusco at 1400-3400 m. Regular on upper parts of Manu Road. Recorded along La Peca Nueva trail and above San Cristóbal (Amazonas) at 1800 m; in Río Abiseo Nat. Park; and at Mashua (La Libertad) at 3300 m. *Humid Andes of Colombia, Ecuador and Peru.*

Painted Parakeet *Pyrrhura picta* Perico Pintado
23 cm (9"). Plate 28. ♪797. A parakeet with a distinctive head pattern. Note the reddish rump, belly and tail. Widespread race *roseifrons* is illustrated. Race *lucianii* (extreme ne Peru) has a dark maroon head with little or no red. Fairly common in humid lowland forests e of Andes to 1200 m. *Patchily distributed from w Panama to Amazonian Brazil.*

Maroon-tailed Parakeet *Pyrrhura melanura* Perico Colimarrón
25 cm (9.8"). Plate 28. The two Peruvian subspecies are similar to Black-capped Parakeet, but Maroon-tailed has a maroon belly and tail is a dark reddish-brown. Race *melanura* (east of Andes) is similar to Huallaga Valley race *berlepschi* (illustrated) but has an even darker tail and chest with red and yellow primary coverts. Uncommon in humid lowland forests e of Andes (*melanura*); uncommon and local on lower east Andean slopes in Huallaga Valley to 1500 m (*berlepschi*). *Venezuela to ne Peru and nw Brazil.*

Black-capped (Rock) Parakeet *Pyrrhura rupicola* Perico Gorrinegro
27 cm (10.5"). Plate 28. 816CD. Similar to Maroon-tailed Parakeet, but the tail is green; crown is darker and stands out more against the green cheeks. Fairly common in lowland *terra firme* and *várzea* forests e of Andes from s Loreto to Madre de Dios and Puno to 600 m. *Humid forests of e Peru, n Bolivia and w Amazonian Brazil.*

Andean Parakeet *Bolborhynchus orbygnesius* Perico Andino
18 cm (7"). Plate 26. ♪ 797. A stocky, short-tailed, uniformly green parakeet with some bluish on the flight feathers. Cf. in parts of range Mountain Parakeet subspecies *margaritae*. All *Forpus* parrotlets occur at much lower elevations. Locally common in montane and elfin forests north to Cajamarca and La Libertad at 3000-4000 m. *Andes of Peru and w Bolivia.*

Barred Parakeet *Bolborhynchus lineola* Perico Barreteado
18 cm (7"). Plate 28. ♪ 797. No other parakeet has barring on the upperparts (not always easy to see when perched, and almost impossible to see in flight). Uncommon in montane forests in Amazonas, Huánuco, Ayacucho and Cusco at 1600-3300 m. *Humid montane forests of s Mexico to s Peru.*

Mountain Parakeet *Psilopsiagon aurifrons* Perico Cordillerano
20 cm (8"). Plate 28. ♪ 797. Three subspecies occur in Peru. The nominate race on Pacific slope (illustrated) is unmistakable, but female is duller and greener. A very rare subspecies (*robertsi*) in the Marañón Valley has yellow only on the foreface and throat. High-altitude altiplano *margaritae* has very little yellow on underparts (or none at all), and a shorter tail. Similar to sympatric Andean Parakeet, but latter has an even shorter tail and is stockier. Fairly common in montane forests and scrub on Pacific slope of Andes from La Libertad to Arequipa at 1000-2900 m, and to 4500 m on altiplano in Puno. *Andes of Peru to central Argentina and n Chile.*

Blue-winged Parrotlet *Forpus xanthopterygius* Periquito Aliazul
12.5 cm (5"). Plate 28. ♪ 797. A tiny grass-green parrotlet, similar to Dusky-billed, but the latter's maxilla is dusky. Blue-winged's maxilla sometimes has a dusky ridge. Female lacks blue markings, and has more yellow-green on face and underparts. Fairly common in humid lowland forests e of Andes to 1200 m. *Patchily distributed n Colombia to ne Argentina and Brazil.*

Dusky-billed Parrotlet *Forpus sclateri* Periquito Piquioscuro
12.5 cm (5"). Plate 28. ♪ 816CD. A tiny parrotlet, similar to Blue-winged, but maxilla is darker. Overall plumage is darker, with less contrasting blue markings on wings and rump. Female lacks blue markings, and has a yellow-green face and cheeks. Uncommon in humid lowland forests e of Andes to 800 m. *Venezuela and the Guianas to n Bolivia and Amazonian Brazil.*

Pacific Parrotlet *Forpus coelestis* Periquito Esmeralda
12.5 cm (5"). Plate 26. The only *Forpus* in its range. Female lacks blue markings on the rump, wings and head, and has a grass-green rump and wing-patch. Gray-cheeked Parakeet is larger, longer-tailed, and has gray cheeks. Common in arid coastal lowlands and on Pacific slope south to La Libertad from sea level to 1000 m; recorded to 2150 m at Huancabamba (e Piura). *Arid w Ecuador and nw Peru.*

*Yellow-faced Parrotlet *Forpus xanthops* Periquito Cariamarillo
14 cm (5.5"). Plate 26. Distinctive. Cf. very rare and localized race *robertsi* of Mountain Parakeet has a much longer tail and green rump. Uncommon and local in upper Marañón Valley (s Amazonas, Cajamarca and La Libertad) at 1000-1600 m, with extremes at 500 m and 2745 m. Recent records from Balsas and Corral Quemado. Reported fairly common by TSS at Soquián (La Libertad). *Endemic to Peru.*

Canary-winged Parakeet *Brotogeris versicolurus* Perico Aliamarillo
23 cm (9"). Plate 28. No other parakeet has a similar wing pattern (yellow on median coverts, white on secondaries). Common in humid lowland forests e of Andes to 1200 m. Feral populations in Lima. *Lowlands of se Colombia to e Peru and Amazonian Brazil.*

*Gray-cheeked Parakeet *Brotogeris pyrrhopterus* Perico Cachetigris (Perico Macareño)
21 cm (8.5"). Plate 26. No other parakeet in its range has gray cheeks and forecrown and a bluish-green crown. Cf. much smaller Pacific Parrotlet. Note the orange underwing lining. Fairly common in arid scrub on Pacific slope in Tumbes and Piura, occasionally to 1500 m. Recorded regularly at Zona Reservada de Tumbes. *Arid scrub of w Ecuador and extreme nw Peru.*

Cobalt-winged Parakeet *Brotogeris cyanoptera* Perico Alicobalto
20 cm (8"). Plate 28. ♪797. Similar to sympatric Tui Parakeet. Two subspecies in Peru (*gustavi* in upper Huallaga Valley, illustrated, may represent a separate species). Widespread nominate form lacks yellow wing band but otherwise is similar. Common in lowland forests e of Andes to 1000 m, occasionally to 1350 m in San Martín. *Lowlands of w Amazon basin.*

Tui Parakeet *Brotogeris sanctithomae* Perico Tui
14 cm (5.5"). Plate 28. Similar to Cobalt-winged Parakeet, but lacks the cobalt-blue on the flight feathers. Also lacks Cobalt-winged's orange chin, and yellow crown is larger and more prominent. Common in humid lowland forests e of Andes to 300 m. *Mainly along rivers in w Amazon basin.*

Amazonian Parrotlet *Nannopsittaca dachilleae* Periquito Amazónico
12.5 cm (5"). Plate 26. ♪816CD. The only small parrotlet in its range that is green with a bluish crown (more pronounced on the forecrown). Cf. females of *Forpus* parrotlets lack blue on the crown. Fairly common in humid lowlands of Ucayali and Madre de Dios to 300 m. Fairly regular in Manu National Park and Pampas del Heath, with occasional reports in Tambopata region. Recent records from Iquitos area (pers. comm. Charles Munn). *Tropical se Peru and nw Bolivia.*

Scarlet-shouldered Parrotlet *Touit huetii* Periquito Alirroja
15 cm (6"). Plate 28. ♪816CD. Both sexes have blue wing coverts, red underwing linings and yellow undertail coverts. Female has a green tail. Uncommon in lowland *terra firme* forests e of Andes to 1200 m. *Patchily distributed n South America to n Bolivia and n Brazil.*

Sapphire-rumped Parrotlet *Touit purpurata* Periquito Lomizafiro
18 cm (7"). Plate 28. ♪652. Note limited range. A small green parrotlet with conspicuous dark brown scapulars that form a "V" on back. Has green underwings and undertail coverts. Note blue rump and mostly maroon tail. Female has a green terminal tail band. Uncommon in humid lowland forests in Loreto to 400 m. *S Venezuela and the Guianas to Ecuador and n Amazonian Brazil.*

*Spot-winged Parrotlet *Touit stictoptera* Periquito Alipunteado
18 cm (7"). Plate 28. Male has brown wing coverts tipped with white, and a yellow-orange patch on the greater coverts. Female has green wings with dark centers to median and lesser coverts. Rare and local in humid montane forests in Cordillera del Cóndor, lower Río Marañón, and Cordillera de Cutucú, chiefly at 1050-1700 m. Fairly common at Abra Patricia, and recorded at San José de Lourdes at 1200 m. *Locally in Andes of s Colombia to ne Peru.*

Black-headed Parrot *Pionites melanocephala* Loro Cabecinegro
23 cm (9"). Plate 29. ♪542. The black crown, contrasting pale face and underparts are diagnostic. Cf. immature White-bellied Parrot may have a few dark feathers on the crown. Fairly common in humid lowland forests e of Andes south to s Ucayali to 600 m. *S Venezuela and the Guianas to ne Peru and n Brazil.*

White-bellied Parrot *Pionites leucogaster* Loro Ventriblanco
23 cm (9"). Plate 29. ♪797. No other parrot has a peach crown, yellowish cheeks and a white belly. Fairly common in lowland forests e of Andes north to upper Río Ucayali to 800 m. *Tropical forests of Amazon basin s of the Amazon.*

Orange-cheeked Parrot *Pionopsitta barrabandi* Loro Cachetinaranja
25 cm (9.8"). Plate 29. ♪ 816CD. Unmistakable. No other parrot has a black head, an orange cheek patch and red underwing linings. Immature has a golden head. Uncommon and local in humid lowland *terra firme* forests e of Andes to 500 m. *S Venezuela to n Bolivia and w Amazonian Brazil.*

Black-winged Parrot *Hapalopsittaca melanotis* Loro Alinegro
25 cm (9.8"). Plate 26. ♪ 797. The only parrot in its range with extensive black markings on upperwing, and a bluish collar. Note the blue terminal tail band and green wing lining. Rare in humid montane forests on e slope of Andes north to Huánuco, Pasco and Junín at 2800-3450 m. *Andes of central Peru to w Bolivia.*

*Red-faced Parrot *Hapalopsittaca pyrrhops* Loro Carirrojo
23 cm (9"). Plate 26. ♪ LNS. Within its limited range, the only parrot with a red face, red shoulders and a dark blue terminal tail band. Note that in flight leading edge of the underwing is red, and the remainder of underwing is light blue. Rare and local in montane cloud forests on Cerro Chinguela at 2500-3000 m. *Andes of s Ecuador and adjacent nw Peru.*

Short-tailed Parrot *Graydidascalus brachyurus* Loro Colicorto
25 cm (9.8"). Plate 29. ♪ LNS. Note limited range. A stocky, green parrot with a very short, square tail; at close range shows yellow edging to upperwing coverts. In flight shows red at the base of leading edge of upperwing, and red on base of outer tail feathers (no red on tail of immatures). All other small green parrots or parrotlets have longer and more pointed tails. Locally common in lowland *várzea* forests in Loreto to 400 m. Several large roosts along rivers in Iquitos area near ExplorNapo Lodges. *Mainly along rivers in Amazon basin.*

***Pionus* Parrots.** A genus of medium-sized, square-tailed parrots, that all have red undertail coverts.

Blue-headed Parrot *Pionus menstruus* Loro Cabeciazul
27 cm (10.5"). Plate 29. ♪ 797. The blue head of the adult male makes it unmistakable. Immature has a green head with varying amounts of blue. Common to abundant in humid lowland forests e of Andes, occasionally to 1400 m. *Costa Rica to Bolivia, Amazonian and e Brazil.*

Red-billed Parrot *Pionus sordidus* Loro Piquirrojo
27 cm (10.5"). Plate 29. ♪ 797. A green *Pionus* with a red bill and some blue on the throat. In flight note blue outer tail feathers. Immature Blue-headed Parrot is similar, but has a duskier bill and lacks blue on tail. Fairly common in subtrop. montane forests on e slope of Andes in Amazonas and San Martín at 500-1500 m. *Mountains of n Venezuela to w Bolivia.*

Speckle-faced Parrot *Pionus tumultuosus* Loro Tumultuoso
27 cm (10.5"). Plate 26. ♪ 797. Nominate race (illustrated) has a distinctive plum-colored head and is speckled white on cheeks. Head of northern ssp. *seniloides* is heavily speckled with white over pinkish and its underparts are tinged reddish. Both races in flight show red at base of the outer tail feathers. Nominate race uncommon in montane forests north to Carpish Mts. (Huánuco) at 1400-3300 m. Race *seniloides* (sometimes considered a separate species) rare in montane forests in Cajamarca and La Libertad at 2000-2300 m. *Andes of w Venezuela to Peru and w Bolivia.*

Bronze-winged Parrot *Pionus chalcopterus* Loro Alibronceado
27 cm (10.5"). Plate 29. Unlikely to be confused in its limited range. In flight underwing and undertail are sky-blue, and most of underwing lining is bluish-purple. Uncommon in trop. and subtrop. forests in Piura and Tumbes at 1400-2800 m. Fairly common in Zona Reservada de Tumbes. *Humid forests of w Venezuela to nw Peru.*

Amazona **Parrots.** Medium to fairly large, mostly green parrots with square tails and broad wings. Most show some red on the secondaries.

Festive Parrot *Amazona festiva* Loro Lomirrojo
38 cm (15"). Plate 29. ♪ 677. Note limited range. The only *Amazona* that has a red rump. Note also the red lores. Lacks red on wings. Fairly common and local in humid lowland *várzea* and *igapó* forests in Loreto to 500 m. *Riverine forests of Amazon and Orinoco basins.*

Yellow-crowned Parrot *Amazona ochrocephala* Loro Coroniamarilla
35 cm (14"). Plate 29. ♪ 797. Yellow is limited to crown. Note the yellowish terminal tail-band on mostly greenish tail. Fairly common in humid lowland forests and woodlands e of Andes to 500 m. *Tropical n Honduras; Panama to Bolivia and Amazonian Brazil.*

Orange-winged Parrot *Amazona amazonica* Loro Alinaranja
33 cm (13"). Plate 29. ♪ 797. Face pattern is unique, but otherwise similar to higher-elevation Scaly-naped Parrot. Uncommon in humid lowland forests e of Andes to 500 m. *Tropical Amazon basin; Trinidad and Tobago.*

Scaly-naped Parrot *Amazona mercenaria* Loro Nuquiescamosa
33 cm (13"). Plate 29. ♪ 797. Lacks the yellow facial markings of Orange-winged Parrot, and has a smaller red speculum (ranges do not overlap). Note tail pattern. Fairly common in humid montane forests on e slope of Andes at 800-3200 m. *Mountains of nw Venezuela to w Bolivia.*

Mealy Parrot *Amazona farinosa* Loro Harinosa
40 cm (15.5"). Plate 29. ♪ 797. The largest *Amazona*. Neck and mantle are frosty gray-green. Has a conspicuous, wide yellow terminal tail band and bare orbital skin. Shows variable amounts of yellow flecks on forecrown. Fairly common in humid lowland forests e of Andes to 500 m. *Tropical se Mexico to n Bolivia, Amazonian and e Brazil.*

Red-fan Parrot *Deroptyus accipitrinus* Loro de Abanico
35 cm (14"). Plate 29. Note limited range. One of most unique and beautiful New World parrots. Sometimes raises its neck feathers into a fan. Very local on upper Río Pastaza in n Loreto. *Humid lowland forests of n Amazon basin to the Guianas.*

Cuculidae (Cuckoos; Cuclillos). Species: World 138; Peru 17
The family is comprised of three subfamilies (formerly regarded as separate families), the Cuckoos, Anis and Ground-Cuckoos. New World cuckoos are slender, short-legged birds with long, graduated tails, that range from southern Canada to southern South America, including islands in the Caribbean and the Galápagos. Most are sedentary, but northern breeders regularly migrate to warmer climates during the northern winter. Their diet consists mainly of insects; and at least some species of *Coccyzus* take hairy caterpillars by beating them on a branch, extracting and eating the viscera, and discarding the remainder. The coccyzids usually raise their own young, but some species of *Coccyzus* occasionally are brood parasites.

Ash-colored Cuckoo *Coccyzus cinereus* Cuclillo Gris
23 cm (9"). Plate 30. A small, dull grayish cuckoo with a relatively short, ungraduated tail, black bill and red eye-ring. Resembles Black-billed Cuckoo, but Ash-colored has a pale grayish throat and chest. Rare in humid lowland forests in s Peru (possibly vagrants or migrants), with recent records from Pampas del Heath. *S Brazil to n Argentina, Paraguay, Bolivia and extreme se Peru.*

Black-billed Cuckoo *Coccyzus erythropthalmus* Cuclillo Piquinegro
28 cm (10.9"). Plate 30. ♪ 626. Like Dark-billed Cuckoo, but tail spots are small, base of tail is gray, and face lacks a black mask. Black-billed's eye-ring is red and underparts are whiter. Rare northern-winter migrant in lowlands e of Andes, rarely to lower limit of temp. zone. Recently recorded at Campo Verde (Whiffen and Sadgrove 2000). *Breeds e North America; winters to Bolivia.*

Yellow-billed Cuckoo *Coccyzus americanus* Cuclillo Piquiamarillo
30 cm (11.7"). Plate 30. ♪ 626. The only Peruvian cuckoo with yellow on lower mandible and white underparts. Rufous primaries prominent in flight. Uncommon migrant in humid lowland forests e of Andes. *Breeds Canada to Mexico and West Indies; winters to n Argentina.*

Dark-billed Cuckoo *Coccyzus melacoryphus* Cuclillo Piquioscuro
26 cm (10.1"). Plate 30. ♪ 797. A cuckoo with a blackish mask, gray sides of neck and buff underparts. Gray-capped Cuckoo is similar, but is cinnamon below and darker above. Uncommon in humid lowlands e of Andes; rarely to 2800 m in semiarid e Andean valleys. *Venezuela and the Guianas to n Argentina; Galápagos Is.*

Gray-capped Cuckoo *Coccyzus lansbergi* Cuclillo Gorrigris
25 cm (9.8"). Plate 30. ♪ 624. Cinnamon below, gray head contrasts with ruddy back. Cf. Dark-billed Cuckoo. Rare migrant in arid w subtrop. zone. Accidental at Bosque de Ampay at 4000 m. *Forests of w Colombia to nw Venezuela; winters to w Peru.*

Squirrel Cuckoo *Piaya cayana* Cuco Ardilla
40 cm (15.5"). Plate 30. ♪ 797. A cuckoo with a very long tail, yellow bill, a conspicuous red orbital ring, and a broad, light-gray band on the mid-belly. Cf. Black-bellied Cuckoo and Little Cuckoo. Fairly common on Pacific slope south to Piura. Common in humid trop. and subtrop. forests e of Andes, occasionally to 2550 m along e slope of Andes. *Mexico to s Brazil and n Argentina.*

Black-bellied Cuckoo *Piaya melanogaster* Cuco Ventrinegro
36 cm (14"). Plate 30. ♪ 816CD. Similar to Squirrel Cuckoo, but has a red bill, gray cap and yellow supraloral spot. Ruddy chest gradually blends into black belly. Uncommon in humid lowland primary forests e of Andes. *S Venezuela and the Guianas to e Peru and w Amazonian Brazil.*

Little Cuckoo *Piaya minuta* Cuco Menudo
27 cm (10.5"). Plate 30. ♪ 797. Similar to Squirrel Cuckoo, but smaller, with a much shorter tail and bill, and more uniform underparts. Uncommon in humid lowland forests e of Andes. *Lowlands of e Panama to n Bolivia and Amazonian Brazil.*

***Crotophaga* Anis.** Anis are black, short-winged, long-tailed, sociable cuckoos with deep, laterally compressed black bills. Their diet consists primarily of insects, but they may take animal prey as large as lizards.

Greater Ani *Crotophaga major* Garrapatero Grande (Locrero)
48 cm (19"). Plate 30. ♪ 797. A large, long-tailed, glossy-blue cuckoo with a ridged bill and pale eyes. Sympatric Smooth-billed Ani is smaller, dark eyed and blacker. Cf. Giant Cowbird (different body shape). Locally common in lowland aquatic habitats e of Andes. *E Panama and South America e of Andes to n Argentina.*

Smooth-billed Ani *Crotophaga ani* Garrapatero Piquiliso
33 cm (13"). Plate 30. ♪ 797. Similar to Groove-billed Ani, but bill has a high-arched ridge on the maxilla. Common in humid lowland and subtrop. forests e of Andes; occasionally to 2800 m in central Andean valleys. *Southern US to Brazil and n Argentina; West Indies.*

Groove-billed Ani *Crotophaga sulcirostris* Garrapatero Piquiestriado (Guardacaballo)
33 cm (13"). Plate 30. ♪ 626. The only ani on the Pacific Coast. In contact zone with Smooth-billed Ani note that bill lacks a ridge. Deep grooves on maxilla are visible at close range. Common in arid trop. and subtrop. zones; locally to 2700 m in n Peru. Accidental near Laguna Huacarpay (Cusco) at 3100 m (Fjeldså and Krabbe 1990). *Texas to n Chile and Argentina.*

Ground-Cuckoos and Roadrunners. Long-legged, long-tailed, short-winged, terrestrial cuckoos. Their diet consists primarily of insects and small vertebrates, but roadrunners frequently kill and eat snakes, including some venomous species. The roadrunners (*Geococcyx*) and ground-cuckoos (*Morococcyx* and *Neomorphus*) are self-brooders, whereas the Striped, Pheasant and Pavonine Cuckoos are brood parasites.

Striped Cuckoo *Tapera naevia* Cuclillo Listado
28 cm (10.9"). Plate 30. ♪ 797. Distinguished from *Dromococcyx* cuckoos by its streaked crown and back. Uncommon in arid trop. zone and fairly common in trop. and lower subtrop. zones e of Andes. *Mexico to Brazil and n Argentina.*

***Dromococcyx* Cuckoos.** A pair of extremely shy and secretive cuckoos with long, lightly tipped wide tails and pointed crests.

Pheasant Cuckoo *Dromococcyx phasianellus* Cuco Faisán
38 cm (15"). Plate 30. ♪ 797. Note the white postocular stripe and streaked neck and chest. Pavonine has buffier head and breast and unstreaked chest. Cf. Striped Cuckoo. Rare in humid lowland forests e of Andes. *Lowlands of s Mexico to se Brazil and ne Argentina.*

Pavonine Cuckoo *Dromococcyx pavoninus* Cuco Pavonino
25 cm (9.8"). Plate 30. ♪ 797. Like Pheasant Cuckoo, but entire head area has unstreaked rich buff tones. Rare in humid lowland forests e of Andes. *South America e of the Andes to ne Argentina.*

***Neomorphus* Ground-Cuckoos.** Two terrestrial cuckoos, shaped like roadrunners; both Peruvian species are forest birds. A loud bill-clacking, often heard when accompanied by antbirds in a mixed-species flock.

Rufous-vented Ground-Cuckoo *Neomorphus geoffroyi* Cuco-Terrestre Ventrirrufo
45 cm (17.5"). Plate 30. ♪ LNS. Similar to Red-billed Ground-Cuckoo, but bill is yellow and vent is rufous. Rare in humid lowland forests e of Andes. Recently reported from Lago Sándoval (PC). *Nicaragua to n Bolivia and se Brazil.*

Red-billed Ground-Cuckoo *Neomorphus pucheranii* Cuco-Terrestre Piquirrojo
45 cm (17.5"). Facing Plate 30. The only ground-cuckoo with a fairly thick, red bill. Possible overlap (?) with Rufous-vented in ne Peru. Regularly recorded near Tahuayo Lodge, and recently recorded at Caño Pichana, Loreto (Ascanio 1998). Rare in humid lowland forests e of Andes. *NE Peru and w Amazonian Brazil.*

Tytonidae (Barn Owls; Lechuzas de Campanario). Species: World 16; Peru 1
The Barn Owl (*Tyto alba*) is perhaps the world's most widely distributed species, with an almost cosmopolitan distribution. Barn Owls are characterized by their white, heart-shaped faces. They are extremely efficient nocturnal hunters, and take a variety of small mammals, birds, bats and insects.

Barn Owl *Tyto alba* Lechuza Campanaria
38 cm (15"). Plate 31. ♪ 797. An unmistakable owl with a white heart-shaped face. Note that some populations have buffy underparts. Uncommon from arid trop. to temp. zones. *Cosmopolitan; wide distribution worldwide.*

Strigidae (Typical Owls; Búhos). Species: World 189; Peru 30
Like Barn Owls, typical strigids have soft, dense plumage that renders them virtually soundless in flight. Most species have patterns that match the lichen-covered trunks and branches of their abodes, and are difficult to see when roosting during the day. Most are nocturnal, but *Glaucidium* species are often heard and seen during daylight hours. Strigid owls have a wide distribution, from the Arctic to the high latitudes of the southern hemisphere. As with Barn Owls, they take a variety of animal food, depending upon the size of the owl and its habitat.

Otus **Screech Owls.** A large genus of 64 species, well represented in Peru with nine species, but usually with only two to three species in any locale. They are fairly small owls, often with small to prominent ear tufts. Like many nocturnal birds, their vocalizations are often the most reliable clue to identification. Many members are polymorphic and have a typical gray or rufous morph, and occasionally a brown morph.

Tropical Screech-Owl *Otus choliba* Lechuza Tropical
24 cm (9.4"). Plate 31. ♪ 654. The most widespread screech-owl. Note the yellow eyes and prominent black rim around the face. Similar to West Peruvian and Koepcke's Screech-Owls, but no known overlap. Sympatric with Tawny-bellied and Vermiculated Screech-Owls. Fairly common in humid trop. and subtrop. forests e of the Andes to 2500 m. *Costa Rica to n Argentina and s Brazil.*

Peruvian Screech-Owl *Otus roboratus* Lechuza Peruana
25 cm (9.8"). Plate 32. Two races occur in Peru and may represent separate species. Nominate race *roboratus* (drainage of Río Chinchipe and Río Marañón) is significantly larger than *pacificus* (arid tropical lowlands south to Lambayeque and Lima). Both races have yellow eyes and black facial rims, but *pacificus*' facial rim is not as pronounced. Both are relatively dark (*pacificus* slightly paler). Both races have a rufous morph, which is more common in *pacificus*. Cf. Koepcke's Screech-Owl. Fairly common and local in arid woodlands south to Lima from sea level to 2500 m. *NW Peru and adjacent sw Ecuador.*

Koepcke's Screech-Owl *Otus koepckeae* Lechuza de Koepcke
24 cm (9.4"). Plate 32. Larger than West Peruvian Screech-Owl, with coarser "fishbone" markings on the underparts. Not known to overlap but comes close to range of West Peruvian Screech-Owl race *pacificus*. Rare and poorly known in arid montane forests in Amazonas, Ancash and Ayacucho at 1500-3200 m. *Disjunct in Andes of n Peru and central Bolivia.*

Rufescent Screech-Owl *Otus ingens* Lechuza Rojiza
26 cm (10.1"). Plate 31. ♪ 654. A fairly large, dark-eyed screech-owl, that lacks a black facial rim. Plumage varies from rufescent to sandy-brown and grayish. Fairly coarse "fishbone" markings on underparts. Cf. highly local Cinnamon and Cloud-forest Screech-Owls. Fairly common in montane forests on e slope of Andes at 1500-3400 m. Recorded on Manu Road at 1600-2200 m. *Andes of w Venezuela to w Bolivia.*

Cinnamon Screech-Owl *Otus petersoni* Lechuza Canela
26 cm (10.1"). Plate 32. ♪ 654. A fairly small screech-owl with dark eyes, cinnamon underparts and a narrow black facial rim. Has narrow "fishbone" markings on cinnamon underparts (including lower belly). Rufescent Screech-Owl is paler and larger, has a whitish lower belly, and lacks the black rim. Cloud-forest Screech-Owl has boldly marked underparts. Rare and local in cloud forests of Cordillera del Cóndor. Recently recorded in La Peca Nueva region at 1900-2500 m. *S Ecuador (Cordillera de Cutucú) and ne Peru.*

Cloud-forest Screech-Owl *Otus marshalli* Lechuza de Bosque Neblina
25 cm (9.8"). Plate 32. ♪ 654. A dark-eyed screech-owl with a cinnamon face surrounded by a dark rim and bold markings on whitish underparts. Other sympatric screech-owls (Cinnamon, Rufescent, White-throated) lack such markings. Uncommon in cloud forests in Cordillera Yanachaga and Cordillera Vilcabamba at 1650-2450 m. *Endemic to Peru.*

Tawny-bellied Screech-Owl *Otus watsonii* Lechuza Ventrileonada
23 cm (9"). Plate 31. ♪ 654. A common screech-owl with many color morphs (rufous morph illustrated), all of which share dark eyes, pronounced ear-tufts, and buffy to tawny underparts with "fishbone" markings. Tropical Screech-Owl has yellow eyes and a thicker black rim on face. Vermiculated Screech-Owl has fine vermiculations on underparts, and lacks a dark rim on face. Note: König *et al.* (1999) regard *O. w. usta* (Southern Tawny-bellied Screech-Owl) as a distinct species. Common in humid lowland and foothill forests along e slope of Andes to 900 m. *Tropical e Colombia to Bolivia, ne Argentina and Amazonian Brazil.*

Vermiculated Screech-Owl *Otus vermiculatus* Lechuza Vermiculada
26 cm (10.1"). Plate 33. ♪ 654. A screech-owl that lacks a dark rim to face, and has fine vermiculations on underparts. Eyes are yellow to brown. Tropical Screech-Owl has a black facial rim. Cf. Tawny-bellied Screech-Owl. Taxonomic classification of the species is problematic. König *et al.* (1999) regard the ssp. *helleri* that occurs in Peru, and the ssp. *napensis* that may occur in n Peru, as a distinct species (Río Napo Screech-Owl). Hardy recognized them as part of *Otus roraimae* (Tepui Screech-Owl). Fairly common in humid lowland and foothill forests on e slope of Andes from 250 to 1500 m. *Costa Rica to Venezuela, Brazil, Peru and n Bolivia.*

White-throated Screech-Owl *Otus albogularis* Lechuza Gargantiblanca
28 cm (10.9"). Plate 31. ♪ 654. A fairly large screech-owl with orange-yellow eyes, almost no ear-tufts, a dark face, and a broad chest band with a contrasting white throat. Fairly common in temp. and subtrop. montane forests at 2200-3000 m. *Andes of w Venezuela to w Bolivia.*

Great Horned Owl *Bubo virginianus* Búho Americano
53 cm (21"). Plate 33. ♪ 654. A very large owl with conspicuous ear tufts. In contact zone cf. Magellanic Horned Owl. Uncommon in arid subtrop. and temp. zones; in *puna* zone mainly above 3000 m. *Alaska to the Guianas, Bolivia and central Argentina.*

Magellanic Horned Owl *Bubo magellanicus* Búho Magallánico
48 cm (19"). Plate 31. ♪ 797. Similar to Great Horned Owl, but smaller, with weaker bill and talons. Underparts are vermiculated (not barred) and lack the dark chest area typical of Great Horned Owl. Recent split from Great Horned Owl (del Hoyo *et al.* 1999). Uncommon in rocky upland pastures south from central Peru at 2500-4500 m. *Central Peru to w Bolivia and w Argentina south to Tierra del Fuego and Cape Horn.*

Ciccaba **Owls.** Four species of medium-sized owls that have rounded heads and lack ear tufts. The genus is sometimes merged with Old World genus *Strix*.

Mottled Owl *Ciccaba virgata* Búho Café
33 cm (13"). Plate 31. ♪ 654. Note the dark eyes. Mostly dark face contrasts with whitish rim and spectacles. Underparts streaked, heavier on chest. All other *Ciccaba* are barred below. Upperparts mottled. Variable, light morph is illustrated. Cf. Rufous-banded Owl. Rare in humid lowland forests e of Andes. *N Mexico to ne Argentina and Brazil.*

Black-and-white Owl *Ciccaba nigrolineata* Búho Blanquinegro
38 cm (15"). Plate 33. ♪ 654. Note limited range. Similar to Black-banded Owl, but underparts are white barred narrowly with black. Upperparts and crown are unbarred black. Rare in extreme northern arid trop. zone. Recorded in Tumbes at Campo Verde (Whiffen and Sadgrove 2000). *Lowlands of s Mexico to nw Peru.*

Black-banded Owl *Ciccaba huhula* Búho Negribandeado
38 cm (15"). Plate 33. ♪ 654. A very dark *Ciccaba* that appears all black but has narrow white barring on underparts, crown and upperparts. Rare in humid lowland forests e of Andes to 700 m. Pair recorded in March 1998 at Lago Sándoval (JFC and PC). *S Venezuela, Guianas and Amazon basin.*

Rufous-banded Owl *Ciccaba albitarsus* Búho Rufibandeado
39 cm (15.5"). Plate 31. ♪ 654. Note the amber eyes. Rather rufescent above, streaks on whitish underparts have a thick crossbar "fishbone pattern". Sympatric Band-bellied Owl has conspicuous white spectacles and banded underparts. Mottled Owl's (usually at lower elevation) belly streaks lack crossbar. Cf. smaller White-throated Screech-Owl. Fairly common in humid Andean montane forests at 1700-3000 m. *Andes of w Venezuela to w Bolivia.*

Crested Owl *Lophostrix cristata* Búho Penachudo
40 cm (15.5"). Plate 33. ♪ 654. No other owl has such prominent long white eyebrows (which extend to the ear tufts). Uncommon in humid lowland forests e of Andes. *S Mexico to n Bolivia and w Amazonian Brazil.*

Spectacled Owl *Pulsatrix perspicillata* Búho de Anteojos
45 cm (17.5"). Plate 31. ♪ 654. A distinctive large owl with yellow eyes, unbanded belly, a dark chest-band, white throat and spectacled face. Band-bellied Owl has dark eyes and barred underparts. Rare along Pacific slope south to Cajamarca; fairly common in humid lowland forests e of Andes. *S Mexico to nw Argentina and s Brazil.*

Band-bellied Owl *Pulsatrix melanota* Búho Ventribandeado
42 cm (16.5"). Plate 31. ♪ 654. Note the dark eyes and striking spectacled face. Whitish belly is banded with rufous. Cf. Spectacled and Rufous-banded Owls. Fairly common in humid lowland and foothill forests e of Andes to 2000 m. *SE Colombia to w Bolivia.*

Glaucidium **Pygmy-Owls.** Six species of small, very similar owls. Best told by voice. All have rounded heads without ear tufts, yellow eyes, and dark spots (false eyes) on the back of the head. The tail is fairly long (for an owl) and usually banded. Identification of silent birds can be very difficult. Often more than one species is present. Most are polymorphic, and brown, gray and rufous morphs occur. Recent DNA and studies of vocalizations have led to major revisions in the genus.

Andean Pygmy-Owl *Glaucidium jardinii* Lechucita Andina
16 cm (6.5"). Plate 31. ♪ 654. Can be distinguished from other *Glaucidium* by heavily mottled chest band, spotted mantle and crown, medium-sized rather evenly banded tail, and its fairly long pointed wings (at rest note comparatively longer primaries). Possibly sympatric Yungas Pygmy-Owl (smaller crown spots less visible, longer tail), Subtropical Pygmy-Owl (much shorter tail, streaked underparts), and Ferruginous Pygmy-Owl (streaked not spotted crown, more streaked flanks and tail is more evenly banded). Fairly common in montane forests and scrub, mainly at 2000-3500 m, but locally to 4000 m north of Río Marañón. *Montane forests of Colombia to Venezuela and c Peru.*

Yungas Pygmy-Owl *Glaucidium bolivianum* Lechucita de las Yungas
17 cm (6.6"). Plate 32. ♪ 797. Very similar to Andean Pygmy-Owl and probably allopatric. Yungas Pygmy-Owl has shorter extension of the primaries (hence more rounded wings) and a longer tail. Also cf. Subtropical (much shorter tail, streaked below, unspotted mantle), Ferruginous (more streaked flanks, and tail is more evenly banded) and Peruvian (more conspicuously spotted mantle). Fairly common in Andes from Amazonas to Puno, mainly at 1700-2900 m but up to 3300 m. Recorded from elfin (cloud) forest on Manu Road at 1825-2900 m. *Humid Andes of central Peru, Bolivia and nw Argentina.*

Subtropical Pygmy-Owl *Glaucidium parkeri* Lechucita Subtropical
18 cm (7"). Plate 32. ♪ 797. Slightly shorter-tailed than other *Glaucidium,* and crown, scapulars and wing coverts are more broadly spotted with white. Uncommon in humid montane forests on e slope of Andes at 1450-2000 m. *E slope of Andes of Ecuador and Peru, locally to n Bolivia.*

Amazonian Pygmy-Owl *Glaucidium hardyi* Lechucita Amazónica
14 cm (5.5"). Plate 32. ♪ 654. Very small with a short tail and unspotted mantle. Head is often gray, contrasting with cinnamon–rufous body. Sympatric with Ferruginous Pygmy-Owl, but latter is larger and has a longer tail that is either evenly banded or plain. Fairly common in humid lowland forests e of Andes to 350 m. *Amazonian Brazil, adjacent e Peru and Bolivia.*

Ferruginous Pygmy-Owl *Glaucidium brasilianum* Lechucita Ferruginosa
16 cm (6.5"). Plate 31. ♪ 654. Widespread and variable. Slightly larger and longer-tailed than any sympatric *Glaucidium.* Crown is finely streaked. Amazonian and Subtropical Pygmy-Owls have shorter tails and unspotted mantles. Yungas and Andean Pygmy-Owls have spotted crowns, and usually range at higher elevations. Allopatric Peruvian Pygmy-Owl (formerly a ssp. of Ferruginous) is almost identical, but has a tawny nuchal collar just below the "false eyes". Common in arid trop. and subtrop. zones; fairly common in humid lowland forests and lowland forests e of Andes. *SE Arizona to Tierra del Fuego.*

Peruvian Pygmy-Owl *Glaucidium peruanum* Lechucita Peruana (Paca Paca)
18 cm (7"). Plate 32. ♪ 654. The only pygmy-owl on the Pacific slope. In the eastern portion of its range cf. Andean and Yungas Pygmy-Owls. Nearly identical to allopatric Ferruginous Pygmy-Owl. Uncommon in lowlands and foothills south to Tacna and Apurímac to 2400 m; fairly common in drainage of Río Marañón and Cusco Valley. *SW Ecuador and Peru.*

*Long-whiskered Owlet *Xenoglaux loweryi* Lechucita Bigotona
12.5 cm (5"). Plate 32. A very small, fairly dark owl, with amber eyes and whitish eyebrows. Long whiskers surrounding the facial disc are distinctive. If seen unlikely to be confused. An almost unknown tiny owlet discovered in 1976, and known from two localities in the cloud forests of subtrop. east Andes in Amazonas and San Martín. Only three specimens have been recorded. Species was discovered 10 km ne of Abra Patricia (San Martín) at 1890 m, and another specimen collected east of Bagua in Cordillera de Colán (Amazonas) at 2165 m. *Endemic to Peru.*

Burrowing Owl *Athene cunicularia* Lechuza Terrestre
23 cm (9"). Plate 31. ♪ 654. The only owl in open country with long legs, a stubby tail, and large yellow eyes. Almost exclusively terrestrial and usually diurnal. Fairly common from arid trop. to *puna* zone. *S Canada to s Argentina.*

Buff-fronted Owl *Aegolius harrisii* Lechucita Frentianteada
21 cm (8.5"). Plate 33. ♪ 654. A small owl with a distinctive pattern of buffy underparts and face, and dark upperparts with white spots on wings. Rare and local in temp. zone at 1700-3100 m; recorded at Yurinaqui Alto (Junín), Cushi (Pasco), Cajamarca and Huancabamba deflection. *Patchily distributed South America south to n Argentina and Uruguay.*

Striped Owl *Asio clamator* Búho Listado
38 cm (15"). Plate 33. ♪ 654. A medium-sized owl with long ear tufts, dark eyes, a whitish face with a dark rim, and striped underparts. Cf. Short-eared Owl and larger *Bubo* owls. Rare in arid trop. zone and uncommon in humid lowland forests. *Tropical s Mexico to Brazil and n Argentina.*

Stygian Owl *Asio stygius* Búho Estigio
38-46 cm (15-18"). Plate 33. ♪ 654. A large, dark owl with prominent ear tufts. Recalls Striped Owl but has a dark (not whitish) face, and "fish bone" pattern on underparts (not stripes). Recently recorded in extreme n Peru in Bosque de Cuyas (Piura) at 2200-2900 m (Flanagan and Vellinga 2000). *Mexico to se Brazil, Paraguay and n Argentina; West Indies.*

Short-eared Owl *Asio flammeus* Lechuza de Orejicorta
43 cm (17"). Plate 33. ♪654. Open country and marshes. Medium sized with yellow eyes and almost no ear tufts. Striped Owl (limited overlap at best) has dark eyes and long ear tufts. Rare along coast; uncommon in *puna* zone. *Eurasia, North and South America; Hawaiian Is.*

Steatornithidae (Oilbird; Guácharo). Species: World 1
Oilbirds are residents of caves in northern South America and Trinidad. The Oilbird is the only exclusively nocturnal frugivore, feeding mainly on the fruits of palms and members of the *Lauraceae*. The fruit is plucked on the wing with the strong, hooked bill, brought back to their nesting caves, and digested there during the day. They have a highly developed olfactory sense, which probably serves as an aid in locating aromatic fruits in the dark. Although Oilbirds use echolocation inside their caves, they evidently have acute night vision.

Oilbird *Steatornis caripensis* Guácharo
45 cm (17.5"). Plate 31. ♪797. A large night bird, shaped like a nightjar that perches horizontally. When seen away from roosting caves can be identified by its rufous-buff plumage and strongly hooked bill. Cf. Rufous Potoo. Uncommon and local from trop. to temp. zones. Large colony at Cueva de las Lechuzas, Tingo Maria (Huánuco). *Locally in n South America to w Bolivia; Trinidad.*

Nyctibiidae (Potoos; Nictibios). Species: World 7; Peru 6
Potoos are close relatives of the nightjars, and are found only in the Neotropics. Their drab coloration, coupled with elaborate barring and mottling, creates an excellent camouflage when they characteristically perch on the end of a broken-off stump. Their diet consists of plant bugs, moths, beetles, crickets, termites and other flying insects obtained by flycatcher-like flights from an exposed perch. After an insect is captured it is carried back to the original perch and consumed there. At night their eyes are highly reflective, and eye shine can be seen a long distance away. Note vocalizations, body size and structure, head markings, and pattern on wing coverts.

Great Potoo *Nyctibius grandis* Nictibio Grande
50 cm (19.5"). Plate 33. ♪797. The largest and bulkiest potoo. Usually appears very pale. Long-tailed Potoo is slimmer, obviously proportionately longer-tailed and darker. Common Potoo is much smaller and sometimes has a dark malar stripe. Fairly common in humid lowland forests e of Andes to 500 m. *Guatemala to n Bolivia and se Brazil.*

Long-tailed Potoo *Nyctibius aethereus* Nictibio Colilargo
45 cm (17.5"). Plate 33. ♪655. The long and graduated tail gives it a slender appearance. Note the dark crown, pale malar stripe and pale median wing coverts. Fairly common in humid lowland forests e of Andes to 700 m. *Locally in tropical and foothill forests of South America.*

Common Potoo *Nyctibius griseus* Nictibio Común
38 cm (15"). Plate 33. ♪655. Widespread. A medium-sized potoo with various color morphs. Lacks distinctive markings. Dark malar stripe bordered by white above is sometimes conspicuous. Common in humid lowland forests e of Andes; rare along Pacific slope south to Lambayeque to 1300 m. *Tropical e Nicaragua to n Argentina and Brazil.*

Andean Potoo *Nyctibius maculosus* Nictibio Andino
36 cm (14"). Plate 33. ♪655. Generally the only potoo in its altitudinal range, but possible limited overlap with Common Potoo. Andean has conspicuous whitish shoulders. Rare in humid subtrop. Andes at 1800-2800 m. Recorded on Manu Road at 1700-2800 m. *Locally in Andes of w Venezuela to w Bolivia.*

White-winged Potoo *Nyctibius leucopterus* Nictibio Aliblanco.
27 cm (10.5"). Plate 33. ♪ 655. Note limited range. Similar to Andean Potoo (no overlap) but smaller and with largely white wing coverts. No sympatric potoo has extensive white in the wings (Long-tailed Potoo is much larger and has pale shoulders). To 500m. Recent sight records and tape recordings from white-sand forests in Iquitos area. *Amazonian Brazil and adjacent Peru; e Brazil (Bahia)*

Rufous Potoo *Nyctibius bracteatus* Nictibio Rufo
23 cm (9"). Plate 33. ♪ 655. The smallest potoo and the only one that is unstreaked rufous with bold white spots on underparts. Cf. Oilbird. Rare in humid lowland forests e of Andes to 500 m. Recorded at Lago Sándoval (PC). *Locally in Guyana and w Amazon basin.*

Caprimulgidae (Nightjars and Allies; Añaperos y Chotacabras). Species: World 89; Peru 20
Nightjars and nighthawks are medium-sized birds of worldwide distribution. They are mostly nocturnal, and feed mainly on insects caught in flight, especially moths, beetles and crickets. As would be expected of birds that feed largely on flying insects, the greatest diversity of species occurs in tropical and subtropical regions. Many nightjars are migratory, and it has recently been discovered that the Common Poorwill (*Phalaenoptilus nuttallii*) is among the few birds that is known to hibernate. The family is comprised of two groups. The nighthawks (7 species in Peru) tend to forage on the wing—often in flocks. The 13 Peruvian nightjars usually sally forth to capture prey from a perch or from the ground, and are mostly solitary. Note vocalization, habitat, shape, tail and wing patterns (often visible only in flight), presence of nuchal collar, and a breast collar.

Short-tailed (Semicollared) Nighthawk *Lurocalis semitorquatus* Chotacabras Colicorta
25 cm (9.8"). Plate 34. ♪ 1015CD. Shaped like Rufous-bellied Nighthawk (limited if any overlap). The very long wings and extremely short tail give both species a distinctive silhouette. When perched note that long wings project beyond the tail. Lacks markings on wings or tail. Rare in humid lowland and subtrop. forests e of Andes to 1800 m. *Extreme s Mexico to s Brazil and ne Argentina.*

Rufous-bellied Nighthawk *Lurocalis rufiventris* Chotacabras Ventrirrufo
25 cm (9.8"). Plate 34. ♪ 1015CD. Similar to previous species (limited overlap in lower limit of range). Lacks markings on wings or tail. When seen in good light note rufous belly. Upperwing is dotted with buff. Uncommon in montane forests and scrub at 1500-3300 m. *Mountains of Colombia to Bolivia.*

Sand-colored Nighthawk *Chordeiles rupestris* Chotacabras Arenisco
21 cm (8.5"). Plate 34. ♪ 1015CD. Note distinctive habitat. A pale, buffy nighthawk. Tail is largely white with a dark terminal band. In flight shows mostly white underwing. Locally common to abundant along lowland sandbars and river banks e of Andes. *Sandbars and river banks of Amazon basin.*

Lesser Nighthawk *Chordeiles acutipennis* Chotacabra Menor
20 cm (8"). Plate 34. ♪ 1015CD. Note the falcon-like shape and notched tail. Male has a white subterminal tail band and a white band close to wingtip. Female lacks tail band and wing band is buff. Coastal populations are paler. Cf. very similar Common Nighthawk. Fairly common in arid trop. and subtrop. zones south to Arequipa and lowlands e of Andes. *Open country of w US to s Brazil and n Chile.*

Common Nighthawk *Chordeiles minor* Chotacabras Migratorio
23 cm (9"). Plate 34 ♪ 1015CD. Very similar to smaller and paler Lesser Nighthawk but wings are more pointed and wing band is placed farther from wingtip. Female has a smaller wing band and lacks tail band. Common Nighthawk usually flies higher than Lesser Nighthawk. Rare migrant along Pacific slope south to Lambayeque. *Breeds Alaska to Panama; winters to n Argentina.*

Nacunda Nighthawk *Podager nacunda* Chotacabras Ventriblanco
27 cm (10.5"). Plate 34. ♪ 1015CD. A large, distinctive nighthawk. No other nighthawk has a white belly and contrasting dark breast. In flight shows a conspicuous white wing band, white underwing coverts and a white terminal tail band. Uncommon and very local in lowlands e of Andes to 300 m, especially in savanna and open country (Jeberos, Pampas del Heath). *Tropical South America e of the Andes to n Argentina.*

Band-tailed Nighthawk *Nyctiprogne leucopyga* Chotacabras Colibandeada
18 cm (7"). Plate 34. ♪ 1015CD. A dark nighthawk with a white band close to the base of the tail. Lacks wing band. Rare and local along lowland rivers and streams in Loreto. Recently recorded at Pacaya Samiria National Reserve (Begazo and Valqui 1998). *Locally from the Guianas to Amazon basin.*

Pauraque *Nyctidromus albicollis* Chotacabras Común
27 cm (10.5"). Plate 35. Appendix A. ♪ 1015CD. Widespread. Both sexes have a long tail and a band close to the tip of the wing. Tail pattern of male is diagnostic—dark outermost feather and white on the third and fourth (as counted from outside). Female has whitish tips to outer tail. Common in humid trop. and subtrop. forests to 2500 m (occasionally higher with a record at Bosque de Cuyas at 2800 m). *S Texas to n Argentina and s Brazil.*

Ocellated Poorwill *Nyctiphrynus ocellatus* Chotacabras Ocelado
21 cm (8.5"). Plate 35. ♪ 1015CD. Very dark, with only a white band on lower throat and narrow white tips to tail feathers. Mostly arboreal. Cf. Blackish Nightjar (more mottled plumage, incomplete collar, mostly terrestrial). Locally fairly common in humid trop. and subtrop. forests e of Andes to 2500 m. *N Nicaragua; w Colombia to ne Argentina.*

Rufous Nightjar *Caprimulgus rufus* Chotacabras Rufo
26 cm (10.1"). Plate 35. Appendix A. ♪ 1015CD. A large and robust rather rufescent nightjar. Both sexes lack a wing band. Male has white spots on the inner webs of outer tail feathers (seen in flight). Female lacks tail markings. Cf. Pauraque (wing band, longer tail), and Silky-tailed Nightjar (white to buffy corners on tail). Rare in humid lowland forests e of Andes to 1100 m. Recent records from Jesus del Monte (Begazo et. al. 2001) and Tambopata Candamo Reserve. *Locally from Costa Rica to n Argentina; St. Lucia.*

Silky-tailed Nightjar *Caprimulgus sericocaudatus* Chotacabras Coladeseda
25 cm (9.8"). Plate 35. Appendix A. ♪ 1015CD. A large and robust nightjar. Both sexes have white (or buffy in female) tips to outer tail feathers, a buffy nuchal collar, blackish breast and white pectoral band. Lacks wing band. Rare in humid lowland forests e of Andes to 400 m; recorded at Yarinacocha (Ucayali); uncommon in *terra firme* forests in Manu area. *E Peru to ne Argentina.*

Band-winged Nightjar *Caprimulgus longirostris* Chotacabras Alifajeado
21.5 cm (8.4"). Plate 35. Appendix A. ♪ 1015CD. Both sexes have wing bands (white in male, buffy in female), a buffy nuchal collar and a pectoral band. Male has white tips to outer tail feathers. Note that coastal race *decussatus* is smaller and paler, and has reduced pale corners to the tail. Cf. Little and Scrub Nightjars. Fairly common along arid Pacific littoral, and to 3600 m in *puna* zone. *Venezuela through w South America to Argentina and e Brazil.*

Spot-tailed Nightjar *Caprimulgus maculicaudus* Chotacabras Colipunteada
20 cm (8"). Plate 35. Appendix A. ♪ 1015CD. Both sexes have a distinctive face pattern: buffy throat and a dark malar stripe, pale superciliary and a tawny nuchal collar. Scapulars and wing coverts boldly tipped with large buff spots. Lacks a wing band. Male has white tips to outer tail feathers. Locally fairly common in lowlands e of Andes to 500 m in Pampas del Heath and Tambopata, especially near marshes and savanna. Recently recorded near Jesus del Monte (Begazo *et al.* 2001). *Locally from tropical s Mexico to n Bolivia and se Brazil.*

Little Nightjar *Caprimulgus parvulus* Chotacabras Chico
20 cm (8"). Plate 34. Appendix A. ♪ 1015CD. Both sexes have a white throat. Male has a white wing band and narrow tips to outer tail feathers. Female lacks wing band and tail tips. Sympatric Spot-tailed Nightjar lacks white throat. Band-winged Nightjar (possible limited overlap) has more prominent tail tips (male) and less white on throat. Rare in humid lowlands e of Andes, occasionally to 1000 m. *Venezuela and n Colombia; e Peru and s Amazonia to n Argentina.*

Scrub (Anthony's) Nightjar *Caprimulgus anthonyi* Chotacabras de Matorral
8.5" (21 cm). Plate 34. Appendix A. ♪ 1015CD. Similar to Little Nightjar (no overlap). Both sexes have white throats. Male has a white wing band and narrow buff tips to outer tail feathers. Female has a buffy wing band and reduced tail tips. Band-winged Nightjar has more prominent tail tips (male) and less white on throat. Uncommon along Pacific slope south to Lambayeque and an isolated population in Marañón Valley. *Lowlands of sw Ecuador to nw Peru.*

Blackish Nightjar *Caprimulgus nigrescens* Chotacabras Negruzco
20 cm (8"). Plate 35. Appendix A. ♪ 1015CD. A blackish, almost unmarked nightjar. Both sexes have a white spot on the side of the neck. Male has a very short white wing band and very narrow white tips to the tail feathers (female lacks such markings). Cf. Ocellated Poorwill. Locally fairly common in lowlands e of Andes to 1100 m, especially along rocky river banks and sandy savanna. *S Venezuela, the Guianas and Amazon basin.*

Ladder-tailed Nightjar *Hydropsalis climacocerca* Chotacabras Coliescalera
26 cm (10.1"). Plate 34. Appendix A. ♪ 1015CD. Tail shape is diagnostic of the genus (outermost and central tail feathers are longer than the rest, and much more pronounced in the male). Male's inner webs of outer tail feathers are white (cf. Pauraque), much reduced in female. Both sexes have a wing band but lack a nuchal collar. Cf. Scissor-tailed Nightjar. Locally fairly common in humid lowlands e of Andes to 500 m. *Along rivers from s Venezuela, the Guianas and the Amazon basin.*

Scissor-tailed Nightjar *Hydropsalis torquata* Chotacabras Colitijereta
Male 40 cm (15.5"); female 29 cm (11.3"). Plate 34. ♪ 1015CD. Note limited range. Male's tail shape recalls that of Ladder-tailed Nightjar but outermost tail feathers are much longer. Female's tail is like that of Ladder-tailed. Both sexes lack a wing band and have a tawny nuchal collar. Rare along humid lowland rivers and margins e of Andes in Junín, Cusco and Madre de Dios (Pampas del Heath) to 500 m. *Tropical e Peru and Amazonian Brazil to central Argentina.*

***Uropsalis* Nightjars.** In both members of the genus the males possess almost unbelievably long outermost tail feathers. The two species are sometimes sympatric (Manu Road near Pillahuata). Often arboreal. Females recall that of Band-winged Nightjar (another high-elevation nightjar) but lack wing band and white collar.

Swallow-tailed Nightjar *Uropsalis segmentata* Chotacabras Colihorquillada
Male 64 cm (25"); female 23 cm (9"). Plate 35. ♪ 1015CD. Both sexes are similar to respective sexes of Lyre-tailed Nightjar, but lack a nuchal collar. Crown color is mostly rufous in Swallow-tailed and mostly gray in Lyre-tailed. Male's tail is different. Swallow-tailed's long tail feathers are dark with white shafts. Lyre-tailed's is longer and dark with pale tips. Uncommon in cloud and elfin forests on e slope of Andes at 2300-3600 m. *Temp. and páramo zones in Andes of Colombia to w Bolivia.*

Lyre-tailed Nightjar *Uropsalis lyra* Chotacabras Colilira
Male 78 cm (30.5"); female 25 cm (9.8"). Plate 35. ♪ 1015CD. Both sexes are similar to respective sexes of Swallow-tailed Nightjar but have a tawny nuchal collar. Uncommon in humid montane forests on e slope of Andes at 800-3500 m. Regularly seen displaying near El Mirador (Cusco) at 1825 m. *Andes of w Venezuela to nw Argentina.*

Apodidae (Swifts; Vencejos). Species: World 99; Peru 15
Swifts are the most aerial of birds, far surpassing any swallow or hawk in their ability to continue rapid flight for days on end. They collect nesting material, copulate, drink and bathe while flying— and even pass the night on the wing. They have a worldwide range, but like the nightjars are more heavily distributed in the tropics, where flying insects are more abundant. Their food consists almost entirely of small insects taken in the air, and includes flies, beetles, flying ants, aphids and even tiny spiders. Swiftlets of the genus *Collocalia* nest in caves, and their saliva nests have been a source of bird's-nest soup for centuries. Some species nest in pitch-black caves, where they navigate by means of echolocation similar to bats. Identification of Peruvian swifts can be very challenging, especially *Cypseloides* and *Chaetura* groups. Good light on both upper and lower parts is essential. Note the body and tail shapes (but remember that notched tails may look almost round when fanned, and a square tail may look almost notched when closed) and any contrast (on chin, throat or rump).

[White-chested Swift] *Cypseloides lemosi* Vencejo Pechiblanco
14 cm (5.5"). Plate 36. No other swift is all blackish with a white patch on the chest. Female has a reduced and blurry chest patch. White-collared Swift is much larger and has a complete white collar around the neck. Sight records in Cordillera del Cóndor in Amazonas at ca 1600 m. *Andes of sw Colombia and adjacent Ecuador.*

Rothschild's Swift *Cypseloides rothschildi* Vencejo de Rothschild
15 cm (6"). Plate 36. ♫ 797. An obscure, dark swift with a square tail that lacks any prominent field marks. Nearly identical to White-chinned Swift, but the latter is darker and blacker and has a whitish chin. Female and young Chestnut-collared Swift are nearly identical but have longer notched tails. Rare (vagrant?) in montane foothill forests on e slope of Andes in Cusco at 700-2100 m. *Yungas and forests of nw Argentina, adjacent s Bolivia and Peru.*

White-chinned Swift *Cypseloides cryptus* Vencejo Barbiblanco
15 cm (6"). Plate 36. Accidental?. An obscure, blackish swift with a square tail. Lacks any prominent field marks. In optimal view note whitish chin. Nearly identical to female and young Chestnut-collared Swift, but they have slightly longer notched tails. See also rare Rothschild's Swift. Almost certainly overlooked due to problems in identification. Single Peru specimen from Inca Mine (Puno) at 1690 m. *Locally in mountains of nw South America; winters to Honduras.*

Chestnut-collared Swift *Streptoprocne rutila* Vencejo Cuellicastaño
15 cm (6"). Plate 36. ♫ 797. In good light the rufous collar and throat of male are diagnostic. Female and immature lack the collar, and tail is less notched than illustrated male. Cf. rare Rothschild's and White-chinned Swifts. Locally uncommon along e slope of Andes at 900-3000 m, occasionally to 3400 m in Pasco and Ayacucho. *Lowlands and mountains of Mexico to w Bolivia.*

White-collared Swift *Streptoprocne zonaris* Vencejo Cuelliblanco
21 cm (8.5"). Plate 36. ♫ 797. The largest swift in the country. White collar is conspicuous. Locally common along coast (May-August); common east of the Andes up to *puna* zone at 4400 m. *S Mexico to Brazil and n Argentina; Greater Antilles.*

***Chaetura* Swifts.** Small, "cigar-with-wings" shaped swifts that have short to very short tails (at extremely close view show tail "spines").

Gray-rumped Swift *Chaetura cinereiventris* Vencejo Lomigris
11 cm (4.5"). Plate 36. ♫ 797. Very similar to, and often flies together with, Pale-rumped Swift (which offers a direct comparison), but rump and uppertail coverts are mouse-gray and not whitish, showing less contrast with the blackish back. Mouse-gray underparts have almost no contrast with slightly paler throat, unlike Pale-rumped Swift that has dark underparts contrasting with a whitish throat. When seen together note that Gray-rumped Swift has proportionately shorter wings. Fairly common along Pacific slope south to Piura and common in humid lowlands e of Andes. *Nicaragua to Brazil and ne Argentina.*

Pale-rumped Swift *Chaetura egregia* Vencejo Lomipálido
12.5 cm (5"). Plate 36. Similar to sympatric Gray-rumped Swift. Rare in humid lowlands south to Madre de Dios to 900 m. *Lowlands of e Ecuador to n Bolivia and w Amazonian Brazil.*

Chimney Swift *Chaetura pelagica* Vencejo de Chimenea
13 cm (5.2"). Plate 36. ♪ 626. The only *Chaetura* that does not have a contrasting pale rump. Mainly dark and uniform except for a whitish throat and darker cap. Common northern-winter visitor along coast from La Libertad to Lima and in Amazonian Peru; rare in *puna* zone (recorded at 3600 m in Cusco). *Breeds e North America; winters Amazonia to s Peru.*

Chapman's Swift *Chaetura chapmani* Vencejo de Chapman
13 cm (5.2"). Plate 36. A dark and uniform *Chaetura* that lacks the whitish throat and darker cap of very similar migratory Chimney Swift. Chapman's rump and uppertail coverts are buffy and paler than the back (almost concolor in Chimney Swift), but not as contrasting as in Gray-rumped and Pale-rumped Swifts. *Cypseloides* swifts have longer tails. Rare in humid lowland forests e of Andes to 900 m. The only race (*viridipennis*) that occurs in Peru is possibly a valid species (Amazonian Swift) but considered a race of *chapmani* by del Hoyo *et al.* 1999. *Locally in Panama and n South America to Amazon basin.*

Short-tailed Swift *Chaetura brachyura* Vencejo Colicorto
11 cm (4.5"). Plate 36. ♪ 797. The very short tail and unique wing shape (broad wings are pinched at the base and hooked at the tip) give this *Chaetura* a distinctive silhouette. Note the pale rump and uppertail coverts. Common in humid lowlands e of Andes to 900 m. *Panama to Amazonian Brazil and n Bolivia; s Lesser Antilles.*

Tumbes Swift *Chaetura ocypetes* Vencejo de Tumbes
11 cm (4.5"). Plate 36. Note limited range. Recent split from almost identical Short-tailed Swift (Ridgely and Greenfield 2001a). Uncommon along Pacific slope south to Piura in deciduous woodlands to 1000. *Southwest Ecuador and adjacent nw Peru.*

White-tipped Swift *Aeronautes montivagus* Vencejo Montañés
13 cm (5.2"). Plate 36. ♪ 797. Similar to Andean Swift but belly and rump are dark. Tail tips are white in male but dark in female. Color pattern recalls that of Lesser Swallow-tailed Swift, but body shape is very different. Locally common on Andean slopes and forests at 500-2700 m. *Locally in mountains of n Venezuela to w Bolivia.*

Andean Swift *Aeronautes andecolus* Vencejo Andino
14 cm (5.5"). Plate 36. ♪ 797. The only swift with mostly white underparts and a white rump. Cf. White-tipped Swift. Common on Pacific slope of Andes south to Tacna and on e slope north to Huancavelica, mostly at 2500-3550 m, but has been recorded at 340-3900 m. *Andes of Peru to n Chile and w Argentina.*

Fork-tailed Palm-Swift *Tachornis squamata* Vencejo Tijereta de Palmeras
14 cm (5.5"). Plate 36. ♪ 677. Note the thin, long wings and long deeply forked tail. Lacks bold pattern of Lesser Swallow-tailed Swift. Common in humid lowlands e of Andes, rarely to 1000 m; usually associated with *Mauritia* palms. *Venezuela and the Guianas to Amazonia.*

Lesser Swallow-tailed Swift *Panyptila cayennensis* Vencejo Tijereta Menor
13 cm (5.2"). Plate 36. Easily recognized by its bold pattern and slender, streamlined silhouette. Pattern recalls that of White-tipped Swift. Rare along Pacific slope south to Piura; uncommon in humid lowlands e of Andes to 900 m. *Humid lowlands of s Mexico to n Bolivia and Brazil.*

Trochilidae (Hummingbirds; Colibríes y Picaflores). Species: World 337; Peru 127
Hummingbirds are tiny, nectar-drinking birds related to the swifts. They are entirely dependent on their wings for locomotion, since their legs and feet are too weak for anything but perching. They range from Alaska to Tierra del Fuego, from sea level to over 4500 m (15,000 feet) in the Andes. In order to conserve energy, some of the high-altitude hillstars of the genus *Oreotrochilus* undergo a torpor-like state, during which they lower their basic metabolism rate. The variety of bills in hummingbirds indicates their adaptation to different types of flowers as sources of food. To supplement their nectar diet with protein, hummingbirds are often seen hawking small insects in the air. Several species regularly engage in kleptoparisitism by stealing tiny insects caught in spider webs.

Eutoxeres **Sicklebills.** Two species, both of which have extremely decurved bills and heavily streaked underparts.

White-tipped Sicklebill *Eutoxeres aquila* Picohoz Puntiblanco
12.5 cm (5"). Plate 37. Limited overlap with Buff-tailed Sicklebill and lacks buff outer tail feathers. Uncommon in humid lower montane forests e of Andes south to the Río Marañón, occasionally to 2100 m. Recently recorded in Cordillera de Colán at 2300 m, which extends its known range south of the deep gap formed by the Marañón Valley (Barnes 1997). *Humid foothills of Costa Rica to n Peru.*

Buff-tailed Sicklebill *Eutoxeres condamini* Picohoz Colicanela
12.5 cm (5"). Plate 40. Note buff outer tail feathers. Uncommon in trop. and upper trop. forests e of Andes to 1300 m, rarely to 3300 m. *Lowlands of se Colombia to n Bolivia.*

Glaucis, Threnetes and *Phaethornis* **Hermits and Barbthroat.** Fourteen species of relatively dull-plumaged hummingbirds. Most have decurved bills and a facial pattern, and are inhabitants of the forest interiors. There are two types of *Phaethornis*—large, with the sexes similar, and a long graduated tail with the two elongated central tail feathers tipped white; and small, in which the male usually has a black pectoral band and a shorter tail.

Rufous-breasted Hermit *Glaucis hirsuta* Ermitaño Pechicanelo
10.7 cm (4.2"). Plate 37. The only hermit with a plain face, dull rufous breast and a rounded tail (rufous on basal half). Common in humid lowland forests e of Andes to 1100 m. *Tropical central Panama to Brazil and n Bolivia; Grenada.*

Pale-tailed Barbthroat *Threnetes niger* Ermitaño Colipálida
10.2 cm (4"). Plate 37. Note the strong facial pattern and pale whitish base to the rounded tail. Uncommon in humid lowland and upper tropical forests e of Andes to 1600 m. *S Venezuela and the Guianas to n Bolivia and Amazonian Brazil.*

Green Hermit *Phaethornis guy* Ermitaño Verde
11 cm (4.5"). Plate 37. ♪613. The only hermit with uniformly dark green upperparts and dark dusky-green underparts. Tail is graduated but rather short. Note pale-buff facial pattern. Uncommon in lowlands and foothills south to Cusco and Madre de Dios, rarely to 3000 m. *Mainly subtropical Costa Rica to ne Venezuela and s Peru.*

White-bearded Hermit *Phaethornis hispidus* Ermitaño Barbiblanco
13 cm (5.2") Plate 37. The only large hermit with a white "beard" chin stripe. Cf. Great-billed Hermit. Fairly common in humid lowland forests e of Andes to 900 m. *Tropical s Venezuela to n Bolivia and w Amazonian Brazil.*

Western Long-tailed Hermit *Phaethornis longirostris* Ermitaño Colilargo Occidental
11 cm (4.5"). Plate 37. ♪542. The only large, long-billed, long-tailed hermit in its range. W Ecuador and nw Peru race *baroni* (illustrated) may represent a separate species (Baron's Hermit). Fairly common on Pacific slope of Andes south to Lambayeque to 1700 m. *W Mexico to nw Peru.*

Great-billed Hermit *Phaethornis malaris* Ermitaño Picogrande
15 cm (6"). Plate 37. Note the long decurved bill and long tail. Cf. White-bearded (grayer below with a white beard), Straight-billed (bill shape), Koepcke's, Tawny-bellied, and Needle-billed (tawny underparts). Fairly common in humid lowland *terra firme* forests e of Andes to 600 m, occasionally to 1500 m. *E Colombia to Venezuela, the Guianas, Brazil, Peru and Bolivia.*

Tawny-bellied Hermit *Phaethornis syrmatophorus* Ermitaño Ventrileonado
12.5 cm (5"). Plate 37. ♪EC007T. The only hermit in its range with a rufous-cinnamon rump and mostly tawny underparts (some irregular white feathers on underparts). Koepcke's Hermit is very similar (lower elevations and very limited overlap at best), but Koepcke's rump is not as rufous. Common in humid foothill and montane forests south to San Martín at 800-3100 m. *Mainly subtropical Colombia, Ecuador and n Peru.*

Koepcke's Hermit *Phaethornis koepckeae* Ermitaño de Koepcke
11 cm (4.5"). Plate 38. Note the combination of rufous rump, tawny underparts and white chin stripe. Similar to Tawny-bellied (higher elevation) and Needle-billed Hermit (lower elevation, bill fairly straight). Locally fairly common in foothill forest undergrowth from Amazonas to Madre de Dios at 500-1300 m. Frequents *Heliconia* patches at Amazonia Lodge. *Endemic to Peru.*

Needle-billed Hermit *Phaethornis philippii* Ermitaño Picoaguja
12 cm (4.7"). Plate 38. The only large hermit in its elevation with tawny underparts. Cf. Koepcke's Hermit. Uncommon in humid lowland forests e of Andes to 325 m. *Tropical e Peru, n Bolivia and w Amazonian Brazil.*

Straight-billed Hermit *Phaethornis bourcieri* Ermitaño Piquirrecto
10.7 cm (4.2"). Plate 37. The only large, dull hermit with an almost straight bill. Cf. Great-billed (decurved bill) and Needle-billed (more tawny underparts). Uncommon in humid lowland forests e of Andes in Loreto to 200 m. *S Venezuela and the Guianas to ne Peru and n Amazonian Brazil.*

Reddish Hermit *Phaethornis ruber* Ermitaño Rojizo
7.7 cm (3"). Plate 37. ♪797. Small, with reddish-rufous underparts and rufous rump. Male has a prominent black breast-band (lacking in female or with a trace of it). Cf. localized White-browed Hermit. In north cf. Gray-chinned Hermit. Locally common in humid lowland forests e of Andes to 1100 m. *S Venezuela and the Guianas to n Bolivia and se Brazil.*

White-browed Hermit *Phaethornis stuarti* Ermitaño Cejiblanco
8 cm (3.3"). Plate 38. ♪797. Very similar to Reddish Hermit but tips of central tail feathers are white (not rufous). Female lacks a breast-band. Uncommon in humid lowland forests e of Andes north to Cusco at 500-1500 m. *Foothills of se Peru and w Bolivia.*

Black-throated Hermit *Phaethornis atrimentalis* Ermitaño Gargantinegro
9.2 cm (3.6"). Plate 37. A small hermit with cinnamon underparts and a buffy throat with dark streaks. Sympatric races of Gray-chinned Hermit have dark streaks on a deep rufous-brown throat. Cf. also Reddish Hermit (cinnamon throat). Formerly considered a race of Little Hermit (*P. longuemareus*). Locally fairly common in lowland forests e of Andes, rarely to 1700 m. *E Andes of Colombia to central Peru.*

Gray-chinned Hermit *Phaethornis griseogularis* Ermitaño Barbigris
7.7 cm (3"). Plate 37. Three ssp. occur in Peru. Race *porcullae* in Andes of Tumbes, Piura and Lambayeque is the only small hermit on Pacific slope, and may represent a separate species. It is larger with paler underparts than races *zonura* (Pacific slope of Cajamarca and adjacent Amazonas) and nominate race (illustrated, east of Andes south to Amazonas). The two latter races recall Reddish Hermit but note the gray chin, and longer, darker tail than in Reddish Hermit (usually at lower ele-

vations). See also Black-throated Hermit. Rare on Pacific slope of w Andes in nw Peru); uncommon in montane forests on e slope of Andes south to Amazonas to 2100 m. *Locally from s and w Venezuela to n Peru.*

***Doryfera* Lancebills.** A pair of small, dark hummingbirds characterized by very long, straight lance-like bills.

Green-fronted Lancebill *Doryfera ludovicae* Picolanza Frentiverde
10.2 cm (4"). Plate 37. Larger and longer-billed than Blue-fronted Lancebill. Both sexes have a green forecrown (smaller or sometimes lacking in female), a rusty-brown head (duller in female) and gray tips to the outer tail feathers. Uncommon in foothill and subtropical forests on e slope of Andes at 900-2200 m, occasionally to 2850 m. *Humid montane forests of Costa Rica to w Bolivia.*

Blue-fronted Lancebill *Doryfera johannae* Picolanza Frentiazul
9.2 cm (3.6"). Plate 37. Very small. Male has a violet-blue forecrown. Dull female has a small green forecrown (sometimes lacking), a coppery nape and narrow gray tips to outer tail feathers. Cf. Green-fronted Lancebill (rusty-brown crown, larger gray tips to tail). Uncommon in upper trop. forests e of Andes, occasionally to 2000 m. *Humid foothills of Venezuela and Guyana to ne Peru.*

Gray-breasted Sabrewing *Campylopterus largipennis* Ala-Sable Pechigris
11 cm (4.5"). Plate 37. ♪ 797. A large, gray-breasted hummingbird with a white postocular spot and broad white tips to the outer tail feathers. Female Napo Sabrewing has a similar shape but has narrow white tips to tail. Female Fork-tailed Woodnymph is smaller, lacks pronounced postocular spot and has narrow white tips to tail. Uncommon in humid lowland forests e of Andes, occasionally to 1650 m. *S Venezuela and the Guianas to n Bolivia and Brazil.*

Napo Sabrewing *Campylopterus villaviscensio* Ala-Sable del Napo
11 cm (4.5"). Plate 38. Both sexes are large and have dark-blue outer tail feathers. Male is dark and has a dark-blue throat and some iridescent green on crown. Female is similar to Gray-breasted Sabrewing. Rare in humid foothill forests near Jesús del Monte at 1500 m and at Abra Patricia. *Foothills of e Ecuador and adjacent Peru.*

Swallow-tailed Hummingbird *Campylopterus macrourus* Ala-Sable Golondrina
14 cm (5.5"). Plate 40. ♪ 797. Note limited range. Unmistakable with its deeply forked tail and violet-blue hood. Uncommon and local in lowland forests e of Andes in Pampas del Heath and Quillabamba Valley. *Guianas to e Brazil, Paraguay and n Bolivia.*

White-necked Jacobin *Florisuga mellivora* Colibrí Nuquiblanca
10.2 cm (4"). Plate 40. ♪ 797. Male is unmistakable. Female has white underparts with dark spots on throat, upper breast and vent. Tail is mostly dark with narrow white tips. Uncommon in humid lowland forests e of Andes, occasionally to 1600 m. *Trop. s Mexico to n Bolivia and Amazonian Brazil.*

Brown Violetear *Colibri delphinae* Orejivioleta Parda
11 cm (4.5"). Plate 41. ♪ 797. The only dull-brown hummingbird with a violet ear patch. In good light shows a small green gorget and rusty rump. Rare in humid foothill and montane forests on e slope of Andes at 900-2500 m. *Locally from Belize and Guatemala to Brazil and Bolivia.*

Green Violetear *Colibri thalassinus* Orejivioleta Verde
10.2 cm (4"). Plate 41. ♪ 797. Smaller than sometimes sympatric Sparkling Violetear, but in Peruvian races belly is green (not violet-blue) and violet is restricted to the ear (does not extend to the chin). Fairly common in montane forests throughout Andes, mainly at 600-2800 m. *Open mountain slopes of s Mexico to nw Argentina.*

Sparkling Violetear *Colibri coruscans* Orejivioleta Ventriazul
13 cm (5.2"). Plate 41. ♫ 797. A tireless singer. Note the violet-blue on belly, and violet ear that extends to chin. Cf. smaller Green Violetear. Common in montane forests and scrub, mainly at 2000-3000 m in austral winter, but to 4500 m during breeding season. Most common hummingbird in Cusco gardens. *Mts. of Venezuela to nw Argentina.*

Green-breasted Mango *Anthracothorax prevostii* Mango Pechiverde
10.2 cm (4"). Plate 41. Note limited range. Male has mostly green underparts, a black throat that extends as a wide stripe down to upper belly, and purple outer tail feathers (maroon in poor light). Female has a distinctive black stripe on the underparts and maroon outer tail feathers (rufous at the base). No overlap with Black-throated Mango. Uncommon on Pacific slope in Tumbes. *S Mexico to Colombia, Venezuela and extreme nw Peru.*

Black-throated Mango *Anthracothorax nigricollis* Mango Gargantinegro
10.2 cm (4"). Plate 41. Similar to allopatric Green-breasted Mango, but black on the male's underparts is more extensive. Female is like that of Green-breasted Mango. Fairly common in lowlands east of Andes. *Panama and Colombia east of Andes to ne Argentina and Brazil.*

Fiery Topaz *Topaza pyra* Topacio de Fuego
18 cm (7"). Plate 41. Note limited range. Very large male is unmistakable. Female is green with a rufous throat and tail. Rare in humid lowland forests along Río Napo and Río Corrientes (Loreto) to 500 m. Considered conspecific with Crimson Topaz (del Hoyo *et al.* 1999) but elevated to species status (Hu *et al.* 2000). *SE Colombia, e Ecuador and ne Peru to nw Brazil and s Venezuela.*

Violet-headed Hummingbird *Klais guimeti* Colibrí Cabecivioleta
9.2 cm (3.6"). Plate 39. ♫ 797. Small. Both sexes have a conspicuous white postocular spot, a fairly short, dark bill, and a green tail with narrow white tips. Cf. female *Urosticte*. Uncommon in upper trop. forests on e slope of Andes, rarely to 1800 m. *Honduras to w Bolivia and extreme w Brazil.*

***Lophornis* Coquettes and *Discosura* Thorntails.** Tiny hummingbirds (some have insect-like flights) with short bills and a white band on lower back. Male coquettes have some of the most unusual adornments in the avian world. Male thorntails have a wire-like tail.

Rufous-crested Coquette *Lophornis delattrei* Coqueta Crestirrufa
6.9 cm (2.7"). Plate 39. Male has a long rufous crest and a red bill. Female has a rufous forehead, throat and rufous on inner webs of outer tail feathers. In Loreto and Amazonas cf. Spangled Coquette. Uncommon in lowland and foothill forests on e slope of Andes to 2000 m. *Locally from central Costa Rica to w Bolivia.*

Spangled Coquette *Lophornis stictolophus* Coqueta Coronada
6.9 cm (2.7"). Plate 39. Very similar to Rufous-crested Coquette, but male has a fuller crest with black dots on the tips of crest feathers (Rufous-crested has a longer, skinnier crest with black points to the tips, but they are nearly invisible in the field). Outer tail feathers on Spangled are rufous at the base and tip—unlike Rufous-crested. Females are probably not separable in the field. Rare in humid lowland and foothill forests in Loreto and Amazonas. *Andes of Venezuela to n Peru.*

Festive Coquette *Lophornis chalybeus* Coqueta Verde
8 cm (3.3"). Plate 39. Male is crested with an iridescent green forecrown and elongated, white-tipped throat feathers. Female can be told by its dark upperparts and rounded dark tail (lacks rufous) divided by a white band on the rump. Female thorntails have pointed white-tipped tails. Rare in humid lowland *terra firme* forests e of Andes to 1000 m. Fairly common at Manu Wildlife Center. *S Venezuela to n Bolivia and Amazonian Brazil; coastal se Brazil.*

Wire-crested Thorntail *Discosura popelairii* Coliespina Crestada
Male 11 cm (4.5"); female 8 cm (3.2"). Plate 38. Male has a long pointed crest and long wire-like tail. Female has mostly black underparts and a white moustache. Cf. female Festive Coquette and Black-bellied Thorntail. Uncommon in lowland and foothill forests e of Andes south to Madre de Dios at 500-1600 m. *E Colombia to e Peru.*

Black-bellied Thorntail *Discosura langsdorffi* Coliespina Ventrinegro
Male 14 cm (5.5"); female 7.7 cm (3"). Plate 39. Male is similar to Wire-crested Thorntail but lacks a crest. Female is similar but has more mottled underparts. Cf. female Festive Coquette. Rare and local in humid lowland forests e of Andes to 800 m. *S Venezuela to n Bolivia and Amazonian Brazil.*

Blue-chinned Sapphire *Chlorostilbon notatus* Zafiro Barbiazul
9.2 cm (3.6"). Plate 39. Similar to more widespread Blue-tailed Emerald, but larger and has reddish at base of the bill. Sapphire-spangled Emerald has a much brighter gorget. Female Glittering-throated Emerald has a greener tail and more solid green on sides. Locally fairly common in humid lowland forests e of Andes south to Loreto to 1000 m. *Tropical n South America to e Peru and e Brazil.*

Blue-tailed Emerald *Chlorostilbon mellisugus* Esmeralda Coliazul
6.9 cm (2.7"). Plate 39. ♪797. The only tiny, fairly uniformly green hummingbird with a blue tail and a black bill. Cf. larger Blue-chinned Sapphire. Fairly common in lowland forests e of Andes, rarely to 2700 m. *S Venezuela and the Guianas to n Bolivia and Amazonian Brazil.*

[Short-tailed Emerald] *Chlorostilbon poortmani* Esmeralda Colicorta
6.9 cm (2.7"). Not illustrated. Small; recalls Blue-tailed Emerald but tail is short and shining green. Known from an old specimen labeled "*C. auratus*, Peru". Montane forests of w Colombia and nw Venezuela. *Andes of Colombia and w Venezuela.*

Green-crowned Woodnymph *Thalurania fannyi* Ninfa Coroniverde
10.5 cm (4.3"). Plate 39. Note limited range. Rare and has an extremely limited range in n Peru. Male resembles Fork-tailed Woodnymph (no overlap) but crown is iridescent green and underparts mostly green (some violet on shoulders). Female is similar to female Fork-tailed Woodnymph. Rare in extreme nw Peru. Recorded at Zona Reservada de Tumbes. *E Panama to w Colombia, n Ecuador and extreme nw Peru.*

Fork-tailed Woodnymph *Thalurania furcata* Ninfa Colihorquillada
10.5 cm (4.3"). Plate 39. ♪797. Male is unmistakable in its range. Female has grayish underparts, white tips to tail and a slightly decurved bill. Cf. Gray-breasted Sabrewing. Fairly common in humid trop. and subtrop. forests e of Andes. *Venezuela and the Guianas to n Argentina, Amazonian and e Brazil.*

Violet-bellied Hummingbird *Damophila julie* Colibrí Ventrivioleta
7.7 cm (3"). Plate 39. Note limited range. Male is the only hummingbird in its range with a violet belly, iridescent green throat and crown, and a reddish lower mandible. Female is dark green with a whitish throat and reddish lower mandible. Fairly common in lowland and foothill forests in Tumbes to 1000 m. *Central Panama to extreme nw Peru.*

Rufous-throated Sapphire *Hylocharis sapphirina* Zafiro Gargantirufa
8.7 cm (3.4"). Plate 39. ♪797. Male is the only small hummingbird with a golden tail and violet throat. Note the bright-red bill and rufous chin. Female is mostly white below with a diagnostic rufous chin. Rare in humid lowland forests e of Andes in Loreto. *S Venezuela and the Guianas to ne Argentina, Amazonian and se Brazil.*

White-chinned Sapphire *Hylocharis cyanus* Zafiro Barbiblanco
8.7 cm (3.4"). Plate 39. ♪ 797. Male is the only small hummingbird with a golden-rufous rump, a contrasting dark tail, a violet throat and extensive violet on the face. Note the bright-red bill. Female is mostly white below with a diagnostic golden-rufous rump. Uncommon in humid lowland forests e of Andes to 300 m. *S Venezuela and the Guianas to n Bolivia, Amazonian and se Brazil.*

Golden-tailed Sapphire *Chrysuronia oenone* Zafiro Colidorada
8.7 cm (3.4"). Plate 39. ♪ 797. Male is the only small hummingbird with a golden tail and entirely blue head (race *oenone* in Loreto) or blue crown and sides of head (race *josephinae* in most of e Peru). Female recalls Rufous-throated Sapphire but lacks rufous chin. Uncommon in humid lowland and montane forests on e slope of Andes to 1650 m. *N Venezuela to n Bolivia and extreme w Brazil.*

White-tailed Goldenthroat *Polytmus guainumbi* Gargantioro Coliblanco
10.5 cm (4.1"). Plate 41. ♪ 797. Note savanna habitat. The only hummingbird in its range and habitat that is golden-olive above, golden-green below (buffy in female), has a postocular spot and a short white malar stripe. Male shows white on inner web of outer tail feathers and an incomplete tail band. Female has white tail tips. Fairly common in extreme se humid lowlands in Pampas del Heath (Graham *et al.* 1980). *Savanna of trop. South America south to s Brazil and ne Argentina.*

Green-tailed Goldenthroat *Polytmus theresiae* Gargantioro Coliverde
8.7 cm (3.4"). Plate 41. The only hummingbird in its range and habitat (savanna) that is very green above and below (sexes are similar, but female's underparts are more mottled) with a white vent and a white postocular spot. Fairly common but very local in e savannas (Jeberos and Pampas del Heath) to 500 m. *Savanna of n South America to Amazonian Brazil and e Peru.*

Leucippus **Hummingbirds.** Seven species of dull hummingbirds with female-like plumage. Sexes alike. Fortunately most are allopatric.

Tumbes Hummingbird *Leucippus baeri* Colibrí de Tumbes
9.4 cm (3.7"). Plate 38. Note limited range. A very dull hummingbird, olive above and pale dingy below, becoming whiter on belly. Cf. Spot-throated Hummingbird (no overlap but range comes close) has golden-green "flecks" on throat. Common and local in arid scrub in Tumbes, Piura and Lambayeque to 1300 m. *Arid nw Peru and extreme s Ecuador.*

Spot-throated Hummingbird *Leucippus taczanowskii* Colibrí de Taczanowski
10.2 cm (4"). Plate 38. Note limited range. A very dull hummingbird, olive above and pale dingy below, with a spotted throat. Cf. Tumbes Hummingbird. Fairly common in arid scrub from Piura to Ancash at 350-1000 m, but occasionally to 3000 m. *Endemic to Peru.*

Olive-spotted Hummingbird *Leucippus chlorocercus* Colibrí Blanquioliva
9.2 cm (3.6"). Plate 38. Note limited range. A very dull hummingbird, olive above and pale-gray below, with limited green spotting on neck and malar area. Cf. female Fork-tailed Woodnymph (not as olive and lacks postocular spot). Rare in humid valleys of Ucayali, Marañón and lower Río Napo to 450 m. *River islands in Ecuador, n Peru and w Amazonian Brazil.*

White-bellied Hummingbird *Leucippus chionogaster* Colibrí Ventriblanco
9.4 cm (3.7"). Plates 38, 40. ♪ 797. Green above and white below. Similar to Green-and-white Hummingbird. Uppertail is green. Outer tail feathers (at least basally) are white. Overlaps with similar Andean Emerald but female Andean's uppertail is coppery. Cf. female Booted Racket-tail. Fairly common in montane scrub in Andes at 800-3000 m. *E Peru to nw Argentina and sw Brazil.*

"Ampay" Hummingbird *Leucippus sp.* Colibrí de Ampay
11 cm (4.5"). Plate 41. An unnamed form of *Leucippus* hummingbird collected in *Podocarpus* forest at Bosque de Ampay (Apurímac) at 2800-3400 m (Fjeldså and Krabbe 1990). Very similar to Many-spotted Hummingbird (no overlap) but slightly buffier below and vent is unspotted. Blue-green tail has a purplish-blue subterminal band and a gray terminal band. Cf. Speckled Hummingbird. This bird was originally placed in *Taphrospilus* but that genus has been submerged in *Leucippus* (del Hoyo et al. 1999). *Endemic to Peru.*

Green-and-white Hummingbird *Leucippus viridicauda* Colibrí Verdiblanco
9.4 cm (3.7"). Plate 38. Similar to widespread and often sympatric White-bellied Hummingbird, but base of undertail is all dark; White-bellied has whitish base at least to the outer undertail feathers (usually shows mostly whitish undertail). Uncommon and poorly known in humid montane scrub in Pasco and Cusco at 900 to 2800 m. Regularly recorded near Machu Picchu. *Endemic to Peru.*

Many-spotted Hummingbird *Leucippus hypostictus* Colibrí Multipunteado
11 cm (4.5"). Plate 38. White underparts are heavily spotted with green. Cf. Speckled Hummingbird (strong facial pattern). Rare in foothill forests north to Amazonas at 750-1400 m. Often recorded near Cock-of-the-rock Lodge. *E slope of Andes from Ecuador to sw Brazil and nw Argentina.*

Amazilia Hummingbird *Amazilia amazilia* Colibrí Ventrirufa
9.2 cm (3.6"). Plate 38. The only hummingbird in its range with rufous tail and belly and a bright-red bill (dark on tip). In widespread nominate race (illustrated) the white chest patch is often replaced by green. The patch is blue in *caeruleigularis* (Ica), or extends to the chin in *dumerilii* and *leucophaea* (n Peru). The most common hummingbird in gardens of Lima. Common in arid Pacific lowlands to 2000 m; sight record from Volcán El Misti (Arequipa) at 2850 m (BPW). *W Ecuador and w Peru.*

Versicolored Emerald *Agyrtria versicolor* Colibrí Versicolor
8.5 cm (3.3"). Not illustrated. Accidental. Sexes similar. Recalls Andean Emerald (no overlap). Both sexes can be recognized by combination of mostly pure white underparts (including throat), green sides of breast, whitish tips to tail and (in good light) bluish malar. Lower mandible of straight bill is reddish. Recalls female of various sympatric hummingbirds but none has a white throat or is as white below. Known from a single specimen from near Iquitos but there are records from adjacent Colombia (pers. comm. K. Schuchmann). *S Venezuela and e Colombia to ne Argentina and Brazil.*

Andean Emerald *Agyrtria franciae* Colibrí Andino
9 .2cm (3.6"). Plate 41. Both sexes can be recognized by the combination of white underparts and coppery uppertail and rump (brighter golden-copper on rump). Male has a blue crown. Cf. sympatric White-bellied Hummingbird and female Booted Racket-tail. Fairly common in Andes south to Cajamarca at 1000-2000 m. *Andes of Colombia to n Peru.*

Sapphire-spangled Emerald *Polyerata lactea* Colibrí Pechizafiro
9 cm (3.6"). Plate 40. The male's extensive sapphire (violet-blue) gorget is replaced in the female by a gray throat with shiny light-blue flecks. Cf. White-chinned Sapphire (coppery rump). Fairly common in humid lowland forests e of Andes. *S Venezuela to Peru and n Bolivia; se Brazil.*

Glittering-throated Emerald *Polyerata fimbriata* Colibrí Gargantibrillante
8 cm (3.2"). Plate 41. ♪ 677. Male has a shiny green throat, replaced in female with a white throat spotted with green flecks. Both sexes have a reddish bill, green upperparts and a white belly with green sides. Female resembles female Blue-chinned Sapphire. Uncommon in humid lowland forests e of Andes, occasionally to 1200 m. *Tropical South America e of the Andes to n Bolivia and s Brazil.*

White-vented Plumeleteer *Chalybura buffonii* Colibrí de Buffon
10.2 cm (4"). Plate 41. Note limited range. Tail is dark blue (not bronzy); female has gray tips to tail. Both sexes have a white crissum and pinkish lower mandible. Pink feet (when visible) are diagnostic. Uncommon in humid foothill forests in Tumbes to 1000 m. The geographically isolated race *intermedia* that occurs in nw Peru may represent a separate species (Loja Plumeleteer). *Central Panama to Venezuela and extreme nw Peru.*

Ecuadorian Piedtail *Phlogophilus hemileucurus* Colipinto Ecuatoriano
7.7 cm (3"). Plate 38. The tail pattern is distinctive. Also note the white semicollar. Fairly common near humid headwaters of Río Napo at 800-1500 m; recently recorded at Abra Patricia at 1890 m. *Locally in foothills of e Ecuador and n Peru.*

Peruvian Piedtail *Phlogophilus harterti* Colipinto Peruano
7.7 cm (3"). Plate 38. Tail pattern is distinctive. Similar to Ecuadorian Piedtail (no overlap) but chin and belly are tinged rufous. Rare in Andean foothills in Huánuco, Pasco, Cusco and Puno at 750-1200 m. Photographed near Cock-of-the-rock Lodge (RC). *Endemic to Peru.*

Speckled Hummingbird *Adelomyia melanogenys* Colibrí Jaspeado
8.7 cm (3.4"). Plate 39. ♪ 797. A dull hummingbird, brownish-green above and pale-buff below with a strong facial pattern (dark ear coverts bordered above by a white postocular stripe are reminiscent of a hermit or woodstar), bronzy rump and buffy tail tips. The three ssp. that occur in Peru differ in the amount of speckling on underparts. Cf. Many-spotted Hummingbird. Fairly common in humid montane forests on e slope of Andes at 1000-3000 m. *Mountains of w South America from n Venezuela to nw Argentina.*

Gould's Jewelfront *Heliodoxa aurescens* Brillante Pechicastaño
11 cm (4.5"). Plate 42. ♪ 797. Both sexes have a rufous breast patch and mostly dark-rufous tail. Female has a heavily spotted pale throat. Uncommon in humid lowland forests e of Andes to 900 m. *Venezuela to n Bolivia and w Amazonian Brazil.*

Fawn-breasted Brilliant *Heliodoxa rubinoides* Brillante Pechianteado
10.2 cm (4"). Plate 43. ♪ 742CD. No other hummingbird has lightly spotted, dull-buff underparts, cinnamon-buff undertail and green upperparts. Male has a small pink patch on the throat. Females of other brilliants are grayer below and have darker undertails. Uncommon in montane forests on e slope of Andes south to Cusco at 1750-2700 m. *Colombia, Ecuador and Peru.*

Violet-fronted Brilliant *Heliodoxa leadbeateri* Brillante Frentivioleta
13.5 cm (5.3"). Plate 43. ♪ 797. Sympatric with most other brilliants. Male has a violet-blue forecrown and green gorget (all other brilliants have green forecrowns). Both sexes of Pink-throated and Rufous-webbed Brilliants have white vents. Cf. Black-throated Brilliant. Fairly common in foothill and montane forests on e slope of Andes at 700-2400 m. *Venezuela to w Bolivia.*

Black-throated Brilliant *Heliodoxa schreibersii* Brillante Gargantirosada
12 cm (4.7"). Plate 42. ♪ 652. Both sexes have long forked tails (more deeply forked in male), blackish belly and a glittering violet patch on lower throat. Female has a white malar stripe. Nominate ssp. (illustrated) occurs n of Amazon. Race *whitelyana* (s of Amazon) lacks shiny green forecrown and has only a violet breast-band (lacks green). Compare Violet-fronted and Pink-throated Brilliants. Uncommon to rare in humid trop. and upper trop. forests e of Andes south to n Ucayali to 1450 m. *Colombia to e Peru and nw Amazonian Brazil.*

Pink-throated Brilliant *Heliodoxa gularis* Brillante Gargantirosado
10.2 cm (4"). Plates 42, 43. The only brilliant in its limited range with a white vent. Rare in humid upper trop. forests in Loreto to 1050 m. *S Colombia, Ecuador and adjacent n Peru.*

Rufous-webbed Brilliant *Heliodoxa branickii* Brillante Alicanela
10.2 cm (4"). Plate 42. The only brilliant in its range with a white vent. Uncommon in Andean foothills in Huánuco, Pasco, Cusco and Madre de Dios at 750-1550 m. Recorded near Cock-of-the-rock Lodge. *Endemic to Peru.*

White-tailed Hillstar *Urochroa bougueri* Estrella Coliblanca
12 cm (4.7"). Plate 43. Note limited range. No other hummingbird in its range has a similar tail pattern (black central and outermost feathers, mostly white between). Rare in humid upper trop. forests in Amazonas and San Martín at 900-1500 m. *Andes of Colombia, Ecuador and ne Peru.*

Chestnut-breasted Coronet *Boissonneaua matthewsii* Colibrí Pechicastaño
10.7 cm (4.2"). Plate 43. ♪ EC007T. Sexes alike. Almost all rufous-chestnut underparts (throat heavily spotted with green) and green upperparts. Female Great Sapphirewing is much larger and has blue on underwing. Starfrontlets (especially females and immatures) have much longer bills. Fairly common in humid montane forests south to Cusco at 1550-2700 m. *Colombia, Ecuador and e Peru.*

Shining Sunbeam *Aglaeactis cupripennis* Rayo-de-Sol Brillante
10.2 cm (4"). Plate 40. ♪ LNS. A medium-sized hummingbird with cinnamon underparts and head. In good light colors of rump are iridescent. Cf. sympatric and local White-tufted Sunbeam. Note that tail color varies from rufous to dark brown. Southern ssp. *caumatonotus* (north to Junín) has purple on upper-tail coverts that almost completely replaces the green in nominate ssp. (illustrated). Locally common in montane scrub at 2200-4300 m. *Andes of Colombia, Ecuador and Peru.*

White-tufted Sunbeam *Aglaeactis castelnaudii* Rayo-de-Sol Acanelado
10.2 cm (4"). Plate 42. Similar to, and often sympatric with, Shining Sunbeam, but white tufts on breast are conspicuous. Also note that dark upper throat contrasts with dark cinnamon-rufous chest. Locally fairly common in montane shrubbery and *Polylepis* and *Escallonia* at 2500 to 4300 m in woodlands in Huánuco, Pasco, Apurímac and Cusco. *Endemic to Peru.*

*Purple-backed Sunbeam *Aglaeactis aliciae* Rayo-de-Sol de Dorso Púrpura
11.7 cm (4.6"). Plate 42. Note limited range. Recalls Shining Sunbeam but note large white patch on lower throat and center of breast, and remaining dark underparts. Rare in montane shrubbery in upper Marañón Valley (La Libertad and Ancash) at 3,000-3500 m. Reported feeding from mistletoe that parasitize alders and other trees. All records within a 20-km radius, mainly near El Molino on road from Trujillo to Río Marañón at 3000 m (Begazo *et al.* 2001). *Endemic to Peru.*

Andean Hillstar *Oreotrochilus estella* Estrella Andina
11.7 cm (4.6"). Plate 40. ♪ 797. Male is unmistakable in its range (no overlap with Green-headed Hillstar). Female is dull-green above and dingy-gray below with a spotted throat. In female outermost rectrix has entirely white inner web and entirely black outer. Bases and tips of remaining outer rectrices are evenly white. Cf. female Black-breasted Hillstar. Fairly common on rocky Andean slopes from Ayacucho south at 2400-5000 m. *Andes of c Peru to nw Argentina and n Chile.*

Green-headed Hillstar *Oreotrochilus stolzmanni* Estrella Cabeciverde
13 cm (5.2"). Plate 43. Male is similar to Andean Hillstar (no overlap) but median belly stripe is black. Female is also similar, but outer tail feathers have white bases and white tips, giving tail a banded look. Locally common in montane *Puya* and *Polylepis* forests in Cajamarca and Huánuco at 3600-4200. *Andes of n Peru; recently recorded in adjacent s Ecuador.*

Black-breasted Hillstar *Oreotrochilus melanogaster* Estrella Pechinegro
10.2 cm (4"). Plates 43, 45. Note limited range. Almost all black male is unmistakable. Female similar to female Andean Hillstar but base of outer rectrices is black. Uncommon on alpine slopes of Andes in Junín, Lima and Huancavelica at 3500-4500 m. Frequents *Chuquiragua* shrubs with sheltered places among rocks. *Endemic to Peru.*

Mountain Velvetbreast *Lafresnaya lafresnayi* Colibrí Aterciopelado
9 .2 cm (3.6"). Plate 43. ♪ LNS. Both sexes have a decurved bill and mostly white tail. Male has a mostly black belly; female mostly whitish underparts with a spotted throat and streaked breast. Uncommon in arid montane shrubbery south to Junín at 1500-3700 m. *Andes of nw Venezuela to s Peru.*

***Coeligena* Incas and Starfrontlets.** Six species of medium-sized to large hummingbirds that inhabit humid montane forests. They all have long, straight bills.

Bronzy Inca *Coeligena coeligena* Inca Bronceado
4.9" (11.7 cm). Plate 43. ♪ EC007T. Blackish-bronze above and brownish below (grayish throat is spotted). Immature starfrontlets do not look as dark and colorless. Fairly common in humid montane forests on e slope of Andes at 950-3000 m. *Venezuela to w Bolivia.*

Gould's Inca *Coeligena inca* Inca de Gould
11 cm (4.5"). Plate 43. Similar to Collared Inca except collar is rufous instead of white. Common in humid montane forests at 1600-3200 m from Cordillera Urubamba to Puno. *Andes of se Peru to n Bolivia.*

Collared Inca *Coeligena torquata* Inca Acollarado
11 cm (4.5"). Plate 40. ♪ EC007T. Easily recognized by distinctive combination of white breast-band and mostly white tail. Common in humid montane forests on e slope of Andes at 2200-3000 m (rarely down to 1500 m) south to Cordillera Vilcabamba. *Venezuela to se Peru.*

Buff-winged Starfrontlet *Coeligena lutetiae* Inca Alianteada
11.7 cm (4.6"). Plate 43. ♪ LNS. Note limited range. Both sexes have a diagnostic buff patch on secondaries. Common in montane forests and *páramo* on Cerro Chinguela at 2600-3300 m. *Colombia to nw Peru.*

Violet-throated Starfrontlet *Coeligena violifer* Inca Gargantivioleta
11.5 cm (4.8"). Plates 42, 43. ♪ 797. Three ssp. occur in Peru. All have a dark terminal band on the tail and the male has a violet patch on the throat and a shining blue forecrown. Southeast race *osculans* is only starfrontlet in its range with an orange-buff tail. Race *albicaudata* (Ayacucho and Apurímac) is duller and has a whitish tail. Race *dichroura* (Ayacucho northward, locally on Pacific slope) is similar to *osculans*, but central tail feathers are dark and terminal tail band is broader. Possible overlap with Rainbow Starfrontlet, but latter's tail is a brighter orange-red, lacks a terminal band and is forked. Females of all ssp. are pale-buff below and heavily spotted with green on throat and breast. Common in montane forests and *páramo* at 1500-3700 m. *Andes of s Ecuador, Peru and w Bolivia.*

Rainbow Starfrontlet *Coeligena iris* Inca Arcoiris
10.9 cm (4.3"). Plate 42, 43. ♪ LNS. Five ssp. occur in Peru. All can be identified by the fairly long, forked, orange-rufous tail and lower back (sometimes upper back as well). Note absence of terminal tail band. Cf. Violet-throated Starfrontlet. Males have a colorful head pattern (varies between ssp.). Females have a pale breast and heavily spotted green throat. Common in montane forests south to La Libertad at 1500-3500 m. Accidental in Ancash. *S Ecuador and n Peru.*

Sword-billed Hummingbird *Ensifera ensifera* Colibrí Pico Espada
13 cm (5.2"). Plate 40. ♪ LNS. Unmistakable with its amazingly long bill. Uncommon in montane and elfin forests at 1700-3600 m. *Venezuela to w Bolivia.*

Great Sapphirewing *Pterophanes cyanopterus* Alizafiro Grande
16.5 cm (6.5"). Plate 40. ♪ LNS. A very large hummingbird. Both sexes have iridescent blue underwings; female has cinnamon-rufous underparts. Cf. smaller Chestnut-breasted Coronet. Fairly common in montane scrub at 1600-3700 m. *Colombia to w Bolivia.*

Giant Hummingbird *Patagona gigas* Colibrí Gigante
18.5 cm (7.2"). Plate 40. ♪ LNS. The largest hummingbird in the world. Note the white rump on both sexes. Female's underparts are dingy to buffy and often mottled. Fairly common in montane scrub at 1000-4500 m. *Andes of Ecuador to s Chile and nw Argentina.*

Amethyst-throated Sunangel *Heliangelus amethysticollis* Angel-del-Sol Gargantiamatista
9.4 cm (3.7"). Plate 44. ♪ 797. Crescent-shaped chest band is often conspicuous and diagnostic. Ssp. differ in color of male's gorget (amethyst to violet) and color of chest band (white to pale-buff). Female's rusty-orange throat may cause confusion with Little Sunangel but the latter lacks a chest band. Cf. female Royal Sunangel (very local, blue forked tail and spotted throat). Common in humid montane forests at 1800-3300 m. *NE Colombia and Venezuela; s Ecuador to w Bolivia.*

Little Sunangel *Heliangelus micraster* Angel-del-Sol Chico
10.2 cm (4"). Plate 44. Note limited range. Recalls widespread Amethyst-throated Sunangel but lacks chest band and gorget color ranges from orange-yellow (nominate, illustrated) to reddish-orange in *cutervensis* (Cajamarca). Female has orange spots on throat. Compare female Purple-throated Sunangel. Fairly common in humid montane forests south to Cerros de Amachongo (Cajamarca) at 1500-3400 m. *Andes of se Ecuador and n Peru.*

Purple-throated Sunangel *Heliangelus viola* Angel-del-Sol Gargantipúrpura
12 cm (4.7"). Plate 42. ♪ LNS. Note limited range. Larger than similar Amethyst-throated Sunangel but lacks pale crescent on chest. Male's head pattern is distinctive (purple gorget and a blue chest band). Both sexes have fairly long, forked tails. Female similar but duller. Common in montane forests south to Marañón Valley (Cajamarca) at 1900-3100 m. *W Ecuador and n Peru.*

*Royal Sunangel *Heliangelus regalis* Angel-del-Sol Real
12 cm (4.7"). Plate 42. Male is unmistakable. Both sexes have long blue, deeply forked tails. Female looks like a large Amethyst-throated Sunangel but latter's tail is shorter, greener and only notched. An extremely localized hummingbird discovered in 1975. Rare to locally (seasonally?) fairly common in montane forest edge and shrubbery. Known from only four localities: above San José de Lourdes in Cordillera del Cóndor (Cajamarca) at 1800-2200 m; on Balsapuerta trail ne of Jirillo (San Martín) at 1450 m; Abra Patricia (San Martín) at 1900 m; and above San Cristóbal in Cordillera de Colán (Amazonas) at 1600-1950 m. Favors flowers of the melastome *Brachyotum quinquenerve*. *Endemic to Peru.*

Glowing Puffleg *Eriocnemis vestitus* Calzadito Reluciente
9.2 cm (3.6"). Plate 44. ♪ LNS. The male is the only hummingbird with large white "puffs", a violet vent and throat. Female is similar to female Coppery-naped Puffleg (limited overlap) but latter is larger, has a coppery nape and lacks purple on throat and rusty on breast. Common in montane shrubbery and *páramo* south to Cajamarca at 2200-3900 m. *Andes of w Venezuela and Colombia to extreme n Peru.*

Coppery-naped Puffleg *Eriocnemis sapphiropygia* Calzadito Colilargo Sureño
11 cm (4.5"). Plate 44. Over most of its range the only hummingbird with white "puffs" and a violet vent. Male of nominate race (illustrated) has a green lower belly, which is blue in northern race *catharina* (Piura, Amazonas). In extreme north cf. Glowing Puffleg. Sometimes regarded as conspecific with Sapphire-vented Puffleg (*E. luciani*) from Ecuador and s Colombia. Uncommon in montane and elfin forests at 2800-4800 m. *Endemic to Peru.*

Emerald-bellied Puffleg *Eriocnemis alinae* Calzadito Ventriesmeralda
7.7 cm (3"). Plate 44. Unmistakable with its huge white "puffs", emerald-green belly and undertail. Uncommon in subtrop. and montane forests on e slope of Andes south to Huánuco at 2000-2800 m. *E Andes of Colombia to n Peru.*

Buff-thighed Puffleg *Haplophaedia assimilis* Calzadito Verdoso Sureño
9.2 cm (3.6"). Plate 44. A dark-green hummingbird with a dark-blue tail and bronzy rump. "Puffs" are small pale-buff (nominate, Pasco southward) to cinnamon-buff (*affinis*, illustrated). Female Booted Racket-tail lacks blue tones on tail. Sometimes considered conspecific with Greenish Puffleg (*H. aureliae*) from Colombia and Ecuador. Uncommon in subtrop. montane forests on e slope of Andes at 900-3100 m. *Andes of Peru to nw Bolivia.*

Purple-bibbed Whitetip *Urosticte benjamini* Colibrí Pechipúrpura
9.4 cm (3.7"). Plate 44. Note limited range. Both sexes have forked tails and a noticeable white postocular spot. Male has diagnostic large white tips to central tail feathers and a magenta patch on breast. Female has white tips to outer tail feathers, and white underparts are heavily spotted with green. Cf. female Violet-headed Hummingbird (dingy, unspotted underparts). Uncommon and local in Andes of Piura at 700-1600m. *Andes of s Colombia to sw Ecuador and nw Peru.*

Rufous-vented Whitetip *Urosticte ruficrissa* Colibrí Ventrirrufa
3.7" (9.5 cm). Plate 44. Note limited range. Both sexes differ from similar respective Purple-bibbed Whitetip by having smaller tail spots. Male has a green (not magenta) bib. Uncommon and local in humid montane forests in Amazonas at 1600-2400. Recently recorded at Jesus del Monte. *E slope of Andes from Colombia to extreme n Peru.*

Booted Racket-tail *Ocreatus underwoodii* Colibrí Colaespátula
Male 11.4-12.5 cm (4.8"-5"); female 7.7 cm (3"). Plate 44. ♪742CD. A very small-bodied hummingbird. Male's cinnamon "puffs" and racket-like tail make it unmistakable. Female's combination of pale-buff "puffs" and mostly white underparts is diagnostic. Male of ne race *peruanus* has slightly longer tail rackets (that do not cross each other) than *annae* (illustrated, c and s Peru). Both Peruvian races *peruanus* and *annae* may represent separate species. Uncommon in montane forests on e slope of Andes at 850-3100 m. *Andes of Venezuela to s Bolivia.*

Lesbia **Trainbearers.** A pair of attractive, high-elevation hummingbirds with deeply forked, extremely long tails. Note the proportion between body size and tail, uppertail colors and if possible shape of gorget. Cf. Long-tailed Sylph.

Black-tailed Trainbearer *Lesbia victoriae* Colibrí Colilarga Negra
Male 24 cm (9.4"); female 14 cm (5.5"). Plate 44. ♪LNS. Male's tail is very long (double the size of body), and from above is almost all black except for narrow greenish-bronze tips to tail feathers. Gorget extends to lower breast where it tapers. In both sexes bill is slightly decurved (bill is shorter in southern race *berlepschi* than in illustrated *juliae*). In good light note upper parts are bronzy-green, darker than bright-green upperparts of Green-tailed Trainbearer. Females of both trainbearers are very similar, with spotted underparts. Female Black-tailed has a blacker and longer tail (as long as the body) compared with female Green-tailed, which has a greener uppertail (only about 3/4 length of body) and a straighter bill. Fairly common in montane scrub and forest edge at 2500-4000 m. *Andes of Colombia, Ecuador and Peru.*

Green-tailed Trainbearer *Lesbia nuna* Colacintillo Colilarga Verde
Male 15.5 cm (6.3"); female 11.2 cm (4.4"). Plate 40. ♪797. Male has a long tail, but usually shorter than 1-1/2 times the size of the body; uppertail is mostly green and gorget is rounded. Bill is rather short and straight. Female is similar to that of Black-tailed Trainbearer. Fairly common in montane scrub and forest edge at 1700-3800 m. *Andes of w Venezuela to w Bolivia.*

[Red-tailed Comet] *Sappho sparganura* Cometa Coliroja
16.5 cm (6.5"). Plate 44. ♪797. Accidental? The fiery-red back and long tail make this spectacular hummingbird unmistakable. Undocumented old sight record from montane scrub in Puno. *Andes of Bolivia, w Argentina and n Chile.*

Bronze-tailed Comet *Polyonymus caroli* Cometa Colibronceada
12 cm (4.7"). Plate 42. Both sexes can be identified by the bronzy, forked tail and magenta-red gorget. Female's gorget is less developed. Cf. very rare Gray-bellied Comet (much larger, etc.). Uncommon to locally common on semiarid slopes of w Andes from Cajamarca to Arequipa at 2000-3400 m. Common at Huaytará (Huancavelica) at 2925 m. Commonly seen feeding on flowers of *Phrygilanthus* mistletoes and *Mutisia*. Often difficult to observe if aggressive violetears are feeding in same area. *Endemic to Peru*.

Purple-backed Thornbill *Ramphomicron microrhynchum* Picoespina Dorsipúrpura
8 cm (3.2"). Plate 46. ♪ LNS. Male is unlikely to be confused. Female recalls a female metaltail but Purple-backed Thornbill's longer tail is tipped white. Rare in montane and elfin forests on e slope of Andes at 1700-3750 m. Recorded at Bosque de Ampay and above Pillahuata. *Andes of w Venezuela to w Bolivia*.

Bearded Mountaineer *Oreonympha nobilis* Montañés Barbudo
13.5 cm (5.3"). Plate 42. A magnificent, unmistakable hummingbird. Female is duller with slightly shorter tail than male. Uncommon in dry Andean valleys of central Peru at 2500-3800 m. Feeds on flowers of columnar cacti, agaves, occasionally *Eucalyptus*, and especially on the yellow flowers of the tobacco plant *Nicotiana*. Seen regularly in various sites around city of Cusco (especially Laguna Huacarpay) and in parts of Apurímac Valley. *Endemic to Peru*.

Metallura **Metaltails.** Six species of small, short-billed hummingbirds that generally inhabit high-elevation forests. Tyrian Metaltail is widespread, and four of the species are allopatric. As they open and close their tail, a flash of iridescent color is visible. Note colors of upper and under tail, underparts and gorget.

Tyrian Metaltail *Metallura tyrianthina* Colibrí Tirio
9.2 cm (3.6"). Plate 46. ♪ 797. A widespread metaltail with a dark blue (or coppery) tail and green gorget. Compare with sympatric metaltails. Three ssp occur in Peru. Race *septentrionalis* (w of Río Marañón) and *smaragdinicollis* (e slopes) have a darker, more violet tail. In extreme north nominate *tyrianthina* has a coppery tail. Females usually have a buff throat, sometimes spotted with green. Cf. female Rufous-capped Thornbill and Mountain Avocetbill. Common in humid montane forests and scrub at 2500-3800 m. *Andes of Venezuela to w Bolivia*.

Scaled Metaltail *Metallura aeneocauda* Colibrí Escamoso
10.2 cm (4"). Plates 45, 46. ♪ 797. Note the green undertail and flash of blue on uppertail. Feathers on underparts are green with buff edges, creating a heavily scaled appearance. Sympatric Tyrian Metaltail has blue undertail (underparts on molting birds may appear scaled). Female Scaled Metaltail has very reduced (or no) gorget and dull buff underparts with green sides. Fairly common in cloud forests south from Cordillera Vilcabamba at 1950-4000 m. *Andes of s Peru and w Bolivia*.

Fire-throated Metaltail *Metallura eupogon* Colibrí Barbafuego
10.2 cm (4"). Plate 45. Within its limited range the only metaltail with a fiery-red gorget (reduced to a red spot in female) bordered with metallic green. Uppertail is metallic-blue. Uncommon and local in dwarf and elfin Andean forests in Huánuco, Junín, Ayacucho and Apurímac at 3000 to 3700 m. Recorded at Bosque de Ampay. *Endemic to Peru*.

Coppery Metaltail *Metallura theresiae* Colibrí Cobrizo
9.4 cm (3.7"). Plate 45. Within its limited range the only metaltail with coppery-rufous underparts. Uppertail is metallic violet. Female is similar but gorget is reduced. Nominate ssp *theresiae* (illustrated) has blue undertail. Ssp. male *parkeri* (Cordillera de Colán) lacks bright-red border to green gorget and has greenish undertail. Locally common in dwarf and elfin forest in Cordillera de Colán in Amazonas, and south locally to Carpish Mts. north of Río Huallaga (Huánuco) at 3100-3700 m. Recorded at Bosque de Unchog. Feeds mostly on melastome flowers. *Endemic to Peru*.

Neblina Metaltail *Metallura odomae* Colibrí de Neblina
9.2 cm (3.6"). Plate 45. ♪ LNS. Within its limited range the only metaltail with a red gorget (spotted red in female). Tail is metallic-blue above and often tipped whitish. Fairly common and local in *pajonal* of humid elfin forest at tree-line on Cerro Chinguela (Piura). *Andes of n Peru and adjacent Ecuador.*

Black Metaltail *Metallura phoebe* Colibrí Negro
12 cm (4.7"). Plate 45. A fairly large metaltail, mostly black with a coppery tail. Female is similar and slightly duller. Common in montane scrub from Cajamarca to Tacna at 1800-4300 m. *Endemic to Peru.*

Rufous-capped Thornbill *Chalcostigma ruficeps* Picoespina Gorrirufo
9.2 cm (3.6"). Plate 40. Note the very short bill. Male can be identified by its rufous cap, narrow gorget and bronzy tail. Female resembles female Tyrian Metaltail but tail is bronzy (not blue). Cf. also Rainbow-bearded Thornbill (blackish with large white tips to tail). Uncommon in humid montane forest and scrub in Andes at 1900-3800 m. *Andes of s Ecuador, e Peru and w Bolivia.*

Olivaceous Thornbill *Chalcostigma olivaceum* Picoespina Oliváceo
13.5 cm (5.3"). Plate 42. Note habitat. Uniform dull olivaceous-brown with a multicolored narrow gorget. Female is even duller. Told from Blue-mantled Thornbill by lack of blue on back and tail. Uncommon in *puna* grasslands from Ancash south at 3150-4600 m. *Andes of central Peru to w Bolivia.*

Blue-mantled Thornbill *Chalcostigma stanleyi* Picoespina Dorsiazul
12 cm (4.7"). Plate 42. ♪ LNS. A dark thornbill with a blue back and forked tail. Gorget is multicolored in race *versigularis* n of Río Huallaga (illustrated) but mostly green in *vulcani* (s of Río Huallaga). Cf. Rainbow-bearded Thornbill (smaller, chestnut crown, white tips to tail). Female is similar but tail is shorter and throat is pale and spotted. Told from Olivaceous Thornbill by its blue tail and back. Fairly common in *Polylepis* woodlands and montane scrub in Andes at 3300-4300 m. *Páramo of Ecuador, Peru and w Bolivia.*

Rainbow-bearded Thornbill *Chalcostigma herrani* Picoespina Arcoiris
10.2 cm (4"). Plate 46. ♪ LNS. Note limited range. A small, dark thornbill with large white tips to tail and a chestnut crown. Cf. other *Chalcostigma*. Fairly common in montane scrub near Huancabamba deflection at 2700-3700 m. *Andes of Colombia to extreme n Peru.*

Mountain Avocetbill *Opisthoprora euryptera* Colibrí Piquiavoceta
10.2 cm (4"). Plate 40. ♪ LNS. Note limited range. Short bill is slightly upturned. Note heavily streaked underparts, brownish cast to head, prominent white postocular spot, and cinnamon on lower belly. Recalls female metaltail or thornbill but none is as streaked below. Locally uncommon in humid montane forests and scrub in Cordillera de Colán at 1700-3800 m. *Andes of Colombia to n Peru.*

*Gray-bellied Comet *Taphrolesbia griseiventris* Cometa Ventrigris
15 cm (6"). Plate 45. A large hummingbird with a fairly long, deeply forked tail and gray underparts. Tail is bronzy-green above and dark blue below. Female lacks blue gorget. Cf. smaller Bronze-tailed Comet. Rare in semiarid scrub in Cajamarca and Huánuco. Found on barren hills surrounding towns of Cajamarca at 2900 m and Cajabamba at 2655 m. Recently found nesting 7 km from Cajamarca airport at Quebrada Sangal (Garrigues 2001). Shows considerable altitudinal variation, with specimens recorded from 200 m to 3170 m (but most records above 2750 m) along Río Marañón. TSS reported a bird at Cullcui (Huánuco) at 3200 m. *Endemic to Peru.*

Long-tailed Sylph *Aglaiocercus kingi* Silfo Colilargo
Male 16 cm (6.3"); female 9.7 cm (3.8"). Plate 46. ♪ 797. Male's iridescent long tail and blue-green forecrown are diagnostic (cf. *Lesbia* trainbearers). Female identified by its iridescent blue uppertail, cinnamon belly and white throat spotted with green. Fairly common in humid montane forests and scrub along e slope of Andes at 900-3000 m. *Mountains of Venezuela to w Bolivia.*

Wedge-billed Hummingbird *Augastes geoffroyi* Colibrí Piquicuña
8.9 cm (3.5"). Plate 46. ♪ 742CD. Best identified by the combination of broken, white pectoral band, white postocular stripe and dark subterminal band to tail. Note also the pointed bill and dark cheeks. Female has a white throat spotted with green. Uncommon in humid montane forests along e slope of Andes at 800-2500 m. *Andes of w Venezuela to w Bolivia.*

Black-eared Fairy *Heliothryx aurita* Colibrí-Hada Orejinegra
10.2 cm (4"). Plate 46. No other Peruvian hummingbird has pure white underparts, black "ears" and white outer tail feathers. Uncommon in humid lowland forests and along e slope of Andes to 1300 m. *S Venezuela and the Guianas to n Bolivia and Amazonian Brazil.*

***Marvelous Spatuletail** *Loddigesia mirabilis* Colibrí Maravilloso
12.5 cm (5"). Back cover and Plate 45. The spectacular male is unmistakable. The only hummingbird with only four tail feathers. Female lacks a gorget, dark median breast stripe, and highly modified tail of male. Female's tail is fairly long, and mostly white from below. Confined to the e bank of Río Utcubamba at extreme south end of Cordillera del Colán. Most records are from shrubs around La Florida, but additional populations have been recorded near Leimebamba and Chachapoyas. Known to feed on the red tubular flowers of *Satureja sericea* and orange blossoms of *Bomarea formosissima* (known locally as *romero*) but often difficult to observe if dominant Green Violetears and Long-tailed Sylphs are present. A male recorded near Jusús del Monte (San Martín) may suggest an additional population. Most records are from 2100-2900 m, with 1700-3700 m as the extremes. *Endemic to Peru.*

Long-billed Starthroat *Heliomaster longirostris* Colibrí Piquilargo
9.2 cm (3.6"). Plate 46. Identified by the combination of very long bill, white "moustache" and a white stripe on the back. Male has an iridescent blue crown and magenta-red gorget but female's crown and gorget are duller. Uncommon along arid Pacific slope to 1500 m and in dry lowland forests e of Andes. *S Mexico to n Bolivia and Amazonian Brazil.*

Oasis Hummingbird *Rhodopis vesper* Colibrí de Oasis
10.7 cm (4.2"). Plates 45, 46. Decurved bill's length varies greatly, medium in extreme nw *koepckeae* (illustrated) to long (nominate *vesper*, illustrated, south of Piura). Best identified by its rufous rump. Male has a fairly long, deeply forked tail and a magenta gorget. Female's underparts are dingy gray, and its forked tail is shorter than male's. Uncommon along arid Pacific slope and in montane scrub to 3350 m. *Arid w Peru and n Chile.*

Peruvian Sheartail *Thaumastura cora* Colibrí de Cora
Male 12.5 cm (5"); female 7 cm (2.75"). Plates 45, 46. Note the short, straight bill. Male in breeding plumage is easily recognized with mostly white tail streamers. Non-breeding male lacks streamers but outer tail feathers are tipped white. Female is buffy below and has a fairly short, white-tipped tail. Fairly common in lowlands and mountains along Pacific slope from Piura and Lambayeque to Tacna to 3350 m. *Arid w Peru and extreme n Chile.*

***Calliphlox*, *Myrtis* and *Chaetocercus* Woodstars.** A group of small to tiny hummingbirds that hovers in insect-like fashion. Females are often difficult to identify. Carefully note tail pattern.

Amethyst Woodstar *Calliphlox amethystina* Estrellita Amatista
7.7 cm (3"). Plate 46. A tiny hummingbird. Male told from possibly sympatric White-bellied Woodstar by longer, deeply forked tail. Female can be told by the short, square tail with green central feathers and outer tail feathers with a black subterminal band and cinnamon tips. Usually the only woodstar in its range (White-bellied Woodstar is found higher). Uncommon in humid lowland forests e of Andes, occasionally to 1500 m. *Tropical South America to ne Argentina and s Brazil.*

Purple-collared Woodstar *Myrtis fanny* Estrellita Collaripúrpura
7.7 cm (3"). Plates 45, 46. ♪ LNS. Male is only woodstar with a turquoise gorget. Medium-length tail is forked. Female is cinnamon-buff below; black outer tail feathers have a rufous base and broad white tips; central tail feathers green. The only woodstar over most of its range, but possible overlap with Short-tailed and White-bellied Woodstars. Fairly common along arid Pacific slope and in montane scrub to 4000 m. *Arid lowlands and mountains of w Ecuador and w Peru.*

*Chilean Woodstar *Myrtis yarrellii* Estrellita Chilena
7.9 cm (3.1"). Plate 45. Note limited range. Male is similar to Purple-collared Woodstar but gorget is magenta (not turquoise). Female like that of Purple-collared but outer tail feathers lack rufous base. Rare (vagrant?) and local in arid lowlands in Tacna and Moquegua, occasionally to 800 m. *S Peru and n Chile.*

Short-tailed Woodstar *Myrmia micrura* Estrellita Colicorta
6.4 cm (2.5"). Plate 45. Note limited range. Male is similar to Purple-collared Woodstar but gorget is red (not turquoise) and tail is very short. Female's tail has black subterminal band and white tips. Uncommon in arid coastal lowlands south to La Libertad to 800 m. *SW Ecuador and nw Peru.*

White-bellied Woodstar *Chaetocercus mulsant* Estrellita Ventriblanca
7.7 cm (3"). Plates 40, 46. ♪ LNS. Male has a magenta gorget and white pectoral band. Lower belly is separated by a complete (or incomplete) green band on mid-belly. Shows a white patch on flanks; tail is short and forked. Female has a white belly, with rufous sides, a green pectoral band and buffy throat. Rufous tail is rounded, with a black subterminal band. Fairly common in montane forests and scrub in Andes at 900-4000 m. *Andes of Colombia to w Bolivia.*

*Little Woodstar *Chaetocercus bombus* Estrellita Chica
6.4 cm (2.5"). Plate 45. Smaller than White-bellied Woodstar. Male has a buff pectoral band and a rosy gorget. Female is uniform cinnamon below; rufous tail has a black subterminal band. Rare and local in lowlands and Andes south to middle Río Marañón (La Libertad) and upper Río Huallaga drainage (Huánuco) to 3050 m. Recorded at 150 m at Las Pampas, at Soquián (La Libertad) at 1050 m and at Chinchao (Huánuco) at 2000 m. *Forests and scrub of Ecuador and n Peru.*

Trogonidae (Quetzals and Trogons; Quetzales y Trogones). Species: World 39; Peru 10
Trogons and quetzals are a group of highly colorful birds that anatomically show only distant relationships to any other bird family. They are distributed throughout the Neotropical, Afrotropical and Oriental regions, with the highest concentration in the Americas. Most members of the family are sedentary. New World trogons are mainly frugivores, and obtain their fruit by hovering and plucking berries and small fruits. They supplement their diet with insects and spiders.

Trogon **Trogons.** Attractive forest birds with long, square tails. Note the undertail pattern, color of underparts, color of bill and eye-ring.

White-tailed Trogon *Trogon viridis* Trogón Coliblanco
26 cm (10.1"). Plate 47. ♪ 624. The male is the only trogon with yellow underparts and white undertail. Female has a gray hood, yellow belly and a complete bluish eye-ring. Cf. Violaceous and Black-throated Trogons. Common in humid *terra firme* and humid lowland forests e of Andes. *W Panama to Amazonian Brazil and n Bolivia.*

Violaceous Trogon *Trogon violaceus* Trogón Violáceo
23 cm (9"). Plate 47. ♪ 624. The male is the only trogon with a violet head, yellow underparts and barred tail. Female has a gray hood and a broken eye-ring. Cf. Black–throated and White-tailed Trogons. Rare along Pacific slope south to Piura; fairly common in humid lowland forests e of Andes. *S Mexico to n Bolivia and Amazonian Brazil.*

Collared Trogon *Trogon collaris* Trogón Acollarado
26 cm (10.1"). Plate 47. ♪ 624. The male has a green head and mostly barred undertail. Tail pattern is similar to that of smaller Blue-crowned Trogon, but latter has a bluish head. Undertail is noticeably barred (equal width of black and white bars). Female has a brown hood and bicolored bill (dusky upper mandible and yellow lower). Cf. Masked Trogon. Common in humid *terra firme* and humid lowland forests e of Andes, rarely to 2700 m. *E Mexico to n Bolivia and Amazonian Brazil.*

Masked Trogon *Trogon personatus* Trogón Enmascarado
26 cm (10.1"). Plate 47. ♪ 624. Similar to sympatric Collared Trogon, but barring on the undertail is finer, the black bars are thicker than white bars and tail appears blackish. Female has a brown hood, a yellow bill and a black mask. Fairly common in humid montane forests along e slope of Andes at 700-3600 m. *Venezuela and Guyana to w Bolivia.*

Black-throated Trogon *Trogon rufus* Trogón Gargantinegro
26 cm (10.1"). Plate 47. ♪ 624. Both sexes are similar respectively to Violaceous Trogon. Male's head is green (not violet-blue), eye-ring is bluish (not yellow) and bill is yellow (not dusky). Female has a brown (not gray) hood and a broken eye-ring. Rare in humid lowland forests e of Andes, occasionally to 1100 m. *Honduras to s Brazil and ne Argentina.*

Blue-crowned Trogon *Trogon curucui* Trogón Coroniazul
23 cm (9"). Plate 47. ♪ 624. The male is the only trogon with a blue head, red eye-ring, pale yellow bill, barred undertail and red underparts. Cf. Collared Trogon. Female is the only trogon with a gray hood, red belly, yellow bill and a broken eye-ring. Locally fairly common in humid lowland forests e of Andes, occasionally to 1600 m. *Colombia to w Brazil and n Argentina.*

Black-tailed Trogon *Trogon melanurus* Trogón Colinegro
28 cm (10.9"). Plate 47. ♪ 624. The only trogon in its range with red underparts and black undertail. Cf. Pavonine and Golden-headed Quetzals (wedge-shaped tail and green shoulders). Rare in arid Pacific lowlands s to Piura to 1500 m; fairly common in humid lowland forests e of Andes. *Central Panama to n Bolivia and Amazonian Brazil.*

Pharomachrus **Quetzals.** A trio of spectacular trogons. Males have elongated wing and tail coverts and all have wedged tails. Note the color of the bill and undertail.

Crested Quetzal *Pharomachrus antisianus* Quetzal Crestado
34 cm (13.5"). Plate 47. ♪ 624. The male is the only quetzal with a white undertail. Female has a black bill and barred undertail. Uncommon in humid montane forests along e slope of Andes at 1100-3000 m. *Andes of w Venezuela to w Bolivia.*

Golden-headed Quetzal *Pharomachrus auriceps* Quetzal Cabecidorado
34 cm (13.5"). Plate 47. ♪ 624. The male is the only quetzal with black undertail and a yellow bill. Note the golden-green head. Female is similar to female Pavonine Quetzal but has a dusky black bill and black undertail. Fairly common in humid montane forests at 500-3100 m. *Panama to w Bolivia.*

Pavonine Quetzal *Pharomachrus pavoninus* Quetzal Pavonino
34 cm (13.5"). Plate 47. ♪ 624. The male is the only quetzal with black undertail and a red bill. Female has a reddish bill tipped dark, and black undertail with barring on outer feathers. Uncommon in humid lowland forests e of Andes, occasionally to 1200 m. *Venezuela to n Bolivia and Amazonian Brazil.*

Alcedinidae (Kingfishers; Martines Pescadores). Species: World 93; Peru 5
Kingfishers are widely distributed throughout the world, with the New World species being almost exclusively piscivorous (although the American Pygmy Kingfisher feeds mostly on insects caught on the wing) and are found mainly along unpolluted rivers, lakes and streams. They nest in burrows dug in river banks. Many African, Asian and Australian species are forest kingfishers, and subsist on a diet of insects, often being found miles from the nearest water.

Ringed Kingfisher *Ceryle torquata* Martín Pescador Grande
38 cm (15"). Plate 48. ♪ 797. A very large kingfisher with a blue-gray back. Female has a gray breast-band. Fairly common along lowland rivers and oxbow lakes e of Andes, occasionally to 2600 m; rare on Pacific slope south to Lambayeque. *Mexico to Tierra del Fuego; Lesser Antilles and Trinidad.*

Amazon Kingfisher *Chloroceryle amazona* Martín Pescador Amazónico
27 cm (10.5"). Plate 48. ♪ 797. Similar to Green Kingfisher but much larger, with a longer crest, heavier bill and no white in the wings. Female has a green chest-band. Fairly common along lowland rivers and oxbow lakes e of Andes. *Mexico to n Argentina, mainly e of the Andes.*

Green Kingfisher *Chloroceryle americana* Martín Pescador Verde
20 cm (9"). Plate 48. ♪ 797. A small, green-backed kingfisher with a short crest, small white spots on the wings, and a rufous pectoral band (male) or two green breast-bands (female). Compare with larger Amazon Kingfisher. Rare along rivers on Pacific slope to 2500 m; fairly common along lowland rivers and oxbow lakes e of Andes. *Texas to n Argentina and n Chile.*

Green-and-rufous Kingfisher *Chloroceryle inda* Martín Pescador Verdirrufo
23 cm (9"). Plate 48. ♪ 797. Similar to American Pygmy Kingfisher but much larger, with a rufous vent and white spots on the wings. Male is all rufous below; female has a green chest-band spotted with white. Uncommon along lowland streams, swamps and oxbow lakes e of Andes. *Nicaragua to n Bolivia and Brazil.*

American Pygmy Kingfisher *Chloroceryle aenea* Martín Pescador Pigmeo
13.5 cm (5.3"). Plate 48. ♪ 797. A tiny sparrow-sized kingfisher. Note the white lower belly and vent. Compare with much larger Green-and-rufous Kingfisher. Female has a narrow green chest-band. Uncommon along lowland streams, swamps and oxbow lakes e of Andes. *Mexico to n Bolivia and Brazil.*

Momotidae (Motmots; Momotos y Relojeros). Species: World 10; Peru 4
Motmots are a small family of medium-sized, highly colored birds restricted to the Neotropics. In some species the tail is long, graduated and racket-tipped, and is often swung like a pendulum. They feed mainly on insects, including beetles, caterpillars, butterflies, spiders and worms, and occasionally supplement their diet with lizards and fruit.

Blue-crowned Motmot *Momotus momota* Relojero Coroniazul
41 cm (16"). Plate 48. ♪ 797. Similar to larger Highland Motmot (limited range overlap at best) but underparts are cinnamon brown (Highland's underparts are green). Fairly common along Pacific slope south to Tumbes and Piura to 1500 m, and in humid lowland forests e of Andes. *Mexico to nw Argentina and Brazil.*

Highland Motmot *Momotus aequatorialis* Relojero Montañero
48 cm (19"). Plate 48. ♪EC007T. A large motmot with a turquoise-blue forecrown. Similar to smaller Blue Crowned Motmot but underparts are green. Often perches along streamside boulders. Fairly common in humid montane forests in Andes at 1500-2400 m, rarely to 3100 m. *Subtropical Andes of Colombia to e Peru.*

Rufous Motmot *Baryphthengus martii* Relojero Rufo
45 cm (17.5"). Plate 48. ♪797. A large motmot with a rufous head and mostly rufous underparts. Compare with smaller Broad-billed Motmot. Fairly common in humid *terra firme* forests e of Andes. *Honduras to n Bolivia and Amazonian Brazil.*

Broad-billed Motmot *Electron platyrhynchum* Relojero Piquiancho
35 cm (14"). Plate 48. ♪797. Similar to Rufous Motmot but smaller, has a green chin-patch, rufous extends only to lower breast, larger breast spots and a shorter tail. Fairly common in humid *terra firme* forests e of Andes to 900 m. *Honduras to n Bolivia and Amazonian Brazil.*

Galbulidae (Jacamars; Jacamares). Species: World 18; Peru 12
Jacamars are a streamlined group of birds confined to the American tropics. They somewhat resemble oversized hummingbirds with their iridescent plumage, long pointed bills and long tails. They typically feed on insects, including bees, wasps and flying ants, which they pursue in deft aerial chases.

White-eared Jacamar *Galbalcyrhynchus leucotis* Jacamar Orejiblanco
20 cm (8"). ♪677. Plate 49. Unmistakable in its limited range with its huge red bill and white ear patch. No overlap with Purus Jacamar. Locally fairly common in humid lowland forests e of Andes in Loreto to 500 m. *Colombia e of the Andes to ne Peru and w Amazonian Brazil.*

Purus (Chestnut) Jacamar *Galbalcyrhynchus purusianus* Jacamar Castaño
20 cm (8"). Plate 51. Unmistakable with its huge red bill and uniform maroon-purple coloration. Rare in humid lowland riverine forests in s Ucayali, Madre de Dios and Puno. Recorded at Manu Wildlife Center. *Tropical e Peru to n Bolivia and w Amazonian Brazil.*

Brown Jacamar *Brachygalba lugubris* Jacamar Pardo
16.3 cm (6.7"). Plate 49. A dull, uniform brown jacamar with a black bill, whitish on throat and on lower belly. Cf. White-throated Jacamar. Uncommon in lowland forests and second growth e of Andes. *S Venezuela, the Guianas and Amazon basin.*

White-throated Jacamar *Brachygalba albogularis* Jacamar Gargantiblanco
16 cm (6.2"). Plate 51. ♪816CD. Note the yellow bill, chestnut lower belly, extensive white on throat (extends to sides of head) and contrasting dark brown breast-band. Cf. Brown Jacamar. Rare along humid lowland tropical rivers in Loreto, Madre de Dios and possibly Cajamarca. *E Peru to n Bolivia and sw Amazonian Brazil.*

Yellow-billed Jacamar *Galbula albirostris* Jacamar Piquiamarillo
18.5 cm (7.2"). Plate 49. The only jacamar with a yellow bill (sometimes dusky on upper mandible), mostly rufous underparts and undertail, and a white throat (buff in female). Cf. Blue-cheeked Jacamar. Fairly common in humid lowland forests e of Andes in Loreto. *S Venezuela and the Guianas to ne Peru and Amazonian Brazil.*

Blue-cheeked Jacamar *Galbula cyanicollis* Jacamar Cachetiazul
18.5 cm (7.2"). Plate 49. Similar to Yellow-billed Jacamar, but throat is same rufous color as underparts, and side of head is bluish (not green). Common and local in humid *terra firme* forests e of Andes south to upper Río Ucayali to 900 m. *NE Peru and Brazil south of the Amazon.*

*Coppery-chested Jacamar *Galbula pastazae* Jacamar Pechicobrizo
24 cm (9.4"). Plate 49. Note limited range. Similar to White-chinned Jacamar but has a conspicuous yellow eye-ring. Female has a rufous chin (always white in White-chinned), but eye-ring is less pronounced. Only known Peru records are from humid montane forests in Cordillera del Cóndor near Ecuador border at 900-1700 m (pers. comm. TSS). *SE Colombia and e Ecuador.*

Bluish-fronted Jacamar *Galbula cyanescens* Jacamar Frentiazulada
22.3 cm (8.8"). Plate 51. ♪816CD. Over most of its range the only jacamar with a small white chin-patch (sometimes scaled), rufous belly and undertail, and green breast. Forecrown is blue. Cf. White-chinned Jacamar. Fairly common in humid lowland *terra firme* forests e of Andes to 1450 m. *E Peru to n Bolivia and w Amazonian Brazil.*

White-chinned Jacamar *Galbula tombacea* Jacamar Barbiblanco
22 cm (8.6"). Plate 49. ♪677. Similar to Bluish-fronted Jacamar (both have a small white chin-patch, rufous belly and undertail, and green breast), but forecrown is brown (not blue). Rare in humid lowland riverine forests in e Loreto north of the Amazon. *SE Colombia to ne Peru and w Amazonian Brazil.*

Purplish Jacamar *Galbula chalcothorax* Jacamar Purpúreo
21 cm (8.5"). Plate 49. ♪542. The only Peruvian jacamar with a black bill, greenish head, copper-green upperparts and copper breast. Lower belly and throat are white (female has a buffy throat). Undertail blackish. Rare in humid lowland riverine forests e of Andes to 800 m. *Colombia to n Bolivia and sw Amazonian Brazil.*

Paradise Jacamar *Galbula dea* Jacamar Paraíso
31 cm (12"). Plate 49. ♪797. A large dark jacamar with a white throat and a distinctive long and pointed tail. Rare to uncommon in humid lowland forests e of Andes south to Cusco to 500 m. *S Venezuela and the Guianas to n Bolivia and Amazonian Brazil.*

Great Jacamar *Jacamerops aurea* Jacamar Grande
30 cm (11.7"). Plate 49. ♪613. A large rufous-bellied jacamar with a thick, slightly decurved bill. Coloration recalls smaller Bluish-fronted Jacamar but undertail is black (not rufous). Uncommon in humid lowland forests e of Andes to 1000 m. *Costa Rica to n Bolivia and Amazonian Brazil.*

Bucconidae (Puffbirds; Bucos). Species: World 33; Peru 22
Puffbirds are a group of medium-sized Neotropical birds related to the jacamars. Many are clad in soft shades of brown and buff, and they blend inconspicuously into their forest backgrounds. Most puffbirds perch motionless for long periods, waiting patiently for a large insect to pass, rather than sallying forth after any tiny morsel. Their prey consists mainly of large insects, supplemented with small frogs and lizards. The Swallow-wing (*Chelidoptera tenebrosa*), commonly seen perched along lowland rivers, has become completely dependent upon aerial prey.

Notharchus **Puffbirds.** A trio of mostly black-and-white puffbirds that perch high, often on snags.

White-necked Puffbird *Notharchus macrorhynchos* Buco Cuelliblanco
25 cm (9.8"). Plate 50. ♪797. A large black-and-white puffbird with a white forehead. See smaller Pied and Brown-banded Puffbirds. Uncommon in humid *terra firme* and humid lowland forests e of Andes, occasionally to 1200 m. *Mexico to ne Argentina and Brazil.*

Brown-banded Puffbird *Notharchus ordii* Buco Pardibandeado
20 cm (8"). Plate 50. Smaller than White-necked Puffbird and lacks white forecrown. Has a brown band on lower breast. Rare in humid lowland forests e of Andes in Madre de Dios and Puno. Two records from Explorers Inn. Recently recorded in white sand forests in Iquitos area (RAR and RW). *S Venezuela to n Amazonian Brazil, se Peru and n Bolivia.*

Pied Puffbird *Notharchus tectus* Buco Pinto
15 cm (6"). Plate 50. ♪ 613. A small puffbird with a narrow white superciliary and white spots on undertail. Rare in humid lowland forest edge and second growth e of Andes to 1000 m. *Costa Rica to n Bolivia and Amazonian Brazil.*

Chestnut-capped Puffbird *Bucco macrodactylus* Buco Gorricastaño
13.5 cm (5.3"). Plate 50. ♪ 816CD. The only puffbird with the combination of rufous crown, white superciliary, dark mask and black chest-band. Uncommon in humid lowland forests and second growth e of Andes to 1000 m. *Venezuela to n Bolivia and w Amazonian Brazil.*

Spotted Puffbird *Bucco tamatia* Buco Moteado
18 cm (7"). Plate 50. ♪ 797. The only puffbird with a cinnamon forecrown and throat, black moustache and spotted breast. Uncommon in humid lowland forests e of Andes to 1400 m. *S Venezuela and the Guianas to e Peru and Amazonian Brazil.*

Collared Puffbird *Bucco capensis* Buco Acollarado
18.5 cm (7.2"). Plate 50. ♪ 652. The only puffbird with a cinnamon-orange head and orange bill. Rare in humid lowland *terra firme* forests e of Andes, occasionally to 1700 m. Recently recorded in Iquitos area (RW and RAR). *S Venezuela and the Guianas to e Peru and Amazonian Brazil.*

White-eared Puffbird *Nystalus chacuru* Buco Orejiblanco
21.5 cm (8."). Plate 50. ♪ 797. Note the distinctive facial pattern and red bill. Uncommon in dry savanna and scrub e of Andes to 2500 m. Recorded in Pampas del Heath and dry intermontane valleys in lower Urubamba Valley (Cusco) and at Moyobamba (San Martín). *Brazil to se Peru, Paraguay and ne Argentina.*

Striolated Puffbird *Nystalus striolatus* Buco Estriolado
21.5 cm (8.4"). Plate 51. ♪ 797. The only puffbird with a buffy breast (streaked black) and collar. Note the yellow bill, yellowish eye and banded tail. Cf. *Malacoptila,* especially White-chested Puffbird (no collar and no bands on tail). Uncommon in humid lowland and foothill forests e of Andes to 1700 m. *Ecuador to n Bolivia and sw Amazonian Brazil.*

Malacoptila **Puffbirds.** Four species of puffbirds with a white area around the bill and streaked underparts. They favor the lower and middle strata of the forest.

White-chested Puffbird *Malacoptila fusca* Buco Pechiblanco
18.5 cm (7.2"). Plate 50. ♪ 652. Note the orange-yellow bill with white around base of bill and a white crescent on the chest (sometimes obscure). Compare Semicollared (rufous semicollar), Black-streaked (black bill) and Striolated Puffbirds. Uncommon in humid lowland forests e of Andes south to Ucayali to 900 m. *S Venezuela and the Guianas to e Peru and w Amazonian Brazil.*

Semicollared Puffbird *Malacoptila semicincta* Buco Semiacollarado
18.5 cm (7.2"). Plate 51. ♪ 816CD. A dark-blackish puffbird with a contrasting rufous semicollar and orange-red bill. Uncommon in humid lowland forests in Cusco, Madre de Dios and Puno to 1050 m. *SE Peru, sw Brazil and n Bolivia.*

Black-streaked Puffbird *Malacoptila fulvogularis* Buco Negrilistado
23 cm (9"). Plate 50. ♪ 741CD. A higher-elevation puffbird with a black bill, buff throat and heavily streaked underparts. Cf. Striolated Puffbird (limited overlap at best). Uncommon in humid subtrop. foothills on e slope of Andes at 1700-2100 m. *Andean foothills of s Colombia to w Bolivia.*

Rufous-necked Puffbird *Malacoptila rufa* Buco Cuellirufo
20 cm (8"). Plate 50. The only puffbird with a gray head, contrasting rufous cheeks and a semicollar. Cf. White-chested Puffbird. Rare in humid lowland forests e of Andes in Loreto to 900 m. Recently recorded at Pacaya Samiria National Reserve (Begazo and Valqui 1998) and near Tahuayo Lodge. *NE Peru and Amazonian Brazil.*

Lanceolated Monklet *Micromonacha lanceolata* Monjecito Lanceolado
13.5 cm (5.3"). Plate 50. ♪741CD. Note tiny size and distinctive spotted underparts. Rare and local in humid forests on e slope of Andes at 300-2100 m. Recorded at 1100 m on Manu Road and recently in Iquitos area (RAR and RW). *Costa Rica to e Peru and w Amazonian Brazil.*

Nonnula **Nunlets.** Four species of small dull-colored puffbirds with long, slender, slightly decurved bills. They favor thickets in forest edge.

Fulvous-chinned Nunlet *Nonnula sclateri* Monjita Barbifulva
15 cm (6"). Plate 50. ♪.816CD. Similar to Brown Nunlet (no known overlap) but chin and forehead are fulvous-buff (not rufous). Rare and local in humid lowland forests in Cusco, Madre de Dios and Puno to 900 m. *SE Peru, n Bolivia and sw Amazonian Brazil.*

Rusty-breasted Nunlet *Nonnula rubecula* Monjita Pechirrojizo
16 cm (6.5"). Plate 50. The only nunlet in its range with a conspicuous white eye-ring and whitish lores. The pale-rufous breast contrasts with whitish belly. Rare and local in humid lowland forests in Loreto to 1000 m. Recorded near Tahuayo Lodge. *S Venezuela to s Brazil, ne Argentina and e Paraguay.*

Brown Nunlet *Nonnula brunnea* Monjita Parda
15 cm (6"). Plate 50. ♪652. A uniformly rufous-brown nunlet with rufous forehead and chin. Cf. Fulvous-chinned and Rusty-breasted Nunlets. Rare in humid lowland *terra firme* forests along e slope of Andes south to Ucayali. *SE Colombia, e Ecuador and ne Peru.*

Rufous-capped (Gray-cheeked) Nunlet *Nonnula ruficapilla* Monjita Gorrirrufa
15 cm (6"). Plate 51. ♪816CD. The only Peruvian nunlet with gray cheeks and a contrasting rufous cap. Uncommon in humid thickets and second growth in lowlands and foothills e of Andes to 1650 m. *E Peru, n Bolivia and Amazonian Brazil.*

White-faced Nunbird *Hapaloptila castanea* Monja Cariblanca
25 cm (9.8"). Plate 50. ♪EC007T. The only puffbird in its range with unstreaked rufous underparts and white around the bill. Rare in humid montane forests south to Huánuco at 2400-2900 m. *Andes of s Colombia to n Peru.*

Monasa **Nunbirds.** A trio of black, active and noisy puffbirds that often accompany canopy flocks.

Black-fronted Nunbird *Monasa nigrifrons* Monja Frentinegra
28.5 cm (11.1"). Plate 50. ♪797. Note the red bill and black face. Common in humid lowland forests and second growth e of Andes to 1000 m. *SE Colombia to n Bolivia and Brazil.*

White-fronted Nunbird *Monasa morphoeus* Monja Frentiblanca
28.5 cm (11.1"). Plate 50. ♪797. Similar to Black-fronted Nunbird but has white around base of red bill. Common in humid lowland forests e of Andes to 1350 m. *Nicaragua to n Bolivia and Brazil.*

Yellow-billed Nunbird *Monasa flavirostris* Monja Piquiamarilla
26 cm (10.1"). Plate 50. ♪797. The only *Monasa* with a yellow bill and white shoulders. Rare in humid lowland forests and second growth e of Andes to 1400 m. *Colombia to e Peru and w Amazonian Brazil.*

Swallow-wing *Chelidoptera tenebrosa* Buco Golondrina
16 cm (6.6"). Plate 50. ♪ 677. A dark flycatcher-like puffbird with very broad wings and white rump. Commonly seen perched on snags along tropical waterways. Common along tropical rivers and margins e of Andes to 1200 m. *Tropical South America e of the Andes to n Bolivia and Brazil.*

Capitonidae (Barbets; Barbudos). World: 83; Peru 7
A family of stocky, medium-sized birds closely related to woodpeckers with a wide distribution in the tropical forests of the world. The 15 New World species are restricted to Central and South America, and are basically non-migratory, having seasonal movements in search of food. Their diet consists primarily of fruits, berries and buds, which is supplemented with some insect food. Most of the family have rather uncomplicated metallic hoots, and in many parts of their range are the only bird vocalizations heard during the heat of the day.

Scarlet-crowned Barbet *Capito aurovirens* Barbudo Coroniescarlata
7.2" (18.3 cm). Plate 49. ♪ 619. A barbet with a heavy black bill, olive-green back and lower belly, and an orange-yellow breast. Crown is red in male or whitish in female. Recalls similar-sized Black-spotted Barbet but latter always has some black spots on flanks, and upperparts are never uniform olive. Fairly common in humid lowland forests e of Andes south to Ucayali to 500 m. *SE Colombia to e Peru and w Amazonian Brazil.*

Scarlet-banded Barbet *Capito wallacei* Barbudo Franjiescarlata
19 cm (7.5"). Plate 52. ♪ LSN. Note limited range. Unmistakable. A recently discovered species in ne Peru (O'Neill *et al.* 2000). Fairly common in isolated cloud forests at ca 1600 m on outlying ridges near headwaters of upper Río Cushabatay, 77 km nw of Contamana (Loreto). *Endemic to Peru.*

Gilded Barbet *Capito auratus* Barbudo Brilloso
19 cm (7.5"). Plate 49. ♪ 797. Variable. In all plumages note the black spots on flanks and yellow stripes on back. Throat color varies from scarlet to orange. Females are heavily spotted below and heavily streaked above. Female's throat may be spotted or unspotted. Cf. Scarlet-crowned and Lemon-throated Barbets. Formerly considered a race of the Black-spotted Barbet (*Capito niger*) but differences in song and color of plumage suggest species level (Daniel F Lane, *in litt.*). Uncommon in humid lowland forests e of Andes to 1500 m. *S Venezuela and Guianas to n Bolivia and Amazonian Brazil.*

***Eubucco* Barbets.** All four species have pale, conical bills and green backs. Underparts and head pattern are important for identification.

Lemon-throated Barbet *Eubucco richardsoni* Barbudo Gargantilimón
15 cm (6"). Plate 49. ♪ 797. Male has a yellow bill, yellow throat and a red pectoral band. Northern race *aurantiicollis* lacks the blue nuchal collar (as in nominate race, illustrated). Female has a black mask, olive crown and white throat. Usually distinctive but in n Peru cf. Versicolored Barbet (usually at higher elevations) and in s Peru cf. female Scarlet-hooded Barbet. Uncommon in humid lowland forests e of Andes to 1200 m. *E Colombia to n Bolivia and w Amazonian Brazil.*

Red-headed Barbet *Eubucco bourcierii* Barbudo Cabecirrojo
16 cm (6.5"). Plate 49. ♪ 613. Male is the only barbet in its range with a red hood and a yellow bill. Female has a blue mask and yellow throat. Rare and local in humid foothill and subtropical montane forests south to n Cajamarca to 2400 m. *Highlands of Costa Rica to n Peru.*

Scarlet-hooded Barbet *Eubucco tucinkae* Barbudo Capuchiescarlata
16 cm (6.5"). Plate 52. ♪816CD. Male similar to Red-headed Barbet (no overlap). Female recalls male Lemon-throated Barbet (yellow throat and orange pectoral band) but has a yellow nuchal collar. Rare in humid lowland forests e of Andes north to Ucayali to 850 m. Regularly recorded at Manu Wildlife Center. *E Peru to n Bolivia and w Amazonian Brazil.*

Versicolored Barbet *Eubucco versicolor* Barbudo Versicolor
16 cm (6.5"). Plate 52. ♪797. Three ssp. occur in Peru. Nominate male (s Peru, illustrated) has a blue malar area and red throat. Central Peru race *glaucogularis* has a yellow malar area, red chin and blue throat. Northern Peru race *steerii* has a yellow malar and a red chin. All females have blue throats and breasts with a red pectoral band. Uncommon in humid montane forests on e slope of Andes at 750-2500 m. *Andes of e Peru and w Bolivia.*

Ramphastidae (Toucans; Tucanes). Species: World 41; Peru 19
Toucans are among the few tropical birds well known to the general public, primarily because of their outrageous bills. They are residents of the Neotropics, ranging from s Mexico to n Argentina. Most species inhabit mature lowland forests, but some species, especially the mountain-toucans of the genus *Andigena*, occur as high as 3400 meters in the montane forests of the Andes. Toucans are omnivorous, and supplement their diet of fruit with insects and bird eggs.

Aulacorhynchus **Toucanets.** Four species of small green toucans that typically inhabit humid montane forests. Note color of bill, tail, vent and rump. Emerald Toucanet is widespread, but the others are scarce.

Emerald Toucanet *Aulacorhynchus prasinus* Tucancillo Esmeralda
30 cm (11.7"). Plate 53. ♪797. Note the dark bill with a yellow ridge, rufous vent and undertail. Three ssp. occur. Northern race *cyanolaemus* has a blue throat; humid montane eastern *atrogularis* (illustrated) and subtropical eastern *dimidiatus* both have black throats. All other toucanets have green or yellow vents and at least the basal half of the undertail is green. Fairly common in humid montane forests on e slope of Andes at 800-3700 m. Accidental at Tambopata Candamo Reserve at 230 m. *S Mexico to nw Bolivia.*

Chestnut-tipped Toucanet *Aulacorhynchus derbianus* Tucancillo Punticastaña
33 cm (13"). Plate 53. ♪797. A toucanet with a green rump, reddish ridge on the bill and red base to lower mandible. Cf. Blue-banded Toucanet (red rump, different bill color). Rare in humid montane forests on e slope of Andes at 600-2400 m. *Venezuela and Guyana to w Bolivia.*

*Yellow-browed Toucanet *Aulacorhynchus huallagae* Tucancillo Cejiamarillo
35 cm (14"). Plate 53. The only toucanet with a yellow vent. Cf. Blue-banded Toucanet. Known from several specimens from cloud forests (especially with *Clusia*) of e slope of Andes in San Martín and se La Libertad at 1800-2500 m. Recently recorded at Río Abiseo National Park at 2500 m, the only protected area in this region. Four collected at Cumpang (La Libertad) at 2400 m (Schulenberg and Parker 1997). *Endemic to Peru.*

Blue-banded Toucanet *Aulacorhynchus coeruleicinctis* Tucancillo Franjiceleste
35 cm (14"). Plate 53. ♪797. A toucanet with a dark bill with a pale tip. Has a green vent, red rump and chestnut tips to tail. Distinctive blue breast-band is often diffused. Uncommon in humid montane forests on e slope of Andes north to Huánuco at 1500-2700 m. *Andes of e Peru and w Bolivia.*

Pteroglossus **Aracaris.** Seven species of medium-sized toucans, all with red rumps and olive backs. Note bill color and pattern on underparts.

Lettered Aracari *Pteroglossus inscriptus* Arasari Letreado
27 cm (10.5"). Plate 53. ♪ 817CD. Note the black head, bicolored bill (at close view shows "letters" on upper mandible) and absence of belly bands. Fairly common in humid lowland forests e of Andes to 700 m. *Colombia to n Bolivia and Amazonian Brazil.*

Ivory-billed Aracari *Pteroglossus azara* Arasari Piquimarfil
30 cm (11.7"). Plate 53. ♪ 817CD. Note limited range. Replaces similar Brown-mandibled Aracari north of the Amazon. Note the all ivory bill. Fairly common in humid *terra firme* forests in Loreto to 900 m. *Venezuela to ne Peru and nw Amazonian Brazil.*

Brown-mandibled Aracari *Pteroglossus mariae* Arasari Piquipardo
30 cm (11.7"). Plate 53. Over most of its range the combination of dark brown neck, and red and black breast-bands, is distinctive. Has a bicolored bill with lower mandible darker than the upper. Ivory-billed Aracari (limited overlap in Loreto) is similar but note bill color. Fairly common in humid lowland forests e of Andes, occasionally to 1300 m. *E Peru, n Bolivia and w Amazonian Brazil south of the Amazon.*

Chestnut-eared Aracari *Pteroglossus castanotis* Arasari Orejicastaño
43 cm (17"). Plate 53. ♪ 797. The only aracari with a single belly band and a dark hood. Common in humid lowlands and riverine forests e of Andes to 1300 m. *E Colombia to ne Argentina, Amazonian and se Brazil.*

Pale-mandibled Aracari *Pteroglossus erythropygius* Arasari Piquipálido
41 cm (16"). Plate 53. The only aracari with a pale-yellow bill, a black spot on center of chest and a narrow band on belly. Recent sight record and tape recordings of a small group of five of this Ecuador endemic in Tumbes at control post at Campo Verde (Whiffin and Sadgrove 2000). *Pacific lowlands of w Ecuador and immediately adjacent Peru.*

Many-banded Aracari *Pteroglossus pluricinctus* Arasari Multibandeado
34.3 cm (13.5"). Plate 53. ♪ 542. Note limited range. The only aracari with two dark belly bands and a bicolored bill. Fairly common in humid *terra firme* forests e of Andes in Loreto to 900 m. *Venezuela to ne Peru and nw Amazonian Brazil.*

Curl-crested Aracari *Pteroglossus beauharnaesii* Arasari Encrespado
38 cm (15"). Plate 53. ♪ 797. The only aracari that lacks a dark hood. Note the red band on yellow belly. Modified curly crown feathers are visible at close range. Uncommon in humid *terra firme* forests e of Andes to 800 m. *E Peru, n Bolivia and w Amazonian Brazil south of the Amazon.*

Gray-breasted Mountain-Toucan *Andigena hypoglauca* Tucán-Andino Pechigris
46 cm (18"). Plate 54. ♪ LNS. Distinctive. Mostly gray below with a very colorful bill. Compare Hooded Mountain-Toucan. Uncommon in humid montane forests on e slope of Andes south to Cusco at 2000-3400 m. *Andes of s Colombia to s Peru.*

Hooded Mountain-Toucan *Andigena cucullata* Tucán-Andino Encapuchado
50 cm (19.5"). Plate 54. ♪ 797. Note limited range. A high-elevation toucan with a dark hood and a green bill with a yellow spot on base of lower mandible. Uncommon in humid Andean forests in Puno at 2000-3300 m. *Andes of se Peru and w Bolivia.*

Black-billed Mountain-Toucan *Andigena nigrirostris* Tucán-Andino Piquinegro
50 cm (19.5"). Plate 54. Recalls Gray-breasted Mountain-Toucan but bill is all black (some reddish on upper mandible), underparts light blue, throat white. Recorded near Chontalí, Cajamarca (unpublished specimen LSUMZ). *Andes of nw Venezuela to Colombia and Ecuador.*

Golden-collared Toucanet *Selenidera reinwardtii* Tucancillo Collardorado
26.6 cm (10.5"). Plate 53. ♪ 797. Both sexes have yellow tufts on cheeks. Note that in southern populations bill is blacker. Fairly common in humid *terra firme* and subtrop. forests along e slope of Andes to 1550 m. *SE Colombia to e Peru and w Amazonian Brazil.*

Yellow-ridged Toucan *Ramphastos culminatus* Tucán Rabadilla Dorada
48 cm (19"). Plate 54. ♪ 542. Note the yellow rump. Mimics sympatric and larger Cuvier's Toucan, but has proportionately smaller bill. Best told by voice (Yellow-ridged gives a croak, Cuvier's a yelp). Fairly common in humid lowland *terra firme* forests e of Andes to 1700 m. *W Venezuela to n Bolivia and w Amazonian Brazil.*

Black-mandibled Toucan *Ramphastos ambiguus* Tucán Mandíbula Negra
61 cm (24"). Plate 54. Unmistakable. Uncommon in humid montane forests on e slope of Andes south to Huánuco at 800-2400 m. *W Venezuela and e slope of Andes of Colombia to Peru.*

Cuvier's Toucan *Ramphastos cuvieri* Tucán de Cuvier
61 cm (24"). Plate 54. ♪ 542. Very similar to Yellow-ridged Toucan. Best told by voice. Common in humid lowland forests e of Andes to 900 m. *Colombia to n Bolivia and Amazonian Brazil.*

Toco Toucan *Ramphastos toco* Tucán Toco
55 cm (21.5"). Plate 54. ♪ 797. A large toucan with an orange-yellow bill with a black spot on tip. Rare in humid lowland forests e of Andes in s Madre de Dios and Puno to 1200 m. *The Guianas and e Brazil to Paraguay, n Argentina and n Bolivia.*

Picidae (Woodpeckers and Allies; Carpinteros). Species: World 217; Peru 38
A large family of birds highly specialized for digging prey out of wood or the bark of trees. The most remarkable feature of woodpeckers is the long protrusible tongue, which in flickers of the genus *Colaptes* can extend 5 cm beyond the bill. They are distributed throughout forested regions of the world, where they range from sea level to over 5000 meters (16,400 feet) in the Andes. Flickers spend considerable time on the ground, where they feed on ants and other small insects.

Picumnus **Piculets.** A large genus comprised of 26 tiny Neotropical woodpeckers, well represented in Peru with nine species. They usually inhabit tangles in forest edge where they give "telegraph messages" using their fairly short, pointed bills. Sexually dimorphic, all have black crowns spotted white, but the forecrown color of males is often red. Note facial pattern and pattern of underparts.

Bar-breasted Piculet *Picumnus aurifrons* Carpinterito Pechirayado
9.2 cm (3.6"). Plate 52. ♪ 797. The only piculet with a pattern of bars on the breast and a striped yellowish belly. Uncommon in humid lowland forests e of Andes to 1100 m. *E Peru, n Bolivia and Amazonian Brazil s of the Amazon.*

Lafresnaye's Piculet *Picumnus lafresnayi* Carpinterito de Lafresnaye
9.2 cm (3.6"). Plate 52. ♪ EC008T. Three ssp. Nominate race (illustrated) and *punctifrons* have fine pale barring on a greenish back, but latter sometimes lacks blackish barring on underparts. Nominate race and *taczanowskii* have blackish barring on underparts, but latter lacks barring on upperparts. Other piculets in its range lack barring altogether. Rare in humid lowland forests e of Andes south to Huánuco to 1400 m. *SE Colombia to e Peru and w Amazonian Brazil.*

Ecuadorian Piculet *Picumnus sclateri* Carpinterito Ecuatoriano
9.2 cm (3.6"). Plate 52. The only piculet in its range with fine barring on underparts. Uncommon in dry forests along Pacific slope south to n Lambayeque to 1400 m (rarely to 2100 m). *Arid scrub of w Ecuador and nw Peru.*

Speckle-chested Piculet *Picumnus steindachneri* Carpinterito Pechijaspeado
9.2 cm (3.6"). Plate 52. The only piculet with a black breast with white spots and a barred belly. Uncommon in humid lower montane forests in Río Huallaga drainage of Amazonas and San Martín at 1150-2000 m. *Endemic to Peru.*

Ocellated Piculet *Picumnus dorbygnianus* Carpinterito Ocelado
9.2 cm (3.6"). Plate 52. ♪742CD. The only piculet with scaled underparts. Note the rather dull upperparts. Uncommon and local in humid montane forests on e slope of Andes at 1100-2200 m. Regularly recorded near Machu Picchu. *Andes of e Peru, Bolivia and extreme nw Argentina.*

Rufous-breasted Piculet *Picumnus rufiventris* Carpinterito Pechirrufo
10.2 cm (4"). Plate 52. ♪817CD. The largest piculet, and the only one with rufous underparts. Uncommon and local in humid lowland bamboo stands e of Andes to 900 m. Recorded at Amazonia Lodge and Tambopata Research Center. *SE Colombia to n Bolivia.*

Plain-breasted Piculet *Picumnus castelnau* Carpinterito Pechillano
9.2 cm (3.6"). Plate 52. A piculet with unmarked underparts. Sympatric Fine-barred Piculet is similar, but Plain-breasted has a white spot behind the eye, and red crown is more extensive with fewer white spots. Female's crown is unspotted. Uncommon and local in humid lowland forests e of Andes south to Pucallpa (Ucayali) to 900 m. *Locally along rivers in se Colombia, e Ecuador and ne Peru.*

Fine-barred Piculet *Picumnus subtilis* Carpinterito de Barras Finas
9.2 cm (3.6"). Plate 52. Sympatric with similar Plain-breasted Piculet, but bars are often invisible. Female's crown is spotted white. Rare in eastern lowlands from Río Ucayali in Loreto to Marcapata (Cusco). Ranges from base of Andes to 1000 m. Recorded at Amazonia Lodge. *Endemic to Peru.*

Olivaceous Piculet *Picumnus olivaceus* Carpinterito Oliváceo
9.2 cm (3.6"). Plate 52. Note limited range. The only piculet in its range that has a crown spotted with white, and pale-olive underparts. Rare resident in Tumbes (recorded at Cotrina at 600-750 m). *Guatemala to nw Venezuela and w Ecuador.*

White Woodpecker *Melanerpes candidus* Carpintero Blanco
26 cm (10.1"). Plate 55. ♪797. Unmistakable in its limited range. Black above and white below, with an almost entirely white head (male has a narrow black line behind the eye). Rare in savanna and scrub in Pampas del Heath. *South America e of Andes to n Argentina.*

Yellow-tufted Woodpecker *Melanerpes cruentatus* Carpintero Penachiamarillo
20 cm (8"). Plate 55. ♪797. Unmistakable. Female lacks the red crown. Note that some individuals lack the yellow tufts. Common in humid lowland forests and second growth e of Andes to 1350 m. *S Venezuela and the Guianas to e Bolivia and Amazonian Brazil.*

[White-fronted Woodpecker] *Melanerpes cactorum* Carpintero Frentiblanco
18 cm (7"). Plate 55. ♪797. No other Peruvian woodpecker has spotted wings, buffy-white underparts and a white forecrown. Throat color varies from white to yellow. Reported in the literature (Meyer de Schauensee 1982; Short 1970a, 1982; Winkler *et al.* 1995) as rare in arid foothills and montane scrub in "se Peru" with no specific locality records. *SE Peru to n Argentina, Paraguay and sw Brazil.*

***Veniliornis* Woodpeckers.** A genus of small, chunky woodpeckers with seven species in Peru. Some have similar color patterns to members of the genus *Piculus*, but *Veniliornis* have a relatively shorter bill and tail. In all species the males have red crowns and females black.

Scarlet-backed Woodpecker *Veniliornis callonotus* Carpintero Dorsiescarlata
14 cm (5.5"). Plate 51. Unmistakable. No other woodpecker has red upperparts and white underparts. Female has a black crown. Fairly common in arid lowland scrub on Pacific slope to 1500 m, extending inland to arid upper Marañón Valley. *SW Colombia to nw Peru.*

Yellow-vented Woodpecker *Veniliornis dignus* Carpintero Ventriamarillo
18 cm (7"). Plate 55. Like Bar-bellied Woodpecker, but belly and vent yellow and unmarked. The blackish cheeks contrast with whitish-buff superciliary and malar stripe. Rare in humid montane forests on e slope of Andes at 700-2700 m. *Andes of w Venezuela to e Peru.*

Bar-bellied Woodpecker *Veniliornis nigriceps* Carpintero Ventrirrayado
20 cm (8"). Plate 55. ♪797. The only small woodpecker in its elevation with completely barred underparts. Cf. Yellow-vented Woodpecker. Uncommon in montane and elfin forests of Andes at 2000-3600 m. *Andes of Colombia to w Bolivia.*

Smoky-brown Woodpecker *Veniliornis fumigatus* Carpintero Pardo
18 cm (7"). Plate 55. ♪797. The only small, uniformly dark-brown woodpecker. Note the pale cheeks. Fairly common in lowlands and foothills along both slopes of Andes, mainly at 1200-2800 m. *Mexico to Andes of nw Argentina.*

Little Woodpecker *Veniliornis passerinus* Carpintero Chico
15 cm (6"). Plate 55. ♪797. Similar to Red-stained Woodpecker, but lacks latter's golden-yellow hind collar. At close range Little Woodpecker shows a few pale spots on wing coverts. Bar-bellied is similar but larger, and found at higher elevations. Fairly common along trop. river margins and second growth e of Andes to 900 m. *Venezuela and the Guianas to ne Argentina and s Brazil.*

Red-rumped Woodpecker *Veniliornis kirkii* Carpintero Lomirrojo
18 cm (7"). Plate 55. Note limited range. Similar to Little Woodpecker (no overlap) but rump is red. Face is plain (lacks pale superciliary and pale malar stripe). Uncommon in dry forests on Pacific slope in Tumbes to 1500 m. *Costa Rica to nw South America.*

Red-stained Woodpecker *Veniliornis affinis* Carpintero Rojoteñido
18 cm (7"). Plate 55. ♪797. A *Veniliornis* with a golden-yellow hind collar. At close range wing coverts show rusty stain spots. Cf. sympatric Little Woodpecker. Uncommon in humid lowland *terra firme* and *várzea* forests e of Andes to 1300 m. *N and central South America e of Andes.*

Piculus **Woodpeckers.** A group of medium-sized woodpeckers with fairly long bills and tails. Often barred or scaled below.

White-throated Woodpecker *Piculus leucolaemus* Carpintero Gargantiblanco
20 cm (8"). Plate 55. ♪797. The only medium-sized woodpecker with a white throat, scaly breast and barred belly. Note the yellow line above the malar stripe. Cf. Golden-green Woodpecker. Uncommon in humid lowland *terra firme* and *várzea* forests e of Andes to 1400 m. *Ecuador to n Bolivia and w Amazonian Brazil.*

Yellow-throated Woodpecker *Piculus flavigula* Carpintero Gargantiamarillo
20 cm (8"). Plate 55. ♪797. The only medium-sized woodpecker with scaled underparts and yellow sides of head (cheeks). Male has a red crown; female an olive crown and red hindcrown. Rare in humid lowland *terra firme* and *várzea* forests e of Andes to 500 m. *S Venezuela and the Guianas to n Bolivia, Amazonian and e Brazil.*

Golden-green Woodpecker *Piculus chrysochloros* Carpintero Verdidorado
23 cm (9"). Plate 55. ♪797. No other medium-sized woodpecker has a yellow malar stripe (may look whitish in a distance) and barred underparts. Cf. sympatric White-throated Woodpecker (white throat and scaly breast) and Golden-olive Woodpecker (no yellow malar stripe, no bars on lower belly). Uncommon in humid lowland *terra firme* and *várzea* forests e of Andes to 650 m. *Panama to the Guianas, Brazil and n Argentina.*

Golden-olive Woodpecker *Piculus rubiginosus* Carpintero Olividorado
23 cm (9"). Plate 55. ♪797. The only medium-sized woodpecker with whitish cheeks and a plain back. Three ssp. occur, with varied amounts of barring on underparts. Race *chrysogaster* (central Peru, illustrated) has the least; similar *coloratus* (north-central) has little red on crown; *rubripileus* (northwest) has entire underparts barred with little or no yellow on belly, thicker black bars on breast and a black throat. Cf. Golden-green Woodpecker. Recalls Black-necked Woodpecker (especially in northwest), but latter's back is barred and throat is black. Fairly common in dry forests on Pacific slope to 1500 m, occasionally to 2300 m; uncommon in humid foothill forests e of Andes to 1500 m. *NE Mexico to n Argentina.*

Crimson-mantled Woodpecker *Piculus rivolii* Carpintero Dorsicarmesi
27 cm (10.5"). Plate 55. ♪797. Two ssp. occur in Peru. Male of illustrated race *brevirostris* (south to central Peru) is unmistakable. Female has black hind crown and throat. Race *atriceps* (se Peru) has mostly olive wings (crimson is restricted to hind neck and mantle), a black crown and duller underparts. Fairly common in humid montane forests at 700-3700 m. *Andes of w Venezuela to w Bolivia.*

Black-necked Woodpecker *Colaptes atricollis* Carpintero Cuellinegro
27 cm (10.5"). Plate 51. A woodpecker with a heavily barred chest, black throat and barred back. Female has black forecrown. Two ssp. recognized, nominate (w Peru, illustrated) and *peruvianus* (e Peru), which has less barred whitish underparts and somewhat scaled browner upperparts. Recalls Golden-olive Woodpecker. Uncommon in Andes from La Libertad and Ancash to w Arequipa at 500-2800 m, and from Piura to w Huánuco around Río Marañón Valley at 1700-4300 m. Seen regularly on Santa Eulalia road above Lima ca 2500 m; from xeric slopes above Balsas; and in Colca Canyon at 3600 m. Recent southern range extensions to Moquegua and Tacna (Høgsås *et al.* in prep.). *Endemic to Peru.*

Spot-breasted Woodpecker *Colaptes (Chrysoptilus) punctigula* Carpintero Pechipunteado
20 cm (8"). Plate 55. ♪652. The only medium-sized woodpecker with a spotted breast and barred back. Often forages on the ground. Fairly common in humid lowland forests and palm savanna e of Andes to 900 m. *E Panama to the Guianas, Amazonian Brazil and n Bolivia.*

Andean Flicker *Colaptes rupicola* Carpintero Andino
35 cm (14"). Plate 56. ♪797. An unmistakable, mainly terrestrial woodpecker with a very long bill. Fairly common in *puna, páramo* and montane scrub of high Andes at 2000-5000 m, rarely down to 800 m. *Peru to n Argentina and n Chile.*

Celeus **Woodpeckers.** Medium-sized to large woodpeckers with pointed crests. Females lack the male's red moustache.

Scaly-breasted Woodpecker *Celeus grammicus* Carpintero Pechiescamoso
23 cm (9"). Plate 56. ♪797. Note the rufous body barred black above and below. Northern races (nominate and *verreauxi*) are darker overall than southern *latifasciatus* (illustrated). Chestnut Woodpecker lacks barring and has a conspicuous pale rump. Uncommon in humid lowland forests e of Andes to 900 m. *S Venezuela to n Bolivia and w Amazonian Brazil.*

Chestnut Woodpecker *Celeus elegans* Carpintero Castaño
27 cm (10.5"). Plate 56. ♪ 677. Note the uniform rufous body and pale rump. Cf. Scaly-breasted Woodpecker. Uncommon in humid lowland *terra firme* forests e of Andes to 1100 m. *S Venezuela and the Guianas to n Bolivia and Amazonian Brazil.*

Cream-colored Woodpecker *Celeus flavus* Carpintero Crema
26 cm (10.1"). Plate 56. ♪ 797. Unmistakable. Uncommon in humid lowland forests e of Andes to 700 m. *S Venezuela and the Guianas to n Bolivia and Amazonian Brazil.*

Rufous-headed Woodpecker *Celeus spectabilis* Carpintero Cabecirrufo
27 cm (10.5"). Plate 51. ♪ 817CD. Unmistakable. Ringed Woodpecker has similar pattern but has a rufous back. Rare in humid lowland forests e of Andes, especially along rivers and river islands to 300 m. Regularly recorded in *Guadua* bamboo thickets in Manu Wildlife Center and Tambopata Research Center. *Locally from e Ecuador to n Bolivia.*

Ringed Woodpecker *Celeus torquatus* Carpintero Anillado
24 cm (9.5"). Plate 56. ♪ 797. The only *Celeus* with a black breast and rufous upperparts. Barred above (including rump and tail) and on lower underparts. Fairly common but local in humid lowland forests to 725 m. *S Venezuela and the Guianas to n Bolivia, Amazonian and e Brazil.*

Lineated Woodpecker *Dryocopus lineatus* Carpintero Lineado
35 cm (14"). Plate 56. ♪ 797. Recalls some *Campephilus* but Lineated's white lines on back do not meet. Both sexes have a diagnostic streaked chin (looks gray from a distance). Male has a red malar stripe. Female's head pattern recalls that of male Powerful Woodpecker. Nominate ssp. (illustrated) occurs east of the Andes. On Pacific slope *fuscipennis* is browner, with almost unbarred dingy buff underparts. Uncommon along Pacific slope south to Lambayeque, and fairly common in humid tropical lowlands e of Andes to 900 m. *Mexico to the Guianas, s Brazil and n Argentina.*

Powerful Woodpecker *Campephilus pollens* Carpintero Poderoso
35 cm (14"). Plate 56. ♪ EC007T. Similar to Lineated Woodpecker (limited overlap) but white lines on back meet to form a "V". Rump is white, barred with cinnamon. Male's head is similar to that of Lineated Woodpecker, but throat is all black (no red and gray). Female has a black crest. Rare in humid montane forests south to Pasco at 900-3750 m. *Andes of w Venezuela to n Peru.*

Crimson-bellied Woodpecker *Campephilus haematogaster* Carpintero Ventrirrojo
37 cm (14.5"). Plate 56. ♪ 742CD. Unmistakable. Note the red underparts, striped face and red rump. Rare in humid montane forests on e slope of Andes at 900-2200 m. *Panama to e Peru.*

Red-necked Woodpecker *Campephilus rubricollis* Carpintero Cuellirrojo
34 cm (13.5"). Plate 56. ♪ 797. The only large woodpecker with a red head and neck, cinnamon underparts and a uniform dark-brown back. Fairly common in humid lowland forests e of Andes to 600 m. *S Venezuela and the Guianas to n Bolivia and Amazonian Brazil.*

Crimson-crested Woodpecker *Campephilus melanoleucos* Carpintero Crestirrojo
35 cm (14"). Plate 56. ♪ 797. White lines on back meet to form a "V". Head pattern is distinctive; rump is white. Guayaquil Woodpecker (no overlap) has barred rump. Cf. Lineated Woodpecker. Fairly common in humid lowlands and savanna e of Andes to 1500 m. *Panama to ne Argentina (mainly e of Andes).*

Guayaquil Woodpecker *Campephilus gayaquilensis* Carpintero Guayaquileño
35 cm (14"). Plate 56. White lines on back meet to form a "V". Head pattern is like that of Crimson-crested (no overlap) but rump is barred and primaries are brownish. Cf. Powerful and Lineated Woodpeckers (both have black cheeks). Uncommon in Pacific lowlands and on Pacific slope south to Cajamarca to 1500 m. *Colombia to nw Peru.*

Passerines

Furnariidae (Ovenbirds and Allies; Horneros). Species: World 240; Peru 120
The furnariids (ovenbirds) represent one of the largest passerine families in the New World. They are an incredibly diverse assemblage of birds that differ widely in appearance and habits, ranging in size from the diminutive 11.5 cm (4-inch) Orange-fronted Plushcrown to the 27 cm (10.5-inch) Brown Cacholote of the pampas. They inhabit almost every conceivable niche in Peru, from the wave-washed rocks at Paracas to over 5,000 meters (16,350 feet) on the bleak altiplano, as well as temperate and tropical rainforests and the arid cactus belt. Their nests are often constructed of mud and shaped like ovens (horneros), from which the common name *ovenbird* was derived. Ovenbirds are primarily insectivorous, but the types of insects taken vary widely due to the tremendous range of habitats they occupy. The seaside-cinclodes are the only passerines that obtain their food exclusively from a marine environment.

Geositta **Miners.** Terrestrial birds that inhabit open terrain, sometimes near boulders, mostly in the coastal regions or arid higher elevations. They are colored mostly in earth tones, often with a rufous band on the short wings.

Coastal Miner *Geositta peruviana* Minero Peruano
16.5 cm (6.5"). Plate 57. A pale miner with a pale wing band and whitish underparts. Common Miner has a pale rump and dusky streaks on breast. Common in arid coastal Peru from Tumbes to Ica below 400 m. Common along road into Lachay Nature Reserve. *Endemic to Peru.*

Grayish Miner *Geositta maritima* Minero Gris
14 cm (5.5"). Plate 57. The only miner in its range without a band on the wings. Has uniform gray upperparts and pinkish flanks. Fairly common and local in arid Pacific littoral north to Ancash to about 2500 m. *Arid coast of Peru and n Chile.*

Common Miner *Geositta cunicularia* Minero Común
15 cm (6"). Plates 57, 58. ♪797. The only miner with a streaky breast. Shows a rufous band on the wings, dark tip to tail and a pale rump. Altiplano races *juninensis* (Junín and Huancavelica), *titicacae* (Andes of se Peru) and *frobeni* (Andes of Arequipa and Tacna) have a noticeably paler rump (especially *titicacae*). Coastal races *deserticolor* and *georgei* (arid littoral in Arequipa and coastal lomas of s Peru) are paler and smaller (14 cm), and may represent a separate species (Lomas Miner). Common in *puna* zone of Andes north to Junín to 4800 m and along coast north to Ica. *Central Peru to Tierra del Fuego and extreme se Brazil.*

Puna Miner *Geositta punensis* Minero de la Puna
14.5 cm (5.75"). Plate 58. ♪797. Like Common Miner but paler overall with a shorter bill. Rump is concolor to back and breast is unstreaked. Common in *puna* and montane scrub north to Moquegua and Puno at 3000-5000 m. *Altiplano of extreme s Peru to n Argentina and n Chile.*

Dark-winged Miner *Geositta saxicolina* Minero Andino
16 cm (6.5"). Plate 57. The only miner in its range that lacks a rufous band on the wing. Has a blackish tail, and off-white rump and base of the tail. Locally common on high Andean slopes in Junín, Lima, Pasco and Huancavelica at 4000-4900 m. *Endemic to Peru.*

Thick-billed Miner *Geositta crassirostris* Minero Piquigrueso
18 cm (7"). Plate 57. The only miner with a heavy, thick, long bill. Legs are whitish, and rump and tail rufous. Uncommon in coastal lomas usually around rocks and boulders at 600-800 m. Regularly recorded at Lomas de Lachay. Also in Lima and w Ayacucho at 1500-3000 m, and on Pampa de Nazca (Arequipa) where it has been recorded at 3850 m. *Endemic to Peru.*

Slender-billed Miner *Geositta tenuirostris* Minero Piquilargo
19 cm (7.5"). Plate 58. ♪ 797. The only miner with a long, thin, decurved bill. Earthcreepers have longer tails and mostly strongly decurved bills. Fairly common in bare fields and grassy flats north to Cajamarca at 2500-4600 m. *Andes of n Peru to nw Argentina; central Ecuador.*

Upucerthia **Earthcreepers.** Five mostly terrestrial species found at higher elevations of the Andes; often run with their tail cocked. Most of the genus have strongly decurved bills. Their plumage is mostly brown but some have a scaly or striated pattern to the underparts.

Scale-throated Earthcreeper *Upucerthia dumetaria* Bandurrita Gargantiescamosa
21.5 cm (8.4"). Plate 58. ♪ 797. The only earthcreeper with a scaly effect on the chest (in some individuals on throat). Tail feathers are paler at the tip. Rare in montane scrub of Andes in extreme s Peru to 3900 m. *S Peru to Tierra del Fuego.*

Plain-breasted Earthcreeper *Upucerthia jelskii* Bandurrita de Jelski
19 cm (7.5"). Plate 58. ♪ 797. A brownish earthcreeper with a strongly decurved bill and uniform plain-buff underparts (cf. White-throated Earthcreeper where ranges overlap). Fairly common in montane scrub and *puna* from Ancash south at 3500-4600 m. *Andes of Peru to n Chile and extreme nw Argentina.*

White-throated Earthcreeper *Upucerthia albigula* Bandurrita Gargantiblanca
20 cm (8"). Plate 57. Very similar to Plain-breasted Earthcreeper, but with brighter rufous primaries and a whiter throat that is in sharper contrast to the chest. Uncommon and local along Pacific slope of Andes north to the Nazca-Puquio road at 2500-4000 m. Regularly recorded near Chihuata (Arequipa). *Andes of sw Peru and extreme n Chile.*

Striated Earthcreeper *Upucerthia serrana* Bandurrita Peruana
20 cm (8"). Plate 57. The only earthcreeper with bold white streaks over gray underparts and on mantle. Wings and tail rufous. Fairly common on rocky slopes and *Polylepis* woodlands in Andes from Cajamarca to Huancavelica at 2800-4300 m. *Endemic to Peru.*

Straight-billed Earthcreeper *Upucerthia ruficauda* Bandurrita Piquirrecto
19 cm (7.5"). Plate 58. ♪ 797. The only earthcreeper with a nearly straight bill and unstreaked mantle. Has a rufous tail, white throat, and remaining underparts are buff with whitish streaks. Fairly common in montane scrub north to Arequipa at 2300-4300 m. *Andes of s Peru to c Argentina and Chile.*

Cinclodes **Cinclodes.** The five Peruvian species are usually associated with water. Four inhabit high-elevation habitats and one rocky shorelines. Most *Cinclodes* have prominent wingbars.

Peruvian Seaside Cinclodes *Cinclodes taczanowskii* Churrete Marisquero
21.5 cm (8.4"). Plate 57. A sooty cinclodes with a rufous wingbar. Unmistakable in its range and habitat. Locally fairly common along rocky coasts from Ancash to Tacna. Readily seen on wave-washed rocks at Paracas Peninsula, Ancon and Pucusana. *Endemic to Peru.*

Bar-winged Cinclodes *Cinclodes fuscus* Churrete Alibandeado
18 cm (7"). Plate 58. ♪ 797. A widespread cinclodes with white outer tail feathers. The three Peruvian ssp., *longipennis* (south to Huánuco, illustrated), *rivularis* (Junín to Puno) and *albiventris* (Tacna) vary in wingbar color (from buff to almost white, respectively). Sympatric White-winged Cinclodes is larger, has more rufous back, a longer bill, and the longer tail has white only at the corners. Common in *puna* zone and around montane lakes and streams at 2500-5000 m. *Andes of w Venezuela to Tierra del Fuego and extreme s Brazil.*

*Royal Cinclodes *Cinclodes aricomae* Churrete Real
20 cm (8"). Plate 57. Larger and darker below than more widespread Bar-winged Cinclodes. Bill is heavier, longer and slightly decurved. Wingbar is rufous. Rare and local in *Polylepis* woodlands adjacent to steep, rocky slopes in Apurímac, Cusco and Puno. Recorded at 3600 m in *Polylepis* woodland near Abra Málaga road and in *Polylepis-Gynoxys* forest on Cerro Runtacocha southeast of Abancay at 4100-4550 m. *Páramo of se Peru and w Bolivia.*

White-winged Cinclodes *Cinclodes atacamensis* Churrete Aliblanca
19.8 cm (7.7"). Plate 58. A cinclodes with a prominent white wingbar and white tips to the outer tail feathers. Has a proportionately longer tail and bill than smaller and duller Bar-winged Cinclodes. Fairly common along montane lakes and streams at 2200-4500 m in Andes north to Ancash and Pasco. *Andes of Peru to central Argentina and Chile.*

*White-bellied Cinclodes *Cinclodes palliatus* Churrete Ventriblanco
23 cm (9"). Plate 57. A large cinclodes with totally white underparts and a white wingbar. Very rare and local in *Distichia* bogs with adjacent rocky outcrops in Junín, Lima and Huancavelica at 4400-5000 m. World population 24 individuals in 2001 (pers. comm. GE). Most easily seen on road to Laguna Marcapomacocha (Junín) at 4415 m. Recently reported west of Pampa Pucacocha at 4450 m on Lima-Junín border and sw of Yaulí (Huancavelica) at 4940 m. *Endemic to Peru.*

***Furnarius* Horneros.** The three Peruvian species all inhabit lowlands, often near water. All have predominantly rufous upperparts and a conspicuous white superciliary.

Lesser Hornero *Furnarius minor* Hornero Menor
15.5 cm (6"). Plate 58. ♪ 677. The smallest and dullest of the Peruvian horneros. Legs are dark gray (sympatric horneros have flesh-colored legs). Rare along lowland river islands south to lower Río Huallaga at Santa Cruz (Loreto) to 300 m. Regularly recorded at ExplorNapo. *River islands in Amazon basin.*

Pale-legged Hornero *Furnarius leucopus* Hornero Patipálida
18 cm (7"). Plate 58. ♪ 797. The only hornero in most of its range, but two other species occur in upper Amazonia. Race *tricolor* (illustrated) has flesh-colored legs and is uncommon along lowland trop. rivers and margins e of Andes from Loreto to Puno and Madre de Dios to 1100 m. Race *cinnamomeus* (common on Pacific slope south to Ancash at 2300 m) has grayer legs and is sometimes considered a separate species (Pacific Hornero). *Guyana to w Ecuador, n Bolivia and Amazonian Brazil.*

Bay Hornero *Furnarius torridus* Hornero Bayo
19 cm (7.5"). Plate 65. Similar to Pale-legged Hornero but darker (especially on the underparts). Rare along lowland river islands on Río Ucayali, lower Río Huallaga and Río Napo. Regularly recorded at ExplorNapo. *Riverine habitats of ne Amazonian Peru and w Brazil.*

***Leptasthenura* Tit-Spinetails.** Six species occur in Peru, mostly at higher elevations, but also in coastal lomas. A group of small, active birds. Their very long tail is "spiny" looking; most species are heavily streaked.

Andean Tit-Spinetail *Leptasthenura andicola* Tijeral Andino
16.5 cm (6.5"). Plate 62. ♪ JM. The only tit-spinetail with heavy white streaks on its dark underparts and upperparts. Other tit-spinetails may have dark streaks on pale underparts. Uncommon in *Polylepis* woodlands and montane scrub of Andes from Ancash south to Arequipa and Puno at 3000-4500 m. *Andes of w Venezuela to w Bolivia.*

Streaked Tit-Spinetail *Leptasthenura striata* Tijeral Listado
16.5 cm (6.5"). Plate 62. The only tit-spinetail with a streaked back and rufous wing-patch. The three races that occur differ in the amount of streaking on the underparts. Nominate *striata* (Arequipa and Tacna) has a streaked throat and breast; *superciliaris* (Ancash to Lima) has a streaked throat and *albigularis* (Huancavelica) has unmarked underparts. Fairly common in montane scrub on Pacific slope north to Ancash at 1500-4000 m. Also recorded at Lomas de Lachay. *Andes of central Peru to n Chile.*

Rusty-crowned Tit-Spinetail *Leptasthenura pileata* Tijeral Coronicastaño
18 cm (7"). Plate 62. A tit-spinetail with a bright rusty crown. Crown is streaked in *cajabambae* (Andes of Cajamarca to Junín and Huancavelica) or unstreaked in *pileata* (Lima) and *latistriata* (Ayacucho). Note checkered throat and mottled underparts and lack of rufous wing-patch. Race *cajabambae* may represent a separate species. Fairly common in *Polylepis* woodlands and montane scrub in w Andes from Cajamarca to Ayacucho, mostly at 2500-4300 m. *Endemic to Peru.*

*White-browed Tit-Spinetail *Leptasthenura xenothorax* Tijeral Cejiblanco
18 cm (7"). Plate 62. A tit-spinetail with a bright rusty crown, and unstreaked gray belly and breast. Very similar to previous species (no overlap). Uncommon and local in *Polylepis* woodlands southeast of Abancay and in Cordillera Vilcanota above right bank of upper Urubamba Valley at 3680-4500 m. Fairly regular along Abra Málaga road above Ollantaytambo, at Yanacocha lakes at 3800 m, and a large population 35 km se of Abra Málaga on Nevada Chaiñapuerto. *Endemic to Peru.*

Plain-mantled Tit-Spinetail *Leptasthenura aegithaloides* Tijeral Lomillano
16.5 cm (6.5"). Plate 61. ♪797. A pale tit-spinetail with an unstreaked mantle and underparts, a rufous wing-patch, and a streaked crown. High-elevation *berlepschi* is larger and buffier below than illustrated coastal race *grisescens*, and may represent a separate species. Fairly common in arid brush and cactus along coast north to Arequipa and Moquegua and on altiplano north to Puno to 4300 m. *S Peru to s Argentina and Chile.*

Tawny Tit-Spinetail *Leptasthenura yanacensis* Tijeral Leonado
16.5 cm (6.5"). Plate 62. ♪797. Mostly tawny with rufous wings and tail. The only tit-spinetail without any streaking. Uncommon in montane *Polylepis* woodlands in Cordillera Blanca (Ancash and n Lima), and above treeline on e slope of Andes in Cusco and Puno at 3200-4600 m. *Andes of n Peru and w Bolivia.*

Wren-like Rushbird *Phleocryptes melanops* Junquero (Totorero)
13.5 cm (5.3"). Plate 63. ♪797. Unmistakable in its habitat. A small brown bird with a large buff superciliary, white streaks on the back and much rufous in the wings. Common in coastal marshes north to Lambayeque and along montane lake and stream margins north to Junín to 4300 m. *Marshes of Peru and s Brazil to s Argentina.*

Synallaxis **Spinetails** A large group (19 species in Peru) of furnariids found in many habitats, ranging from lowlands to mountains. Most of the species skulk in dense undergrowth and scrub. All have rather long, graduated tails. Note crown and wing color, presence or lack of throat-patch, and color and pattern of tail and head.

*Russet-bellied Spinetail *Synallaxis zimmeri* Colaespina Ventrirrojiza
16.5 cm (6.5"). Plate 60. The only spinetail in its range with a gray head, rufous wings, reddish underparts and a dark tail with rufous outer feathers. Rare to uncommon and local in montane scrub on Pacific slope of Andes in Casma and Huarmey Valleys of Cordillera Negra (Ancash) at 1800-2900 m. Reported from Bosque San Damián at 1800-2400 m, Bosque de Noquo at 2850 m, and above Chaccan in dense *Croton* scrub at 2830-2900 m (NK). *Endemic to Peru.*

Rufous Spinetail *Synallaxis unirufa* Colaespina Rufa
18 cm (7"). Plate 61. ♪ EC007T. A uniformly rufous spinetail with black lores. Cf. Rufous Wren. Fairly common in undergrowth of humid montane forests in Andes south to Cordillera Vilcabamba at 1650-3200 m. Recently recorded at Quebrada Frejolillo at 800 m (Pyhälä and Brightsmith 1999). *Andes of w Venezuela to s Peru.*

Azara's Spinetail *Synallaxis azarae* Colaespina de Azara
18 cm (7"). Plate 61. ♪ 797. A common *Synallaxis* with a combination of rufous crown, gray forecrown, rufous wings and tail. The five ssp. that occur in Peru can be grouped into two types, and are sometimes considered two separate species. The "Elegant Spinetail" type, with races *ochracea* (nw Peru), *fruticicola* (Amazonas to San Martín) and *infumata* (illustrated, San Martín to Junín) have olive-brown backs, pale-gray breasts and whitish bellies. "Azara's Spinetail" type, with races *urubambae* (Cusco) and *carabayae* (Puno) have shorter and darker chestnut tails, darker upperparts and grayish underparts. Most similar spinetails are found at lower elevations. Common in humid montane scrub, mostly at 1500-3200 m. *Andes of w Venezuela to nw Argentina.*

*Apurímac Spinetail *Synallaxis courseni* Colaespina de Apurímac
19 cm (7.5"). Plate 60. ♪ JFC. Note limited range. Similar to Azara's Spinetail, but tail is longer and browner. Uncommon in humid montane *Podocarpus*, bamboo and streamside vegetation in Bosque de Ampay at 2800-3500 m. Recently recorded above Pasaje, Cusco. *Endemic to Peru.*

Cinereous-breasted Spinetail *Synallaxis hypospodia* Colaespina Pechocinéreo
15.5 cm (6"). Plate 61. ♪ 797. Note limited range. A spinetail with grayish underparts, rufous crown (gray forecrown), mostly rufous wings and dark, dusky tail. Tail feathers have rounded tips. Dark-breasted Spinetail (limited overlap at best) is very similar but has a shorter tail with pointed "spines" to tail feathers. Similar Pale-breasted Spinetail has paler underparts and only rufous shoulders. Fairly common and local in humid lowland scrub and tropical savanna in Santa Ana and Pampas del Heath. *Locally in s Peru and n Bolivia to central and ne Brazil.*

Pale-breasted Spinetail *Synallaxis albescens* Colaespina Pechiblanco
16.5 cm (6.5"). Plate 61. ♪ 797. Note limited range. A spinetail with whitish underparts, rufous crown (gray forecrown), rufous wing coverts and a dusky tail. Tail feathers have slightly pointed tips. Rare in humid lowland forests along tropical rivers, oxbow lakes and margins in Tambopata Candamo Reserve. *SW Costa Rica to central Argentina and e Brazil.*

Dark-breasted Spinetail *Synallaxis albigularis* Colaespina Pechioscuro
15.5 cm (6"). Plate 61. ♪ 677. A spinetail with a rufous crown (gray forecrown), rufous wing coverts, gray underparts, and a short, dusky, "spiny" tail. Tail feathers are noticeably pointed. Cf. Pale-breasted, Cinereous-bellied and Dusky Spinetails. Common in humid lowland forests e of Andes south to Madre de Dios to 1200 m. *W Amazonian Brazil, e Ecuador, se Colombia and e Peru.*

Slaty Spinetail *Synallaxis brachyura* Colaespina Pizarrosa
15.5 cm (6"). Plate 61. ♪ 603. Note limited range. A mostly slate-gray spinetail with rufous crown, rufous wing coverts and a dark tail. Sympatric Azara's Spinetail has paler underparts. Fairly common in second growth and forest edge in Tumbes to 1400 m. *E Honduras to extreme nw Peru.*

Cabanis' Spinetail *Synallaxis cabanisi* Colaespina de Cabanis
15.5 cm (6"). Plate 60. ♪ 797. A brown-backed spinetail with a rufous crown (rufous reaches the bill), rufous wings and chestnut tail. Similar Dark-breasted Spinetail has a gray forecrown. Uncommon in undergrowth of humid lowlands and foothills, river margins and oxbow lakes e of Andes north to Huánuco at 200-1350 m. *N Peru to w Bolivia.*

Dusky Spinetail *Synallaxis moesta* Colaespina Oscura
15.5 cm (6"). Plate 61. ♪ 542. A mostly dark-gray spinetail with a rufous crown, wings and tail. Dark-breasted Spinetail has a dusky tail. Uncommon in undergrowth of humid lowland forests e of Andes at 200-1200 m in Loreto and San Martín. *E Colombia to n Peru.*

Plain-crowned Spinetail *Synallaxis gujanensis* Colaespina Coroniparda
16.5 cm (6.5"). Plate 61. ♪ 797. A spinetail with rufous wings and tail, buff underparts and a crown that is the same color as the back. Fairly common in humid lowland open forests, scrub, tropical river margins and oxbow lakes e of Andes to 600 m. *Generally distributed e of Andes to n Bolivia, Paraguay and Brazil.*

*Marañón Spinetail *Synallaxis maranonica* Colaespina del Marañón
15.5 cm (6"). Plate 60. The only spinetail in its limited range with rufous wings and tail, buff underparts, and a crown that is the same color as the back. Grayer below than very similar Plain-crowned Spinetail (no overlap). Uncommon in undergrowth of semi-deciduous forests in Río Marañón Valley at 500-1100 m. Recorded near Tamborapa (Begazo et al. 2001). *Upper Marañón drainage of n Peru and adjacent Ecuador.*

White-bellied Spinetail *Synallaxis propinqua* Colaespina Ventriblanca
16 cm (6.5"). Plate 61. ♪ 677. Note limited range and habitat. A spinetail with rufous wings, rufous tail and olive-brown back and crown. Chin is blackish, breast light gray and belly is white. Plain-crowned Spinetail also lacks a rufous crown but has a white throat and buff underparts. Uncommon on river islands along the Amazon, Napo and Ucayali south to Lagarto to 300 m. *River islands from French Guiana to e Ecuador, e Peru and n Bolivia.*

*Blackish-headed (Black-faced) Spinetail *Synallaxis tithys* Colaespina Cabecinegra
14.5 cm (5.75"). Plate 60. Note limited range. A gray spinetail with blackish head, rufous wings and dark tail. Uncommon in deciduous forests and adjacent scrub in Tumbes to 1100 m. Recorded in Zona Reservada de Tumbes (TAP). *SW Ecuador to extreme nw Peru.*

Ruddy Spinetail *Synallaxis rutilans* Colaespina Rojiza
15.5 cm (6"). Plate 61. ♪ 797. A dark, uniformly chestnut spinetail with a blackish tail and a black throat-patch. Uncommon and local in humid lowland *terra firme* forests e of Andes to 900 m. *S Venezuela and the Guianas to n Bolivia and Amazonian Brazil.*

Chestnut-throated Spinetail *Synallaxis cherriei* Colaespina Garganticastaña
14 cm (5.5"). Plate 61. Similar to Ruddy Spinetail but lacks black throat-patch. Chestnut-throated Spinetail has a rufous breast and throat that contrasts strongly with gray belly. Uncommon and local in humid woodland and *terra firme* forest edge (especially bamboo) at Moyobamba (San Martín) and at Hacienda Luisiana (Ayacucho). Recently recorded at 1450 m near Jerillo (Begazo et al. 2001). *Locally in e Ecuador, e Peru and Amazonian Brazil.*

Necklaced Spinetail *Synallaxis stictothorax* Colaespina Acollarada
12.5 cm (5"). Plate 60. The only spinetail in its range and habitat with a white throat and streaked breast. Tail and much of wings are rufous. No overlap with similar Chinchipe Spinetail. Fairly common in arid scrub on Pacific slope south to La Libertad to 400 m. *Arid sw Ecuador to nw Peru.*

Chinchipe Spinetail *Synallaxis chinchipensis* Colaespina de Chinchipe
13.5 cm (5.3"). Plate 60. The only spinetail in its range and habitat with a white throat and mottled breast. Similar to coastal Necklaced Spinetail (no overlap) but central tail feathers are dark (not rufous). Common in arid scrub in upper Río Marañón Valley to about 700 m, mainly in drainage of Río Chinchipe. *Endemic to Peru.*

*Great Spinetail *Siptornopsis hypochondriacus* Colaespina Grande
18.5 cm (7.2"). Plate 60. A notorious skulker. The only spinetail in its range and habitat with a white throat and streaked breast. Much larger than Necklaced Spinetail, and found at much higher elevations. Rare in montane scrub in upper Río Marañón Valley from 2000-3000 m. Recorded 3 km north of San Marcos (Begazo *et al.* 2001) and reported above w bank of Río Marañón near Balsas at 2300 m. *Endemic to Peru.*

White-browed Spinetail *Hellmayrea gularis* Colaespina Cejiblanca
13.5 cm (5.3"). Plate 61. ♪ JM. The only uniformly rufous-brown spinetail with a white throat-patch and superciliary. Has a much shorter tail than other sympatric spinetails. Uncommon in undergrowth of humid montane elfin forests (especially *Chusquea* bamboo) south to Junín at 2500-3500 m. *Andes of w Venezuela to central Peru.*

Cranioleuca **Spinetails.** A fairly large group of furnariids (8 species in Peru). More arboreal than *Synallaxis* spinetails. Often seen climbing tree trunks, in tangles, or foraging acrobatically at mid-level to canopy crowns. Closed tail usually appears forked.

Creamy-crested Spinetail *Cranioleuca albicapilla* Colaespina Cresticremosa
18 cm (7"). Plate 60. ♪ JFC. Pale bill and creamy crest are distinctive. Mantle is olive-brown. Nominate race (Junín to Apurímac) is paler with whiter crest than race *albigula* (Cusco, illustrated). Fairly common in middle level of montane scrub and *Podocarpus* woodlands in semiarid Andean valleys and slopes from Junín to Cusco at 2500-3600 m. Regular above Ollantaytambo and at Bosque de Ampay. *Endemic to Peru.*

Light-crowned Spinetail *Cranioleuca albiceps* Colaespina Coronipálida
15.5 cm (6"). Plate 60. ♪ 797. Note limited range. The only spinetail in its limited range with rufous wings, back and tail, and a whitish to buffy crown. Similar to Marcapata Spinetail race *weskei* (no range overlap) but crown and chin are white; neck, nape and superciliary are gray. Fairly common in middle and lower level of humid Andean bamboo forests in Valcón (s Puno) at 2400-3300 m. *Andes of sw Peru to w Bolivia.*

Marcapata Spinetail *Cranioleuca marcapatae* Colaespina de Marcapata
15.5 cm (6"). Plate 60. ♪ LNS. The only spinetail in its range with rufous wings, back and tail. Nominate *marcapatae* (Cusco, illustrated) has a rufous crown and *weskei* (Cordillera Vilcabamba) has a white crown. Fairly common in middle level of humid montane and elfin forests at 2400-3400 m. Frequents *Chusquea* bamboo. Recorded on Abra Málaga road above Ollantaytambo and on e slope of Cordillera Vilcanota and Cordillera Carabaya at 2800 m. *Endemic to Peru.*

Baron's Spinetail *Cranioleuca baroni* Colaespina de Baron
18 cm (7"). Plate 60. Like a larger version of Line-cheeked Spinetail (no known overlap) but Baron's has grayer mantle, and white throat contrasts with mottled grayish sides and belly. Fairly common in *Polylepis* woodlands, scrub and thorn forests from s Amazonas to n Lima and Pasco at 1650-4500 m. *Endemic to Peru.*

Line-cheeked Spinetail *Cranioleuca antisiensis* Colaespina Cachetilineado
14 cm (5.5"). Plate 60. The only spinetail in its range that has a rufous crown bordered with a white superciliary, and contrasting buffy-brown back and belly. Fairly common and local in humid montane forests in Andes south to n Cajamarca and Lambayeque at 1100-2900 m. *Andes of s Ecuador to n Peru.*

Color Plates

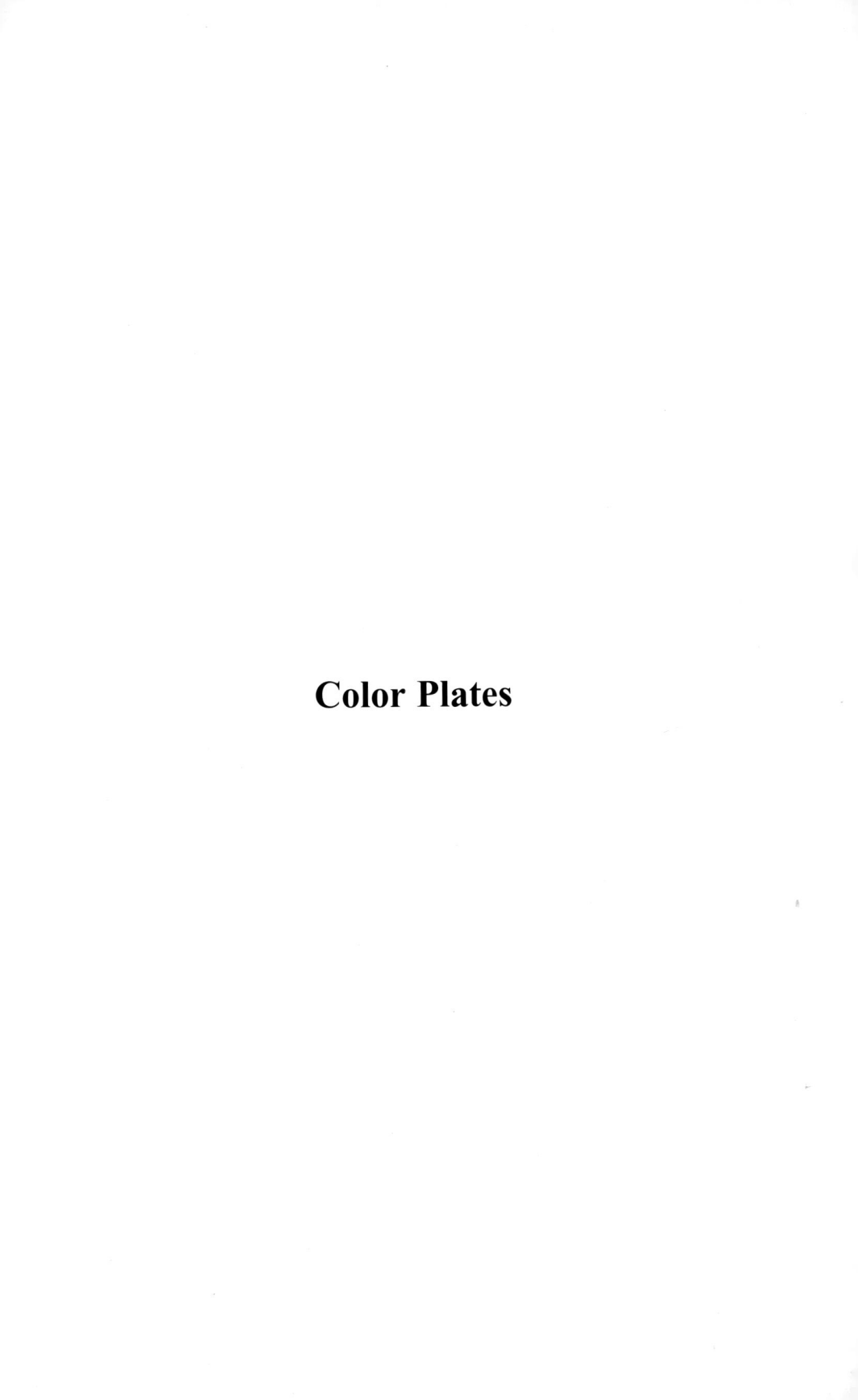

Plate 1

1. Kalinowski's Tinamou *Nothoprocta kalinowskii* p. 4

2. Ornate Tinamou *Nothoprocta ornata* p. 4

3. Black Tinamou *Tinamus osgoodi* p. 1

4. Taczanowski's Tinamou *Nothoprocta taczanowskii* p. 4

5. Darwin's Nothura *Nothura darwinii* p. 4

6. Andean Tinamou *Nothoprocta pentlandii* p. 4

7. Hooded Tinamou *Nothocercus nigrocapillus* p. 2

8. Curve-billed Tinamou *Nothoprocta curvirostris* p. 4

9. Puna Tinamou *Tinamotis pentlandii* p. 4

10. Lesser Rhea *Rhea pennata* p. 1

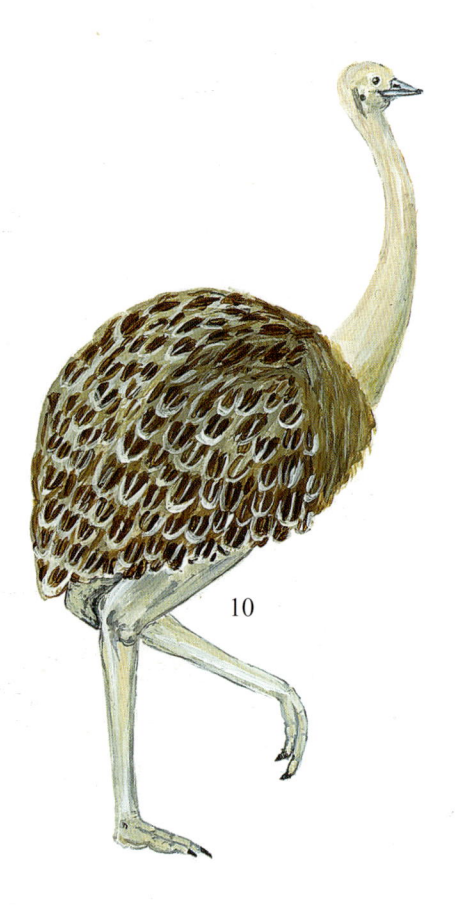

1

Plate 2

1. Gray Tinamou *Tinamus tao* p. 1

2. Great Tinamou *Tinamus major* p. 1

3. Highland Tinamou *Nothocercus bonapartei* p. 2

4. White-throated Tinamou *Tinamus guttatus* p. 1

5. Tawny-breasted Tinamou *Nothocercus julius* p. 2

6. Cinereous Tinamou *Crypturellus cinereus* p. 2

7. Little Tinamou *Crypturellus soui* p. 2

8. Brown Tinamou *Crypturellus obsoletus* p. 2

9. Undulated Tinamou *Crypturellus undulatus yapura* p. 2

10. Pale-browed Tinamou *Crypturellus transfasciatus* p. 3
    a. ♀   b. ♂

11. Black-capped Tinamou *Crypturellus atrocapillus* p. 3

12. Variegated Tinamou *Crypturellus variegatus* p. 3

13. Brazilian Tinamou *Crypturellus strigulosus*

14. Bartlett's Tinamou *Crypturellus bartletti* p. 3

15. Small-billed Tinamou *Crypturellus parvirostris* p. 3

16. Tataupa Tinamou *Crypturellus tataupa* p. 3

17. Red-winged Tinamou *Nothoprocta curvirostris* p. 3

2

Plate 3

1. Royal Albatross *Diomedea epomophora* p. 6

2. Black-browed Albatross *Thalassarche melanophris* p. 6
   a. Adult head   b. Immature head

3. Shy Albatross *Thalassarche cauta salvini* p. 7
   a. *T. c. salvini*   b. *T. c. eremita*
   c. *T. c. cauta*   d. *Immature*

4. Waved Albatross *Phoebastria irrorata* p. 6

5. Antarctic Giant Petrel *Macronectes giganteus* p. 7

6. Buller's Albatross *Thalassarche bulleri* p. 7

7. Gray-headed Albatross *Thalassarche chrysostoma* p. 7

8. Wedge-rumped Storm-Petrel *Oceanodroma tethys* p. 11

9. Ringed Storm-Petrel *Oceanodroma hornbyi* p. 12

10. Leach's Storm-Petrel *Oceanodroma leucorhoa* p. 12

11. Band-rumped Storm-Petrel *Oceanodroma castro* p. 11

12. Markham's Storm-Petrel *Oceanodroma markhami* p. 12

13. Black Storm-Petrel *Oceanodroma melania* p. 12

14. White-faced Storm-Petrel *Pelagodroma marina* p. 11

15. White-vented Storm-Petrel *Oceanites gracilis* p. 11

16. Black-bellied Storm-Petrel *Fregetta tropica* p. 11

17. White-bellied Storm-Petrel *Fregetta grallaria* p. 11

18. Wilson's Storm-Petrel *Oceanites oceanicus* p. 11

19. Least Storm-Petrel *Oceanodroma microsoma* p. 11

20. Wandering Albatross *Diomedea exulans* p. 6

Inserts not to scale

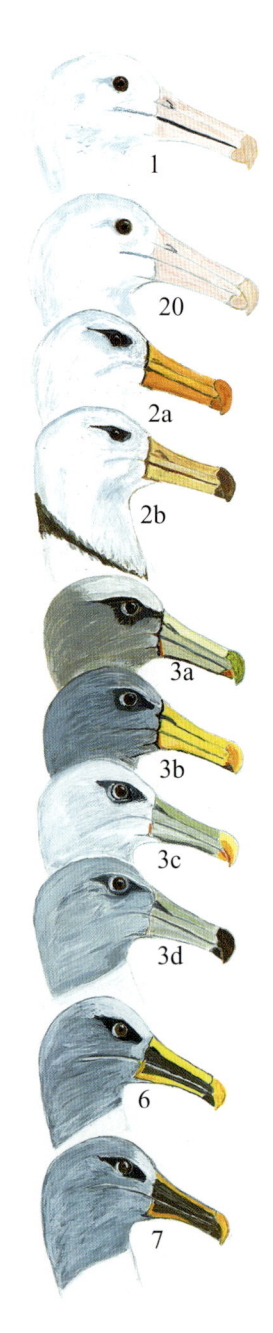

3

Plate 4

1. Cook's Petrel *Pterodroma cookii* p. 8

2. Defilippe's Petrel *Pterodroma defilippiana* p. 8

3. Dark-rumped Petrel *Pterodroma phaeopygia* p. 8

4. Black-winged Petrel *Pterodroma nigripennis* p. 8

5. Stejneger's Petrel *Pterodroma longirostris.* p. 9

6. Murphy's Petrel *Pterodroma ultima* p. 8

7. Kermadec Petrel *Pterodroma neglecta* p. 8

8. Juan Fernández Petrel *Pterodroma externa* p. 8

9. Slender-billed Prion *Pachyptila belcheri* p. 9

10. Antarctic Prion *Pachyptila desolata* p. 9

11. Fairy Prion *Pachyptila turtur* p. 9

12. Broad-billed Prion *Pachyptila vittata* p. 9

13. White-chinned Petrel *Procellaria aequinoctialis* P. 9

14. Westland Petrel *Procellaria westlandica* p. 10

15. Parkinson's Petrel *Procellaria parkinsoni* p. 10

16. Gray Petrel *Procellaria cinerea* p. 9

17. Blue Petrel *Halobaena* caerulea p. 9

18. Wedge-rumped Storm-Petrel *Oceanodroma tethys* P. 11

19. Little Shearwater *Puffinis assimilis* p. 10

20. Sooty Shearwater *Puffinus griseus* p. 10

21. Flesh-footed Shearwater *Puffinus carneipes* p. 10

22. Audubon's Shearwater *Puffinus lherminieri* p. 10

23. Buller's Shearwater *Puffinus bulleri* p. 10

24. Pink-footed Shearwater *Puffinus creatopus* p. 10

25. Southern Fulmar *Fulmarus glacialoides* p. 7

26. Cape Petrel *Daption capense* p. 7

4

Inserts not to scale

Plate 5

1. Peruvian Pelican *Pelecanus thagus* p. 13
       a. Breeding   b. Non-breeding

2. Brown Pelican *Pelecanus occidentalis* p. 13
       a. Breeding   b. Non-breeding

3. Great Grebe *Podiceps major* p. 6

4. Neotropic Cormorant *Phalacrocorax brasilianus* p. 14
       a. Immature   b. Adult

5. Least Grebe *Tachybaptus dominicus* p. 5

6. White-tufted Grebe *Rollandia rolland* p. 5

7. Junín Grebe *Podiceps taczanowskii* p. 6

8. Silvery Grebe *Podiceps occipitalis* p. 6

9. Short-winged Grebe *Rollandia microptera* p. 5

10. Pied-billed Grebe *Podilymbus podiceps* p. 5
        a. Breeding   b. Non-breeding

5

Plate 6

1. Peruvian Pelican *Pelecanus thagus* p. 13

2. Peruvian Booby *Sula variegata* p. 13

3. Chilean Flamingo *Phoenicopterus chilensis* p. 19

4. Guanay Cormorant *Phalacrocorax bougainvillii* p. 14

5. Red-legged Cormorant *Phalacrocorax gaimardi* p. 14

6. Peruvian Diving-Petrel *Pelecanoides garnotii* p. 12

7. Wilson's Storm-Petrel *Oceanites oceanicus* p. 11

8. Gray Gull *Larus modestus* p. 48

9. Kelp Gull *Larus dominicanus* p. 48
    a. Adult   b. Immature

10. Inca Tern *Larosterna inca* p. 52

11. Peruvian Tern *Sterna lorata* p. 51

12. Blackish Oystercatcher *Haematopus ater* p. 39

13. Black Skimmer *Rynchops niger* p. 52

14. Humboldt Penguin *Spheniscus humboldti* p. 5

15. White-cheeked Pintail *Anas bahamensis* p. 21

16. Cinnamon Teal *Anas cyanoptera* p. 21
    a. ♂   b. ♀

17. Andean Coot *Fulica ardesiaca* p. 38
    a. Red-fronted morph   b. White-fronted morph

6

Plate 7

1. Great Egret *Ardea alba* p. 15

2. Snowy Egret *Egretta thula* p. 16

3. Little Blue Heron *Egretta caerulea* p. 16

4. Yellow-crowned Night-Heron *Nyctanassa violacea* p. 16

5. Black-crowned Night-Heron *Nycticorax nycticorax* p. 16
   a. Adult   b. Immature

6. Tricolored Heron *Egretta tricolor* p. 16

7. Pinnated Bittern *Botaurus pinnatus* p. 17

8. Bare-throated Tiger-Heron *Tigrisoma mexicanum* p. 17

9. Striated Heron *Butorides striatus* p. 16

10. Stripe-backed Bittern *Ixobrychus involucris* p. 17

11. Least Bittern *Ixobrychus exilis* ♂ p. 17

7

Plate 8

1. Sunbittern *Eurypyga helias* p. 39

2. Boat-billed Heron *Cochlearius cochlearius* p. 16

3. Capped Heron *Pilherodius pileatus* p. 15

4. Cattle Egret *Bubulcus ibis* p. 16
      a. Non-breeding   b. Breeding

5. Hoatzin *Opisthocomus hoazin* p. 35

6. Sungrebe *Heliornis fulica* ♀ p. 39

7. Zigzag Heron *Zebrilus undulatus* p. 17

8. Fasciated Tiger-Heron *Tigrisoma fasciatum* p. 17
      a. Immature   b. Adult

9. Rufescent Tiger-Heron *Tigrisoma lineatum* p. 17
      a. Immature   b. Adult

10. Agami Heron *Agamia agami* p. 16

11. Puna Flamingo *Phoenicopterus jamesi* p. 19

12. Andean Flamingo *Phoenicopterus andinus* p. 19

13. Chilean Flamingo *Phoenicopterus chilensis* p. 19

14. Cocoi Heron *Ardea cocoi* p. 15

8

Plate 9

1. Large-billed Tern *Phaetusa simplex* p. 52

2. Yellow-billed Tern *Sterna superciliaris* p. 51

3. Torrent Duck *Merganetta armata* p. 20
    a. *M. a. leucogenis* ♀
    b. *M. a. leucogenis* ♂
    c. *M. a. turneri* ♂

4. Masked Duck *Oxyura dominica* p. 22
    a. ♂   b. ♀

5. Puna Teal *Anas puna* p. 21

6. Crested Duck *Anas specularioides* p. 21

7. Red Shoveler *Anas platalea* ♂ p. 22

8. Anhinga *Anhinga anhinga* p. 14
    a. ♀   b. ♂

9. Muscovy Duck *Cairina moschata* ♂ p. 20

10. Andean Goose *Chloephaga melanoptera* p. 20

11. Horned Screamer *Anhima cornuta* p. 19

12. Limpkin *Aramus guarauna* p. 35

13. Orinoco Goose *Neochen jubata* p. 20

14. Southern Screamer *Chauna torquata* p. 19

9

Plate 10

1. Fulvous Whistling-Duck *Dendrocygna bicolor* p. 20

2. White-faced Whistling-Duck *Dendrocygna viduata* p. 20

3. Black-bellied Whistling-Duck *Dendrocygna autumnalis* p. 20

4. Comb Duck *Sarkidiornis melanotos* p. 20
    a. ♂ b. ♀

5. Yellow-billed Pintail *Anas georgica* p. 21

6. Speckled Teal *Anas flavirostris* p. 21

7. Chiloe Wigeon *Anas sibilatrix* p. 21
    a. ♂ b. ♀

8. Blue-winged Teal *Anas discors* p. 21
    a. ♀ b. ♂

9. Rosy-billed Pochard *Netta peposaca* p. 22
    a. ♂ b. ♀

10. Southern Pochard *Netta erythrophthalma* p. 22
    a. ♂ b. ♀

11. Andean Duck *Oxyura ferruginea* p. 22
    a. ♂ b. ♀

12. Nazca Booby *Sula granti* p. 13

13. Masked Booby *Sula dactylatra* p. 13

14. Red-footed Booby *Sula sula* p. 14

15. Red-billed Tropicbird *Phaethon aethereus* p. 12
    a. Adult b. Immature

16. Blue-footed Booby *Sula nebouxii* p. 13
    a. Immature b. Adult

17. Red-tailed Tropicbird *Phaethon rubricauda* p. 13

18. Magnificent Frigatebird *Fregata magnificens* p. 15
    a. Immature b. ♂ c. ♀

19. Great Frigatebird *Fregata minor* p. 15
    a. Immature b. ♂

20. Brown Booby *Sula leucogaster* p. 14

1
2
3
4a
4b
5
6
7a
7b
8a
8b
9a
9b
10a
10b
11a
11b
12
13
14
15a
15b
16a
16b
17
18a
18b
18c
19a
19b
20

Plate 11

1. Greater Yellow-headed Vulture *Cathartes melambrotus* p. 23

2. Zone-tailed Hawk *Buteo albonotatus* p. 29

3. Black Vulture *Coragyps atratus* p. 22

4. Andean Condor *Vultur gryphus* p. 23

5. Turkey Vulture *Cathartes aura* p. 22

6. Lesser Yellow-headed Vulture *Cathartes burrovianus* p. 23

7. King Vulture *Sarcoramphus papa* p. 23

8. Green Ibis *Mesembrinibis cayennensis* p. 18

9. White-faced Ibis *Plegadis chihi* p. 18

10. Puna Ibis *Plegadis ridgwayi* p. 18

11. Black-faced Ibis *Theristicus melanopis* p. 18

12. Andean Ibis *Theristicus branickii* p. 18

13. White Ibis *Eudocimus albus* p. 18
        a. Immature   b. Adult

14. Roseate Spoonbill *Ajaia ajaja* p. 19

15. Maguari Stork *Ciconia maguari* p. 18

16. Wood Stork *Mycteria americana* p. 17

17. Jabiru *Jabiru mycteria* p. 18

11

Plate 12

1. Gray-headed Kite *Leptodon cayanensis* p. 24
    a. Immature   b. Adult

2. Double-toothed Kite *Harpagus bidentatus* p. 24

3. Pearl Kite *Gampsonyx swainsonii* p. 24

4. Hook-billed Kite *Chondrohierax uncinatus* p. 24
    a. ♂   b. ♀   c. Immature   d. Dark morph

5. Swallow-tailed Kite *Elanoides forficatus* p. 24

6. Slate-colored Hawk *Leucopternis schistacea* p. 26

7. Crane Hawk *Geranospiza caerulescens* p. 26

8. Snail Kite *Rostrhamus sociabilis* p. 24

9. Slender-billed Kite *Rostrhamus hamatus* p. 24

10. Barred Forest-Falcon *Micrastur ruficollis* p. 31

11. Lined Forest-Falcon *Micrastur gilvicollis* p. 31

12. Slaty-backed Forest-Falcon *Micrastur mirandollei* p. 31

13. Collared Forest-Falcon *Micrastur semitorquatus* p. 31

14. Buckley's Forest-Falcon *Micrastur buckleyi* p. 31

15. Mississippi Kite *Ictinia mississippiensis* p. 25

12

Plate 13

1. Snail Kite *Rostrhamus sociabilis* p. 24
    a. ♂   1b. ♀

2. Variable Hawk *Buteo polyosoma* p. 29
    a. "Red-chested" morph
    b. "Red-backed" morph
    c. Pale morph

3. Plumbeous Kite *Ictinia plumbea* p. 25

4. Bicolored Hawk *Accipiter bicolor* p. 26

5. Semicollared Hawk *Accipiter collaris* p. 25

6. Tiny Hawk *Accipiter superciliosus* p. 25

7. Plain-breasted Hawk *Accipiter ventralis* p. 25

8. Roadside Hawk *Buteo magnirostris* p. 28

9. Cinereous Harrier *Circus cinereus* p. 25
    a. ♀   b. ♂

10. Savanna Hawk *Buteogallus meridionalis* p. 27

11. Harris' Hawk *Parabuteo unicinctus* p. 27

12. Gray-backed Hawk *Leucopternis occidentalis* p. 26

13. White-browed Hawk *Leucopternis kuhli* p. 26

14. Mangrove Black-Hawk *Buteogallus subtilis* p. 27

15. Great Black-Hawk *Buteogallus urubitinga* p. 27

16. Osprey *Pandion haliaetus* p. 23

13

Plate 14

1. Black Caracara *Daptrius ater* p. 30

2. Red-throated Caracara *Ibycter americanus* p. 30

3. Mountain Caracara *Phalcoboenus megalopterus* p. 30

4. Southern Caracara *Caracara cheriway* p. 30

5. Bat Falcon *Falco rufigularis* p. 32

6. Orange-breasted Falcon *Falco deiroleucus* p. 32

7. Laughing Falcon *Herpetotheres cachinnans* p. 31

8. Yellow-headed Caracara *Milvago chimachima* p. 30

9. American Kestrel *Falco sparverius* p. 31
    a. ♂   b. ♀

10. Black-collared Hawk *Busarellus nigricollis* p. 27

11. Merlin *Falco columbarius* ♂ p. 32

12. Peregrine Falcon *Falco peregrinus* p. 32

13. Aplomado Falcon *Falco femoralis* p. 32

14. Harpy Eagle *Harpia harpyja* p. 29

15. Black-chested Buzzard-Eagle *Geranoaetus melanoleucus* p. 27

14

Plate 15

1. Gray-bellied Goshawk *Accipiter poliogaster* p. 25

2. Long-winged Harrier *Circus buffoni* p. 25

3. Plumbeous Hawk *Leucopternis plumbea* p. 26

4. Barred Hawk *Leucopternis princeps* p. 26

5. White-rumped Hawk *Buteo leucorrhous* p. 28

6. Broad-winged Hawk *Buteo platypterus* p. 28

7. Gray Hawk *Asturina nitida* p. 27

8. White Hawk *Leucopternis albicollis* p. 26

9. Black-faced Hawk *Leucopternis melanops* p. 26

10. Short-tailed Hawk *Buteo brachyurus* p. 28

11. Swainson's Hawk *Buteo swainsoni* p. 28

12. White-throated Hawk *Buteo albigula* p. 28

13. White-tailed Hawk *Buteo albicaudatus* p. 28

14. Zone-tailed Hawk *Buteo albonotatus* p. 29

15. Solitary Eagle *Harpyhaliaetus solitarius* p. 27

16. Black-and-chestnut Eagle *Oroaetus isidori* p. 30

17. Crested Eagle *Morphnus guianensis* p. 29

18. Black-and-white Hawk-Eagle *Spizastur melanoleucus* p. 29

19. Black Hawk-Eagle *Spizaetus tyrannus* p. 29

20. Ornate Hawk-Eagle *Spizaetus ornatus* p. 29

15

Plate 16

1. Osprey *Pandion haliaetus* p. 23

2. Gray-headed Kite *Leptodon cayanensis* p. 24

3. Hook-billed Kite *Chondrohierax uncinatus* p. 24

4. Bicolored Hawk *Accipiter bicolor* p. 26

5. Roadside Hawk *Buteo magnirostris* p. 28

6. Plumbeous Kite *Ictinia plumbea* p. 25

7. Cinereous Harrier *Circus cinereus* p. 25

8. Double-toothed Kite *Harpagus bidentatus* p. 24

9. Great Black-Hawk *Buteogallus urubitinga* p. 27

10. Variable Hawk *Buteo polyosoma* 29
    a. Dark morph "Puna" Hawk
    b. Light morph "Puna" Hawk
    c. Dark morph "Red-backed" Hawk

11. Crane Hawk *Geranospiza caerulescens* p. 26

12. Collared Forest-Falcon *Micrastur semitorquatus* p. 31

13. Harris' Hawk *Parabuteo unicinctus* p. 27

14. Yellow-headed Caracara *Milvago chimachima* p. 30

15. Harpy Eagle *Harpia harpyja* p. 29

16. Black-chested Buzzard-Eagle *Geranoaetus melanoleucus*

17. Mountain Caracara *Phalcoboenus megalopterus* p. 30

18. Crested Caracara *Caracara cheriway* p. 30

19. Aplomado Falcon *Falco femoralis* p. 32

16

Plate 17

1. Speckled Chachalaca *Ortalis guttata* p. 32

2. Blue-throated Piping-Guan *Pipile cumanensis* p. 33

3. White-winged Guan *Penelope albipennis* p. 33

4. Rufous-headed Chachalaca *Ortalis erythroptera* p. 32

5. Andean Guan *Penelope montagnii* p. 33

6. Bearded Guan *Penelope barbata* p. 32

7. Spix's Guan *Penelope jacquacu* p. 33

8. Sickle-winged Guan *Chamaepetes goudotii* p. 33

9. Wattled Guan *Aburria aburri* p. 33

10. Nocturnal Curassow *Nothocrax urumutum* p. 33

11. Wattled Curassow *Crax globulosa* ♂ p. 34

12. Razor-billed Curassow *Mitu tuberosa* p. 34

13. Salvin's Curassow *Mitu salvini* p. 33

14. Horned Curassow *Pauxi unicornis* p. 34

17

Plate 18

1. Rufous-breasted Wood-Quail *Odontophorus speciosus* p. 34
   a. ♂   b. ♀

2. Stripe-faced Wood-Quail *Odontophorus balliviani* p. 34

3. Starred Wood-Quail *Odontophorus stellatus* ♂ p. 34

4. Marbled Wood-Quail *Odontophorus gujanensis* p. 34

5. Puna Snipe *Gallinago andina* p. 42
   Also: South American Snipe *Gallinago paraguiae* p. 42
   Common snipe *Gallinago gallinago* p.42

6. Andean Snipe *Gallinago jamesoni* p. 43

7. Imperial Snipe *Gallinago imperialis* p. 43

8. Noble Snipe *Gallinago nobilis* p. 42

9. Rufous-necked Wood-Rail *Aramides axillaris* p. 37

10. Red-winged Wood-Rail *Aramides calopterus* p. 37

11. Red-fronted Coot *Fulica rufifrons* p. 38

12. Gray-winged Trumpeter *Psophia crepitans* p. 35

13. Pale-winged Trumpeter *Psophia leucoptera* p. 35

14. Giant Coot *Fulica gigantea* p. 38

18

Plate 19

1. Chestnut-headed Crake *Anurolimnas castaneiceps* p. 35

2. Ocellated Crake *Micropygia schomburgkii* p. 35

3. Russet-crowned Crake *Anurolimnas viridis* p. 36

4. Black-banded Crake *Anurolimnas fasciatus* p. 36

5. Junín Rail *Laterallus tuerosi* p. 36

6. Uniform Crake *Amaurolimnas concolor* p. 37

7. Rufous-sided Crake *Laterallus melanophaius* p. 36

8. Black Rail *Laterallus jamaicensis* p. 36

9. Gray-breasted Crake *Laterallus exilis* p. 36

10. Ash-throated Crake *Porzana albicollis* p. 37

11. Sora *Porzana carolina* p. 37

12. Paint-billed Crake *Neocrex erythrops* p. 37

13. Bogotá Rail *Rallus semiplumbeus* p. 36

14. Virginia Rail *Rallus Limicola* p. 36

15. Clapper Rail *Rallus longirostris* p. 36

16. Gray-necked Wood-Rail *Aramides cajanea* p. 37

17 Brown Wood-Rail *Aramides wolfi* p. 37

18. Spotted Rail *Pardirallus maculatus* p. 37

19. Purple Gallinule *Porphyrula martinica* p. 38

20. Azure Gallinule *Porphyrula flavirostris* p. 38

21. Blackish Rail *Pardirallus nigricans* p. 37

22. Spot-flanked Gallinule *Gallinula melanops* p. 38

23 Common Moorhen *Gallinula chloropus* p. 38

24. Plumbeous Rail *Pardirallus sanguinolentus* p. 38

25. Wattled Jacana *Jacana jacana* p. 39
    a. Immature   b. Adult

19

Plate 20

1. Rufous-bellied Seedsnipe *Attagis gayi* p. 47

2. Gray-breasted Seedsnipe *Thinocorus orbignyianus* p. 47
   a. ♀   b. ♂

3. Least Seedsnipe *Thinocorus rumicivorus* p. 47

4. Tawny-throated Dotterel *Oreopholus ruficollis* p. 42

5. Andean Lapwing *Vanellus resplendens* p. 40

6. Southern Lapwing *Vanellus chilensis* p. 40

7. Pied Lapwing *Vanellus cayanus* p. 40

8. Rufous-chested Dotterel *Charadrius modestus* p. 42
   a. Non-breeding   b. Breeding

9. Collared Plover *Charadrius collaris* p. 41

10. Puna Plover *Charadrius alticola* p. 42

11. Wilson's Plover *Charadrius wilsonia* p. 41

12. Killdeer *Charadrius vociferus* p. 41

13. Semipalmated Plover *Charadrius semipalmatus* p. 41

14. Snowy (Kentish) Plover *Charadrius alexandrinus* p. 41

15. Diademed Sandpiper-Plover *Phegornis mitchellii* p. 42

16. Wilson's Phalarope *Phalaropus tricolor* p. 46
    a. Non-breeding   b. Breeding

17. White-backed Stilt *Himantopus melanurus* p. 40

18. Andean Avocet *Recurvirostra andina* p. 40

19. Black-necked Stilt *Himantopus mexicanus* p. 40

20. Peruvian Thick-knee *Burhinus superciliaris* p. 40

20

Plate 21

1. Spotted Sandpiper *Actitis macularia* p. 44

2. Wandering Tattler *Heteroscelus incanus* p. 44

3. Ruddy Turnstone *Arenaria interpres* p. 44

4. Sanderling *Calidris alba* p. 44

5. Red Knot *Calidris canutus* p. 44

6. Least Sandpiper *Calidris minutilla* p. 45

7. Surfbird *Aphriza virgata* p. 44

8. White-rumped Sandpiper *Calidris fuscicollis* p. 45

9. Baird's Sandpiper *Calidris bairdii* p. 45

10. Western Sandpiper *Calidris mauri* p. 45

11. Dunlin *Calidris alpina* p. 46

12. Curlew Sandpiper *Calidris ferruginea* p. 46

13. Pectoral Sandpiper *Calidris melanotos* p. 45

14. Semipalmated Sandpiper *Calidris pusilla* p. 44

15. Ruff *Philomachus pugnax* p. 46

16. Stilt Sandpiper *Calidris himantopus* p. 46

17. Red-necked Stint *Calidris ruficollis* p. 45

18. Red Phalarope *Phalaropus fulicaria* p. 46

19. Red-necked Phalarope *Phalaropus lobatus* p. 46

20. Buff-breasted Sandpiper *Tryngites subruficollis* p. 46

21

Plate 22

1. American Oystercatcher *Haematopus palliatus* p. 39

2. Upland Sandpiper *Bartramia longicauda* p. 43

3. Short-billed Dowitcher *Limnodromus griseus* p. 43

4. Willet *Catoptrophorus semipalmatus* p. 44

5. Black-bellied (Gray) Plover *Pluvialis squatarola* p. 41

6. American Golden-Plover *Pluvialis dominica* p. 41

7. Greater Yellowlegs *Tringa melanoleuca* p. 43

8. Lesser Yellowlegs *Tringa flavipes* p. 43

9. Solitary Sandpiper *Tringa solitaria* p. 44

10. Marbled Godwit *Limosa fedoa* p. 43

11. Hudsonian Godwit *Limosa haemastica* p. 43

12. Whimbrel *Numenius phaeopus* p. 43

13. Chilean Skua *Stercorarius chilensis* p. 47
    a. Adult   b. Immature

14. South Polar Skua *Stercorarius maccormicki* p. 47

15. Long-tailed Jaeger *Stercorarius longicaudus* p. 48
    a. Adult   b. Immature

16. Pomarine Jaeger *Stercorarius pomarinus* p. 48
    a. Adult   b. Immature

17. Parasitic Jaeger *Stercorarius parasiticus* p. 48
    a. Adult light morph   b. Immature

22

Plate 23

1. Band-tailed Gull *Larus belcheri* p. 48
       a. Breeding   b. Juvenile   c. Non-breeding

2. Herring Gull *Larus argentatus* p. 49

3. Gray-headed Gull *Larus cirrocephalus* p. 49
       a. Bbreeding   b. First winter   3c. Non-breeding

4. Swallow-tailed Gull *Creagrus furcatus* p. 50

5. Franklin's Gull *Larus pipixcan* p. 49
       a. Breeding   b. Non-breeding

6. Laughing Gull *Larus atricilla* p. 49
       a. Breeding   b. Non-breeding

7. Sabine's Gull *Xema sabini* p. 49

8. Black-legged Kittiwake *Rissa tridactyla* p. 50

9. Andean Gull *Larus serranus* p. 49
       a. Breeding   b. Non-breeding

10. South American Tern *Sterna hirundinacea* p. 50
        a. Non-breeding   b. Breeding

11. Arctic Tern *Sterna paradisaea* p. 51

12. Snowy-crowned Tern *Sterna trudeaui* p. 51
        a. Non-breeding b. Breeding

13. Sooty Tern *Sterna fuscata* p. 51

14. Least Tern *Sterna antillarum* p. 51

15. Common Tern *Sterna hirundo* p. 51

16. Sandwich Tern *Sterna sandvicensis* p. 50

17. Royal Tern *Sterna maxima* p. 50

18. Elegant Tern *Sterna elegans* p. 50

19. Gull-billed Tern *Sterna nilotica* p. 50

20. Black Tern *Chlidonias niger* p. 51
        a. Breeding   b. Non-breeding

23

Plate 24

1. Spot-winged Pigeon *Columba maculosa* p. 52

2. Band-tailed Pigeon *Columba fasciata* p. 53

3. Rock Dove *Columba livia* p. 52

4. Ruddy Pigeon *Columba subvinacea* p. 53

5. Plumbeous Pigeon *Columba plumbea* p. 53

6. Pale-vented Pigeon *Columba cayennensis* p. 53

7. Scaled Pigeon *Columba speciosa* p. 52

8. Pacific Dove *Zenaida meloda* p. 53

9. Eared Dove *Zenaida auriculata* p. 53

10. Black-winged Ground-Dove *Metriopelia melanoptera* p. 54

11. Golden-spotted Ground-Dove *Metriopelia aymara* p. 54

12. Bare-faced Ground-Dove *Metriopelia ceciliae* p. 54

24

Plate 25

1. Croaking Ground-Dove *Columbina cruziana* ♂ p. 54

2. Plain-breasted Ground-Dove *Columbina minuta* ♂ p. 53

3. Ecuadorian Ground-Dove *Columbina buckleyi* ♂ p. 53

4. Picui Ground-Dove *Columbina picui* p. 54

5. Ruddy Ground-Dove *Columbina talpacoti* p. 54
    a. ♀   b. ♂

6. Blue Ground-Dove *Claravis pretiosa* p. 54
    a. ♂   b. ♀

7. Maroon-chested Ground-Dove *Claravis mondetoura* p. 54
    a. ♂   b. ♀

8. White-throated Quail-Dove *Geotrygon frenata* p. 55

9. Sapphire Quail-Dove *Geotrygon saphirina* p. 55

10. Ruddy Quail-Dove *Geotrygon montana* p. 55
    a. ♂   b. ♀

11. Violaceous Quail-Dove *Geotrygon violacea* p. 55

12. White-tipped Dove *Leptotila verreauxi* p. 55

13. Gray-fronted Dove *Leptotila rufaxilla* p. 55

25

Plate 26

1. Red-faced Parrot *Hapalopsittaca pyrrhops* p. 60

2. Black-winged Parrot *Hapalopsittaca melanotis* p. 60

3. Speckle-faced Parrot *Pionus t. tumultuosus* p. 60

4. Red-masked Parakeet *Aratinga erythrogenys* p. 57

5. Gray-cheeked Parakeet *Brotogeris pyrrhopterus* p. 59

6. Andean Parakeet *Bolborhynchus orbygnesius* p. 58

7. Peruvian Pigeon *Columba oenops* p. 53

8. Golden-plumed Parakeet *Leptosittaca branickii* p. 57

9. Ochre-bellied Dove *Leptotila ochraceiventris* p. 55

10. Blue-headed Macaw *Propyrrhura couloni* p. 56

11. Amazonian Parrotlet *Nannopsittaca dachilleae* p. 60

12. Pacific Parrotlet *Forpus coelestis* p. 58

13. Yellow-faced Parrotlet *Forpus xanthops* p. 58

26

Plate 27

1. Military Macaw *Ara militaris* p. 56

2. Blue-and-yellow Macaw *Ara ararauna* p. 56

3. Scarlet Macaw *Ara macao* p. 56

4. Red-and-green Macaw *Ara chloropterus* p. 56

5. Red-shouldered Macaw *Diopsittaca nobilis* p. 56

6. Chestnut-fronted Macaw *Ara severa* p. 56

7. Red-bellied Macaw *Orthopsittaca manilata* p. 56

8. Scarlet-fronted Parakeet *Aratinga wagleri* p. 56

9. White-eyed Parakeet *Aratinga leucophthalmus* p. 57

10. Mitred Parakeet *Aratinga mitrata* p. 56
        a. *A. m. mitrata*   b. *A. m. alticola*

11. Peach-fronted Parakeet *Aratinga aurea* p. 57

12. Dusky-headed Parakeet *Aratinga weddellii* p. 57

27

Plate 28

1. Dusky-billed Parrotlet *Forpus sclateri*   p. 58

2. Blue-winged Parrotlet *Forpus xanthopterygius*   p. 58

3. Scarlet-shouldered Parrotlet *Touit huetii*   p. 59

4. Barred Parakeet *Bolborhynchus lineola*   p. 58

5. Spot-winged Parrotlet *Touit stictoptera*   p. 59

6. Sapphire-rumped Parrotlet *Touit purpurata*   p. 59

7. Tui Parakeet *Brotogeris sanctithomae*   p. 59

8. Mountain Parakeet *Psilopsiagon aurifrons*   p. 58

9. Black-capped Parakeet *Pyrrhura rupicola*   p. 57

10. Cobalt-winged Parakeet *Brotogeris cyanoptera*   p. 59

11. Painted Parakeet *Pyrrhura picta*   p. 57

12. Maroon-tailed Parakeet *Pyrrhura melanura berlepschi*   p. 57

13. Canary-winged Parakeet *Brotogeris versicolurus*   p. 58

28

Plate 29

1. Blue-headed Parrot *Pionus menstruus* p. 60

2. Red-billed Parrot *Pionus sordidus* p. 60

3. Bronze-winged Parrot *Pionus chalcopterus* p. 60

4. Short-tailed Parrot *Graydidascalus brachyurus* p. 60

5. Orange-cheeked Parrot *Pionopsitta barrabandi* p. 60

6. White-bellied Parrot *Pionites leucogaster* p. 59

7. Black-headed Parrot *Pionites melanocephala* p. 59

8. Orange-winged Parrot *Amazona amazonica* p. 61

9. Scaly-naped Parrot *Amazona mercenaria* p. 61

10. Red-fan Parrot *Deroptyus accipitrinus* p. 61

11. Mealy Parrot *Amazona farinosa* p. 61

12. Festive Parrot *Amazona festiva* p. 61

13. Yellow-crowned Parrot *Amazona ochrocephala* p. 61

29

Plate 30

1. Pheasant Cuckoo *Dromococcyx phasianellus* p. 63

2. Pavonine Cuckoo *Dromococcyx pavoninus* p. 63

3. Gray-capped Cuckoo *Coccyzus lansbergi* p. 62

4. Dark-billed Cuckoo *Coccyzus melacoryphus* p. 62

5. Ash-colored Cuckoo *Coccyzus cinereus* p. 61

6. Yellow-billed Cuckoo *Coccyzus americanus* p. 62

7. Black-billed Cuckoo *Coccyzus erythropthalmus* p. 62

8. Striped Cuckoo *Tapera naevia* p. 63

9. Little Cuckoo *Piaya minuta* p. 62

10. Squirrel Cuckoo *Piaya cayana* p. 62

11. Black-bellied Cuckoo *Piaya melanogaster* p. 62

12. Greater Ani *Crotophaga major* p. 62

13. Groove-billed Ani *Crotophaga sulcirostris* p. 63

14. Smooth-billed Ani *Crotophaga ani* p. 62

15. Rufous-vented Ground-Cuckoo *Neomorphus geoffroyi* p. 63

16. Red-billed Ground-Cuckoo *Neomorphus pucheranii* p. 63

30

Plate 31

1. Ferruginous Pygmy-Owl *Glaucidium brasilianum* p. 67

2. Andean Pygmy-Owl *Glaucidium jardinii* p. 66

3. Oilbird *Steatornis caripensis* p. 68

4. White-throated Screech-Owl *Otus albogularis* p. 65

5. Rufescent Screech-Owl *Otus ingens* p. 64

6. Tropical Screech-Owl *Otus choliba* p. 64

7. Tawny-bellied Screech-Owl *Otus watsonii* p. 65

8. Burrowing Owl *Athene cunicularia* p. 67

9. Rufous-banded Owl *Ciccaba albitarsus* p. 66

10. Barn Owl *Tyto alba* p. 63

11. Mottled Owl *Ciccaba virgata* p. 65

12. Spectacled Owl *Pulsatrix perspicillata* p. 66

13. Band-bellied Owl *Pulsatrix melanota* p. 66

14. Magellanic Horned Owl *Bubo magellanicus* p. 65

31

Plate 32

1. Koepcke's Screech-Owl *Otus koepckeae* p. 64

2. Long-whiskered Owlet *Xenoglaux loweryi* p. 67

3. Peruvian Screech-Owl *Otus roboratus* p. 64
    a. *O. r. roboratus*   b. *O. r. pacificus*

4. Cinnamon Screech-Owl *Otus petersoni* p. 64

5. Cloud-forest Screech-Owl *Otus marshalli* p. 65

6. Peruvian Pygmy-Owl *Glaucidium peruanum* p. 67

7. Yungas Pygmy-Owl *Glaucidium bolivianum* p. 66

8. Subtropical Pygmy-Owl *Glaucidium parkeri* p. 67

9. Amazonian Pygmy-Owl *Glaucidium hardyi* p. 67

32

Plate 33

1. Great Horned Owl *Bubo virginianus* p. 65

2. Andean Potoo *Nyctibius maculosus* p. 68

3. Common Potoo *Nyctibius griseus* p. 68

4. Great Potoo *Nyctibius grandis* 68

5. Rufous Potoo *Nyctibius bracteatus* p. 69

6. Long-tailed Potoo *Nyctibius aethereus* p. 68

7. Crested Owl *Lophostrix cristata* p. 66

8. White-winged Potoo *Nyctibius leucopterus* p. 69

9. Buff-fronted Owl *Aegolius harrisii* p. 67

10. Vermiculated Screech-Owl *Otus vermiculatus* p. 65

11. Short-eared Owl *Asio flammeus* p. 68

12. Striped Owl *Asio clamator* p. 67

13. Stygian Owl *Asio stygius* p. 67

14. Black-banded Owl *Ciccaba huhula* p. 66

15. Black-and-white Owl *Ciccaba nigrolineata* p. 65

33

Plate 34

1. Lesser Nighthawk *Chordeiles acutipennis* p. 69

2. Common Nighthawk *Chordeiles minor* p. 69

3. Ladder-tailed Nightjar *Hydropsalis climacocerca* p. 71
   a. ♀   b. ♂

4. Short-tailed Nighthawk *Lurocalis semitorquatus* p. 69

5. Nacunda Nighthawk *Podager nacunda* p. 70

6. Rufous-bellied Nighthawk *Lurocalis rufiventris* p. 69

7. Band-tailed Nighthawk *Nyctiprogne leucopyga* p. 70

8. Scissor-tailed Nightjar *Hydropsalis torquata* p. 71
   a. ♂   b. ♀

9. Scrub Nightjar *Caprimulgus anthonyi* p. 71

10. Little Nightjar *Caprimulgus parvulus* p. 71

11. Sand-colored Nighthawk *Chordeiles rupestris* p. 69

34

Plate 35

1. Swallow-tailed Nightjar *Uropsalis segmentata* p. 71
    a. ♂   b. ♀

2. Band-winged Nightjar *Caprimulgus longirostris* p. 70

3. Lyre-tailed Nightjar *Uropsalis lyra* p. 71
    a. ♂   b. ♀

4. Silky-tailed Nightjar *Caprimulgus sericocaudatus* p. 70

5. Pauraque *Nyctidromus albicollis* p. 70
    a. Gray morph   b. Rufous morph

6. Blackish Nightjar *Caprimulgus nigrescens* p. 71
    a. ♂   b. ♀

7. Ocellated Poorwill *Nyctiphrynus ocellatus* p. 70

8. Spot-tailed Nightjar *Caprimulgus maculicaudus* p. 70
    a. ♂   b. ♀

9. Rufous Nightjar *Caprimulgus rufus* p. 70

35

Plate 36

1. White-collared Swift *Streptoprocne zonaris* p. 72

2. White-tipped Swift *Aeronautes montivagus* p. 73

3. Andean Swift *Aeronautes andecolus* p. 73

4. White-chested Swift *Cypseloides lemosi* p. 72

5. Lesser Swallow-tailed Swift *Panyptila cayennensis* p. 73

6. White-chinned Swift *Cypseloides cryptus* p. 72

7. Chestnut-collared Swift *Streptoprocne rutila* p. 72

8. Rothschild's Swift *Cypseloides rothschildi* p. 72

9. Fork-tailed Palm-Swift *Tachornis squamata* p. 73

10. Gray-rumped Swift *Chaetura cinereiventris* p. 72

11. Pale-rumped Swift *Chaetura egregia* p. 73

12. Short-tailed Swift *Chaetura brachyura* p. 73

13. Tumbes Swift *Chaetura ocypetes* p. 73

14. Chimney Swift *Chaetura pelagica* p. 73

15. Chapman's Swift *Chaetura chapmani* p. 73

36

Plate 37

1. Great-billed Hermit *Phaethornis malaris* p. 75

2. Green Hermit *Phaethornis guy* p. 74

3. Pale-tailed Barbthroat *Threnetes niger* p. 74

4. White-tipped Sicklebill *Eutoxeres aquila* p. 74

5. Western Long-tailed Hermit *Phaethornis longirostris* p. 74
    a. ♂   b. ♀

6. White-bearded Hermit *Phaethornis hispidus* p. 74

7. Tawny-bellied Hermit *Phaethornis syrmatophorus* p. 75

8. Rufous-breasted Hermit *Glaucis hirsuta* p. 74

9. Straight-billed Hermit *Phaethornis bourcieri* p. 75

10. Reddish Hermit *Phaethornis ruber* p. 75
    a. ♀   b. ♂

11. Gray-chinned Hermit *Phaethornis g. griseogularis* p. 75

12. Black-throated Hermit *Phaethornis atrimentalis* p. 75

13. Blue-fronted Lancebill *Doryfera johannae* p. 76
    a. ♂   b. ♀

14. Green-fronted Lancebill *Doryfera ludovicae* p. 76
    a. ♂   b. ♀

15. Gray-breasted Sabrewing *Campylopterus largipennis* p. 76

37

Plate 38

1. Needle-billed Hermit *Phaethornis philippii* p. 75

2. Koepcke's Hermit *Phaethornis koepckeae* p. 75

3. White-browed Hermit *Phaethornis stuarti* p. 75

4. Many-spotted Hummingbird *Leucippus hypostictus* p. 80

5. Olive-spotted Hummingbird *Leucippus chlorocercus* p. 79

6. Tumbes Hummingbird *Leucippus baeri* p. 79

7. Wire-crested Thorntail *Discosura popelairii* ♂ p. 78

8. Napo Sabrewing *Campylopterus villaviscensio* ♂ p. 76

9. Spot-throated Hummingbird *Leucippus taczanowskii* p. 79

10. Ecuadorian Piedtail *Phlogophilus hemileucurus* p. 81

11. Peruvian Piedtail *Phlogophilus harterti* p. 81

12. Amazilia Hummingbird *Amazilia amazilia* p. 80

13. White-bellied Hummingbird *Leucippus chionogaster* p. 79

14. Green-and-white Hummingbird *Leucippus viridicauda* p. 80

38

Plate 39

1. Violet-headed Hummingbird *Klais guimeti* p. 77
   a. ♂   b. ♀

2. Rufous-crested Coquette *Lophornis delattrei* p. 77
   a. ♂   b. ♀

3. Spangled Coquette *Lophornis stictolophus* ♂ p. 77

4. Festive Coquette *Lophornis chalybeus* p. 77
   a. ♂   b. ♀

5. Black-bellied Thorntail *Discosura langsdorffi* p. 78
   a. ♂   b. ♀

6. Blue-chinned Sapphire *Chlorostilbon notatus* ♂ p. 78

7. Green-crowned Woodnymph *Thalurania fannyi* ♂ p. 78

8. Blue-tailed Emerald *Chlorostilbon mellisugus* p. 78
   a. ♂   b. ♀

9. Fork-tailed Woodnymph *Thalurania furcata* p. 78
   a. *T. f. jelskii* ♂
   b. *T. f. jelskii* ♀
   c. *T. f. viridipectus* ♂

10. Violet-bellied Hummingbird *Damophila julie* p. 78
    a. ♂   b. ♀

11. Rufous-throated Sapphire *Hylocharis sapphirina* ♂ p. 78

12. White-chinned Sapphire *Hylocharis cyanus* p. 79
    a. ♂   b. ♀

13. Golden-tailed Sapphire *Chrysuronia oenone* p. 79
    a. *C. o. josephinae* ♂
    b. *C. o. oenone* ♀
    c. *C. o. oenone* ♂

14. Speckled Hummingbird *Adelomyia melanogenys* p. 81

39

Plate 40

1. Shining Sunbeam *Aglaeactis cupripennis* p. 82

2. Green-tailed Trainbearer *Lesbia nuna* ♂ p. 85

3. White-bellied Woodstar *Chaetocercus mulsant* ♂ p. 89

4. Sword-billed Hummingbird *Ensifera ensifera* p. 83

5. White-bellied Hummingbird *Leucippus chionogaster* p. 79

6. Sapphire-spangled Emerald *Polyerata lactea* ♂ p. 80

7. Rufous-capped Thornbill *Chalcostigma ruficeps* ♂ p. 87

8. Mountain Avocetbill *Opisthoprora euryptera* p. 87

9. Giant Hummingbird *Patagona gigas* p. 85

10. Andean Hillstar *Oreotrochilus estella* ♂ p. 82

11. Great Sapphirewing *Pterophanes cyanopterus* ♂ p. 83

12. White-necked Jacobin *Florisuga mellivora* ♂ p. 76

13. Swallow-tailed Hummingbird *Campylopterus macrourus* p. 76

14. Collared Inca *Coeligena torquata* p. 83

15. Buff-tailed Sicklebill *Eutoxeres condamini* p. 74

40

Plate 41

1. Green Violetear *Colibri thalassinus* p. 76

2. Brown Violetear *Colibri delphinae* p. 76

3. Sparkling Violetear *Colibri coruscans* p. 77

4. Green-breasted Mango *Anthracothorax prevostii* p. 77
    a. ♂   b. ♀

5. Fiery Topaz *Topaza pyra* p. 77
    a. ♀   b. ♂

6. Black-throated Mango *Anthracothorax nigricollis* p. 77
    a. ♀   b.. ♂

7. Green-tailed Goldenthroat *Polytmus theresiae* p. 79
    a. ♂   b. ♀

8. White-tailed Goldenthroat *Polytmus guainumbi* p. 79
    a. ♂   b. ♀

9. Glittering-throated Emerald *Polyerata fimbriata* p. 80
    a. ♂   b. ♀

10. Andean Emerald *Agyrtria franciae* p. 80
    a. ♂   b. ♀

11. "Ampay" Hummingbird *Leucippus sp.* p. 80

12. White-vented Plumeleteer *Chalybura buffonii* p. 81
    a. ♀   b. ♂

41

Plate 42

1. Black-throated Brilliant *Heliodoxa s. schreibersii* ♂ p. 81

2. Gould's Jewelfront *Heliodoxa aurescens* ♂ p. 81

3. Pink-throated Brilliant *Heliodoxa gularis* ♂ p. 81

4. Rufous-webbed Brilliant *Heliodoxa branickii* ♂ p. 82

5. Rainbow Starfrontlet *Coeligena i. iris* ♂ p. 83

6. White-tufted Sunbeam *Aglaeactis castelnaudii* p. 82

7. Violet-throated Starfrontlet *Coeligena violifer osculans* ♂ p. 83

8. Purple-throated Sunangel *Heliangelus viola* ♂ p. 84

9. Royal Sunangel *Heliangelus regalis* ♂ p. 84

10. Purple-backed Sunbeam *Aglaeactis aliciae* p. 82

11. Blue-mantled Thornbill *Chalcostigma stanleyi* ♂ p. 87

12. Olivaceous Thornbill *Chalcostigma olivaceum* p. 87

13. Bronze-tailed Comet *Polyonymus caroli* ♂ p. 86

14. Bearded Mountaineer *Oreonympha nobilis* ♂ p. 86

42

Plate 43

1. Fawn-breasted Brilliant *Heliodoxa rubinoides* ♂ p. 81

2. Violet-fronted Brilliant *Heliodoxa leadbeateri* p. 81
    a. ♂   b. ♀

3. Pink-throated Brilliant *Heliodoxa gularis* ♀ p. 81

4. Chestnut-breasted Coronet *Boissonneaua matthewsii* p. 82

5. White-tailed Hillstar *Urochroa bougueri* ♂ p. 82

6. Buff-winged Starfrontlet *Coeligena lutetiae* p. 83
    8a. ♂   8b. ♀

7. Black-breasted Hillstar *Oreotrochilus melanogaster* ♀ p. 82

8. Violet-throated Starfrontlet *Coeligena violifer* p. 83
    a. *C. v. dichroura* ♂
    b. *C. v. albicaudata* ♂
    c. *C. v. albicaudata* ♀

9. Green-headed Hillstar *Oreotrochilus stolzmanni* p. 82
    a. ♀   b. ♂

10. Rainbow Starfrontlet *Coeligena iris*
    a. *C. i. eva* ♂
    b. *C. i. aurora* ♀
    c. *C. i. aurora* ♂

11. Bronzy Inca *Coeligena coeligena* p. 83

12. Gould's Inca *Coeligena inca* p. 83

13. Mountain Velvetbreast *Lafresnaya lafresnayi* p. 83
    a. ♂   b. ♀

43

Plate 44

1. Amethyst-throated Sunangel *Heliangelus amethysticollis decolor* p. 84
   a. ♂   b. ♀

2. Little Sunangel *Heliangelus m. micraster* p. 84
   a. ♂   b. ♀

3. Glowing Puffleg *Eriocnemis vestitus* ♂ p. 84

4. Coppery-naped Puffleg *Eriocnemis sapphiropygia* p. 84
   a. ♂   b. ♀

5. Black-tailed Trainbearer *Lesbia victoriae juliae* p. 85
   a. ♂   b. ♀

6. Red-tailed Comet *Sappho sparganura* ♂ p. 85

7. Emerald-bellied Puffleg *Eriocnemis alinae* p. 84

8. Booted Racket-tail *Ocreatus underwoodii annae* p. 85
   a. ♂   b. ♀

9. Buff-thighed Puffleg *Haplophaedia assimilis* p. 85

10. Rufous-vented Whitetip *Urosticte ruficrissa* ♂ p. 85

11. Purple-bibbed Whitetip *Urosticte benjamini* p. 85
    a. ♂   b. ♀

44

Plate 45

1. Black Metaltail *Metallura phoebe* p. 87

2. Neblina Metaltail *Metallura odomae* ♂ p. 87

3. Fire-throated Metaltail *Metallura eupogon* ♂ p. 86

4. Coppery Metaltail *Metallura t. theresiae* ♂ p. 86

5. Scaled Metaltail *Metallura aeneocauda* ♂ p.86

6. Oasis Hummingbird *Rhodopis vesper* ♂ p.88

7. Marvelous Spatuletail *Loddigesia mirabilis* ♂ p. 88

8. Chilean Woodstar *Myrtis yarrellii* ♂ p. 89

9. Purple-collared Woodstar *Myrtis fanny* ♂ p. 89

10. Gray-bellied Comet *Taphrolesbia griseiventris* ♂ p. 87

11. Peruvian Sheartail *Thaumastura cora* ♂ p. 88

12. Little Woodstar *Chaetocercus bombus* ♂ p. 89

13. Black-breasted Hillstar *Oreotrochilus melanogaster* ♂ p. 82

14. Short-tailed Woodstar *Myrmia micrura* ♂ p. 89

45

Plate 46

1. Purple-backed Thornbill *Ramphomicron microrhynchum* p. 86
   a. ♂   b. ♀

2. Tyrian Metaltail *Metallura tyrianthina* p. 86
   a. *M. t. tyrianthina* ♂
   b. *M. t. tyrianthina* ♀
   c. *M. t. smaragdinicollis* ♂

3. Rainbow-bearded Thornbill *Chalcostigma herrani* p. 87
   a. ♂   b. ♀

4. Long-tailed Sylph *Aglaiocercus kingi* p. 88
   a. ♂   b. ♀

5. Scaled Metaltail *Metallura aeneocauda* ♂ p. 86

6. Long-billed Starthroat *Heliomaster longirostris* ♂ p. 88

7. Amethyst Woodstar *Calliphlox amethystina* p. 89
   a. ♂   b. ♀

8. Wedge-billed Hummingbird *Augastes geoffroyi* p. 88

9. Black-eared Fairy *Heliothryx aurita* p. 88

10. Oasis Hummingbird *Rhodopis vesper* p. 88
    a. ♂   b. ♀

11. Peruvian Sheartail *Thaumastura cora* ♀ p. 88

12. Purple-collared Woodstar *Myrtis fanny* ♀ p. 89

13. White-bellied Woodstar *Chaetocercus mulsant* ♀ p. 89

46

Plate 47

1. Golden-headed Quetzal *Pharomachrus auriceps* ♂   p. 90

2. Crested Quetzal *Pharomachrus antisianus* p. 90
   a. ♂   b. ♀

3. Pavonine Quetzal *Pharomachrus pavoninus* p. 91
   a. ♂   b. ♀

4. Collared Trogon *Trogon collaris* p. 90
   a. ♂   b. ♀

5. Masked Trogon *Trogon personatus* p. 90
   a. ♂   b. ♀

6. Black-tailed Trogon *Trogon melanurus* p. 90
   a. ♂   b. ♀

7. Blue-crowned Trogon *Trogon curucui* p. 90
   a. ♂   b. ♀

8. White-tailed Trogon *Trogon viridis* p. 89

9. Violaceous Trogon *Trogon violaceus* p. 90
   a. ♂   b. ♀

10. Black-throated Trogon *Trogon rufus* p. 90
    a. ♂   b. ♀

47

Plate 48

1. Highland Motmot *Momotus aequatorialis* p. 92

2. Blue-crowned Motmot *Momotus momota* p. 91

3. Rufous Motmot *Baryphthengus martii* p. 92

4. Broad-billed Motmot *Electron platyrhynchum* p. 92

5. Green Kingfisher *Chloroceryle americana* p. 91
    a. ♂   b. ♀

6. Green-and-rufous Kingfisher *Chloroceryle inda* ♀ p. 91

7. American Pygmy Kingfisher *Chloroceryle aenea* p. 91
    a. ♀   b. ♂

8. Amazon Kingfisher *Chloroceryle amazona* p. 91
    a. ♂   b. ♀

9. Ringed Kingfisher *Ceryle torquata* p. 91
    a. ♀   b. ♂

48

Plate 49

1. Gilded Barbet *Capito auratus* p. 96
   a. ♂   b. ♀

2. Lemon-throated Barbet *Eubucco r. richardsoni* p. 96
   a. ♂   b ♀

3. Scarlet-crowned Barbet *Capito aurovirens* p. 96
   a. ♂   b. ♀

4. Red-headed Barbet *Eubucco bourcierii* p. 96
   a. ♂   b. ♀

5. White-eared Jacamar *Galbalcyrhynchus leucotis* p. 92

6. Purplish Jacamar *Galbula chalcothorax* p. 93

7. White-chinned Jacamar *Galbula tombacea* p. 93

8. Brown Jacamar *Brachygalba lugubris* p. 92

9. Great Jacamar *Jacamerops aurea* ♂ p. 93

10. Paradise Jacamar *Galbula dea* p. 93

11. Coppery-chested Jacamar *Galbula pastazae* ♂ p. 93

12. Blue-cheeked Jacamar *Galbula cyanicollis* p. 92

13. Yellow-billed Jacamar *Galbula albirostris* ♂ p. 92

49

1a 1b
2a 2b
3a 3b
4a 4b
5
6
7
8
9
10
11
12
13

Plate 50

1. Swallow-wing *Chelidoptera tenebrosa* p. 96

2. Yellow-billed Nunbird *Monasa flavirostris* p. 95

3. White-fronted Nunbird *Monasa morphoeus* p. 95

4. Black-fronted Nunbird *Monasa nigrifrons* p. 95

5. White-necked Puffbird *Notharchus macrorhynchos* p. 93

6. Pied Puffbird *Notharchus tectus* p. 94

7. Brown-banded Puffbird *Notharchus ordii* p. 93

8. White-faced Nunbird *Hapaloptila castanea* p. 95

9. White-eared Puffbird *Nystalus chacuru* p. 94

10. Collared Puffbird *Bucco capensis* p. 94

11. Chestnut-capped Puffbird *Bucco macrodactylus* p. 94

12. Spotted Puffbird *Bucco tamatia* p. 94

13. White-chested Puffbird *Malacoptila fusca* p. 94

14. Black-streaked Puffbird *Malacoptila fulvogularis* p. 94

15. Rufous-necked Puffbird *Malacoptila rufa* p. 95

16. Lanceolated Monklet *Micromonacha lanceolata* p. 95

17. Rusty-breasted Nunlet *Nonnula rubecula* p. 95

18. Fulvous-chinned Nunlet *Nonnula sclateri* p. 95

19. Brown Nunlet *Nonnula brunnea* p. 95

50

Plate 51

1. Rufous-headed Woodpecker *Celeus spectabilis* ♂ p. 103

2. Scarlet-backed Woodpecker *Veniliornis callonotus* ♂ p. 101

3. Black-necked Woodpecker *Colaptes a. atricollis* ♂ p. 102

4. Semicollared Puffbird *Malacoptila semicincta* p. 94

5. Striolated Puffbird *Nystalus striolatus* p. 94

6. White-throated Jacamar *Brachygalba albogularis* p. 92

7. Rufous-capped Nunlet *Nonnula ruficapilla* p. 95

8. Purus Jacamar *Galbalcyrhynchus purusianus* p. 92

9. Bluish-fronted Jacamar *Galbula cyanescens* p. 93

51

Plate 52

1. Scarlet-hooded Barbet *Eubucco tucinkae* ♂ p. 97

2. Versicolored Barbet *Eubucco versicolor* ♂ p. 97

3. Scarlet-banded Barbet *Capito wallacei* ♂ p. 96

4. Bar-breasted Piculet *Picumnus aurifrons* ♂ p. 99

5. Plain-breasted Piculet *Picumnus castelnau* ♂ p. 100

6. Fine-barred Piculet *Picumnus subtilis* ♂ p. 100

7. Ocellated Piculet *Picumnus dorbygnianus* ♂ p. 100

8. Rufous-breasted Piculet *Picumnus rufiventris* ♂ p. 100

9. Speckle-chested Piculet *Picumnus steindachneri* ♂ p. 100

10. Olivaceous Piculet *Picumnus olivaceus* ♂ p. 100

11. Lafresnaye's Piculet *Picumnus lafresnayi* ♂ p. 99

12. Ecuadorian Piculet *Picumnus sclateri* ♂ p. 99

52

Plate 53

[handwritten: Black-throated Toucanet (split)]

1. Emerald Toucanet *Aulacorhynchus prasinus* p. 97

2. Chestnut-tipped Toucanet *Aulacorhynchus derbianus* p. 97

3. Blue-banded Toucanet *Aulacorhynchus coeruleicinctis* p. 97

4. Yellow-browed Toucanet *Aulacorhynchus huallagae* p. 97

5. Curl-crested Aracari *Pteroglossus beauharnaesii* p. 98

6. Pale-mandibled Aracari *Pteroglossus erythropygius* p. 98

7. Lettered Aracari *Pteroglossus inscriptus* p. 98

8. Ivory-billed Aracari *Pteroglossus azara* p. 98

9. Chestnut-eared Aracari *Pteroglossus castanotis* p. 98

10. Many-banded Aracari *Pteroglossus pluricinctus* p. 98

11. Golden-collared Toucanet *Selenidera reinwardtii* p. 99
    a. ♂   b. ♀

12. Brown-mandibled Aracari *Pteroglossus mariae* p. 98

53

Plate 54

1. Black-billed Mountain-Toucan *Andigena nigrirostris* p. 98

2. Toco Toucan *Ramphastos toco* p. 99

3. Hooded Mountain-Toucan *Andigena cucullata* p. 98

4. Gray-breasted Mountain-Toucan *Andigena hypoglauca* p. 98

5. Black-mandibled Toucan *Ramphastos ambiguus* p. 99

6. Yellow-ridged Toucan *Ramphastos culminatus* p. 99

7. Cuvier's Toucan *Ramphastos cuvieri* p. 99

54

Plate 55

1. Smoky-brown Woodpecker *Veniliornis fumigatus* ♂ p. 101

2. Little Woodpecker *Veniliornis passerinus* ♂ p. 101

3. Yellow-vented Woodpecker *Veniliornis dignus* ♂ p. 101

4. Red-rumped Woodpecker *Veniliornis kirkii* ♂ p. 101

5. Red-stained Woodpecker *Veniliornis affinis* ♂ p. 101

6. Golden-olive Woodpecker *Piculus rubiginosus chrysogaster* ♂ p. 102

7. Bar-bellied Woodpecker *Veniliornis nigriceps* ♂ p. 101

8. Yellow-throated Woodpecker *Piculus flavigula* ♂ p. 101

9. Golden-green Woodpecker *Piculus chrysochloros* p. 102
    a. ♀   b. ♂

10. White-fronted Woodpecker *Melanerpes cactorum* ♂ p. 100

11. White-throated Woodpecker *Piculus leucolaemus* p. 101
    a. ♀   b. ♂

12. Spot-breasted Woodpecker *Colaptes punctigula* ♂ p. 102

13. Yellow-tufted Woodpecker *Melanerpes cruentatus* ♂ p. 100

14. White Woodpecker *Melanerpes candidus* ♂ p. 100

15. Crimson-mantled Woodpecker *Piculus rivolii brevirostris* ♂ p. 102

55

Plate 56

1. Chestnut Woodpecker *Celeus elegans* ♂ p. 103

2. Cream-colored Woodpecker *Celeus flavus* ♂ p. 103

3. Ringed Woodpecker *Celeus torquatus* ♂ p. 103

4. Scaly-breasted Woodpecker *Celeus grammicus* ♂ p. 102

5. Lineated Woodpecker *Dryocopus lineatus* p. 103
   a. ♂   b. ♀

6. Guayaquil Woodpecker *Campephilus gayaquilensis* p. 103
   a. ♂   b. ♀

7. Crimson-crested Woodpecker *Campephilus melanoleucos* p. 103
   a. ♂   b. ♀

8. Crimson-bellied Woodpecker *Campephilus haematogaster* p. 103
   a. ♂   b. ♀

9. Powerful Woodpecker *Campephilus pollens* p. 103
   a. ♂   b. ♀

10. Red-necked Woodpecker *Campephilus rubricollis* p. 103
    a. ♂   b. ♀

11. Andean Flicker *Colaptes rupicola* ♂ p. 102

56

Plate 57

1. Thick-billed Miner *Geositta crassirostris* p. 104

2. Coastal Miner *Geositta peruviana* p. 104

3. Common Miner *Geositta cunicularia deserticolor* p. 104

4. Grayish Miner *Geositta maritima* p. 104

5. White-throated Earthcreeper *Upucerthia albigula* p. 105

6. Dark-winged Miner *Geositta saxicolina* p. 104

7. Striated Earthcreeper *Upucerthia serrana* p. 105

8. White-bellied Cinclodes *Cinclodes palliatus* p. 106

9. Peruvian Seaside Cinclodes *Cinclodes taczanowskii* p. 105

10. Royal Cinclodes *Cinclodes aricomae* p. 106

57

Plate 58

1. Lesser Hornero *Furnarius minor* p. 106

2. Pale-legged Hornero *Furnarius leucopus tricolor* p. 106

3. Common Thornbird *Phacellodomus rufifrons* p. 114

4. Plain Softtail *Phacellodomus fusciceps* p. 114

5. Streak-fronted Thornbird *Phacellodomus striaticeps* p. 114

6. Puna Canastero *Asthenes sclateri* p. 113

7. Many-striped Canastero *Asthenes flammulata* p. 113

8. Puna Miner *Geositta punensis* p. 104

9. Streak-backed Canastero *Asthenes wyatti* p. 113

10. Common Miner *Geositta cunicularia juninensis* p. 104

11. Slender-billed Miner *Geositta tenuirostris* p. 105

12. Cordilleran Canastero *Asthenes modesta proxima* p. 112

13. Bar-winged Cinclodes *Cinclodes fuscus longipennis* p. 105

14. White-winged Cinclodes *Cinclodes atacamensis* p. 106

15. Plain-breasted Earthcreeper *Upucerthia jelskii* p. 105

16. Scale-throated Earthcreeper *Upucerthia dumetaria* p. 105

17. Straight-billed Earthcreeper *Upucerthia ruficauda* p. 105

58

Plate 59

1. Canyon Canastero *Asthenes pudibunda* p. 112

2. Streak-throated Canastero *Asthenes humilis* p. 113

3. Rusty-fronted Canastero *Asthenes ottonis* p. 112

4. Dark-winged Canastero *Asthenes arequipae* p. 112

5. Cactus Canastero *Asthenes cactorum* p. 113

6. Pale-tailed Canastero *Asthenes huancavelicae* p. 112
    a. *A. h. usheri*
    b. Undescribed cinnamon-tailed race

7. Scribble-tailed Canastero *Asthenes maculicauda* p. 113

8. Junín Canastero *Asthenes virgata* p. 113

9. Line-fronted Canastero *Asthenes urubambensis* p. 113

59

Plate 60

1. Russet-bellied Spinetail *Synallaxis zimmeri* p. 107

2. Marcapata Spinetail *Cranioleuca marcapatae* p. 110

3. Creamy-crested Spinetail *Cranioleuca albicapilla albigula* p. 110

4. Marañón Spinetail *Synallaxis maranonica* p. 109

5 Light-crowned Spinetail *Cranioleuca albiceps* p. 110

6. Baron's Spinetail *Cranioleuca baroni* p. 110

7. Line-cheeked Spinetail *Cranioleuca antisiensis* p. 110

8. Blackish-headed Spinetail *Synallaxis tithys* p. 109

9. Great Spinetail *Siptornopsis hypochondriacus* p. 110

10. Necklaced Spinetail *Synallaxis stictothorax* p. 109

11. Chinchipe Spinetail *Synallaxis chinchipensis* p. 109

12. Apurímac Spinetail *Synallaxis courseni* p. 108

13. Cabanis' Spinetail *Synallaxis cabanisi* p. 108

60

Plate 61

1. Equatorial Graytail *Xenerpestes singularis* p. 114

2. Red-and-white Spinetail *Certhiaxis mustelina* p. 111

3. Yellow-chinned Spinetail *Certhiaxis cinnamomea* p. 111

4. Plain-mantled Tit-Spinetail *Leptasthenura aegithaloides grisescens* p. 107

5. White-browed Spinetail *Hellmayrea gularis* p. 110

6. Speckled Spinetail *Cranioleuca gutturata* p. 111

7. Parker's Spinetail *Cranioleuca vulpecula* p. 111

8. Ash-browed Spinetail *Cranioleuca curtata* p. 111

9. Rufous Spinetail *Synallaxis unirufa* p. 108

10. Ruddy Spinetail *Synallaxis rutilans* p. 109

11. Chestnut-throated Spinetail *Synallaxis cherriei* p. 109

12. Slaty Spinetail *Synallaxis brachyura* p. 108

13. Dusky Spinetail *Synallaxis moesta* p. 109

14. Dark-breasted Spinetail *Synallaxis albigularis* p. 108

15. Cinereous-breasted Spinetail *Synallaxis hypospodia* p. 108

16. Pale-breasted Spinetail *Synallaxis albescens* p. 108

17. Azara's Spinetail *Synallaxis azarae infumata* p. 108

18. White-bellied Spinetail *Synallaxis propinqua* p. 109

19. Plain-crowned Spinetail *Synallaxis gujanensis* p. 109

61

Plate 62

1. Streaked Tit-Spinetail *Leptasthenura striata* p. 107
    a. *L. s. albogularis*
    b. *L. s. superciliaris*
    c. *L. s. striata*

2. Rusty-crowned Tit-Spinetail *Leptasthenura pileata* p. 107
    a. *L. p. pileata*
    b. *L. p. cajabambae*

3. White-browed Tit-Spinetail *Leptasthenura xenothorax* p. 107

4. Andean Tit-Spinetail *Leptasthenura andicola peruviana* p. 106

5. Vilcabamba Thistletail *Schizoeaca vilcabambae* p. 112
    a. *S. v. vilcabambae*
    b. *S. v. ayacuchensis*

6. White-chinned Thistletail *Schizoeaca fuliginosa* p. 111
    a. *S. f. peruviana*
    b. *S. f. plengei*

7. Tawny Tit-Spinetail *Leptasthenura yanacensis* p. 107

8. Puna Thistletail *Schizoeaca h. helleri* p. 112

9. Eye-ringed Thistletail *Schizoeaca palpebralis* p. 111

10. Mouse-colored Thistletail *Schizoeaca griseomurina* p. 111

62

Plate 63

1. Streaked Xenops *Xenops rutilans* p. 115

2. Slender-billed Xenops *Xenops tenuirostris* p. 115

3. Streaked Tuftedcheek *Pseudocolaptes boissonneautii* p. 115

4. Pearled Treerunner *Margarornis squamiger* p. 115

5. Rufous-tailed Xenops *Xenops milleri* p. 115

6. Plain Xenops *Xenops minutus* p. 115

7. Spotted Barbtail *Premnoplex brunnescens* p. 115

8. Orange-fronted Plushcrown *Metopothrix aurantiacus* p. 114

9. Spectacled Prickletail *Siptornis striaticollis* p. 114

10. Wren-like Rushbird *Phleocryptes melanops* p. 107

11. Point-tailed Palmcreeper *Berlepschia rikeri* p. 116

12. Rusty-winged Barbtail *Premnornis guttuligera* p. 114

13. Gray-throated Leaftosser *Sclerurus albigularis* p. 119

14. Short-billed Leaftosser *Sclerurus rufigularis* p. 119

15. Tawny-throated Leaftosser *Sclerurus mexicanus* p. 119

16. Black-tailed Leaftosser *Sclerurus caudacutus* p. 119

17. Sharp-tailed Streamcreeper *Lochmias nematura* p. 119

63

Plate 64

1. Montane Foliage-gleaner *Anabacerthia striaticollis* p. 115

2. Chestnut-winged Hookbill *Ancistrops strigilatus* p. 117

3. Buff-browed Foliage-gleaner *Syndactyla rufosuperciliata* p. 116

4. Lineated Foliage-gleaner *Syndactyla subalaris* p. 116

5. Striped Woodhaunter *Hyloctistes subulatus* p. 117

6. Flammulated Treehunter *Thripadectes flammulatus* p. 116

7. Black-billed Treehunter *Thripadectes melanorhynchus* p. 116

8. Striped Treehunter *Thripadectes holostictus* p. 116

9. Ruddy Foliage-gleaner *Automolus rubiginosus moderatus* p. 119

10. Chestnut-crowned Foliage-gleaner *Automolus rufipileatus* p. 118

11. Olive-backed Foliage-gleaner *Automolus infuscatus* p. 118

12. Brown-rumped Foliage-gleaner *Automolus melanopezus* p. 118

13. Dusky-cheeked Foliage-gleaner *Automolus dorsalis* p. 118

14. Buff-throated Foliage-gleaner *Automolus ochrolaemus* p. 118

15. Buff-fronted Foliage-gleaner *Philydor rufus* p. 118

16. Chestnut-winged Foliage-gleaner *Philydor erythropterus* p. 117

17. Rufous-rumped Foliage-gleaner *Philydor erythrocercus lyra* p. 117

18. Rufous-tailed Foliage-gleaner *Philydor ruficaudatus* p. 117

19. Cinnamon-rumped Foliage-gleaner *Philydor pyrrhodes* p. 118

64

Plate 65

1. Greater Scythebill *Campylorhamphus pucherani* p. 123

2. Rufous-necked Foliage-gleaner *Syndactyla ruficollis* p. 116

3. Buff-throated Treehunter *Thripadectes scrutator* p. 116

4. Henna-hooded Foliage-gleaner *Hylocryptus erythrocephalus* p. 119

5. Chestnut-backed Thornbird *Phacellodomus dorsalis* p. 114

6. Tyrannine Woodcreeper *Dendrocincla tyrannina* p. 119

7. Peruvian Recurvebill *Simoxenops ucayalae* p. 117

8. Bay Hornero *Furnarius torridus* p. 106

9. Russet-mantled Softtail *Phacellodomus berlepschi* p. 115

65

Plate 66

1. Amazonian Barred-Woodcreeper *Dendrocolaptes certhia juruanus* p. 120

2. Bar-bellied Woodcreeper *Hylexetastes stresemanni* p. 120

3. Strong-billed Woodcreeper *Xiphocolaptes promeropirhynchus lineatocephalus* p. 120

4. Striped Woodcreeper *Xiphorhynchus obsoletus* p. 122

5. Elegant Woodcreeper *Xiphorhynchus elegans* p. 122

6. Buff-throated Woodcreeper *Xiphorhynchus guttatus* p. 122

7. Black-banded Woodcreeper *Dendrocolaptes picumnus* p. 120

8. Ocellated Woodcreeper *Xiphorhynchus ocellatus brevirostris* p. 122

9. Zimmer's Woodcreeper *Xiphorhynchus necopinus* p. 122

10. Straight-billed Woodcreeper *Xiphorhynchus picus* p. 122

11. Long-tailed Woodcreeper *Deconychura longicauda pallida* p. 120

12. Spot-throated Woodcreeper *Deconychura stictolaema* p. 120

66

Plate 67

1. Cinnamon-throated Woodcreeper *Dendrexetastes rufigula* p. 120

2. Montane Woodcreeper *Lepidocolaptes lacrymiger carabayae* p. 123

3. Olive-backed Woodcreeper *Xiphorhynchus triangularis* p. 122

4. Long-billed Woodcreeper *Nasica longirostris* p. 120

5. Wedge-billed Woodcreeper *Glyphorynchus spirurus albigularis* p. 121

6. Lineated Woodcreeper *Lepidocolaptes albolineatus* p. 123

7. Curve-billed Scythebill *Campylorhamphus procurvoides* p. 123

8. Streak-headed Woodcreeper *Lepidocolaptes souleyetii* p. 123

9. Olivaceous Woodcreeper *Sittasomus griseicapillus aequatorialis* p. 120

10. Plain-brown Woodcreeper *Dendrocincla fuliginosa* p. 120

11. White-chinned Woodcreeper *Dendrocincla merula* p. 120

12. Brown-billed Scythebill *Campylorhamphus pusillus* p. 123

13. Red-billed Scythebill *Campylorhamphus trochilirostris napensis* p. 123

67

Plate 68

1. Black-crested Antshrike *Sakesphorus canadensis* p. 124
   a. ♀   b. ♂

2. Rufous-capped Antshrike *Thamnophilus ruficapillus jaczewskii* p. 126
   a. ♀   b. ♂

3. Russet Antshrike *Thamnistes anabatinus* p. 127

4. Fasciated Antshrike *Cymbilaimus lineatus* p. 124
   a. ♀   b. ♂

5. Pearly Antshrike *Megastictus margaritatus* ♂ p. 127

6. Black Bushbird *Neoctantes niger* ♀ p. 127

7. Barred Antshrike *Thamnophilus doliatus* p. 124
   a. ♀   b. ♂

8. Lined Antshrike *Thamnophilus tenuepunctatus* p. 125
   a. ♂   b. ♀

9. Great Antshrike *Taraba major* p. 124
   a. ♀   b. ♂

10. Undulated Antshrike *Frederickena unduligera* ♂ p. 124

68

Plate 69

1. White-lined Antbird *Percnostola lophotes* ♂   p. 136

2. Manu Antbird *Cercomacra manu* ♂   p. 134

3. Rufous-capped Antshrike *Thamnophilus ruficapillus marcapatae* ♂   p. 126

4. Striated Antbird *Drymophila devillei* ♂   p. 132

5. Dot-winged Antwren *Microrhopias quixensis albicauda* ♀   p. 132

6. Hairy-crested Antbird *Rhegmatorhina melanosticta brunneiceps* ♀   p. 138

7. Bamboo Antshrike *Cymbilaimus sanctaemariae* ♂   p. 124

8. Lunulated Antbird *Gymnopithys lunulata*   p. 137
   a. ♂   b. ♀

9. Slaty Gnateater *Conopophaga ardesiaca* ♂   p. 143

10. Goeldi's Antbird *Myrmeciza goeldii* ♂   p. 136

11. Amazonian Antbird *Percnostola minor* ♀   p. 136

12. Rufous-fronted Antthrush *Formicarius rufifrons*   p. 139

69

Plate 70

1. Variable Antshrike *Thamnophilus caerulescens* p. 126
   a. ♀   b. ♂

2. Spot-winged Antshrike *Pygiptila stellaris* p. 126
   a. ♂   b. ♀

3. Plain-winged Antshrike *Thamnophilus schistaceus* ♂ p. 125

4. White-shouldered Antshrike *Thamnophilus aethiops kapouni* p. 125
   a. ♂   b. ♀

5. Western Slaty-Antshrike *Thamnophilus atrinucha* ♂ p. 126

6. Amazonian Antshrike *Thamnophilus amazonicus* p. 126
   a. ♂   b. ♀

7. Bluish-slate Antshrike *Thamnomanes schistogynus* p. 128
   a. ♀   b. ♂

8. Cinereous Antshrike *Thamnomanes caesius* p. 128
   a. ♀   b. ♂

9. Uniform Antshrike *Thamnophilus unicolor* p. 125
   a. ♂   b. ♀

10. Dusky-throated Antshrike *Thamnomanes ardesiacus* p. 128
    a. ♂   b. ♀

11. Saturnine Antshrike *Thamnomanes saturninus* ♂ p. 127

12. Mouse-colored Antshrike *Thamnophilus murinus* p. 125
    a. ♂   b. ♀

70

Plate 71

1. Collared Antshrike *Sakesphorus bernardi* ♂   p. 124

2. Chapman's Antshrike *Thamnophilus zarumae* ♂   p. 124

3. Bluish-slate Antshrike *Thamnomanes schistogynus* ♀   p. 128

4. Upland Antshrike *Thamnophilus aroyae* ♂   p. 125

5. Chestnut-backed Antshrike *Thamnophilus palliatus* ♂   p. 125

6. Gray-headed Antbird *Myrmeciza griseiceps* ♂   p. 137

7. Marañón Slaty-Antshrike *Thamnophilus leucogaster* ♂   p. 126
    a. *T. l. leucogaster*   b. *T. l. huallagae*

8. Black-tailed Antbird *Myrmoborus melanurus* ♂   p. 135

9. Castelnau's Antshrike *Thamnophilus cryptoleucus* ♂   p. 125

10. Marañón Crescent-chest *Melanopareia maranonica*   p. 144

71

Plate 72

1. White-streaked Antvireo *Dysithamnus leucostictus* ♀ p. 127

2. Pygmy Antwren *Myrmotherula brachyura* ♂ p. 128

3. Short-billed Antwren *Myrmotherula obscura* ♂ p. 128

4. Plain Antvireo *Dysithamnus mentalis* p. 127
   a. ♀   b. ♂

5. Amazonian-Streaked Antwren *Myrmotherula multostriata* p. 129
   a. ♂   b. ♀

6. White-flanked Antwren *Myrmotherula axillaris* p. 130
   a. ♂   b. ♀

7. Cherrie's Antwren *Myrmotherula cherriei* ♂ p. 129

8. Stripe-chested Antwren *Myrmotherula longicauda* p. 129
   a. ♂   b. ♀

9. Slaty Antwren *Myrmotherula schisticolor* p. 130
   a. ♀   b. ♂

10. White-eyed Antwren *Myrmotherula leucophthalma* ♂ p. 129

11. Long-winged Antwren *Myrmotherula longipennis* ♂ p. 131

12. Plain-throated Antwren *Myrmotherula hauxwelli* ♂ p. 129

13. Gray Antwren *Myrmotherula menetriesii* p. 131
    a. ♂   b. ♀

14. Rufous-tailed Antwren *Myrmotherula erythrura* ♂ p. 130

15. Leaden Antwren *Myrmotherula assimilis* ♂ p. 131

72

Plate 73

1. Ash-throated Antwren *Herpsilochmus parkeri* ♂ p. 131

2. Yellow-rumped Antwren *Terenura sharpei* ♂ p. 133

3. Dugand's Antwren *Herpsilochmus dugandi* ♂ p. 132

4. Ancient Antwren *Herpsilochmus gentryi* ♂ p. 132

5. Sclater's Antwren *Myrmotherula sclateri* ♂ p. 129

6. Creamy-bellied Antwren *Herpsilochmus motacilloides* ♂ p. 132

7. Foothill Antwren *Myrmotherula spodionota* ♂ p. 130

8. Ihering's Antwren *Myrmotherula iheringi* ♂ p. 131

9. Rio Suno Antwren *Myrmotherula sunensis* ♂ p. 130

10. Brown-backed Antwren *Myrmotherula fjeldsaai* ♂ p. 129

11. Ornate Antwren *Myrmotherula ornata atrogularis* ♂ p. 130

12. White-eyed Antwren *Myrmotherula leucophthalma* ♂ p. 129

13. Stipple-throated Antwren *Myrmotherula haematonota* ♂ p. 130

73

Plate 74

1. Rufous-winged Antwren *Herpsilochmus rufimarginatus* p. 132
    a. ♀   b. ♂

2. Yellow-breasted Antwren *Herpsilochmus axillaris* p. 132
    a. ♂   b. ♀

3. Rusty-backed Antwren *Formicivora rufa* p. 132
    a. ♀   b. ♂

4. Rufous-rumped Antwren *Terenura callinota* ♂ p. 133

5. Chestnut-shouldered Antwren *Terenura humeralis* ♂ p. 133

6. Long-tailed Antbird *Drymophila caudata* p. 133

7. Yellow-browed Antbird *Hypocnemis hypoxantha* p. 135

8. Black-and-white Antbird *Myrmochanes hemileucus* p. 135

9. Warbling Antbird *Hypocnemis cantator* p. 135
    a. *H. c. subflava*   b. *H. c. peruviana*

10. Black-chinned Antbird *Hypocnemoides melanopogon* p. 135
    a. ♀   b. ♂

11. Band-tailed Antbird *Hypocnemoides maculicauda* ♂ p. 135

12. Spot-winged Antbird *Percnostola leucostigma* p. 136
    a. ♂   b. ♀

13. Slate-colored Antbird *Percnostola schistacea* p. 136
    a. ♀   b. ♂

74

Plate 75

1. Gray Antbird *Cercomacra cinerascens* p. 133
     a. ♂ b. ♀

2. Black Antbird *Cercomacra serva* p. 134
     a. ♀ b. ♂

3. Blackish Antbird *Cercomacra nigrescens* ♀ p. 133

4. Black-throated Antbird *Myrmeciza atrothorax* p. 137
     a. ♀ b. ♂

5. Chestnut-tailed Antbird *Myrmeciza hemimelaena* ♂ p. 136

6. Sooty Antbird *Myrmeciza fortis* p. 137
     a. ♂ b. ♀

7. White-lined Antbird *Percnostola lophotes* p. 136
     a. ♀ b. ♂

8. Plumbeous Antbird *Myrmeciza hyperythra* p. 136
     a. ♂ b. ♀

9. White-shouldered Antbird *Myrmeciza melanoceps* p. 136
     a. ♀ b. ♂

10. Goeldi's Antbird *Myrmeciza goeldii* p. 136
     a. ♀ b. ♂

11. White-backed Fire-eye *Pyriglena leuconota* p. 134
     a. *P. l. marcapatensis* ♀
     b. *P. l. picea* ♀
     c. ♂ all subspecies

75

Plate 76

1. Banded Antbird *Dichrozona cincta* p. 131

2. Spot-backed Antbird *Hylophylax naevia* ♂ p. 138

3. Dot-backed Antbird *Hylophylax punctulata* ♂ p. 138

4. Scale-backed Antbird *Hylophylax poecilinota lepidonota* p. 138
    a. ♂   b. ♀

5. Ash-breasted Antbird *Myrmoborus lugubris* p. 134
    a. ♂   b. ♀

6. Bicolored Antbird *Gymnopithys leucaspis* ♂ p. 137

7. Black-faced Antbird *Myrmoborus myotherinus* p. 134
    a. ♂   b. ♀

8. White-throated Antbird *Gymnopithys salvini* p. 138
    a. ♂   b. ♀

9. White-browed Antbird *Myrmoborus leucophrys* p. 134
    a. ♂   b. ♀

10. Silvered Antbird *Sclateria naevia* p. 135

76

Plate 77

1. Reddish-winged Bare-eye *Phlegopsis erythroptera* ♂ p. 138

2. Black-spotted Bare-eye *Phlegopsis nigromaculata* p. 138

3. Barred Antthrush *Chamaeza mollissima* p. 139

4. Wing-banded Antbird *Myrmornis torquata* ♂ p. 138

5. White-plumed Antbird *Pithys albifrons* p. 137

6. Black-faced Antthrush *Formicarius analis* p. 139

7. Rufous-capped Antthrush *Formicarius colma* p. 139

8. Rufous-breasted Antthrush *Formicarius rufipectus* p. 139

9. Striated Antthrush *Chamaeza nobilis* p. 139

10. Short-tailed Antthrush *Chamaeza campanisona* p. 139

11. Rufous-fronted Antthrush *Formicarius rufifrons* p. 139

12. White-masked Antbird *Pithys castanea* p. 137

77

Plate 78

1. White-bellied Antpitta *Grallaria hypoleuca* p. 141

2. White-lored Antpitta *Hylopezus fulviventris* p. 142

3. Slate-crowned Antpitta *Grallaricula nana* p. 143

4. Chestnut-crowned Antpitta *Grallaria ruficapilla* p. 140

5. Thrush-like Antpitta *Myrmothera campanisona* p. 142

6. Spotted Antpitta *Hylopezus macularius* p. 142

7. Scaled Antpitta *Grallaria guatimalensis* p. 140

8. Tawny Antpitta *Grallaria quitensis* p. 142

9. Ochre-striped Antpitta *Grallaria dignissima* p. 140

10. White-throated Antpitta *Grallaria albigula* p. 141

11. Variegated Antpitta *Grallaria varia* p. 140

12. Undulated Antpitta *Grallaria squamigera* p. 140

13. Chestnut-naped Antpitta *Grallaria nuchalis* p. 141

14. Jocotoco Antpitta *Grallaria ridgelyi* p. 141

78

Plate 79

1. Pale-billed Antpitta *Grallaria carrikeri* p. 141

2. Bay Antpitta *Grallaria capitalis* p. 141

3. Rufous Antpitta *Grallaria rufula* p. 141
    a. *G. r. occabambae*   b. *G. r. cajamarcae*

4. Chestnut Antpitta *Grallaria blakei* p. 142

5. Red-and-white Antpitta *Grallaria erythroleuca* p. 141

6. Rusty-tinged Antpitta *Grallaria przewalskii* p. 141

7. Watkins' Antpitta *Grallaria watkinsi* p. 140

8. Amazonian Antpitta *Hylopezus berlepschi* p. 142

9. Ochre-fronted Antpitta *Grallaricula ochraceifrons* ♂ p. 143

10. Stripe-headed Antpitta *Grallaria andicola* p. 140

11. Peruvian Antpitta *Grallaricula peruviana* ♂ p. 143

12. Ochre-breasted Antpitta *Grallaricula flavirostris boliviana* p. 142

13. Rusty-breasted Antpitta *Grallaricula ferrugineipectus leymebambae* p. 142

14. Elusive Antpitta *Grallaria eludens* p. 140

79

Plate 80

1. Chestnut-crowned Gnateater *Conopophaga castaneiceps* ♂ p. 143

2. Ash-throated Gnateater *Conopophaga peruviana* p. 143
   a. ♂   b. ♀
3. Elegant Crescentchest *Melanopareia elegans* ♂ p. 144

4. Chestnut-belted Gnateater *Conopophaga aurita* ♂ p. 143

5. Rusty-belted Tapaculo *Liosceles thoracicus* p. 144

6. Unicolored Tapaculo *Scytalopus unicolor* p. 144
   a. Juvenile   b. ♀   c. ♂
   Also: Blackish Tapaculo *Scytalopus latrans* p. 144
   Trilling Tapaculo *Scytalopus parvirostris* p. 145
   Páramo Tapaculo *Scytalopus canus* 146

7. Ash-colored Tapaculo *Myornis senilis* p. 144

8. Ancash Tapaculo *Scytalopus affinis* p. 146

9. Large-footed Tapaculo *Scytalopus macropus* p. 145

10. Rufous-vented Tapaculo *Scytalopus femoralis* p. 145
    Also: Long-tailed Tapaculo *Scytalopus micropterus* p. 145
    Chusquea Tapaculo *Scytalopus parkeri* p. 146

11. Vilcabamba Tapaculo *Scytalopus urubambae* p. 145

12. Tschudi's Tapaculo *Scytalopus acutirostris* p. 146
    Also: Puna Tapaculo *Scytalopus simonsi* p. 145
    Neblina Tapaculo Scytalopus altirostris p. 145

13. Diademed Tapaculo *Scytalopus schulenbergi* p. 146

14. White-crowned Tapaculo *Scytalopus atratus* p. 145
    Also: Bolivian Tapaculo *Scytalopus bolivianus* p. 145

13. Ocellated Tapaculo *Acropternis orthonyx* p. 146

80

Plate 81

1. Shrike-like Cotinga *Laniisoma elegans* ♂ p. 147

2. Fiery-throated Fruiteater *Pipreola chlorolepidota* p. 148
    a. ♀   b. ♂

3. White-browed Purpletuft *Iodopleura isabellae* ♂ p. 149

4. Scarlet-breasted Fruiteater *Pipreola f. frontalis* p. 148
    a. ♀   b. ♂

5. Masked Fruiteater *Pipreola pulchra* p. 148
    a. ♂   b. ♀

6. Black-chested Fruiteater *Pipreola lubomirskii* ♂ p. 148

7. Green-and-black Fruiteater *Pipreola riefferii* p. 148
    a. *P. r. tallmanorum* ♂
    b. *P. r. chachapoyas* ♂
    c. *P. r. chachapoyas* ♀

8. Scaled Fruiteater *Ampelioides tschudii* p. 148
    a. ♀   b. ♂

9. Barred Fruiteater *Pipreola arcuata* ♂ p. 148

10. Band-tailed Fruiteater *Pipreola intermedia* ♂ p. 148

81

Plate 82

1. Spangled Cotinga *Cotinga cayana* p. 159
    a. ♀   b. ♂

2. Plum-throated Cotinga *Cotinga maynana* ♂ p. 149

3. Purple-throated Cotinga *Porphyrolaema porphyrolaema* p. 149
    a. ♂   b. ♀

4. Purple-breasted Cotinga *Cotinga cotinga.* ♂ p. 149

5. Pompadour Cotinga *Xipholena punicea* p. 150
    a. ♀   b. ♂

6. Peruvian Plantcutter *Phytotoma raimondii* p. 146
    a. ♀   b. ♂

7. Chestnut-crested Cotinga *Ampelion rufaxilla* p. 147

8. White-cheeked Cotinga *Zaratornis stresemanni* p. 147

9. Red-crested Cotinga *Ampelion rubrocristata* p. 147

10. Chestnut-bellied Cotinga *Doliornis remseni* ♂ p. 147

11. Bay-vented Cotinga *Doliornis sclateri* p. 147

12. Black-faced Cotinga *Conioptilon mcilhennyi* p. 150

82

Plate 83

1. Cinereous Mourner *Laniocera hypopyrra* p. 147

2. Gray-tailed Piha *Lipaugus subalaris* p. 149

3. Scimitar-winged Piha *Lipaugus uropygialis* p. 149

4. Screaming Piha *Lipaugus vociferans* p. 149

5. Dusky Piha *Lipaugus fuscocinereus*p. p. 149

6. Olivaceous Piha *Lipaugus cryptolophus* p. p. 149

7. Grayish Mourner *Rhytipterna simplex* p. 179

8. Purple-throated Fruitcrow *Querula purpurata* ♂ p. 150

9. Andean Cock-of-the-rock *Rupicola peruviana* p. 150
   a. ♀   b. ♂

10. Black-necked Red Cotinga *Phoenicircus nigricollis* p. 147
    a. ♂   b. ♀

11. Amazonian Umbrellabird *Cephalopterus ornatus* ♂ p. 150

12. Red-ruffed Fruitcrow *Pyroderus scutatus* p. 150

13. Bare-necked Fruitcrow *Gymnoderus foetidus* ♂ p. 150

83

Plate 84

1. Jet Manakin *Chloropipo unicolor* ♂ p. 151

2. Sulphur-bellied Tyrant-Manakin *Neopelma sulphureiventer* p. 153

3. Flame-crested Manakin *Heterocercus linteatus* ♂ p. 153

4. Orange-crested Manakin *Heterocercus aurantiivertex* ♂ p. 153

5. Fiery-capped Manakin *Machaeropterus pyrocephalus* ♂ p. 152

6. Yungas Manakin *Chiroxiphia boliviana* ♂ p. 151

7. Blue-backed Manakin *Chiroxiphia pareola regina* ♂ p. 151

8. Blue-crowned Manakin *Pipra coronata exquisita* ♂ p. 152

9. Blue-rumped Manakin *Pipra isidorei leucopygia* ♂ p. 152

10. Cerulean-capped Manakin *Pipra coeruleocapilla* p. 152
    a. ♂   b. ♀

11. Red-headed Manakin *Pipra rubrocapilla* ♂ p. 152

12. Round-tailed Manakin *Pipra chloromeros* ♂ p. 152

13. Band-tailed Manakin *Pipra fasciicauda* ♂ p. 151

84

Plate 85

1. Green Manakin *Chloropipo holochlora* p. 151

2. White-bearded Manakin *Manacus manacus* p. 151
   a. ♂   b. ♀

3. Wire-tailed Manakin *Pipra filicauda* p. 151
   a. ♂   b. ♀

4. White-crowned Manakin *Pipra pipra* p. 151
   a. ♂   b. ♀

5. Golden-headed Manakin *Pipra erythrocephala* p. 152
   a. ♂   b. ♀

6. Band-tailed Manakin *Pipra fasciicauda* p. 151
   a. ♂   b. ♀

7. Blue-crowned Manakin *Pipra coronata coronata* p. 152
   a. ♀   b. ♂

8. Round-tailed Manakin *Pipra chloromeros* p. 152
   a. ♀   b. ♂

9. Blue-backed Manakin *Chiroxiphia pareola napensis* p. 151
   a. ♂   b. ♀

10. Golden-winged Manakin *Masius chrysopterus* ♂ p. 152

11. Striped Manakin *Machaeropterus regulus* p. 152
    a. ♂   b. ♀

12. Saffron-crested Tyrant-Manakin *Neopelma chrysocephalum* p. 153

13. Wing-barred Piprites *Piprites chloris* p. 153

14. Dwarf Tyrant-Manakin *Tyranneutes stolzmanni* p. 153

15. Black Manakin *Xenopipo atronitens* p. 153
    a. ♀   b. ♂

85

Plate 86

1. Mouse-colored Tyrannulet *Phaeomyias murina wagae* p. 154
2. Southern Beardless-Tyrannulet *Camptostoma obsoletum* p. 154
3. White-lored Tyrannulet *Ornithion inerme* p. 154
4. Yellow-crowned Tyrannulet *Tyrannulus elatus* p. 154
5. Yellow Tyrannulet *Capsiempis flaveola* p. 154
6. Torrent Tyrannulet *Serpophaga cinerea* p. 157
7. Rufous-tailed Flatbill *Ramphotrigon ruficauda* p. 167
8. Olivaceous Flatbill *Rhynchocyclus olivaceus* p. 167
9. Yellow-breasted Flycatcher *Tolmomyias flaviventris* p. 168
10. Fulvous-breasted Flatbill *Rhynchocyclus fulvipectus* p. 167
11. Yellow-margined Flycatcher *Tolmomyias assimilis* p. 167
12. Yellow-olive Flycatcher *Tolmomyias sulphurescens* p. 167
13. Gray-crowned Flycatcher *Tolmomyias poliocephalus* p. 168
14. Plain-crested Elaenia *Elaenia cristata* p. 156
15. Gray Elaenia *Myiopagis caniceps* ♂ p. 155
16. Foothill Elaenia *Myiopagis olallai* p. 154
17. White-crested Elaenia *Elaenia albiceps chilensis* p. 156
18. Greenish Elaenia *Myiopagis viridicata* p. 155
19. Forest Elaenia *Myiopagis gaimardii* p. 154
20. Ringed Antpipit *Corythopis torquata* p. 166
21. Mottle-backed Elaenia *Elaenia gigas* p. 156
22. Brownish Flycatcher *Cnipodectes subbrunneus* p. 166
23. Amazonian Royal-Flycatcher *Onychorhynchus coronatus* p. 168
24. Pacific Royal-Flycatcher *Onychorhynchus occidentalis* p. 168

86

Plate 87

1. Rufous-winged Tyrannulet *Mecocerculus calopterus* p. 162

2. White-tailed Tyrannulet *Mecocerculus poecilocercus* p. 161

3. Sulphur-bellied Tyrannulet *Mecocerculus minor* p. 162

4. White-throated Tyrannulet *Mecocerculus leucophrys* p. 161

5. Sooty-headed Tyrannulet *Phyllomyias griseiceps* p. 160

6. White-banded Tyrannulet *Mecocerculus stictopterus* p. 162

7. Ashy-headed Tyrannulet *Phyllomyias cinereiceps* p. 160

8. Black-capped Tyrannulet *Phyllomyias nigrocapillus* p. 160

9. Plumbeous-crowned Tyrannulet *Phyllomyias plumbeiceps* p. 160

10. Tawny-rumped Tyrannulet *Phyllomyias uropygialis* p. 160

11. Golden-faced Tyrannulet *Zimmerius chrysops* p. 161

12. Mishana Tyrannulet *Zimmerius villarejoi* p. 161

13. Variegated Bristle-Tyrant *Phylloscartes poecilotis* p. 159

14. Marble-faced Bristle-Tyrant *Phylloscartes ophthalmicus* p. 158

15. Rufous-breasted Flycatcher *Leptopogon rufipectus* p. 157

16. Slender-footed Tyrannulet *Zimmerius gracilipes* p. 161

17. Sepia-capped Flycatcher *Leptopogon amaurocephalus* p. 158

18. Amazonian Scrub-Flycatcher *Sublegatus obscurior* p. 161

19. Southern Scrub-Flycatcher *Sublegatus modestus* p. 161

20. Rufous-headed Pygmy-Tyrant *Pseudotriccus ruficeps* p. 158

21. Slaty-capped Flycatcher *Leptopogon superciliaris* p. 158

22. Ochre-bellied Flycatcher *Mionectes oleagineus* p. 157

23. Olive-striped Flycatcher *Mionectes olivaceus* p. 157

24. Streak-necked Flycatcher *Mionectes striaticollis* p. 157

87

Plate 88

1. Spectacled Bristle-Tyrant *Phylloscartes orbitalis* p. 158

2. McConnell's Flycatcher *Mionectes macconnelli* p. 157

3. Dusky-tailed Flatbill *Ramphotrigon fuscicauda* p. 167

4. Plain Tyrannulet *Inezia inornata* p. 162

5. Yellow-crowned Elaenia *Myiopagis flavivertex* p. 155

6. Citron-bellied Attila *Attila citriniventris* p. 178

7. River Tyrannulet *Serpophaga hypoleuca* p. 157

8. Large-headed Flatbill *Ramphotrigon megacephala* p. 167

9. White-fronted Tyrannulet *Phyllomyias zeledoni* p. 159

10. Euler's Flycatcher *Lathrotriccus euleri* p. 171

11. Mottle-cheeked Tyrannulet *Phylloscartes ventralis* p. 159

12. Ecuadorian Tyrannulet *Phylloscartes gualaquizae* p. 159

13. Sclater's Tyrannulet *Phyllomyias sclateri* p. 159

14. Buff-banded Tyrannulet *Mecocerculus hellmayri* p. 162

15. Orange-eyed Flycatcher *Tolmomyias traylori* p. 168

16. Rufous-browed Tyrannulet *Phylloscartes superciliaris* p. 159

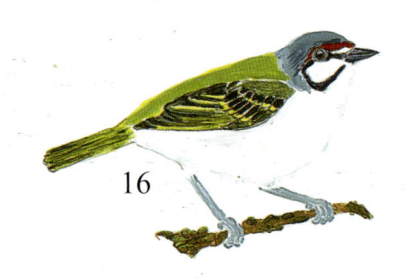

88

Plate 89

1. White-bellied Pygmy-Tyrant *Myiornis albiventris* p. 163

2. Johannes' Tody-Tyrant *Hemitriccus iohannis* p. 165

3. Long-crested Pygmy-Tyrant *Lophotriccus eulophotes* p. 164

4. Flammulated Bamboo-Tyrant *Hemitriccus flammulatus* p. 164

5. Cinnamon-breasted Tody-Tyrant *Hemitriccus cinnamomeipectus* p. 165

6. Buff-throated Tody-Tyrant *Hemitriccus rufigularis* p. 165

7. Ochre-faced Tody-Flycatcher *Todirostrum plumbeiceps* p. 166

8. Lulu's Tody-Tyrant *Poecilotriccus luluae* p. 164

9. Black-backed Tody-Flycatcher *Todirostrum pulchellum* ♂ p. 166

10. Hazel-fronted Pygmy-Tyrant *Pseudotriccus simplex* p. 158

11. Black-and-white Tody-Tyrant *Poecilotriccus capitalis* ♂ p. 164

12. White-cheeked Tody-Tyrant *Poecilotriccus albifacies* p. 164

13. Golden-winged Tody-Flycatcher *Todirostrum calopterum* p. 166

14. Rufous-crowned Tody-Tyrant *Poecilotriccus ruficeps* p. 164

89

Plate 90

1. Zimmer's Tody-Tyrant *Hemitriccus minimus* p. 165

2. Spotted Tody-Flycatcher *Todirostrum maculatum* p. 166

3. Yellow-browed Tody-Flycatcher *Todirostrum chrysocrotaphum* p. 166
    a. *T. c. neglectum*   b. *T. c. chrysocrotaphum*

4. Common Tody-Flycatcher *Todirostrum cinereum* p. 166

5. White-eyed Tody-Tyrant *Hemitriccus zosterops* p. 165
    a. *H. z. flaviviridis*   b. *H. z. griseipectus*

6. Black-throated Tody-Tyrant *Hemitriccus granadensis* p. 165

7. Rusty-fronted Tody-Flycatcher *Todirostrum latirostre* p. 166

8. Pearly-vented Tody-Tyrant *Hemitriccus margaritaceiventer* p. 165

9. Stripe-necked Tody-Tyrant *Hemitriccus striaticollis* p. 165

10. White-throated Spadebill *Platyrinchus mystaceus* p. 168

11. Golden-crowned Spadebill *Platyrinchus coronatus* p. 168

12. Lesser Wagtail-Tyrant *Stigmatura napensis* p. 162

13. Cinnamon-crested Spadebill *Platyrinchus saturatus* p. 168

14. Yellow-throated Spadebill *Platyrinchus flavigularis* p. 168

15. White-crested Spadebill *Platyrinchus platyrhynchos* p. 168

16. Subtropical Doradito *Pseudocolopteryx acutipennis* p. 163

17. Short-tailed Pygmy-Tyrant *Myiornis ecaudatus* p. 163

18. Tufted Tit-Tyrant *Anairetes parulus* p. 163

19. Yellow-billed Tit-Tyrant *Anairetes flavirostris* p. 163

20. Many-colored Rush-Tyrant *Tachuris rubrigastra* p. 163

21. Bronze-olive Pygmy-Tyrant *Pseudotriccus pelzelni* p. 158

22. Scale-crested Pygmy-Tyrant *Lophotriccus pileatus* p. 164

23. Double-banded Pygmy-Tyrant *Lophotriccus vitiosus* p. 164

24. Helmeted Pygmy-Tyrant *Lophotriccus galeatus* p. 164

90

Plate 91

1. Pied-crested Tit-Tyrant *Anairetes reguloides* ♂ p. 163

2. Black-crested Tit-Tyrant *Anairetes nigrocristatus* ♂ p. 162

3. Ash-breasted Tit-Tyrant *Anairetes alpinus* p. 162

4. D'Orbigny's Chat-Tyrant *Ochthoeca oenanthoides polionota* p. 173

5. Unstreaked Tit-Tyrant *Uromyias agraphia* p. 162

6. Golden-browed Chat-Tyrant *Ochthoeca pulchella* p. 173

7. Brown-backed Chat-Tyrant *Ochthoeca fumicolor berlepschi* p. 174

8. Maroon-chested Chat-Tyrant *Ochthoeca thoracica* p. 173

9. Peruvian Chat-Tyrant *Ochthoeca spodionota* p. 173

10. Jelski's Chat-Tyrant *Ochthoeca jelskii* p. 173

11. Andean Tyrant *Knipolegus s. signatus* ♂ p. 177

12. Piura Chat-Tyrant *Ochthoeca piurae* p. 173

13. Andean Negrito *Lessonia oreas* ♂ p. 177

14. White-browed Chat-Tyrant *Ochthoeca leucophrys* p. 174

91

Plate 92

1. Bran-colored Flycatcher *Myiophobus fasciatus* p. 170

2. Tawny-breasted Flycatcher *Myiobius villosus* p. 170

3. Whiskered Flycatcher *Myiobius barbatus* p. 170

4. Black-tailed Flycatcher *Myiobius atricaudus* p. 170

5. Ruddy-tailed Flycatcher *Terenotriccus erythrurus* p. 170

6. Fuscous Flycatcher *Cnemotriccus fuscatus* p. 171

7. Ornate Flycatcher *Myiotriccus ornatus* p. 169

8. Cinnamon Flycatcher *Pyrrhomyias cinnamomea* p. 171

9. Cinnamon Tyrant *Neopipo cinnamomea* p. 171

10. Little Ground-Tyrant *Muscisaxicola fluviatilis* p. 175

11. Vermilion Flycatcher *Pyrocephalus rubinus* p. 172
    a. ♀   b. ♂

12. Cliff Flycatcher *Hirundinea ferruginea* p. 171

13. Drab Water-Tyrant *Ochthornis littoralis* p. 174

14. Yellow-bellied Chat-Tyrant *Ochthoeca diadema* p. 173

15. Crowned Chat-Tyrant *Ochthoeca frontalis* p. 172

16. Slaty-backed Chat-Tyrant *Ochthoeca cinnamomeiventris* p. 173

17. Rufous-breasted Chat-Tyrant *Ochthoeca rufipectoralis rufipectoralis* p. 173

18. Gray Monjita *Xolmis cinerea* p. 174

19. Red-rumped Bush-Tyrant *Cnemarchus erythropygius* p. 174

20. Streak-throated Bush-Tyrant *Myiotheretes striaticollis* p. 174

21. Smoky Bush-Tyrant *Myiotheretes fumigatus* p. 174

92

Plate 93

1. Gray-bellied Shrike-Tyrant *Agriornis microptera* p. 175

2. White-tailed Shrike-Tyrant *Agriornis andicola* p. 175

3. Rufous-webbed Tyrant *Polioxolmis rufipennis* p. 175

4. Rufous-bellied Bush-Tyrant *Myiotheretes fuscorufus* p. 174

5. Black-billed Shrike-Tyrant *Agriornis montana* p. 175

6. Yellow-bellied Elaenia *Elaenia flavogaster* p. 156

7. Small-billed Elaenia *Elaenia parvirostris* p. 156

8. Brownish Elaenia *Elaenia pelzelni* p. 156

9. Highland Elaenia *Elaenia obscura* p. 157

10. Lesser Elaenia *Elaenia chiriquensis* p. 156

11. White-crested Elaenia *Elaenia albiceps modesta* p. 156

12. Sierran Elaenia *Elaenia pallatangae* p. 157

13. Large Elaenia *Elaenia spectabilis* p. 155

14. Slaty Elaenia *Elaenia strepera* ♂ p. 156

93

Plate 94

1. Roraiman Flycatcher *Myiophobus roraimae* p. 169

2. Flavescent Flycatcher *Myiophobus flavicans* p. 169

3. Ochraceous-breasted Flycatcher *Myiophobus ochraceiventris* p. 170

4. Orange-banded Flycatcher *Myiophobus lintoni* p. 169

5. Unadorned Flycatcher *Myiophobus inornatus* p. 169

6. Handsome Flycatcher *Myiophobus pulcher* p. 169

7. Orange-crested Flycatcher *Myiophobus phoenicomitra* p. 169

8. Olive-chested Flycatcher *Myiophobus cryptoxanthus* p. 170

9. Inca Flycatcher *Leptopogon taczanowskii* p. 159

10. Red-billed Tyrannulet *Zimmerius cinereicapillus* p. 160

11. Peruvian Tyrannulet *Zimmerius viridiflavus* p. 161

12. Cinnamon-faced Tyrannulet *Phylloscartes parkeri* p. 159

13. Bolivian Tyrannulet *Zimmerius bolivianus* p. 160

14. Olive-tufted Flycatcher *Mitrephanes olivaceus* p. 171

94

Plate 95

1. Mouse-colored Tyrannulet *Phaeomyias murina* p. 154

2. Gray-breasted Flycatcher *Lathrotriccus griseipectus* p. 171

3. Snowy-throated Kingbird *Tyrannus niveigularis* p. 182

4. Tawny-crowned Pygmy-Tyrant *Euscarthmus meloryphus fulviceps* p. 163

5. Short-tailed Field-Tyrant *Muscigralla brevicauda* p. 176

6. Pacific Elaenia *Myiopagis subplacens* p. 155

7. Gray-and-white Tyrannulet *Pseudelaenia leucospodia* p. 155

8. Baird's Flycatcher *Myiodynastes bairdii* p. 181

9. Rufous Flycatcher *Myiarchus semirufus* p. 179

10. Slaty Becard *Pachyramphus spodiurus* ♂ p. 184

11. Vermilion Flycatcher *Pyrocephalus rubinus obscurus* ♂ p. 172

12. Sooty-crowned Flycatcher *Myiarchus phaeocephalus* p. 180

13. Tumbes Tyrant *Tumbezia salvini* p. 174

14. Ochraceous Attila *Attila torridus* p. 178

15. Bran-colored Flycatcher *Myiophobus fasciatus rufescens* p. 170

16. Masked Water-Tyrant *Fluvicola nengeta* p. 178

95

Plate 96

1. Spot-billed Ground-Tyrant *Muscisaxicola maculirostris* p. 175

2. Rufous-naped Ground-Tyrant *Muscisaxicola rufivertex* p. 176

3. Puna Ground-Tyrant *Muscisaxicola juninensis* p. 176

4. White-browed Ground-Tyrant *Muscisaxicola albilora* p. 176

5. Dark-faced Ground-Tyrant *Muscisaxicola macloviana* p. 175

6. Cinnamon-bellied Ground-Tyrant *Muscisaxicola capistrata* p. 176

7. Plain-capped Ground-Tyrant *Muscisaxicola alpina* p. 176

8. Cinereous Ground-Tyrant *Muscisaxicola cinerea* p. 176

9. Black-fronted Ground-Tyrant *Muscisaxicola frontalis* p. 176

10. Ochre-naped Ground-Tyrant *Muscisaxicola flavinucha* p. 176

11. White-fronted Ground-Tyrant *Muscisaxicola albifrons* p. 176

96

Plate 97

1. White-winged Black-Tyrant *Knipolegus aterrimus anthracinus* p. 177
    a. ♀   b. ♂

2. Riverside Tyrant *Knipolegus orenocensis* ♂ p. 177

3. Rufous-tailed Tyrant *Knipolegus poecilurus* p. 177

4. Yellow-browed Tyrant *Satrapa icterophrys* p. 178

5. White-headed Marsh-Tyrant *Arundinicola leucocephala* ♂ p. 178

6. Hudson's Black-Tyrant *Knipolegus hudsoni* p. 177

7. Amazonian Black-Tyrant *Knipolegus poecilocercus* ♂ p. 177

8. Black-backed Water-Tyrant *Fluvicola albiventer* p. 178

9. Blackish Pewee *Contopus nigrescens* p. 172

10. Black Phoebe *Sayornis nigricans* p. 172

11. Spectacled Tyrant *Hymenops perspicillatus* p. 178
    a. ♂   b. ♀

12. Long-tailed Tyrant *Colonia colonus* p. 178

13. Alder Flycatcher *Empidonax alnorum* p. 172

14. Western/Eastern Wood-Pewee *Contopus sordidulus/virens* p. 172

15. Tropical Pewee *Contopus cinereus* p. 172

16. Olive-sided Flycatcher *Contopus cooperi* p. 171

17. Smoke-colored Pewee *Contopus fumigatus* p. 177

18. Short-crested Flycatcher *Myiarchus ferox* p. 180

19. Pale-edged Flycatcher *Myiarchus cephalotes* p. 180

20. Dusky-capped Flycatcher *Myiarchus tuberculifer* p. 179

21. Swainson's Flycatcher *Myiarchus swainsoni* p. 179

22. Brown-crested Flycatcher *Myiarchus tyrannulus* p. 180

97

Plate 98

1. Tropical Kingbird *Tyrannus melancholicus* p. 182

2. White-throated Kingbird *Tyrannus albogularis* p. 182

3. Fork-tailed Flycatcher *Tyrannus savana* p. 183

4. Eastern Kingbird *Tyrannus tyrannus* p. 182

5. Crowned Slaty-Flycatcher *Griseotyrannus aurantioatrocristatus* p. 182

6. Three-striped Flycatcher *Conopias trivirgata* p. 181

7. Boat-billed Flycatcher *Megarynchus pitangua* p. 180

8. Great Kiskadee *Pitangus sulphuratus* p. 180

9. Lesser Kiskadee *Philohydor lictor* p. 180

10. Sulphury Flycatcher *Tyrannopsis sulphurea* p. 182

11. Lemon-browed Flycatcher *Conopias cinchoneti* p. 181

12. Yellow-throated Flycatcher *Conopias parva* p. 181

13. Piratic Flycatcher *Legatus leucophaius* p. 182

14. Variegated Flycatcher *Empidonomus varius* p. 182

15. Rusty-margined Flycatcher *Myiozetetes cayanensis* p. 180

16. Gray-capped Flycatcher *Myiozetetes granadensis* p. 181

17. Social Flycatcher *Myiozetetes similis* p. 181

18. Dusky-chested Flycatcher *Myiozetetes luteiventris* p. 181

19. Sulphur-bellied Flycatcher *Myiodynastes luteiventris* p. 182

20. Streaked Flycatcher *Myiodynastes maculatus* p. 181

21. Golden-crowned Flycatcher *Myiodynastes chrysocephalus* p. 181

98

Plate 99

1. Sharpbill *Oxyruncus cristatus* p. 185

2. Greater Schiffornis *Schiffornis major* p. 183

3. Thrush-like Schiffornis *Schiffornis turdinus* p. 183

4. Bright-rumped Attila *Attila spadiceus* p. 179

5. Cinnamon Attila *Attila cinnamomeus* p. 178

6. Rufous Casiornis *Casiornis rufa* p. 179

7. Sirystes *Sirystes sibilator* p. 179

8. Chestnut-crowned Becard *Pachyramphus castaneus* p. 183

9. Yellow-cheeked Becard *Pachyramphus xanthogenys* ♂ p. 183

10. White-eyed Attila *Attila bolivianus* p. 179

11. Crested Becard *Pachyramphus validus* p. 184
    a. ♂ b. ♀

12. Pink-throated Becard *Pachyramphus minor* p. 184
    11a. ♂ 11b. ♀

13. White-winged Becard *Pachyramphus polychopterus* p. 183
    a. ♀ b. ♂

14. One-colored Becard *Pachyramphus homochrous* p. 184
    a. ♂ b. ♀

15. Black-and-white Becard *Pachyramphus albogriseus* p. 183
    a. ♀ b. ♂

16. Cinereous Becard *Pachyramphus rufus* ♂ p. 184

17. Barred Becard *Pachyramphus versicolor* p. 183
    a. ♂ b. ♀

18. Black-capped Becard *Pachyramphus marginatus* p. 184
    a. ♀ b. ♂

99

Plate 100

1. Black-crowned Tityra *Tityra inquisitor* ♂ p. 184

2. Masked Tityra *Tityra semifasciata* ♂ p. 184

3. Violaceous Jay *Cyanocorax violaceus* p. 197

4. Purplish Jay *Cyanocorax cyanomelas* p. 197

5. Black-tailed Tityra *Tityra cayana* ♂ p. 184

6. White-tailed Jay *Cyanocorax mystacalis* p. 197

7. Green Jay *Cyanocorax yncas* p. 197

8. White-collared Jay *Cyanolyca viridicyana* p. 197

9. Turquoise Jay *Cyanolyca turcosa* p. 197

100

Plate 101

1. White-rumped Swallow *Tachycineta leucorrhoa* p. 186

2. White-winged Swallow *Tachycineta albiventer* p. 186

3. Tumbes Swallow *Tachycineta stolzmanni* p. 186

4. Andean Swallow *Stelgidopteryx andecola* p. 187

5. Peruvian Martin *Progne murphyi* a. ♂ p. 186

6. Chilean Swallow *Tachycineta meyeni* p. 186

7. Blue-and-white Swallow *Pygochelidon cyanoleuca* p. 186

8. Pale-footed Swallow *Notiochelidon flavipes* p. 187

9. Chestnut-collared Swallow *Petrochelidon rufocollaris* p. 187

10. Southern Rough-winged Swallow *Stelgidopteryx ruficollis* p. 187

11. White-banded Swallow *Atticora fasciata* p. 187

101

Plate 102

1. Brown-chested Martin *Phaeoprogne tapera* p. 185

2. Purple Martin *Progne subis* p. 185
   a. ♂   b. ♀

3. Gray-breasted Martin *Progne chalybea* p. 185

4. Caribbean Martin *Progne dominicensis* p. 185

5. Southern Martin *Progne elegans* p. 186
   a. ♂   b. ♀

6. Brown-bellied Swallow *Notiochelidon murina* p. 187

7. White-thighed Swallow *Neochelidon tibialis* p. 187

8. Tawny-headed Swallow *Stelgidopteryx fucata* p. 187

9. Bank Swallow (Sand Martin) *Riparia riparia* p. 187

10. Cliff Swallow *Petrochelidon pyrrhonota* p. 187

11. Barn Swallow *Hirundo rustica* p. 188

12. Páramo Pipit *Anthus bogotensis* p. 188

13. Yellowish Pipit *Anthus lutescens* p. 188

14. Correndera Pipit *Anthus correndera* p. 188

15. Short-billed Pipit *Anthus furcatus* p. 188

16. Hellmayr's Pipit *Anthus hellmayri* p. 188

102

Plate 103

1. Fasciated Wren *Campylorhynchus fasciatus* p. 189

2. Inca Wren *Thryothorus eisenmanni* p. 190

3. Rufous Wren *Cinnycerthia unirufa* p. 189

4. Plain-tailed Wren *Thryothorus euophrys schulenbergi* p. 190

5. Sharpe's Wren *Cinnycerthia olivascens* p. 189

6. Bar-winged Wood-Wren *Henicorhina leucoptera* p. 191

7. Peruvian Wren *Cinnycerthia peruana* p. 190

8. Chestnut-breasted Wren *Cyphorhinus thoracicus* p. 192

9. Fulvous Wren *Cinnycerthia fulva* p. 190

10. Superciliated Wren *Thryothorus superciliaris* p. 191

11. Speckle-breasted Wren *Thryothorus sclateri maranonica* p. 190

103

Plate 104

1. Collared Gnatwren *Microbates collaris* p. 196

2. Long-billed Gnatwren *Ramphocaenus melanurus* p. 196

3. House Wren *Troglodytes aedon* p. 191

4. Mountain Wren *Troglodytes solstitialis* p. 191

5. Tawny-faced Gnatwren *Microbates cinereiventris* p. 196

6. Gray-mantled Wren *Odontorchilus branickii* p. 189

7. Buff-breasted Wren *Thryothorus leucotis* p. 190

8. Sedge Wren *Cistothorus platensis* p. 191

9. White-breasted Wood-Wren *Henicorhina leucosticta* p. 191

10. Moustached Wren *Thryothorus genibarbis* p. 191

11. Coraya Wren *Thryothorus coraya* p. 190

12. Gray-breasted Wood-Wren *Henicorhina leucophrys* p. 191

13. Scaly-breasted Wren *Microcerculus marginatus* p. 191

14. Musician Wren *Cyphorhinus aradus* p. 192

15. Wing-banded Wren *Microcerculus bambla* 191

16. Black-capped Donacobius *Donacobius atricapillus* p. 189

17. Thrush-like Wren *Campylorhynchus turdinus* p. 189

104

Plate 105

1. Lawrence's Thrush *Turdus lawrencii* p. 195

2. White-eared Solitaire *Entomodestes leucotis* p. 193

3. Rufous-brown Solitaire *Cichlopsis leucogenys* p. 193

4. Creamy-bellied Thrush *Turdus amaurochalinus* p. 195

5. Black-billed Thrush *Turdus ignobilis* p. 195

6. Hauxwell's Thrush *Turdus hauxwelli* p. 195

7. Ecuadorian Thrush *Turdus maculirostris* p. 195

8. Andean Slaty-Thrush *Turdus nigriceps* ♂ p. 194

9. Chiguanco Thrush *Turdus chiguanco* p. 194

10. Great Thrush *Turdus fuscater gigantoides* ♂ p. 194

11. Marañón Thrush *Turdus maranonicus* p. 194

12. Plumbeous-backed Thrush *Turdus reevei* p. 194

13. Long-tailed Mockingbird *Mimus longicaudatus* p. 192

105

Plate 106

1. White-capped Dipper *Cinclus leucocephalus* p. 189

2. Swainson's Thrush *Catharus ustulatus* p. 193

3. Gray-cheeked Thrush *Catharus minimus* p. 193

4. Andean Solitaire *Myadestes ralloides venezuelensis* p. 192

5. Veery *Catharus fuscescens* p. 193

6. Spotted Nightingale-Thrush *Catharus dryas* p. 193

7. Slaty-backed Nightingale-Thrush *Catharus fuscater* p. 193

8. Pale-breasted Thrush *Turdus leucomelas* p. 195

9. White-necked Thrush *Turdus albicollis* p. 195

10. Chestnut-bellied Thrush *Turdus fulviventris* p. 194

11. Pale-eyed Thrush *Platycichla leucops* p. 193
    a. ♂   b ♀

12. Glossy-black Thrush *Turdus serranus* p. 194
    a. ♀   b. ♂

106

Plate 107

1. Slaty-capped Shrike-Vireo *Vireolanius leucotis* p. 199
2. Black-whiskered Vireo *Vireo altiloquus* 198
3. Rufous-browed Peppershrike *Cyclarhis gujanensis* p. 199
   a. *C. g. saturatus*   b. *C. g. virenticeps*   c. *C. g. gujanensis*
4. Yellow-green Vireo *Vireo flavoviridis* p. 198
5. Red-eyed Vireo *Vireo olivaceus* p. 198
6. Dusky-capped Greenlet *Hylophilus hypoxanthus* p. 198
7. Ashy-headed Greenlet *Hylophilus pectoralis* p. 198
8. Brown-capped Vireo *Vireo leucophrys* p. 197
9. Tawny-crowned Greenlet *Hylophilus ochraceiceps* p. 199
10. Rufous-naped Greenlet *Hylophilus semibrunneus* p. 198
11. Lesser Greenlet *Hylophilus decurtatus* p. 199
12. Olivaceous Greenlet *Hylophilus olivaceus* p. 198
13. Lemon-chested Greenlet *Hylophilus thoracicus* p. 198
14. Gray-chested Greenlet *Hylophilus semicinereus* p. 198
15. Tropical Parula *Parula pitiayumi* p. 200
16. Yellow Warbler *Dendroica petechia* p. 201
    a. Migrant *D. p. aestiva* ♀   b. *D. p. peruviana* ♂
17. Slate-throated Redstart *Myioborus miniatus* p. 202
18. Spectacled Redstart *Myioborus melanocephalus* p. 202
19. Northern Waterthrush *Seiurus noveboracensis* p. 201
20. Connecticut Warbler *Oporornis agilis* p. 201
21. Blackpoll Warbler *Dendroica striata* p. 201
    a. ♀   b. ♂
22. Golden-winged Warbler *Vermivora chrysoptera* p. 200
23. American Redstart *Setophaga ruticilla* p. 201
    a. ♂   b. ♀
24. Canada Warbler *Wilsonia canadensis* p. 202
25. Blackburnian Warbler *Dendroica fusca* p. 201
    a. ♀   b. ♂
26. Cerulean Warbler *Dendroica cerulea* p. 201
    a. ♂   b. ♀
27. Black-and-white Warbler *Mniotilta varia* p. 201

107

Plate 108

1. Citrine Warbler *Basileuterus luteoviridis* p. 203
   a. *B. l. striaticeps*   b. *B. l. euophrys*

2. Pale-legged Warbler *Basileuterus signatus flavovirens* p. 203

3. Three-banded Warbler *Basileuterus trifasciatus* p. 203

4. Three-striped Warbler *Basileuterus tristriatus* p. 203

5. Black-crested Warbler *Basileuterus nigrocristatus* p. 203

6. Russet-crowned Warbler *Basileuterus coronatus* p. 203
   a. *B. c. coronatus*   b. *B. c. castaneiceps*

7. Masked Yellowthroat *Geothlypis aequinoctialis auricularis* ♂ p. 202

8. Gray-and-gold Warbler *Basileuterus fraseri* p. 202

9. Tropical Gnatcatcher *Polioptila plumbea* p. 196
   a. *P. p. maior* (sexes alike)
   b. *P. p. parvirostris* ♀
   c. *P. p. parvirostris* ♂

10. Golden-bellied Warbler *Basileuterus chrysogaster* p. 202

11. Two-banded Warbler *Basileuterus bivittatus* p. 202

12. Buff-rumped Warbler *Basileuterus fulvicauda* p. 203

108

Plate 109

1. Cinereous Conebill *Conirostrum cinereum* p. 204

2. Chestnut-vented Conebill *Conirostrum speciosum* ♂ p. 204

3. Bananaquit *Coereba flaveola pacifica* p. 204

4. Capped Conebill *Conirostrum albifrons* p. 205
   a. ♀   b. ♂

5. Bicolored Conebill *Conirostrum bicolor* p. 204

6. Rufous-collared Sparrow *Zonotrichia capensis* p. 231
   a. Adult   b. Immature

7. Blue-backed Conebill *Conirostrum sitticolor* p. 205

8. Band-tailed Seedeater *Catamenia analis* p. 225
   a. ♀   b. ♂

9. Plain-colored Seedeater *Catamenia inornata* ♂ p. 225

10. Chestnut-throated Seedeater *Sporophila telasco* ♂ p. 225

11. Yellow-browed Sparrow *Ammodramus aurifrons* p. 231

12. Grassland Sparrow *Ammodramus humeralis* p. 231

13. Double-collared Seedeater *Sporophila caerulescens* p. 224
    a. ♀   b. ♂

14. Lined Seedeater *Sporophila lineola* ♂ p. 224

15. Variable Seedeater *Sporophila corvina* ♂ p. 223

16. Yellow-bellied Seedeater *Sporophila nigricollis* ♂ p. 224

17. Chestnut-bellied Seedeater *Sporophila castaneiventris* ♂ p. 225

18. Black-and-white Seedeater *Sporophila luctuosa* ♂ p. 224

19. Caqueta Seedeater *Sporophila murallae* ♂ p. 223

20. Chestnut-bellied Seed-Finch *Oryzoborus angolensis* ♂ p. 225

21. Large-billed Seed-Finch *Oryzoborus crassirostris* ♂ p. 225

109

Plate 110

1. Buff-breasted Mountain-Tanager *Dubusia taeniata stictocephala* p. 213

2. Lacrimose Mountain-Tanager *Anisognathus lacrymosus lachymosus* p. 213

3. Blue-winged Mountain-Tanager *Anisognathus somptuosus* p. 213

4. Hooded Mountain-Tanager *Buthraupis montana* p. 212

5. Black-chested Mountain-Tanager *Buthraupis eximia* p. 212

6. Masked Mountain-Tanager *Buthraupis wetmorei* p. 212

7. Scarlet-bellied Mountain-Tanager *Anisognathus igniventris* p. 213

8. Black-faced Tanager *Schistochlamys melanopis* p. 205

9. Magpie Tanager *Cissopis leveriana* p. 205

10. Red-billed Pied Tanager *Lamprospiza melanoleuca* ♂ p. 205

11. Blue-and-yellow Tanager *Thraupis bonariensis* ♂ p. 212

12. Masked Crimson Tanager *Ramphocelus nigrogularis* p. 211

13. Silver-beaked Tanager *Ramphocelus carbo* ♂ p. 211

14. Sayaca Tanager *Thraupis sayaca* p. 211

15. Blue-gray Tanager *Thraupis episcopus* p. 211
    a. *T. e. quaesita*   b. *T. e. urubambae*

16. Palm Tanager *Thraupis palmarum* p. 212

17. Blue-capped Tanager *Thraupis cyanocephala* 212

110

Plate 111

1. White-capped Tanager *Sericossypha albocristata* p. 205

2. Golden-backed Mountain-Tanager *Buthraupis aureodorsalis* p. 212

3. Chestnut-bellied Mountain-Tanager *Delothraupis castaneoventris* p. 213

4. Orange-throated Tanager *Wetmorethraupis sterrhopteron* p. 212

5. Golden-collared Tanager *Iridosornis jelskii* p. 213

6. Vermilion Tanager *Calochaetes coccineus* p. 211

7. Yellow-throated Tanager *Iridosornis analis* p. 213

8. Huallaga Tanager *Ramphocelus melanogaster* p. 211
   a. ♂   b. ♀

9. Yellow-crested Tanager *Tachyphonus rufiventer* ♂ p. 209

10. Black-and-white Tanager *Conothraupis speculigera* ♂ p. 205

111

Plate 112

1. Hooded Tanager *Nemosia pileata* ♂ p. 208

2. Ashy-throated Bush-Tanager *Chlorospingus canigularis* p. 206

3. Common Bush-Tanager *Chlorospingus ophthalmicus* p. 206
   a. *C. o. peruvianus* b. *C. o. cinereocephalus*

4. Gray-hooded Bush-Tanager *Cnemoscopus rubrirostris chrysogaster* p. 206

5. Yellow-whiskered Bush-Tanager *Chlorospingus parvirostris* p. 206

6. Yellow-throated Bush-Tanager *Chlorospingus flavigularis* p. 206

7. Guira Tanager *Hemithraupis guira* p. 208

8. Rust-and-yellow Tanager *Thlypopsis ruficeps* p. 208

9. Orange-headed Tanager *Thlypopsis sordida* p. 208

10. Rufous-chested Tanager *Thlypopsis ornata* p. 208

11. Superciliaried Hemispingus *Hemispingus superciliaris* p. 207
    a. *H. s. leucogaster* b. *H. s. urubambae*

12. Black-capped Hemispingus *Hemispingus atropileus auricularis* p. 206

13. Black-eared Hemispingus *Hemispingus melanotis berlepschi* p. 207

14. Oleaginous Hemispingus *Hemispingus frontalis* p. 207

15. Black-headed Hemispingus *Hemispingus verticalis* p. 207

112

Plate 113

1. Rusty Flowerpiercer *Diglossa sittoides* ♂ p. 226

2. White-sided Flowerpiercer *Diglossa albilatera* ♂ p. 226

3. Glossy Flowerpiercer *Diglossa lafresnayii* p. 226

4. Black Flowerpiercer *Diglossa humeralis* p. 227

5. Masked Flowerpiercer *Diglossopis cyanea* p. 227

6. Deep-blue Flowerpiercer *Diglossopis glauca* p. 227

7. Bluish Flowerpiercer *Diglossopis caerulescens* p. 227

8. Moustached Flowerpiercer *Diglossa mystacalis* p. 226
    a. *D. m. unicincta*   b. *D. m. albilinea*

9. Slaty Finch *Haplospiza rustica* ♂ p. 226

10. Blue Seedeater *Amaurospiza concolor* ♂ p. 225

11. Orange-browed Hemispingus *Hemispingus calophrys* p. 206

12. Parodi's Hemispingus *Hemispingus parodii* p. 206

13. Rufous-browed Hemispingus *Hemispingus rufosuperciliaris* p. 207

14. Drab Hemispingus *Hemispingus xanthophthalmus* p. 207

15. Three-striped Hemispingus *Hemispingus trifasciatus* p. 207

113

Plate 114

1. Yellow-backed Tanager *Hemithraupis flavicollis* ♂ p. 208

2. Fulvous Shrike-Tanager *Lanio fulvus* ♂ p. 209

3. White-winged Shrike-Tanager *Lanio versicolor* ♂ p. 209

4. Rufous-crested Tanager *Creurgops verticalis* p. 209
    a. ♀   b. ♂

5. White-shouldered Tanager *Tachyphonus luctuosus* ♂ p. 209

6. Flame-crested Tanager *Tachyphonus cristatus* ♂ p. 209

7. Fulvous-crested Tanager *Tachyphonus surinamus* ♂ p. 209

8. Slaty Tanager *Creurgops dentata* p. 209
    a. ♀   b. ♂

9. White-lined Tanager *Tachyphonus rufus* p. 210
    a. ♀   b. ♂

10. Red-shouldered Tanager *Tachyphonus phoenicius* p. 210
    a. ♂   b. ♀

11. Black-goggled Tanager *Trichothraupis melanops* ♂ p. 210

12. Hepatic Tanager *Piranga flava* p. 210
    a. ♂   b. ♀

13. Olive Tanager *Chlorothraupis carmioli* p. 208

14. Red-crowned Ant-Tanager *Habia rubica* ♂ p. 210

15. Summer Tanager *Piranga rubra* p. 210
    a. ♂   b. ♀

16. Scarlet Tanager *Piranga olivacea* p. 210
    a. ♂   b. ♀

17. White-winged Tanager *Piranga leucoptera* p. 210
    a. ♀   b. ♂

18. Red-hooded Tanager *Piranga rubriceps* ♂ p. 211

19. Gray-headed Tanager *Eucometis penicillata* p. 208

114

Plate 115

1. Straw-backed Tanager *Tangara argyrofenges* ♂ p. 218

2. Brown-flanked Tanager *Thlypopsis pectoralis* p. 208

3. Buff-bellied Tanager *Thlypopsis inornata* p. 208

4. Tit-like Dacnis *Xenodacnis parina petersi* ♂ p. 219

5. Silver-backed Tanager *Tangara viridicollis* ♂ p. 218

6. Giant Conebill *Oreomanes fraseri* p. 205

7. Tamarugo Conebill *Conirostrum tamarugense* ♂ p. 204

8. Sira Tanager *Tangara phillipsi* ♂ p. 218

9. White-browed Conebill *Conirostrum ferrugineiventre* p. 205

10. Pardusco *Nephelornis oneilli* p. 220

11. Black-throated Flowerpiercer *Diglossa brunneiventris* p. 227

12. Green-capped Tanager *Tangara meyerdeschauenseei* ♂ p. 217

13. Pearly-breasted Conebill *Conirostrum margaritae* p. 204

14. Moustached Flowerpiercer *Diglossa mystacalis pectoralis* p. 226

115

Plate 116

1. Black-faced Dacnis *Dacnis lineata* p. 219
   a. ♀   b. ♂

2. Blue Dacnis *Dacnis cayana* p. 219
   a. ♀   b. ♂

3. White-bellied Dacnis *Dacnis albiventris* ♂   p. 218

4. Red-legged Honeycreeper *Cyanerpes cyaneus* p. 219
   a. ♀   b. ♂

5. Purple Honeycreeper *Cyanerpes caeruleus* p. 219
   a. ♀   b. ♂

6. Short-billed Honeycreeper *Cyanerpes nitidus* ♂   p. 219

7. Yellow-bellied Dacnis *Dacnis flaviventer* p. 219
   a. ♂   b. ♀

8. Golden-rumped Euphonia *Euphonia cyanocephala* p. 214
   a. ♀   b. ♂

9. Thick-billed Euphonia *Euphonia laniirostris* p. 214
   a. ♀   b. ♂

10. Green Honeycreeper *Chlorophanes spiza exsul* p. 219
    a. ♀   b. ♂

11. White-vented Euphonia *Euphonia minuta* p. 215
    a. ♀   b. ♂

12. Orange-crowned Euphonia *Euphonia saturata* ♂   p. 214

13. Bronze-green Euphonia *Euphonia mesochrysa* ♂   p. 214

14. White-lored Euphonia *Euphonia chrysopasta* ♂   p. 214

15. Orange-bellied Euphonia *Euphonia xanthogaster brevirostris* p. 215
    a. ♀   b. ♂

16. Rufous-bellied Euphonia *Euphonia rufiventris* p. 215
    a. ♀   b. ♂

17. Purple-throated Euphonia *Euphonia chlorotica* p. 214
    a. ♀   b. ♂

18. Plumbeous Euphonia *Euphonia plumbea* ♂   p. 214

116

Plate 117

1. Orange-eared Tanager *Chlorochrysa calliparaea boucieri* ♂ p. 215

2. Grass-green Tanager *Chlorornis riefferii* p. 205

3. Blue-naped Chlorophonia *Chlorophonia cyanea* p. 215

4. Chestnut-breasted Chlorophonia *Chlorophonia pyrrhophrys* ♂ p. 215

5. Green-and-gold Tanager *Tangara schrankii* ♂ p. 216

6. Golden Tanager *Tangara arthus* p. 216

7. Paradise Tanager *Tangara c. chilensis* p. 216

8. Saffron-crowned Tanager *Tangara xanthocephala* p. 216

9. Golden-eared Tanager *Tangara chrysotis* p. 216

10. Yellow-bellied Tanager *Tangara xanthogastra* p. 216

11. Flame-faced Tanager *Tangara parzudakii* p. 216

12. Spotted Tanager *Tangara punctata* p. 216

13. Metallic-green Tanager *Tangara labradorides* p. 217

14. Dotted Tanager *Tangara varia* ♂ p. 216

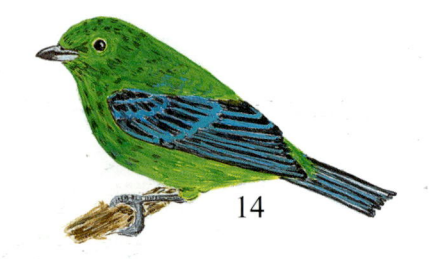

117

Plate 118

1. Swallow-Tanager *Tersina viridis* p. 220
   a. ♂   b. ♀

2. Burnished-buff Tanager *Tangara cayana* ♂ p. 217

3. Golden-collared Honeycreeper *Iridophanes pulcherrima* ♂ p. 218

4. Blue-browed Tanager *Tangara cyanotis* p. 217

5. Fawn-breasted Tanager *Pipraeidea melanonota* p. 213

6. Blue-necked Tanager *Tangara cyanicollis* p. 217

7. Blue-and-black Tanager *Tangara vassorii atrocaerulea* p. 218

8. Bay-headed Tanager *Tangara gyrola* p. 217

9. Masked Tanager *Tangara nigrocincta* p. 217

10. Beryl-spangled Tanager *Tangara nigroviridis* p. 217

11. Opal-rumped Tanager *Tangara velia* p. 218

12. Turquoise Tanager *Tangara mexicana* p. 215

13. Golden-naped Tanager *Tangara ruficervix inca* p. 217

14. Opal-crowned Tanager *Tangara callophrys* p. 218

15. Golden-crowned Tanager *Iridosornis rufivertex* p. 213

16. Yellow-scarfed Tanager *Iridosornis reinhardti* p. 213

118

Plate 119

1. Great Inca-Finch *Incaspiza pulchra* p. 222

2. Gray-winged Inca-Finch *Incaspiza ortizi* p. 222

3. Buff-bridled Inca-Finch *Incaspiza laeta* p. 222

4. Little Inca-Finch *Incaspiza watkinsi* p. 222

5. Rufous-backed Inca-Finch *Incaspiza personata* p. 222

6. Collared Warbling-Finch *Poospiza hispaniolensis* ♂ p. 223

7. Plain-tailed Warbling-Finch *Poospiza alticola* p. 222

8. Rufous-breasted Warbling-Finch *Poospiza rubecula* p. 223

9. Chestnut-breasted Mountain-Finch *Poospiza caesar* p. 223

119

Plate 120

1. Cusco Brush-Finch *Atlapetes canigenis* p. 230

2. Bay-crowned Brush-Finch *Atlapetes seebohmi* p. 230

3. White-headed Brush-Finch *Atlapetes albiceps* p. 230

4. Cloud-forest Brush-Finch *Atlapetes latinuchus* p. 229
    a. *A. l. baroni*   b. *A. l. latinuchus*

5. Tricolored Brush-Finch *Atlapetes tricolor* p. 229

6. White-winged Brush-Finch *Atlapetes leucopterus* p. 230
    a. *A. l. dresseri*   b. *A. l. paynteri*

7. Rusty-bellied Brush-Finch *Atlapetes nationi* p. 230

8. Apurímac Brush-Finch *Atlapetes forbesi* p. 229

9. Rufous-eared Brush-Finch *Atlapetes rufigenis rufigenis* p. 229

10. Black-spectacled Brush-Finch *Atlapetes melanops* p. 229

11. Vilcabamba Brush-Finch *Atlapetes terborghi* p. 230

12. Dark-faced Brush-Finch *Atlapetes melanolaemus* p. 230

13. Slaty Brush-Finch *Atlapetes schistaceus* p. 229

14. Pale-naped Brush-Finch *Atlapetes pallidinucha* p. 229

120

Plate 121

1. Yellow-shouldered Grosbeak *Caryothraustes humeralis* p. 232

2. Red-capped Cardinal *Paroaria gularis* p. 228

3. Orange-billed Sparrow *Arremon aurantiirostris* p. 231

4. Pectoral Sparrow *Arremon taciturnus* p. 231

5. Stripe-headed Brush-Finch *Buarremon torquatus poliophrys* p. 230

6. Blue-black Grosbeak *Cyanocompsa cyanoides* p. 233
    a. ♀   b. ♂

7. Slate-colored Grosbeak *Saltator grossus* p. 232

8. Chestnut-capped Brush-Finch *Buarremon brunneinucha* p. 230

9. Streaked Saltator *Saltator striatipectus flavidicollis* p. 232

10. Golden-billed Saltator *Saltator aurantiirostris* ♂ p. 232

11. Buff-throated Saltator *Saltator maximus* p. 232

12. Grayish Saltator *Saltator coerulescens* p. 232

13. Rose-breasted Grosbeak *Pheucticus ludovicianus* p. 233
    a. ♀   b. ♂

14. Golden-bellied Grosbeak *Pheucticus chrysogaster* ♂ p. 233

15. Black-backed Grosbeak *Pheucticus aureoventris* ♂ p. 233

121

Plate 122

1. Crimson-breasted Finch *Rhodospingus cruentus* p. 220
    a. ♂ b. ♀

2. White-throated Sierra-Finch *Phrygilus erythronotus* p. 221

3. Cinereous Finch *Piezorhina cinerea* p. 222

4. Short-tailed Finch *Idiopsar brachyurus* p. 221

5. Peruvian Sierra-Finch *Phrygilus punensis* p. 221
    a. ♂ b. ♀

6. Slender-billed Finch *Xenospingus concolor* p. 222

7. Slate-colored Seedeater *Sporophila schistacea* ♂ p. 223

8. Plumbeous Seedeater *Sporophila plumbea* ♂ p. 223

9. Lesson's Seedeater *Sporophila bouvronides* ♂ p. 224

10. Drab Seedeater *Sporophila simplex* p. 224

11. White-bellied Seedeater *Sporophila leucoptera* ♂ p. 224

12. Parrot-billed Seedeater *Sporophila peruviana* p. 224
    a. ♀ b. ♂

13. Tawny-bellied Seedeater *Sporophila hypoxantha* ♂ p. 224

14. Dark-throated Seedeater *Sporophila ruficollis* ♂ p. 224

15. Dull-colored Grassquit *Tiaris obscura* p. 226

16. Black-billed Seed-Finch *Oryzoborus atrirostris* ♂ p. 225

17. Páramo Seedeater *Catamenia homochroa* ♂ p. 226

18. Black-striped Sparrow *Arremonops conirostris* p. 231

19. Wedge-tailed Grass-Finch *Emberizoides herbicola* p. 228

20. Olive Finch *Lysurus castaneiceps* p. 228

21. Black-capped Sparrow *Arremon abeillei* p. 231
    a. *A. a. abeillei* b. *A. a. nigriceps*

22. Tumbes Sparrow *Aimophila stolzmanni* p. 231

122

Plate 123

1. Thick-billed Siskin *Carduelis crassirostris* p. 199
    a. ♀   b. ♂

2. Black Siskin *Carduelis atrata* ♂   p. 200

3. Yellow-rumped Siskin *Carduelis uropygialis* ♂   p. 200

4. Yellow-bellied Siskin *Carduelis xanthogastra* ♂   p. 200

5. Saffron Siskin *Carduelis siemiradzkii* ♂   p. 200

6. Hooded Siskin *Carduelis magellanica* p. 199
    a. *C. m. capitalis* ♂   b. *C. m. peruana* ♂   c. ♀

7. Olivaceous Siskin *Carduelis olivacea* ♂   p. 200

8. Lesser Goldfinch *Carduelis psaltria* ♂   p. 200

9. Sulphur-throated Finch *Sicalis taczanowskii* p. 228

10. Orange-fronted Yellow-Finch *Sicalis columbiana* ♂   p. 228

11. Raimondi's Yellow-Finch *Sicalis raimondii* p. 228
    a. Non-breeding ♂   b. Breeding ♂   c. ♀

12. Stripe-tailed Yellow-Finch *Sicalis citrina* p. 228
    a. ♂   b. ♀   c. Undertail

13. Grassland Yellow-Finch *Sicalis luteola* p. 227
    a. ♂   b. Immature

14. House Sparrow *Passer domesticus* p. 197
    a. ♂   b. ♀

123

Plate 124

1. Blue-black Grassquit *Volatinia jacarina* p. 223
    a. ♀   b. ♂

2. Plush-capped Finch *Catamblyrhynchus diadema* p. 220

3. Black-masked Finch *Coryphaspiza melanotis* ♂ p. 220

4. Red-crested Finch *Coryphospingus cucullatus* ♂ p. 220

5. Bright-rumped Yellow-Finch *Sicalis uropygialis connectens* p. 228

6. Greenish Yellow-Finch *Sicalis olivascens* p. 228

7. Puna Yellow-Finch *Sicalis lutea* p. 227

8. Saffron Finch *Sicalis flaveola* p. 227
    a. Adult   b. Immature

9. Plumbeous Sierra-Finch *Phrygilus unicolor* ♂ p. 221

10. Band-tailed Sierra-Finch *Phrygilus alaudinus* ♂ p. 221

11. Ash-breasted Sierra-Finch *Phrygilus plebejus* ♂ p. 221

12. Black-hooded Sierra-Finch *Phrygilus atriceps* ♂ p. 221

13. Mourning Sierra-Finch *Phrygilus fruticeti* ♂ p. 221

14. White-winged Diuca-Finch *Diuca speculifera* p. 221

124

Plate 125

1. Pale-eyed Blackbird *Agelaius xanthophthalmus* p. 233

2. Selva Cacique *Cacicus koepckeae* p. 236

3. Ecuadorian Cacique *Cacicus sclateri* p. 236

4. Scrub Blackbird *Dives warszewiczi kalinowskii* p. 234

5. Dusky-green Oropendola *Psarocolius atrovirens* p. 236

6. Black-cowled Saltator *Saltator nigriceps* p. 232

7. White-edged Oriole *Icterus graceannae* p. 235

8. Masked Saltator *Saltator cinctus* p. 232

125

Plate 126

1. Casqued Oropendola *Psarocolius oseryi* p. 236

2. Green Oropendola *Psarocolius viridis* p. 236

3. Crested Oropendola *Psarocolius decumanus* p. 236

4. Band-tailed Oropendola *Ocyalus latirostris* p. 237

5. Amazonian Oropendola *Gymnostinops bifasciatus* p. 237

6. Russet-backed Oropendola *Psarocolius angustifrons* p. 237
    a. *P. a. alfredi*   b. *P. a. angustifrons*

7. Subtropical Cacique *Cacicus uropygialis* p. 235

8. Yellow-rumped Cacique *Cacicus cela* p. 235

9. Mountain Cacique *Cacicus chrysonotus chrysonotus* p. 236

10. Red-rumped Cacique *Cacicus haemorrhous* p. 235

11. Yellow-billed Cacique *Amblycercus holosericeus* p. 235

12. Solitary Cacique *Cacicus solitarius* p. 236

126

Plate 127

1. Moriche Oriole *Icterus chrysocephalus* p. 235

2. Epaulet Oriole *Icterus cayanensis* p. 235

3. Yellow-tailed Oriole *Icterus mesomelas* p. 235

4. Oriole Blackbird *Gymnomystax mexicanus* p. 237

5. Troupial *Icterus icterus* p. 235

6. Peruvian Meadowlark *Sturnella bellicosa* ♂ p. 234

7. Yellow-hooded Blackbird *Agelaius icterocephalus* p. 234
    a. ♂   b. ♀

8. Yellow-winged Blackbird *Agelaius thilius* p. 233
    a. ♂   b. ♀

9. Red-breasted Blackbird *Sturnella militaris* ♂ p. 234

10. White-browed Blackbird *Sturnella superciliaris* p. 234
    a. ♂   b. ♀

11. Chopi Blackbird *Gnorimopsar chopi* p. 237

12. Velvet-fronted Grackle *Lampropsar tanagrinus* p. 237

13. Bobolink *Dolichonyx oryzivorus* (non-breeding) p. 233

14. Shiny Cowbird *Molothrus bonariensis* p. 234
    a. ♀   b. ♂

15. Great-tailed Grackle *Quiscalus mexicanus* p. 234
    a. ♂   b. ♀

16. Giant Cowbird *Scaphidura oryzivora* ♂ p. 234

127

Wingtips and Tail Patterns of Nightjars

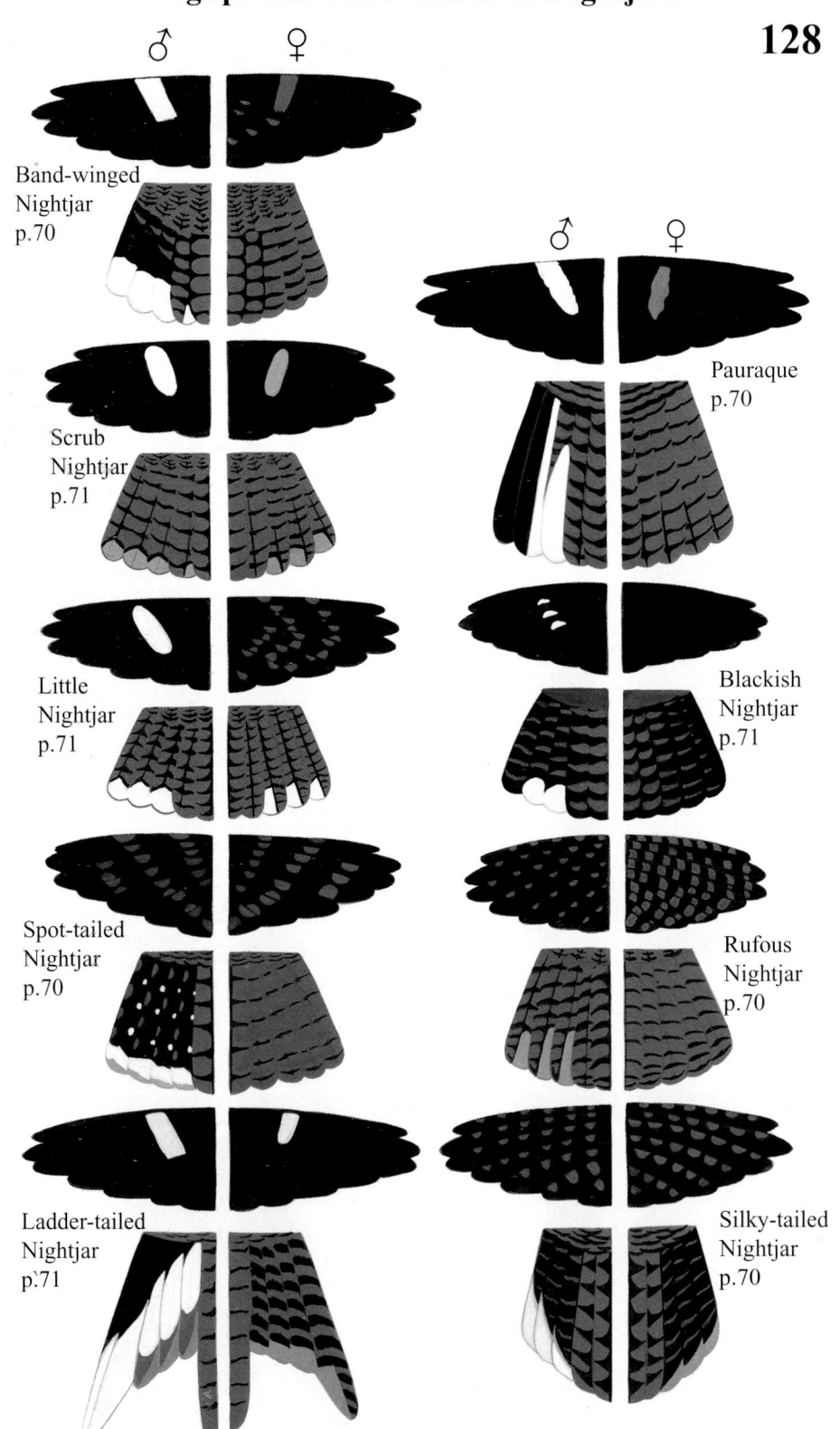

128

Band-winged Nightjar p.70

Scrub Nightjar p.71

Little Nightjar p.71

Spot-tailed Nightjar p.70

Ladder-tailed Nightjar p.71

Pauraque p.70

Blackish Nightjar p.71

Rufous Nightjar p.70

Silky-tailed Nightjar p.70

Ash-browed Spinetail *Cranioleuca curtata* Colaespina Cejiceniza
14 cm (5.5"). Plate 61. ♪ 797. Often found in tangles and vines. A dark olive-brown *Cranioleuca* with a rufous crown, wings and tail, and an ash-gray superciliary. Line-cheeked Spinetail (possible limited overlap at best on Cerro Chinguela) has paler underparts and a more prominent whitish superciliary. Uncommon in humid subtrop. forest borders on e slope of Andes at 900-2500 m. *E Andes of Colombia to w Bolivia.*

Parker's (White-breasted) Spinetail *Cranioleuca vulpecula* Colaespina de Parker
13.5 cm (5.3"). Plate 61. ♪ LNS. Note limited range and habitat. A spinetail with rufous upperparts and whitish underparts, with some indistinct mottling on chest. Has a narrow light superciliary. Both species of *Certhiaxis* have much whiter and cleaner underparts. Uncommon in lower growth of forest edge and second growth (especially on river islands) in lowlands e of Andes south along Río Ucayali to Lagarto to 500 m. (Formerly considered a race of Rusty-backed Spinetail *C. vulpina*, but see Zimmer 1997). *River islands in Amazon system from e Peru to e Brazil.*

Speckled Spinetail *Cranioleuca gutturata* Colaespina Jaspeada
14 cm (5.5"). Plate 61. ♪ 817CD. The only spinetail in its range with black speckling on its breast. Has a rufous crown, olive-brown mantle and yellowish chin. Uncommon in tangles and lower growth of lowland *várzea* (and occasionally *terra firme*) forests e of Andes to 750 m. *Venezuela and the Guianas to Amazonian Brazil and n Bolivia.*

Red-and-white Spinetail *Certhiaxis mustelina* Colaespina Rojiblanca
13.5 cm (5.3"). Plate 61. A bicolored spinetail with bright rufous upperparts and white underparts. Lores are black and forehead is same color as rest of crown. Cf. Parker's and Yellow-chinned Spinetails. Fairly common in scrub, especially on river islands and oxbow lakes, along Amazon and upper Río Ucayali to 300 m. *Widespread in Amazon basin.*

Yellow-chinned Spinetail *Certhiaxis cinnamomea* Colaespina Barbiamarilla
14 cm (5.5"). ♪ 797. Plate 61. Note wet habitat. Similar to Red-and-white Spinetail but has gray forehead, grayish superciliary and an indistinct yellow chin. Red-and-white Spinetail has prominent black lores and lacks a superciliary. Parker's Spinetail's underparts are not as white and it lacks a yellow chin spot. Uncommon in wet habitats (often on floating vegetation) along tropical rivers, oxbow lakes and margins e of Andes to 500 m. *Tropical n South America to n Argentina and Brazil.*

Schizoeaca Thistletails. The five Peruvian species are allopatric and all inhabit dense undergrowth in high montane regions near treeline. The tails of these small birds are very long, narrow and pointed, and tips often appear worn.

White-chinned Thistletail *Schizoeaca fuliginosa* Colicardo Barbiblanca
19 cm (7.5"). Plate 62. ♪ JM. The only thistletail in its range, but Mouse-colored Thistletail may be in close proximity. White-chinned's upperparts are more rufous, and it has a conspicuous superciliary. Race *peruviana* (Andes of n Peru) and *plengei* (Carpish Mts.) have been considered separate species. Fairly common in *páramo* and *pajonal* of Andes in Amazonas, San Martín and Huánuco (Carpish Mts.) at 2400-3500 m. *Andes of w Venezuela to n Ecuador and central Peru.*

Mouse-colored Thistletail *Schizoeaca griseomurina* Colicardo Murino
19 cm (7.5"). Plate 62. ♪ JM. Grayer and duller overall than White-chinned Thistletail. Uncommon in humid montane treeline woodlands (especially *Polylepis*) in n Piura and nw Cajamarca at 2800-4000 m. *Andes of s Ecuador and extreme n Peru.*

Eye-ringed Thistletail *Schizoeaca palpebralis* Colicardo Ojianillado
19 cm (7.5"). Plate 62. The only thistletail in its range. Rare and poorly known from *páramo* of Andes of Junín at 2100-3300 m. *Endemic to Peru.*

Vilcabamba Thistletail *Schizoeaca vilcabambae* Colicardo de Vilcabamba
19 cm (7.5"). Plate 62. Race *ayacuchensis* (Andes of Ayacucho) has been considered a separate species (Ayacucho Thistletail). Fairly common in Andes w of Río Apurímac near Puncu (n Ayacucho), and in Cusco on north end of Cordillera Vilcabamba at 2500-3500 m. Birds resident in Bosque de Ampay are tentatively assigned to this species, but possibly represent an undescribed taxon. *Endemic to Peru.*

Puna Thistletail *Schizoeaca helleri* Colicardo de la Puna
18 cm (7"). Plate 62. ♪797. The only thistletail in its range. An unnamed ssp. from near Limbani (Puno) may be a separate species. Uncommon in humid montane and elfin forests near treeline in s Cusco and Puno. Recorded along upper Manu road at 2800-3600 m. *Endemic to Peru.*

Asthenes **Canasteros.** Canasteros are small furnariids, often with long tails that are held cocked. They inhabit open and semi-open regions, grasslands, shrubbery and rocky terrain. For identification note pattern of tail, presence of streaking on upperparts or underparts, and presence of a chin spot. They are named after the large basket-like nest (canasta) that some of them build.

Dark-winged Canastero *Asthenes arequipae* Canastero Alioscura
15.5 cm (6"). Plate 59. ♪JFC. The only canastero in its range with a bright rufous rump and vent combined with a mostly black tail (outermost rectrices are rufous). The creamy-white breast and dark blackish wings are also distinctive. An unnamed ssp. from Ayacucho and s Lima lacks almost any rufous on rump, wings or chin. Fairly common and local in *Polylepis* woodlands and montane scrub in Andes north to s Lima and adjacent Ayacucho, mainly at 3500-4800 m. *Andes of w Peru to w Bolivia and n Chile.*

*Pale-tailed Canastero *Asthenes huancavelicae* Canastero Colipálida
15.5 cm (6"). Plate 59. ♪JFC. Like a dull version of Dark-winged Canastero (no overlap). Wings show much cinnamon. The three widely disjunct ssp. may represent separate taxa. They vary mostly in tail coloration—tawny with pink sides in nominate *huancavelicae* from Huancavelica and Ayacucho; almost white with dark central feathers in *usheri* (Ninabamba and Mutca, Apurímac, illustrated); or mostly cinnamon in unnamed ssp. (illustrated) from drainage of Río Santa (Ancash). Fairly common to rare and local in arid intermontane valleys at 1830-4200 m. *Endemic to Peru.*

Canyon Canastero *Asthenes pudibunda* Canastero de Quebradas
16.5 cm (6.5"). Plate 59. ♪JFC. Within its range the only canastero with all rufous tail and wings. Has an indistinct whitish superciliary and grayish underparts. Fairly common in rocky montane scrub, semiarid cloud forests and *Polylepis* with scattered cacti from La Libertad and Ancash south to Tacna at 2500-3700 m. Recorded on upper parts of Santa Eulalia road and at Colca Canyon. Recently recorded in adjacent Chile in Putre (Van der Gaast 1997). *Endemic to Peru.*

Rusty-fronted Canastero *Asthenes ottonis* Canastero Frentirrojiza
18 cm (7"). Plate 59. A skulking canastero with a long rufous tail, rufous wings and rufous forehead. Cf. Streak-fronted Thornbird. Fairly common in montane scrub in inter-Andean valleys in Huancavelica, Ayacucho, Apurímac and Cusco at 2750-4000 m. Reported from Laguna Huacarpay, above Ollantaytambo, and around Urpicancha Lakes. *Endemic to Peru.*

Cordilleran Canastero *Asthenes modesta* Canastero Cordillerano
15.5 cm (6"). Plate 58. ♪797. A plain-backed canastero with streaks on throat, upper breast and sides of head. Has a small rufous chin spot (often hard to see), dark central tail feathers and rufous outer ones. Nominate *modesta* (s Peru) is less streaked below than illustrated race *proxima* (central Peru). Cf. Streak-throated Canastero. No overlap with similar Cactus Canastero. Common in *puna* grasslands north to Junín at 2600-4500 m. *Andes of Peru to s Argentina and Chile.*

Cactus Canastero *Asthenes cactorum* Canastero de los Cactus
14.5 cm (5.75"). Plate 59. ♪ JFC. Similar to Cordilleran Canastero (no overlap) but bill is longer and it lacks streaks on underparts. Fairly common in stands of large cacti (*Haageocereus lachayensis*) in rocky, hilly country from Lima to Arequipa at 2200-2400 m. Ranges from 250-300 m in Lachay Nature Reserve and 50-1680 m in Loma de Atico (n Arequipa). *Endemic to Peru.*

Streak-throated Canastero *Asthenes humilis* Canastero Gargantilistado
15.5 cm (6"). Plate 59. Similar to Cordilleran Canastero but back is faintly streaked and lacks rufous on the tail. Streaks on the throat and sides of head are more prominent than in Cordilleran Canastero. Common in arid *puna* grasslands from s Cajamarca to Ayacucho, Cusco and Puno at 2650-4800 m. *Puna grasslands of Peru to w Bolivia.*

Streak-backed Canastero *Asthenes wyatti* Canastero Dorsilistado
16.5 cm (6.5"). Plate 58. ♪ 797. A tawny canastero with black streaks on back and crown. Dark tail has rufous outer feathers. Puna Canastero is nearly identical (ranges overlap in Puno). Uncommon and disjunct in *puna* grasslands in Piura and Cajamarca, and from Ancash to Puno at 3000-4500 m. *Andes of w Venezuela to s Peru.*

Puna Canastero *Asthenes sclateri* Canastero de la Puna
18 cm (7"). Plate 58. ♪ 797. Note limited range. Very similar to Streak-backed Canastero (sympatric in extreme s Peru) but base of outer tail feathers is dark and not rufous (a detail not easily seen in the field). Uncommon and local in *puna* grasslands in Puno at 2150-4000 m. Recent records from Lampa and Lake Titicaca environs. *Andes of s Peru to nw Argentina.*

Scribble-tailed Canastero *Asthenes maculicauda* Canastero Estriado
18 cm (7"). Plate 59. ♪ 797. Note limited range. A heavily streaked (above and below) canastero, with rufous crown and broken black streaks on the rufous tail. Cf. Junín Canastero (range overlaps in extreme s Peru). Uncommon in *puna* grasslands in Cordillera de Carabaya south of Limbani at 3000-4300 m. *Disjunct in Andes of s Peru, w Bolivia and nw Argentina.*

Junín Canastero *Asthenes virgata* Canastero de Junín
18 cm (7"). Plate 59. A heavily streaked (above and below) canastero with rufous wings and rump and a pale chin. Outer tail feathers are mostly rufous. Many-striped Canastero has streaked rump, whitish throat and blacker streaks on underparts. Cf. Scribble-tailed Canastero (whitish throat, streaked tail). Uncommon and very local in *páramo* and *puna* grasslands in Lima, Junín, Ayacucho, Cusco and Puno at 3300-4300 m. Frequents bunchgrass with scattered small bushes adjacent to forest and *Polylepis* woodlands. Recorded on Abra Málaga road. *Endemic to Peru.*

Line-fronted Canastero *Asthenes urubambensis* Canastero Frentilistada
15.5 cm (6"). Plate 59. ♪ 797. The only canastero in its range with an unstreaked brown back, streaked underparts and an orange chin-patch. Uncommon and local in montane *Polylepis* woodlands and elfin forests on e slope of Andes from s San Martín to Puno at 2750-4300 m. *Locally in Andes of Peru and w Bolivia.*

Many-striped Canastero *Asthenes flammulata* Canastero Multilistado
15.5 cm (6"). Plate 58. ♪ JM. The only heavily streaked (above and below) canastero in most of its range. In southern part of range cf. similar Junín Canastero. Uncommon in *páramo* and *puna* grasslands of Andes south to Ancash and Junín at 3000-4500 m. *Locally distributed in páramo from Colombia to central Peru.*

***Phacellodomus* Thornbirds/Softtails.** The five Peruvian species of this ill-defined genus are rather nondescript furnariids that range from the lowlands to high elevations. Thornbirds are mostly birds of open country with rather dull attire, and their large nests of sticks are conspicuous. The softtails inhabit thick vegetation and are both rare. The softtails are often placed in the genus *Thripophaga*, and each may deserve to be classified in a monotypic genus.

Plain Softtail *Phacellodomus fusciceps* Colasuave Simple
18 cm (7"). ♪797. Plate 58. Found in mid-level and subcanopy. A uniformly dull buff-brown furnariid with rufous wings, tail and lower back. Chin yellowish. Cf. various foliage-gleaners (all have longer bills, more prominent field marks and different behavior). Rare in lowland *várzea* forests e of Andes from Pasco to Madre de Dios and Puno to 500 m. Recorded at Manu Wildlife Center and Amazonia Lodge. *Locally in Amazon basin.*

*Russet-mantled Softtail *Phacellodomus berlepschi* Colasuave Dorsirojizo
18 cm (7"). Plate 65. Frequents dense understory, especially with bamboo. The only furnariid in its limited range and habitat that is mostly rufous with a whitish-buff crown. Rare in humid montane and elfin forests from Cordillera de Colán to e La Libertad at 2450-3350 m. Recorded at Cerro Chinguela, Leimebamba, Atuén and Lluy. Also recorded along La Peca Nueva trail at 2500 m, above San Cristóbal at 1800-1950 m, at Abra Patricia, and at Mashua at 3300 m. *Endemic to Peru.*

Common Thornbird *Phacellodomus rufifrons* Espinero Común
15.5 cm (6"). Plate 58. ♪797. Brown above with rufous forecrown, a pale superciliary and whitish underparts. Often conspicuous around the large nest. Common in arid scrub in Amazonas, Cajamarca and San Martín to 1300 m. *Discontinuously distributed in campos of South America.*

Streak-fronted Thornbird *Phacellodomus striaticeps* Espinero Frentirrayada
16.5 cm (6.5"). Plate 58. Shy. Similar to Common Thornbird (no overlap), and has rufous on wings, rump and outer tail feathers. Cf. Rusty-fronted Canastero (tail is more rufous, longer and graduated). Uncommon in arid montane scrub in inter-Andean valleys north to Apurímac and Cusco at 2800-4200 m. *Andes of s Peru to nw Argentina.*

*Chestnut-backed Thornbird *Phacellodomus dorsalis* Espinero Dorsicastaño
19.5 cm (7.75"). Plate 65. A large, mostly rufous thornbird (back brighter) with grayish on sides of head and nape, a somewhat rusty crown and whitish throat. Uncommon in dense montane scrub of upper Río Marañón Valley in s Cajamarca and La Libertad at 2000-3400 m. One sighting from Ancash (JF). Frequents dense shrubs and bushy slopes with *Prosopis* trees. *Endemic to Peru.*

Orange-fronted Plushcrown *Metopothrix aurantiacus* Coronifelpa Frentinaranja
11.5 cm (4.5"). Plate 63. ♪677. A monotypic genus that looks more like a warbler than a furnariid. Often found in mixed-species flocks and easily mistaken for a tanager, but its orange legs, yellowish throat and orange forecrown identify this small arboreal furnariid. Fairly common in mid-level and tangles of humid secondary forests e of Andes south to Madre de Dios to 1000 m. *SE Colombia to n Bolivia and w Amazonian Brazil.*

Equatorial Graytail *Xenerpestes singularis* Colagris Ecuatorial
11.5 cm (4.5"). Plate 61. A small, warbler-like gray bird with a rufous forecrown, streaky underparts and no wingbars. Usually feeds actively near the canopy. Uncommon and local in humid foothill forests of Andes in Cajamarca and San Martín at 1000-1680 m. *Foothills of e Ecuador and n Peru.*

Spectacled Prickletail *Siptornis striaticollis* Colapúa Frontino
11.5 cm (4.5"). Plate 63. White pattern on face is distinctive (broken eye-ring and short postocular stripe); rufous above and grayish below. Tail is double-pointed. Often joins mixed feeding flocks. Uncommon and local in humid montane forests in n Cajamarca at 1300-2300 m. *Locally in Andes of s Colombia to n Peru.*

Rusty-winged Barbtail *Premnornis guttuligera* Colapúa Alirrojiza
14.5 cm (5.75"). Plate 63. ♪797. A brownish furnariid with rufous tail, rusty wings, buff streaks on the breast, and some streaking on the back. Often accompanies mixed flocks. Despite its English name it doesn't have a barbed tail, nor does it use its tail for support. Spotted Barbtail has brown flight feathers, tawny throat and stiffened rectrices. Uncommon in lower growth of humid montane forests on e slope of Andes at 1300-2500 m. *Andes of extreme nw Venezuela to s Peru.*

Spotted Barbtail *Premnoplex brunnescens* Colapúa Moteada
13.5 cm (5.3"). Plate 63. ♪797. Look for the tawny throat, buff spots on underparts, buff superciliary, and dark brown upperparts. Uncommon in undergrowth of humid montane forests of Andes at 900-2500 m. *Costa Rica to w Bolivia.*

Pearled Treerunner *Margarornis squamiger* Subepalo Perlado
15.5 cm (6"). Plate 63. ♪797. Resembles a woodcreeper in its arboreal behavior. Beautifully patterned below, with brown underparts profusely marked with tear-shaped, black-edged buffy spots. Has a white throat, prominent creamy-white superciliary, and rufous upperparts and tail. Fairly common in humid montane and elfin forests on e slope of Andes, and south on Pacific slope to Piura and Cajamarca at 1800-4100 m. *NW Venezuela to w Bolivia.*

Xenops **Xenops**. Four small acrobatic, arboreal furnariids very similar to each other. Most have an upturned lower mandible and a conspicuous white malar stripe. All have rufous wingbars.

Rufous-tailed Xenops *Xenops milleri* Pico-Lezna Colirrufa
10.7 cm (4.2"). Plate 63. ♪817CD. The only xenops that has a straight bill and lacks a white malar stripe. Lacks any black in tail. Mantle, crown and underparts are streaked. Uncommon in humid lowland forests e of Andes south to Madre de Dios to 600 m. *Venezuela and the Guianas to e Peru and Amazonian Brazil.*

Slender-billed Xenops *Xenops tenuirostris* Pico-Lezna Piquifino
10.7 cm (4.2"). Plate 63. Note the slender, slightly upturned bill, white malar stripe and black lines on rufous tail (at least two inner rectrices are dark). Streaked Xenops (higher elevation) has almost no black on tail. Rufous-tailed Xenops lacks white malar and has no black on tail. Rare in humid lowland forests e of Andes to 1000 m. Recorded at Amazonia Lodge and Manu National Park. *S Venezuela and the Guianas to n Bolivia and Amazonian Brazil.*

Plain Xenops *Xenops minutus* Pico-Lezna Simple
12.5 cm (5"). Plate 63. ♪797. The only xenops with an unstreaked mantle and underparts. Fairly common in humid lowland forests e of Andes, and w of Andes in Tumbes to 1000 m. *S Mexico to ne Argentina and se Brazil.*

Streaked Xenops *Xenops rutilans* Pico-Lezna Rayado
12.5 cm (5"). Plate 63. ♪797. Similar to Slender-billed Xenops, but usually found at higher elevations. Tail has very little black (only on outer web of one rectris). Uncommon in humid forests e of Andes and on Pacific slope south to Piura to 2400 m . *Costa Rica to n Argentina and s Brazil.*

Montane Foliage-gleaner *Anabacerthia striaticollis* Limpia-follaje Montano
16.5 cm (6.5"). Plate 64. ♪797. Arboreal: in canopy and borders. A "spectacled" foliage-gleaner. The buff eye-ring and superciliary are conspicuous. Where range overlaps with Rufous-rumped Foliage-gleaner, latter has brighter rufous upperparts and a darker, more richly colored throat. Fairly common in humid montane forests on e slope of Andes at 900-2300 m. *Andes of Venezuela to w Bolivia.*

Streaked Tuftedcheek *Pseudocolaptes boissonneautii* Barbablanca Rayado
20 cm (8"). Plate 63. ♪797. A large furnariid that often accompanies mixed flocks as it gleans through the mossy bromeliads. Recalls treehunters, but the puffy white cheek feathers make this attractive bird unmistakable. Common in humid montane and elfin forests at 1650-3100 m. *Andes of Venezuela to w Bolivia.*

Thripadectes **Treehunters**. Four species of fairly large foliage-gleaners with stout, hooked bills. They mostly inhabit mossy undergrowth of montane forests. All have streaked mantles and crowns. Note carefully the extent of streaking on underparts and upperparts.

Flammulated Treehunter *Thripadectes flammulatus* Trepamusgo Flamulado
24 cm (9.4"). Plate 64. ♫ JM. Note limited range. A large furnariid with prominent streaks on blackish upperparts and entire underparts. Sympatric with Striped Treehunter, but latter's belly and crissum are unmarked. Very similar to allopatric Buff-throated Treehunter, but latter's lower belly is almost unstreaked. Rare in humid montane forests (especially *Chusquea* bamboo) on Cerro Chinguela and Cordillera del Cóndor at 2000-3500 m. *Humid Andes of w Venezuela to extreme n Peru.*

Buff-throated (Peruvian) Treehunter *Thripadectes scrutator* Trepamusgo Peruano
24 cm (9.5"). Plate 65. A large furnariid with prominent buff streaks on its dark breast, upper belly and crissum. Sympatric with Striped Treehunter, but latter's streaks do not extend to the upper belly, and its breast is not as dark. Uncommon and local in humid montane forests on e slope of Andes south to Cusco (possibly Puno) at 2450-3200 m. *Andes of Peru and w Bolivia.*

Striped Treehunter *Thripadectes holostictus* Trepamusgo Listado
20 cm (8"). Plate 64. ♫ 797. Throat and breast are boldly streaked, but belly is unmarked. Black-billed Treehunter lacks bold streaks on breast. Buff-throated Treehunter is larger and has bolder, more contrasting streaks on upper belly. Cf. localized Flammulated Treehunter. Uncommon and local in humid montane forests south of Río Marañón at 1500-2500 m. *Andes of extreme sw Venezuela to w Bolivia.*

Black-billed Treehunter *Thripadectes melanorhynchus* Trepamusgo Piquinegro
20 cm (8"). Plate 64. ♫ 741CD. The least streaked of the treehunters. Throat is streaked, but breast and belly are almost unstreaked. Uncommon in humid subtropical forests on e slope of Andes south to Puno at 1000-1700 m. *Andes of Colombia to se Peru.*

Syndactyla **Foliage-gleaners.** The three species of *Syndactyla* foliage-gleaners in Peru inhabit mostly lower (sometimes middle) level of subtropical and montane forests, woodlands and borders. All have streaked underparts and straight bills.

Lineated Foliage-gleaner *Syndactyla subalaris* Limpia-follaje Lineado
18 cm (7"). Plate 64. ♫ 603. Crown and mantle are heavily streaked. Underparts are yellowish and mostly streaked. Chin is unstreaked yellowish, and wings and tail are rufous. Distinguished from any treehunter by its thinner bill. Buff-browed Foliage-gleaner has unstreaked mantle. Less conspicuously streaked Striped Woodhaunter has darker chin, longer bill and is generally duller. Uncommon in humid montane forests along e slope of Andes south to Cordillera Vilcabamba at 1000-2000 m. *Montane forests of Costa Rica to s Peru.*

Buff-browed Foliage-gleaner *Syndactyla rufosuperciliata* Limpia-follaje Cejianteada
18 cm (7"). Plate 64. ♫ 797. A foliage-gleaner with a prominent buff superciliary, a plain unstreaked olive-brown back and crown, a white chin, and whitish streaks on underparts and sides of neck. Uncommon in humid montane forests on e slope of Andes at 1300-2500 m. *Andes of s Ecuador to ne Argentina; disjuntly se Brazil to ne Argentina.*

*Rufous-necked Foliage-gleaner *Syndactyla ruficollis* Limpia-follaje Cuellirrufo
18 cm (7"). Plate 65. Within its limited range, the only foliage-gleaner that is mostly rufescent above with a bright rufous neck and superciliary. Rare to fairly common in humid montane forests on Pacific slope of Andes south to Lambayeque and Cajamarca at 600-2900 m. *Humid forests of sw Ecuador and nw Peru.*

Point-tailed Palmcreeper *Berlepschia rikeri* Trepador de Palmeras (Palmero)
21.5 cm (8.4"). Plate 63. ♫ 609. Associated with stands of *Mauritia* palms, where it creeps inconspicuously among the fronds. Black head, neck and underparts are conspicuously streaked with white. Unlikely to be confused in its limited habitat. Rare and local e of Andes to 600 m. Recent records from Tambopata Candamo Reserve, Lago Sándoval, Manu Wildlife Center and in suburbs of Iquitos. *Locally in Guyanas and Amazon basin.*

Peruvian Recurvebill *Simoxenops ucayalae* Pico-recurvo Peruano
19 cm (7.5"). Plate 65. ♪ 817CD. Undergrowth of *Guadua* bamboo thickets. A uniformly rufous furnariid with a pale superciliary, easily recognized by its massive bill with upturned lower mandible. Chestnut-crowned and Brown-rumped Foliage-Gleaners both have normal bills. Uncommon in humid *Guadua* bamboo forests and occasionally *Gynerium* canebrakes in s Ucayali and Madre de Dios to 1300 m. Regularly recorded at Tambopata Candamo Reserve. *Locally in se Peru and adjacent Amazonian Brazil.*

Striped Woodhaunter *Hyloctistes subulatus* Rondabosque Rayado
18 cm (7"). Plate 64. ♪ 797. A rather dull understory foliage-gleaner with a long, slender bill, and diffused streaks on mantle, crown and underparts. Very similar to Lineated Foliage-gleaner, but latter's streaks are bolder and more pronounced (limited elevation overlap). Distinguished from treehunters by its longer, more slender bill. Uncommon in humid lowland forests e of Andes to 1100 m. *Nicaragua to n Bolivia and Amazonian Brazil.*

Chestnut-winged Hookbill *Ancistrops strigilatus* Picogancho Alicastaño
19 cm (7.5"). Plate 64. ♪ 797. Frequents canopy and subcanopy. A heavy-billed furnariid with chestnut wings and tail combined with a grayish back and crown, heavily streaked with white, and pale underparts. Cf. Chestnut-winged Foliage-gleaner (unstreaked back and crown). Uncommon in humid lowland *terra firme* forests e of Andes, occasionally to 900m. *W and central Amazon basin.*

Philydor **Foliage-gleaners.** Five species of medium-sized foliage-gleaners that inhabit primary humid lowland forests, mostly in canopy and mid-level. Most are sympatric. All accompany mixed flocks; two or three species are occasionally seen foraging together. Identification can be difficult.

Chestnut-winged Foliage-gleaner *Philydor erythropterus* Limpia-follaje Alicastaña
18.5 cm (7.2"). Plate 64. ♪ 817CD. No other foliage-gleaner has the combination of rufous wings and tail contrasting with an unstreaked olive-gray mantle and crown, and buffy-yellow superciliary, lores and throat. Chestnut-winged Hookbill's mantle and crown are streaked. Buff-fronted Foliage-gleaner's mantle and wings are similar in color but underparts are buff. Uncommon in humid lowland *terra firme* forests e of Andes to 1200 m. *S Venezuela to n Bolivia and Amazonian Brazil.*

Rufous-rumped Foliage-gleaner *Philydor erythrocercus* Limpia-follaje Lomirrufo
16.5 cm (6.5"). Plate 64. ♪ 741CD. Three ssp. occur in Peru. All share olivaceous-brown mantle and wings, whitish-buff superciliary, and rufous uppertail coverts and tail. The ssp. differ in extent of rufous on rump and color of underparts. Race *subfulvus* (ne Peru) and *lyra* (illustrated, most of e Peru) have pale olive-buff underparts, darker on the flanks and buffier on the throat. Race *ochrogaster* has ochre-buff underparts, brighter buff on throat (cf. Buff-throated and Buff-fronted Foliage-Gleaners). Rufous in *lyra* and *ochrogaster* extends to rump, but in *subfulvus* is limited only to uppertail coverts. Very similar to sympatric Rufous-tailed Foliage-Gleaner. Fairly common in humid lowland *terra firme* forests and foothills e of Andes to 1600 m. Race *ochrogaster* of central Peru to Bolivia has been treated as a separate species (Ochre-bellied Foliage-gleaner). *Tropical se Colombia to the Guianas, Amazonian Brazil and n Bolivia.*

Rufous-tailed Foliage-gleaner *Philydor ruficaudatus* Limpia-follaje Colirrufa
18 cm (7"). Plate 64. ♪ 817CD. Very similar to Rufous-rumped Foliage-Gleaner, but only tail and uppertail coverts are rufous (as in *P. e. subfulvus*), and underparts have indistinct pale-buff streaks. Rufous-tailed is likely to accompany understory flocks, while Rufous-rumped is associated with canopy flocks (which provides a good clue for separating them). Uncommon in humid lowland *terra firme* forests e of Andes to 800 m. *S Venezuela and the Guianas to n Bolivia and Amazonian Brazil.*

Buff-fronted Foliage-gleaner *Philydor rufus* Limpia-follaje Frentianteada
19 cm (7.5"). Plate 64. ♪ 797. A *Philydor* with a conspicuous bright buff superciliary and throat, buff forecrown, rufous wings and tail, rufous-brown mantle and ochre-buff underparts. Compare Rufous-rumped (no rufous on wings), Chestnut-winged (grayer mantle, grayer rump, dingy underparts) and Buff-throated (conspicuous eye-ring, no rufous on wings). Uncommon in humid subtrop. forests along e slope of Andes to 1800 m, ranging to lowlands in Madre de Dios. *Mts. of Costa Rica to ne Argentina and se Brazil.*

Cinnamon-rumped Foliage-gleaner *Philydor pyrrhodes* Limpia-follaje Lomicanela
16.5 cm (6.5"). Plate 64. ♪ 797. No other *Philydor* has the combination of cinnamon rump and tail, cinnamon underparts and superciliary, blackish wings and yellowish legs. Cf. Chestnut-crowned Foliage-gleaner (rufous wings and crown). Uncommon in humid lowland forests e of Andes to 700 m. *S Venezuela and the Guianas to n Bolivia and e Brazil.*

Automolus **Foliage-gleaners.** Six species of bulky foliage-gleaners that usually inhabit the dense undergrowth of lowland forests. Subtle differences in plumage and their skulking habits make identification challenging.

Dusky-cheeked (Crested) Foliage-gleaner *Automolus dorsalis* Rascahojas Cachetioscuro
18 cm (7"). Plate 64. ♪ 817CD. An *Automolus* with a white throat, whitish superciliary (hence a "dark-cheeked" look), dingy whitish underparts, and dull rufous-brown upperparts. Olive-backed Foliage-Gleaner is similar (and sometimes shares same habitat) but has a brownish superciliary (cheeks don't stand out), and most of underparts are darker (contrasting with white throat). Uncommon and local in humid lowlands and foothills (mostly with bamboo) e of Andes from Loreto to Madre de Dios to 1200 m. Recorded at Amazonia Lodge. *SE Colombia to e Peru.*

Buff-throated Foliage-gleaner *Automolus ochrolaemus* Rascahojas Gargantianteada
19 cm (7.5"). Plate 64. ♪ 797. The only *Automolus* with a buff throat, bold buff eye-ring and a narrow superciliary. Cf. Buff-fronted Foliage-Gleaner. Common in humid lowland *terra firme* forests e of Andes to 1300 m. *S Mexico to n Bolivia and Amazonian Brazil.*

Chestnut-crowned Foliage-gleaner *Automolus rufipileatus* Rascahojas Coronicastaña
19.5 cm (7.75"). Plate 64. ♪ 817CD. A mostly uniform rufous-brown *Automolus* with orange eyes and uniform cinnamon-rufous underparts (throat is similar color to rest of underparts). Wings, crown and tail are slightly brighter rufous. Cf. Brown-rumped and Ruddy Foliage-gleaners and leaftossers. Fairly common in lowland *várzea* and riparian forests e of Andes, usually below 500 m. *Venezuela and the Guianas to n Bolivia and Amazonian Brazil.*

Olive-backed Foliage-gleaner *Automolus infuscatus* Rascahojas Dorsioliva
19 cm (7.5"). Plate 64. ♪ 797. A dull *Automolus* with a white throat; remaining underparts dingy-brown; olivaceous-brown upperparts. Cf. Dusky-cheeked Foliage-Gleaner. See also Rufous-tailed Foliage-gleaner (more arboreal, buff superciliary and dingy-buff underparts). Fairly common in humid lowland forests e of Andes to 700 m. *S Venezuela and the Guianas to e Peru and Brazil.*

Brown-rumped Foliage-gleaner *Automolus melanopezus* Rascahojas Lomipardo
18.5 cm (7.2"). Plate 64. ♪ 817CD. A mostly rufous-brown *Automolus* with red eyes and broad, orange malar area (center of throat is paler). Similar to, and often sympatric with, Ruddy (dark eyes, darker underparts) and Chestnut-crowned (more rufous underparts, crown and wings). Cf. Peruvian Recurvebill. Rare in lowland *Guadua* bamboo stands in s Ucayali, Madre de Dios and adjacent Cusco to 500 m. Recorded at Manu Wildlife Center. *Locally from se Colombia to se Peru and w Amazonian Brazil.*

Ruddy Foliage-gleaner *Automolus rubiginosus* Rascahojas Rojizo
18.5 cm (7.2"). Plate 64. ♪817CD. Four ssp. occur in Peru. All are fairly uniformly dark rufous-brown, with a somewhat brighter cinnamon throat. Race *brunnescens* (extreme ne Loreto) and *moderatus* (illustrated, Loreto to San Martin) have rufous-brown crowns and tails, but *watkinsi* (locally in Huánuco, Madre de Dios and Puno) has chestnut crown and tail. Tail is nearly black in race *nigricauda* that was recently recorded in Zona Reservada de Tumbes (Wust *in litt.*). Cf. Brown-rumped and Chestnut-crowned Foliage-gleaners. Uncommon and local in humid lowland and montane *terra firme* forests to 1300 m. *S Mexico to w Bolivia.*

*Henna-hooded Foliage-gleaner *Hylocryptus erythrocephalus* Rascahojas Capuchirrufo
21.5 cm (8.4"). Plate 65. Note restricted range. The only foliage-gleaner with an orange-rufous hood, wings and tail. Rare and local in dry deciduous forests in Tumbes, Lambayeque and Piura at 400-1900 m. Recorded at Zona Reservada de Tumbes. *SW Ecuador to nw Peru.*

Sclerurus **Leaftossers.** Four species of short-legged, terrestrial furnariids. All are plump and dark with fairly short, black tails. They forage inconspicuously away from mixed flocks by tossing leaves from side to side. Note bill shape and length and color of throat and chin. Superficially resemble Sharp-tailed Streamcreeper.

Short-billed Leaftosser *Sclerurus rufigularis* Tirahojas Piquicorto
15.5 cm (6"). Plate 63. ♪632. Note the fairly short straight bill and rufous throat. Tawny-throated Leaftosser has a longer, slightly decurved bill. Black-tailed Leaftosser has a longer bill, whitish chin and dark rump. Rare and local in humid lowland *terra firme* forests in Loreto and Amazonas. *S Venezuela and the Guianas to n Bolivia and Amazonian Brazil.*

Tawny-throated Leaftosser *Sclerurus mexicanus* Tirahojas Gargantianteado
16 cm (6.5"). Plate 63. ♪797. Note the long, slender, slightly decurved bill, tawny throat and rump. Other leaftossers have straight bills, and most lack a tawny throat. Uncommon in humid lowland and foothill forests e of Andes to 1500 m. *S Mexico to w Bolivia and e Brazil.*

Gray-throated Leaftosser *Sclerurus albigularis* Tirahojas Gargantigris
18 cm (7"). Plate 63. ♪797. Note the long, straight bill, and gray throat sharply bordered by a tawny chest. Limited overlap with Tawny-throated Leaftosser (tawny throat, decurved bill). Rare in humid montane forests on e slope of Andes at 1000-2000 m. *Costa Rica to Bolivia; Trinidad and Tobago.*

Black-tailed Leaftosser *Sclerurus caudacutus* Tirahojas Colinegro
18 cm (7"). Plate 63. ♪817CD. The only leaftosser with combination of long straight bill, whitish chin and dark rump. Uncommon in humid lowland *terra firme* forests e of Andes to 500 m. *S Venezuela and the Guianas to n Bolivia, Amazonian and e Brazil.*

Sharp-tailed Streamcreeper *Lochmias nematura* Riachuelero
15.5 cm (6"). Plate 63. ♪797. A shy, plump, mostly terrestrial furnariid that favors thick vegetation near mountain streams. The only bird in its range and habitat that is dark brown above and spotted with white below. Cf. Spotted Barbtail. Rare in montane forests along streams and rivers on e slope of Andes to 1700 m. Recorded at Manu Cloud-forest Lodge at 1660 m. *E Panama and Venezuela to n Argentina, Uruguay and se Brazil.*

Dendrocolaptidae (Woodcreepers; Trepadores). Species: World 51; Peru 27
A family of climbing birds closely related to the New World furnariids that inhabits tropical forests from Mexico to central Argentina. They are mostly medium-sized birds, and display an enormous variation in bill size and shape. This allows many species to have sympatric distributions in the tropical rainforests. Like woodpeckers, woodcreepers usually perch vertically with the spines at the tips

of the tails resting on the tree trunks. Most woodcreepers are insectivores, and climb trees in mixed-species flocks in search of insects on trunks and limbs. They spend a great deal of time rummaging in lianas, epiphytes, leaf litter and crevices. Identification is often challenging. Note size, bill (shape, color and size), presence of spots or streaks on mantle and crown, and pattern of underparts.

Dendrocincla **Woodcreepers.** Three medium to large woodcreepers, mostly uniform brown with straight bills.

Tyrannine Woodcreeper *Dendrocincla tyrannina* Trepador Tiranino
25 cm (9.8"). Plate 65. ♪658. The only large uniformly reddish-brown woodcreeper in its range that has a straight bill and lacks facial markings. Sympatric Strong-billed Woodcreeper has a longer slightly decurved bill and some facial markings. Rare in montane and cloud forests south to Cusco at 1800-3000 m. Recorded 18 km from Botoquín on Bagua Grande road and at 2100-2900 m on Manu road. *Andes of nw Venezuela to s Peru.*

Plain-brown Woodcreeper *Dendrocincla fuliginosa* Trepador Pardo
20 cm (8"). Plate 67. ♪658. A uniformly dark-brown woodcreeper with dark eyes. Cheeks are slightly paler, chin often pale but never white. Often follows army ants. Cf. White-chinned and Cinnamon-throated Woodcreepers. Rare in dry forests on Pacific slope south to Lambayeque; fairly common in humid lowland forests e of Andes to 1300 m. *Honduras to Amazonian Brazil; Trinidad and Tobago.*

White-chinned Woodcreeper *Dendrocincla merula* Trepador Barbiblanco
19 cm (7.5"). Plate 67. ♪658. Similar to Plain-brown Woodcreeper but has pale-blue eyes and a white chin. Rarely seen away from flocks attending army ant swarms. Uncommon in lowland *terra firme* forests e of Andes to 300 m. *S Venezuela and the Guianas to n Bolivia and Amazonian Brazil.*

Deconychura **Woodcreepers.** A pair of slim, medium-sized woodcreepers with comparitively short, straight bills and proportionately longer tails. In both species the male is considerably larger than the female.

Long-tailed Woodcreeper *Deconychura longicauda* Trepador Colilargo
Male 21.5 cm (8.4"); female 19 cm (7.5"). Plate 66. *658.* Typical of the genus; a long-tailed, straight-billed woodcreeper. Has a faint facial pattern, narrow buffy streaks on crown, slightly more pronounced buffy postocular stripe, and buffy "arrowhead" spots (*connectens* in most of e Peru) or buffy streaks on the breast (*pallida* in Madre de Dios and Puno, illustrated). Very similar to Spot-throated Woodcreeper. Cf. Wedge-billed Woodcreeper (very different bill, more pronounced markings). Uncommon in humid lowlands and foothills on e slope of Andes to 1700 m. *SE Honduras to n Bolivia and Amazonian Brazil.*

Spot-throated Woodcreeper *Deconychura stictolaema* Trepador Gargantipunteada
Male 17.5 cm (6.8") female 16.5 cm (6.5"). Plate 66. ♪658. Similar to Long-tailed Woodcreeper but smaller (note size difference between sexes), rump and tail are rufous, contrasting with browner back (rump in Long-tailed same color as back) and buffy "arrowhead" markings on breast. Rare and local in humid lowland *terra firme* forests e of Andes south to n Ucayali. *S Venezuela and the Guianas to ne Peru and Amazonian Brazil.*

Olivaceous Woodcreeper *Sittasomus griseicapillus* Trepador Oliváceo
12.5 cm (5"). Plate 67. ♪658. A small, distinctive woodcreeper with a plain gray head. Olivaceous-gray back contrasts with rufous secondaries in e Peru race *amazonus*, or olive-gray back contrasts with pale-cinnamon secondaries in extreme nw race *aequatorialis* (illustrated) in Tumbes. Fairly common in humid lowland and upper trop. forests to 1500 m. *Mexico to n Argentina, Paraguay and s Brazil.*

Wedge-billed Woodcreeper *Glyphorynchus spirurus* Trepador Piquicuña
14 cm (5.5"). Plate 67. ♪ 658. Note the small, unique wedge-shaped bill and conspicuous buffy postocular stripe. Other small woodcreepers have "normal" bills. Common in humid lowland and upper trop. forests e of Andes to 1000 m. *S Mexico to n Bolivia, Amazonian and e Brazil.*

Long-billed Woodcreeper *Nasica longirostris* Trepador Piquilargo
35 cm (14"). Plate 67. ♪ 658. A large, distinctive woodcreeper with a very long, whitish bill and white throat. Rare in humid lowland *várzea* and riparian forests e of Andes to 500 m. Frequently recorded at Manu Wildlife Center and Tambato Candamo. *S Venezuela and French Guiana to n Bolivia and Amazonian Brazil.*

Cinnamon-throated Woodcreeper *Dendrexetastes rufigula* Trepador Garganticanela
24 cm (9.5"). Plate 67. ♪ 658. No other large woodcreeper has a heavy, straight yellowish bill. Fairly uniform rufous-brown with a necklace of white streaks on the chest. Cf. *Dendrocincla* (dark bill, smaller size, no necklace), Barred Woodcreeper (densely barred, dark bill), and Strong-billed Woodcreeper. Fairly common in humid lowland forests e of Andes, mostly below 500 m but rarely to 950 m. *The Guianas to n Bolivia and Amazonian Brazil.*

Bar-bellied Woodcreeper *Hylexetastes stresemanni* Trepador Ventrirrayado
27 cm (10.5"). Plate 66. ♪ 658. A large woodcreeper with a long, heavy reddish bill, unmarked mantle and barred belly. Similar Amazonian Barred-Woodcreeper is barred on mantle and entire underparts, and its bill is darker and more slender. Rare (known from four records) in humid lowland forests in s Ucayali and Madre de Dios to 300 m. *E Peru and w Brazil.*

Strong-billed Woodcreeper *Xiphocolaptes promeropirhynchus* Trepador Piquifuerte
30 cm (11.7"). Plate 66. ♪ 658. A large woodcreeper with a long, very heavy, slightly decurved bill. At least seven ssp. occur in Peru, which differ in size and color of the bill (paler and longer in lowlands, darker and slightly shorter in highlands); also different head and underpart markings. All have a dark malar area, buffy postocular stripe, and narrow buffy streaking on the crown. Other similarly patterned woodcreepers have more slender bills. Lowland races *orenocensis* and *berlepschi* may represent separate species. Uncommon to rare and widespread in humid lowland *várzea* and montane forests e of Andes to 2800 m (w of Andes only in Tumbes and n Piura). *Mexico to n Bolivia and Amazonian Brazil.*

Amazonian Barred-Woodcreeper *Dendrocolaptes certhia* Trepador Barreteado
26.5 cm (10.3"). Plate 66. ♪ 658. A large woodcreeper, heavily barred above and below, with a straight dusky-reddish bill. Cf. Black-banded (buffy streaks on breast and crown), Strong-billed (no barring and much heavier, slightly decurved bill) and Cinnamon-throated (yellowish bill, not barred). Uncommon in humid lowland forests (especially secondary and *várzea*) e of Andes to 900 m. *S Venezuela to n Bolivia, Amazonian and e Brazil.*

Black-banded Woodcreeper *Dendrocolaptes picumnus* Trepador Ventribandeado
27 cm (10.5"). Plate 66. ♪ 658. A large woodcreeper with a long, dark, straight bill, dark barring on the belly, and buff streaks on throat, breast and crown. Cf. Amazonian-Barred, Strong-billed (heavier bill, stronger facial pattern) and Buff-throated (streaked underparts and unstreaked buff throat). Uncommon in humid montane and lowland *terra firme* forests e of Andes to 2000 m. *Mexico to n Argentina and Amazonian Brazil.*

Xiphorhynchus **Woodcreepers**. Seven species of mostly medium-sized, very similar looking woodcreepers. Bills are straight or slightly decurved. Mantle and breast can be spotted or streaked with buff or white (often with a dark frame to each spot).

Straight-billed Woodcreeper *Xiphorhynchus picus* Trepador Piquirrecto
21.5 cm (8.4"). Plate 66. ♪658. Whitish bill is very straight (especially the culmen and cutting edge). Crown is streaked with white but mantle is largely unstreaked; throat is white and breast has conspicuous white spots edged black. Similar Striped Woodcreeper has a striped back, and bill is slightly decurved. See also very rare and almost identical Zimmer's Woodcreeper. Fairly common mainly in lowland *várzea* forests e of Andes to 1100 m. *Panama to n Bolivia, central and ne Brazil.*

*Zimmer's Woodcreeper *Xiphorhynchus necopinus* Trepador de Zimmer
21 cm (8.5"). Plate 66. Apparently almost identical to Straight-billed, though said to be duller brown above; spots on breast are slightly narrower—without conspicuous black edges—giving a more streaked appearance. First identification of this rare woodcreeper in life has been reported by Bret Whitney. Previously known only from Amazonian Brazil (Ridgely and Tudor 1994). Whitney and José Alvarez (pers. comm.) have recently confirmed its presence in Peru (tape recordings and specimens) in flooded forests along the Amazon and major tributaries, including the Marañón, Ucayali and lower Río Napo. *Flooded forests along Amazon River and major tributaries.*

Striped Woodcreeper *Xiphorhynchus obsoletus* Trepador Listado
19 cm (7.5"). Plate 66. ♪658. A woodcreeper with a very slightly decurved, whitish bill, whitish streaks on crown and mantle, a whitish throat and conspicuous white spots on breast. Cf. Straight-billed Woodcreeper. Uncommon in lowland *várzea* forests e of Andes to 500 m. *S Venezuela and the Guianas to n Bolivia and Amazonian Brazil.*

Ocellated Woodcreeper *Xiphorhynchus ocellatus* Trepador Ocelado
21.5 cm (8.4"). Plate 66. ♪658. Note the slightly decurved, dark bill, buff spots on the breast, and buff streaks on crown and mantle, with only a few narrow buff streaks. Very similar to Spix's Woodcreeper, but latter has conspicuous streaks on mantle. Cf. Buff-throated Woodcreeper (larger, longer bill, more prominent buff throat, streaks on mantle). Fairly common in lower and middle level in humid *terra firme* and foothill forests on e slope of Andes to 1500 m. *Amazonian Brazil to se Colombia, e Ecuador, e Peru and n Bolivia.*

Elegant Woodcreeper *Xiphorhynchus elegans* Trepador Elegante
21.5 cm (8.4"). Plate 66. ♪658. Note the slightly decurved, dark bill, buff spots on breast, and buff streaks on crown and mantle. Cf. Ocellated and Buff-throated (larger, longer bill, more prominent buff throat). Fairly common in humid lowland forests e of Andes to 1400 m. Formerly considered conspecific with Spix's Woodcreeper *X. spixii* (Ridgely and Tudor 1994), but see Haffer (1997). *Colombia to n Bolivia and Amazonian Brazil.*

Buff-throated Woodcreeper *Xiphorhynchus guttatus* Trepador Gargantianteado
27 cm (10.5"). Plate 66. ♪658. A large woodcreeper with a long bill, prominent buff throat, and buff streaks on breast, crown and mantle. Larger than any other *Xiphorhynchus*. Cf. Black-banded (streaked throat, barred belly) and Strong-billed (larger, very heavy bill, dark malar stripe). Common in humid lowland forests e of Andes to 1100 m. *E Guatemala to n Bolivia and e Brazil.*

Olive-backed Woodcreeper *Xiphorhynchus triangularis* Trepador Dorsioliva
23 cm (9"). Plate 67. ♪658. Olive-brown crown and underparts are spotted with whitish, and throat is scaly. In good light note olive-brown back. Fairly common to uncommon in humid montane forests on e slope of Andes at 1000-2500 m. *Andes of Venezuela to w Bolivia.*

Lepidocolaptes **Woodcreepeers.** Three species of mostly allopatric, medium-sized woodcreepers with slender, decurved bills; more decurved than in *Xiphorhynchus*. Conspicuous white streaks (with dark frame to each streak) on entire underparts.

Streak-headed Woodcreeper *Lepidocolaptes souleyetii* Trepador Cabecirrayado
21 cm (8.3"). Plate 67. ♪ 658. The only *Lepidocolaptes* in its range and habitat. Note the narrow buffy streaks on crown and underparts. Fairly common in dry forests on Pacific slope south to Lambayeque to 1500 m. *Mexico to nw Peru and extreme n Brazil.*

Montane Woodcreeper *Lepidocolaptes lacrymiger* Trepador Montano
20 cm (8"). Plate 67. ♪ 797. A *Lepidocolaptes* with an unspotted mantle, and crown spotted with buff. Cf. Lineated Woodcreeper (crown is unspotted). Formerly considered conspecific with Spot-crowned Woodcreeper (*L. affinis*) of Central America. Fairly common in humid montane forests on e slope of Andes at 1500-3000 m. *Mountains of w Venezuela to n Bolivia.*

Lineated Woodcreeper *Lepidocolaptes albolineatus* Trepador Lineado
21 cm (8"). Plate 67. ♪ 658. Often accompanies mixed-canopy flocks. The only woodcreeper with boldly streaked underparts and unmarked upperparts. Cf. Montane Woodcreeper (limited overlap at best). Uncommon in humid lowland *terra firme* forests mostly to 1000 m, occasionally higher. *S Venezuela and the Guianas to n Bolivia and Amazonian Brazil.*

Campylorhamphus **Scythebills.** Four species of fairly large woodcreepers with very long, slender, deeply decurved bills. Note color and location of streaks, bill color and facial pattern.

Greater Scythebill *Campylorhamphus pucherani* Picoguadaña Grande
29 cm (11.3"). Plate 65. ♪ JM. A scythebill with a relatively short, whitish bill, conspicuous whitish malar and postocular stripes, and an almost unstreaked dark body. Rare and local in humid montane forests from Amazonas to Cusco at 1500-3000 m. *W Andes of Colombia to se Peru.*

Red-billed Scythebill *Campylorhamphus trochilirostris* Picoguadaña Piquirrojo
30 cm (11.7"). Plate 67. ♪ 658. Note the conspicuous, long reddish bill, and whitish streaks on mantle, crown and underparts. Cf. Brown-billed (darker bill, buffier streaks) and Curve-billed (unstreaked mantle, buffier streaks on crown). Uncommon on Pacific slope south to Piura, and in lowlands e of Andes to 1000 m. *E Panama to n Argentina and e Brazil.*

Brown-billed Scythebill *Campylorhamphus pusillus* Picoguadaña Piquipardo
25 cm (9.8"). Plate 67. ♪ 658. A scythebill with a long, dusky bill, and buff streaks on mantle, crown and underparts. Cf. Red-billed Scythebill. Rare in humid montane forests on e slope of Andes south to San Martín and Cajamarca at 600-1700 m. *Costa Rica to nw Venezuela and n Peru.*

Curve-billed Scythebill *Campylorhamphus procurvoides* Picoguadaña Piquicurvo
26 cm (10.1"). Plate 67. ♪ 658. Very similar to Red-billed Scythebill, but mantle is unstreaked; underparts are more spotted than streaked. Bill is relatively shorter and slightly darker. A single record (overlooked due to identification problems?) from humid lowland forests near e bank of Río Napo (n Loreto). *E Colombia to s Venezuela, the Guianas and Amazonian Brazil.*

Thamnophilidae (Typical Antbirds; Hermigueros Tipicos). Species: World 208; Peru 105
Typical antbirds comprise another large family of birds restricted mainly to lowland tropical forests from Mexico to central Argentina. Some species associate with army ants, but most do not. They vary greatly in size and color, often being combinations of black, rufous, white, brown or yellow, and range in size from the minuscule 7.5-cm Pygmy Antwren to the 35-cm Giant Antshrike. They feed primarily on insects, spiders, lizards, frogs and other small animals. Some species follow army ants to capture prey flushed by the ants.

Fasciated Antshrike *Cymbilaimus lineatus* Batará Lineado
18 cm (7"). Plate 68. ♪ 797. Mostly in mid-level and high-level subcanopy of tangles and forest clearings. Both sexes are dark with fine light barring (black and white in male, brown and buff in female), have red eyes, and fairly short, compressed crests (black in male, rufous in female). In southeast compare to very similar Bamboo Antshrike (Fasciated Antshrike is sometimes found in bamboo). Similar *Thamnophilus* (especially Lined and Barred Antshrikes) have yellowish eyes. Uncommon in humid lowland and foothill forests e of Andes to 1000 m. *SE Honduras to n Bolivia and Amazonian Brazil.*

Bamboo Antshrike *Cymbilaimus sanctaemariae* Batará de Bambú
17 cm (6.6"). Plate 69. ♪ 797. Local in mid-level, usually associated with bamboo. Both sexes have dark-brown eyes and a fairly long, shaggy crest. Cf. Fasciated Antshrike. Fairly common and local in *Guadua* bamboo thickets in Madre de Dios and Cusco at 300-1200 m. *SE Peru, n Bolivia and sw Amazonian Brazil.*

Undulated Antshrike *Frederickena unduligera* Batará Ondulado
23 cm (9"). Plate 68. ♪ 817CD. Largest Peruvian antshrike; stocky and heavy-billed. Throat is black in male, and barred black and rufous in female. Rare in undergrowth of humid lowland and foothill *terra firme* forests e of Andes to 1050 m. *W Amazon basin.*

Great Antshrike *Taraba major* Batará Grande
20 cm (8"). Plate 68. ♪ 797. Undergrowth of borders of humid second-growth thickets. Note the stout, hooked bill and red eyes. The only antshrike that is black (male) or rufous (female) above and white below. Uncommon along Pacific slope in Tumbes and Piura; fairly common e of Andes to 900 m. *S Mexico to n Argentina and se Brazil.*

Collared Antshrike *Sakesphorus bernardi* Batará Acollarado
18 cm (7"). Plate 71. Unmistakable in its range. Female is like that of Black-crested Antshrike, but underparts are unstreaked. Common in lower level of deciduous forests and arid scrub on Pacific slope south to La Libertad to 1500 m. Disjunct population in Río Marañón Valley. *W Ecuador to nw Peru.*

Black-crested Antshrike *Sakesphorus canadensis* Batará Copetón
16.5 cm (6.5"). Plate 68. ♪ 622. No overlap with similar Collared Antshrike. Female has a rufous crown, streaked grayish cheeks, a short crest, buffy edges to wing coverts and a rufous tail. Rare and local in humid lowlands e of Andes, especially blackwater lake margins along lower Río Ucayali and lower Río Marañón (Loreto). *S Venezuela and the Guianas to ne Peru and nw Amazonian Brazil.*

Thamnophilus **Antshrikes.** A large genus of medium-sized, sexually dimorphic antshrikes. Can be divided into two large groups by male's plumage—species with barred underparts (sometimes upperparts as well) and mostly slaty or black antshrikes. Most females are browner with rufous caps.

Barred Antshrike *Thamnophilus doliatus* Batará Barreteado
16.5 cm (6.5"). Plate 68. ♪ 797. Male is barred above and below, has a fairly long black crest and yellow eyes. Eyes of similar Chapman's Antshrike (no overlap) are brownish to grayish-yellow (not yellow). Female is mostly rufous, with stripes on neck and sides of head. Male Lined Antshrike (limited overlap) is similar, but much darker, especially on underparts. Cf. darker red-eyed Fasciated Antshrike. Fairly common in forest edge and second growth in humid lowlands e of Andes to 1500 m. *E Mexico to nw Argentina, central and e Brazil.*

Chapman's Antshrike *Thamnophilus zarumae* Batará de Chapman
15.5 cm (6"). Plate 71. The only barred antshrike in its limited range. Female similar to female Barred Antshrike. Fairly common in scrub and secondary woodlands on Pacific slope south to Lambayeque at 500-2200 m, but to 2625 m at Ayabaca, Piura (Best *et al.* 1993). Formerly considered conspecific with Barred Antshrike. *SW Ecuador and nw Peru.*

Lined Antshrike *Thamnophilus tenuepunctatus* Batará Listado
16.5 cm (6.5"). Plate 68. Male is similar to male Barred Antshrike (bars are thicker giving a darker look). Male Fasciated Antshrike has barred throat and red (not yellow) eyes. Female similar to female Chestnut-backed Antshrike (no overlap). Fairly common along humid thickets and forest borders along e slope of Andes south to San Martín at 500-1400 m. *E Colombia to ne Peru.*

Chestnut-backed Antshrike *Thamnophilus palliatus* Batará Dorsicastaño
16.5 cm (6.5"). Plate 71. ♪ 797. The only antshrike in its range with a bright rufous back and barred underparts. Crown is black in male, rufous in female. Formerly considered a race of Lined Antshrike. Uncommon in thickets and forest borders in humid lowlands and subtrop. forests north to Huánuco at 500-2000 m. *Amazon basin and s Brazil.*

Castelnau's Antshrike *Thamnophilus cryptoleucus* Batará de Castelnau
18 cm (7"). Plate 71. ♪ 677. Closely associated with island riverside vegetation. A very large, mostly black antshrike with red eyes, a heavy bill and white edges to wing coverts. All other black antshrikes are smaller, smaller-billed, and none is as black. Female is all black (lacks white on wing coverts). Uncommon in undergrowth of river island thickets in Loreto and Ucayali south to Lagarto to 300 m. *SE Colombia, e Ecuador, ne Peru and w Amazonian Brazil.*

White-shouldered Antshrike *Thamnophilus aethiops* Batará Hombriblanco
16 cm (6.5"). Plate 70. ♪ 797. Male is gray, with sparsely dotted wings in *kapouni* (e Peru, illustrated) or nearly all black with narrow white shoulders in *aethiops* (ne Peru). Eyes usually red. Plain-winged Antshrike is similar but lacks white dots on wing coverts. Female is uniformly rufous and has red eyes. Nominate *aethiops* of s Ecuador and ne Peru may represent a separate species. Uncommon in lowland and foothill *terra firme* forests e of Andes south of the Amazon, and in extreme n La Libertad to 1100 m. *S Venezuela to n Bolivia and Brazil.*

Uniform Antshrike *Thamnophilus unicolor* Batará Unicolor
15.5 cm (6"). Plate 70. Male is the only uniform dark lead-gray antshrike in its elevation. Lacks any markings on wing and tail and has gray eyes. Cf. Variable Antshrike. Female is rufous-brown with gray cheeks and gray eyes. Uncommon in humid montane forests along e slope of Andes south to n Cusco at 1400-2300 m. *Andes of se Colombia to central Peru.*

Upland Antshrike *Thamnophilus aroyae* Batará de Altura
15.5 cm (6"). Plate 71. ♪ 797. Male is the only gray antshrike in its limited range with narrow white edges to wing coverts and narrow white tips to tail. Other gray antshrikes in its range either lack wing and tail markings or have bolder markings. Female is rufous-brown with chestnut-rufous crown and grayish cheeks. Fairly common on lower Andean slopes and foothills in s Cusco and Puno at 800-1700 m. *S Peru to n Bolivia.*

Plain-winged Antshrike *Thamnophilus schistaceus* Batará Alillano
14 cm (5.5"). Plate 70. ♪ 797. A uniformly gray, unmarked antshrike with red eyes. Ssp. *capitalis* in Loreto has a black crown. Nominate (illustrated) and *dubius* have gray crowns. No other *Thamnophilus* in the lowlands lacks any markings. Cf. Bluish-slate and Cinereous Antshrikes (both have rather upright postures, thinner bills, and are closely associated with mixed flocks, unlike Plain-winged Antshrike). Cf. Mouse-colored Antshrike. Female is rufous-brown with a chestnut-rufous crown, grayish cheeks and red eyes. Fairly common, mostly in mid-level of humid lowland forests e of Andes, occasionally to 1200 m. *SE Colombia to n Bolivia and w Amazonian Brazil.*

Mouse-colored Antshrike *Thamnophilus murinus* Batará Murino
14 cm (5.5"). Plate 70. ♪ 797. Male is gray, has dark eyes, narrow whitish edges to wing coverts, and narrow whitish tips to undertail. Other gray antshrikes in its range either lack wing and tail markings or have bolder markings. Cf. especially Plain-winged Antshrike. Female like female Plain-

winged, but former has a dark (not red) eye. Fairly common and local, mostly in mid-level of humid lowland forests e of Andes south to Madre de Dios to 500 m. *S Venezuela and the Guianas to e Peru and Amazonian Brazil.*

Slaty-Antshrikes. A complex of dark antshrikes with conspicuous white spots on tail and wing. We follow the taxonomy suggested by Isler *et al.* 2001.

Western Slaty-Antshrike *Thamnophilus atrinucha* Batará-Pizarroso Occidental
15.5 cm (6"). Plate 70. Very similar to Marañón Slaty-Antshrike (no overlap). Similar tail and wing markings and pale-gray underparts, but male's crown is spotted with gray (not solid black). Female similar to female Marañón Slaty-Antshrike but duller. Recent sight records and tape recordings in Tumbes at Quebrada Faical, Pozo del Pato and between Campo Verde and Cotrina (Whiffen and Sadgrove 2000). *S Belize and Guatemala to nw Venezuela, w Ecuador and n Peru.*

Marañón Slaty-Antshrike *Thamnophilus leucogaster* Batará-Pizarroso de Marañón
15.5 cm (6"). Plate 71. Nominate *leucogaster* and allopatric *huallagae* (Huallaga Slaty-Antshrike) may represent two distinct species (Isler *et al.* 1997; 2001). Race *leucogaster* is notably whiter on belly. Amazonian Antshrike is similar to *huallagae,* but smaller and even darker on the back and belly. Female of *leucogaster* is similar to male but gray is replaced by buffy-rufous. Female of *huallagae* has an olive-gray back and rufous crown; underparts are dusky-gray. Fairly common in riparian thickets and dry forests in middle Marañón Valley in Cajamarca and Amazonas, and on w slope of middle Río Huallaga Valley in San Martín to 1100 m. *N Peru and adjacent s Ecuador.*

Amazonian Antshrike *Thamnophilus amazonicus* Batará Amazónico
15.5 cm (6"). Plate 70. ♫ 797. Male is similar to male Marañón Slaty-Antshrike (no overlap) but is smaller and darker with a gray forecrown. Female has rufous-orange underparts and head, bold wing and tail markings. Cf. Pearly Antshrike (blue-gray eyes and white spots on tertials). Uncommon and local in lower level of humid lowland riverine woodlands e of Andes from Loreto south to Madre de Dios to 1300 m. *S Venezuela and the Guianas to n Bolivia, Amazonian and central Brazil.*

Variable Antshrike *Thamnophilus caerulescens* Batará Variable
14.5 cm (5.75"). Plate 70. ♫ 797. Within its range, the male is the only black *Thamnophilus* with white edges to wing coverts and white tail tips. Female is olive-brown above, tawny below and has a grayish head. Cf. some *Cercomacra*. Both Peruvian races *subandinus* and *melanochrous* together with Bolivian *aspersiventer* may represent a separate species. Fairly common along e slope of Andes north to s Amazonas to 2500 m. *E Peru to n Argentina, Uruguay and Brazil.*

Rufous-capped Antshrike *Thamnophilus ruficapillus* Batará Gorrirrufo
16.5 cm (6.5"). Plate 68, 69. ♫ 797. Two ssp. occur, males of both have dark reddish eyes, rufous caps and black and white barring on underparts. Color of upperparts varies from olive-gray back and face (*marcapatae*, Cusco and Puno) to brown with grayish-brown on face (*jaczewskii*, Amazonas and Cajamarca). Chestnut-backed and female Lined Antshrikes have yellow eyes, barring on face and bright rufous backs. Female *marcapatae* is olive above, unbarred tawny below and has a rufous crown. Female *jaczewskii* is similar but upperparts are rufous brown. Uncommon and disjunct in scrub in humid Andes at 2000-2800 m. The Peruvian races have been treated as a separate species (Marcapata Antshrike). *E Peru to n Argentina, Paraguay and se Brazil.*

Spot-winged Antshrike *Pygiptila stellaris* Batará Alimoteado
13.5 cm (5.3"). Plate 70. ♫ 797. Chunky and shorter-tailed than any other gray antshrike. Hooked bill is especially heavy. Fairly common in subcanopy of humid lowland forests e of Andes to 500 m. *S Venezuela and the Guianas to n Bolivia and Amazonian Brazil.*

Pearly Antshrike *Megastictus margaritatus* Batará Perlado
14 cm (5.5"). Plate 68. ♪ 677. The wing coverts and tertials have large round white spots. No other gray antshrike has such wing spots, white tail tips, white spots on uppertail and blue-gray eyes. Female is brown with large round buffy spots on wing coverts, tertials and tail. Uncommon and local in lower level of humid lowland forests in Loreto and Ucayali to 400 m. *S Venezuela to e Peru and w Amazonian Brazil.*

Black Bushbird *Neoctantes niger* Arbustero Negro
16.5 cm (6.5"). Plate 68. ♪ 677. An antbird with a uniquely shaped bill—the lower mandible is decidedly upturned. Male is uniformly black. Female is dull black with a chestnut breast and upper belly. Uncommon and local in undergrowth of humid lowland forests e of Andes from Loreto to Madre de Dios and adjacent Cusco to 500 m. *W Amazon basin.*

Russet Antshrike *Thamnistes anabatinus* Batará Rojizo
15.5 cm (6"). Plate 68. ♪ 741CD. Both sexes are mostly rufous-brown. They resemble foliage-gleaners but the bill is heavy and hooked. A dark line runs from the lores to ear coverts and is bordered by a pale-brown superciliary. Note the russet wings, crown and tail. Peruvian and Bolivian race *rufescens* may represent a separate species. Joins mixed flocks in canopy and subcanopy. Uncommon in canopy of humid Andean foothill and lowland forests from Amazonas south, to 1700 m. *Gulf-Caribbean slope of se Mexico to w Bolivia.*

Dysithamnus **Antvireos.** A pair of rather chunky, short-tailed antbirds with stout, vireo-like bills. Both Peruvian species inhabit mostly mid-elevation humid forests.

Plain Antvireo *Dysithamnus mentalis* Batarito Cabecigris
11.5 cm (4.5"). Plate 72. ♪ 797. Four ssp. occur in Peru (*tavarae*, illustrated). Male: back color varies from olive to dark gray, and belly color ranges from pale-gray to pale-yellow; ear coverts are often darker. Female is rather dull with a darker patch on the ear and a rufous crown. Female superficially recalls a Tawny-crowned Greenlet. Fairly common in Pacific lowlands in Tumbes and Piura to 900 m; common along e slope of Andes to 2000 m. *SE Mexico to ne Argentina, Paraguay and Brazil; Trinidad and Tobago.*

White-streaked Antvireo *Dysithamnus leucostictus* Batarito Albirrayado
12.5 cm (5"). Plate 72. Note limited range. Male is rather uniform slate-gray, blacker on chest; larger and blacker than Plain Antvireo. Similar *Myrmotherula* antwrens have thinner bills. Female pattern is unique, with white streaks on underparts and a rufous crown. Often seen in pairs (where presence of female provides a good clue for identification). Rare in humid foothill and montane forests on e slope of Andes along Peru-Ecuador border at 900-1900 m. *E Colombia, Venezuela and e Ecuador to extreme n Peru.*

Thamnomanes **Antshrikes.** Four species of antshrikes with upright posture and relatively thin bills (versus *Thamnophilus*). Closely associated with lower-level mixed flocks. All members of the genus are very similar to each other and some are sympatric. Males are mostly gray, and sometimes have a black throat. Females are usually dull (except distinctive female Bluish-slate). For identification note especially: presence of black on throat, white dorsal patch, posture and body structure. Some *Thamnophilus* and *Cercomacra* are similar in color, but have different posture and behavior.

Saturnine Antshrike *Thamnomanes saturninus* Batará Saturnino
14.5 cm (5.75"). Plate 70. ♪ 797. A bull-headed, short-tailed *Thamnomanes* with a semi-concealed white dorsal patch. Male has extensive black on throat and upper chest. Sympatric Cinereous and Dusky-throated Antshrikes lack black on throat. Female is rather dull-brown, with more rufous on wings and tail, like that of Dusky-throated Antshrike (latter lacks a white dorsal patch). Note: possibly a ssp. of Dusky-throated. Rare in humid lowland *terra firme* forests from Loreto south to Río Ucayali to 300 m. *NE Peru, extreme ne Bolivia and w Amazonian Brazil.*

Dusky-throated Antshrike *Thamnomanes ardesiacus* Batará Gargantioscura
14 cm (5.5"). Plate 70. ♪817CD. A bull-headed, short-tailed *Thamnomanes* without a white dorsal patch. In most cases males do not have black throats (in southern part of range may have a little black on throat). Sympatric Cinereous and Bluish-slate Antshrikes have longer tails, more slender builds and a semi-concealed white dorsal patch. In Loreto, cf. Saturnine Antshrike. Dull female similar to Saturnine Antshrike. Other female *Thamnomanes* have brighter rufous bellies. Uncommon in humid lowland *terra firme* forests e of Andes to 500 m. *S Venezuela and the Guianas to e Peru and Amazonian Brazil.*

Cinereous Antshrike *Thamnomanes caesius* Batará Cinéreo
14.5 cm (5.75"). Plate 70. ♪797. Note limited range. Sits more upright and is longer-tailed than sympatric Dusky-throated and Saturnine Antshrikes. Male has a white dorsal patch, but lacks any black on throat. Female is rather dull brown, but belly and crissum are rufous. Fairly common in humid lowland forests in Loreto n of the Amazon to 800 m. Recently recorded in s Loreto along Río Cushabatay and at Orellana (TSS). *S Venezuela and the Guianas to n Bolivia, Amazonian and e Brazil.*

Bluish-slate Antshrike *Thamnomanes schistogynus* Batará Azulino
14.5 cm (5.75"). Plate 70, 71. ♪797. A nuclear species in understory mixed flocks. Sympatric only with Dusky-throated Antshrike, but sits more upright and is longer-tailed. Female's gray hood and rufous belly combination is distinctive. Fairly common in humid lowland forests from Loreto south of the Amazon and east of Río Ucayali to Madre de Dios. *E Peru, n Bolivia and sw Amazonian Brazil.*

Myrmotherula **Antwrens.** A very large genus, represented in Peru by 20 (plus one hypothetical) species. All are small and short-tailed. Some species accompany mixed flocks and others don't. Some inhabit forest interiors and others live on the forest edge. They can be divided into three groups based on plumage (note Ornate Antwren is included in two groups):

Streaked mantle and crown group. Six species. Pay attention to color of underparts, amount of streaking on the crown and upperparts, and tail length.

"Brown" with checkered-throat group. Six species. Pay attention especially to color of wingbars, and to contrast between mantle and crown. Female's throat pattern is often faint. Eye color often varies.

"Gray" group. Nine species plus one hypothetical. Males are gray, slate-gray or black. Pay attention to presence (or lack) and amount of black on the throat, presence (or lack) and amount of white on tips of tail, amount of white on wings, and length of tail. Females usually dull brown.

Pygmy Antwren *Myrmotherula brachyura* Hormiguerito Pigmeo
7.7 cm (3"). Plate 72. ♪797. A streaked antwren with very short tail, yellowish belly and a white throat. Crown is streaked with white (male) or pale yellow (female). Very similar to Short-billed Antwren. but latter's mantle and crown are blacker with very narrow, pale streaks. Sclater's Antwren has a longer tail and yellow throat. Fairly common high in humid lowland forests e of Andes to 500 m. *Panama to n Bolivia and Amazonian Brazil.*

Short-billed Antwren *Myrmotherula obscura* Hormiguerito Piquicorto
7.7 cm (3"). Plate 72. ♪619. A streaked antwren with a very short tail, yellowish belly, white throat and a conspicuous black malar stripe. Crown is narrowly streaked with white (male) or with pale-yellow (female). Similar to Pygmy Antwren, but latter has wider, more conspicuous pale streaks on crown and mantle. Sclater's Antwren has a longer tail and yellow throat. Uncommon high in humid *várzea* and *terra firme* forests south to upper Río Ucayali valley to 600 m. *E Colombia to ne Peru and w Amazonian Brazil.*

Sclater's Antwren *Myrmotherula sclateri* Hormiguerito de Sclater
8.9 cm (3.5"). Plate 73. ♪ 797. The only streaked antwren with a yellow belly and yellow throat. Longer tailed than Pygmy and Short-billed Antwrens. Fairly common high in humid lowland forests from Loreto south to Madre de Dios to 700 m. *E Peru, n Bolivia and Amaz. Brazil s of the Amazon.*

Cherrie's Antwren *Myrmotherula cherriei* Hormiguerito de Cherrie
10.2 cm (4"). Plate 72. ♪ MS. Note limited range. Slightly larger than very similar widespread Amazonian Streaked-Antwren, but streaks on chest are wider (both sexes respectively) giving a blacker impression. Throat is unstreaked. Cherrie's Antwren lacks a concealed dorsal patch. Female like female Amazonian but belly is brownish-buff (Amazonian has a whitish belly). Recent sight records and tape recordings in white sands area of Río Tigre (Loreto). *Northeast Colombia to sw Venezuela and n Amazonian Brazil.*

Amazonian Streaked-Antwren *Myrmotherula multostriata* Hormiguerito-Rayado Amazónico
9.6 cm (3.75"). Plate 72. ♪ 797. Often in borders near water. Male is a streaked antwren with fine black streaks on white underparts. Similar Striped-chested and Cherrie's Antwrens have coarser streaks that are more confined to the chest and don't reach the belly. Female is equally streaked, but buffy, with a brighter tawny frontlet. Uncommon along oxbow lakes and margins e of the Andes to 900 m. *E Colombia to n Bolivia and Amazonian Brazil south of the Amazon.*

Stripe-chested Antwren *Myrmotherula longicauda* Hormiguerito Pechilistado
10.2 cm (4"). Plate 72. ♪ 797. A streaked antwren of the foothills, usually above the range of Amazonian. Male has white underparts with black streaks on chest, but not on throat or belly. Amazonian has a streaked throat and upper belly. Female: crown and upperparts are streaked with buff and black, unstreaked underparts; buffy breast is sharply bordered by a white belly. Fairly common in disturbed/successional upper trop. woodlands along e base of Andes at 400-1300 m. *SE Colombia to w Bolivia.*

Plain-throated Antwren *Myrmotherula hauxwelli* Hormiguerito Gargantillano
10.2 cm (4"). Plate 72. ♪ 797. Mainly terrestrial. Male is a gray antwren with two white wingbars, white spots on the tertials, and a white terminal tail band; lacks black on throat. Female has similar pattern but wingbars and tertial spots are buff. Mostly brownish above and ochre below. No other *Myrmotherula* has similar markings on the tertials. Fairly common low in humid lowland forests e of Andes to 600 m. *SE Colombia to n Bolivia and Amazonian Brazil.*

White-eyed Antwren *Myrmotherula leucophthalma* Hormiguerito Ojiblanco
11.5 cm (4.5"). Plate 72, 73. ♪ 797. A checker-throated, brown antwren with a brown back, buff wingbars and a rufous-brown tail. Stipple-throated Antwren has a brighter rufous back and white wing spots. Female Ornate Antwren has brownish underparts and whiter wingbars. Foothill Antwren (limited overlap at best) has a grayer mantle and underparts. Female White-eyed Antwren is pale-cinnamon below with buff wing spots and unmarked throat. Fairly common low in humid lowland forests in Ucayali, Madre de Dios and Puno to 800 m. *SE Peru to n Bolivia and Amazonian Brazil.*

Brown-backed (Yasuni) Antwren *Myrmotherula fjeldsaai* Hormiguerito Dorsipardo
11.5 cm (4.5"). Plate 73. Note limited range. Very similar to White-eyed Antwren (no overlap) but male has more extensive gray on underparts (reaching mid belly) and a browner tail. Sympatric Stipple-throated Antwren has a rufous back and whiter wingbars. Cf. Foothill Antwren (higher elevation, gray mantle). Similar Ornate Antwren has mostly brownish-buff underparts. Female Brown-backed like White-eyed, but throat is streaked. Uncommon and local low in humid primary *terra firme* forest and adjacent tongues of *várzea* forest in nw Loreto. Recorded from upper Río Tigre, Río Curaray and Río Corrientes (Loreto). A recently described species (Krabbe *et al.* 1999). *Lower tropical zone of e Ecuador and immediately adjacent Peru.*

Stipple-throated Antwren *Myrmotherula haematonota* Hormiguerito Gargantipunteada
11.5 cm (4.5"). Plate 73. ♪797. Male is the only checker-throated, brown antwren with a rufous back, grayish underparts and white wingbars. Female has a rufous back, buffy wingbars, pale-cinnamon underparts and pale streaks on throat. Cf. female Ornate Antwren (brown back, checkered throat, white wingbars). Cf. Brown-backed, Foothill and White-eyed Antwrens. Uncommon and local low in humid *terra firme* forests from Loreto to Madre de Dios to 500 m. *S Venezuela to se Colombia, n Bolivia and w Amazonian Brazil.*

Foothill Antwren *Myrmotherula spodionota* Hormiguerito Submontano
11.5 cm (4.5"). Plate 73. ♪741CD. Usually found at higher elevations than other checker-throated, brown antwrens. Male is the only checker-throated brown antwren with a grayish mantle and white wingbars. Cf. female Ornate Antwren (brownish underparts). Female Foothill Antwren is brownish below with buff wingbars and an unmarked throat. Uncommon in foothills along e base of Andes south to Cusco at 650-1300 m. *E Ecuador and e Peru.*

Ornate Antwren *Myrmotherula ornata* Hormiguerito Adornado
11.5 cm (4.5"). Plate 73. ♪797. Note bold white wingbars. In races *atrogularis* (drainage of Río Huallaga and Río Ucayali, illustrated) and *meridionalis* (Madre de Dios and Puno) the black on the throat of the gray male is limited to upper throat (does not extend down to chest). Tail lacks white tips. Female has rich ochre underparts, a brown back, and black throat checkered with white. Both sexes of race *saturata* (extreme northeast) have rufous back and rump. Cf. male Foothill, Stipple-throated and White-eyed Antwrens (all have gray on underparts). Race *atrogularis* (with *meridionalis*) may represent a separate species. Uncommon in humid lowland forests to 1250 m (usually associated with bamboo). *SE Colombia to n Bolivia and Brazil s of the Amazon.*

Rufous-tailed Antwren *Myrmotherula erythrura* Hormiguerito Colirrufo
11.5 cm (4.5"). Plate 72. ♪677. Tail is fairly long and rufous. Male is the only checker-throated, brown antwren with a gray (only faintly checkered) throat, rufous mantle and buff wingbars. Female is the only brown antwren with a rufous back, rufous tail and an orange-rufous throat. Uncommon low in humid lowland *terra firme* forests south to Puno to 900 m. *SE Colombia to e Peru and w Amazonian Brazil.*

White-flanked Antwren *Myrmotherula axillaris* Hormiguerito Flanquiblanco
11.5 cm (4.5"). Plate 72. ♪797. White flanks are often conspicuous in both sexes. Female is dull olive-brown above and mostly buff below. Mostly in mixed understory flocks. Common in humid lowland forests e of Andes to 900 m. *NE Honduras to n Bolivia, Amazonian and e Brazil.*

Slaty Antwren *Myrmotherula schisticolor* Hormiguerito Pizarroso
10.2 cm (4"). Plate 72. ♪742CD. Dark gray male has an extensive black bib that extends down to mid-belly. Río Suno and Ihering's Antwrens are very similar but have shorter tails. Cf. Long-winged Antwren (lighter gray, sharp contrast between gray belly and black bib, white tips to tail). Female Slaty Antwren is brownish above and ochre below, with two faint rufous wingbars. Common in lower growth of humid montane forests on e slope of Andes south to Puno at 900-1800 m. *S Mexico to s Peru.*

Río Suno Antwren *Myrmotherula sunensis* Hormiguerito del Suno
9.2 cm (3.6"). Plate 73. Male is like a short-tailed version of Slaty Antwren (no known overlap). Ihering's Antwren is very similar (no overlap), but has a more defined black bib. Sympatric Long-winged Antwren is larger, longer tailed, has a smaller bib and white tips to tail. Female is olivaceous above and ochre below. Rare and local low in humid lowland *terra firme* forests in Loreto, Huánuco and Pasco to 900 m. *SE Colombia to ne Peru and w Amazonian Brazil.*

Long-winged Antwren *Myrmotherula longipennis* Hormiguerito Alilargo
11.5 cm (4.5"). Plate 72. ♪817CD. Male has a fairly long tail, tipped with white, and a well-defined black bib that contrasts sharply with gray belly. Most other gray antwrens lack white tips to the tail or lack the black bib. Female is brownish-gray above, buff below, has buff wingbars and buffy tail tips. Fairly common low in humid lowland forests e of Andes to 500 m. *S Venezuela and the Guianas to e Peru and Amazonian Brazil.*

[Salvadori's Antwren] *Myrmotherula minor* Hormiguerito de Salvadori
9.2 cm (3.6"). Not illustrated. Male is very similar to Río Suno and Ihering's Antwrens, but the crissum is narrowly barred with black (not unbarred gray). The few Peruvian records are all questionable (Ridgely and Tudor 1994). *SE Brazil (n Espírito Santo to central São Paulo) and possibly w Amazonia.*

Ihering's Antwren *Myrmotherula iheringi* Hormiguerito de Ihering
9.2 cm (3.6"). Plate 73. ♪817CD. Within its range the only gray antwren with a black bib, that has an all black tail (no white tips). Sympatric Long-winged Antwren is larger, and has a longer tail with white tips. Cf. Slaty and Gray Antwrens. Female Ihering's is grayish above, buff below and has buff wingbars. Rare to uncommon low in humid lowland *várzea* forests and *Guadua* bamboo thickets in Madre de Dios to 650 m. Recorded at Tambopata Candamo Reserve and Manu National Park. *SE Peru and w Brazil.*

Gray Antwren *Myrmotherula menetriesii* Hormiguerito Gris
10.2 cm (4"). Plate 72. ♪797. Mostly in mid-level and subcanopy. Male has white edging to gray wing coverts (at close range note black subterminal band on coverts). Male lacks dorsal patch; usually has a small black throat-patch confined to middle of throat (lacking in birds n of Amazon). Cf. Long-winged (more extensive black bib), and Leaden (different wing pattern, white dorsal patch). Female is brownish above and ochre below, with plain wings. Fairly common in humid lowland (mostly *terra firme*) forests e of Andes to 900 m. *S Venezuela and the Guianas to n Bolivia and Amazonian Brazil.*

Leaden Antwren *Myrmotherula assimilis* Hormiguerito Plomizo
10.2 cm (4"). Plate 72. ♪797. Confined to river islands. Male is the only gray antwren in its limited habitat. Has a white dorsal patch, faint whitish edges to wing coverts, and lacks black throat-patch. Female is olivaceous above and buff below with buff wingbars. Fairly common in humid *várzea* forests along the Amazon and tributaries in Loreto. *River islands of Amazon system.*

Banded Antbird (Antwren) *Dichrozona cincta* Hormiguerito Bandeado
10.2cm (4"). Plate 76. ♪817CD. Mostly terrestrial. No other antbird has a white (buff in female) band on the back. Note two wingbars and short tail. Compare Spot-backed and Dot-backed Antbirds (spotted back, no white band on back). Rare in humid *terra firme* forests e of Andes to 900 m. *SE Colombia and sw Venezuela to n Bolivia and Amazonian Brazil.*

***Herpsilochmus* Antwrens.** Mostly canopy-dwelling antwrens of montane, foothill and Amazonian forests. They have a bold white superciliary and a longer tail than *Myrmotherula*. Male's crown is usually black (sometimes spotted with white) while the female's is spotted or rufous.

*Ash-throated Antwren *Herpsilochmus parkeri* Hormiguerito Garganticeniza
12 cm (4.75"). Plate 73. The only gray *Herpsilochmus* in its limited range. Underparts are grayer than in similar Creamy-bellied Antwren. Recently described species reported as relatively common at Jesús del Monte (San Martín) ca 1450 m (Begazo *et al.* 2001). *Endemic to Peru.*

Creamy-bellied Antwren *Herpsilochmus motacilloides* Hormiguerito Ventricremoso
12 cm (4.75"). Plate 73. ♪742CD. The only gray *Herpsilochmus* in its range. Yellow-breasted Antwren is yellower below and olive above. Fairly common in humid montane forests on e slope of Andes from Junín to n Cusco at 1000-2200 m. *Endemic to Peru.*

Dugand's Antwren *Herpsilochmus dugandi* Hormiguerito de Dugand
11.5 cm (4.5"). Plate 73. ♪677. The only gray *Herpsilochmus* in its limited range. Lengthwise white spots on central tail feathers are diagnostic. Female has rufous crown and white spots on tail. Ancient Antwren lacks tail spots and is olive above and yellowish below. Uncommon and local in humid lowland *terra firme* forests in Loreto north of the Amazon to 400 m. Often recorded along ExplorNapo canopy walk. *SE Colombia, e Ecuador and ne Peru.*

Ancient Antwren *Herpsilochmus gentryi* Hormiguerito Antiguo
11.5 cm (4.5"). Plate 73. The only *Herpsilochmus* in its limited range that is olive above and yellowish below. Cf. Dugand's Antwren. Fairly common recently described species found in canopy of lowland *terra firme* white-sand forests in Loreto. Recorded regularly in Allpahuayo-Mishana forest near Iquitos. *N Amazonian Peru and adjacent Ecuador.*

Yellow-breasted Antwren *Herpsilochmus axillaris* Hormiguerito Pechiamarillo
12 cm (4.75"). Plate 74. ♪741CD. A *Herpsilochmus* with yellowish underparts and mostly olive upperparts. Crown is spotted (male) or rufous (female). Creamy-bellied Antwren is gray above. Fairly common in humid montane forests along e slope of Andes south to Puno at 900-1800 m. *Disjunct in sw Colombia; se Colombia to s Peru.*

Rufous-winged Antwren *Herpsilochmus rufimarginatus* Hormiguerito Alirrufo
11.5 cm (4.5"). Plate 74. ♪797. The only *Herpsilochmus* with rufous on its primaries and much of the secondaries. Male has a solid black crown, and female has a rufous crown. Fairly common in humid lowland and foothill forests e of Andes to 1000 m. *E Panama to ne Argentina, e Paraguay, e and s Brazil.*

Dot-winged Antwren *Microrhopias quixensis* Hormiguerito Alipunteado
12 cm (4.75"). Plate 69. ♪817CD. Fairly long tail has conspicuous and diagnostic white tips. Four ssp. occur in Peru. In all races male is mostly black except for white tips to tail (seen from above and below), white wingbars and white dots on wing coverts. In all races female's upperparts as in male, but pattern of underparts varies. Race *quixensis* (south to north bank of Río Marañón) has a black throat and rufous underparts; *intercedens* (lower Río Ucayali and adjacent s bank of Amazon) has completely rufous underparts; *nigriventris* (San Martin, Junín and Cusco) has a black throat, dark rufous breast and black belly; *albicauda* (Madre del Dios and Puno, illustrated) has all rufous underparts and mostly white undertail. Rare low in humid lowland and foothill forests e of Andes to 900 m. Locally common in bamboo. *Mexico to n Bolivia, Amazonian Brazil and the Guianas.*

Rusty-backed Antwren *Formicivora rufa* Hormiguerito Dorsirrufa
12.5 cm (5"). Plate 74. ♪797. Male is the only antwren with black underparts and face bordered with white, combined with a rufous back. Female has streaked face and underparts. Fairly common and local in savanna and scrub on e slope of Andes in San Martín, Cusco and Madre de Dios (Pampas del Heath) to 1450 m. *Suriname and Brazil to n Bolivia, Paraguay and e Peru.*

Striated Antbird *Drymophila devillei* Hormiguero Estriado
13.5 cm (5.3"). Plate 69. ♪797. A slender antbird with large white tips to the long tail. Crown, mantle and throat are streaked. Crissum is rufous and remainder of underparts white. Long-tailed Antbird is larger (limited overlap at best) streakier on underparts, and rufous on crissum extends to mid-belly. Warbling Antbird color pattern is similar, but it has a shorter tail that lacks white tips and tail spots. Fairly common low in humid *Guadua* bamboo stands on e slope of Andes north to Pasco and s Ucayali to 1050 m. *Disjunct from ne Ecuador to n Bolivia and s Amazonian Brazil.*

Long-tailed Antbird *Drymophila caudata* Hormiguero Colilargo
15.5 cm (6"). Plate 74. ♪797. A long-tailed antbird with streaked throat and breast, and rufous crissum and lower belly. Longer-tailed than similar Striated Antbird and lacks spots on upper central tail feathers. Cf. much shorter-tailed Warbling Antbird. Fairly common low in humid montane forests on e slope of Andes at 1200-2700 m. *N Venezuela to w Bolivia.*

Terenura **Antwrens.** Four species of slender-bodied, canopy-dwelling antwrens that resemble gnatcatchers. Most have yellowish wingbars and bright-colored rumps. Females have an olive cap.

Rufous-rumped Antwren *Terenura callinota* Hormiguerito Lomirrufo
11.5 cm (4.5"). Plate 74. A *Terenura* with a rufous rump, yellowish belly and yellow shoulders (hard to see). Females have an olive cap and whitish throat. Similar (especially females) to Chestnut-shouldered Antwren (limited overlap at best) but latter has chestnut shoulders (sometimes lacking in females). Uncommon in humid foothill and premontane forests on e slope of Andes south to Cusco at 800-2000 m. *Costa Rica to s Peru.*

Chestnut-shouldered Antwren *Terenura humeralis* Hormiguerito Hombricastaño
11.5 cm (4.5"). Plate 74. ♪632. The only *Terenura* in its range. Male has a chestnut rump, whitish belly and chestnut shoulders. Female sometimes lacks color on shoulders, and has an olive cap and buff throat. Cf. Rufous-rumped Antwren. Uncommon in humid lowland forests in Loreto and Madre de Dios. *E Ecuador to n Bolivia and w Amazonian Brazil.*

***Yellow-rumped Antwren** *Terenura sharpei* Hormiguerito Lomiamarillo
11.5 cm (4.5"). Plate 73. ♪741CD. Note limited range. No other *Terenura* has a yellow rump. Rare in humid subtropical montane forests in Puno and Cusco at 1100-1800 m. Recorded at Inca Mine 19 km north of Oroya on the Limbani-Astillero road (Puno). Recently recorded near San Pedro on Manu Road at ca 1800 m (EB). *SE Peru and w Bolivia.*

Ash-winged Antwren *Terenura spodioptila* Hormiguerito Aliceniza
10 cm (4") Not illustrated. Known from a single sight record from Río Napo, Loreto. Similar to Rufous-rumped Antwren but grayer (lacks yellow tones), and lower back and mantle are chestnut. Wings are gray with two white wingbars. Crown is dark gray in male or brown in female. *The Guianas, s Venezuela, se Colombia and n Brazil.*

Cercomacra **Antbirds.** Four species of medium-sized gray to black antbirds. All have long tails (sometimes with white tips). Bill is fairly long and slender. Males are very similar, but the usually present females are somewhat easier to identify.

Gray Antbird *Cercomacra cinerascens* Hormiguero Gris
15.5 cm (6"). Plate 75. ♪797. The only gray *Cercomacra* with conspicuous white spots on the tip of tail feathers (best seen from below). Note small white dots on wing coverts. Female is olivaceous above, ochre below, and has white tips to tail. In vines and tangles; more arboreal than other *Cercomacra,* and thus recalls various *Thamnomanes.* Fairly common in humid lowland forests e of Andes to 700 m, occasionally to 1150 m. *S Venezuela and the Guianas to n Bolivia and Brazil.*

Blackish Antbird *Cercomacra nigrescens* Hormiguero Negruzco
15.5 cm (6"). Plate 75. ♪797. Male is slate-gray below and lacks any white on tail. Wing coverts are edged white and has a white dorsal patch. Very similar to Black Antbird but latter has blacker underparts. Female is rufous below and brown above with a conspicuous rufous forehead. Two species may be involved with *aequatorialis* and *notata* representing the upland, and *fuscicauda* the lowland forms in Peru. Uncommon in lower growth of secondary forests in humid trop. and upper trop. slopes, and lowland islands on e slope of Andes to 1600 m. *Suriname and the Guianas to n Bolivia and Amazonian Brazil.*

Black Antbird *Cercomacra serva* Hormiguero Negro
15.5 cm (6"). Plate 75. ♫ 797. Sympatric with, and very similar to, Blackish Antbird (sometimes indistinguishable). Male Manu Antbird has small white spots on undertail. Female is similar to that of Blackish Antbird, but rufous forehead is duller (doesn't stand out). Rare in secondary forest and edges of humid lowlands and foothills, and along tropical rivers e of Andes to 1100 m. *SE Colombia to n Bolivia and w Amazonian Brazil.*

Manu Antbird *Cercomacra manu* Hormiguero del Manu
15.5 cm (6"). Plate 69. ♫ 817CD. Closely associated with bamboo. Male is only *Cercomacra* with small white tips to tail (often hard to discern). Males of Blackish and Black Antbirds are very similar, but they lack white on tail, and do not favor bamboo. Female is gray below and olive above, wing coverts are edged white and tail is tipped white. Uncommon in *Guadua* bamboo thickets (often close to rivers) in Ucayali, Cusco and Madre de Dios to 1200 m. *SE Peru, adjacent sw Brazil and extreme nw Bolivia.*

White-backed Fire-eye *Pyriglena leuconota* Ojo-de-Fuego Dorsiblanco
18 cm (7"). Plate 75. ♫ 797. Four ssp. occur in Peru. Males of all ssp. are uniformly black (except for a white dorsal patch) and have bright red eyes. In se Peru cf. Goeldi's Antbird, but latter is plumper and has a heavier bill. Females vary, but always have bright-red eyes. In *castanoptera* (e slope south to Cajamarca) head and most of underparts are black and back is rufous. In *picea* (Loreto, Huanuco and Junín, illustrated) head is black, but body is rufous-brown. Race *marcapatensis* (Cusco and Puno, illustrated) is brown above and tawny below, with a white patch on back and a short superciliary. Isolated *pacifica* (Pacific slope of Tumbes and Piura) is brown above and dingy buff below, and may be a separate species (Pacific Fire-eye). Fairly common along humid e slope of Andes at 1000-2000 m. *Disjunct from se Colombia to sw Brazil, Paraguay and lower Amazonian Brazil.*

Myrmoborus **Antbirds.** Four species of chunky, short-tailed antbirds that inhabit lowland forest undergrowth. Most males have a black mask. Note facial pattern, eye color and presence (or lack) of wingbars.

White-browed Antbird *Myrmoborus leucophrys* Hormiguero Cejiblanco
13.5 cm (5.3"). Plate 76. ♫ 797. Male can be identified by a combination of black mask, conspicuous white superciliary, no wingbars and dark eyes. Female has a black mask, cinnamon eyebrows, rufous-brown back and whitish underparts. Common in humid lowland forests e of Andes to 900 m (local in foothills in ne Peru; absent from Iquitos area). *S Venezuela and the Guianas to n Bolivia and Amazonian Brazil.*

Ash-breasted Antbird *Myrmoborus lugubris* Hormiguero Pechicenizo
13.5 cm (5.3"). Plate 71. Note habitat. Male has a black mask (no white superciliary), ashy-gray underparts, plain wings and bright-red eyes. Cf. White-browed and Black-faced Antbirds. Female has white underparts, rufous brown upperparts, buffy edges on wing coverts and red eyes. Fairly common in *várzea* and river island forests along the Amazon, Napo, Marañón and Ucayali rivers to 900 m. *River islands of Amazon system.*

Black-faced Antbird *Myrmoborus myotherinus* Hormiguero Carinegro
12.5 cm (5"). Plate 76. ♫ 797. Male can be identified by the combination of black mask, narrow white superciliary, wingbars and red eyes. Female's combination of black mask, white throat, and tawny underparts is unique. Common in humid lowland *terra firme* forests e of Andes to 700 m. *SE Colombia and s Venezuela to n Bolivia and Amazonian Brazil.*

Black-tailed Antbird *Myrmoborus melanurus* Hormiguero Colinegro
12.5 cm (5"). Plate 71. Very local. Male is a dark *Myrmorborus* that appears almost black, is slightly lighter on the underparts, lacks a contrasting mask, and has red eyes and white wingbars. Recalls a darker version of Black-faced Antbird. Various antbirds are dark with red eyes, but they are not shaped—and do not behave—like *Myrmorborus*. Female has whitish underparts, brown upperparts, white edges on dark wing coverts and red eyes. Rare and poorly known in *várzea* forests south of the Amazon and east of Río Ucayali (Loreto), and south to n Ucayali to 125 m. Recently recorded at Pacaya Samiria National Reserve (Begazo and Valqui 1998), in Iquitos area (Field Guides tour) and at Yarinacocha (Ucayali). *Endemic to Peru.*

Warbling Antbird *Hypocnemis cantator* Hormiguero Gorjeador
12 cm (4.75"). Plate 74. ♪ 797. A widespread but variable species, four ssp. of which occur in Peru. All ssp. share a white superciliary, spotted (white in male, buff in female) crown, streaked mantle, and rufous flanks. Tail is fairly short. Underparts of races *saturata* and *peruviana* (n and most of e Peru, illustrated) are dingy-whitish. Underparts of *subflava* (illustrated) and *collinsi* (some overlap in se Peru) are yellowish. Long-tailed and Striated Antbirds have longer tails. Cf. Yellow-browed Antbird. Tropical se races (*subflava* and *collinsi*) may represent a separate species. Common in edge shrubbery and successional habitats in humid lowlands and foothills e of Andes to 1100 m. *S Venezuela and the Guianas to n Bolivia and Amazonian Brazil.*

Yellow-browed Antbird *Hypocnemis hypoxantha* Hormiguero Cejiamarillo
12 cm (4.75"). Plate 74. ♪ 609. The combination of yellow underparts, yellow superciliary, spotted crown, and olive back is distinctive. Sympatric populations of Warbling Antbirds have rufous flanks, whitish underparts, white superciliary, etc. Uncommon low in humid *terra firme* forests in Loreto south to lower Río Ucayali to 400 m. *SE Colombia to e Peru and Amazonian Brazil.*

***Hypocnemoides* Antbirds.** A pair of small, gray, mostly allopatric antbirds, found low in tangles near water. Both resemble gray *Myrmotherula*, but are slightly larger and have gray eyes.

Black-chinned Antbird *Hypocnemoides melanopogon* Hormiguero Barbinegro
11.5 cm (4.5"). Plate 74. ♪ 677. Female's underparts are whitish, faintly scalloped with gray. Cf. Band-tailed Antbird. Uncommon and local in lowland *várzea* forests in Loreto north of the Amazon and Río Marañón to 500 m. *S Venezuela and the Guianas to ne Peru and Amazonian Brazil.*

Band-tailed Antbird *Hypocnemoides maculicauda* Hormiguero Colifajeado
12 cm (4.75"). Plate 74. ♪ 797. Note the prominent white terminal tail band. Female's underparts are whitish (lacks black throat), faintly scalloped with gray. Very similar (both sexes respectively) to Black-chinned Antbird (limited overlap), but latter lacks a white dorsal patch and has a slightly narrower terminal tail band. Cf. Silvered Antbird (flesh-colored legs). Uncommon in lowland *várzea* forests and along oxbow lakes south of the Amazon from Loreto to Madre de Dios to 500 m. *E Peru, e Bolivia and Amazonian Brazil s of Amazon.*

Black-and-white Antbird *Myrmochanes hemileucus* Hormiguero Negriblanco
11.5 cm (4.5"). Plate 74. ♪ 797. Note habitat. Mostly black above and white below. Fairly common in grass and scrub along lowland river islands in Loreto and on Río Ucayali as far south as Lagarto (Ucayali) to 300 m. *River islands of Amazon system.*

Silvered Antbird *Sclateria naevia* Hormiguero Plateado
15.5 cm (6"). Plate 76. ♪ 797. Invariably found near water. Within its habitat, the only antbird with flesh-colored legs that is mostly gray above (female browner) and whitish below. Compare *Hypocnemoides* (gray legs). Fairly common in humid lowland forests and along oxbow lakes e of Andes to 500 m. *S Venezuela and the Guianas to n Bolivia and Amazonian Brazil; Trinidad.*

Amazonian Antbird *Percnostola minor* Hormiguero Amazónico
15.5 cm (6"). Plate 69. Note limited range. Male is a gray antbird with gray eyes, black crown, black chin and white edges to wing coverts. Recalls Band-tailed Antbird. Spot-winged and Slate-colored Antbirds have spots on wings and lack black bib. Female has rufous-ochre underparts, head and wingbars, with a darker cap. Recent split from Black-headed Antbird *P. rufifrons* (Capparella *et al.* 1997). Uncommon and local low in borders of humid lowland forests in ne Loreto to 500 m. *E Colombia to sw Venzuela and ne Peru.*

Slate-colored Antbird *Percnostola schistacea* Hormiguero Pizarroso
12 cm (4.75"). Plate 74. Male is very similar to male Spot-winged Antbird but darker overall, has gray eyes, and bill is all black. Female similar to female Spot-winged Antbird, but head is rufous-brown (not gray). Both sexes of Amazonian Antbird have white edges to wing coverts. Uncommon and local low in humid *terra firme* forests from Loreto to Puno to 300 m. *SE Colombia, e Peru and w Amazonian Brazil.*

Spot-winged Antbird *Percnostola leucostigma* Hormiguero Alimoteado
15.5 cm (6"). Plate 74. ♪ 677. Both sexes have pale lower mandibles and spotted wing coverts (white in male, cinnamon in female). Compare respective sexes of Slate-colored Antbird. Female is similar to that of Black-throated Antbird, but latter has a white dorsal patch and whitish throat. Uncommon low in humid lowland *terra firme* and montane forests on e slope of Andes to 1650 m. *S Venezuela and the Guianas to n Bolivia and Amazonian Brazil.*

White-lined Antbird *Percnostola lophotes* Hormiguero Lineado Blanco
14.5 cm (5.75"). Plate 69, 75. ♪ 817CD. Both sexes have a long, conspicuous crest that is often raised. Male is black except for white wingbars. Female has rufous upperparts, dusky cheeks, and white underparts. No other crested antbird is similar. Uncommon in humid lowlands e of Andes, especially in *Guadua* bamboo and *Gynerium* cane stands from Ucayali to Madre de Dios to 700 m. Recorded regularly at Amazonia Lodge and Tambopata Candamo Reserve. *E Peru and n Bolivia.*

Myrmeciza **Antbirds.** The seven Peruvian species inhabit mostly the understory of lowland forests. They are quite variable in size, appearance and behavior; some have conspicuous blue orbital skin.

Chestnut-tailed Antbird *Myrmeciza hemimelaena* Hormiguero Colicastaño
12 cm (4.75"). Plate 75. ♪ 797. Both sexes have a diagnostic combination of chestnut tail and gray head. Male has a black throat; female's throat is buff to rufous. Common in humid *terra firme* and secondary woodlands e of Andes to 1500 m. *SE Colombia to n Bolivia and s Amazonian Brazil.*

Plumbeous Antbird *Myrmeciza hyperythra* Hormiguero Plomizo
18 cm (7"). Plate 75. ♪ 797. No other antbird (both sexes) has the combination of a large blue orbital skin patch and spots on wing coverts. Cf. Slate-colored and Spot-winged Antbirds (both lack bare skin around the eye). Fairly common in lowland *várzea* forests and along oxbow lakes e of Andes to 400 m. *SE Colombia to n Bolivia and w Amazonian Brazil.*

White-shouldered Antbird *Myrmeciza melanoceps* Hormiguero Hombriblanco
18 cm (7"). Plate 75. ♪ 632. Male is the only black antbird with a blue orbital skin patch and white on shoulder (often concealed). Cf. Sooty Antbird (lacks white on shoulder, near ants) or Goeldi's Antbird (red eye, small bluish orbital skin, dorsal patch). Female's combination of rufous body, black hood and blue orbital skin is distinctive. Fairly common in humid *várzea* forests south to Lagarto on upper Río Ucayali to 500 m. *E Colombia to ne Peru and w Amazonian Brazil.*

Goeldi's Antbird *Myrmeciza goeldii* Hormiguero de Goeldi
18 cm (7"). Plate 69, 75. ♪ 797. Male is all black except for a small bluish orbital skin patch, a white dorsal patch and bright red eyes. Recalls males of White-shouldered (limited overlap at best, much

larger orbital skin, dark eyes, no dorsal patch) and Sooty (much larger orbital skin, grayer). Male resembles White-backed Fire-eye, but latter is more slender-bodied with a slimmer bill. Female can be identified by the combination of red eyes, rufous back, mostly cinnamon underparts, gray head and white throat. Fairly common and local in *Heliconia* and bamboo thickets in s Ucayali, Madre de Dios and adjacent Cusco to 550 m. Recorded regularly at Tambopata Candamo Reserve and Amazonia Lodge. *SE Peru, n Bolivia and sw Amazonian Brazil.*

Sooty Antbird *Myrmeciza fortis* Hormiguero Tiznado
18.5 cm (7.2"). Plate 75. ♪ 817CD. An army ant follower. Male may have white at bend of wing, and is similar to blacker male White-shouldered Antbird. Cf. local Goeldi's Antbird. Female has blue orbital skin, gray underparts, brown back and chestnut crown. Fairly common in humid lowland *terra firme* and secondary forests e of Andes to 1050 m. *SE Colombia to n Bolivia and w Amazonian Brazil.*

*Gray-headed Antbird *Myrmeciza griseiceps* Hormiguero Cabecigris
14 cm (5.5"). Plate 71. Distinctive in its limited range. Has a gray head, wingbars, dorsal patch and white tips to tail. Male has a black chest; female a pale-gray chest. Rare to locally uncommon in understory in lower montane forests (especially *Chusquea* bamboo) in Tumbes, Piura and Lambayeque at 600-2500 m. *Andes of sw Ecuador and nw Peru.*

Black-throated Antbird *Myrmeciza atrothorax* Hormiguero Gargantinegra
14 cm (5.5"). Plate 75. ♪ 797. Males of *maynana* and *obscurata* (south of the Amazon, illustrated) can be recognized by the combination of black throat, gray underparts, dark tail, brown back, and whitish spots on wing coverts. North of the Amazon, race *tenebrosa* is very dark gray above and below, except for black throat, white dorsal patch and whitish dots on wing coverts. All females have whitish throats (rest of underparts are cinnamon), brown upperparts, buff wing spots and a white dorsal patch. Cf. female Spot-winged Antbird (lacks whitish throat). Common in borders and secondary growth in humid lowlands e of Andes to 500 m. *S Venezuela and the Guianas to n Bolivia and Amazonian Brazil.*

White-plumed Antbird *Pithys albifrons* Hormiguero de Plumón Blanco
12.5 cm (5"). Plate 77. ♪ 632. An unmistakable attendant at ant swarms. Fairly common low in humid lowland *terra firme* forests e of Andes south to Cordillera Vilcabamba to 1100 m. *S Venezuela and the Guianas to e Peru and w Amazonian Brazil.*

White-masked Antbird *Pithys castanea* Hormiguero de Mascara Blanca
14 cm (5.5"). Facing Plate 77. Larger than White-plumed Antbird and lacks plumes. Can be identified by mostly uniform chestnut body, black head and white surrounding bill and eyes. Known from a single 1937 male specimen from Andoas on Río Pastaza (extreme n Loreto) at 250 m; recently rediscovered. *Endemic to Peru.*

Bicolored Antbird *Gymnopithys leucaspis* Hormiguero Bicolor
14 cm (5.5"). Plate 76. ♪ 603. An unmistakable attendant at ant swarms. No other antbird has rufous-brown upperparts and mostly white underparts and cheeks. Fairly common in humid lowland forests in Amazonas, San Martín and Loreto to 750 m. One of most common birds in mixed-antbird flocks in Iquitos area. Peruvian and all Amazonian races sometimes considered a separate species (White-cheeked Antbird, *Gymnopithys bicolor*). *Honduras to w Ecuador, ne Peru and nw Amazonian Brazil.*

Lunulated Antbird *Gymnopithys lunulata* Hormiguero Lunado
14.5 cm (5.75"). Plate 69. ♪ EC008T. Associated with ant swarms. Male is similar to male White-throated Antbird (no overlap), but tail is all black. Female is mostly brown, except for a white throat, short superciliary, dark scales on mantle and white barring on tail. Fairly common in undergrowth of humid *várzea* forests north of the Amazon and west of Río Ucayali in Loreto and Ucayali to 300 m. Reported to be numerous at Yarinacocha (E. O. Willis). *E Ecuador and e Peru.*

White-throated Antbird *Gymnopithys salvini* Hormiguero Gargantiblanca
14.5 cm (5.75"). Plate 76. ♪797. Follows ant swarms. Male: no other gray antbird has the pattern of barring on tail and white throat. Female has brown upperparts, dark scales on mantle, darker crown, rufous underparts and dark barring on a rufous tail. Fairly common in humid lowland *terra firme* and transitional forests from Loreto south to Madre de Dios and Puno to 500 m. *E Peru, n Bolivia and w Amazonian Brazil.*

Wing-banded Antbird *Myrmornis torquata* Hormiguero Alifranjeado
15.5 cm (6"). Plate 77. Unmistakable in its limited range. Female is similar to male but has a chestnut throat. Uncommon low in humid lowland forests in ne Loreto to 300 m. *Nicaragua to e Ecuador, Amazonian and central Brazil.*

Hairy-crested Antbird *Rhegmatorhina melanosticta* Hormiguero Cresticanoso
15.5 cm (6"). Plate 69. ♪797. Associated with ant swarms. Easily recognized by its hairy-like crest, black face and blue orbital skin. Male's back and wings are unmarked. The three ssp. that occur in Peru differ mostly by color of crest. Race *brunneiceps* (mostly in foothills from San Martin to n Cusco, illustrated) has a blond crest and may be a separate species. Races *purusiana* (most of lowlands of e Peru) and *badia* (Puno) have ashy crests. Uncommon low in humid lowland *terra firme* forests e of Andes to 1050 m. *SE Colombia to n Bolivia and w Amazonian Brazil.*

Spot-backed Antbird *Hylophylax naevia* Hormiguero Dorsipunteado
11.5 cm (4.5"). Plate 76. ♪797. Both sexes have similar bold and attractive plumage; female has a black malar stripe (not a black throat) and is yellower below. Both sexes have brown rumps, gray eyes and gray cheeks. Cf. Dot-backed Antbird (spotted rump, brown eyes and whitish cheeks) and Banded Antbird (white band on back, no spots on back). Uncommon low in humid trop. and upper trop. forests e of Andes to 1100 m. *S Venezuela and the Guianas to n Bolivia and Amazonian Brazil.*

Dot-backed Antbird *Hylophylax punctulata* Hormiguero Lomipunteado
11.5 cm (4.5"). Plate 76. ♪632. Note habitat. Similar to widespread Spot-backed Antbird. Dot-backed's rump is spotted (plain in Spot-backed), eyes are brown (not pale-gray), and cheeks whitish (not gray). Female is similar but has a black malar stripe (and no black throat). Cf. Banded Antbird. Uncommon low in lowland *várzea* and flooded oxbow lake edges south along Río Ucayali to Sarayacu (Loreto). Recent record from Manu National Park. *S Venezuela to e Ecuador, n Bolivia and Amazonian Brazil.*

Scale-backed Antbird *Hylophylax poecilinota* Hormiguero Dorsiescamado
12.5 cm (5"). Plate 76. ♪797. Over most of its range both sexes have diagnostic white scales on back and white spots on mid-tail and tail tips. Males of race *lepidonota* (most of e Peru, illustrated) and *griseiventris* (Cusco and Puno) are similar. Male of *gutturalis* (south of Amazon in Loreto) has a black throat. Females of *lepidonota* and *gutturalis* are similar. Female *griseiventris* lacks scales on the back, spots on mid-tail, and is rufescent-brown above and gray below. Common low in humid lowland *terra firme* forests e of Andes to 1100 m. *S Venezuela and the Guianas to n Bolivia and Amazonian Brazil.*

Black-spotted Bare-eye *Phlegopsis nigromaculata* Ojipelado Negripunteado
18 cm (7"). Plate 77. ♪797. Follows army ants. Unmistakable. Sexes alike. Uncommon mainly in lowland *várzea* forests to 500 m. *E Colombia to n Bolivia and Amazonian Brazil.*

Reddish-winged Bare-eye *Phlegopsis erythroptera* Ojipelado Alirrojiza
18.5 cm (7.2"). Plate 77. ♪797. Follows army ants. Male unmistakable. Chestnut-brown female has bold buff wingbars, and only a small red orbital skin patch. Uncommon mostly in lowland *terra firme* forests in Loreto and Ucayali to 600 m. Common in mixed-species antbird flocks around Iquitos. *SW Venezuela to ne Peru and w Amazonian Brazil.*

Formicariidae (Antthrushes and Antpittas; Formicarios). Species: World 57; Peru 35
Ground antbirds are residents of the humid forest understory, and range from central Mexico to ne Argentina. The rounded, almost tailless antpittas resemble Old World pittas, and the antthrushes have the long legs and body form of ground-dwelling thrushes. The antthrushes walk like small rails on the forest floor, usually with their tails cocked, ofen vocalizing as they walk. They are primarily insectivorous, but some species feed on small vertebrates. Some ground antbirds follow army ant columns to feed on flushed insects and other animals. They range from the lowlands to the *páramo*, and are equipped with long, strong legs. They are shy and often very difficult to observe, but their presence is usually evident by their loud calls, which are often audible from a long distance.

Rufous-capped Antthrush *Formicarius colma* Gallito-Hormiguero Gorrirufo
18 cm (7"). Plate 77. ♪ 797. The only antthrush in its range with an all rufous cap and black on the side of the head. Fairly common to common in lowland *terra firme* forests e of Andes to 500 m. *S Venezuela and the Guianas to n Bolivia, Amazonian and e Brazil.*

Black-faced Antthrush *Formicarius analis* Gallito-Hormiguero Carinegra
18 cm (7"). Plate 77. ♪ 797. Note the black face and throat and gray underparts, and lack of any rufous on crown or forecrown. Common in humid lowland forests e of Andes, occasionally to 1000 m. *Mexico to n Bolivia and Amazonian Brazil; Trinidad.*

Rufous-fronted Antthrush *Formicarius rufifrons* Gallito-Hormiguero Frentirrufo
18 cm (7"). Plate 69, 77. ♪ 797. Shows rufous only on the forehead. Lacks black on sides of head. Uncommon and extremely local in lowland *Heliconia* and *Guadua* bamboo thickets in Madre de Dios at 350-400 m. Regularly recorded at Cocha Cashu research station, Manu Wildlife Center, Boca de Manu and Cocha Juárez in Manu National Park. Recorded from *ccolpa de guacamayos* along Río Tambopata and Lago Sálvador. *SE Peru; recently recorded in adjacent Brazil and Bolivia.*

Rufous-breasted Antthrush *Formicarius rufipectus* Gallito-Hormiguero Pechirrufo
19 cm (7.5"). Plate 77. ♪ 603. Note rufous breast and belly, and black sides of head and throat. Rare to uncommon in humid montane forests on e slope of Andes south to Cusco at 1100-2200 m. Recorded near Cock-of-the-rock Lodge. *Costa Rica to w Venezuela and s Peru.*

Striated (Noble) Antthrush *Chamaeza nobilis* Rasconzuelo Estriado
22.5 cm (8.8"). Plate 77. ♪ 797. A fairly large antthrush with a brown back and scalloped underparts. Very similar to Short-tailed Antthrush. Uncommon to fairly common in humid lowland forests e of Andes to 700 m. *SE Colombia to n Bolivia and w Amazonian Brazil.*

Short-tailed Antthrush *Chamaeza campanisona* Rasconzuelo Colicorta
19 cm (7.5"). Plate 77. ♪ 797. Smaller than Striated Antthrush (limited overlap at best). Short-tailed Antthrush underparts are yellowish (sometimes ochre) and scalloped with black (especially on chest), where Striated Antthrush has more contrasting white and black scalloping. Uncommon in humid upper tropical forests along e slope of Andes at 900-1800 m. *S Venezuela and the Guianas to ne Argentina, e Paraguay and e Brazil.*

Barred Antthrush *Chamaeza mollissima* Rasconzuelo Barreteado
20 cm (8"). Plate 77. ♪ 797. The only antthrush with barred underparts (best seen on chest). Rare and local in humid montane forests on Cerro Chinguela, Cordillera de Colán, Cordillera de Vilcabamba and Puno at 1800-3000 m. *Andes of Colombia to w Bolivia.*

***Grallaria* Antpittas.** A genus well represented in Peru (19 species) of large to fairly small, mostly terrestrial antpittas. Some are streaked or scaled while others are plain. They hop around the undergrowth, and often vocalize from a slightly higher perch.

Undulated Antpitta *Grallaria squamigera* Tororoi Ondulado
21.5 cm (8.4"). Plate 78. ♪ 797. A large antpitta with a black malar stripe and slate-gray upperparts; ochraceous underparts are scaled black. Other antpittas that are scaled or scalloped below are smaller and not gray above. Uncommon in humid montane and elfin forests at 1800-3700 m. *Andes of w Venezuela to w Bolivia*

Variegated Antpitta *Grallaria varia* Tororoi Variegado
20 cm (8"). Plate 78. Note limited range. Like a larger version of Scaled Antpitta (no known overlap) but back feathers have light shafts, giving the back a streaked appearance. Rare in humid lowland forests on n bank of lower Río Napo (Loreto) to 600 m. *S Venezuela and the Guianas to ne Argentina, e Paraguay and Brazil.*

Scaled Antpitta *Grallaria guatimalensis* Tororoi Escamoso
16.5 cm (6.5"). Plate 78. ♪ 797. A medium-sized antpitta, heavily scaled above and mostly rufous-brown below. Note the white "moustache," white crescent on chest, brown back and gray crown. Similar to very local and larger Variegated Antpitta (no known overlap). Uncommon and local in humid foothill and montane forests on e slope of Andes at 500-2500 m; south on Pacific slope to Lambayeque and nw Cajamarca. *Mexico to w Bolivia; Trinidad.*

Plain-backed Antpitta *Grallaria haplonota* Tororoi Dorsillano
17 cm (6.6"). Not illustrated. Note limited range. Similar to Scaled Antpitta, but throat is whitish-buff (instead of dark bordered by pale malar area and whitish crescent on the chest); only vaguely scaled on back. Tape recorded in Cordillera del Condor, Amazonas and in Jerillo (San Martín). *Highlands of n Venezuela to w and se Ecuador.*

Ochre-striped Antpitta *Grallaria dignissima* Tororoi Ocrelistado
19 cm (7.5"). Plate 78. ♪ 632 Recalls Elusive Antpitta (no overlap) but throat and breast are ochre-rufous (Elusive has a white throat). No other antpitta in its limited range has a rufous throat. Rare in humid lowland forests east to mouth of Río Napo (Loreto) to 400 m; uncommon at ExplorNapo. *SE Colombia, e Ecuador and n Peru.*

Elusive Antpitta *Grallaria eludens* Tororoi Evasivo
19 cm (7.5"). Plate 79. ♪ 818CD. No other antpitta in its range has an ochre to buff breast, white throat and streaks on flanks. Uncommon in humid *terra firme* forest in lowlands e of Andes near Balta (Ucayali); recently recorded at Manu Wildlife Center. *Lowlands of e Peru (Ucayali and Madre de Dios) and immediately adjacent Brazil.*

Chestnut-crowned Antpitta *Grallaria ruficapilla* Tororoi Coronicastaña
19 cm (7.5"). Plate 78. ♪ EC007T. The only *Grallaria* in its range with a bright rufous crown and sides of head, bold streaks on white underparts, and grayish legs. Fairly common in montane forests south to Cajamarca and San Martín at 2000-2900 m. *Venezuela to n Peru.*

Watkins' (Scrub) Antpitta *Grallaria watkinsi* Tororoi de Watkins
18 cm (7"). Plate 79. No other antpitta in its limited range has a rufous crown, whitish sides of head, pinkish legs and buff streaks on underparts. Cf. higher-elevation Chestnut-crowned Antpitta. Fairly common in deciduous woodlands at 600-900 m in Tumbes. Recorded in Zona Reservada de Tumbes *SE Ecuador and nw Peru.*

Stripe-headed Antpitta *Grallaria andicola* Torotoi Cabecilistada
16.5 cm (6.5"). Plate 79. ♪ 797. Note habitat. No other *Grallaria* is as streaked below and none has such streaks on head. Locally common in *Gynoxys-Polylepis* woodlands from Cajamarca south at 3000-4300 m. *Andes of Peru and w Bolivia.*

Chestnut-naped Antpitta *Grallaria nuchalis* Tororoi Nuquicastaña
20 cm (8"). Plate 78. ♪ EC007T. Note limited range. A large, dark antpitta, lead-gray below with a brown back, chestnut crown, and a bare postocular spot. The only antpitta in its limited range with dark gray underparts. (The recently discovered Jocotoco Antpitta *Grallaria ridgleyi* [Plate 78] may occur in extreme northern Peru). Fairly common, mostly in montane forest bamboo thickets, on Cerro Chinguela at 2200-3000 m. *Andes of Colombia to n Peru.*

Pale-billed Antpitta *Grallaria carrikeri* Tororoi Piquipálido
19 cm (7.5"). Plate 79. No other antpitta in its limited range has a black hood and a horn-colored bill. Fairly common and local in bamboo thickets in e Andes south of Río Marañón, in Cordillera de Colán and Cumpang at 2350-2900 m. Reported from 33 km ne of Ingenio. This is another of those puzzling species (Yellow-browed Toucanet, Russet-mantled Softtail and Rusty-tinged Antpitta) whose range is limited on the north by Río Marañón, but surprisingly does not occur in the comparatively well-known Carpish Mts. *Endemic to Peru.*

White-bellied Antpitta *Grallaria hypoleuca* Tororoi Ventriblanco
17 cm (6.6"). Plate 78. ♪ EC007T. No other antpitta in its limited range is chestnut-brown above and white below. Uncommon in humid montane forests and second growth on Cerro Chinguela and Chaupe at 1500-2250 m. *Andes of Colombia to n Peru.*

Rusty-tinged Antpitta *Grallaria przewalskii* Tororoi Rojizo
17 cm (6.6"). Plate 79. No other antpitta in its limited range has the combination of rusty-rufous back, sides of head, throat and chest, dark-gray crown and pale-gray belly. Fairly common in humid montane and cloud forests on e slope of Andes south of Río Marañón in Amazonas, e La Libertad and San Martín at 2200-2750 m. Reported as fairly common 2.0 km west of Abra Patricia at 2200 m; and in Cordillera de Colán at 1680-2650 m (Barnes *et al.* 1997). *Endemic to Peru.*

Bay Antpitta *Grallaria capitalis* Tororoi Bayo
17 cm (6.6"). Plate 79. Like a larger, stronger-billed version of Rufous and Chestnut Antpittas. Sympatric ssp. of Rufous Antpitta is duller brown. Chestnut Antpitta (lower elevation) has dark barring on belly. Fairly common on bamboo-covered hillsides and cloud forest edge on e slope of Andes from Huánuco to Junín at 2600-3000 m. Recorded on upper upper parts of Paty trail in Carpish Mts. (Huánuco). *Endemic to Peru.*

Red-and-white Antpitta *Grallaria erythroleuca* Tororoi Rojiblanco
18 cm (7"). Plate 79. ♪ JFC. The only antpitta in its range with bright rufous upperparts and mostly snowy-white underparts. Cf. White-throated Antpitta. Uncommon to locally fairly common in montane woodlands along se slope of Andes in Cusco at 2100-3000 m. Recorded regularly from Pillahuata and from north slope of Abra Málaga road at 2800 m. *Endemic to Peru.*

White-throated Antpitta *Grallaria albigula* Tororoi Gargantiblanca
18.5 cm (7.2"). Plate 78. ♪ 797. Resembles Red-and-white Antpitta (latter is found higher, limited overlap at best) but White-throated Antpitta's back is browner than the crown and sides of underparts are grayish. Note the white eye-ring. No overlap with White-bellied Antpitta. Fairly common in humid montane forests on e slope of Andes at 800-1700 m on Cerro de Pantiacolla and in Puno. *Andes of s Peru to extreme nw Argentina.*

Rufous Antpitta *Grallaria rufula* Tororoi Rufo
15.5 cm (6"). Plate 79. ♪ 797. A fairly small, uniformly colored *Grallaria*. Races *rufula* from north of Río Marañón, and *occabambae* (illustrated) from Cusco and Puno, are uniformly rufous-brown; races *cajamarcae* from south of Río Marañón (illustrated) and *obscura* from Huanuco and Junín are duller brown. Cf. Bay, Chestnut and Tawny Antpittas. Fairly common in humid Andean montane forests at 2300-3600 m. *Andes of w Venezuela to w Bolivia.*

Chestnut Antpitta *Grallaria blakei* Tororoi Castaño
14.5 cm (5.75"). Plate 79. A fairly small, uniformly chestnut *Grallaria* with dark barring on the belly and no eye-ring. Sympatric ssp. of Rufous Antpitta is duller and paler, and lacks barring on the belly. Cf. Bay Antpitta. Birds from Pasco lack dark barring on belly and may represent an undescribed race or species. Uncommon and local in dense cloud forests at Abra Patricia and Cordillera de Colán (Amazonas), Carpish Mts. (Huánuco), Cordillera de Yanachaga and Playa Pampa (Pasco) at 1650-2500 m. *Endemic to Peru.*

Tawny Antpitta *Grallaria quitensis* Tororoi Leonado
18 cm (7"). Plate 78. ♪ JM. No other antpitta in highlands is so plain. Cf. Rufous Antpitta (smaller, finer bill and browner, especially on the underparts). Not particularly shy. Fairly common in *páramo* and elfin forests south to Piura and La Libertad at 2800-4000 m. *Andes of Colombia to n Peru.*

Spotted Antpitta *Hylopezus macularius* Tororoi Moteado
14 cm (5.5"). Plate 78. Note distinctive pattern of gray crown, brown back, spotted breast, buff wingbars and conspicuous ochre eye-ring. Cf. White-lored Antpitta (no overlap). Uncommon and local in humid lowland forests west to Pacaya Samiria Reserve (Loreto) to 500 m. *S Venezuela and the Guianas to n Bolivia and w Amazonian Brazil.*

White-lored Antpitta *Hylopezus fulviventris* Tororoi Loriblanco
14.5 cm (5.75"). Plate 78. ♪ 677. Note limited range. Like Spotted Antpitta, but White-lored lacks eye-ring and wingbars, and has a streaked (not spotted) chest. Rare in humid lowland forests near Pantoja (Loreto) on Río Napo at 150 m. Recorded at ExplorNapo Lodge. *SE Colombia to e Ecuador and extreme ne Peru.*

Amazonian Antpitta *Hylopezus berlepschi* Tororoi Amazónico
14.5 cm (5.75"). Plate 79. ♪ 797. The only antpitta in its range with a streaked breast and fairly plain face. Thrush-like Antpitta is plain-looking and has indistinct breast streaking at best. Ochre-breasted Antpitta is much smaller with patterned face. Rare in humid lowland forests e of Andes north to Junín to 500 m (regularly recorded at Amazonia and Pantiacolla Lodges). *W Amazonian Brazil, se Peru, n and e Bolivia.*

Thrush-like Antpitta *Myrmothera campanisona* Tororoi Campanero
15.5 cm (6"). Plate 78. ♪ 797. The only plain-looking antpitta in the lowlands. Cf. Amazonian Antpitta. Uncommon in humid lowland forests e of Andes to 700 m. *S Venezuela and the Guianas to n Bolivia and Amazonian Brazil.*

Grallaricula **Antpittas.** Very small antpittas, more arboreal than *Grallaria*. Often have eye-rings and pale lores.

Ochre-breasted Antpitta *Grallaricula flavirostris* Tororoi Pechiocráceo
10.2 cm (4"). Plate 79. ♪ 797. The only *Grallaricula* with an ochre breast scalloped with black. Three ssp. occur: illustrated *boliviana* (se Peru); *similis* (central Peru) has darker underparts, darker crown, and a yellow-tipped, black maxilla; *zarumae* (Piura) has unmarked ochre breast. Compare with very localized Ochre-fronted and Peruvian Antpittas (no known overlap). Uncommon in humid montane forests on e slope of Andes at 800-2200 m; on Pacific slope only in Piura. *Costa Rica to w Bolivia.*

Rusty-breasted Antpitta *Grallaricula ferrugineipectus* Tororoi Pechirrojizo
10.2 cm (4"). Plate 79. ♪ 797. Note limited range. Has unmarked underparts and a pale postocular spot. Crown same color as back. Cf. Slate-crowned Antpitta. Fairly common in humid subtrop. montane forests on e slope of Andes from Amazonas south at 600-2200 m. *N Venezuela to w Bolivia.*

Slate-crowned Antpitta *Grallaricula nana* Tororoi Coronipizarrosa
11.5 cm (4.5"). Plate 78. ♪EC007T. Note limited range. Similar to Rusty-breasted Antpitta, but slate-gray crown contrasts with brown back. Fairly common and local in humid montane and elfin forests on Cerro Chinguela at 2000-2900 m. *Venezuela to n Peru.*

Peruvian Antpitta *Grallaricula peruviana* Tororoi Peruano
10.2 cm (4"). Plate 79. Note limited range. Sexes different. Both sexes have black scalloping on a white breast (not buff or ochre as in Ochre-breasted Antpitta). Crown on male is rufous; female brown. No known overlap with Ochre-breasted Antpitta. Rare and local in humid montane forests on e slope of Andes in Cajamarca and Piura at 1650-2100 m. Reported from e side of Cerro Chinguela at 1660-2050 m (TAP). *SE Ecuador and n Peru.*

*Ochre-fronted Antpitta *Grallaricula ochraceifrons* Tororoi Frentiocrácea
10.5 cm (4.75 "). Plate 79. Note limited range. Sexes different. Both sexes have similar pattern on underparts; ochre sides heavily streaked with black, white in center of underparts. Male has ochre-rufous forecrown. Female has brown crown and forecrown. Very rare in dwarf montane forests on e slope of Andes below Abra Patricia (San Martín) and Cordillera de Colán at 1890-1980 m. Known from only a few specimens (BirdLife International 2000). *Endemic to Peru.*

Conopophagidae (Gnateaters; Jejeneros). Species: World 8; Peru 4
A family of small, plump, long-legged birds restricted to the Neotropics that inhabit the humid forest undergrowth from Colombia to Peru, Bolivia, Paraguay, Brazil and northeastern Argentina. They resemble *Grallaricula* antpittas and all Peruvian species have a long white (or gray in females) postocular stripe. Gnateaters feed mainly on insects and small invertebrates, and forage by dropping from a perch to the ground, or by scratching in the litter.

Chestnut-belted Gnateater *Conopophaga aurita* Jejenero Fajicastaña
12 cm (4.75"). Plate 80. Male is unmistakable. Female is similar, but sides of head and throat are chestnut. Cf. Female Ash-throated and Chestnut crowned Gnateaters. Note that in both sexes bill is black. Uncommon and local in humid lowland forests north of Amazon and east of Río Napo to 700 m. *SE Colombia to e Peru, Amazonian Brazil and Guyana.*

Ash-throated Gnateater *Conopophaga peruviana* Jejenero Garganticeniza
12 cm (4.75"). Plate 80. ♪818CD. Both sexes have diagnostic brown wings, with coverts tipped with buff spots. Male has an ashy-gray throat and breast, and dark gray, scaled mantle. Female is similar, but has rufous underparts and browner mantle. Rare to uncommon in humid lowland forests e of Andes to 850 m. Uncommon at Pacaya Samiria National Reserve (Begazo and Valqui 1998) and in Manu National Park. *E Ecuador, e Peru and w Amazonian Brazil.*

Slaty Gnateater *Conopophaga ardesiaca* Jejenero Pizarroso
12.5 cm (5"). Plate 69. ♪797. Male is gray below and brown above. Female has a tawny-buff forecrown and resembles male Chestnut-crowned Gnateater (very limited overlap on Manu road), but the rufous on crown of latter is brighter and more extensive. Uncommon in humid montane forests on e slope of Andes north to Cusco at 800-2450 m. *S Peru and Bolivia.*

Chestnut-crowned Gnateater *Conopophaga castaneiceps* Jejenero Coronicastaña
12.5 cm (5"). Plate 80. ♪741CD. The only gnateater over most of its altitudinal range. Male has a bright rufous forecrown and gray underparts. Female Slaty Gnateater (limited overlap) is similar but has a duller forecrown. Uncommon in humid montane forests on e slope of Andes s to Cordillera Vilcanota at 1200-2000 m. Recently recorded on Manu road at ca 2200 m (EB). *Andes of Colombia to s Peru.*

Rhinocryptidae (Tapaculos). Species: World 56; Peru 21
A family of small to mid-sized, mainly terrestrial birds that ranges from mountains of Costa Rica to Argentina and Chile, and occupies a variety of habitats from sea level to over 4000 meters in the Andes. They reach their greatest diversity in the Andes, where several species coexist at numerous localities. The tail feathers are usually carried erect, which led to their common name *tapaculo* (Spanish for *cover your ass*).

Rusty-belted Tapaculo *Liosceles thoracicus* Tapaculo Fajirrojiza
19 cm (7.5"). Plate 80. ♪ 797. The only tapaculo in Amazonian lowlands. Fairly large (for a tapaculo), long-tailed, brown above, noticeable white superciliary, mostly white throat and breast (in good views note rusty pectoral belt) and barred flanks. Uncommon or locally common in humid *terra firme* e of Andes south to Madre de Dios to 1000 m. *SE Colombia to e Peru and w Amazonian Brazil.*

Elegant Crescentchest *Melanopareia elegans* Pecholuna Elegante
14.5 cm (5.75"). Plate 80. Boldly patterned, similar to Marañón Crescentchest (no known overlap), but Elegant has rufous edging to wing coverts and secondaries; chestnut below pectoral band conrasts with buff belly. Female lacks chestnut below black crescent on chest. Uncommon in dense arid scrub south to La Libertad to about 1700 m. *Arid sw Ecuador and nw Peru.*

Marañón Crescentchest *Melanopareia maranonica* Pecholuna del Marañón
16 cm (6.5"). Plate 71. A tapaculo with a boldly patterned head. Sexes similar. Resembles Elegant Crescentchest (no known overlap), but wing coverts are edged white, and underparts below crescent are uniform rufous. Uncommon and local in dense scrub in upper Río Marañón Valley at 200-750 m. *Marañón valley of n-central Peru and adjacent Ecuador.*

Ash-colored Tapaculo *Myornis senilis* Tapaculo Cenizo
14 cm (5.5"). Plate 80. ♪ EC007T. Tail is noticeably longer than in similar *Scytalopus* tapaculos. Juvenile differs from *Scytalopus* in being fairly bright-rufous above and cinnamon below. Fairly common and local in humid montane forests (especially *Chusquea* bamboo thickets) south to Pasco at 2300-3700 m. *Colombia to n Peru.*

Scytalopus **Tapaculos.** This predominant genus in Peru is comprised of 17 secretive species, that tunnel mouse-like through the dense understory of humid forests. They are sedentary and confined to dense cover; and are one of the most complicated and difficult of all Neotropical bird genera. They use their large feet and strong claws to scratch for food in the loose soil and leaf litter, which consists mainly of insects, including larvae, but seeds and spiders also form part of their diet. We follow Krabbe and Schulenberg (1997) revision of the genus. Identification to species level of the genus based on morphological characters alone is often impossible. Vocalization is the best means of separating them. It is helpful to learn the basic ingredients of their song—tempo, pitch, duration and intervals (even though vocalizations can vary within the species almost as much as among them). Few visual features are sometimes apparent in the field. Try to determine color—whether uniformly black or gray (what shade of gray); whether the bird has barred brown posterior underparts or unbarred brown; and whether any white head markings are present (forecrown, supraloral or superciliary). Bear in mind that juveniles of all species are brown and heavily scaled with dark.

Unicolored Tapaculo *Scytalopus unicolor* Tapaculo Unicolor
12.5 cm (5"). Plate 80. ♪ EC007T. Adult is uniform dark gray. Voice is a single frog-like note. No overlap with Blackish. Very similar to Páramo Tapaculo. Fairly common in humid montane forests on Pacific slope of Andes in Cajamarca and La Libertad at 2000-3150 m. *Endemic to Peru.*

Blackish Tapaculo *Scytalopus latrans* Tapaculo Negruzco
12.5 cm (5"). Like Plate 80 (6), but darker. Adult is uniform black. Typical song is a repetitive double note in slow tempo. No overlap with Unicolored. Fairly common in Andes of n Peru south to Lambayeque and in Utcubamba drainage in Amazonia mostly at 1500-3200 m. *Andes of Colombia and w Venezuela to n Peru.*

Trilling Tapaculo *Scytalopus parvirostris* Tapaculo Trinador
12.5 cm (5"). Like Plate 80 (6). ♪ 742CD. Adult is uniform dark gray. Vocalization is a long, very fast, medium-pitched, machine-gun like song. Overlaps with Large-footed and Tschudi's Tapaculos. Uncommon in humid montane elfin and cloud forests south and east of Río Marañón from Cordillera de Colán south at 1850-2500 m. *Andes of Peru and Bolivia.*

Large-footed Tapaculo *Scytalopus macropus* Tapaculo Patigrande
14.5 cm (5.75"). Plate 80. ♪ JFC. A uniform slate-gray tapaculo, and the largest member of the genus. Typical song is a slow repetition (3 per second) of a low-pitched note. Uncommon and local in mossy montane and elfin cloud forests south and east of Río Marañón from Amazonas to Junín at 2400-3500 m (occasionally lower). *Endemic to Peru.*

Rufous-vented Tapaculo *Scytalopus femoralis* Tapaculo Ventrirrufo
13.5 cm (5.3"). Plate 80. A dark-gray tapaculo with a dark crown, and heavily barred, dark rufous vent. Averages larger than most other similar-plumaged tapaculos. Single note delivered at an interval of about one per second. Common in humid montane forests on e slope of Andes from Amazonas south to Ayacucho at 1000-2050 m. *Endemic to Peru.*

Long-tailed Tapaculo *Scytalopus micropterus* Tapaculo Colilarga
12.5 cm (5"). Like Plate 80 (10). ♪ EC007T. Similar to Rufous-vented Tapaculo (overlap?). Double note delivered at intervals of about one per second. Uncommon and local in humid montane forests on e slope of Andes south to just north of Río Marañón at 1650-1950 m. *Andes of Colombia, Ecuador and n Peru.*

Bolivian Tapaculo *Scytalopus bolivianus* Tapaculo Boliviano
12.5 cm (5"). ♪ 741CD. Like Plate 80 (14). A dark-gray tapaculo with a small white patch on the forecrown and heavily barred, dark-rufous vent. Song is a long fairly fast trill. Uncommon in humid montane forests on e slope of Andes north to Puno at 1000-2300 m. *Andes of s Peru and w Bolivia.*

White-crowned Tapaculo *Scytalopus atratus* Tapaculo Coroniblanca
12.5 cm (5"). Plate 80. A dark-gray tapaculo with a small white patch on the forecrown and heavily barred, dark-rufous vent. Song is series of short trills. Fairly common in humid montane forests south to central Peru at 900-1800 m. *Andes of w Venezuela and Ecuador to central Peru.*

Puna Tapaculo *Scytalopus simonsi* Tapaculo de la Puna
11.5 cm (4.5"). ♪ 797. Like Plate 80 (12). A small tapaculo that sometimes shows a short, whitish superciliary. Posterior underparts are pale-rufous and barred. Song consists of a rising series of *chihuu* (first note louder). Uncommon in humid montane forests at and above treeline (often in *Polylepis*) north to Cordillera Vilcanota at 3000-4300 m. *Andes of s Peru and Bolivia.*

Vilcabamba Tapaculo *Scytalopus urubambae* Tapaculo de Vilcabamba
10.2 cm (4"). Plate 80. Male is deep-gray above with a faint brownish wash; below dark-gray with bright rufous unbarred flanks. Lacks a superciliary. Female is generally paler. Fairly common in humid montane and elfin forests, often in areas dominated by moss and boulders near treeline, in Cordillera Vilcabamba at 3500-4100 m. Can be seen along Inca Trail between Sayacmarca and Phuyupatamarca. *Endemic to Peru.*

Neblina Tapaculo *Scytalopus altirostris* Tapaculo de Neblina
10.5 cm (4.3"). Like Plate 80 (12). Vocalization consists of sharp, even, high-pitched notes, about 4 per second. Uncommon in humid montane forests on e slope of Andes from La Libertad and Amazonas s to Huánuco. Recorded in Cordillera Colán and Carpish Mts. at 2450-3300 m. *Endemic to Peru.*

Ancash Tapaculo *Scytalopus affinis* Tapaculo de Ancash
10.5 cm (4.3"). Plate 80. The only member of the genus in its range with rufous posterior underparts. Cf. immature Unicolored Tapaculo. Song is a chain of fairly short trills, descending toward the end. Uncommon in humid montane forests in Cordillera Blanca (Ancash) at 3050-4000 m. *Endemic to Peru.*

Páramo Tapaculo *Scytalopus canus* Tapaculo del Páramo
10.2 cm (4"). Like Plate 80 (6). ♪ JM. A small, uniformly slate-gray tapaculo. Like sympatric Unicolored Tapaculo, but proportionatly shorter-tailed, with a dark-brown vent. Female has rufous-brown back and barred, ochraceous posterior underparts. Song is a long, very fast trill. Uncommon in humid montane forests (mainly *Chusquea* bamboo) on Cerro Chinguela on Piura-Cajamarca border at 2600-3500 m. *Andes of n Colombia to n Peru.*

Tschudi's Tapaculo *Scytalopus acutirostris* Tapaculo de Tschudi
10.5 cm (4.3"). Plate 80. A small, uniformly slate-gray tapaculo with dark, rufous-barred posterior underparts. Song is a series of short trills (about 0.5 second long, at one-second intervals), usually beginning with a louder introductory note. Fairly common in humid cloud forests of Carpish Mts. (Huánuco) and e of Panao (Pasco) at 2675-3500 m. *Endemic to Peru.*

Diademed Tapaculo *Scytalopus schulenbergi* Tapaculo Diademado
10.5 cm (4.3"). Plate 80. ♪ 797. A tapaculo with a pale-gray head, often with a white superciliary. Song is a long trill in medium tempo. Uncommon in humid temp. cloud and elfin forests on e slope of Andes north to Abra Málaga and Valcón (Puno) at 2950-3400 m. *Andes of s Peru and n Bolivia.*

Chusquea Tapaculo *Scytalopus parkeri* Tapaculo de Chusquea
10.5 cm (4.3"). Like Plate 80 (10). ♪ JM. A pale-gray tapaculo with ochraceous posterior underparts and unbarred rufous rump. Song is a trill (1-9 seconds long) delivered in medium tempo and fading towards the end. Uncommon along continental divide of Andes in n Cajamarca and adjacent Piura on Cerro Chinguela at 2550-2900 m. *Andes of s Ecuador to extreme n Peru.*

Ocellated Tapaculo *Acropternis orthonyx* Tapaculo Ocelado
21.5 cm (8.4"). Plate 80. ♪ JM. Note limited range. A very attractive tapaculo, with most of the body spotted white (except for the rufous face, rump and crissum). Rare in montane forests on Cerro Chinguela and Cordillera de Colán at 1900-3650 m. *Andes of nw Venezuela to n Peru.*

Phytotomidae (Plantcutters; Cortahojas). Species: World 3; Peru 1
A family of three medium-sized birds with grosbeak-like bills that resemble finches, but their syrinx muscles and foot structure show a clear relationship to the cotingas (with which they are often included). They earn their name by their manner of feeding—clipping off leaves, buds, fruits and shoots with their serrated bills, and even severing small plants at the base—wasting far more food than they eat.

*Peruvian Plantcutter *Phytotoma raimondii* Cortarrama Peruana
18.5 cm (7.2"). Plate 82. Unmistakable in its limited range. Gray male has a conspicuous white wingbar, white tips to tail, and rufous lower belly. Grayish-buff female is heavily streaked. Rare and local in sandy coastal desert scrub from Tumbes to n Lima below 550 m. The two largest populations are from Quebrada Salada to Quebrada Ancha in Talará area, and Reque and Rafan area (especially in Murales forest.). *Endemic to Peru.*

Cotingidae (Cotingas). Species: World 66; Peru 33
An extremely diverse family of arboreal birds, ranging in size from the 8-cm Kinglet Calyptura of Brazil to the crow-sized Amazonian Umbrellabird. The cotingas range from extreme southern Mexico to ne Argentina, from sea level to over 4000 meters in the Andes. Most cotingas are frugivorus, and some species supplement their diet with insects. Some members of the family, especially the cocks-of-the-rock, have elaborate courtship displays in communal leks. The purpletufts are adept at capturing flying insects in flycatcher-like fashion.

Black-necked Red Cotinga *Phoenicircus nigricollis* Cotinga-Roja Cuellinegro
23 cm (9"). Plate 83. ♪ 632. A stunning and unmistakable cotinga. Uncommon in humid *terra firme* forests e of Andes in Loreto and San Martín. Seen regularly at leks at ExplorNapo Lodge on lower Río Napo near Iquitos. *SE Colombia to sw Venezuela, ne Peru and Amazonian Brazil.*

Shrike-like Cotinga *Laniisoma elegans* Plañidero Elegante
17.5 cm (6.8"). Plate 81. ♪741CD. An inconspicuous cotinga, olive-green above and yellow below. Male has a black crown; female similar, but crown is concolor to back and underparts are scaled. Cf. various female fruiteaters. Rare in lower level of humid lowland and foothill forests e of Andes from Amazonas to Pasco at 400-1350 m (once at 1800 m). *W Venezuela to w Bolivia; se Brazil.*

Cinereous Mourner *Laniocera hypopyrra* Plañidero Cinéreo
20 cm (8"). Plate 83. ♪ 797. The only cotinga-like bird that is gray with cinnamon-rufous spots on wing coverts. Cf. Screaming Piha. Uncommon low in humid *terra firme* forests e of Andes to 500 m, occasionally to 900 m. *E Colombia to e Brazil and Amazon basin.*

Red-crested Cotinga *Ampelion rubrocristata* Cotinga Crestirroja
21.5 cm (8.4"). Plate 82. ♪ 797. The only high-altitude cotinga with a white subterminal band to tail (seen from below and in flight), a whitish bill tipped black, white crissum streaked with black, and dark-gray body. Sometimes raises crest. Immature is streaked gray and tan. Fairly common in montane scrub, *Polylepis*, and elfin forests on e slope of Andes and on Pacific slope south to Lima at 2500-3700 m. *W Venezuela to w Bolivia.*

Chestnut-crested Cotinga *Ampelion rufaxilla* Cotinga Cresticastaña
21 cm (8.5"). Plate 82. ♪797. Unmistakable. Rare and local in humid montane forests on e slope of Andes at 1750-2700 m. Recorded along Paty Trail in Carpish Mts.; recently recorded near Río Pauya (Loreto) by TSS. *Colombia to w Bolivia.*

*Chestnut-bellied Cotinga *Doliornis remseni* Cotinga Ventricastaño
21 cm (8.5"). Plate 82. Told from also rare Bay-vented Cotinga by its dark iris and mostly chestnut underparts. Rare in montane forests in Cordillera de Lagunillas at 3100-3650 m. *S Ecuador and adjacent n Peru.*

Bay-vented Cotinga *Doliornis sclateri* Cotinga Ventribayo
21.5 cm (8.4"). Plate 82. The only high-altitude cotinga with pale-gray eyes and rufous crissum. Cf. Chestnut-bellied and Red-crested Cotingas. Rare to uncommon in montane elfin forests (especially *Escallonia* and *Weinmannia*) on e slope of Andes in Puerto del Monte (San Martín), near Tayabamba (e La Libertad), Carpish Mts. (Huánuco), Pozuco-Chaglla trail (Pasco), and Maraynioc (Junín) at 2500-3500 m. *Endemic to Peru.*

*White-cheeked Cotinga *Zaratornis stresemanni* Cotinga Cachetiblanco
21 cm (8.5"). Plate 82. Note distinctive facial pattern. The only high-altitude cotinga with white cheeks. Cf. immature Red-crested Cotinga (lacks white cheeks and has a white subterminal band to tail). Uncommon in *Polylepis-Gynoxys* woodlands in w Andes in La Libertad, Ancash, Lima and Ayacucho at 3250-4250 m. Largest-known concentration is at Pueblo Quichas, where an estimated 500 individuals were reported in 1987 (JF). *Endemic to Peru.*

Green-and-black Fruiteater *Pipreola riefferii* Frutero Verdinegro
18 cm (7"). Plate 81. ♪ 797. Three ssp. occur in Peru. "Typical" race *chachapoyas* (illustrated, San Martín) and *confusa* (n Amazonas) have red bills and legs, dark eyes, and dark streaks on yellow belly (especially on sides) Cf. Band-tailed and Black-chested Fruiteaters. Race *tallmanorum* (illustrated, Andes of Huánuco) at 2100-2300 m is smaller (16 cm, 6.5"), has red iris and mostly unstreaked yellow underparts, and may possibly represent a separate species (Huánuco Fruiteater). Fairly common in humid montane forests on e slope of Andes south to Huánuco at 1500-2700 m. *Mountains of Venezuela to n Peru.*

Band-tailed Fruiteater *Pipreola intermedia* Frutero Colifajeado
19 cm (7.5"). Plate 81. ♪ 797. Recalls a "typical" Green-and-black Fruiteater but larger; both sexes have a black subterminal band and white tips to tail. Two ssp. occur. Nominate (illustrated, La Libertad to Junín) has blackish chevron markings on underparts. Race *signata* (Cusco and Puno) has cleaner yellow underparts. Fairly common in humid montane forests on e slope of Andes north to La Libertad at 2300-3000 m. *Andes of Peru and w Bolivia.*

Barred Fruiteater *Pipreola arcuata* Frutero Barreteado
23 cm (9"). Plate 81. ♪ 797. A large fruiteater with barred underparts. Male has black hood. Female has a green head and barred throat. Fairly common in humid montane and elfin forests on e slope of Andes at 2000-3300 m. *Andes of w Venezuela to w Bolivia.*

Black-chested Fruiteater *Pipreola lubomirskii* Frutero Pechinegro
17 cm (6.6"). Facing Plate 81. ♪ EC007T. Note limited range. Both sexes are similar to respective sexes of Green-and-black Fruiteater, but eyes are yellow, legs gray, and they lack white tips to tertials. Male lacks yellow border to sides of black head. Rare in humid montane forests west of Río Marañón at 1500-2300 m. Recently recorded in elfin forest in Cordillera de Colán at 1750-1900 m (Barnes *et al.* 1997). *Andes of se Colombia to extreme n Peru.*

Masked Fruiteater *Pipreola pulchra* Frutero Enmascarado
18 cm (7"). Plate 81. ♪ 742CD. Male is unmistakable. Female's yellow breast is streaked greenish (unlike female Scarlet-breasted Fruiteater's unstreaked green breast). Rare to uncommon in humid montane forests on e slope of Andes from Amazonas to Cordillera Vilcabamba at 1500-2200 m. Regularly seen in Divisoria area east of Tingo Maria (Huánuco) and at Machu Picchu. *Endemic to Peru.*

Fiery-throated Fruiteater *Pipreola chlorolepidota* Frutero Gargantifuego
12.5 cm (5"). Plate 81. The smallest fruiteater. Male has red throat bordered by green breast. Female can be recognized by its small size, yellow eyes, red legs, and yellow underparts streaked with green. Rare in humid foothill forests along e slope of Andes south to Pasco at 600-1200 m. *Andean foothills of se Colombia to central Peru.*

Scarlet-breasted Fruiteater *Pipreola frontalis* Frutero Pechiescarlata
16 cm (6.5"). Plate 81. ♪ 797. The beautiful male is unmistakable. Female has a yellow foreface, a green breast and yellow eyes. Cf. Masked Fruiteater. Female Green-and-black Fruiteater has a dark eye. Race *squamipectus* (from Huánuco south) has an iridescent bluish crown, is smaller than illustrated nominate (south to San Martín), and may represent a separate species. Uncommon and disjunct in humid montane and foothill forests on e slope of Andes in San Martín, and from Huánuco south at 650-2000 m. *Andes of e Ecuador to w Bolivia.*

Scaled Fruiteater *Ampelioides tschudii* Frutero Escamoso
19 cm (7.5"). Plate 81. ♪ 797. Unlikely to be confused. Fairly common and local in humid montane forests on e slope of Andes south to Cerros de Pantiacolla at 900-2000 m. *Andes of w Venezuela to w Bolivia.*

White-browed Purpletuft *Iodopleura isabellae* Iodopleura Cejiblanca
11.5 cm (4.5"). Plate 81. ♪ 677. Perches on bare branches in canopy. A small cotinga with a diagnostic face pattern and white rump The purple tufts are hard to see in the field (female has white tufts). Uncommon (overlooked?) in humid lowland forests to 500 m. *SE Colombia to s Venezuela, n Bolivia and Amazonian Brazil.*

Gray-tailed Piha *Snowornis subalaris* Piha Coligris
23.5 cm (9.5"). Plate 83. ♪ 741CD. Similar to Olivaceous Piha, but rump and uppertail are gray and lower belly is whitish. Rare and local in middle and lower level of humid foothill forests northeast of Jerillo (San Martín), Enenas (Pasco) and on Cerros de Pantiacolla at 600-1400 m. *Foothills of e Ecuador and e Peru.*

Olivaceous Piha *Snowornis cryptolophus* Piha Olivácea
23.5 cm (9.5"). Plate 83. A fairly uniform olive-green piha, with a yellow-green lower belly. Cf. Gray-tailed Piha. Uncommon in middle and lower level of humid montane forests on e slope of Andes south to Huánuco at 1200-2200 m. *Andes of s Colombia to e Peru.*

Dusky Piha *Lipaugus fuscocinereus* Piha Oscura
32.5 cm (12.7"). Plate 83. ♪ EC007T. A large, uniformly dusky-gray piha with a long tail. Gray-tailed Piha is smaller and greener. Rare and local in humid montane forests on Cerro Chinguela at 2000-3000 m. *Andes of Colombia to n Peru.*

*Scimitar-winged Piha *Lipaugus uropygialis* Piha Alicimatarra
30 cm (11.7"). Plate 83. Note limited range. No other long-tailed bird is gray with a chestnut rump and crissum. At close range note highly modified (very narrow and curved) primaries. Rare in humid montane forests in Cordillera Apolobamba and Abra de Maruncunca at 1800-2560 m. *Andes of extreme s Peru and w Bolivia.*

Screaming Piha *Lipaugus vociferans* Piha Gritona
25 cm (9.8"). Plate 83. ♪ 797. Most often seen after tracking down its ear-splitting call. If quiet, cf. very similar Grayish Mourner. Screaming Piha is larger and has dark eyes (Grayish Mourner has reddish eyes). Common in humid lowland forests e of Andes to 500 m, occasionally in foothills to 1000 m. *S Venezuela and the Guianas to e Bolivia, Amazonian and e Brazil.*

Purple-throated Cotinga *Porphyrolaema porphyrolaema* Cotinga Gargantipúrpura
18 cm (7"). Plate 82. ♪ 632. Male is unmistakable. Dark female can be recognized by its rufous throat and barred underparts. Uncommon in humid lowland forests e of Andes south to Madre de Dios to 400 m, rarely to 900 m. *SE Colombia to se Peru and w Amazonian Brazil.*

Plum-throated Cotinga *Cotinga maynana* Cotinga Gargantimorada
19.5 cm (7.75"). Plate 82. ♪ 677. Male is an intensely blue cotinga. It lacks the black spangles that characterize Spangled Cotinga. Eyes are usually yellow, but color may vary. Female is like that of Spangled Cotinga, but a warmer buff-color, especially on lower belly and crissum. Uncommon in humid lowland forests e of Andes to 700 m. *SE Colombia to n Bolivia and w Amazonian Brazil.*

Purple-breasted Cotinga *Cotinga cotinga* Cotinga Pechipúrpura
18 cm (7"). Plate 82. Male has a dark-blue body with a dark-purple throat and breast. Female is more boldly scaled than that of larger Spangled and Plum-throated Cotingas. Recent sight records from Jesus del Monte (Begazo et al. 2001) and on "Wetmorethraupis" ridge out of Bagua Chica (EB). Occurrence of this "sandy-belt" cotinga marks a considerable extension westward from its previously published range (Ridgely and Tudor 1994). *S Venezuela and the Guianas to n Amazonian Brazil.*

Spangled Cotinga *Cotinga cayana* Cotinga Lentejuelada
20 cm (8"). Plate 82. Male is easily recognized by its heavily scaled "spangled" body, especially on back, head and sides of breast. Female is grayish-buff, scaled above and on chest, but lower belly is unscaled gray. Uncommon in humid lowland forests e of Andes to 600 m. *S Venezuela and the Guianas to n Bolivia and Amazonian Brazil.*

Pompadour Cotinga *Xipholena punicea* Cotinga Pomposa
19.5 cm (7.75"). Plate 82. ♪ MS. Both sexes have whitish eyes. Male has a crimson-purple body, elongated wing coverts, and white flight feathers. Female is gray, paler on underparts; wings are darker with strong white edging to wing coverts and secondaries. Other female *Cotingas* are browner, more scaled and dark-eyed. A small population recently found in white sand forests in Iquitos area. This is a considerable westward extension from its published range (Ridgely and Tudor 1994). *Extreme e Colombia to the Guianas, Amazonian Brazil and ne Bolivia.*

Black-faced Cotinga *Conioptilon mcilhennyi* Cotinga Carinegra
23 cm (9"). Plate 82. ♪ 818CD. Unmistakable in its limited range. Locally common in humid lowland forests in Ucayali, Cusco and Madre de Dios. Usually found in subcanopy of river-edge forest, swampy or seasonally flooded forest habitats, and along lake or river margins to e of Andes to 350 m, with one record at 700 m along Río Caimisea (Lloyd 2000). *SE Peru; recently recorded in immediately adjacent Brazil and Bolivia.*

Bare-necked Fruitcrow *Gymnoderus foetidus* Cuervo-Frutero Cuellipelado
38 cm (15"). Plate 83. Unmistakable. Female is similar to male but has dark wings (lacking the pale-gray upperwing), and neck wattles are much reduced. Fairly common in humid lowland forests e of Andes to 500 m. *S Venezuela and the Guianas to n Bolivia and Amazonian Brazil.*

Purple-throated Fruitcrow *Querula purpurata* Cuervo-Frutero Gargantipúrpura
27 cm (10.5"). Plate 83. ♪ 797. Black male with its plum-purple throat is distinctive. Female is uniformly black and lacks purple on throat. Female umbrellabird is larger, with a small crest and heavier bill. Common in humid lowland forests e of Andes to 700 m. *Costa Rica to n Bolivia and Amazonian Brazil.*

Red-ruffed Fruitcrow *Pyroderus scutatus* Cuervo-Frutero Gargantirroja
40 cm (15.5"). Plate 83. Unlikely to be confused. Purple-throated Fruitcrow is much smaller, with a darker, smaller throat-patch. Uncommon in humid montane forests on e slope of Andes south to Junín at 1200-2200 m. *Venezuela and Guyana to e Peru; se Brazil to ne Argentina.*

Amazonian Umbrellabird *Cephalopterus ornatus* Pájero-Paraguas Amazónico
48 cm (19"). Plate 83. ♪ 797. Male is distinctive. Glossy-black female has only a short crest and is rather crow-like. Cf. female Purple-throated Fruitcrow. Uncommon in humid lowland forests and along e base of Andes to 1500 m. *S Venezuela and Guyana to n Bolivia and Amazonian Brazil.*

Andean Cock-of-the-rock *Rupicola peruviana* Gallito de las Rocas Andino
30 cm (11.7"). Plate 83. ♪ 797. One of Peru's most beloved and spectacular birds. Unmistakable. Uncommon in humid montane ravines and forests at 500-2400 m. Frequently seen along railroad tracks below Machu Picchu train station, and large lek near Cock-of-the-rock Lodge. *Andes of w Venezuela to w Bolivia.*

Pipridae (Manakins; Saltarines). Species: World 52; Peru 24
Manakins are small, forest-dwelling birds of the New World tropics that are closely related to the cotingas and tyrant-flycatchers. Many manakins have courtship displays that are among the most elaborate of any family of birds, especially those in the genera *Manacus*, *Pipra* and *Chiroxiphia*. They are omnivorous, feeding on both fruits and insects, which they pluck (or catch) in flight by rapid sallies from a perch.

Jet Manakin *Chloropipo unicolor* Saltarín Azabache
12 cm (4.75"). Plate 84. Male is the only all "black" manakin in its range. In flight shows white underwing lining. The glossy-black male superficially resembles Andean Tyrant, but latter lacks gloss. Female is dark olive-gray, grayer on belly, with pale lores, eye-ring and blackish legs. Fairly common in humid montane forests on e slope of Andes south to Puno at 900-1900 m. *Andes from e Ecuador to central Peru.*

Green Manakin *Chloropipo holochlora* Saltarín Verde
12 cm (4.75"). Plate 85. Sexes alike. Yellowish-olive with yellow on belly and vent. Blackish legs. Recalls a few female manakins, especially much smaller and shorter-tailed Blue-crowned, and similar-sized Blue-backed (pale-orange legs). Fairly common in humid *terra firme* forests e of Andes south to Puno at 500-1100 m. *E Panama to s Peru.*

White-bearded Manakin *Manacus manacus* Saltarín Barbiblanca
10.2 cm (4"). Plate 85. ♪797. Male's black and white pattern is distinctive. Female is olive above and paler below. Both sexes have orange legs. Common in lowland forests e of Andes in Loreto and San Martín to 1000 m. Rare on Pacific slope in Tumbes. *Colombia to ne Argentina, Amazonian and se Brazil.*

Blue-backed Manakin *Chiroxiphia pareola* Saltarín Dorsiazul
12.5 cm (5"). Plates 84, 85. ♪797. Two ssp. occur in Peru. Race *napensis* (ne Peru) has red on crown as in Yungas Manakin (no overlap). Where yellow-crowned race *regina* (e and se Peru) overlaps with Yungas, latter is usually found at higher elevations. Female has dark eyes, uniform pale-olive on belly, and pale-orange legs. Female Jet and Black Manakins are darker with grayer legs. Common and local in humid lowland forests e of Andes in Loreto and Cerros de Pantiacolla (Madre de Dios) to 750 m. *S Venezuela and the Guianas to n Bolivia, Amazonian and e Brazil.*

Yungas Manakin *Chiroxiphia boliviana* Saltarín de Yungas
12.5 cm (5"). Plate 84. ♪797. Sympatric race of Blue-backed Manakin has a yellow crown. Female is like that of Blue-backed Manakin but Yungas' legs are darker and browner. Occurs higher than Blue-backed Manakin. Fairly common and local in humid montane forests in Cusco, Cerros de Pantiacolla and Puno at 650-2150 m. Regularly recorded near Cock-of-the-rock Lodge. *Yungas of w Bolivia and se Peru.*

Band-tailed Manakin *Pipra fasciicauda* Saltarín Colifajeado
11.5 cm (4.5"). Plates 84, 85. ♪797. Male is easily recognized. Female is olive, yellower on belly and has white eyes. Cf. female Wire-tailed Manakin (different tail structure). Fairly common in lowland *várzea* forests north to San Martín and s Loreto to 600 m. *E Peru to ne Argentina, e Paraguay and s Amazonian Brazil.*

Wire-tailed Manakin *Pipra filicauda* Saltarín Cola-de-Alambre
11.5 cm (4.5"). Plate 85. ♪542. Both sexes have wire-like tail ends. Female is like that of Band-tailed Manakin, but tail structure is diagnostic. Fairly common in humid lowland forests e of Andes south to lower Río Huallaga (San Martín) and along lower Río Ucayali (s Loreto) to 500 m. *W Venezuela to ne Peru and w Amazonian Brazil.*

White-crowned Manakin *Pipra pipra* Saltarín Coroniblanca
10.2 cm (4"). Plate 85. ♪677. Male is all black with a white crown and reddish eyes. Cf. Blue-rumped Manakin. Female can be recognized by its gray crown, red eyes, olive-green upperparts and greenish-yellow underparts. Uncommon in humid lowland and foothill forests along e base of Andes south to Cusco to 1600 m. *Costa Rica to e Peru, the Guianas, Amazonian and e Brazil.*

Blue-crowned Manakin *Pipra coronata* Saltarín Coroniazul
9.2 cm (3.6"). Plate 84, 85. ♪797. Three ssp. occur. Males of *exquisita* (s of Loreto to Cusco, illustrated) and *caelestipileata* (Puno) have a mostly green body, yellow belly and blue crown. Northern race *coronata* (Loreto, illustrated) has a black body with a blue crown. Females of all ssp. are similar—bluish-green above and yellow-green on belly. Similar to female Cerulean-capped (darker, especially on the belly) and that of Blue-rumped (yellower on crown). Fairly common in humid *terra firme* forests e of Andes to 1000 m. *Costa Rica to s Venezuela, n Bolivia and w Amazonian Brazil.*

Golden-headed Manakin *Pipra erythrocephala* Saltarín Cabecidorada
9.2 cm (3.6"). Plate 85. ♪609. Male has a black body, golden-orange head and white eyes. Female like that of Red-headed Manakin, but bill is pale. Fairly common in humid and deciduous lowland forests e of Andes south to n San Martín and s Loreto to 1100 m. *Panama to ne Peru, the Guianas and Amazonian Brazil.*

Red-headed Manakin *Pipra rubrocapilla* Saltarín Cabecirroja
10.2 cm (4"). Plate 84. ♪797. Male's dark eye, red and white thighs, and square tail separate it from Round-tailed Manakin. Female is dingy olive, dark-eyed and dark-billed. Female Round-tailed Manakin has a rounded tail and is larger. Female Golden-headed Manakin has a pale bill. Fairly common but disjunct in humid lowland forests in drainage of lower Río Ucayali and Río Huallaga (s Loreto) and in se Madre de Dios. *E Peru, n Bolivia and s Amazonian Brazil.*

Round-tailed Manakin *Pipra chloromeros* Saltarín Coliredonda
11.5 cm (4.5"). Plate 84, 85. ♪797. The red on male's head creates a short crest. Male has pale eyes and yellow thighs. Female is similar to female Red-headed Manakin. Fairly common in humid lowland and foothill forests on e slope of Andes north to s Amazonas to 1400 m. *E Peru and n Bolivia.*

Blue-rumped Manakin *Pipra isidorei* Saltarín Lomiazul
7.7 cm (3"). Plate 84. Combination of male's white crown and light-blue rump is diagnostic. Female is like that of Blue-crowned Manakin, but yellower on crown. Rare in humid foothill forests on e slope of Andes in San Martín and n Huánuco at 700-1700 m. Peruvian race *leucopygia* may represent a separate species (Milky-rumped Manakin). *Andean foothills of Colombia to n Peru.*

Cerulean-capped Manakin *Pipra coeruleocapilla* Saltarín de Gorricerúleo
8.9 cm (3.5"). Plate 84. ♪741CD. Male's blue crown and blue rump are diagnostic. Female is similar to Blue-crowned Manakin (longer tail, usually found at lower elevations). Uncommon to locally fairly common in humid foothill forests on e slope of Andes from Huánuco south to Puno at 500-2100 m. Recorded near Cock-of-the-rock Lodge. *Endemic to Peru.*

Golden-winged Manakin *Masius chrysopterus* Saltarín Alidorada
11.5 cm (4.5"). Plate 85. Note that tail is exceptionally long for a manakin. Male is distinctive. Female is greenish-olive with a yellow patch on lower throat. Fairly common in humid montane forests in Cajamarca and San Martín at 1200-2300 m. *Andes of nw Venezuela to ne Peru.*

Fiery-capped Manakin *Machaeropterus pyrocephalus* Saltarín Gorrifuego
9.2 cm (3.6"). Plate 84. ♪797. Male with his red and yellow crown and streaked underparts is distinctive. Female is olive-green above and paler below, with olive streaking on breast. Some overlap (in ne Peru) with Striped Manakin, but latter's female has reddish streaks on belly. Uncommon and local in humid lowland forests e of Andes from San Martín south to Puno and Madre de Dios to 1200 m. *Disjunct in s Venezuela, e Peru, n Bolivia, ne and central Brazil.*

Striped Manakin *Machaeropterus regulus* Saltarín Rayado
9.2 cm (3.6"). Plate 85. ♪609. Male resembles male Fiery-capped Manakin, but crown is entirely red. Female is olive-brown above, yellowish below with reddish streaks. Uncommon in humid *terra firme* forests e of Andes south to Pucallpa (n Ucayali) to 1300 m. *Venezuela to ne Peru, w Amazonian and e Brazil.*

Black Manakin *Xenopipo atronitens* Saltarín Negro
12 cm (4.75"). Plate 85. The only all black manakin in its limited range. Similar to Jet Manakin (no overlap). Some resemblance to larger *Knipolegus* black-tyrants. Female is similar to female Blue-backed Manakin, but has blackish legs. Rare in humid lowland savanna and scrub in Pampas del Heath. *S Venezuela to extreme ne Bolivia and Amazonian Brazil.*

Orange-crested Manakin *Heterocercus aurantiivertex* Saltarín Crestinaranja
14 cm (5.5"). Plate 84. Note limited range. Male has a white throat, grayish cheeks, orange coronal stripe, mostly olive-brown upperparts and cinnamon-buff underparts. Female is similar but lacks coronal stripe. Cf. Flame-crested Manakin. Rare and local in *várzea* forests near Chamicuros (sw Loreto) at ca 300 m. Recently recorded in white sand forests in Iquitos area and several sites along middle and lower Río Tigre (Alvarez 2000). *Lowlands of e Ecuador and adjacent ne Peru.*

Flame-crested Manakin *Heterocercus linteatus* Saltarín Crestifuego
14 cm (5.5"). Plate 84. Male has a black head, conspicuous white throat, a narrow blackish pectoral band and rich rufous underparts. Female is olivaceous above, cinnamon below, and has a gray throat and blackish cheeks. Cf. Orange-crested Manakin. Two sight records from Madre de Dios (Pampas del Heath and Río Palma Real). Original specimen from Puerto Indiana (Loreto) might represent a female Orange-crested Manakin, which was unknown at the time (pers. comm. TSS). *S Amazonian Brazil, e Peru and extreme ne Bolivia.*

Saffron-crested Tyrant-Manakin *Neopelma chrysocephalum* Tirano-Saltarín Coroniazafrán
12.5 cm (5"). Plate 85. ♪ MS. Very similar to Sulphur-bellied Tyrant-Manakin (occurs together near Iquitos) but coronal stripe is broader, longer and brighter in color. Recent sight records and tape recordings from white sands forest in Iquitos area. This is a westward extension of its Amazon basin range (Ridgely and Tudor 1994). *Extreme e Colombia to s Venezuela and n Brazil.*

Sulphur-bellied Tyrant-Manakin *Neopelma sulphureiventer* Tirano-Saltarín Ventriazufrado
12.5 cm (5"). Plate 84. ♪ 797. A very plain, nondescript manakin that recalls a *Myiopagis* elaenia, but lacks wingbars or facial markings. Note yellow eyes. Much smaller Dwarf Tyrant-Manakin's tail is shorter. See recently recorded Saffron-crested Tyrant-Manakin. Uncommon along tropical rivers and margins from San Martín to Ucayali to 450 m. *E Peru, n Bolivia and sw Amazonian Brazil.*

Dwarf Tyrant-Manakin *Tyranneutes stolzmanni* Tirano-Saltarincillo Enano
9.2 cm (3.6"). Plate 85. ♪ 797. A tiny, short-tailed manakin, light olive above and yellowish below with a pale eye. Cf. Sulphur-bellied Tyrant-Manakin. Fairly common in humid *terra firme* forests e of Andes to 800 m. *S Venezuela to n Bolivia and Amazonian Brazil.*

Wing-barred Piprites *Piprites chloris* Piprites Alibandeada
12.5 cm (5"). Plate 85. ♪ 797. A chunky, greenish manakin, grayer on nape and yellower on face. Has conspicuous wingbars and pale edging to tertials. No other manakin has wingbars. Recalls a flycatcher but is shaped like a true manakin. Uncommon in humid lowland and foothill forests e of Andes to 1000 m. *Venezuela and the Guianas to ne Argentina and s Brazil.*

Tyrannidae (Tyrant Flycatchers; Tiranos y Mosqueros). Species: World 435; Peru 254
The tyrant-flycatchers form the largest group of New World perching birds. They are most numerous in the tropics, and are the largest family of birds found in Peru, ranging in every habitat from sea level to over 5000 meters. They vary in size from the tiny 6.5-cm Short-tailed Pygmy-Tyrant to the 40-cm Fork-tailed Flycatcher. They are mostly arboreal, and feed chiefly on insects caught on the wing, although tropical species often glean food from twigs and leaves in the manner of warblers, or feed on berries. Recent studies have shown that many North American migrants become partially frugivorus during their annual stay in the tropics. The tropical species tend to be sedentary, with their ranks swelled alternately with visiting northern migrants from October to March, and austral migrants from May to September.

White-lored Tyrannulet *Ornithion inerme* Moscareta Loriblanca
9.2 cm (3.6"). Plate 86. ♪797. No other small flycatcher has two wingbars composed of large whitish spots. Uncommon in humid lowland forests e of Andes south to Madre de Dios to 900 m. *S Venezuela and the Guianas to n Bolivia, Amazonian and e Brazil.*

Southern Beardless-Tyrannulet *Camptostoma obsoletum* Mosquerito Silbador
10.2 cm (4"). Plate 86. ♪797. Four ssp. occur in Peru. All are dull with two yellowish-buff to ochre wingbars. They often raise a distinctive crest, and the tail is held cocked. Ssp. *sclateri* (nw) and *olivaceum* (ne, illustrated) are olive-gray above with a yellowish belly, but *maranonicum* (middle Marañón Valley) and *griseum* (arid coast) are grayer above with a whitish belly. Cf. Mouse-colored Tyrannulet (lacks crest), Gray-and-white Tyrannulet (limited range, white on crest). Uncommon in lowland forests e of Andes; common on Pacific slope south to Lima, and in arid intermontane Andean valleys to 2500 m. *SW Costa Rica to n Argentina and Uruguay.*

Mouse-colored Tyrannulet *Phaeomyias murina* Moscareta Murino
12 cm (4.75"). Plate 86, 95. ♪797. Four ssp. occur in Peru. All are dull with a whitish superciliary and pale on base of lower mandible. The three Pacific slope ssp. (*tumbezana, maranonica* and illustrated *inflava*) have ochre wingbars and whitish to pale-yellowish bellies. Race *wagae* (illustrated) of Amazon basin has buff wingbars. Cf. Southern Beardless-Tyrannulet and Gray-and-white Tyrannulet. Race *tumbezana* (s Ecuador and n Peru) may possibly be a separate species (Tumbes Tyrannulet). Rare in lowland forests e of Andes; common on arid Pacific slope south to Lima and in intermontane Andean valleys to 2000 m. *Panama to nw Argentina and Brazil; Trinidad.*

Yellow Tyrannulet *Capsiempis flaveola* Moscareta Amarilla
11.5 cm (4.5"). Plate 86. ♪797. No other tyrannulet is as yellow—yellow below, yellow wingbars and superciliary, and yellow-olive above. Cf. Yellow-breasted Flycatcher (wider bill, weaker face pattern). Known from three records: Isla Pasto, 80 km ne of Iquitos (Loreto) at 80 m; Pakitza (Madre de Dios) at 356 m; and Tono (Cusco) at 780 m (Servat 1993). *Nicaragua to ne Argentina and Brazil.*

Yellow-crowned Tyrannulet *Tyrannulus elatus* Moscareta Coroniamarilla
11 cm (4.5"). Plate 86. ♪797. A small tyrannid with two white wingbars and a dark gray head with a yellow coronal stripe. Note the short black bill. Cf. Slender-footed Tyrannulet and Forest Elaenia. Fairly common high in humid lowland forests, and along tropical rivers e of Andes to 1000 m. *Costa Rica to n Bolivia and Amazonian Brazil.*

***Myiopagis* Elaenias.** A genus of six mid-sized (slightly smaller than *Elaenia*) confusing flycatchers. Some have wingbars and others don't. On most the crown is darker than the back and has a concealed coronal stripe. Normally perch less upright than *Elaenia*, and do not tend to perch on exposed branches.

Forest Elaenia *Myiopagis gaimardii* Elainia de la Selva
12.5 cm (5"). Plate 86. ♪797. A *Myiopagis* with two prominent yellowish wingbars, yellowish edging to secondaries, and a whitish coronal stripe. Mantle and nape are concolor olive-green. Yellowish underparts. The newly described Foothill Elaenia is similar, but has three wingbars. Female Gray Elaenia has contrasting crown and mantle, and whitish underparts. Sympatric with similarly plumaged members of *Zimmerius* (no coronal stripe), *Tolmomyias* (no coronal stripe, broader, flatter bill) and *Tyrannulus* (yellow crown stripe, white wingbars). Common in humid forests along e base of Andes to 1000 m. *Panama to e Bolivia, Amazonian and ne Brazil; Trinidad.*

Foothill Elaenia *Myiopagis olallai* Elainia Submontana
12.5 cm (5"). Plate 86. ♪LNS. A *Myiopagis* with three yellowish wingbars, yellowish edging to secondaries, a pure white coronal stripe, yellowish throat, and dark olive-green mantle contrasting with dark gray crown and nape. Very similar to Forest Elaenia (two wingbars, concolor nape and mantle)

and female Gray Elaenia (white throat). A recently described species collected in Peru 6 km east of Luisiana (Ayacucho) at 890 m (Coopmans and Krabbe 2000). Probably will be found in intervening foothills between Ayacucho and Ecuador border. *Disjunct in foothills on e slope of Andes of Ecuador and Peru.*

Gray Elaenia *Myiopagis caniceps* Elainia Gris
12.5 cm (5"). Plate 86. ♪ 797. Sexually dimorphic. Both sexes have bold wingbars, wing edging and coronal stripe (white in male and yellowish in female), whitish belly and white throat. Male has pure gray back and crown. Recalls Slaty Elaenia (no wingbars). Female has olive mantle sharply bordered by a gray nape and crown, otherwise similar to Forest Elaenia. Rare and local in humid lowland and foothill forests e of Andes in Loreto, Ucayali and Madre de Dios to 1200 m. Recently recorded at Pacaya Samiria National Reserve (Begazo and Valqui 1998). *Panama to n Argentina, Brazil and the Guianas.*

Pacific Elaenia *Myiopagis subplacens* Elainia del Pacífico
13.5 cm (5.3"). Plate 95. Note limited range. A *Myiopagis* without wingbars with a bright yellow coronal stripe. Note the dark auricular, bordered behind by grizzled gray. The dark-brown crown contrasts with olive back, grayish breast and yellowish belly. It is likely that very similar Greenish Elaenia race *implacens* from w Ecuador will be recorded in nw Peru. The latter is even duller, lacks contrast between crown and back, and has less pronounced grayish breast-band. Fairly common in deciduous woodlands in Tumbes, Piura and Lambayeque to 1500 m. *W Ecuador and nw Peru.*

Yellow-crowned Elaenia *Myiopagis flavivertex* Elainia Coroniamarilla
12.5 cm (5"). Plate 88. ♪ 677. A dull-olive *Myiopagis* with a bright-yellow coronal stripe, whitish superciliary and two yellowish wingbars. Forest Elaenia has a whitish coronal stripe; female Gray Elaenia has a gray crown and whiter underparts; Greenish Elaenia lacks wingbars. Uncommon in humid lowland forests e of Andes in Loreto and Ucayali to 300 m. *S Venezuela and the Guianas to ne Peru and Amazonian Brazil.*

Greenish Elaenia *Myiopagis viridicata* Elainia Verdosa
13.5 cm (5.3"). Plate 86. ♪ 797. A dull, nondescript *Myiopagis* without wingbars with a yellow coronal stripe. Note white supraloral spot, yellowish belly and grayish-olive breast. Back and crown have similar olive-green tone. Uncommon in humid lowland and foothill forests e of Andes from Madre de Dios north to Ucayali to 1300 m. *Mexico to n Argentina, e Paraguay and Brazil.*

Gray-and-white Tyrannulet *Pseudelaenia leucospodia* Moscareta Gris y Blanco
12.5 cm (5"). Plate 95. A very plain, crested tyrannulet, often with a visible white coronal patch. Mouse-colored Tyrannulet lacks crest or white on crown. Southern Beardless-Tyrannulet lacks white coronal patch. Fairly common in arid scrub and riparian thickets from Tumbes to La Libertad to 300 m. *SW Ecuador and nw Peru.*

Elaenia **Elaenias.** Eleven species in Peru. Field identification is extremely difficult (in many cases almost impossible). They tend to perch vertically on exposed branches. Some are crested, and many have a concealed crown patch. Note size, crest (shape and size), coronal patch (if visible), wingbars, color of underparts, and absence or presence of an eye-ring.

Large Elaenia *Elaenia spectabilis* Elenia Grande
18 cm (7"). Plate 93. ♪ 797. Very similar to Yellow-bellied Elaenia but has a third wingbar (not always visible) and a smaller crest. The breast is often grayish. When crest is compressed recalls a *Myiarchus*. Uncommon austral-winter visitor along tropical rivers and oxbow lakes e of Andes to 500 m. *SE Colombia to n Argentina and Brazil.*

Yellow-bellied Elaenia *Elaenia flavogaster* Elenia Ventriamarillo
16 cm (6.5"). Plate 93. ♫ 797. The bushy crest is often conspicuously raised (white coronal patch is often visible). Unlike the name, the belly isn't always yellow, or yellower than other yellow-bellied elaenias. Cf. migratory Large Elaenia (larger, three wingbars, crest is smaller and not conspicuous). Lesser Elaenia is smaller, with a considerably smaller crest. Mottle-backed Elaenia is larger with a dark, mottled back, and an obvious crest that is divided into two "horns". Uncommon in woodlands and scrub on e slope of Andes to 2500 m. *Mexico to n Argentina, e Paraguay and s Brazil.*

White-crested Elaenia *Elaenia albiceps* Elenia Crestiblanca
15.5 cm (6"). Plate 86, 93. ♫ 797. The white coronal patch is often prominent. Underparts are whitish to dingy grayish and lack yellow tones. Several ssp. occur. Race *modesta* (arid tropical Pacific slope, illustrated), has the least pronounced wingbars and may be a separate species (Peruvian Elaenia). Races *diversa* of central Andes, *urubambae* of Cusco, *albiceps* of Puno and *griseogularis* of nw Peru are very much like Lesser Elaenia (which has some yellowish on belly). Sierran Elaenia also has yellowish underparts and wingbars. Migratory race *chilensis* has a conspicuous white crown patch and a bold eye-ring. East of Andes cf. near-identical migratory Small-billed Elaenia, which always has a conspicuous eye-ring (not all ssp. of White-crested Elaenia do), a marginally shorter bill, and a small, third wingbar. They often can be told safely only by voice. Fairly common on Pacific slope, mostly below 3000 m (single record at 5100 m). *Colombia to Tierra del Fuego and Brazil.*

Small-billed Elaenia *Elaenia parvirostris* Elenia Piquichico
14.5 cm (5.75"). Plate 93. ♫ 797. Nearly identical to White-crested Elaenia. Lesser Elaenia is similar but has a yellowish belly. Uncommon austral-winter visitor along tropical rivers and forest edge to 2000 m. *S Brazil to Bolivia, Paraguay and central Argentina; winters north to the Guianas.*

Slaty Elaenia *Elaenia strepera* Elenia Pizarrosa
15.5 cm (6"). Plate 93. ♫ 797. Sexually dimorphic. Male is gray with indistinct gray edging to the plain wings. Female is olive-gray with fairly prominent buff wingbars. Cf. Smoke-colored Pewee (longer, bicolored bill and no eye-ring). Rare austral-winter visitor in humid forests in Loreto and Madre de Dios to 400 m. *Bolivia and nw Argentina; austral-winter visitor to e Peru.*

Mottle-backed Elaenia *Elaenia gigas* Elenia Moteada
18 cm (7"). Plate 86. ♫ 797. No other elaenia has such a divided "two-horned" crest. Note the dark mottling on the back. Cf. Yellow-bellied Elaenia. Rare in humid upper tropical forests on e slope of Andes at 250-1000 m. *SE Colombia to w Bolivia.*

Brownish Elaenia *Elaenia pelzelni* Elenia Parda
18 cm (7"). Plate 93. Canopy of river island woodlands. Browner than any other large elaenia (no olive or gray tinge). Rounded head shows no crest, and concealed crown patch is small and rarely visible (sometimes lacking altogether). Uncommon along lowland riverine forests in Loreto and Amazonas to 200 m. *River islands of Amazon system.*

Plain-crested Elaenia *Elaenia cristata* Elenia Crestisimple
14.5 cm (5.75"). Plate 86. Accidental. Very similar to White-crested, Small-billed and Lesser Elaenias, but lacks any white on crown. Recorded in arid Andean rain-shadow valley near Santa Ana (Cusco) and Pampas del Heath. *S Venezuela and the Guianas to Amazonian and e Brazil.*

Lesser Elaenia *Elaenia chiriquensis* Elenia Menor
13.5 cm (5.3"). Plate 91. Very similar to White-crested and Small-billed Elaenias, but eye-ring is not prominent, belly is yellowish and chest is grayish. Also similar to yellower Sierran Elaenia. Fairly common in humid lowland forests e of Andes to 2000 m (rarely to 2800 m); uncommon on Pacific slope south to Cajamarca. *Costa Rica to n Argentina, the Guianas and Brazil.*

Highland Elaenia *Elaenia obscura* Elainia Oscura
18 cm (7"). Plate 93. ♪797. A large elaenia, mostly dark-olive above with a pale-yellow belly and dull olive breast and flanks. Lacks a coronal stripe or a crest. Note the short bill. Similar to Sierran Elaenia, but latter is smaller and has a white coronal stripe (sometimes concealed). Large Elaenia has a slight crest and is not as yellow. Fairly common in humid montane forests on e slope of Andes at 1650-3000 m. *E slope of Andes of s Ecuador to Bolivia, Paraguay, nw Argentina and se Brazil.*

Sierran Elaenia *Elaenia pallatangae* Elainia Serrana
14.5 cm (5.75"). Plate 93. ♪797. The only medium-sized elaenia with a yellow belly. Cf. White-crested and Highland Elaenias. Fairly common in humid montane forests on e slope of Andes at 1500-3000 m. *Andes of s Ecuador to n Argentina, e Paraguay and se Brazil.*

Torrent Tyrannulet *Serpophaga cinerea* Moscareta de los Torrentes
11.5 cm (4.5"). Plate 86. ♪EC007T. Invariably found near water. No other flycatcher has an ash-gray back, blackish head and wings, and smoke-gray underparts. Common along fast-flowing Andean streams and lakes on e slope at 600-2500 m; rare on Pacific slope south to Lima. *Costa Rica to w Bolivia.*

River Tyrannulet *Serpophaga hypoleuca* Moscareta de los Ríos
11.5 cm (4.5"). Plate 88. Often found on rocks near water. Dusky-gray above and white below, with a light gray head. Little Ground-Tyrant (runs on ground) and Drab Water-Tyrant (pale rump) are sympatric but browner and dingier. Rare and local on humid river islands from Loreto south to Cusco to 600 m. *S Venezuela to n Bolivia, w and central Amazonian Brazil.*

Streak-necked Flycatcher *Mionectes striaticollis* Mosquerito Cuellilistado
13.5 cm (5.3"). Plate 87. ♪797. Three ssp. occur in Peru, all of which have grayer heads and throats than similar Olive-striped Flycatcher. All ssp. have fine streaks on throat but differ in amount of streaking and color of underparts (gray to yellow). Fairly common in humid montane forests and woodlands on e slope of Andes, and on Pacific slope south to Lambayeque at 1200-2700 m. *Andes of Colombia to w Bolivia.*

Olive-striped Flycatcher *Mionectes olivaceus* Mosquerito Olivirrayado
13.5 cm (5.3"). Plate 87. ♪741CD. Like Streaked-necked Flycatcher, but throat is yellowish streaked with olive and head is olive-green (not gray and does not connect with upperparts). Lower mandible is completely black (not pale with a dark tip). Uncommon in humid lowlands along e slope of Andes at 500-1600 m. *Costa Rica to se Peru and Venezuela.*

Ochre-bellied Flycatcher *Mionectes oleagineus* Mosquerito Ventriocráceo
12.5 cm (5"). Plate 87. ♪797. Over most of its range the only flycatcher with an ochre belly. Wingbars and tertial edging vary in intensity. Where sympatric cf. very similar McConnell's Flycatcher. Fairly common in lowland forests e of Andes to 1000 m; uncommon on Pacific slope in Tumbes and Piura. *Mexico to e Bolivia and Amazonian Brazil; Trinidad.*

McConnell's Flycatcher *Mionectes macconnelli* Mosquerito de McConnell
12.5 cm (5"). Plate 88. ♪797. Very similar to Ochre-bellied Flycatcher, but lacks wingbars and edging to tertials. Rare low in disturbed humid *terra firme* forests e of Andes north to Junín and s Ucayali to 500 m. *S Venezuela and the Guianas to n Bolivia and Amazonian Brazil.*

Rufous-breasted Flycatcher *Leptopogon rufipectus* Mosquerito Pechirrufo
13.5 cm (5.3"). Plate 87. ♪EC007T. Within its limited range the only flycatcher with rich rufous on the throat and breast and a yellow belly. Fairly common in humid montane forests on Cerro Chinguela at 1500-2400 m. *Andes of w Venezuela to extreme n Peru.*

Inca Flycatcher *Leptopogon taczanowskii* Mosquerito Inca
13.5 cm (5.3"). Plate 94. ♪742CD. Within its range the only flycatcher with a gray face and rufous wingbars. Slaty-capped Flycatcher's face is whiter, postocular spot is more noticeable, and wingbars are never rufous. Fairly common in humid montane forests on e slope of Andes from central Amazonas to Cusco at 1350-2650 m. *Endemic to Peru.*

Sepia-capped Flycatcher *Leptopogon amaurocephalus* Mosquerito Gorrisepia
13.5 cm (5.3"). Plate 87. ♪797. Similar to Slaty-capped Flycatcher but crown is brown (not gray), face is brownish (not gray and white) and wingbars are tawny. Uncommon in humid lowland forests e of Andes to 1100 m. *Mexico to n Argentina and s Brazil.*

Slaty-capped Flycatcher *Leptopogon superciliaris* Mosquerito Gorripizarroso
13.5 cm (5.3"). Plate 87. ♪797. The only *Leptopogon* with a slate-gray cap, pale-grayish face and a conspicuous postocular spot. Some *Phylloscartes* (especially Variegated and Marbled-faced Bristle-Tyrants) are similar, but smaller, and have shorter bills. Note that wingbar of Slaty-capped varies from yellow to tawny-buff. Fairly common in humid montane forests on e slope of Andes at 500-1800 m. Rare on Pacific slope in Tumbes. *Costa Rica to w Bolivia.*

Pseudotriccus **Pygmy-Tyrants.** A trio of small flycatchers that forage near the montane forest floor. They can often be detected by wing- and bill-snapping sounds.

Bronze-olive Pygmy-Tyrant *Pseudotriccus pelzelni* Tirano-Pigmeo Bronceado
11.5 cm (4.5"). Plate 90. ♪EC007T. A rather nondescript tyrannid. Resembles a female manakin, but bill and body shape are different. Cf. Hazel-fronted Pygmy-Tyrant (no known overlap). Uncommon and local in humid montane forests along e slope of Andes south to Cusco at 650-2000 m. *Panama to s Peru.*

Hazel-fronted Pygmy-Tyrant *Pseudotriccus simplex* Tirano-Pigmeo Frentiavellanada
11.5 cm (4.5"). Plate 89. ♪797. Allopatric with Bronze-olive Pygmy-Tyrant. The rufous forecrown is not easily seen. Immature Rufous-headed Pygmy-Tyrant has more rufous on wings and head. Uncommon in humid montane forests on e slope of Andes on Cerro de Pantiacola and in Puno at 1300-2000 m. *S Peru and w Bolivia.*

Rufous-headed Pygmy-Tyrant *Pseudotriccus ruficeps* Tirano-Pigmeo Cabecirrufa
11.5 cm (4.5"). Plate 87. ♪EC007T. The only small flycatcher of higher elevations with rufous wings and an entire rufous head. Cf. Lulu's Tody-Tyrant in n Peru. Common in humid montane forests on e slope of Andes at 2000-3300 m. *Colombia to w Bolivia.*

Phylloscartes **Bristle-Tyrants.** Typical posture is upright. They have a gray crown, wingbars, and a dark crescent-shaped border to rear of auricular. Marble-faced and Variegated also have a whitish border behind the crescent. Carefully note color of wingbars, head and bill coloration.

Marble-faced Bristle-Tyrant *Phylloscartes ophthalmicus* Moscareta Carijaspeada
11.5 cm (4.5"). Plate 87. ♪797. Note entirely black bill and yellow wingbars (cf. Variegated Bristle-Tyrant), black-and-white marbled face, and white border behind black postocular crescent (cf. Spectacled Bristle-Tyrant). Cf. Slaty-capped Flycatcher (longer bill, lacks white behind black postocular crescent) and Plumbeous-crowned Tyrannulet (much shorter bill, different posture). Fairly common in humid montane forests on e slope of Andes at 800-2200 m. *N Venezuela to w Bolivia.*

Spectacled Bristle-Tyrant *Phylloscartes orbitalis* Moscareta de Anteojos
11.5 cm (4.5"). Plate 88. ♪741CD. The only bristle-tyrant with a yellow face. Has bold eye-ring and lacks a white border behind the weak postocular crescent. Note yellow wingbars and pale lower mandible. Uncommon in humid foothill forests on e slope of Andes at 600-1200 m. *Andes of s Colombia to w Bolivia.*

Variegated Bristle-Tyrant *Phylloscartes poecilotis* Moscareta Variegada
11.5 cm (4.5"). Plate 87. ♫ EC007T. Similar to Marble-faced Bristle-Tyrant but cinnamon wingbars contrast with yellow edging to flight feathers. Lower mandible is yellow (sometimes almost orange). Cf. Spectacled Bristle-Tyrant. Uncommon in humid montane forests on e slope of Andes south to Puno at 1500-2300 m. *W Venezuela to s Peru.*

Phylloscartes **Tyrannulets.** More horizontal posture, and more active than bristle-tyrants. Some have rufous to chestnut on face and others recall various *Phyllomyias* tyrannulets.

Ecuadorian Tyrannulet *Phylloscartes gualaquizae* Moscareta Ecuatoriana
11.5 cm (4.5"). Plate 88. Note limited range. A tyrannulet with a grayish face, dark crown and a small dark postocular crescent. Slightly longer-billed than any similar *Phyllomyias* (especially the higher-elevation Plumbeous-crowned Tyrannulet), and grayer on throat than any sympatric *Phylloscartes*. Rare and local in humid foothill forests along e slope of Andes in n San Martín at 800-1200 m. Recently recorded at Agua Verde below Abra Patricia. Reported as fairly common in Río Afluente region (MS). *E Ecuador and n Peru.*

Cinnamon-faced Tyrannulet *Phylloscartes parkeri* Moscareta Caricanela
11.5 cm (4.5"). Plate 94. ♫ 741CD. The only gray-crowned tyrannulet that shows so much rufous on the face (around the eyes, lores and forecrown). Fairly common in foothill forests on e slope of Andes from Pasco south at 650-1200 m. Recorded along Río Urubamba below Machu Picchu, and on lower part of Manu Road. *SE Peru and adjacent n Bolivia.*

Mottle-cheeked Tyrannulet *Phylloscartes ventralis* Moscareta Cachetimoteada
12 cm (4.75"). Plate 88. ♫ 797. A tyrannulet with yellow underparts, yellow-olive upperparts and two yellowish wingbars. Face pattern: whitish to pale-yellow supraloral and eye-ring, with a dark line extending behind eye. Cheeks in fresh plumage may show mottled effect, but otherwise cheeks are whitish. Closely resembles *Phyllomyias* (Sclater's and Plumbeous-crowned Tyrannulets), but they have shorter, stubbier bills and grayer crowns. Uncommon in humid montane forests on e slope of Andes north to San Martín at 1000-2200 m. *E Peru to n Argentina, e Paraguay and se Brazil.*

Rufous-browed Tyrannulet *Phylloscartes superciliaris* Moscareta Cejirrufa
11.5 cm (4.5"). Facing Plate 88. Note limited range. Has a distinctive face pattern—a short rufous superciliary and white cheeks framed by a black line. Recently recorded along border with Ecuador in Cordillera del Cóndor (Fitzpatrick and Stotz 1997). *Mountains of Costa Rica to Colombia, w Venezuela and extreme n Peru.*

Phyllomyias **Tyrannulets.** A group of five tyrannulets with stubby bills and a pale superciliary. Four of the species inhabit montane forest and have wingbars. Sooty-crowned Tyrannulet lacks wingbars and is found mostly in the lowlands.

White-fronted Tyrannulet *Phyllomyias zeledoni* Moscareta Frentiblanca
11.5 cm (4.5"). Plate 88 ♫ 603. Very similar to Sclater's Tyrannulet but superciliary is wider in front of eye than behind the eye. Crown is darker than that of Sclater's Tyrannulet. Rare and local, with single records from three locations in humid foothill and lower montane forests in San Martín, Cusco and Madre de Dios at 600-1600 m. *Costa Rica to e Peru and Venezuela.*

Sclater's Tyrannulet *Phyllomyias sclateri* Moscareta de Sclater
12 cm (4.75"). Plate 88. ♫ 797. A small tyrannulet with a combination of short, bicolored bill (black on upper mandible and pale on lower), gray crown, white superciliary, plain face, two yellowish-white wingbars and yellowish edging to flight feathers. Mostly whitish underparts. Cf. Slender-footed (light eye, wing coverts edged yellow but no wingbars, yellower below), Plumbeous-crowned (darker ocular area, yellower wingbars, yellower below) and Buff-banded (darker crown and darker

face create a greater contrast with superciliary). Mottled-cheeked has a longer bill and is usually yellower. Rare in humid montane forests on e slope of Andes in Cusco and Puno at 1000-2200 m. Regularly reported from near base of Machu Picchu. *SE Peru to nw Argentina.*

Sooty-headed Tyrannulet *Phyllomyias griseiceps* Moscareta Cabecizitiznada
10.2 cm (4"). Plate 87. Unique among tyrannulets in having no wingbars or edging to wing coverts. Facial pattern is relatively plain. Rare and local in humid lowland and foothill forests along e base of Andes from San Martín to Junín and Ayacucho to 1800 m. *E Panama to e Peru and Amazonian basin.*

Plumbeous-crowned Tyrannulet *Phyllomyias plumbeiceps* Moscareta Coroniplomiza
11.5 cm (4.5"). Plate 87. ♪742CD. A small tyrannulet with a combination of short, black bill, gray crown, whitish superciliary, dark crescent on rear auricular, two yellow wingbars and edging to greater coverts, and mostly yellowish underparts. Has a habit of lifting one wing. In extreme n Peru nearly identical Ecuadorian Tyrannulet is found at lower elevations. Ashy-headed Tyrannulet has a blacker crescent to auriculars, and lacks yellow edging to greater coverts. Cf. local Sclater's and White-fronted Tyrannulets. Uncommon and local in humid montane forests on e slope of Andes south to Cusco at 1300-2200 m. *Andes of Colombia to s Peru.*

Black-capped Tyrannulet *Phyllomyias nigrocapillus* Moscareta Gorrinegra
11.5 cm (4.5"). Plate 87. ♪JM. Note black crown that contrasts with white superciliary, short black bill, two yellowish wingbars and edging to flight feathers. Tawny-rumped Tyrannulet is similar but has a tawny rump and buff wingbars. Sulphur-bellied Tyrannulet's crown is dark gray, and bill is thinner and longer, wingbars buffier, etc. Uncommon in humid montane and elfin forests on e slope of Andes south to Cusco at 1800-3300 m. *Andes of w Venezuela to central Peru.*

Ashy-headed Tyrannulet *Phyllomyias cinereiceps* Moscareta Cabeciceniza
11.5 cm (4.5"). Plate 87. ♪EC007T. A small tyrannulet with a dark-gray crown, a black crescent to rear auricular, two clearly defined yellow wingbars, and faint streaking on yellow underparts. Similar to Plumbeous-crowned Tyrannulet and some *Phylloscartes,* especially Variegated and Marbled-faced Bristle-Tyrants (longer bills), but none has faint streaking on breast. Rare in humid montane forests on e slope of Andes south to Puno at 1400-2700 m. *Andes of Colombia to s Peru.*

Tawny-rumped Tyrannulet *Phyllomyias uropygialis* Moscareta Lomileonada
11.5 cm (4.5"). Plate 87. ♪797. No other small flycatcher has a tawny rump. Cf. Black-capped Tyrannulet. Uncommon in humid montane forests on e slope of Andes at 1800-3100 m. Three records from Pacific slope in Piura, Lima and Arequipa. *Andes of w Venezuela to s Bolivia.*

***Zimmerius* Tyrannulets.** A group of five mostly dull tyrannulets with stubby bills, and pronounced edging to wing coverts and flight feathers (but no wingbars). They tend to perch horizontally with tail slightly cocked.

Bolivian Tyrannulet *Zimmerius bolivianus* Moscareta Boliviana
11.5 cm (4.5"). Plate 94. ♪742CD. The only small, pale-eyed flycatcher in its range that lacks facial markings and wingbars. Crown is olive. Lower-elevation Slender-footed Tyrannulet has a grayer crown. Fairly common in humid montane forests on e slope of Andes north to Cerros del Sira (Huánuco) at 1000-2600 m. *Andes of se Peru and w Bolivia.*

Red-billed Tyrannulet *Zimmerius cinereicapillus* Moscareta Piquirrojo
11.5 cm (4.5"). Plate 94. ♪797. A tyrannid with the combination of yellow eyes, gray crown and a reddish lower mandible. Normally found at higher elevation than Slender-footed Tyrannulet, but range may overlap. Latter has a white supraloral, a black bill, and eyes are not as yellow. Uncommon in humid foothill forests along e base of Andes from Huánuco to Cusco and Madre de Dios at 750-1200 m. Recorded in elfin forests in Cordillera de Colán at 1800 m (Barnes *et al.* 1997). *E Ecuador and e Peru.*

Mishana Tyrannulet *Zimmerius villarejoi* Moscarete de Mishana
10.2 cm (4"). Plate 87. ♪LNS. Note limited range. Similar to locally common Slender-footed Tyrannulet but differs in having a pinkish lower mandible. Recently described from white sand forests in Allpahuayo-Mishana Reserve near Iquitos (Alvarez and Whitney 2001). *Endemic to Peru.*

Slender-footed Tyrannulet *Zimmerius gracilipes* Moscareta Patidelgada
10.2 cm (4"). Plate 87. ♪797. A small tyrannulet with pale eyes, gray crown and a narrow white supraloral. Wing coverts and flight feathers are edged yellow. Most other members of the genus are found at higher elevations. Cf. newly described Mishana Tyrannulet. Yellow-crowned Tyrannulet has a yellow coronal stripe, and wingbars are whiter and more pronounced. Fairly common in humid lowland forests e of Andes to 850 m. *S Venezuela and the Guianas to n Bolivia, Amazonian and ne Brazil.*

Golden-faced Tyrannulet *Zimmerius chrysops* Moscareta Caridorada
11.5 cm (4.5"). Plate 87. ♪632. The only tyrannulet in its range with a yellow supraloral and extensive gold on face. Race *flavidifrons* from Piura and Cajamarca (adjacent to Ecuadorian border west of Río Marañón) has a paler yellowish face, and is sometimes regarded as a separate species (Loja Tyrannulet). Cf. Peruvian Tyrannulet. Fairly common in humid foothill and montane forests e of Andes south to San Martín at 300-2400 m. *N Venezuela to n Peru.*

Peruvian Tyrannulet *Zimmerius viridiflavus* Moscareta Peruana
11.5 cm (4.5"). Plate 94. A small, dull tyrannulet with dark eyes, a yellow supraloral and yellowish underparts. Cf. Slender-footed Tyrannulet. Golden-faced Tyrannulet shows more yellow on face and whitish (not yellow) on belly (no range overlap). Fairly common in montane forests on e slope of Andes from Huánuco to Junín at 1000-2500 m. Mts. *Endemic to Peru.*

Amazonian Scrub-Flycatcher *Sublegatus obscurior* Mosquerito-Matorralero Amazónico
14 cm (5.5"). Plate 87. Color pattern recalls a small *Myiarchus*, but with a much shorter bill and a conspicuous white supraloral. Similar-sized elaenias have a coronal patch (often concealed), a slightly longer bill and an inconspicuous supraloral. In southern part of range during austral winter cf. Southern Scrub-Flycatcher. Rare in humid *terra firme* forests e of Andes to 400 m. *South America e of Andes from Peru to s Brazil and c Argentina.*

Southern Scrub-Flycatcher *Sublegatus modestus* Mosquerito-Matorralero Sureño
14 cm (5.5"). Plate 87. ♪797. Very similar to Amazonian Scrub-Flycatcher, but bill is slightly shorter, wingbars are whitish and more pronounced, and underparts are more clearly divided (grayish breast and yellow belly). Uncommon austral-winter visitor in humid lowland forests e of Andes north to s Ucayali to 1000 m. *S Venezuela and the Guianas to central Argentina and Brazil.*

Mecocerculus **Tyrannulets.** Six species of mostly montane tyrannulets. All have bold wingbars and most have a prominent superciliary. All but White-throated Tyrannulet perch horizontally.

White-throated Tyrannulet *Mecocerculus leucophrys* Tiranillo Gargantiblanca
14 cm (5.5"). Plate 87. ♪797. A larger tyrannulet with a white throat that is sharply separated from the grayish breast. Note also upright posture and two prominent rufous wingbars. Common in humid montane and elfin forests on e slope of Andes at 2500-4000 m and south on Pacific slope to Ancash. *Venezuela and extreme n Brazil to nw Argentina.*

White-tailed Tyrannulet *Mecocerculus poecilocercus* Tiranillo Coliblanca
11.5 cm (4.5"). Plate 87. ♪EC007T. The only tyrannulet with the two outermost tail feathers mostly white, so tail looks all white from below. Similar to White-banded Tyrannulet but smaller, shorter-tailed, has a weaker superciliary and a pale yellow-green rump. Fairly common in humid montane forests on e slope of Andes south to Cusco at 1500-2500 m. *Andes of Colombia to s Peru.*

Buff-banded Tyrannulet *Mecocerculus hellmayri* Tiranillo Bandeado
11.5 cm (4.5"). Plate 88. ♫ 797. Note limited range. Recalls allopatric White-tailed Tyrannulet but lacks white on tail; inconspicuous rump patch. Cf. Sclater's Tyrannulet (no recorded overlap). Rare in humid montane forests in Puno at 1100-2600 m. *Andes of se Peru, Bolivia and nw Argentina.*

Rufous-winged Tyrannulet *Mecocerculus calopterus* Tiranillo Alirrufo
11.5 cm (4.5"). Plate 87. No other tyrannulet has such conspicuous rufous flight feathers. Otherwise recalls White-banded Tyrannulet. Rare in foothill and montane forests on lower Pacific slope of Andes south to Lambayeque, and on e slope south to e La Libertad at 400-1500 m. *Andes of Ecuador and nw Peru.*

Sulphur-bellied Tyrannulet *Mecocerculus minor* Tiranillo Ventriazufrado
11.5 cm (4.5"). Plate 87. ♫ EC007T. Resembles White-banded Tyrannulet but underparts and wingbars are yellow. Fairly common in humid montane forests on e slope of Andes south to Huánuco at 1600-2700 m. *Andes of extreme w Venezuela to central Peru.*

White-banded Tyrannulet *Mecocerculus stictopterus* Tiranillo Alibandeado
12.5 cm (5"). Plate 87. ♫ 797. A long-tailed tyrannulet with olive upperparts, two bold white wingbars, and yellow edging to the flight feathers. Underparts whitish. Gray crown is bordered by a white superciliary. Cf. White-tailed Tyrannulet. Common in humid montane forests on e slope of Andes at 2300-3300 m. *Andes of w Venezuela to w Bolivia.*

Plain Tyrannulet *Inezia inornata* Inezia Simple
10.2 cm (4"). Plate 88. ♫ 797. Note limited range. Recalls allopatric Sclater's Tyrannulet but white supraloral reaches only to the eye; breast is grayish, belly yellowish and bill is more slender. Cf. White-fronted Tyrannulet. Uncommon austral-winter visitor along tropical rivers in Madre de Dios to 700 m. *S Peru to Bolivia, s-central Brazil, Paraguay and nw Argentina.*

Lesser Wagtail-Tyrant *Stigmatura napensis* Mosquereta-Coleador Menor
12.5 cm (5"). Plate 90. ♫ 677. Distinctive. No other flycatcher has such a long, graduated tail with white at its tip and base. Arboreal. Uncommon and local on river islands along Amazon, lower Río Ucayali and Río Napo to 500 m. *River islands in Amazon system; ne Brazil.*

***Uromyias* and *Anairetes* Tit-Tyrants.** Six species of small, active, crested flycatchers, found mostly in high-elevation woodlands.

Unstreaked Tit-Tyrant *Uromyias agraphia* Torito Llano
12.5 cm (5"). Plate 91. The only tit-tyrant that lacks wingbars. The short black crest is often compressed. Note the long white superciliary. Uncommon and local in elfin forest and *Chusquea* bamboo-covered hillsides from central Amazonas to Cordillera Vilcanota at 2600-3600 m. Recorded in Carpish Mts. and along north slope of Abra Málaga road. *Endemic to Peru.*

*Ash-breasted Tit-Tyrant *Anairetes alpinus* Torito Pechicenizo
13.5 cm (6.5"). Plate 91. ♫ 797. Unmistakable. The only tit-tyrant with an unstreaked ash-gray breast. Rare and local in high *Polylepis* woodlands in Andes at 3600-4600 m. Recorded above Yurac Coral in Huascarán National Park at 4285 m, near Abra Málaga, and southeast of Abancay. *N Peru; se Peru and w Bolivia.*

Black-crested Tit-Tyrant *Anairetes nigrocristatus* Torito Crestinegra
12.5 cm (5"). Plate 91. ♫ JM. Similar to smaller Pied-crested Tit-Tyrant (limited overlap) but crest is even longer, and tail is broadly tipped with white. Pied-crested has narrower white tips to tail (seen from below). Entire lower mandible is bright red (dull reddish in Pied-crested). Females of both species are duller, with a smaller crest, and best told apart by tail tips. Cf. also Tufted and Yellow-

billed Tit-Tyrants (smaller with much shorter crests). Uncommon in montane scrub and *Polylepis* woodlands from Piura and Cajamarca south to Ancash, Huánuco and w Pasco at 2300-4200 m. *Andes of n Peru and extreme s Ecuador.*

Pied-crested Tit-Tyrant *Anairetes reguloides* Torito Crestipintada
11.5 cm (4.5"). Plate 91. Similar to Black-crested Tit-Tyrant (limited overlap at best). Sympatric with Yellow-billed and Tufted Tit-Tyrants, but they have shorter crests and much paler faces. Fairly common in montane hillsides on Pacific slope north to Ancash to 3000 m. *W Peru and extreme n Chile.*

Yellow-billed Tit-Tyrant *Anairetes flavirostris* Torito Piquiamarillo
11.5 cm (4.5"). Plate 90. ♪ 797. Similar to Tufted Tit-Tyrant but bill is yellow at base and iris is dark. Prefers more arid regions, but frequents riparian habitats in such areas. Fairly common in montane scrub north to Piura and Cajamarca at 1000-4000 m, but recorded down to sea level on coast. *Andes of Peru, Bolivia and Argentina.*

Tufted Tit-Tyrant *Anairetes parulus* Torito Copetón
11.5 cm (4.5"). Plate 90. ♪ 797. The only tit-tyrant with a pale eye. Fairly common in elfin forest and *Polylepis* woodlands on e slope of Andes at 1800-4200 m (occasionally lower). Recorded on Pacific slope south to Pampa Galeras at 3900 m. *Andes of s Colombia to Tierra del Fuego.*

Many-colored Rush-Tyrant *Tachuris rubrigastra* Siete Colores de la Totora
11.5 cm (4.5"). Plate 90. ♪ 797. Adult is unmistakable. Juvenile is olive above, yellowish below, and has a black mask, a white throat and a buffy wingbar. Fairly common in coastal marshes and reedbeds from La Libertad to Arequipa and along montane lakes and streams from Junín south to 4100 m. *N Peru to s Argentina and Chile.*

Subtropical Doradito *Pseudocolopteryx acutipennis* Doradito Subtropical
11.5 cm (4.5"). Plate 90. ♪ 797. The only flycatcher in its habitat that is olivaceous above (slightly grayer on crown), and clear yellow below. Note indistinct olive edging to wing coverts. Rare and local along montane lakes and streams on e slope of Andes at 600-2600 m, occasionally to 3500 m. Scattered records from humid lowlands in Madre de Dios. *Colombia to nw Argentina.*

Tawny-crowned Pygmy-Tyrant *Euscarthmus meloryphus* Tirano-Pigmeo Coronileonada
11.5 cm (4.5"). Plate 95. ♪ 797. No other small flycatcher in its range has a cinnamon face (brighter on forecrown) and a rufous coronal stripe. Fairly common in arid scrub and woodlands in upper Río Marañón valley in Amazonas, Cajamarca and La Libertad to 1000 m, and on Pacific slope south to Lima. *N Venezuela to n Argentina, Paraguay, e and s Brazil.*

White-bellied Pygmy-Tyrant *Myiornis albiventris* Tirano-Pigmeo Pechiblanco
7 cm (2.75"). Plate 89. ♪ 741CD. Tiny; no other flycatcher its size has a streaked breast and as short a tail. Note facial pattern and reddish eyes. Cf. Short-tailed Pygmy-Tyrant. Uncommon in humid foothill forests on e slope of Andes north to Huánuco at 400-1200 m. *Central Peru to w Bolivia.*

Short-tailed Pygmy-Tyrant *Myiornis ecaudatus* Tirano-Pigmeo Colicorta
6.4 cm (2.5") Plate 90. ♪ 797. A tiny, almost tailless tyrannid with unstreaked underparts. This minuscule tyrannid has the distinction of being the smallest passerine in the world. Cf. White-bellied Pygmy-Tyrant. Uncommon in humid lowland forests and second growth e of Andes to 900 m. *S Venezuela and the Guianas to n Bolivia and Amazonian Brazil.*

***Lophotriccus* Pygmy-Tyrants.** Crown feathers are unique. Each feather is edged with gray, buffy or red, giving the head a distinctive look. The crest is often raised. All Peruvian species have yellow eyes and streaked breasts. Cf. White-eyed Tody-Tyrant.

Scale-crested Pygmy-Tyrant *Lophotriccus pileatus* Tirano-Pigmeo Crestiescamada
10.cm (4"). Plate 90. ♪741CD. The only pygmy-tyrant with red edging to crown feathers (limited overlap with other *Lophotriccus*). Fairly common in humid foothill and montane forests on e slope of Andes south to Puno at 500-1500 m. Rare on Pacific slope in Tumbes. *Costa Rica to s Peru.*

Double-banded Pygmy-Tyrant *Lophotriccus vitiosus* Tirano-Pigmeo Doblebandeado
10.cm (4"). Plate 90. The only pygmy-tyrant with fairly prominent yellowish wingbars and grayish edging (or buff in *congener*, s of Amazon, e of Río Ucayali) to crown feathers. Limited overlap with other *Lophotriccus*. Uncommon in humid lowland forests e of Andes south to Huánuco to 500 m. *SE Colombia to Venezuela, the Guianas, ne Peru and w Amazonian Brazil.*

Long-crested Pygmy-Tyrant *Lophotriccus eulophotes* Tirano-Pigmeo Crestilarga
10.cm (4"). Plate 89. ♪797. The only pygmy-tyrant in its range that lacks wingbars, and has grayish streaks to whitish underparts (no yellow). Crown feathers edged gray. Rare and local in humid *várzea* forests and bamboo thickets at Balta (se Ucayali), and at Altamira and Pakitza in Manu National Park to 400 m. *Extreme w Amazonian Brazil and adjacent se Peru.*

Helmeted Pygmy-Tyrant *Lophotriccus galeatus* Tirano-Pigmeo de Casquete
10.cm (4"). Plate 90. ♪MS. Note limited range. Like Double-banded Pygmy-Tyrant but has weaker wingbars, and crown feathers are narrower and more pointed. Recent sight records and tape recordings from sandy-belt forest of Río Tigre area (Loreto). *E Colombia to s Venezuela, the Guianas and n Amazonian Brazil.*

Rufous-crowned Tody-Tyrant *Poecilotriccus ruficeps* Tirano-Todi Coronirrufa
10.cm (4"). Facing Plate 89. ♪797. Peruvian race *peruanus* has rufous crown, buffy cheeks and a black malar area. Cf. Lulu's Tody-Tyrant. Rare in humid montane forests in Piura and Cajamarca at 1500-2500 m. *W Venezuela to extreme n Peru.*

Lulu's Pygmy-Tyrant *Poecilotriccus luluae* Tirano-Todi de Lulu
10.cm (4"). Plate 89. Like Rufous-crowned Tody-Tyrant (no overlap) but entire head is rufous. Rare in second growth shrubbery in Cordillera de Colán and nearby mountains at 1800-2200 m. A recently described species (Johnson and Jones 2001). *Endemic to Peru.*

Black-and-white Tody-Tyrant *Poecilotriccus capitalis* Tirano-Todi Negriblanco
9.6 cm (3.75"). Plate 89. Male is unmistakable. Female has a rufous crown, olive back and grayish sides to face and breast. Rare and local in humid lowlands e of Andes south to Cordillera Yanachanga (Pasco) to 1350 m. *SE Colombia, e Ecuador and ne Peru; w Brazil.*

White-cheeked Tody-Tyrant *Poecilotriccus albifacies* Tirano-Todi Cachetiblanco
9.6 cm (3.75"). Plate 89. ♪818CD. Unmistakable. Closely associated with bamboo. Uncommon and local in humid bamboo forests in Madre de Dios and adjacent Cusco to 1050 m. Recorded at Tambopata Candamo Reserve, above Amazonia Lodge and Manu Wildlife Center. *Endemic to Peru.*

Hemitriccus **Bamboo-Tyrant and Tody-Tyrants.** A genus well represented in Peru by 8 species of small flycatchers with somewhat flattened bills, and slim tails that are not held cocked. Identification can be difficult. Note eye color, presence or lack of wingbars, edging to flight feathers, and presence of throat and breast streaking.

Flammulated Bamboo-Tyrant *Hemitriccus flammulatus* Tirano-Bambú Flamulado
11.5 cm (4.5"). Plate 89. ♪797. In its range and habitat the only dark-eyed "tody-tyrant" type flycatcher that is olive-brown above and dingy-white below, with indistinct, dusky streaks on breast and throat. White-bellied Pygmy-Tyrant has a much shorter tail. White-eyed Tody-Tyrant has white eyes and wingbars. Fairly common and local in humid bamboo thickets of w Amazonia north to San Martín to 1300 m. *E Peru, n Bolivia and sw Brazil.*

White-eyed Tody-Tyrant *Hemitriccus zosterops* Tirano-Todi Ojiblanco
11.5 cm (4.5"). Plate 90. ♪797. Two ssp. occur. Both have white eyes, wingbars and indistinct streaking on the throat. Race *flaviviridis* (Cusco northward) has a yellowish belly; *griseipectus* (Cusco and Puno) may represent a separate species (White-bellied Tody-Tyrant). It is duller and has a whitish belly. Johannes' Tody-Tyrant lacks wingbars. Cf. Zimmer's Tody-Tyrant and Flammulated Bamboo-Tyrant. Fairly common in humid lowland and foothill forests e of Andes to 1500 m. *S Venezuela and the Guianas to n Bolivia and Amazonian Brazil.*

Zimmer's Tody-Tyrant *Hemitriccus minimus* Tirano-Todi de Zimmer
10.cm (4"). Plate 90. ♪797. Note limited range. Very similar to White-eyed Tody-Tyrant race *flaviviridis*, but only secondaries and tertials have yellow edging, while all flight feathers of White-eyed Tody-Tyrant have yellow edging. Recently recorded in white sand forests in Iquitos area (RAR, RW and JA). *Disjunct in e Amazonian Brazil and ne Bolivia.*

Johannes' Tody-Tyrant *Hemitriccus iohannis* Tirano-Todi de Johannes
11.5 cm (4.5"). Plate 89. ♪797. A tody-tyrant with yellow underparts, indistinct streaking on throat, a pale eye and indistinct wingbars. Cf. Stripe-necked and White-eyed Tody-Tyrants. Uncommon in humid lowland forests e of Andes from Loreto to Madre de Dios to 500 m. Regularly recorded at Amazonia Lodge. *SE Colombia to n Bolivia and w Amazonian Brazil.*

Stripe-necked Tody-Tyrant *Hemitriccus striaticollis* Tirano-Todi Cuellilistado
11.5 cm (4.5"). Plate 90. ♪797. Very similar to Johannes' Tody-Tyrant but lacks wingbars. Lores and eye-ring are white, throat streaks are stronger and more pronounced over a whiter background. Cf. Spotted Tody-Flycatcher (wingbars, gray crown, even bolder breast streaks and no eye-ring). Uncommon in lowland riparian forests and savanna in Cusco and Madre de Dios to 1000 m; isolated population in Moyobamba (San Martín). *E Colombia to n Bolivia, central and e Brazil.*

Pearly-vented Tody-Tyrant *Hemitriccus margaritaceiventer* Tirano-Todi Ventriperlado
11.5 cm (4.5"). Plate 90 ♪797. A non-forest tody-tyrant with pale eyes, whitish underparts, white vent and buff wingbars. Recalls southern ssp. of White-eyed Tody-Tyrant, but latter is a forest species and has more olive on head, a whiter eye, etc. Spottily distributed in lowland savanna and scrub on e slope of Andes to 2000 m. Most published records are from Chanchamayo/San Ramón region (Junín) and drier portions of Urubamba Valley (Cusco). *N Colombia and Venezuela to n Argentina and s Brazil.*

Black-throated Tody-Tyrant *Hemitriccus granadensis* Tirano-Todi Gargantinegra
10.cm (4"). Plate 90. ♪797. No other small flycatcher has a similar facial pattern. Uncommon in humid montane forests on e slope of Andes at 1500-2800 m. *N Venezuela to w Bolivia.*

Buff-throated Tody-Tyrant *Hemitriccus rufigularis* Tirano-Todi Gargantianteada
12 cm (4.75"). Plate 89. ♪797. A larger tody-tyrant. No other *Hemitriccus* has the combination of whitish eye, grayish crown, pale supraloral spot, buffy wash to indistinctly streaked breast and no wingbars. Uncommon and local in humid foothill forests in San Martín, and from Huánuco south at 800-1450 m. Recently recorded near Río Pauya (Loreto) by TSS. Regularly recorded on slopes above Amazonia Lodge. *Ecuador to w Bolivia.*

Cinnamon-breasted Tody-Tyrant *Hemitriccus cinnamomeipectus* Tirano-Todi Pechicanela
10 cm (4"). Plate 89. A flycatcher with cinnamon throat and breast, red eyes, and broad whitish edging to tertials. Rare and poorly known from mossy montane forests in Cordillera del Cóndor, Cordillera del Colán and Abra Patricia at 1600-2200 m. TSS collected a female near La Peca Nueva that appeared to be associated with a small mixed flock. *N Peru and s Ecuador.*

Todirostrum **Tody-Flycatchers.** A genus of small flycatchers with a long, flattened, spatula-like bill. Posture is often more horizontal than vertical, and tail is often held cocked. Usually found in forest edge, and some species are quiet arboreal.

Ochre-faced Tody-Flycatcher *Todirostrum plumbeiceps* Espatulilla Cariocrácea
10.cm (4"). Plate 89. ♪ 797. No other tody-flycatcher has a similar facial pattern. Cf. Rusty-fronted Tody-Flycatcher (generally found at lower elevations). Often stays very close to ground. Fairly common in montane forests and second growth on e slope of Andes in Cusco and Puno at 1300-2750 m. *SE Peru to n Argentina, e Paraguay and e Brazil.*

Rusty-fronted Tody-Flycatcher *Todirostrum latirostre* Espatulilla Frentirrojiza
9.6 cm (3.75"). Plate 90. ♪ 797. Resembles Ochre-faced Tody-Flycatcher, but rusty on face is restricted to lores and auriculars. Fairly common in humid lowlands e of Andes to 1100 m. *SE Colombia to n Bolivia, Amazonian and s-central Brazil.*

Spotted Tody-Flycatcher *Todirostrum maculatum* Espatulilla Moteada
10.cm (4"). Plate 90. ♪ 797. No other tody-flycatcher has the combination of streaked breast and gray crown. Cf. Stripe-necked Tody-Tyrant. Uncommon along tropical rivers, oxbow lakes and margins e of Andes to 500 m. *S Venezuela and the Guianas to n Bolivia and Amazonian Brazil.*

Golden-winged Tody-Flycatcher *Todirostrum calopterum* Espatulilla Alidorada
9.6 cm (3.75"). Plate 89. No other tody-flycatcher in its limited range has the combination of black head, olive back and a wide, golden band on wing. Uncommon in humid lowland forests and second growth in drainage of Río Napo to its confluence with the Amazon near Iquitos to 1100 m. *SE Colombia to ne Peru.*

Black-backed Tody-Flycatcher *Todirostrum pulchellum* Espatulilla Dorsinegro
9.6 cm (3.75"). Plate 89. No other tody-flycatcher in its range has a combination of black head, black back and a wide, golden band on the wing. Female has a dark-olive back. Uncommon in humid foothill forests in Cusco and Puno at 300-1000 m. Recorded along lower part of Manu road and at Amazonia Lodge. *Endemic to Peru.*

Common Tody-Flycatcher *Todirostrum cinereum* Espatulilla Común
9.6 cm (3.75"). Plate 90. ♪ 797. The only tody-flycatcher that is mostly gray above and yellow below. Note the yellow eye that stands out against a blackish mask. Common on Pacific slope of Andes south to Lambayeque and in lowlands e of Andes to 1200 m. *Mexico to n Bolivia and s Brazil.*

Yellow-browed Tody-Flycatcher *Todirostrum chrysocrotaphum* Espatulilla Cejiamarilla
9.2 cm (3.6"). Plate 90. ♪ 797. No other tody-flycatcher has a prominent golden-yellow postocular stripe. Three ssp. occur. Widespread *neglectum* (illustrated) has a black crown and mask. Nominate and race *guttatum* (n of Río Marañón in Loreto and Amazonas) have bold black streaks on chest and malar area. Fairly common in humid lowland forests e of Andes to 1000 m, occasionally to 1400 m. *E Colombia to n Bolivia and Amazonian Brazil.*

Ringed Antpipit *Corythopis torquata* Coritopis Anillado
14 cm (5.5"). Plate 86. ♪ 797. A strange, unmistakable, mostly terrestrial tyrannid. Fairly common in humid lowland forests e of Andes to 500 m, occasionally to 1300 m. *S Venezuela and the Guianas to n Bolivia and Amazonian Brazil.*

Brownish Flycatcher (Twistwing) *Cnipodectes subbrunneus* Alitorcido Pardo
18 cm (7"). Plate 86. ♪ 818CD. A fairly large, brown flycatcher, with a dark rufous tail and rump, and pale-brown edging to wings. Note heavy, bicolored bill (black above and pale below) and amber eye. Frequently lifts wings. Female is smaller (15.5 cm, 6"). Recalls Thrush-like Schiffornis (shorter tail is not rufous; shorter bill is all black). Uncommon in humid lowland forests e of Andes south to Balta (Ucayali) to 1000 m. *Panama to e Peru and w Amazonian Brazil.*

***Ramphotrigon* and *Rhynchocyclus* Flatbills.** Five species of medium-sized, large-headed flycatchers with wide, flat bills (especially wide in *Rhynchocyclus*). All are mostly dull olive and rather inactive. *Ramphotrigon* have narrower bills, wingbars, and usually some kind of facial pattern (a yellow or whitish supraloral stripe that sometimes extends past the eye). *Rhynchocyclus* have a plain face with an eye-ring, and olive to fulvous edging on wing feathers. Cf. other wide-billed flycatchers (*Tolmomyias*).

Large-headed Flatbill *Ramphotrigon megacephala* Picoplano Cabezón
12.5 cm (5"). Plate 88. ♪ 797. The smallest flatbill, and the only one with the combination of tawny wingbars, a bold, yellowish supraloral and an eye-ring. Cf. Dusky-tailed Flatbill (similar but a bit larger, facial pattern much weaker and streaked underparts). Fairly common in humid bamboo thickets e of Andes in Ucayali and Madre de Dios to 1300 m. *Venezuela to ne Argentina, e Paraguay and Brazil.*

Dusky-tailed Flatbill *Ramphotrigon fuscicauda* Picoplano Colioscura
15.5 cm (6"). Plate 88. ♪ 797. The only flatbill with a combination of tawny wingbars, a weak facial pattern and dusky streaks on chest and upper belly. Cf. smaller Large-headed and Olivaceous Flatbills. Rare in humid forests e of Andes from Junín and Ucayali south to Madre de Dios to 900 m. *SE Colombia to n Bolivia.*

Rufous-tailed Flatbill *Ramphotrigon ruficauda* Picoplano Colirufa
16 cm (6.5"). Plate 86. ♪ 797. The only flatbill with a rufous tail, widespread rufous on wings and streaky underparts. Uncommon in humid lowland forests e of Andes to 300 m. *S Venezuela and the Guianas to n Bolivia and Amazonian Brazil.*

Olivaceous Flatbill *Rhynchocyclus olivaceus* Picoplano Oliváceo
15.5 cm (6"). Plate 86. ♪ 797. A rather dull-plumaged tyrannid with a very wide, bicolored bill (black above and pale below) and indistinct streaking on underparts. Smaller Dusky-tailed Flatbill has a narrower, mostly black bill (pale only on base of lower mandible), and tawny wingbars. Uncommon in humid lowland forests e of Andes to 1000 m. *Panama to n Bolivia, Amazonian and e Brazil.*

Fulvous-breasted Flatbill *Rhynchocyclus fulvipectus* Picoplano Pechifulvo
15.5 cm (6"). Plate 86. ♪ 742CD. The only flatbill with a rich tawny breast (and only flatbill over most of its range). Uncommon in humid montane forests on e slope of Andes at 800-2000 m. *Colombia to w Bolivia.*

***Tolmomyias* Flycatchers.** The five members of the genus are mostly sympatric. All have wide, flat bills, yellow to yellowish underparts, olive upperparts, and strong yellow edging to wing feathers. They are very similar to each other, and to some elaenias (narrower bill, coronal stripe), especially Forest Elaenia. Identification is often impossible (look for head pattern, bill and eye color, and exact wing pattern). Voice often provides the best clue for separating them.

Yellow-olive Flycatcher *Tolmomyias sulphurescens* Picoancho Azufrado
15.5 cm (6"). Plate 86. ♪ 797. The largest member of the genus. Posture is more upright than other *Tolmomyias*. Note the gray crown, pale lower mandible and (usually) pale eyes. Slightly smaller Yellow-margined has dark eyes; Gray-crowned has blacker bill. Local Orange-eyed Flycatcher has ochre supraloral. Uncommon in humid foothill forests on e slope of Andes to 1800 m; on Pacific slope in dry forests south to Piura. *S Mexico to n Argentina and s Brazil.*

Yellow-margined Flycatcher *Tolmomyias assimilis* Picoancho Aliamarilla
13.5 cm (5.3"). Plate 86. ♪ 797. Note gray crown, dark eyes, pale lower mandible, and yellow edges to tertials and coverts. Nearly identical to Yellow-olive Flycatcher. Gray-crowned has blacker bill and pale eyes. Amazonian population sometimes considered a separate species. Fairly common in humid lowland forests e of Andes to 1000 m. *Costa Rica to n Bolivia and Amazonian Brazil.*

Gray-crowned Flycatcher *Tolmomyias poliocephalus* Picoancho Coronigris
12 cm (4.75"). Plate 86. ♪ 797. Note the gray crown, pale eyes, and mostly black bill, with a pale spot at base of lower mandible. Smaller than similar *Tolmomyias*. Fairly common in humid lowland forests e of Andes to 600 m. *S Venezuela and the Guianas to n Bolivia, Amazonian and e Brazil.*

Orange-eyed Flycatcher *Tolmomyias traylori* Picoancho Ojinaranja
12 cm (4.75"). Plate 88. Note limited range. Has pale-orange eyes, ochre supraloral, and bicolored bill (black above, pale below). Uncommon in canopy of riverine and *várzea* forests along e base of Andes north of the Amazon in Loreto and Amazonas to 400 m. Regularly recorded in canopy at ExplorNapo Lodge. *S Colombia and ne Peru.*

Yellow-breasted Flycatcher *Tolmomyias flaviventris* Picoancho Pechiamarillo
12 cm (4.75"). Plate 86. ♪ 797. The only *Tolmomyias* with an olive-yellow crown, black bill and bright yellow underparts. Peruvian birds sometimes treated as a separate species (Olive-faced Flycatcher). Fairly common in humid lowland woodlands e of Andes to 1000 m. *S Venezuela and the Guianas to n Bolivia, Amazonian and e Brazil.*

Platyrinchus **Spadebills.** A group of small, short-tailed flycatchers with very wide bills. Note especially head and color of coronal stripe.

Cinnamon-crested Spadebill *Platyrinchus saturatus* Picochato Cresticanela
9.6 cm (3.75"). Plate 90. Accidental. Recalls White-throated Spadebill of the foothills, but has a weaker facial pattern. Single record from Puerto Indiana on lower Río Napo (Loreto) at 150 m. *S Venezuela, the Guianas and Amazonian Brazil.*

Yellow-throated Spadebill *Platyrinchus flavigularis* Picochato Gargantiamarilla
9.6 cm (3.75"). Plate 90. ♪ 742CD. The only spadebill with yellow underparts and a rufous head. Rare in humid montane forests south to Cordillera Vilcabamba at 750-2300 m. *Venezuela to e Peru.*

Golden-crowned Spadebill *Platyrinchus coronatus* Picochato Coronidorada
9.2 cm (3.6"). Plate 90. ♪ 797. The only spadebill with a large orange crown bordered with black. Strong facial pattern is similar to that of White-crested Spadebill. Uncommon in humid lowland forests e of Andes to 500 m. *Honduras to n Bolivia and Amazonian Brazil.*

White-throated Spadebill *Platyrinchus mystaceus* Picochato Gargantiblanca
10.cm (4"). Plate 90. ♪ 797. The only spadebill in the Andes with a strong facial pattern. Compare with lowland Golden-crowned Spadebill (bright orange crown). Note that underparts of *partridgei* (Puno) have warmer tones, and resemble Golden-crowned Spadebill. Fairly common in humid foothill and montane forests on e slope of Andes at 600-2000 m. *Costa Rica to ne Argentina, e Paraguay and s Brazil.*

White-crested Spadebill *Platyrinchus platyrhynchos* Picochato Crestiblanca
11.5 cm (4.5"). Plate 90. ♪ 797. The largest spadebill (but still a very small tyrannid). The only spadebill with a gray crown, plain face and white throat. White coronal stripe is often concealed. Rare in humid lowland forests e of Andes to 900 m. *S Venezuela and the Guianas to n Bolivia and Amazonian Brazil.*

Amazonian Royal-Flycatcher *Onychorhynchus coronatus* Mosquero-Real Amazónico
15 cm (6"). Plate 86. ♪ 797. The long crest feathers protrude to the rear and give a distinct hammerhead look (the beautiful, fully open, fan-shaped crest is rarely seen in the wild). Uncommon in humid lowland forests e of Andes to 400 m. *Colombia to Venezuela, Bolivia, Amazonian and se Brazil.*

Pacific Royal-Flycatcher *Onychorhynchus occidentalis* Mosquero-Real del Pacifico
16.5 cm (6.5"). Plate 86. Larger and paler than allopatric Amazonian Royal-Flycatcher, and formerly considered conspecific. Underparts are cinnamon, and lack latter's dark mottling. Rare on Pacific slope in Tumbes to 1200. *W Ecuador and nw Peru.*

Ornate Flycatcher *Myiotriccus ornatus* Mosquerito Adornado
12 cm (4.75"). Plate 92. ♪741CD. A colorful and distinctive flycatcher. Fairly common in humid lower montane forests on e slope of Andes at 600-2000 m. *Colombia to s Peru.*

Myiophobus Flycatchers. The nine species of this group are medium-sized *Empidonax*-like flycatchers that inhabit mostly subtropical and montane forests and woodlands (many have a restricted range). All have wingbars (note color) and an eye-ring. Males and some females have a concealed coronal stripe.

Flavescent Flycatcher *Myiophobus flavicans* Mosquerito Amarillento
12.5 cm (5"). Plate 94. ♪EC007T. A medium-sized tyrannid, olive above and yellow below, with a yellow eye-ring and supraloral spot, a black bill and dark eye. The wingbars are very weak in widespread *superciliosus* (illustrated) and buffy in nominate ssp. (only north of Río Marañón). Euler's Flycatcher has a bicolored bill, stronger wingbars and is not as yellow below. Uncommon in humid montane forests on e slope of Andes south to Cusco at 1200-2700 m. *N Venezuela to s Peru.*

Orange-crested Flycatcher *Myiophobus phoenicomitra* Mosquerito Crestinaranja
12 cm (4.75"). Plate 94. Note bicolored bill (black above, pale below), reduced eye-ring and no supraloral spot. Strong cinnamon wingbars. Compare with partly sympatric and similar Flavescent Flycatcher (minor elevation overlap). Uncommon and local in humid foothill and montane forests in San Martín at 500-1300 m. *W Colombia to n Peru.*

Roraiman Flycatcher *Myiophobus roraimae* Mosquerito de Roraima
13.5 cm (5.3"). Plate 94. ♪742CD. A large, dull-colored *Myiophobus* with bold, cinnamon wingbars. Resembles a faded Flavescent Flycatcher, but sympatric race of Flavescent has almost no wingbars. Cf. Unadorned Flycatcher. Rare and local in humid montane forests on e slope of Andes from San Martín to Puno at 1100-1700 m. *S Venezuela, Guyana and n Brazil; e Ecuador and e Peru.*

Unadorned Flycatcher *Myiophobus inornatus* Mosquerito sin Adornos
11.5 cm (4.5"). Plate 94. ♪797. A very dull, aptly named flycatcher. Resembles a faded Flavescent Flycatcher, but lacks the facial pattern. Unadorned has a bicolored bill (black above, pale below) and prominent wing edging. Cf. also larger Roraiman Flycatcher (also dull, but has bold cinnamon wingbars). Rare to uncommon in humid montane forests on e slope of Andes in Cusco and Puno at 1000-2000 m. Seen regularly along Manu road. *S Peru and w Bolivia.*

Handsome Flycatcher *Myiophobus pulcher* Mosquerito Hermoso
11.5 cm (4.5"). Plate 94. ♪EC007T. The only *Myiophobus* with a gray crown, ochre breast and yellow belly. Note bicolored bill (black above, pale below) and tawny wingbars. Recalls a smaller Ochraceous-breasted Flycatcher, but latter's bill is all black. Rare and local in humid montane forests on e slope of Andes in Cusco and Puno at 1500-2500 m. *Colombia to n Ecuador; se Peru.*

Orange-banded Flycatcher *Myiophobus lintoni* Mosquerito Franjinaranja
12.5 cm (5"). Plate 94. ♪JM. An extremely limited-range *Myiophobus* with two bold cinnamon wingbars and a pale-yellow eye. Uncommon in humid montane forests on e slope of Andes on Cerro Chinguela at 2250-2800 m. *SE Ecuador to n Peru.*

Ochraceous-breasted Flycatcher *Myiophobus ochraceiventris* Mosquerito Pechiocráceo
14 cm (5.5"). Plate 94. No other flycatcher shows such contrast between the rich ochre breast and neck, and dark-olive crown. Bill is all black. Cf. Handsome Flycatcher. Locally fairly common in humid montane and elfin forests on e slope of Andes from Amazonas to Puno at 3000-3300 m. *E Peru and w Bolivia.*

Bran-colored Flycatcher *Myiophobus fasciatus* Mosquerito Pechirrayado
12.5 cm (5"). Plate 92, 95. ♪ 797. The various ssp. that occur in the country can be treated as three groups. Populations e of Andes (Plate 92) are dull rufous-brown, with two bold buffy wingbars and streaky breasts. Race *crypterythrus* of Pacific Tumbes is very dull and similar to Olive-chested Flycatcher (no overlap), but lacks latter's yellow belly. Pacific slope population of *rufescens* (possible separate species, Plate 95) lacks breast streaking, has pale-cinnamon underparts and rufous wingbars. In any part of their range they are usually distinctive. Fairly common in lower montane forests at 500-1500 m, occasionally to 2500 m in arid Andean valleys. Ranks swelled in southeast lowlands during austral winter. *Costa Rica to n Argentina.*

Olive-chested Flycatcher *Myiophobus cryptoxanthus* Mosquerito Pechiolaváceo
12 cm (4.75"). Plate 94. Note limited range. Dull, like *crypterythrus* of Bran-colored Flycatcher, but no overlap. No other *Myiophobus* has an olive chest, streaking on flanks, or a buff belly. Wingbars are buff, bill black. Cf. Euler's Flycatcher. Rare in humid foothill and montane forests and second growth in San Martín at 300-1100 m. *E Ecuador and ne Peru.*

Ruddy-tailed Flycatcher *Terenotriccus erythrurus* Mosquerito Colirrojizo
10.cm (4"). Plate 92. ♪ 797. A distinctive small flycatcher of forest interior; upright posture. Very similar to rare Cinnamon Tyrant, but latter has a yellow coronal stripe and gray (not flesh) legs. Fairly common in humid lowland forests e of Andes to 1000 m. *SE Mexico to n Bolivia and Amazonian Brazil.*

Myiobius **Flycatchers.** A trio of similar flycatchers with a bright yellow rump, that contrasts with a dark, rounded tail. Upperparts are dark olive. For separation note color of underparts.

Tawny-breasted Flycatcher *Myiobius villosus* Mosquerito Pechileonado
14 cm (5.5"). Plate 92. ♪ 797. Often the only *Myiobius* in its range, and the only one with tawny across breast (and sometimes most of underparts). Other *Myiobius* (limited overlap) have much duller underparts. Uncommon in humid montane forests on e slope of Andes at 900-2000 m. *E Panama to w Bolivia.*

Whiskered Flycatcher *Myiobius barbatus* Mosquerito Barbudo
12.5 cm (5"). Plate 92. ♪ 632. A *Myiobius* with a dull, grayish-olive breast. Very similar to Black-tailed Flycatcher but breast lacks buffy tones of latter. Has habit of fanning its tail and drooping its wings. Note habitat preference. Uncommon in humid lowland *terra firme* and primary forests e of Andes south to Cerros de Pantiacolla and Manu National Park to 1000 m. A recent split from Sulphur-rumped Flycatcher (*M. sulphureipygius*). *Colombia to the Guianas, Brazil and e Peru.*

Black-tailed Flycatcher *Myiobius atricaudus* Mosquerito Colinegra
12.5 cm (5"). Plate 92. A *Myiobius* with dull grayish-buff breast. Very similar to Whiskered Flycatcher but Black-tailed's breast has somewhat warmer tones. Note habitat preference. Pacific slope race *portovelae* is very similar to depicted Whiskered Flycatcher, but latter isn't known to occur w of Andes. Uncommon in lowland *várzea* and secondary forests e of Andes south to Madre de Dios and on Pacific slope in Tumbes to 1400 m. *Costa Rica to e Peru, Amazonian and se Brazil.*

Cinnamon Tyrant *Neopipo cinnamomea* Tirano Acanelado
9.6 cm (3.75"). Plate 92. Until recently regarded as a manakin. Mostly cinnamon-colored with head and back gray. Wings have much rufous edging on wings. Very similar to more familiar Ruddy-tailed Flycatcher, but Cinnamon Tyrant tends to perch more horizontally, has a yellow coronal stripe (often concealed), bluish legs and a more rounded head. Ruddy-tailed has flesh-colored legs, a thicker bill with bristles around it, somewhat of a crest and a bolder eye-ring. Rare in humid *terra firme* forests from Loreto to Puno to 700 m. *S Venezuela and the Guianas to e Peru and Amazonian Brazil.*

Cinnamon Flycatcher *Pyrrhomyias cinnamomea* Mosquerito Canela
12.5 cm (5"). Plate 92. ♪ 797. No other small flycatcher is as rufous below with so much rufous on the wings and face. Common in humid montane forests on e slope of Andes and south on Pacific slope to Cajamarca at 1200-3000 m. *Colombia and Venezuela to nw Argentina.*

Cliff Flycatcher *Hirundinea ferruginea* Tirano de Riscos
18.5 cm (7.2"). Plate 92. ♪ 797. Distinctive. Fairly common around cliffs and rocky areas south to Cusco to 2000 m. *S Venezuela and the Guianas to n Argentina and Brazil.*

Fuscous Flycatcher *Cnemotriccus fuscatus* Mosquerito Fusco
14.5 cm (5.75"). Plate 92. ♪ 797. No other dull, medium-sized flycatcher in its range and habitat has a long superciliary and cinnamon wingbars. Euler's Flycatcher lacks pale superciliary. Mouse-colored Tyrannulet is smaller, has pale base to lower mandible, and is encountered in different habitat (scrub). Rare in humid lowland forests and along tropical rivers e of Andes to 900 m. *S Venezuela and the Guianas to n Argentina and s Brazil.*

Euler's Flycatcher *Lathrotriccus euleri* Mosquerito de Euler
12.5 cm (5"). Plate 88. ♪ 797. A dull, confusing *Empidonax*-like flycatcher, pale-yellow below, olive back, conspicuous yellowish-buff wingbars, bicolored bill. Very similar to some *Myiophobus*, especially Flavescent Flycatcher. Nearctic migrant Alder Flycatcher is very similar but has whiter wingbars and paler underparts. See Fuscous Flycatcher. Fairly common in humid lowland and foothill forests e of Andes to 1500 m. *S Venezuela and the Guianas to n Argentina and Brazil.*

Gray-breasted Flycatcher *Lathrotriccus griseipectus* Mosquerito Pechigris
12.5 cm (5"). Plate 95. Another exceptionally dull tyrannid. Note the white supraloral and broken eye-ring. Mouse-colored tyrannulet has a pale superciliary. Tropical Pewee has a peaked head and lacks Gray-breasted Flycatcher's face pattern. Rare and local in deciduous woodlands south to Lambayeque and n Cajamarca to 700 m, rarely to 1700 m. Recorded in Zona Reservada de Tumbes. *SW Ecuador and nw Peru.*

Olive-tufted (Olive) Flycatcher *Mitrephanes olivaceus* Mosqueta-Moñudo Oliváceo
13 cm (5.2"). Plate 94. ♪ 797. No other olive flycatcher is as crested. Uncommon in humid montane forests on e slope of Andes at 1000-2000 m. *NE Peru to w Bolivia.*

Olive-sided Flycatcher *Contopus cooperi* Pibí Boreal
17 cm (6.6"). Plate 97. ♪ 576. A rather short-tailed, pewee-type flycatcher with dark sides to the underparts. Unlike wood-pewees, the dark sides are indistinctly streaked and do not meet across chest. Rare northern-winter visitor to lowland and foothill forests e of Andes at 500-2000 m. *Temperate North America; winters south to Bolivia.*

Smoke-colored Pewee *Contopus fumigatus* Pibí Ahumado
17 cm (6.6"). Plate 97. ♪ 797. A dark-gray pewee with a conspicuous crest. Cf. Blackish Pewee. Usually on a high, exposed perch. Fairly common in humid foothill and montane forests on e slope of Andes at 1000-2500 m; on Pacific slope south to Cajamarca at lower elevations. *Venezuela and Guyana to nw Argentina.*

Western Wood-Pewee *Contopus sordidulus* Pibí Occidental
14.5 cm (5.75"). Plate 97. ♪576. Nearly identical to Eastern Wood-Pewee and cannot be separated safely in the field unless heard. Uncommon northern-winter visitor to forests e of Andes to 2500 m. *Breeds w North America; winters s to Bolivia.*

Eastern Wood-Pewee *Contopus virens* Pibí Oriental
14.5 cm (5.75"). Plate 97. ♪576. Nearly identical to Western Wood-Pewee. Safely separated by voice only. Both species similar to Tropical Pewee (limited overlap) but latter has a pale supraloral, and crown appears darker and more peaked. Fairly common northern-winter visitor to lowlands e of Andes south to Madre de Dios to 1500 m. Vagrant west of Andes at Mollendo (Arequipa) at ca. 100 m (Hughes 1968). *Breeds e North America; winters south to n Argentina.*

Tropical Pewee *Contopus cinereus* Pibí Tropical
14 cm (5.5"). Plate 97. ♪797. Race *punensis* (illustrated, Pacific northwest and Marañón Valley south to Junín) is uniform gray above and very dull below. Cf. Gray-breasted Flycatcher (conspicuous white supraloral, broken eye-ring). Austral migrant *pallescens* (Cusco and Madre del Dios) is more olivaceous above and very similar to wood-pewees. Fairly common in deciduous forests on Pacific slope of Andes south to Junín to 1500 m; rare and local in lowland forests e of Andes. *S Mexico to ne Argentina, Paraguay and Brazil.*

Blackish Pewee *Contopus nigrescens* Pibí Negruzco
12.5 cm (5"). Plate 97. Like Smoke-colored Pewee, but smaller, crestless and with a bolder eye-ring. Rare and local in humid foothill and montane forests along e base of Andes from Loreto to Madre de Dios at 400-1200 m. *Disjunct in e Ecuador and e Peru; s Guyana and e Amazonian Brazil.*

Alder Flycatcher *Empidonax alnorum* Mosquerito de Alisos
14 cm (5.5"). Plate 97. ♪797. Greenish-olive above and whitish below with two whitish wingbars and a narrow eye-ring (sometimes absent). Cf. Euler's Flycatcher . Fairly common northern-winter visitor to lowlands e of Andes to 1000 m. *Breeds Alaska to se US; winters w South America.*

Black Phoebe *Sayornis nigricans* Mosquero de Agua
17.5 cm (6.8"). Plate 97. ♪797. An active and familiar, mostly black flycatcher. Cf. Smoke-colored Pewee. Fairly common along montane lakes, streams and marshes on e slope of Andes at 500-2500 m; on Pacific slope south to Lambayeque. *SW US to nw Argentina.*

Vermilion Flycatcher *Pyrocephalus rubinus* Mosquero Bermellón
15 cm (6"). Plate 92, 95. ♪576. Typical male is unmistakable. Typical female has a streaked breast (Cf. Bran-colored Flycatcher) and some pink, red or even yellow on vent and lower belly. In race *obscurus* (Lima to Tacna, Plate 95) a melanistic or partially melanistic morph occurs. The male in this morph can be all dark, or with irregular amounts of red feathering on head and underparts. The female of this morph is all dark, but some pink on vent is visible. Common along arid Pacific slope to 2000 m; uncommon austral-winter visitor in lowland savanna e of Andes. *SW US to n Chile, Argentina, Brazil and Galápagos Is.*

***Ochthoeca* Chat-Tyrants.** Twelve species of attractive flycatchers that inhabit montane woodlands. The superciliary is often long, and its color is an important key to identification. Note the presence and color of wingbars.

Crowned Chat-Tyrant *Ochthoeca frontalis* Pitajo Coronado
12.5 cm (5"). Plate 92. ♪JM. The long superciliary is yellow in front of eye and white behind it. Like Peruvian and Jelski's Chat-Tyrants (no overlap) but lacks wingbars. Cf. also Golden-browed Chat-Tyrant. Fairly common in montane elfin forests on e slope of Andes south to La Libertad at 2500-3500 m. *E Andes of Colombia to n Peru.*

Peruvian Chat-Tyrant *Ochthoeca spodionota* Pitajo Peruano
12.5 cm (5"). Plate 91. ♪ 797. A recent split from similar Crowned Chat-Tyrant (no overlap), but has wingbars. Cf. also Golden-browed Chat-Tyrant. Fairly common in montane elfin forests on e slope of Andes from Huánuco south at 2500-3500 m. *Andes of central Peru to w Bolivia.*

Jelski's Chat-Tyrant *Ochthoeca jelskii* Pitajo de Jelski
12 cm (4.75"). Plate 91. ♪ LNS. Similar to Crowned and Peruvian Chat-Tyrants, but Jelski's has a tawny patch on sides of lower belly, paler underparts, and edging on flight feathers is somewhat buffy (not as rufous). Uncommon in montane forests on Pacific slope south to Huánuco and Lima at 1300-3400 m. *SW Ecuador and w Peru.*

Yellow-bellied Chat-Tyrant *Ochthoeca diadema* Pitajo Ventriamarillo
12 cm (4.75"). Plate 92. ♪ EC007T. The only chat-tyrant with mostly yellow underparts and yellow superciliary. Uncommon in humid montane forests in Piura and Cajamarca at 2000-2900 m. *W Venezuela to n Peru.*

Golden-browed Chat-Tyrant *Ochthoeca pulchella* Pitajo Cejidorada
12 cm (4.75"). Plate 91. ♪ 797. Note entirely yellow superciliary and smoky gray underparts. Peruvian Chat-Tyrant is similar, but has a superciliary that is white behind eye. Uncommon in humid montane forest and scrub on e slope of Andes north to Amazonas at 1700-2800 m. *E Peru and w Bolivia.*

Slaty-backed Chat-Tyrant *Ochthoeca cinnamomeiventris* Pitajo Dorsipizarroso
12.5 cm (5"). Plate 92. ♪ EC007T. The only slate-gray chat-tyrant in its range with a short white superciliary, rufous belly and lower breast. Allopatric Maroon-chested Chat-Tyrant has only rufous pectoral band. Uncommon in humid montane forests on e slope of Andes n of Río Marañón at 1600-3000 m. A small population resident west of Marañón Valley in Piura and Cajamarca. *W Venezuela to Colombia and n Peru.*

Maroon-chested Chat-Tyrant *Ochthoeca thoracica* Pitajo Pechimarrón
12.5 cm (5"). Plate 91. ♪ 797. The only slate-gray chat-tyrant in its range with a short white superciliary and a wide maroon band across chest. A recent split from similar Slaty-backed Chat-Tyrant (no overlap). Uncommon in humid montane forests on e slope of Andes s of Río Marañón at 1600-3000 m. *Andes of central Peru to w Bolivia.*

Piura Chat-Tyrant *Ochthoeca piurae* Pitajo de Piura
12.5 cm (5"). Plate 91. A white-browed chat-tyrant with bold rufous wingbars. Cf. White-browed (larger with weak wingbars at best) and Jelski's (yellow supraloral). Rare and local in arid hillside scrub on Pacific slope from Piura south to Ancash at 1500-2800 m. Known from five localities: Palambla, Porculla, Samne, Colcabamba and San Damián (Fjeldså and Krabbe 1990). *Endemic to Peru.*

D'Orbigny's Chat-Tyrant *Ochthoeca oenanthoides* Pitajo de d'Orbigny
15 cm (6"). Plate 91. ♪ 797. Favors drier habitats. Similar to Brown-backed Chat-Tyrant, but where sympatric, note that D'Orbigny's race *polionota* lacks wingbars and has a conspicuous white superciliary. In Puno and Tacna nominate race has noticeable wingbars. Fairly common in arid montane forests and *Polylepis* woodlands north to La Libertad and w Huánuco at 3200-4400 m. *Peru to nw Argentina and extreme nw Chile.*

Rufous-breasted Chat-Tyrant *Ochthoeca rufipectoralis* Pitajo Pechirrufo
13 cm (5.2"). Plate 92. ♪ 797. The only chat-tyrant with a rufous breast and whitish belly. Populations from central and northern Peru (*obfuscata* and *centralis*) have a rufous wingbar that is absent in nominate southern populations (illustrated). Fairly common in humid montane and *Polylepis* forests on e slope of Andes at 2500-3400 m. *W Venezuela to w Bolivia.*

Brown-backed Chat-Tyrant *Ochthoeca fumicolor* Pitajo Dorsipardo
15 cm (6"). Plate 91. ♪ 797. The only chat-tyrant with two rufous wingbars, cinnamon underparts and brown back (grayer in *berlepschi*, illustrated). Two ssp. occur. Race *brunneifrons* (central Peru northward) has long, conspicuous buff superciliary and strong wingbars. Race *berlepschi* (central Peru southward) has a narrow, whitish superciliary and grayish head. Cf. D'Orbigny's Chat-Tyrant and Rufous-bellied Bush-Tyrant. Fairly common in montane woodlands and scrub in Andes at 2600-4200 m. *W Venezuela to w Bolivia.*

White-browed Chat-Tyrant *Ochthoeca leucophrys* Pitajo Cejiblanca
15 cm (6"). Plate 91. ♪ 797. The only chat-tyrant without (or weak at most) wingbars that is gray above, pale ashy below, and has a conspicuous white superciliary. Common in arid montane forests and *Polylepis* woodlands north to Piura and Cajamarca at 2000-3500 m; occurs to sea level near Arequipa. *Peru to nw Argentina and extreme nw Chile.*

Tumbes Tyrant *Tumbezia salvini* Pitajo de Tumbes
13.5 cm (5.3"). Plate 95. No other chat-tyrant-type flycatcher in its range has a long, bold yellow superciliary, yellow underparts and white wingbars. Uncommon in arid acacia and mesquite groves from Tumbes to La Libertad, generally below 200 m. *Endemic to Peru.*

Drab Water-Tyrant *Ochthornis littoralis* Tirano de Agua Arenisco
13.5 cm (5.3"). Plate 92. ♪ 797. Invariably found near water. A dingy, brown tyrannid with a pale rump, dark lores and whitish supraloral. Shares its habitat with terrestrial Little Ground-Tyrant, but latter has white outer tail feathers and lacks a pale rump. Common along tropical rivers and margins e of Andes to 500 m. *S Venezuela and Guyana to n Bolivia and Amazonian Brazil.*

Red-rumped Bush-Tyrant *Cnemarchus erythropygius* Alirrufa Lomirrojiza
23 cm (9"). Plate 92. ♪ LNS. A large, unmistakable, colorful flycatcher. Uncommon and local in montane scrub and *páramo* of Andes at 3000-4000 m. *N Colombia to w Bolivia.*

Streak-throated Bush-Tyrant *Myiotheretes striaticollis* Alirrufa Gargantilistada
23 cm (9"). Plate 92. ♪ 797. A large flycatcher with a whitish throat with black streaks, mostly rufous underparts and basal half of tail. Cf. Cliff Flycatcher and Rufous-bellied Bush-Tyrant. Uncommon in montane scrub at 2000-3500 m, occasionally down to 500 m in Arequipa. *W Venezuela to nw Argentina.*

Smoky Bush-Tyrant *Myiotheretes fumigatus* Alirrufa Ahumada
20 cm (8"). Plate 92. ♪ EC007T. No other flycatcher in its range is uniformly sooty brown with a pale superciliary and pale streaks on throat. Uncommon in humid montane and elfin forests south to Cusco at 2000-3200 m. *W Venezuela to s Peru.*

Rufous-bellied Bush-Tyrant *Myiotheretes fuscorufus* Alirrufa Ventrirrufo
19 cm (7.5"). Plate 93. ♪ 797. No other bush-tyrant has a combination of unstreaked white throat, rufous underparts and wingbars. Recalls Brown-backed Chat-Tyrant, but latter is smaller, has a conspicuous superciliary, a white crissum, and lacks rufous underwing. Rare to uncommon in humid montane forests on e slope of Andes north to Pasco at 1900-2900 m. Recorded on north side of Abra Málaga road. *S Peru and w Bolivia.*

Gray Monjita *Xolmis cinerea* Monjita Gris
23 cm (9"). Plate 92. ♪ 797. Unmistakable in its limited range. Fairly common in grasslands and savanna in Pampas del Heath. *Suriname, Amazonian and e Brazil to n Argentina.*

Agriornis **Shrike-Tyrants.** A trio of large, high-elevation flycatchers with heavy, hooked bills and streaked throats.

Black-billed Shrike-Tyrant *Agriornis montana* Arriero Piquinegro
24 cm (9.4"). Plate 93. ♪ 797. Bill is black and more slender compared with other shrike-tyrants. Tail (from below) is almost completely white. Note immature Black-billed Shrike-Tyrant's bill is pale at base of lower mandible. Fairly common in arid scrub and *puna* grasslands at 2500-4500 m. *Colombia to s Argentina and adjacent Chile.*

*White-tailed Shrike-Tyrant *Agriornis andicola* Arriero Coliblanca
26.5 cm (10.3"). Plate 93. ♪ LNS. Larger and heavier-billed than Black-billed Shrike-Tyrant (tail is mostly white in both species). Bill is heavily hooked and is dark above with yellowish lower mandible. Gray-bellied has a similar bill, but tail is dark. Rare and local in *páramo*, *puna* and montane scrub of Andes at 2650-4500 m. Reasons not clear for marked reduction in numbers in recent years. *Ecuador to nw Argentina and n Chile.*

Gray-bellied Shrike-Tyrant *Agriornis microptera* Arriero Ventrigris
24.5 cm (9.6"). Plate 93. The only shrike-tyrant with a dark tail. Bill like that of White-tailed Shrike-Tyrant. Rare in arid montane scrub in Cusco and Puno at 2000-4000 m. *S Peru to s Argentina and n Chile.*

Rufous-webbed Tyrant *Polioxolmis rufipennis* Alirrufa Canela
21 cm (8.5"). Plate 93. ♪ 797. At rest, a large uniformly dark-gray flycatcher with a shrike-tyrant bill. In flight shows prominent cinnamon base of flight feathers and underwing coverts, and rufous tail (dark terminal band). In flight recalls Streak-throated Bush-Tyrant but body is gray. Often hovers. Fairly common in semiarid montane slopes north to Cajamarca and Amazonas at 3000-4300 m. *Peru, Bolivia and extreme nw Argentina.*

Muscisaxicola **Ground-Tyrants.** Twelve species of terrestrial flycatchers that inhabit mostly high-elevation open terrain (a few are found at lower elevations). All have black tails with white outer feathers. Most are difficult to identify, and the features to look for are crown or hind-crown patch colors, and face pattern.

Spot-billed Ground-Tyrant *Muscisaxicola maculirostris* Dormilona Chica
14 cm (5.5"). Plate 96. ♪ 797. A small ground-tyrant. The only ground-tyrant in its range with a yellow base to lower mandible. Note the dark line through eye, and short whitish superciliary that just reaches eye. Wing feathers have tawny edging. Cf. Cinereous and Plain-crowned Ground-Tyrants (black bill, longer superciliary, grayer wings). Little Ground-Tyrant (limited overlap at best) is similar, but its pale-brownish breast contrasts markedly with white belly (does not blend in as in Spot-billed Ground-Tyrant). Fairly common in arid montane scrub north to s Amazonas and s Cajamarca at 2000-4000 m, occasionally lower. *Colombia to s Argentina and Chile.*

Little Ground-Tyrant *Muscisaxicola fluviatilis* Dormilona Enana
13.5 cm (5.3"). Plate 92. A small ground-tyrant, generally found near water, and the only ground-tyrant in its range. Wing edging can be less pronounced than illustrated. Cf. Drab and Spot-billed Ground-Tyrants. Uncommon along tropical rivers and margins e of Andes to 800 m, rarely to 1900 m. *E Ecuador to e Bolivia and w Amazonian Brazil.*

Dark-faced Ground-Tyrant *Muscisaxicola macloviana* Dormilona Carioscura
16 cm (6.5"). Plate 96. The only ground-tyrant with a mostly blackish face and ashy underparts. Cf. Cinnamon-bellied Ground-Tyrant. Uncommon austral-winter visitor along coast n to La Libertad. *S Argentina and Chile; winters along coast to Peru and Uruguay.*

Cinnamon-bellied Ground-Tyrant *Muscisaxicola capistrata* Dormilona Ventricanela
18 cm (7"). Plate 96. The only ground-tyrant with a mostly blackish face, pale-cinnamon underparts and a brown back. Uncommon austral-winter visitor to altiplano of Puno and Arequipa at 2000-4000 m. *Breeds s Chile and s Argentina; winters n in Andes to s Peru.*

Rufous-naped Ground-Tyrant *Muscisaxicola rufivertex* Dormilona Nuquirrojiza
18 cm (7"). Plate 96. The well-defined hindcrown (when seen) is bright rufous in *occipitalis* (illustrated) or slightly duller in paler *pallidiceps*. Learn this widespread species well. Note that bill is thin, long and slightly hooked; back is gray, and white supraloral reaches the eye. Ssp. *occipitalis* (possible separate species) fairly common in arid Andes north to Cajamarca at 3000-4500 m. Ssp. *pallidiceps* common in southwest north to Arequipa at 2200-4000 m, moving to lower-elevation *lomas* in winter at 600-1000 m. *N Peru to central Chile and nw Argentina.*

Puna Ground-Tyrant *Muscisaxicola juninensis* Dormilona de Puna
16.5 cm (6.5"). Plate 96. Crown is uniform rufous-brown, and white superciliary reaches just to the rear of eye. Back is slightly browner than that of Rufous-naped and grayer than that of White-browed. Common on stony hillsides north to Junín and Lima at 4200-5000 m, occasionally down to 3200 m. *Peru to n Chile and nw Argentina.*

White-browed Ground-Tyrant *Muscisaxicola albilora* Dormilona Cejiblanca
17 cm (6.6"). Plate 96. No other ground tyrant has the combination of long white superciliary, a brown crown that becomes rufous on the hind crown, and a brown back. Fairly common austral-winter visitor in *puna* grasslands and stony hillsides at 2500-4000 m. *Chile and w Argentina; winters to s Ecuador.*

Plain-capped Ground-Tyrant *Muscisaxicola alpina* Dormilona Gris
19 cm (7.5"). Plate 96. ♪ LNS. Note long white superciliary and very plain, gray plumage. Rufous-naped (when rufous crown patch is not seen) and Cinereous Ground-Tyrants have a supraloral that does not extend past the eye. Fairly common in arid montane scrub and *puna* grasslands at 3300-4700 m. *Colombia to n Bolivia.*

Cinereous Ground-Tyrant *Muscisaxicola cinerea* Dormilona Cinérea
16.5 cm (6.5"). Plate 96. Very similar to Plain-capped Ground-Tyrant, but slightly smaller, with a shorter superciliary. Uncommon in montane scrub and *puna* grasslands in Puno at 3200-5000 m; austral-winter visitor north to Junín and Lima. *S Peru to w Bolivia, n Chile and nw Argentina.*

White-fronted Ground-Tyrant *Muscisaxicola albifrons* Dormilona Frentiblanca
21.5 cm (8.4"). Plate 96. ♪ 797. The largest ground-tyrant. Shows a conspicuous white forecrown, brownish crown and whitish edging to flight feathers. Cf. migrant Ochre-naped Ground-Tyrant. Fairly common in high *puna* grasslands and rocky hillsides north to Ancash at 4100-5200 m. *Central Peru to n Chile.*

Ochre-naped Ground-Tyrant *Muscisaxicola flavinucha* Dormilona Nuquiocrácea
20 cm (8"). Plate 96. ♪ 797. A large ground-tyrant with a conspicuous white forecrown and yellow-ochre hindcrown patch. Cf. White-fronted Ground-Tyrant. Fairly common austral-winter visitor in *puna* grasslands and stony hillsides at 3000-4500 m north to Lima. Accidental in La Libertad. *Chile and Argentina to Tierra del Fuego; winters n to Peru.*

Black-fronted Ground-Tyrant *Muscisaxicola frontalis* Dormilona Frentinegra
18 cm (7"). Plate 96. The only ground-tyrant with a black forecrown and prominent white supraloral. Rare austral-winter visitor in *puna* grasslands and stony hillsides in Arequipa at 2500-4300 m. Recent sight record from Lima. *Chile and adjacent Argentina; winters north in Andes to s Peru.*

Short-tailed Field-Tyrant *Muscigralla brevicauda* Dormilona Colicorta
11.5 cm (4.5"). Plate 95. ♪ 797. Terrestrial, with a distinctive short tail. Note rufous uppertail-coverts, contrasting buffy rump and blackish tail. Fairly common in arid coastal lowlands and in upper Río Marañón Valley to 1300 m. *SW Ecuador to extreme n Chile.*

Andean Negrito *Lessonia oreas* Negrito Andino
12.5 cm (5"). Plate 91. A high-elevation, terrestrial flycatcher. Male is unmistakable. Female is similar but duller. Common along montane lakes and streams north to Huánuco at 3000-4000 m; accidental on coast in Lima and Arequipa. *Andes of Peru to n Chile and nw Argentina.*

***Knipolegus* Tyrants and Black-Tyrants.** Six species occur in Peru, in five of which the male is mostly black. Most species have red or reddish eyes. Females are rather dull and confusing (partly because they don't often associate with the males).

Hudson's Black-Tyrant *Knipolegus hudsoni* Viudita-Negra de Hudson
15.5 cm (6"). Plate 97. ♪797. Both sexes resemble, respectively, those of larger White-winged Black-Tyrant (no overlap), but Hudson's has red (not dark) iris. Shows a white band on wing (like White-winged male in flight). Hudson's sometimes shows a white spot on lower flanks. Recently recorded in savanna and scrub in Pampas del Heath at 200 m (JFC and PC). *Central Argentina; winters to Bolivia, Paraguay and Mato Grosso of Brazil.*

Amazonian Black-Tyrant *Knipolegus poecilocercus* Viudita-Negra Amazónica
13.5 cm (5.3"). Plate 97. Note limited range. Male is glossy-black (glossier on back) and has dark eyes. Riverside Tyrant is slightly larger and duller. Female recalls Bran-colored Flycatcher, but uppertail coverts and inner webs of tail feathers are pale rufous. Rare and local along tropical rivers and margins in Loreto to 300 m. *S Venezuela and Guyana to e Ecuador and Amazonian Brazil.*

Andean (Plumbeous) Tyrant *Knipolegus signatus* Viudita Andina
16 cm (6.5"). Plate 91. ♪797. Two races occur in Peru and may represent separate species. Male of *signatus* (illustrated) north of Río Huallaga to Cajamarca, is all black with a brown or chestnut iris. Cf. Jet Manakin (different shape). Male of *cabanisi* (Cusco and Puno) is dark gray with black wings and tail, a dark-red eye and shiny gray bill. In flight both ssp. show white patch on underwing. Females of both ssp. are similar to female White-winged Black-Tyrant, but have a gray breast with dark streaks. Uncommon in humid montane forests on e slope of Andes at 1900-3100 m. *E Peru to nw Argentina.*

Rufous-tailed Tyrant *Knipolegus poecilurus* Viudita Colirrufa
14.5 cm (5.75"). Plate 97. Sexes alike. Both have red eyes, cinnamon vent and lower belly, gray head and mantle, blackish wings with two wingbars, and rufous on inner webs of tail feathers. Cf. female White-winged Black-Tyrant. Uncommon and local in subtrop. montane forests on e slope of Andes at 900-2200 m. *Venezuela and n Brazil to w Bolivia.*

Riverside Tyrant *Knipolegus orenocensis* Viudita Riverña
15 cm (6"). Plate 97. Note limited range. Male is very similar to Amazonian Black-Tyrant. Female is uniform dull olive above and whitish below, with some indistinct streaking on the breast. Tame and often perches conspicuously in open. Uncommon along Amazon river system in Loreto (west to Iquitos) to 300 m. *Venezuela to ne Peru and Amazonian Brazil.*

White-winged Black-Tyrant *Knipolegus aterrimus* Viudita-Negra Aliblanca
16.5 cm (6.5"). Plate 97. ♪797. The only black flycatcher in its range with a white band on open wing. Males of both ssp. that occur in Peru are similar. Female *anthracinus* (from Ayacucho southward, illustrated) has a conspicuous rufous rump, strong wingbars, and buff underparts with dark streaks on breast. Female *heterogyna* (Marañón Valley to Huánuco) has a buffier rump and is paler below. Uncommon in montane scrub in Andes north to Cajamarca at 1500-3000 m. *Peru to w Argentina and Paraguay; e-central Brazil.*

Spectacled Tyrant *Hymenops perspicillatus* Viudita Piquiplata
15 cm (6"). Plate 97. Accidental. Black male has a bold yellow wattle around eyes, a yellow bill and white primaries. Streaky female has a yellow bill and rufous on primaries. Austral-winter migrant: one record from highlands of Cusco and one from Tambopata Research Center. *Bolivia, Paraguay, s Brazil, n and central Argentina and Chile.*

Black-backed Water-Tyrant *Fluvicola albiventer* Tirano-de-Agua Dorsinegro
14 cm (5.5"). Plate 97. ♪ 797. Unmistakable with its bold black-and-white pattern. Rare austral-winter migrant to humid lowlands e of Andes north to Loreto to 1000 m. *Amazonian and e Brazil to e Bolivia, Paraguay and n Argentina.*

Masked Water-Tyrant *Fluvicola nengeta* Tirano-de-Agua Enmascarado
14.5 cm (5.75"). Plate 95. Note limited range. Unmistakable with its white head and conspicuous black eye line, giving it a masked look. Uncommon in marshes and riparian areas in Tumbes to 800 m. *W Ecuador and nw Peru; e Brazil.*

White-headed Marsh-Tyrant *Arundinicola leucocephala* Tirano-de-Agua Cabeciblanco
12.5 cm (5"). Plate 97. Unmistakable with its white head and black body. Uncommon along tropical rivers and margins in Loreto and Ucayali south to Pucallpa. *S Venezuela and the Guianas to n Argentina and s Brazil; Trinidad.*

Yellow-browed Tyrant *Satrapa icterophrys* Tirano Cejiamarilla
16.5 cm (6.5"). Plate 97. ♪ 797. Like Lemon-browed Flycatcher (possible overlap, share yellow underparts and yellow brow), but has grayish wingbars and pale edges to tertials. Uncommon austral-winter migrant along tropical rivers and forest edges north to Cusco and Madre de Dios. *Venezuela; se Peru to n Argentina, e and s Brazil.*

Long-tailed Tyrant *Colonia colonus* Tirano Colilarga
25 cm (9.8"). Plate 97. ♪ 613. Unmistakable with its long, central tail feathers, black body and pale-gray crown. Fairly common in second growth and forest edge in lowlands e of Andes, occasionally to 1200 m. *Honduras to se Venezuela, the Guianas, s Brazil and ne Argentina*

Attila **Attilas.** Five species of large forest flycatchers with long, sturdy, hooked bills and upturned lower mandible. All are rather inconspicuous in the forest, but are often vocal.

Cinnamon Attila *Attila cinnamomeus* Atila Acanelado
19.5 cm (7.75"). Plate 99. ♪ 797. Uniformly cinnamon. Cf. White-eyed Attila and rufous morph of Bright-rumped Attila (pale edging to wing coverts, streaked breast, etc.). Becards have shorter bills, and Rufous Casiornis has a slender bill. Rare in humid lowlands e of Andes, especially *várzea* forests in Amazonas and Loreto to 500 m. *S Venezuela and the Guianas to n Bolivia and Amazonian Brazil.*

*Ochraceous Attila *Attila torridus.* Atila Ocráceo
20 cm (8"). Plate 95. Accidental. Pacific slope counterpart of Cinnamon Attila, but paler (not as rufous). Three records from Cotrina at ca 650 m, and recorded at Quebrada Faical (Begazo *et al.* 2001). *SW Colombia and w Ecuador.*

Citron-bellied Attila *Attila citriniventris* Atila Ventricitrino
18.5 cm (7.2"). Plate 88. ♪ 677. Note limited range. The only attila with a gray hood and rufous body. Rare and local in canopy of lowland *terra firme* forests in Loreto to 500 m. *S Venezuela to ne Peru and w Amazonian Brazil.*

White-eyed (Dull-capped) Attila *Attila bolivianus* Atila Ojiblanco
19 cm (7.5"). Plate 99. ♪ 818CD. Recalls sympatric Cinnamon Attila, but has a conspicuous white eye, and plumage is browner. Uncommon in lowland *várzea* forests from Loreto to Madre de Dios. *Extreme se Colombia to e Bolivia, Amazonian and sw Brazil.*

Bright-rumped Attila *Attila spadiceus* Atila Polimorfo
18 cm (7"). Plate 99. ♪ 797. Several morphs occur. In typical (illustrated) olive back contrasts with yellow rump and dark-rufous tail. Rare rufous morph is uniformly rufous and similar to Cinnamon Attila, but has a streaked breast. Other morphs occur, all of which can be identified by streaky breast and bright rump. Common in humid *terra firme* and foothill forests e of Andes to 1500 m. *Mexico to e Bolivia, Amazonian and e Brazil.*

Rufous Casiornis *Casiornis rufa* Casiornis Rufa
18 cm (7"). Plate 99. ♪ 797. Fairly uniform rufous (lighter on underparts). Fairly thin bill has a pale base and dark tip. Attilas and becards have different bill shapes. Rare austral migrant in humid lowland and foothill forests e of Andes north to Junín to 1500 m. A recent record from Juan Guerra (Amazonas) extends this species range north of its previous limit in Peru (Begazo *et al.* 2001). *SE Peru to n Argentina, Amazonian and e Brazil.*

Sirystes *Sirystes sibilator* Siristes
18 cm (7"). Plate 99. ♪ 797. A distinctive grayish flycatcher with a black crown and white rump. Fairly common in humid lowland forests and second growth e of Andes to 1000 m. *Panama to ne Argentina, Amazonian and e Brazil.*

Grayish Mourner *Rhytipterna simplex* Plañidero Grisáceo
20 cm (8"). Plate 83. ♪ 797. A large, plain-gray, canopy dweller, nearly identical to Screaming Piha. Best told by voice. If quiet note that Grayish Mourner is slightly smaller and slimmer, with a slightly finer bill, and a reddish eye. Grayish Mourner is a canopy bird, Screaming Piha is a sub-canopy bird. Fairly common in humid lowland forests (especially *terra firme*) e of Andes to 800 m. *S Venezuela and the Guianas to e Bolivia, Amazonian and e Brazil.*

Myiarchus **Flycatchers.** The genus *Myiarchus* presents one of the most difficult Neotropical identification challenges. All but Rufous Flycatcher are quite similar, with shades of olive-gray upperparts, and a gray crown with a short crest that is often raised to give a peaked look. Ash-gray throat is separated from a pale-yellow to yellow belly. Cf. *Sublegatus* scrub-flycatchers. Pay special attention to bill color and color of crown, back and tail. Keep in mind that immatures of all *Myiarchus* have rufous edging to tail feathers and wings. Voice provides the best clue, but even that can be tricky (most widespread Dusky-capped has more than one voice). In Amazonian lowlands four species are often sympatric.

Rufous Flycatcher *Myiarchus semirufus* Copetón Rufo
18 cm (7"). Plate 95. Note limited range. A distinctive *Myiarchus* with cinnamon underparts. Uncommon in arid coastal scrub from Tumbes to n Lima to 200 m. Best known from scattered *Prosopis-Acacia* woodlands near Rafán. *Endemic to Peru.*

Dusky-capped Flycatcher *Myiarchus tuberculifer* Copetón Crestioscura
17 cm (6.6"). Plate 97. ♪ 797. Dark gray (sometimes almost black) crown contrasts with olive back. Secondaries and primaries have some rufous edging (not nearly as defined and bright as in Brown-crested). Uncommon in humid montane forests and agricultural areas on e slope of Andes to 1800 m, and on Pacific slope south to Lima at 1000-2500 m, rarely to 3000 m. *SW US to nw Argentina and Brazil; Trinidad.*

Swainson's Flycatcher *Myiarchus swainsoni* Copetón de Swainson
18 cm (7"). Plate 97. ♪ 797. The palest *Myiarchus* and the only one with a pale, horn-colored lower mandible (amount of pale area varies). Uncommon resident in humid lowland forests in Cusco to 1200 m, with increased numbers in lowland forests e of Andes during austral winter. *S Venezuela and the Guianas to n Argentina and se Brazil.*

Short-crested Flycatcher *Myiarchus ferox* Copetón Cresticorta
18 cm (7"). Plate 95. ♪ 797. Crown is dark gray, back dark brown, and show no contrast. Bill is black, and tail lacks rufous edging. Compare especially with sympatric Dusky-capped (contrasting crown and back), Swainson's (pale lower mandible) and Brown-crested (rufous on primaries and tail). Fairly common in humid lowland forests and savanna e of Andes to 1000 m. *Colombia to ne Argentina, Paraguay and Brazil.*

Pale-edged Flycatcher *Myiarchus cephalotes* Copetón Filipálido
18 cm (7"). Plate 97. ♪ 797. The only *Myiarchus* in most of its range that shows distinct pale edging on outer tail feathers and on wing coverts (forming bold wingbars). Crown and back are olive-brown. Cf. sympatric Dusky-capped Flycatcher (shows contrast between back and crown and lacks tail edging). In extreme north cf. Sooty-crowned Flycatcher. Uncommon in subtrop. montane forests on e slope of Andes at 1500-2500 m. *N Venezuela to w Bolivia.*

Sooty-crowned Flycatcher *Myiarchus phaeocephalus* Copetón Coronitiznada
18 cm (7"). Plate 95. The only *Myiarchus* in most of its range that shows pale outer web and tip to tail. Crown is dark gray, contrasting with lighter gray back. Race *interior* (upper Marañón Valley) has a browner crown (than illustrated nominate) and ranges below Pale-edged (lacks pale tips to tail; back is concolor to crown). Uncommon in arid scrub and woodlands south to Lambayeque and upper Marañón Valley in Cajamarca and Amazonas to 1500 m. *W Ecuador and nw Peru.*

Great Crested Flycatcher *Myiarchus crinitus* Copetón Viajero
20 cm (8"). Not illustrated. Accidental. Very similar to Brown-crested Flycatcher, and has more extensive rufous on the tail. Best told by voice. Seen and tape recorded at Quebrada Sucusari (Loreto) by TAP. *Breeds Canada to Gulf States; winters to nw South America.*

Brown-crested Flycatcher *Myiarchus tyrannulus* Copetón Crestiparda
19.5 cm (7.75"). Plate 97. ♪ 797. A large *Myiarchus,* and the only one with distinct rufous edges to primaries. Note brown crown. Dusky-capped Flycatcher has some dull rufous on primaries, but is smaller, has a blackish crown, etc. Fairly common and local in upper Marañón Valley in Cajamarca and Amazonas to 1700 m. Records from Manu National Park and Tambopata Candamo Reserve are probably austral migrants. *SW US to n Argentina, Brazil and the Guianas.*

Lesser Kiskadee *Philohydor lictor* Bienteveo Menor
17 cm (6.6"). Plate 98. ♪ 797. Much smaller than Great Kiskadee and Boat-billed Flycatcher. Recalls Social and Rusty-margined Flycatchers, but they have much smaller bills and less rufous edging on wings. Fairly common along oxbow lakes and river margins e of Andes to 500 m. *Panama to e Bolivia, Amazonian and e Brazil.*

Great Kiskadee *Pitangus sulphuratus* Bienteveo Grande
23 cm (9"). Plate 98. ♪ 797. A large, vocal and familiar flycatcher. Cf. Boat-billed Flycatcher and Lesser Kiskadee. Common in humid lowlands e of Andes to 1500 m. *S Texas to central Argentina.*

Boat-billed Flycatcher *Megarynchus pitangua* Mosquero Picudo
23 cm (9"). Plate 98. ♪ 797. Like Great Kiskadee, but bill is wider and heavier (culmen is more curved). Wings and tail lack rufous edging. Easily told from Great Kiskadee by totally different vocalization. Fairly common in humid lowland forests e of Andes to 1500 m; uncommon in Tumbes and n Piura. *Mexico to ne Argentina and s Brazil; Trinidad.*

Rusty-margined Flycatcher *Myiozetetes cayanensis* Mosquero Rufomarginado
17 cm (6.6"). Plate 98. ♪ 797. Similar to widespread Social Flycatcher, but mantle is brown (not pure olive) and has a yellow (not red) semiconcealed coronal stripe, and blacker head stripes. Wings narrowly edged rusty (like in some immature Social Flycatchers). Lesser Kiskadee has a much longer bill and more rufous edging on wings. Uncommon along oxbow lakes and margins in Madre de Dios to 1000 m. *Panama to e Bolivia, Amazonian and se Brazil.*

Social Flycatcher *Myiozetetes similis* Mosquero Social
17 cm (6.6"). Plate 98. ♪ 797. A familiar, medium-sized flycatcher with a conspicuous head pattern. Forms a good basis for comparison with similar species. Cf. especially Rusty-margined Flycatcher. Common in humid lowlands e of Andes to 1000 m, and on Pacific slope in Tumbes. *Mexico to ne Argentina, Paraguay and s Brazil.*

Gray-capped Flycatcher *Myiozetetes granadensis* Mosquero Gorrigris
17 cm (6.6"). Plate 98. ♪ 797. Recalls Social Flycatcher, but gray head lacks bordering white superciliary. Sulphury Flycatcher is larger and bulkier. Fairly common in humid lowlands e of Andes to 1100 m; one old record from Tumbes. *Nicaragua to n Bolivia and w Amazonian Brazil.*

Dusky-chested Flycatcher *Myiozetetes luteiventris* Mosquero Pechioscuro
14.5 cm (5.75"). Plate 98. ♪ 818CD. A dark *Myiozetetes* with an olive-brown head that lacks the bold pattern of its congeners. Note the dusky streaks on olive breast. Recalls larger and bulkier Sulphury Flycatcher. Rare in humid lowlands e of Andes in Loreto and Madre de Dios to 600 m. *S Venezuela and Suriname to n Bolivia and Amazonian Brazil.*

Three-striped Flycatcher *Conopias trivirgata* Mosquero Trirayado
14 cm (5.5"). Plate 98. Similar to familiar Social Flycatcher, but throat is yellow. Superciliary does not meet at nape, and lacks coronal stripe. Some possible overlap with Yellow-throated Flycatcher. Rare and local in *várzea* forests in Pacaya Samiria National Reserve (Loreto), Yarinacocha (Ucayali), and Tambopata Candamo Reserve to 300 m. *S Venezuela to ne Argentina, e Paraguay and Amazonian Brazil.*

Yellow-throated Flycatcher *Conopias parva* Mosquero Gargantiamarillo
16.5 cm (6.5"). Plate 98. Note limited range. Has a long white superciliary that meets at the nape. Very similar to potentially sympatric Three-striped Flycatcher, but is larger, blacker on crown, and has a semiconcealed coronal stripe. Rare and local in humid lowland forests south of the Amazon at Santa Cecilia and Nuevo Andoas (n Loreto). *E Colombia to s Venezuela, the Guianas and n Brazil.*

Lemon-browed Flycatcher *Conopias cinchoneti* Mosquero Cejilimón
16 cm (6.5"). Plate 98. ♪ EC007T. The only *Conopias* with a yellow brow and yellow throat. Cf. Yellow-browed Tyrant. Uncommon in humid subtropical forests on e slope of Andes south to Cusco at 700-1700 m. *W Venezuela to s Peru.*

Golden-crowned Flycatcher *Myiodynastes chrysocephalus* Mosquero Coronidorada
20 cm (8"). Plate 98. ♪ 797. A large flycatcher with yellowish underparts, faint olive streaks on breast, a malar stripe and unstreaked back. Uncommon in humid montane forests on e slope of Andes at 1000-2500 m. Recently recorded in w Andes in Bosque de Cuyas (Flanagan and Vellinga 2000). *Extreme e Panama to s Bolivia.*

Baird's Flycatcher *Myiodynastes bairdii* Mosquero de Baird
23 cm (9"). Plate 95. Unmistakable in its range. Fairly common in deciduous woodlands and arid scrub on Pacific slope south to Paramonga, usually below 1000 m. *W Ecuador and nw Peru.*

Streaked Flycatcher *Myiodynastes maculatus* Mosquero Rayado
20 cm (8"). Plate 98. ♪ 797. Similar to Sulphur-bellied Flycatcher. Variegated Flycatcher is smaller and has a black crown. Southern migratory race *solitarius* differs from illustrated *chapmani/maculatus* in having heavier streaking below, darker tail and no rufous on wings. Fairly common in humid *várzea* forests and river islands east of Andes to 1500 m; on Pacific slope south to Piura, with a single record from Arequipa. *Mexico to n Argentina.*

Sulphur-bellied Flycatcher *Myiodynastes luteiventris* Mosquero Ventriazufrado
20 cm (8"). Plate 98. ♪ 797. Similar to Streaked Flycatcher, but malar stripe is broader and blacker and reaches chin. Belly is usually clear yellow. Fairly common northern-winter visitor in humid forests e of Andes to 1000 m. *Arizona to Costa Rica; winters in South America south to Bolivia.*

Piratic Flycatcher *Legatus leucophaius* Mosquero Pirata
14.5 cm (5.75"). Plate 98. ♪ 797. Like Variegated Flycatcher, but smaller, with a dusky tail (lacks rufous edging) and a plain, brown back. Social Flycatcher lacks malar stripe, breast streaking, etc. Common in humid lowland forests e of Andes mostly to 1000 m, occasionally to 2300 m; uncommon on Pacific slope in Tumbes. *Mexico to n Argentina and s Brazil.*

Variegated Flycatcher *Empidonomus varius* Mosquero Variegado
18 cm (7"). Plate 98. ♪ 797. Back is mottled and tail is edged rufous. Sized between Piratic (smaller bill, lacks rufous on tail) and Streaked/Sulphur-bellied Flycatchers (heavier bill, streaked lateral crown stripe). Common austral-winter visitor in humid lowland forests e of Andes to 1200 m. *Venezuela to n Argentina, Brazil and the Guianas.*

Crowned Slaty-Flycatcher *Griseotyrannus aurantioatrocristatus* Mosquero-Pizarroso Coronado
18 cm (7"). Plate 98. Black crown has a semiconcealed, yellow coronal stripe. See Slaty Elaenia (smaller with a smaller bill). Uncommon austral-winter visitor in humid lowland forests e of Andes to 1000 m. For trivia buffs, this rather insignificant flycatcher has the distinction of having the longest scientific name of the almost 10,000 species of birds of the world. *Bolivia to n Argentina and e Brazil; winters n to Venezuela.*

Sulphury Flycatcher *Tyrannopsis sulphurea* Mosquero Azufrado
19 cm (7.5"). Plate 98. ♪ 818CD. Note dusky-gray crown, blackish sides of head and short, square tail. Resembles a short-tailed kingbird. Dusky-chested Flycatcher is smaller and slimmer, and has an olive crown and darker, streaked chest. Uncommon in humid lowlands e of Andes in Loreto, Ucayali and Madre de Dios to 400 m. *S Venezuela and the Guianas to n Bolivia and Amazonian Brazil.*

Snowy-throated Kingbird *Tyrannus niveigularis* Tirano Gargantiníveo
19 cm (7.5"). Plate 95. Note limited range. Like Tropical Kingbird, but white area on throat is whiter, and extends to upper chest, contrasting sharply with yellow upper belly. Uncommon in arid coastal scrub south to Ancash to 500 m. *SW Colombia to w Ecuador and nw Peru.*

White-throated Kingbird *Tyrannus albogularis* Tirano Gargantiblanca
20 cm (8"). Plate 98. Like Tropical Kingbird, but throat is whiter and contrasts sharply with yellow upper breast. Cf. Sulphury Flycatcher. Fairly common austral-winter visitor to Loreto and Ucayali to 1000 m. *S Venezuela and the Guianas to n Bolivia and Amazonian Brazil.*

Tropical Kingbird *Tyrannus melancholicus* Tirano Tropical
20 cm (8"). Plate 98. ♪ 797. An olive band on breast divides grayish throat and yellow belly. See Snowy-throated and White-throated Kingbirds (both lack olive on breast). Common and widespread in lowlands e of Andes to 1000 m; w of Andes south to Lima, occasionally to 2500 m. *SW US to central Argentina.*

Eastern Kingbird *Tyrannus tyrannus* Tirano Norteño
20 cm (8"). Plate 98. ♪ 626. Unmistakable. Note white terminal tail band. Common northern-winter visitor in lowlands e of Andes to 800 m; rare in coastal lowlands south to Mollendo (Arequipa). *E North America; winters mainly in nw South America.*

Fork-tailed Flycatcher *Tyrannus savana* Tijereta Sabanera
38 cm (15"). Plate 98. Unmistakable. Uncommon northern-winter migrant in lowlands e of Andes to 1000 m; vagrant to coastal Lima and Arequipa and on altiplano near Lake Titicaca. *Mexico to s South America.*

***Schiffornis* Schiffornis.** A pair of understory flycatchers with large eyes and rather short tails. Reminiscent of a becard (not found in understory), a large manakin (smaller and even shorter tail) or even a thrush (longer tail and bill). They were formerly assigned to cotingas or manakins, and their previous English names reflect just that (mourner and manakin respectively).

Greater (Várzea) Schiffornis *Schiffornis major* Schiffornis de Várzea
15 cm (6"). Plate 99. ♪ 797. Note the gray cheeks and cinnamon body (somewhat brighter on rump). The amount of gray on cheeks varies. Thrush-like Schiffornis is much darker and browner. Uncommon in humid *várzea* forests e of Andes to 300 m. *S Venezuela to n Bolivia and Amazonian Brazil.*

Thrush-like Schiffornis *Schiffornis turdinus* Schiffornis Pardo
16 cm (6.5"). Plate 99. ♪ 797. A medium-sized, uniformly olivaceous-brown forest species that lacks any prominent field marks, but shape and pronounced large eye provide good clues. Other dull-brown flycatchers (Brownish Elaenia and Brownish Flycatcher) have longer tails, "normal" eyes, etc. Uncommon in humid *terra firme* forests e of Andes to 1500 m. Rare on Pacific slope in Tumbes. *Mexico to e Bolivia and Brazil.*

***Pachyramphus* Becards.** Eleven medium-sized, large-headed flycatchers that were previously placed (together with tityras) in the Cotingidae. Most species are sexually dimorphic. Especially note head and wing patterns.

Chestnut-crowned Becard *Pachyramphus castaneus* Cabezón Coronicastaña
14 cm (5.5"). Plate 99. ♪ 797. Sexes alike. Head pattern is diagnostic, with chestnut crown clearly separated by a bold, gray postocular stripe. Rare in humid lowland forests e of Andes to 1700 m. *N Venezuela to ne Argentina, Amazonian and e Brazil.*

Yellow-cheeked Becard *Pachyramphus xanthogenys* Cabezón Cachetiamarillo
14.5 cm (5.75"). Plate 99. Male's combination of black crown, green back and yellow cheeks is distinctive. Female like male, but yellow on head replaced by gray, and has greenish pectoral band and rufous shoulder. Uncommon in montane and foothill forests along e base of Andes in Huánuco, Pasco and Junín at 800-1400 m. Recently recorded near Tamborapa (Cajamarca) at ca. 600 m (Begazo *et al.* 2001). *E Ecuador and central Peru.*

Barred Becard *Pachyramphus versicolor* Cabezón Barreateado
12.5 cm (5"). Plate 99. ♪ 797. Both sexes have fine barring on underparts. Male has a black crown and back, yellow cheeks, and black wings that are conspicuously edged white. Female has olive upperparts and mostly rufous wings. Cf. localized Yellow-cheeked Becard. Fairly common in humid montane forests on e slope of Andes at 1600-2600 m. *Costa Rica to w Bolivia.*

White-winged Becard *Pachyramphus polychopterus* Cabezón Aliblanco
15 cm (6"). Plate 99. ♪ 797. Male is all blackish with two bold white wingbars and white tail tips. Female has a dull-brown cap, pale supraloral and a broken eye-ring. Fairly common in humid lowland forests e of Andes to 1500 m. *E Guatemala to n Argentina and s Brazil.*

Black-and-white Becard *Pachyramphus albogriseus* Cabezón Blanquinegro
14.5 cm (5.75"). Plate 99. ♪ 613. Over most of its range male is distinctive. Female's head pattern is unmistakable. In Loreto cf. Cinereous Becard. Uncommon in humid montane forests on e slope of Andes south to Ayacucho at 1000-2200 m and in Pacific lowlands south to Lambayeque. *Costa Rica to nw Peru and n Venezuela.*

Black-capped Becard *Pachyramphus marginatus* Cabezón Gorrinegro
14 cm (5.5"). Plate 99. ♫ 797. Male has a variable amount of gray and black on mantle. Female has rufous edging to wings and a chestnut cap. Cf. Cinereous Becard. Uncommon in humid lowland *terra firme* forests e of Andes to 500 m. *Venezuela and the Guianas to n Bolivia, Amazonian and e Brazil.*

Cinereous Becard *Pachyramphus rufus* Cabezón Cinéreo
13.5 cm (5.3"). Plate 99. Note limited range. Male is a pale-gray becard that lacks strong wingbars. May recall Black-capped Becard, but latter has strong wingbars and a darker tail. Female is cinnamon-rufous above and pale below (somewhat buffy breast and whitish belly). Rare in lowland deciduous woodlands in Loreto. *Panama to ne Peru and Amazonian Brazil.*

*Slaty Becard *Pachyramphus spodiurus* Cabezón Pizarroso
14 cm (5.5"). Plate 95. Note limited range. Smaller and smaller-billed than sympatric One-colored Becard. Note that male Slaty Becard has a pale-whitish supraloral and pale-whitish edging to wing feathers (One-colored is grayish around face with an ill-defined supraloral and more uniform wings). Female Slaty Becard (nearly identical to allopatric female Cinereous Becard) can be distinguished with difficulty from One-colored Becard by size and bill. Rare in deciduous woodlands and scrub in Tumbes, Piura and Cajamarca below 750 m. Reported from Quebrada Faical, Campo Verde, southeast of San Ignacio, and near Jaén. *W Ecuador and nw Peru.*

Pink-throated Becard *Pachyramphus minor* Cabezón Gargantirosada
17 cm (6.6"). Plate 99. ♫ 797. If seen, male's pink throat is diagnostic. Otherwise recalls Crested Becard, but latter's underparts are a paler mouse-gray. Pink-throated Becard female is mostly rufous, but has a grayish-brown crown and mantle. Uncommon in humid lowland forests e of Andes to 500 m. *S Venezuela and the Guianas to e Bolivia and Amazonian Brazil.*

One-colored Becard *Pachyramphus homochrous* Cabezón Unicolor
16.5 cm (6.5"). Plate 99. Both sexes can be easily confused with rare Slaty Becard. Common in deciduous woodlands in Tumbes and n Piura to 975 m. *Panama to nw Peru and nw Venezuela.*

Crested Becard *Pachyramphus validus* Cabezón Crestado
18 cm (7"). Plate 99. Cf. lower-elevation Pink-throated Becard. Rare in woodlands and forest borders (especially balsa) along Andean slopes north to Ayacucho, and above Urubamba Valley to 2000 m. *Central Peru to n Argentina and e Brazil.*

Tityra **Tityras.** A trio of large, boldly patterned flycatchers with heavy, hooked bills. Head patterns are best clues for identification.

Black-tailed Tityra *Tityra cayana* Titira Colinegra
21.5 cm (8.4"). Plate 100. ♫ 797. Both sexes have black tails, mostly red bills, and red skin around the eye. Male's crown is black. Female like male, but has dark streaks on gray mantle and breast. Uncommon in humid lowland forests e of Andes to 1000 m. *S Venezuela and the Guianas to e Paraguay and e Brazil.*

Masked Tityra *Tityra semifasciata* Titira Enmascarada
21.5 cm (8.4"). Plate 100. ♫ 797. Both sexes have a diagnostic white terminal tail band. Black on male's head limited to mask and forecrown. Female similar to Black-tailed Tityra, but head is brown, and breast and back are unstreaked. Fairly common in humid lowland forests e of Andes to 1300 m. *Mexico to e Bolivia and Amazonian Brazil.*

Black-crowned Tityra *Tityra inquisitor* Titira Coroninegra
19 cm (7.5"). Plate 100. The only tityra that lacks red on bill and face. Female has a black cap and rusty sides of face. Tail is all black. or white with subterminal black band. Uncommon in humid lowland *várzea* forests e of Andes to 1000 m. *Mexico to ne Argentina and s Brazil.*

Oxyruncidae (Sharpbill; Picoagudo). Species: World 1
A monotypic Neotropical family of uncertain systematic position. Sharpbills seem closest to the tyrant-flycatchers because of their syrinx and foot structure, but they differ markedly from the Tyrannidae in their straight, sharp-pointed, unhooked bills, which are uniquely rimmed at the base with short bristly feathers, instead of with rictal bristles. Some authors (Ridgely and Tudor 1994; Sibley, Lanyon and Ahlquist 1984) place them with the cotingas. Their diet consists of insects and fruits, and they are often encountered singly with mixed-tanager flocks.

Sharpbill *Oxyruncus cristatus* Picoagudo
18 cm (7"). Plate 99. ♫ 797. Note the sharply pointed bill and orange eyes. Olive-green above and yellowish below with black spots. Face is finely scaled. Remotely recalls Shrike-like Cotinga. Rare and local in foothill forests on e slope of Andes in Amazonas, San Martín, Junín and Cerros de Pantiacolla at 500-1000 m. *Costa Rica to Suriname, Paraguay and Brazil.*

Hirundinidae (Swallows; Golondrinas). Species: World: 90; Peru 23
A distinctive and successful family of small to medium-sized birds with a worldwide distribution. All members of the family have long wings and agile flight, and feed almost entirely on insects that they catch in the air. Many of the larger species are called martins, but there is no significant difference between swallows and martins. They perch readily on wires, branches and other vegetation, but due to their foot structure are clumsy on the ground. The broad, flattened bill can be opened to a very wide gape, which forms a highly efficient insect trap, and acts as a trowel for scooping up mud used in nest-building.

Phaeoprogne and *Progne* **Martins.** Large swallows with slightly forked tails. Wings are broad at the base. Some of the species exhibit marked sexual dimorphism.

Brown-chested Martin *Phaeoprogne tapera* Martín Pechipardo
18 cm (7"). Plate 102. ♫ 797. No other martin has a dingy pectoral band and brown upperparts. Gray-breasted Martin has a dark throat. Bank Swallow is much smaller. Uncommon in open lowlands e of Andes; on Pacific slope in Tumbes; vagrant to sw coast in Arequipa. *S Venezuela and the Guianas to n Argentina; winters to Panama.*

Purple Martin *Progne subis* Martín Purpúreo
18.5 cm (7.2"). Plate 102. ♫ 626. The dark male is nearly identical to males of Southern and Peruvian Martins (rarely overlap); if seen together Purple Martin has a shorter, less-forked tail. Female is only martin with gray forehead and collar. Compare with female Southern Martin and Gray-breasted Martin. Rare northern-winter visitor in humid lowlands e of Andes. Three records from coast at Pantanos de Villa—bird photographed in 1997, sight record of 15 birds in August 1998 (González 2001), and sight record in same area Sept. 2000 (pers. comm. MP). *Canada to Mexico; winters in Brazil and Bolivia.*

[Caribbean Martin] *Progne dominicensis* Martin Ventriblanco
19 cm (7.25"). Plate 102. Accidental. A martin with a white belly sharply bordered by a dark chest. Upperparts and chest are dark glossy blue (male), or dark blue with brownish-gray chest and flanks. Female is very similar to Gray-breasted Martin (latter lacks brownish flanks). Sight record 6 km nw of Puerto Maldonado, Madre de Dios (Sorrie *in litt.*). *West Indies (except Cuba and Isle of Pines).*

Gray-breasted Martin *Progne chalybea* Martín Pechigris
19 cm (7.5"). Plate 102. ♫ 797. A martin with dark blue upperparts, dark throat, and breast that contrasts with white belly and vent. Female's vent and belly are dingier. Cf. Female migratory Purple Martin has a gray forecrown, and dark or streaked underparts; female Southern and Peruvian Martins have more uniformly gray underparts. Fairly common in lowlands e of Andes and on coast south to Tumbes and Piura to 1200 m. *Mexico to n Argentina and Brazil.*

Southern Martin *Progne elegans* Martín Sureño
19.5 cm (7.75"). Plate 102. Male is like Peruvian Martin (no overlap), all dark bluish-purple, but even glossier. During migration may occur together with Purple Martin, and cannot be separated safely in the field. Female Southern Martin is dark gray with dark underparts. Cf. Gray-breasted Martin and female Purple Martin. Common austral migrant in lowlands e of Andes. *Bolivia to Paraguay and Argentina; winters north to Colombia.*

Peruvian Martin *Progne murphyi* Martín Peruano
18 cm (7"). Plate 101. The only martin over most of its range, and as such the only all dark swallow. Male is glossy bluish-purple, and female is dark gray with gray and somewhat mottled underparts. In far north overlaps with Gray-breasted Martin (pale belly and vent). Uncommon in coastal Peru from Piura south to Ica. *Pacific coast of Peru, rarely to n Chile (Arica).*

***Tachycineta* Swallows.** All members of the genus that occur in Peru have clean white underparts and glossy blue-green upperparts. Most have white rumps.

[Tree Swallow] *Tachycineta bicolor* Golondrina Bicolor
15 cm (6"). Not illustrated. Accidental? A swallow with glossy blue-green upperparts (no white rump) and white underparts (including undertail coverts). Blue-and-white Swallow is similar, but has black undertail coverts. Reported as an occasional vagrant without further details (Gochfeld *et al.* 1980). *Breeds Alaska to n US; winters to n South America.*

Tumbes Swallow *Tachycineta stolzmanni* Golondrina Peruana
12.5 cm (5"). Plate 101. No other swallow in its limited range has pure white underparts and a white rump. Formerly considered a race of Mangrove Swallow (*T. albilinea*). Fairly common and local along coast from Tumbes south to La Libertad to 100 m. *Endemic to coastal nw Peru and immediately adjacent Ecuador.*

White-winged Swallow *Tachycineta albiventer* Golondrina Aliblanca
13.5 cm (5.3"). Plate 101. ♪ 797. The only swallow with conspicuous white upperwing coverts. Common along lowland rivers and oxbow lakes e of Andes to 500 m. *Venezuela and the Guianas to n Argentina and Brazil.*

White-rumped Swallow *Tachycineta leucorrhoa* Golondrina Lomiblanco
13.5 cm (5.3"). Plate 101. The only swallow with white underparts and deep-blue upperparts with a white supraloral. Cf. Chilean Swallow is nearly identical but lacks the white supraloral. Rare austral-winter migrant in humid lowlands e of Andes north to Junín to 1000 m. *Paraguay, se Brazil and n Argentina; winters north to s Peru.*

Chilean Swallow *Tachycineta meyeni* Golondrina Chilena
13.5 cm (5.3"). Plate 101. Nearly identical at a distance to White-rumped Swallow. It lacks the white supraloral, a detail hard to discern on a distant flying bird. Rare austral-winter migrant in lowlands e of Andes to 1000 m; sight records from Ayacucho and Arequipa were assigned to that species. *S Chile and Argentina; winters n to Bolivia, Brazil and s Peru.*

***Pygochelidon* and *Notiochelidon* Swallows.** A trio of medium to small-sized swallows that share bluish backs, dark tails and undertail coverts, and have somewhat forked tails.

Blue-and-white Swallow *Pygochelidon cyanoleuca* Golondrina Azul y Blanco
12.5 cm (5"). Plate 101. ♪ 797. A blue and white swallow easily recognized by its dark underwing lining. Crissum is black in illustrated nominate (and coastal *peruviana*), but black only on sides of crissum in migratory *patagonica*. Pale-footed Swallow is smaller, with dark flanks, and various degrees of pale rufous on the throat. Immature Blue-and-white is much duller, and may show a buffy throat. Common in open country throughout to 3500 m. *Costa Rica to Tierra del Fuego.*

Brown-bellied Swallow *Notiochelidon murina* Golondrina Ventripardo
13.5 cm (5.5"). Plate 102. ♪797. Dull bluish above and smoky-gray below. Similar to Andean Swallow, but latter has whitish undertail coverts (not dark), and an almost square tail. Common in montane grasslands at 2500-4000 m. *W Venezuela to w Bolivia.*

Pale-footed Swallow *Notiochelidon flavipes* Golondrina Patipálida
12 cm (4.75"). Plate 101. ♪797. Similar to (and often flies together with) Blue-and-white Swallow, but Blue-and-white never shows dark on flanks and at base of wing. Uncommon in montane and elfin forests from Cajamarca and Amazonas to Puno at 2400-3000 m. Regularly recorded along Abra Málaga road. *W Venezuela to w Bolivia.*

White-banded Swallow *Atticora fasciata* Golondrina Fajiblanca
14.5 cm (5.75"). Plate 101. ♪797. The only all dark swallow with a white pectoral band. Common along lowland rivers and streams e of Andes to 1000 m. *S Venezuela and the Guianas to n Bolivia and Amazonian Brazil.*

White-thighed Swallow *Neochelidon tibialis* Golondrina Musliblancos
11.5 cm (4.5"). Plate 102. A very small, dark, sooty-brown swallow with a slightly forked tail. No other dark swallow is as small. The white thighs are visible at close range. Fairly common along forest edge and clearings e of Andes to 1000 m. *Panama to n Bolivia, w Amazonian and e Brazil.*

Andean Swallow *Stelgidopteryx andecola* Golondrina Andina
13.5 cm (5.3"). Plate 101. ♪797. The whitish undertail coverts separate it from any sympatric *Notiochelidon*. Locally common in *puna* grasslands and scrub north to Lima and Junín at 2500-4400 m. *Peru to n Chile.*

Tawny-headed Swallow *Stelgidopteryx fucata* Golondrina Cabecileonada
12 cm (4.75"). Plate 102. A brown swallow with rufous on back of head and on superciliary. Similar to Southern Rough-winged Swallow, but rump is not pale, and tawny color of head is much more extensive. Rare in humid lowlands e of Andes in Cusco to 1600 m. *Venezuela to n Argentina, Paraguay and Brazil.*

Southern Rough-winged Swallow *Stelgidopteryx ruficollis* Golondrina Alirrasposa Sureña
12.5 cm (5"). Plate 101. ♪797. The only uniformly dull-brownish swallow with a conspicuous pale rump and buffy throat. Cf. Cliff Swallow has a pale forehead and collar. Common in humid lowlands e of Andes and on Pacific slope south to Cajamarca to 1000 m. *Honduras to n Argentina.*

Bank Swallow (Sand Martin) *Riparia riparia* Golondrina Ribereña
12 cm (4.75"). Plate 102. ♪626. Dark above and white below (including undertail coverts) with a pectoral band. A small version of Brown-chested Martin. Rare northern-winter visitor in coastal marshes and in lowlands e of Andes to 1000 m. *Holarctic regions; winters in tropics.*

Cliff Swallow *Petrochelidon pyrrhonota* Golondrina Risquera
13.5 cm (5.3"). Plate 102. ♪626. Note the nearly square tail, buff rump, pale collar and forehead. Recalls Southern Rough-winged Swallow but latter lacks a pale forehead, etc. Cf. Chestnut-collared Swallow has a rufous pectoral band. Rare northern-winter visitor and migrant throughout to 1000 m. *Alaska to s Mexico; winters to Argentina and Brazil.*

Chestnut-collared Swallow *Petrochelidon rufocollaris* Golondrina de Cuellicastaño
12 cm (4.75"). Plate 101. The only swallow with a rufous pectoral band, nape and rump. Fairly common over agricultural lands on Pacific slope south to Lima to 1300 m. *SW Ecuador and w Peru.*

Barn Swallow *Hirundo rustica* Golondrina Tijereta
15 cm (6"). Plate 102. ♪797. The only swallow in Peru that has a very deeply forked tail with white tail spots (noticeable in immature birds as well). Uncommon northern-winter visitor and migrant throughout to 1000 m. *Cosmopolitan; almost worldwide distribution.*

Motacillidae (Wagtails and Pipits; Cachirlas). Species: World 62; Peru 5
A fairly large family of terrestrial birds with a large worldwide distribution. They are characterized by long legs, on which they run and walk, rather than hop. Wagtails and pipits feed mainly on small insects, which are actively hunted on the ground. During winter months their diet is supplemented with seeds and other vegetable matter. All members of the only genus found in Peru (*Anthus*) are brownish and streaked birds of fields and grassland. Males often sing in a "flight display" high above the ground. Four species are sympatric in the high Andes. Note tone of underparts, amount and pattern of chest streaking, presence of flank streaking and back pattern.

Correndera Pipit *Anthus correndera* Cachirla Correndera
15 cm (6"). Plate 102. ♪797. A pipit with coarse streaks on breast and flanks and noticeable white longitudinal stripes on back. None of the sympatric pipits has such a coarse pattern on underparts, or similar white stripes on back. Fairly common in *puna* grasslands north to Junín and Lima to 4000 m. This is one of the southernmost-breeding passerines in the world, nesting as far south as latitude 55°. *Peru to Tierra del Fuego and Falkland Is.*

Short-billed Pipit *Anthus furcatus* Cachirla Piquicorto
14.5 cm (5.75"). Plate 102. ♪797. Differs from any other white-bellied pipit by lack of any streaking on flanks. Breast streaks are sharply separated from belly, malar stripe is more pronounced than in most other pipits (except bolder-patterned Correndera Pipit); bill is somewhat shorter. Fairly common in *puna* grasslands north to Huánuco to 4000 m. *Peru to n Argentina, Uruguay and se Brazil.*

Hellmayr's Pipit *Anthus hellmayri* Cachirla de Hellmayr
14.5 cm (5.75"). Plate 102. ♪797. Note limited range. A pipit with very fine breast streaks. Very similar to Short-billed Pipit, but streaks are finer, and gradually merge into belly. Some individuals are buffier below (molt?). Cf. Páramo Pipit. Rare in high-altitude Andean grasslands in Puno to 3700 m. *S Peru to Chile, Argentina and se Brazil.*

Páramo Pipit *Anthus bogotensis* Cachirla del Páramo
15 cm (6"). Plate 102. ♪797. The only pipit with buffy underparts, no streaking on flanks and almost no streaking on breast. Upperparts have a buffy wash; lacks wingbars. Fairly common in *páramo* and *puna* grasslands at 2500-4000 m. *Venezuela to w Argentina.*

Yellowish Pipit *Anthus lutescens* Cachirla Amarillenta
12.5 cm (5"). Plate 102. ♪797. The only pipit in its range. Fairly common along coast north to Lambayeque to 1300 m. *Panama to central Argentina.*

Cinclidae (Dippers; Cinclos). Species: World 5; Peru 1
A small family of five species, with a wide distribution in the mountainous regions of the world. They resemble plump wrens with their short wings and tails, and are anatomically closely related to thrushes. Dippers are highly specialized for feeding in, or under, running water, with the tarsus long and sturdy, and with stout claws for gripping the beds of fast-moving rivers and streams. A flap of skin covers the nostrils while submerged, and translucent eyelids permit underwater sight. Food consists mainly of the larvae of aquatic insects, as well as small aquatic mollusks and crustaceans.

White-capped Dipper *Cinclus leucocephalus* Mirlo Aquático Gorriblanco
15 cm (6"). Plate 106. ♪ JM. Unlikely to be mistaken. Uncommon along rushing mountain streams in the Andes at 1000-3400 m. Readily seen from train between Ollantaytambo and Machu Picchu. *NW Venezuela to w Bolivia.*

Troglodytidae (Wrens; Cucaracheros). Species: World 79; Peru 25
A family of active, small to medium-sized passerines, many of which are gifted vocalists. They range from Alaska to Tierra del Fuego, with one species (Winter Wren) occurring in Eurasia. Wrens are residents of almost every habitat—from coastal scrub to *páramo* and tropical rainforests. All wrens are insectivorous, but supplement their diet with a small amount of vegetable matter, and have even been observed feeding on small fish and tadpoles. The Latin name of the genus *Troglodytes* refers to a cave-dweller, a reference to the wren's predilection for nesting in holes and crevices.

Black-capped Donacobius *Donacobius atricapillus* Donacobio
22 cm (8.6"). Plate 104. ♪ 797. A large unmistakable bicolored wren, usually associated with aquatic vegetation. Common in lowland marshes, along oxbow lakes and margins e of Andes to 600 m. *Panama to ne Argentina, Amazonian and e Brazil.*

Campylorhynchus **Wrens.** A pair of large, long tailed, often conspicuous and vocal wrens that move about in family groups.

Thrush-like Wren *Campylorhynchus turdinus* Cucarachero Zorzal
20 cm (8"). Plate 104. ♪ 797. The only large grayish wren in its range. Note prominent spotted underparts. Fairly common in humid lowland forests e of Andes to 1200 m. *SE Colombia to e Bolivia, Amazonian and sw Brazil.*

Fasciated Wren *Campylorhynchus fasciatus* Cucarachero Ondeado
19 cm (7.5"). Plate 103. ♪ 633. The only large, heavily barred wren in its range. Common along arid Pacific slope south to Ancash (occasionally to n Lima) to 1500 m, rarely to 2500 m. *SW Ecuador and n Peru.*

Gray-mantled Wren *Odontorchilus branickii* Cucarachero Dorsigris
12.5 cm (5"). Plate 104. ♪ 741CD. A small, arboreal, gnatcatcher-like wren, but gnatcatchers lack barring on the tail. Uncommon and local in humid montane forests on e slope of Andes at 1400-2200 m. *S Colombia to w Bolivia.*

Cinnycerthia **Wrens.** Four montane forest species with little range overlap. Sharpe's, Peruvian and Fulvous Wrens were formerly considered a single species (Sepia-brown Wren). They share overall uniformly brown plumage, with the wings and tail barred dark brown.

Rufous Wren *Cinnycerthia unirufa* Cucarachero Rufo
18 cm (7"). Facing Plate 103. ♪ 633. Note limited range. Very similar to Sharpe's Wren. Rufous Wren is more uniformly brighter rufous. Superciliary and barring on tail and wings are not prominent, but blackish lores are pronounced. Usually found at higher elevations than Sharpe's. Rufous Spinetail lacks barring on tail and wings, and has a "double-pointed" tail. Common in humid montane and elfin forests on Cerro Chinguela (Piura-Cajamarca border) at 2700-2900 m. *Venezuela to n Peru.*

Sharpe's Wren *Cinnycerthia olivascens* Cucarachero de Sharpe
18 cm (7"). Plate 103. ♪ EC007T. Some Sharpe's have a white forecrown, but white doesn't extend past the eye. Peruvian Wren shows more white on face. Cf. Rufous Wren. Uncommon in humid montane forests on e slope of Andes south to Amazonas at 2500-3400 m. *Colombia to Ecuador and extreme n Peru.*

Peruvian Wren *Cinnycerthia peruana* Cucarachero Peruano
18 cm (7"). Plate 103. ♪797. The only *Cinnycerthia* with extensive white on face. Fulvous Wren may have a whitish forehead and superciliary, but never as extensive as in Peruvian Wren. Common in humid montane forests along e slope of Andes from Amazonas to Ayacucho at 1500-3300 m. *Endemic to Peru.*

Fulvous Wren *Cinnycerthia fulva* Cucarachero Fulvo
18 cm (7"). Plate 103. ♪742CD. The only *Cinnycerthia* in its range. Sympatric Mountain Wren is much smaller, lacks whitish forehead and has a shorter tail. Fairly common in humid montane forests on e slope of Andes in Cusco and Puno at 1500-3300 m. *Andes of s Peru to w Bolivia.*

Thryothorus Wrens. A large genus, well represented in Peru by seven species of medium-sized wrens. All species share a pronounced superciliary and most have streaked cheeks. Note the presence or lack of barring on wings and tail and of malar stripe.

Inca Wren *Thryothorus eisenmanni* Cucarachero Inca
16 cm (6.5"). Plate 103. ♪633. The only *Thryothorus* in its range with a spotted breast. Locally common in montane *Chusquea* bamboo forests from Cordillera Vilcabamba south to valleys of Río Urubamba and Río Santa María at 1800-3350 m. Recent records from Apurímac drainage south of Cordillera Vilcabamba. Common at Machu Picchu and on far side of Abra Málaga road. *Endemic to Peru.*

Plain-tailed Wren *Thryothorus euophrys* Cucarachero Colillana
16 cm (6.5"). Plate 103. ♪633. The only *Thryothorus* in its range with an unbarred tail. Illustrated *schulenbergi* (most of range) has a spotted breast; *atriceps* (Piura) lacks spots on breast. Inca Wren (no known overlap) has a barred tail. A bird mist-netted 26 April 2001 at the drainage of Río Mantero at 3400 m that had unspotted rufous underparts and an unbarred tail, may represent an isolated population of *atriceps* or a new ssp/species (pers. comm. GE). Fairly common in humid montane forests in Piura, Cajamarca, Amazonas and San Martín at 2000-3300 m. *SW Colombia to n Peru.*

Moustached Wren *Thryothorus genibarbis* Cucarachero Bigotudo
15 cm (6"). Plate 104. ♪797. Similar to (and often sympatric with) Coraya Wren, but has a malar stripe separated by a white moustache from the noticeably streaked cheeks (without the heavy blackish cheeks of Coraya). Buff-breasted Wren lacks malar stripe, has browner (not rufous) upperparts, and buffy (not dingy) gray underparts. Common and local in humid lowlands e of Andes north to Ucayali to 1000 m. *SE Peru, e Bolivia, Amazonian and e Brazil.*

Coraya Wren *Thryothorus coraya* Cucarachero Coraya
14.5 cm (5.75"). Plate 104. ♪633. The only wren in its range with blackish cheeks (often with a few white streaks). Cf. Moustached Wren. Common in humid lowland *várzea* and *terra firme* forests south to Madre de Dios to 1000 m. *S Venezuela and French Guiana to e Peru and Amazonian Brazil.*

Speckle-breasted Wren *Thryothorus sclateri* Cucarachero Pechijaspeado
14 cm (5.5"). Plate 103. ♪633. Note limited range. Two ssp. occur. Nominate *sclateri* (illustrated, upper Marañón Valley) is finely barred on breast and upper belly. Breast and upper belly of *paucimaculatus* (Tumbes) are spotted with black. Fairly common on Pacific slope in Tumbes, Piura and Lambayeque and in upper Marañón Valley to 1600 m. Race *paucimaculatus* may possibly represent a separate species. *S-central Colombia; sw Ecuador to nw Peru.*

Buff-breasted Wren *Thryothorus leucotis* Cucarachero Pechianteado
14 cm (5.5"). Plate 104. ♪797. The only wren with streaked cheeks that has buffy underparts and lacks a malar stripe. Cf. Moustached Wren. Common in humid lowlands e of Andes (especially in *várzea* forests) to 950 m. *Venezuela and the Guianas to Brazil and extreme n Bolivia.*

Superciliated Wren *Thryothorus superciliaris* Cucarachero Cejón
14.5 cm (5.75"). Plate 103. ♪ 633. The only wren in its range with a conspicuous superciliary, white cheeks and pale-whitish underparts. Common in arid coastal lowlands south to Ancash to 1000 m. *SW Ecuador and nw Peru.*

Troglodytes **Wrens.** A pair of small, plain-looking wrens, with barring only on wings and tail. The ubiquitous House Wren occupies nearly every habitat in the country.

House Wren *Troglodytes aedon* Cucarachero Común
11.5 cm (4.5"). Plate 104. ♪ 797. The only plain wren that lacks any obvious field marks. Note: color ranges from dull gray-brown to rufous-brown. Mountain Wren has a prominent buff superciliary. Fairly common and widespread throughout to 4000 m in Andes. *Canada to Tierra del Fuego*

Mountain Wren *Troglodytes solstitialis* Cucarachero Montañés
11.5 cm (4.5"). Plate 104. ♪ 797. The only plain wren with a prominent superciliary. Cf. House Wren (longer tail, and even if superciliary is present it is not conspicuous). Also Fulvous Wren (larger, longer tail, etc.). Common in humid montane forests and second growth at 1500-3500 m, occasionally down to 700 m. *Venezuela to nw Argentina.*

Sedge Wren *Cistothorus platensis* Cucarachero Sabanero
10.cm (4"). Plate 104. ♪ 797. The only wren in its habitat with a streaked mantle. Fairly common and local in *páramo* grasslands, meadows and marshes to 4000 m. *Canada to Tierra del Fuego and Falkland Is.*

Henicorhina **Wood-Wrens.** A trio of mostly terrestrial wrens. All have streaked cheeks, and extremely short tails that are often held in a cocked position.

White-breasted Wood-Wren *Henicorhina leucosticta* Cucarachero-Montés Pechiblanco
11.5 cm (4.5"). Plate 104. ♪ 633. The only wood-wren likely to be found in lowlands, and the only one with white underparts. All *Thryothorus* have longer tails. Common in humid lowland forests e of Andes south to Huánuco to 1100 m. *Mexico to Peru, n Brazil, s Venezuela and Guyana.*

Gray-breasted Wood-Wren *Henicorhina leucophrys* Cucarachero-Montés Pechigris
11.5 cm (4.5"). Plate 104. ♪ 797. Over most of its range the only wood-wren with gray underparts. Cf. Bar-winged Wood-Wren in Marañón area. Common in humid montane forests on e slope of Andes at 1500-3000 m. Uncommon on Pacific slope in Tumbes. *Mexico to w Bolivia.*

Bar-winged Wood-Wren *Henicorhina leucoptera* Cucarachero-Montés Alibandeada
11.5 cm (4.5"). Plate 103. ♪ 633. Note limited range. The only wood-wren with two white wingbars. Otherwise recalls Gray-breasted Wood-Wren. Fairly common and local in heavy montane scrub in Cordillera del Cóndor and at Abra Patricia (e La Libertad) at 1950-2450 m. Recorded as low as 1350 m in e Andes se of Moyobamba. *Andes of ne Peru; recently recorded in adjacent se Ecuador.*

Microcerculus **Wrens.** A pair of shy, terrestrial wrens with short tails and relatively long bills.

Scaly-breasted Wren *Microcerculus marginatus* Cucarachero Ruiseñor Sureño
11.5 cm (4.5"). Plate 104. ♪ 797. The only wren with a clear white throat and breast, and scaled flanks. Lacks white wingbar of Wing-banded Wren. Common in humid lowland *várzea* and *terra firme* forests e of Andes to 1000 m. *S Costa Rica to n Bolivia and Amazonian Brazil.*

Wing-banded Wren *Microcerculus bambla* Cucarachero Alifranjeada
11.5 cm (4.5"). Plate 104. ♪ 633. A brownish wren with a conspicuous white wingbar, and a dingy, somewhat scaly breast. Rare in humid lowland forests on Cerros del Sira (Huánuco), Manu National Park and Cosñipata Valley to 1100 m. *S Venezuela and the Guianas to e Peru and n Amazonian Brazil.*

***Cyphorhinus* Wrens.** A pair of mostly terrestrial wrens with rufous breasts. Both favor forest undergrowth; Chestnut-breasted is found in montane forests, and Musician in humid lowlands. Both are gifted vocalists.

Chestnut-breasted Wren *Cyphorhinus thoracicus* Cucarachero Pechicastaño
15 cm (6"). Plate 103. ♪ 797. No other wren has rufous underparts and a blackish crown. Unlikely to be confused if seen well. Uncommon in humid montane forests on e slope of Andes south to Puno at 1300-2300 m. *Colombia to se Peru.*

Musician Wren *Cyphorhinus aradus* Cucarachero Musical
12.5 cm (5"). Plate 104. ♪ 797. With its upright stance and thick bill, it doesn't look like a wren. Recalls a female antbird (that also has bluish bare skin around the eye), but note barring on wings and tail. Fairly common in humid lowland *várzea* and *terra firme* forests e of Andes to 600 m. *S Venezuela and the Guianas to n Bolivia and Amazonian Brazil.*

Mimidae (Mockingbirds and Thrashers; Calandrias). Species: World 35; Peru 1
The mockingbirds, catbirds and thrashers comprise a small family of birds that ranges from Canada to southern Argentina and Chile, with a single representative in Peru. Many members of the family are superb mimics, and their vocalizations include a wide variety of disparate songs. They are best represented in Central America and the West Indies, with tropical species tending to be sedentary and those from higher latitudes remarkably migratory. Most species feed on fruits and seeds, as well as various invertebrates, including insects, spiders, centipedes and worms. Some mimids tend to be highly terrestrial, which has led to a decreased development of the wings, and a corresponding improvement in their running ability.

Long-tailed Mockingbird *Mimus longicaudatus* Calandria Colilarga
27 cm (10.5"). Plate 105. ♪ 639. The only mockingbird in Peru. Easily identified by its long tail, white wing-patches on wings and tail, and a black malar stripe. Common along arid Pacific slope south to Arequipa and in upper Marañón Valley to 2450 m. Recorded above Huaytará at 2950 m (JFC and TV). *SW Ecuador to sw Peru.*

Turdidae (Thrushes and Allies; Mirlos y Zorzales). Species: World 175; Peru 24
The thrushes, robins and solitaires comprise a large and distinctive group of birds with a vast range that includes all the continents except Antarctica. Some of the birds best known to the general public are included in this assemblage, including the American Robin, European Blackbird and Song Thrush. They range from sea level to the altiplano, and one of the most abundant birds in the high Andes is Chiguanco Thrush. They have a varied diet, consisting of both animal and vegetable matter, with some fruiting trees being particularly favored by members of the genus *Turdus*. Solitaires often capture flying insects and butterflies in flycatcher-like sallies from a perch. Many members of the family are noted for their vocalizations, and some rival the mockingbirds and thrashers in their powers of mimicry. The late Ted Parker's studies of the songs of 30 Lawrence's Thrushes revealed imitations of 173 bird species, as well as those of frogs and insects (Hardy and Parker 1997).

Andean Solitaire *Myadestes ralloides* Solitario Andino
18 cm (7"). Plate 106. ♪ 797. The only thrush with gray underparts, rufous-brown back, wings and upper tail. In flight shows silvery outer tail and wing-patch. Note the short, wide-based bill with a yellow mandible (*venezuelensis*, south to La Libertad, illustrated) or completely black mandible (*ralloides*, south from La Libertad and Huánuco). Common in humid montane forests on e slope of Andes at 1200-2700 m. *N Venezuela to w Bolivia.*

Rufous-brown Solitaire *Cichlopsis leucogenys* Solitario Rufimarrón
20 cm (8"). Plate 105. The combination of rufous underparts with tawny-ochraceous median throat, and a bicolored, broad-based bill (dark upper mandible and yellow lower mandible) is unique in its limited range. Rare in humid lower montane forests on Cerros del Sira (Huánuco) and Río Perené (Junín) at 550-1300 m. *Disjunct in nw Ecuador, s Venezuela, Guyana, se Brazil and e Peru.*

White-eared Solitaire *Entomodestes leucotis* Solitario Orejiblanca
24 cm (9.4"). Plate 105. ♪797. Unmistakable with its black body, chestnut back and white cheeks. Fairly common in montane forests on e slope of Andes north to Amazonas at 1500-2800 m. *Peru and w Bolivia.*

Catharus **Thrushes and Nightingale-Thrushes.** A genus represented in Peru by five species. The two resident nightingale-thrushes are sooty above with orange-red soft parts. They are mostly terrestrial in the forest interior. The three migrants are large-eyed, rather dull brownish-gray above, with some breast streaks and spots.

Slaty-backed Nightingale-Thrush *Catharus fuscater* Zorzal Sombrío
18 cm (7"). Plate 106. ♪797. Underparts are uniformly gray. Glossy-black Thrush has dark eyes, and Pale-eyed Thrush lacks orange eye-ring. They are both larger, more arboreal, and are black rather than slaty. Uncommon in humid montane forests on e slope of Andes at 800-2300 m, and south on Pacific slope to Cajamarca. *Costa Rica to w Bolivia.*

Spotted Nightingale-Thrush *Catharus dryas* Zorzal Moteado
17 cm (6.6"). Plate 106. ♪797. Distinctive. Back is dark olive, head is black and underparts are yellowish with dusky spots on breast. Uncommon in humid montane forests on e slope of Andes at 700-2300 m, and on Pacific slope in Tumbes. *S Mexico to Honduras; Andes of w Venezuela to ne Argentina.*

Veery *Catharus fuscescens* Zorzal Dorsirrojizo
18 cm (7"). Plate 106. ♪797. Accidental. A russet, brown-backed *Catharus* with no eye ring; has indistinct spots on its buffy breast. More common Swainson's Thrush has a noticeable eye-ring and a more spotted breast. Gray-cheeked Thrush is grayer and has a more distinctly spotted breast. Single record from lowlands e of Andes in Madre de Dios. *E North America; winters to n Bolivia and Amazonian Brazil.*

Gray-cheeked Thrush *Catharus minimus* Zorzal Carigris
18 cm (7"). Plate 106. ♪630. A dull gray-brown thrush with grayish cheeks and spotted underparts. Darker than other similar *Catharus*. Lacks a conspicuous eye-ring. Rare migrant and northern-winter visitor in humid lowlands e of Andes to 1500 m. *Siberia and n North America; winters Hispaniola and South America.*

Swainson's Thrush *Catharus ustulatus* Zorzal de Swainson
18 cm (7"). Plate 106. ♪797. A variably colored thrush with olive-brown to russet-brown upperparts and a conspicuous buffy eye-ring. None of the migratory *Catharus* shows such a conspicuous buffy eye-ring. Fairly common northern-winter visitor along e slope of Andes; accidental along coast south to Arequipa. *North America; winters Mexico to n Argentina.*

Pale-eyed Thrush *Platycichla leucops* Zorzal Ojipálido
21.5 cm (8.4"). Plate 106. ♪630. The male is a glossy-black thrush with yellow legs and bill, and white eyes (but without an eye-ring). Glossy-black Thrush has dark eyes. Smaller Slaty-backed Nightingale-Thrush has paler underparts, redder legs and bill, and an eye-ring. Brownish female recalls that of Glossy-black Thrush, but lacks eye-ring and has a grayer lower belly and a dark bill. Uncommon in humid montane forests on e slope of Andes at 900-2000 m. *Venezuela to w Bolivia.*

Turdus **Thrushes.** A cosmopolitan genus of songsters well represented throughout much of the world. The 14 species in Peru occur in almost every habitat. Many of the Peruvian species have dark streaks on the throat.

Chiguanco Thrush *Turdus chiguanco*   Zorzal Chiguanco
27 cm (10.5"). Plate 105. ♪ 797. Both Peruvian races (*chiguanco* in Andes and coastal *conardi*) are similar to, and often sympatric with, Great Thrush. Chiguanco is smaller and proportionately shorter tailed. Chiguanco is usually found in semiarid habitats. Male lacks an eye-ring, has a yellow bill, and is a paler ashy-gray than slate-colored Great Thrush. Female is paler and duskier with a dirty yellowish bill; can be distinguished by size and proportions. Common in montane scrub and second growth at 1500-4000 m (absent on e slope of Andes). *S Ecuador to nw Argentina.*

Great Thrush *Turdus fuscater*   Zorzal Grande
33 cm (13"). Plate 105. ♪ 797. By far the largest of the dark thrushes. Two races occur, *gigantodes* (illustrated, south to Junín) and *ockenderi* (Cusco to Puno). Males of both have a yellow eye-ring and orange bill. Male *ockenderi* is blacker. Female lacks an eye-ring, and is duller and browner with a dull orange-yellow bill. Cf. Glossy-black and Chiguanco Thrushes. Common in humid montane forests and *Polylepis* woodlands on e slope of Andes, and on Pacific slope south to Cajamarca at 1800-4000 m. *NW Venezuela to w Bolivia.*

Glossy-black Thrush *Turdus serranus*   Zorzal Negribrilloso
25 cm (9.8"). Plate 106. ♪ 797. A very black thrush with an orange-red bill, legs and eye-ring. Darker, glossier, smaller and shyer than Great Thrush. Male Pale-eyed Thrush has white eyes. Female is rather uniformly brown with a yellowish eye-ring. Fairly common in humid montane forests on e slope of Andes, and on Pacific slope south to Cajamarca at 1500-2800 m. *Venezuela to extreme nw Argentina.*

Andean Slaty-Thrush *Turdus nigriceps*   Zorzal -Pizarroso Andino
21.5 cm (8.4"). Plate 105. ♪ 797. The slate-gray male has a white throat with black streaks. Other "dark" thrushes have a dark throat. Female is uniformly olive-brown above, paler below, with a whitish belly, whitish throat with black streaks, dark eyes, dark bill and greenish-yellow legs. Female Glossy-black Thrush is darker, especially on underparts, has pale eyes and lacks streaks on throat. Rare in humid montane forests north to Piura, Lambayeque and Amazonas at 500-2000 m. All records on e slope of Andes probably represent austral migrants. *SE Ecuador to n Argentina.*

Plumbeous-backed Thrush *Turdus reevei*   Zorzal Dorsiplomizo
23 cm (9"). Plate 105. ♪ 630. Note limited range. Sexes are similar. No other thrush has bluish-gray upperparts, pale-cream underparts, and pale eyes. Fairly common in deciduous woodlands south to Lambayeque from sea level to 1500 m. *SW Ecuador and nw Peru.*

Marañón Thrush *Turdus maranonicus*   Zorzal del Marañón
21.5 cm (8.4"). Plate 105. ♪ 630. Note limited range. Pattern of underparts is unique—heavily spotted/scaled on breast. Other immature thrushes are either scaled or spotted, but none has a similar pattern. Fairly common and local in deciduous woodlands and arid scrub in drainage of upper Río Marañón in Cajamarca, La Libertad and Piura at 200-2100 m. *N Peru; recorded in adjacent Ecuador.*

Chestnut-bellied Thrush *Turdus fulviventris*   Zorzal Ventricastaño
24 cm (9.4"). Plate 106. ♪ 630. A distinctive thrush that can be recognized by its dark hood and bright rufous belly. Note the yellow bill, legs and eye-ring. Uncommon in humid montane forests in Cajamarca at 1400-2600 m. *NW Venezuela to n Peru.*

Pale-breasted Thrush *Turdus leucomelas* Zorzal Pechipálido
23 cm (9"). Plate 106. ♪ 797. Sexes similar. Within its limited range, the only thrush that has a gray crown with a contrasting cinnamon-brown back. Breast is pale pinkish-brown. Uncommon in lowland savanna and scrub near Moyobamba (San Martín), and Pampas del Heath to 900 m. *S Venezuela and the Guianas to ne Argentina, Amazonian and e Brazil.*

Creamy-bellied Thrush *Turdus amaurochalinus* Zorzal Ventricremoso
23 cm (9"). Plate 105. ♪ 797. The only thrush in its range with pale underparts, a whitish throat with black streaks, and black lores. Male has a yellow bill and female a grayish bill. Somewhat similar to Black-billed Thrush, but latter has a black bill and lacks black lores. Fairly common austral-winter visitor to humid lowlands e of Andes from Puno to 1700 m. *E Peru to Argentina, Paraguay, Amazonian and e Brazil.*

Black-billed Thrush *Turdus ignobilis* Zorzal Piquinegro
23 cm (9"). Plate 105. ♪ 797. A thrush of clearings and forest edge. Sexes similar. Bill black. Very similar to Hauxwell's Thrush, but Black-billed is grayer (not warm brown), especially on underparts. Grayer also than female Lawrence's Thrush, and lacks yellow-orange eye-ring of latter. Common in humid lowland and foothill forests e of Andes to 2000 m. *S Venezuela and the Guianas to n Bolivia and w Amazonian Brazil.*

Lawrence's Thrush *Turdus lawrencii* Zorzal de Lawrence
23 cm (9"). Plate 105. ♪ 797. A thrush of forest canopy. The male is the only *Turdus* in its range that is dark brown with a yellow bill and a conspicuous orange-yellow eye-ring. Female is similar but has a dark bill. Cf. Black-billed, Hauxwell's and White-necked Thrushes. Fairly common in humid lowland forests e of Andes to 500 m. Very vocal and commonly seen along canopy walk at ExplorNapo. *Venezuela to n Bolivia and w Amazonian Brazil.*

[Pale-vented Thrush] *Turdus obsoletus* Zorzal Ventripálido
23 cm (9"). Not illustrated. ♪ 630. Accidental. Similar to Hauxwell's Thrush of Amazonia, but rather dull brown (lacks rufescent tones of latter). Note pure white vent. Two recent sight records from Tumbes (BPW). *Costa Rica to w Colombia and w Ecuador.*

Hauxwell's Thrush *Turdus hauxwelli* Zorzal de Hauxwell
23 cm (9"). Plate 105. ♪ 797. A thrush of forest interiors; mostly dark, rich brown, with a dark bill, and no eye-ring. Sexes similar. Cf. Black-billed, Lawrence's and White-necked Thrushes. Uncommon in humid lowland *várzea* and *terra firme* forests e of Andes to 800 m. *Venezuela to n Bolivia and w Amazonian Brazil.*

Ecuadorian Thrush *Turdus maculirostris* Zorzal Ecuatoriano
23 cm (9"). Plate 105. Note limited range. A rather dull, grayish-brown thrush with a dingy yellowish bill and a yellowish-orange eye-ring. Underparts are paler and become whitish on belly and vent. Cf. female Glossy-black Thrush (more uniformly dark on underparts). Common in woodlands and forests of Tumbes to 1400 m. *W Ecuador and adjacent nw Peru.*

White-necked Thrush *Turdus albicollis* Zorzal Cuelliblanco
23 cm (9"). Plate 106. ♪ 797. The only thrush with a conspicuous white crescent on chest. Also note bold black streaks on white throat, pale-gray breast, and dark-brown upperparts. Narrow eye-ring is usually yellow-orange, but ranges from red to yellow. Fairly common in humid lowland and foothill forests e of Andes to 1500 m. *Venezuela and the Guianas to ne Argentina and Brazil.*

Polioptilidae (Gnatcatchers and Gnatwrens; Perlitas). Species: World 14; Peru 4
The gnatwrens and gnatcatchers form a small family of birds closely related to the wrens and thrushes. They are confined to the New World, and range from northern United States to northern Argentina and Brazil. Gnatwrens inhabit the undergrowth of humid forest, while gnatcatchers are more partial to open, often arid regions. They are basically insectivorous, but vegetable material has been found in the diet of some species.

Microbates and *Ramphocaenus* **Gnatwrens.** The three gnatwrens have the general shape of a wren—tail is held cocked and their behavior is wrenlike. They differ in having a long narrow bill.

Collared Gnatwren *Microbates collaris* Soterillo Acollarado
10.cm (4"). Plate 104. The only gnatwren with a black pectoral band. Uncommon in humid *terra firme* forests in Loreto and San Martín to 500 m. *S Venezuela and the Guianas to ne Peru and Amazonian Brazil.*

Tawny-faced Gnatwren *Microbates cinereiventris* Soterillo Carileonada
10.cm (4"). Plate 104. ♪677. The only gnatwren with a tawny face, black malar stripe and gray underparts. Color pattern recalls that of Ochre-faced Tody-Flycatcher. Uncommon in humid *terra firme* forests in n Loreto, and locally along e base of Andes from Amazonas to Puno to 1000 m. *Nicaragua to se Peru.*

Long-billed Gnatwren *Ramphocaenus melanurus* Soterillo Piquilargo
12 cm (4.75"). Plate 104. ♪797. The only gnatwren that lacks bold head markings. Note the longer bill and tail than *Microbates* gnatwrens. Uncommon in humid *várzea*, *terra firme* and deciduous forests e of Andes, and w of Andes in Tumbes to 1500 m. *Mexico to n Bolivia, Amazonian and se Brazil.*

Tropical Gnatcatcher *Polioptila plumbea* Perlita Tropical
11.5 cm (4.5"). Plate 108. ♪540. A small gray bird with a long tail. Tail is black with prominent white outer rectrices. Three races occur in Peru. In typical *parvirostris* (most of e Peru, illustrated) female has a gray crown. In upper Marañón Valley *maior* (illustrated), both sexes have a black crown and are darker gray. This race is sometimes considered a separate species (Marañón Gnatcatcher). In arid nw Peru, *bilineata* has a white superciliary. Uncommon to locally common in arid scrub and second growth south to Madre de Dios to 1200 m. *Mexico to n Peru and Amazonian Brazil.*

Corvidae (Crows, Jays and Magpies; Cuervos y Urracas). Species: World 119; Peru 6
A large assemblage of robust perching birds with a worldwide distribution. The family includes such disparate members as nutcrackers, magpies, jays, ravens, ground-jays, choughs and crows, but are represented in Peru by only six jays of two genera. Crows are considered to be among the most intelligent of all animals, and the New Caledonian Crow, which shapes a leaf into a barbed tool, is the only bird known to actually make a tool (as opposed to using a ready-made tool such as the cactus spine employed by the Galápagos Woodpecker Finch). Most corvids are opportunistic omnivores, and at times will eat almost anything they can swallow.

Cyanocorax **Jays.** Four species of medium to large jays. Two are essentially dark blue-gray with a black hood, and the other two have black throats and yellow eyes.

Green Jay *Cyanocorax yncas* Urraca Verde
30 cm (11.7"). Plate 100. ♪797. This unique green-and-yellow jay is unmistakable. Most of the South American races are sometimes treated as a separate species (Inca Jay). Fairly common in humid montane forests on e slope of Andes at 1400-2600 m. *S Texas to Venezuela and n Bolivia.*

Purplish Jay *Cyanocorax cyanomelas* Urraca Purpúrea
37 cm (14.5"). Plate 100. ♪797. A dark blue-gray jay with a black hood. Similar and sometimes sympatric with Violaceous Jay. Purplish Jay is duller and darker, and lacks Violaceous Jay's pale nape. Common and local in woodlands and scrub in Cusco and Madre de Dios to 2000 m. *SE Peru to ne Argentina, Paraguay and sw Brazil.*

Violaceous Jay *Cyanocorax violaceus* Urraca Violácea
37 cm (14.5"). Plate 100. ♪638. Over most of its range, the only dark-blue jay with a black head. In southeast Peru cf. Purplish Jay. Common in humid *várzea* forests e of Andes to 1000 m. *S Venezuela to w Amazonian Brazil and extreme n Bolivia.*

White-tailed Jay *Cyanocorax mystacalis* Urraca Coliblanca
32.5 cm (12.7"). Plate 100. ♪638. The only blue-and-white jay with a broad white terminal tail band. Unlikely to be mistaken. Fairly common in arid Pacific littoral south to w La Libertad to 1200 m. *SW Ecuador and nw Peru*

Turquoise Jay *Cyanolyca turcosa* Urraca Turquesa
32 cm (12.5"). Plate 100. ♪638. The only collared jay in its limited range. Fairly common in humid montane forests in nw Cajamarca and n Piura at 1500-3200 m. *SE Colombia to n Peru.*

White-collared Jay *Cyanolyca viridicyana* Urraca Collarblanco
34 cm (13.5"). Plate 100. ♪797. The only collared jay in its range. The white collar is narrow and not always conspicuous. Fairly common in humid montane forests along e slope of Andes north to Amazonas at 1700-3400 m. *E Peru and w Bolivia.*

Passeridae (Old World Sparrows; Gorriones). World: Species 35; Peru 1 (introduced)
A family of sparrow-sized birds widespread in the Palearctic, Oriental and Afrotropical regions. The House Sparrow has been widely introduced in the Americas, Australia and elsewhere, and may be the most widely distributed of all landbird species. Members of the genus *Passer* mainly feed on the seeds of grasses and other herbaceous plants, and supplement their diet with insects. The introduced House Sparrow will consume almost any potentially edible kind of waste that becomes available.

House Sparrow *Passer domesticus* Gorrión Casero
15 cm (6"). Plate 123. ♪797. The male has a gray crown and cheeks and a black throat, usually accompanied by the drab-looking female with her pale superciliary. Fairly common in Pacific lowlands and agricultural areas to 2000 m. *Palearctic and Oriental regions; introduced worldwide and commensal to man.*

Vireonidae (Vireos and Allies; Vireos). Species: World 52; Peru 15
A family of small to medium-sized New World perching birds that ranges from Canada to Brazil and Argentina. Most North American species are migratory, but the tropical species tend to be sedentary. The peppershrikes and shrike-vireos feed on both fruits and insects, but greenlets and vireos feed primarily on insects that they glean from the foliage of bushes and trees. Tawny-crowned Greenlet often follows ant swarms to capture insects disturbed by ants.

Vireo **Vireos.** The four members of the genus that occur in Peru are dull, with a prominent whitish to white superciliary. All lack wingbars. The three "red-eyed" species have a dark eye-line. The red eye is often difficult to discern.

Brown-capped Vireo *Vireo leucophrys* Vireo Gorripardo
12.5 cm (5"). Plate 107. ♪797. The only *Vireo* with a noticeable rufous-brown cap. Common in humid montane forests on e slope of Andes and south on Pacific slope to s Cajamarca at 1300-2500 m. *Mexico to w Bolivia.*

Red-eyed Vireo *Vireo olivaceus* Vireo Ojirrojo 1
5 cm (6"). Plate 107. ♪ 797. A "red-eyed" vireo with a distinct head pattern. The gray crown is bordered by a black stripe, a conspicuous white superciliary, and a black eye line. Cf. Black-whiskered (black malar stripe) and Yellow-green Vireos. Fairly common resident w of Andes south to La Libertad to 1500 m; large influx of migrants and northern-winter visitors to lowlands e of Andes. *Canada to Argentina; West Indies.*

Yellow-green Vireo *Vireo flavoviridis* Vireo Verdiamarillo
15 cm (6"). Plate 107. ♪ 636. A "red-eyed" vireo with a greenish back and yellowish underparts. Superciliary and black lines that border it are not as conspicuous as in similar Red-eyed Vireo. Uncommon northern-winter visitor in humid lowlands e of Andes to 1500 m. *S Texas to Panama; winters to w Brazil and n Bolivia.*

Black-whiskered Vireo *Vireo altiloquus* Vireo Bigotudo
15 cm (6"). Plate 107. ♪ 636. Note limited range. Like Red-eyed Vireo, but has a black malar stripe. Rare northern-winter visitor to open woodlands in Loreto. Recently mist-netted near Hacienda Amazonia (pers. comm. V. Yabar). *Florida and West Indies; winters to Amazon basin.*

***Hylophilus* Greenlets.** A genus of small, dull-looking, arboreal vireos that present difficult identification problems. Note especially eye color.

Lemon-chested Greenlet *Hylophilus thoracicus* Verdillo Pechilimón
12 cm (4.75"). Plate 107. ♪ 636. The only yellow-eyed greenlet with a noticeable yellow band across the chest. Upperparts are bright olive, and bill is dusky. Fairly common and local in humid lowland forests e of Andes from San Martín south to Puno to 600 m. *S Venezuela and the Guianas to n Bolivia, w Amazonian and se Brazil.*

Gray-chested Greenlet *Hylophilus semicinereus* Verdillo Pechigris
12 cm (4.75"). Plate 107. ♪ 636. Similar to Lemon-chested Greenlet, but chest is gray and back is a darker olive. Common in Pacaya Samiria National Reserve (Begazo and Valqui 1998). *S Venezuela to ne Bolivia and Amazonian Brazil.*

Ashy-headed Greenlet *Hylophilus pectoralis* Verdillo Cabeciceniza
12 cm (4.75"). Plate 107. Recalls Lemon-chested Greenlet, but entire crown is gray (versus just nape), and eyes are dark amber. Recorded along Río Heath, Madre de Dios (pers. comm. EB); tape recorded near Tarapoto, San Martín. *Lowlands of Guianas to n Bolivia and Amazonian Brazil.*

Dusky-capped Greenlet *Hylophilus hypoxanthus* Verdillo Gorrioscuro
12 cm (4.75"). Plate 107. ♪ 797. The only greenlet in its range with yellowish underparts, whitish throat, dark eyes and a pale bill. Often a key species in mixed-canopy flocks in Amazonian lowlands. Common in humid lowland *terra firme* forests e of Andes to 500 m. *S Venezuela to n Bolivia and Amazonian Brazil.*

[Rufous-naped Greenlet] *Hylophilus semibrunneus* Verdillo Nuquirrufa
12.5 cm (5"). Plate 107. A dark-eyed greenlet with rufous crown and nape contrasting with whitish face. Cf. Tawny-crowned Greenlet (rufous forecrown, white eyes), female Plain Antvireo (heavier bill, no whitish face). Sight record northeast of Huancabamba, Piura (TAP *in litt.*). *Andes of nw Venezuela to e Ecuador.*

Olivaceous Greenlet *Hylophilus olivaceus* Virdillo Olivácceo
12 cm (4.75"). Plate 107. Over most of its range, the only greenlet with rather dull-olive underparts, pale eyes and a pale bill. Fairly common and local in humid foothills and lower montane forests along e slope of Andes south to Junín at 600-1600 m. *E Ecuador to n Peru.*

Tawny-crowned Greenlet *Hylophilus ochraceiceps* Verdillo Coronileonada
11.5 cm (4.5"). Plate 107. ♪ 797. The only brownish greenlet with a rufous forecrown, white eyes and a pale bill. Often found foraging with mixed-understory flocks (together with antwrens, antvireos, etc.). Cf. female antvireos are dark-eyed. Fairly common in humid lowland forests e of Andes to 800 m. *Mexico to n Bolivia and Amazonian Brazil.*

Lesser Greenlet *Hylophilus decurtatus* Verdillo Menor
10.cm (4"). Plate 107. ♪ 636. The only greenlet in its limited range with an olive back, grayish crown and dark eyes. Also note white eye-ring, white lores, pale bill and white underparts. Fairly common in dry deciduous forests in Tumbes to 1000 m. *Mexico to extreme nw Peru.*

Slaty-capped Shrike-Vireo *Vireolanius leucotis* Vireón Gorriapizarrado
14 cm (5.5"). Plate 107. ♪ 797. A canopy-dwelling vireo with distinctive head pattern, shrike-like bill and yellow underparts. Common in humid *terra firme* and montane forests e of Andes to 1800 m. *S Venezuela and the Guianas to n Bolivia and Amazonian Brazil.*

Rufous-browed Peppershrike *Cyclarhis gujanensis* Vireón Cejirrufa
15 cm (6"). Plate 107. ♪ 797 Four ssp. occur in Peru. All have a heavy shrike-like bill, rufous to chestnut "brows", olive back, white belly and yellowish breast-band. Widespread *gujanensis* (e of Andes) has a gray crown and cheeks. In *virenticeps* (Pacific slope of nw Peru) crown is olive and cheeks and throat are yellow. In *contrerasi* (mts. of n Peru) and *saturatus* (upper Marañón Valley) rufous extends to crown and is often mottled with olive. Fairly common in humid forests e of Andes north to Amazonas, and uncommon along Pacific slope south to Cajamarca to 2000 m. *Mexico to the Guianas, Brazil and n Argentina.*

[Black-billed Peppershrike] *Cyclarhis nigrirostris* Vireón Piquinegro
15 cm (6"). Not illustrated. ♪ EC007T. Similar to race *virenticeps* of Rufous-browed Peppershrike, but bill is black, the yellow chest-band is broken and the rufous is limited to the lores at best. Sight record at El Caucho on Dec. 30, 1998 (Pyhälä *in litt.*). *Andes of Colombia and w Ecuador.*

Fringillidae (Siskins, Crossbills, Canaries and Allies; Jilgueros). Species: World 134; Peru 8
A fairly large family of small songbirds, well represented throughout the world (except for Madagascar and Australia). Their stout, conical bills are ideally adapted for dealing with hard seeds, and the differences in the size and shape of the bill reflect the types of seed-heads they can best exploit. They are mainly sedentary, but often gather in large post-breeding flocks that wander widely in search of food.

Carduelis Siskins. Most have dark wings with prominent yellow markings. Represented in Peru by eight small black and yellow birds. Some present difficult problems in identification.

Thick-billed Siskin *Carduelis crassirostris* Jilguero Piquigrueso
14 cm (5.5"). Plate 123. ♪ 797. Thicker-billed and larger than other siskins. Sympatric with Hooded Siskin. Females, immatures and non-breeding males are sooty in Thick-billed, but greenish in Hooded. In many plumages, there is a diagnostic yellow spot on side of neck. Uncommon and local in montane scrub and *Polylepis* woodlands from Ancash and Pasco south at 3400-4800 m. *Peru to nw Argentina and central Chile.*

Hooded Siskin *Carduelis magellanica* Jilguero Encapuchado
12.5 cm (5"). Plate 123. ♪ 797. Four races occur in Peru, males of which have essentially a black hood and yellow body. Immatures and females are greenish-yellow and lack hood. Males of *capitalis* (illustrated, mts. of nw Peru) and *paula* (trop. and subtrop.nw Peru) have olive backs mottled with varying amounts of black, but *urubambensis* (temperate zone south from Cusco) and *peruana* (illustrated, w slope of Andes in c Peru) have a cleaner olive back. Cf. nearly identical Olivaceous Siskin (no overlap), Thick-billed Siskin and limited-range Saffron Siskin. Common in Pacific lowlands south to Arequipa and in cultivated montane areas to 4000 m. *Widespread and local in South America.*

Yellow-bellied Siskin *Carduelis xanthogastra* Jilguero Ventriamarillo
11.5 cm (4.5"). Plate 123. ♫ 797. The only siskin in its limited range with a black back, black hood and yellow underparts. Cf. Yellow-rumped Siskin. Uncommon in cultivated areas and montane scrub in Puno at 1500-2500 m. *Locally in mts. of Costa Rica to w Bolivia.*

***Saffron Siskin** *Carduelis siemiradzkii* Jilguero Azafranado
11.5 cm (4.5"). Plate 123. Note limited range. Very similar to Hooded Siskin but has a clean yellow-green back. Race *paula* of sympatric Hooded Siskin has an olive back mottled with varying amounts of black. Very rare in semiarid scrub in Tumbes at 400-750 m. *SW Ecuador, Isla Puná and extreme nw Peru.*

Olivaceous Siskin *Carduelis olivacea* Jilguero Oliváceo
11.5 cm (4.5"). Plate 123. ♫ 797. Very similar to Hooded Siskin (no overlap) but underparts have olivaceous tones. Cf. allopatric Hooded Siskin. Uncommon in humid montane forests and second growth on e slope of Andes at 1000-3000 m. *SE Ecuador to w Bolivia.*

Lesser Goldfinch *Carduelis psaltria* Jilguero Menor
10.cm (4"). Plate 123. ♫ 626. Both sexes have narrow white wingbars. The male is the only small finch-like bird that is black above and yellow below. Female is mostly olive-green above and dull yellow below. All other *Carduelis* have prominent yellow wing markings. Uncommon in cultivated areas south to La Libertad, and in Río Marañón Valley drainage at 500-2500 m. *W US to n Peru.*

Black Siskin *Carduelis atrata* Jilguero Negro
12.5 cm (5"). Plate 123. Unmistakable. Mostly black with yellow on wings, lower belly, crissum, and flashes of yellow in tail. Common in *puna* grasslands and montane scrub north to Huánuco and Lima at 3500-4500 m. *Central Peru to n Chile and Argentina.*

Yellow-rumped Siskin *Carduelis uropygialis* Jilguero Cordillerano
12.5 cm (5"). Plate 123. The only siskin that has a dark blackish back, black hood, yellow rump and yellow underparts. Cf. Yellow-bellied Siskin. Rare and local in Andes of Ancash, Lima, Huancavelica, Puno and Arequipa at 2000-4000 m; one record near sea level at Mollendo (Hughes 1970). *Andes of central Peru to nw Argentina and n Chile.*

Parulidae (New World Warblers; Reinitas). Species: World 116; Peru 24
A fairly large family of small, brightly colored songbirds that ranges from Alaska to Argentina and Brazil. The North American species are largely migratory, with many species wintering in the West Indies and northern South America. They occur in a wide variety of habitats, ranging from coastal mangrove swamps to 3400 meters in the Andes. They are mainly insectivorous, with some species catching their prey in flycatcher-like sallies, while others glean insects from tree trunks, branches and foliage. Some species such as Buff-rumped Warbler and the water-thrushes forage on the ground.

Golden-winged Warbler *Vermivora chrysoptera* Reinita Alidorada
12.5 cm (5"). Plate 107. ♫ 627. Accidental. The only warbler in the region that has a combination of bold yellow wing-patch, yellow forehead and black (gray in female) throat and ear-patch. Sight record 2 Dec. 1998 at Pillahuata (Cusco) at 2700 m (Engblom and Nordin 1999). *E North America; winters Guatemala to nw South America and Greater Antilles.*

Tropical Parula *Parula pitiayumi* Parula Tropical
11.5 cm (4.5"). Plate 107. ♫ 797. A distinctive warbler with blue-gray upperparts (mantle is olive), mostly yellow underparts and white wingbars. Male has a small dark mask. Female is duller and lacks a mask. Common and widespread on e slope of Andes and on Pacific slope south to Lambayeque and Cajamarca to 2500 m. Recorded at Chancay, Lima (Pyhälä *in litt*). *Texas to n Argentina and s Brazil.*

Yellow Warbler *Dendroica petechia* Reinita Amarilla
12.5 cm (5"). Plate 107. ♪ 626. Both sexes are the only yellow warblers that show yellow tail spots. Male has chestnut streaks on the breast. Two types occur. In resident race *peruviana* (mangroves in Tumbes) male has a chestnut crown. In migratory race *aestiva* male has a completely yellow head. Female Masked Yellowthroat lacks yellow tail spots. The two types are sometimes regarded as separate species. Fairly common resident in mangroves in Tumbes, and uncommon northern-winter visitor south to central Peru to 2000 m. *North and South America to Bolivia and Brazil; Galápagos Is.*

Blackburnian Warbler *Dendroica fusca* Reinita Gargantinaranja
12.5 cm (5"). Plate 107. ♪ 626. Female and non-breeding male have sulphur-yellow throat and superciliary, dark cheeks and two wingbars. Breeding male has an attractive black-and-orange head pattern, and mostly black wings with a large white wingbar. Fairly common northern-winter visitor to lowland and montane forests at 500-2500 m. *E North America; winters to Bolivia.*

Blackpoll Warbler *Dendroica striata* Reinita Estriada
12.5 cm (5"). Plate 107. ♪ 626. Female and non-breeding male have greenish-olive back (females are slightly grayer), streaked mantle, dingy underparts with greenish-olive streaks on flanks, and two wingbars. Breeding male vaguely recalls Black-and-white Warbler (striped crown, etc.). Uncommon northern-winter visitor in lowlands e of Andes to 1000 m. *Breeds Alaska and Canada; winters to Peru and w Amazonian Brazil.*

Cerulean Warbler *Dendroica cerulea* Reinita Cerúlea
12 cm (4.75"). Plate 107. ♪ 627. Male has cerulean-blue upperparts, white underparts with a narrow black pectoral band, and wingbars. Female has greenish mantle, wingbars, a blue-green crown and yellowish throat. Rare northern-winter visitor on e slope of Andes and adjacent lowlands at 500-2000 m. *E North America; winters Venezuela to Bolivia.*

Black-and-white Warbler *Mniotilta varia* Reinita Trepadora
12.5 cm (5"). Plate 107. ♪ 626. A distinctive warbler with black-and-white stripes on crown and back. Male has a black throat. Rare northern-winter visitor south to Lambayeque, Amazonas and La Libertad to 2000 m. *E North America; winters to Peru and West Indies.*

American Redstart *Setophaga ruticilla* Candelita Americana
12.5 cm (5"). Plate 107. ♪ 626. Male is mostly black with orange wingbars and basal half of outer four tail feathers. Female and immature have orange-yellow wingbars and tail panels. Rare northern-winter visitor in light woods and mangroves south to Apurímac and Arequipa to 1000 m. *Alaska to s US; winters to n South America and West Indies.*

Northern Waterthrush *Seiurus noveboracensis* Reinita-Acuática Norteña
14 cm (5.5"). Plate 107. ♪ 626. A terrestrial warbler usually found near water. Brown above, dingy-white below with dark streaks (heavier on chest) and a white superciliary. Rare northern-winter visitor in humid lowlands near mouth of Río Curaray (Loreto). *North America; winters to n South America and West Indies.*

Connecticut Warbler *Oporornis agilis* Reinita de Connecticut
14 cm (5.5"). Plate 107. ♪ 626. Accidental northern-winter visitor. Male is olive above, yellow below, with a gray hood and a white eye-ring. Female is duller olive above, "dirty" yellow below, with a grayish olive hood and a white eye-ring. Single record from Explorer's Inn. *N North America; winters in Amazonia.*

Masked Yellowthroat *Geothlypis aequinoctialis* Reinita Equinoccial
12.5 cm (5"). Plate 108. ♪ 797. The only warbler that has a black mask, olive back, yellow underparts and a gray crown. Males in populations east of Andes (*velata*) have a black mask, but mask is very reduced in northern and western populations (*peruviana* and *auricularis,* illustrated). Female lacks black mask, but has a yellow supraloral stripe. Marañón race *peruviana* and se Peru race *velata* may represent separate species. Fairly common on Pacific coast south to Ica and in upper Río Marañón Valley (La Libertad and Cajamarca); east of Andes in lowlands north to Ucayali to 1500 m. *Costa Rica to n Argentina and Brazil.*

Canada Warbler *Wilsonia canadensis* Reinita de Canada
13.5 cm (5.3"). Plate 107. ♪ 626. Both sexes are gray above and yellow below, with a yellow eye-ring. The male has a necklace of black streaks; female has faint gray streaks and recalls Gray-and-gold Warbler, but latter has a white supraloral. Uncommon northern-winter visitor in humid lowland and montane forests on e slope of Andes south to Cusco and Madre de Dios to 2000 m. *E North America; winters to nw South America.*

***Myioborus* Redstarts.** A pair of active warblers with conspicuous white outer tail feathers that are often spread like a fan. Because of this field mark some authors in recent works have referred to them as "whitestarts." We follow the American Ornithologists' Union in maintaining this long-established English name. They often accompany mixed flocks.

Slate-throated Redstart *Myioborus miniatus* Candelita Gargantiplomiza
12.5 cm (5"). Plate 107. ♪ 797. The only redstart with a dark throat. Common in humid montane forests on e slope of Andes, and on Pacific slope south to Cajamarca at 700-2500 m. *Mexico to Bolivia.*

Spectacled Redstart *Myioborus melanocephalus* Candelita de Anteojos
12.5 cm (5"). Plate 107. ♪ 797. The only redstart with a yellow throat and prominent yellow spectacles. East-slope populations (illustrated) have black crowns, but Pacific slope race *griseonuchus* has a rufous crown patch, and more extensive black on face. Fairly common in humid montane forests on e slope of Andes and on Pacific slope south to Cajamarca at 2000-3300 m. *Colombia to w Bolivia.*

***Basileuterus* Warblers.** A large genus of 25 Neotropical warblers, well represented in Peru with 10 species. Most have yellow underparts and a prominent superciliary. Many are important components of understory mixed flocks. A few members of the genus closely resemble *Hemispingus* tanagers.

Gray-and-gold Warbler *Basileuterus fraseri* Reinita Grisidorada
14 cm (5.5"). Plate 108. ♪ 563. The only warbler with blue-gray upperparts and yellow underparts that has a white supraloral. Cf. migratory Canada Warbler. Fairly common in deciduous woodlands and scrub south to Lambayeque to 1900 m. *SW Ecuador to nw Peru.*

Two-banded Warbler *Basileuterus bivittatus* Reinita de Dos Bandas
14 cm (5.5"). Plate 108. ♪ 797. A *Basileuterus* with yellow underparts (no olive on flanks), a short yellow supraloral and a broken eye-ring. Sympatric Golden-bellied Warbler lacks broken yellow eye-ring, has olive on flanks, and yellow superciliary that extends well past the eye. Citrine and Pale-legged Warblers also have a yellow supraloral, but lack median rufous crown stripe. Common and local in humid foothill forests and bamboo stands along e slope of Andes in Cusco and Puno at 700-1800 m. *S Venezuela; Peru to nw Argentina.*

Golden-bellied Warbler *Basileuterus chrysogaster* Reinita Ventridorado
12.5 cm (5"). Plate 108. ♪ 563. The only *Basileuterus* with olive flanks and black-and-rufous crown stripes. Compare Two-banded, Citrine and Pale-legged Warblers. Rare in humid lowland and foothill forests on e slope of Andes in Huánuco, and Junín south to Puno at 300-1200 m. *Endemic to Peru.*

Pale-legged Warbler *Basileuterus signatus* Reinita Patipálida
12.5 cm (5"). Plate 108. ♪ 797. Two races in Peru, both similar to sympatric ssp. of Citrine Warbler. Race *flavovirens* (Puno, illustrated) has a yellow supraloral (accented by a black outline) that reaches barely past the eye, and a yellow crescent below the eye. Sympatric Citrine Warbler race *euophrys* has a yellow superciliary that almost reaches the nape, and lacks a yellow crescent below the eye. Race *signatus* (Junín to Cusco) is slightly duller; its superciliary lacks a black upper border and reaches to the rear of the eye. Sympatric Citrine Warbler race *striaticeps* lacks a crescent under the eye and its yellow superciliary reaches past the eye. Race *signatus* can be studied in detail near Machu-Picchu train station. Juvenile is uniformly sooty brown. Fairly common in humid montane forests on e slope of Andes north to Junín at 2000-2800 m. *Central Peru to nw Argentina.*

Citrine Warbler *Basileuterus luteoviridis* Reinita Citrina
14 cm (5.5"). Plate 108. ♪ 797. Two ssp. occur in Peru. Both have a yellow superciliary that tapers behind the eye and both are similar to sympatric Pale-legged Warbler (see above for comparison). Race *striaticeps* (Amazonas to Cusco) is also sympatric with Black-crested Warbler, but latter has a conspicuous black median crown stripe. Cf. Parodi's Hemispingus. Race *euophrys* (Puno) has a long superciliary that almost reaches nape. Common in humid montane forests on e slope of Andes at 2300-3400 m. *Venezuela to w Bolivia.*

Black-crested Warbler *Basileuterus nigrocristatus* Reinita Crestinegra
12.5 cm (5"). Plate 108. ♪ 563. No other warbler in its range has a black median crown stripe bordered with a wide yellow superciliary. Common in montane forests on Pacific slope south to Ancash at 1500-2000 m. *Venezuela to n Peru.*

Russet-crowned Warbler *Basileuterus coronatus* Reinita Coronirrojiza
14 cm (5.5"). Plate 108. ♪ 797. The only warbler that has a gray head with black lateral and rufous median crown stripes. Populations east of Andes (*chapmani, inaequalis, coronatus*) have a yellow breast and belly; in nw Peru ssp. *castaneiceps* has dingy whitish underparts. Common in montane forests on e slope of Andes and on Pacific slope south to Cajamarca at 1500-2500 m. *Venezuela to w Bolivia.*

Three-banded Warbler *Basileuterus trifasciatus* Reinita Tribandeada
12.5 cm (5"). Plate 108. ♪ 563. No other warbler in its range has a black striped, pale-gray head. Median crown stripe is gray. Race *nitidior* (Tumbes) has reduced gray on back (compared with illustrated nominate race), and median crown stripe is sometimes tinged with yellow. Fairly common on e slopes of Cordillera Occidental (western Andes) south to La Libertad at 500-2000 m. *SW Ecuador and nw Peru.*

Three-striped Warbler *Basileuterus tristriatus* Reinita Cabecilistada
12.5 cm (5"). Plate 108. ♪ 797. No other warbler has a similar facial pattern (black cheeks, whitish superciliary, black lateral crown stripe, yellow to buff median stripe, and a white crescent under the eye). There is considerable variation in amount of yellow on underparts. Common in humid montane forests on e slope of Andes at 1000-2000 m. *Costa Rica to Venezuela and w Bolivia.*

Buff-rumped Warbler *Basileuterus fulvicauda* Reinita Lomianteada
12.5 cm (5"). Plate 108. ♪ 797. A primarily terrestrial warbler with a buff rump and basal half of tail; broad dark terminal tail band. Fairly common along lowland rivers and streams e of Andes to 1000 m. *Honduras to n Bolivia and w Amazonian Brazil.*

Coerebidae (Bananaquit; Reinita Mielera). Species: World 1
A taxonomic puzzle which has led to the elevation of this warbler-like tanager to a monotypic family. Some authors place it with the Parulidae.

Bananaquit *Coereba flaveola* Reinita Mielera
11.5 cm (4.5"). Plate 109. ♪797. A small, active, warbler-like bird, easily identified by its short, decurved bill, combined with a prominent white eye-stripe, gray throat and yellow underparts. Four ssp. occur in Peru. Three races—*pacifica* (illustrated), *dispar* and *chloropyga* are quite similar; race *magnirostris* (upper Marañón Valley) has a longer bill. Common in humid lowland forests e of Andes and on Pacific slope south to Ancash to 1500 m. Introduced in Lima in 1990 and very common. *Mexico to ne Argentina and Brazil; West Indies.*

Thraupidae (Tanagers and Allies; Tangaras). Species: World 256; Peru 132
A poorly defined, heterogeneous collection of nine-primaried oscines. It includes the "true" tanagers, dacnises, conebills and honeycreepers. They reach their greatest diversity in the humid tropics, where many species often join together to form the nucleus of mixed-feeding flocks. Most of the "true" tanagers are principally frugivores but regularly obtain insects. The dacnises and conebills are insectivorous, and some, especially the honeycreepers, feed on nectar. Most members of the family are sedentary. Many members are noted for their colorful plumage and few avian families can compete with their broad spectrum of dazzling colors.

Conirostrum **Conebills.** Small tanagers with pointed bills. The eight species found in Peru can be divided into two groups. The first three are Amazon basin species that inhabit forests near river systems. The remaining five species inhabit mostly montane forests and high-elevation woodlands (although widespread Cinereous Conebill ranges from sea-level to the *puna* zone).

Chestnut-vented Conebill *Conirostrum speciosum* Mielerito Ventricastaño
11 cm (4.25"). Plate 109. ♪797. The male is a gray conebill with a chestnut vent and darker underparts than those of Bicolored Conebill. Female has a greenish back, light gray crown and whitish underparts. Fairly common in humid lowland *várzea* forests e of Andes to 1000 m. *S Venezuela and the Guianas to n Argentina, Amazonian and se Brazil.*

Bicolored Conebill *Conirostrum bicolor* Mielerito Bicolor
11.5 cm (4.5"). Plate 109. Note limited range. A conebill with light bluish-gray upperparts and light dirty-gray underparts tinged with buff, and an orange eye. Pearly-breasted Conebill has cleaner and more uniform lighter gray underparts. Hooded Tanager has white lores, yellow legs and iris. Uncommon along river systems and islands in Amazon-Napo system (Loreto) to 200 m. *Venezuela and the Guianas to ne Peru and Amazonian Brazil.*

Pearly-breasted Conebill *Conirostrum margaritae* Mielerito Pechiperlado
11.5 cm (4.5"). Plate 115. Note limited range. A conebill with light bluish-gray upperparts and clean light-gray underparts. Eyes are pale brownish. Cf. Bicolored Conebill. Uncommon in lowland *Cecropia* woodlands near mouth of Río Napo (Loreto) to 100 m. Recorded on river island near Ceiba Tops Lodge. *W Amazonian Brazil and adjacent Peru.*

Cinereous Conebill *Conirostrum cinereum* Mielerito Cinéreo
12.5 cm (5"). Plate 109. ♪797. A familiar conebill with a distinctive wingbar, and a wing speculum combination that creates an "L" shape. Note prominent white superciliary. Pacific slope race *littorale* is darker (more olivaceous above and buffy below) than illustrated nominate race of central Andes. Common in woodlands and scrub on Pacific slope and central Andes from sea level to 4000 m. *Andes of sw Colombia to n Chile and w Bolivia.*

*Tamarugo Conebill *Conirostrum tamarugense* Mielerito de los Tamarugales
12.5 cm (5"). Plate 115. Similar only to Cinereous Conebill, but superciliary is rufous. Only adult male has a rufous throat and vent. Uncommon and local in *Prosopis-Polylepis-Gynoxys* woodlands in Arequipa, Tacna and Moquegua at 3400-4050 m. Recorded 20 km from Chiguata at 3400-3900 m. Recent record from Calientes, Tacna at 1300 m is lowest recorded elevation for this species (GE). A non-breeding austral-winter visitor to s Peru. *Breeds Andes of n Chile; winters to s Peru.*

White-browed Conebill *Conirostrum ferrugineiventre* Mielerito Cejiblanca
12 cm (4.75"). Plate 115. ♪ 797. The combination of long white superciliary, with a bluish back and rufous underparts, will identify this conebill. Fairly common in *Polylepis* and elfin forest north to San Martín at 3000-3700 m (occasionally to 4100 m). *Andes of s Peru and w Bolivia.*

Blue-backed Conebill *Conirostrum sitticolor* Mielerito Dorsiazul
12.5 cm (5"). Plate 109. ♪ 797. The combination of blue back, rufous belly, black face and throat eliminates any other conebill. Common in humid montane forests and forest borders on e slope of Andes and on Pacific slope south to Cajamarca at 2500-3500 m. *Andes of w Venezuela to w Bolivia.*

Capped Conebill *Conirostrum albifrons* Mielerito Coronado
12.5 cm (5"). Plate 109. ♪ 797. Sexually dimorphic. Male is nearly all black with a blue cap and rump. Female is mostly green with a bluish-gray head. Fairly common in humid montane forests on e slope of Andes at 2000-2800 m. *Venezuela to w Bolivia.*

Giant Conebill *Oreomanes fraseri* Piconono Gigante
16.5 cm (6.5"). Plate 115. ♪ 797. A monotypic genus bearing a surprising resemblance to a nuthatch. No other bird in its habitat resembles this species. Fairly common and local in *Polylepis* woodlands north to Ancash at 2700-4850 m. *Andes of s Colombia to w Bolivia.*

Black-faced Tanager *Schistochlamys melanopis* Tangara Carinegra
18 cm (7"). Plate 110. A monotypic genus with a finch-like bill. All gray except for a black face. Fairly common in scrub along e base of Andes from San Martín to Madre de Dios. *Venezuela and the Guianas to e Bolivia and Brazil.*

Black-and-white Tanager *Conothraupis speculigera* Tangara Negriblanca
16.5 cm (6.5"). Plate 111. Male is unmistakable; female is olive above, pale below, with streaky white breast. Rare and local in deciduous woodlands and arid scrub west of Andes south to La Libertad, and east of Andes from Amazonas and Cajamarca to Madre de Dios to 1400 m. *W Ecuador to central Peru.*

Magpie Tanager *Cissopis leveriana* Tangara Urraca
25 cm (9.8"). Plate 110. ♪ 797. A large, unmistakable, long-tailed, pied, jay-like tanager. Common in lowland forests, foothills and clearings east of Andes to 1400 m. *S Venezuela and the Guianas to ne Argentina and Amazonian Brazil.*

Red-billed Pied Tanager *Lamprospiza melanoleuca* Tangara-Pinto Piquirrojo
17 cm (6.6"). Plate 110. Unmistakable. Note the bright red bill. Female has gray mantle. Rare in humid lowland *terra firme* forests north to Río Manití (Loreto) to 600 m. Recorded at Lago Sándoval. *Amazonian Brazil, adjacent n Bolivia, e Peru and the Guianas.*

Grass-green Tanager *Chlorornis riefferii* Tangara Verde Esmeralda
20 cm (8"). Plate 117. ♪ 797. Nothing resembles this beautiful, unique tanager. Fairly common in humid montane forests on e slope of Andes at 2200-2800 m. *Andes of Colombia to w Bolivia.*

White-capped Tanager *Sericossypha albocristata* Tangara Gorriblanco
23 cm (9"). Plate 111. ♪ EC007T. This jay-like tanager is unlikely to be confused. Rare and local in humid montane forests on e slope of Andes south to Junín at 1800-3000 m. *Andes of w Venezuela to se Peru.*

Chlorospingus **Bush-Tanagers.** The four members of this genus inhabit montane and premontane forests on the e slope of the Andes. They are greenish-gray, often with some yellow markings. They travel in small groups, often accompanying understory mixed-species flocks.

Common Bush-Tanager *Chlorospingus ophthalmicus* Tangara-de-Monte Común
14 cm (5.5"). Plate 112. ♪797. Four ssp. occur in Peru. All share an olive back, dark crown and pale iris. Three races, *peruvianus* (se Peru), *hiaticolus* (s of Río Marañón) and *phaeocephalus* (n of Río Marañón) have yellow breast-bands and pale throats (*peruvianus* is brightest and shows the most contrast, becoming duller farther north). Race *cinereocephalus* (Huánuco to Ayacucho) has a gray throat and breast, and lacks a pectoral band. Cf. Ashy-throated Bush-Tanager. Common in humid montane forests on e slope of Andes at 800-2600 m. *Mexico to nw Argentina.*

Yellow-whiskered Bush-Tanager *Chlorospingus parvirostris* Tangara-de-Monte Bigoteamarillo
14.5 cm (5.75"). Plate 112. ♪EC007T. An olive bush-tanager with a broad yellow malar stripe (whisker) and pale iris. Similar to Yellow-throated Bush-Tanager, but generally ranges higher, has a pale iris, and yellow doesn't reach across the throat. Common and local in humid montane forests on e slope of Andes at 1400-2200 m. *Andes of s Colombia to w Bolivia.*

Yellow-throated Bush-Tanager *Chlorospingus flavigularis* Tangara-de-Monte Gargantiamarilla
15 cm (6"). Plate 112. Similar to Yellow-whiskered Bush Tanager, but note that median throat is yellow, lores are gray and iris is hazel. Common in humid foothill and lower subtropical forests on e slope of Andes south to Cordillera Vilcabamba at 700-1600 m. *Panama to Peru.*

Ashy-throated Bush-Tanager *Chlorospingus canigularis* Tangara-de-Monte Garganticeniza
14 cm (5.5"). Plate 112. ♪742CD. Recalls (and often sympatric with) Common Bush-Tanager. Ashy-throated has darker eyes and a white postocular stripe. Fairly common and local in humid montane forests on e slope of Andes south to Cusco at 900-2000 m, and on Pacific slope in Tumbes. *Costa Rica to e Peru.*

Gray-hooded Bush-Tanager *Cnemoscopus rubrirostris* Hemispingo Capuchigris
15 cm (6"). Plate 112. ♪EC007T. A gray-hooded, yellow tanager that often wags its tail. Race *chrysogaster* (illustrated, s of Río Marañón to Cusco and Apurímac) has a dark bill; nominate *rubrirostris* (n Piura and Amazonas) has a reddish bill. Fairly common in humid montane forests on e slope of Andes south to Cordillera Vilcabamba at 2100-3000m. Race *chrysogaster* may represent a separate species. *Andes of Venezuela to central Peru*

Hemispingus Hemispingus. A well-represented genus in Peru with 11 species. The group presents some difficult taxonomic and identification challenges. Some of the species are very similar to *Basileuterus* warblers. Generally *Hemispingus* are small, drab tanagers, but some have distinctive head patterns. They favor cool montane forests, often with *Chusquea* bamboo.

Black-capped Hemispingus *Hemispingus atropileus* Hemispingo Gorrinegro
18 cm (7"). Plate 112. ♪EC007T. Told from any other black-headed hemispingus with yellow underparts by its long and narrow white superciliary. Race *atropileus* (n of Río Marañón) has less black on face (especially on cheeks) than illustrated *auricularis* (s of Río Marañón). Common in humid montane forests with *Chusquea* bamboo on e slope of Andes south to Cusco at 2600-3400m. *Andes of Venezuela to e Peru*

Orange-browed Hemispingus *Hemispingus calophrys* Hemispingo Cejinaranja
16 cm (6.5"). Plate 113. ♪797. Note limited range. The only hemispingus with an orange superciliary and throat, and mostly yellow underparts. Fairly common in montane cloud and bamboo forests in Puno at 3000-3500 m. *Andes of se Peru and w Bolivia.*

Parodi's Hemispingus *Hemispingus parodii* Hemispingo de Parodi
16 cm (6.5"). Plate 113. Note limited range. A hemispingus with a blackish crown and long yellow superciliary that extends almost to the nape. Very similar to Citrine Warbler, but sympatric race of latter has an olive crown, and its superciliary tapers just pass the eye. Uncommon in elfin forests

and dense *Chusquea* bamboo in Cordillera Vilcabamba and Cordillera Vilcanota (Cusco) at 2750-3500m. Recorded along north side of Abra Málaga road and along Inca Trail above Machu Picchu. Endemic to Peru.

Superciliaried Hemispingus *Hemispingus superciliaris* Hemispingo Superciliado
14 cm (5.5"). Plate 112. ♪ JM. The four Peruvian races may represent more than one species. They all share a superciliary that contrasts with a black line of varied thickness that goes through the eye, sometimes creating a black cheek. In central Peru *leucogaster* (illustrated) and *insignis* are grayish with a white belly and superciliary. Cf. Cinereus Conebill (L-shaped wingbar) and Drab Hemispingus (lacks superciliary and has pale eyes). In northernmost Peru *maculifrons* is similar to southwestern ssp. *urubambae*. They are yellow-bellied with a grayish forehead and a white superciliary. Cf. Citrine Warbler. Common in humid montane forests and second growth on e slope of Andes at 2200-3200 m and on Pacific slope south to Cajamarca. *Andes of Venezuela to w Bolivia.*

Oleaginous Hemispingus *Hemispingus frontalis* Hemispingo Oleaginoso
15 cm (6"). Plate 112. ♪ EC007T. A dirty-looking *Hemispingus*. Differs from Citrine Warbler or any yellow hemispingus by lack of pronounced superciliary. Uncommon in humid montane forests on e slope of Andes south to Cusco at 1500-2500 m. *Venezuela to Peru.*

Black-eared Hemispingus *Hemispingus melanotis* Hemispingo Orejinegra
15 cm (6"). Plate 112. ♪ 797. Variable. Four ssp. occur in Peru, all with mostly buffy-ochre underparts and a black ear-patch. Races *piurae* and *macrophrys* (Pacific slope of Piura and La Libertad) have a black crown, black chin, a long, thin white superciliary, and lack contrasting rufous breast. Race *piurae* may represent a separate species (Piura Hemispingus). Race *berlepschi* (illustrated, s of Río Marañón to Cusco) has a rufous throat and breast, contrasting buff belly and gray crown, but lacks a superciliary. Race *castaneicollis* (Puno) has a black chin, gray crown, thin white superciliary and rufous breast. Common and local in humid montane forests on e slope of Andes at 1700-2500m, and on Pacific slope south to s Cajamarca at 1700-3100 m. *Andes of Venezuela to w Bolivia*

*Rufous-browed Hemispingus *Hemispingus rufosuperciliaris* Hemispingo Cejirrufa
15 cm (6"). Plate 113. The only hemispingus with a rufous superciliary and rufous underparts. Rare and local in humid montane elfin forests and bamboo thickets from Cordillera de Colán to Carpish Mts. at 2550-3500 m. *Endemic to Peru.*

Black-headed Hemispingus *Hemispingus verticalis* Hemispingo Cabecinegra
15 cm (6"). Plate 112. ♪ JM. Note limited range. The only gray hemispingus with an all black head. Common in humid montane and elfin forests on Cerro Chinguela on Piura-Cajamarca border at 2700-3600 m. *Andes of Venezuela to n Peru.*

Drab Hemispingus *Hemispingus xanthophthalmus* Hemispingo Simple
14.5 cm (5.75"). Plate 113. The only hemispingus with a gray head and pale eye. Fairly common and local in humid montane and elfin forests in Andes north to central Amazonas (s of Río Marañón) at 2500-3200 m. *Andes of Peru to w Bolivia.*

Three-striped Hemispingus *Hemispingus trifasciatus* Hemispingo Trilistado
14 cm (5.5"). Plate 113. ♪ 797. Recalls Black-capped Hemispingus but has ochre-buff underparts and an olive crown. Black-capped often forages in bamboo and lower-level vegetation; Three-striped tends to forage near canopy. Fairly common in humid montane and elfin forests north to Huánuco at 2900-3600 m. *Andes of central Peru to w Bolivia.*

Thlypopsis **Tanagers.** A group of five species of small tanagers, mostly with gray backs and some rufous on the head.

Rufous-chested Tanager *Thlypopsis ornata* Tangara Pechirfo
12.5 cm (5"). Plate 112. ♪ JM. Over most of its range the only tanager with a combination of gray mantle, completely rufous head and underparts (except for a white belly). Cf. Buff-bellied Tanager and very localized Brown-flanked Tanager. Fairly common in humid montane forests and scrub on e slope of Andes south to Cusco, and on Pacific slope south to Lima at 1800-3200 m. *Andes of s Colombia to Peru.*

Brown-flanked Tanager *Thlypopsis pectoralis* Tangara Flanquipardo
13.5 cm (5.3"). Plate 115. Similar to more widespread Rufous-chested Tanager, but flanks are brownish-gray. Uncommon and local in montane scrub in Huánuco, Pasco and Junín at 1800-3200 m. *Endemic to Peru.*

Orange-headed Tanager *Thlypopsis sordida* Tangara Cabecinaranja
13.5 cm (5.3"). Plate 112. The only gray tanager in its range with an orange hood. Uncommon along lowland rivers and islands e of Andes to 1000 m. *Venezuela to n Argentina, Amazonian and e Brazil.*

Buff-bellied Tanager *Thlypopsis inornata* Tangara Ventrianteado
12.5 cm (5"). Plate 115. Resembles Rufous-chested Tanager but underparts, sides of head and forecrown are buffy (not rufous). Rare in acacia and xeric scrub in drainage of upper Río Marañón in Amazonas and Cajamarca at 600-2000 m. Recently recorded near Tamborapa (Begazo *et al.* 2001). *Endemic to Peru.*

Rust-and-yellow Tanager *Thlypopsis ruficeps* Tangara Rufiamarillo
12.5 cm (5"). Plate 112. ♪ 797. The only yellow tanager with an orange-rufous head and yellow underparts. Immature is almost entirely yellow. Fairly common in montane forests (especially alders) on e slope of Andes north to Huánuco at 1200-3200 m. *Andes of central Peru to nw Argentina.*

Guira Tanager *Hemithraupis guira* Tangara Guira
12.5 cm (5"). Plate 112. ♪ 797. Male plumage is unique. Female is similar to female of sympatric Yellow-backed Tanager. Both are essentially olive above and yellow below. Female Guira has a yellow eye-ring. Female Yellow-backed is darker above and brighter yellow below, showing more contrast. Uncommon in humid lowland forests e of Andes to 1500 m. Recently recorded near Jaén and Manglares de Tumbes (Begazo *et al.* 2001). *S Venezuela and the Guianas to n Argentina and Brazil.*

Yellow-backed Tanager *Hemithraupis flavicollis* Tangara Lomiamarill0
12.5 cm (5"). Plate 114. ♪ 797. Male is unlikely to be confused. Female is similar to female Guira Tanager. Uncommon in humid *terra firme* and *várzea* forests e of Andes to 800 m. *Panama to n Bolivia and Amazonian Brazil.*

Hooded Tanager *Nemosia pileata* Tangara Encapuchada
12.5 cm (5"). Plate 112. ♪ 797. Male's head pattern, yellow eyes and legs are distinctive. Female has blue-gray upperparts, white underparts, white supraloral, pale eyes, pale lower mandible and yellow legs. Cf. Bicolored Conebill (dark eyes and bill and pink legs). Common and local in humid *várzea* and forest borders e of Andes to 600 m. *Venezuela and the Guianas to nw Argentina and Amazonian Brazil.*

Olive (Carmiol's) Tanager *Chlorothraupis carmioli* Tangara Olivácea
17 cm (6.6"). Plate 114. ♪ 797. The only tanager that is uniformly olive. Note the thick, heavy bill. Cf. female Hepatic Tanager. Common in humid forests along e slope of Andes north to Huánuco at 500-1200 m. *Nicaragua to w Bolivia.*

Gray-headed Tanager *Eucometis penicillata* Tangara Cabecigris
18 cm (7"). Plate 114. ♪ 797. A large olive and yellow tanager with a gray head and bushy crest. Cf. female White-shouldered Tanager (smaller, no crest). Fairly common in humid lowland *várzea* forests and woodlands e of Andes to 600 m. *Mexico to ne Argentina and Amazonian Brazil.*

***Lanio* Shrike-Tanagers.** A pair of mostly allopatric species with heavy, hooked bills that often associates with mixed-feeding flocks in humid forests.

Fulvous Shrike-Tanager *Lanio fulvus* Tangara Fulva
17 cm (6.6"). Plate 114. ♪ 677. Male is the only tanager in its range that is cinnamon-yellow with a black head and black wings. Note the tawny breast-band. Tawny female is similar to female Flame-crested Tanager, but has a richer rufescent crissum and rump. Uncommon in humid *terra firme* forests north of the Amazon and west of Río Huallaga to 900 m. *S Venezuela and the Guianas to ne Peru and n Amazonian Brazil.*

White-winged Shrike-Tanager *Lanio versicolor* Tangara Aliblanca
16 cm (6.5"). Plate 114. ♪ 797. Range barely overlaps with previous species, so male should not be confused. Brown female is very similar to female Flame-crested Tanager, but has yellower tones, especially on belly. Fairly common in lowland *terra firme* forests e of Andes south of the Amazon and east of Río Huallaga to 900 m. *W Amazonian Brazil, adjacent Peru and Bolivia.*

Rufous-crested Tanager *Creurgops verticalis* Tangara Crestirrufa
16 cm (6.5"). Plate 114. Unique. Slaty above (except crown in male) and rufous below. Superficially resembles Rusty Flowerpiercer. Uncommon in humid montane forests on e slope of Andes south to Ayacucho at 1400-2700 m. *Andes of sw Venezuela to e Peru.*

Slaty Tanager *Creurgops dentata* Tangara Pizarrosa
15 cm (6"). Plate 114. The slaty male with its rufous crown is distinctive. Female has a thin white superciliary, and white on lower belly and throat. Uncommon in humid montane forests north to Cordillera Vilcabamba at 1600-2200 m. *Andes of se Peru and w Bolivia.*

***Tachyphonus* Tanagers.** A group of six species in Peru, all of which are sexually dimorphic. In flight all males show white underwing linings.

Flame-crested Tanager *Tachyphonus cristatus* Tangara Crestifuego
16.5 cm (6.5"). Plate 114. The crest is conspicuous and varies in color from yellow to almost red. Note buffy throat-patch. Cf. Fulvous-crested Tanager. Female has no distinctive features and can be confused with shrike-tanagers, with other female *Tachyphonus* (but is more uniformly brown) or even various female antshrikes. Fairly common in humid *terra firme* and *várzea* forests in Loreto and Madre de Dios to 800 m. *S Venezuela and the Guianas to e Peru and Amazonian Brazil.*

Yellow-crested Tanager *Tachyphonus rufiventer* Tangara Crestiamarilla
15 cm (6"). Plate 111. Male is the only *Tachyphonus* with tawny underparts and a black pectoral band (sometimes lacking). Female is olive above, with an olive-gray head and yellowish underparts. Resembles female White-shouldered Tanager, but is "dirtier" and less contrasting. Fairly common in humid *terra firme* and *várzea* forests south of Río Marañón and the Amazon to 1200 m. *E Peru to n Bolivia and adjacent w Amazonian Brazil.*

Fulvous-crested Tanager *Tachyphonus surinamus* Tangara Crestifulva
16.5 cm (6.5"). Plate 114. Male's crest is narrow and sometimes concealed. A rufous flank patch is often visible. Lacks the buffy throat-patch of male Flame-crested. Female is similar to female Yellow-crested Tanager, but has a buffy eye-ring. Fairly common in humid *terra firme* and *várzea* forests south to Junín to 500 m. *S Venezuela and the Guianas to e Peru and Amazonian Brazil.*

White-shouldered Tanager *Tachyphonus luctuosus* Tangara Hombriblanco
12.5 cm (5"). Plate 114. ♪ 797. Male's conspicuous white shoulder is diagnostic. White-lined Tanager's white wing lining is sometimes visible at rest. Female is olive above and yellow below with a gray hood. Cf. female Yellow-crested Tanager (underparts not as yellow and not so hooded). Fairly common in humid *terra firme* and *várzea* forests e of Andes and w of Andes in Tumbes to 800 m. *Honduras to n Bolivia, Amazonian Brazil.*

White-lined Tanager *Tachyphonus rufus* Tangara Filiblanca
18 cm (7"). Plate 114. ♪ 797. Less arboreal than White-shouldered Tanager, and white of underwing is shown mostly in flight. Similar to local Red-shouldered Tanager, but larger and without any red. Female is reddish brown with paler underparts, and can be confused with many brown birds, but note general shape and bill. Common and local in humid lowland forests e of Andes south to Cusco to 1500 m. *Costa Rica to n Argentina and Amazonian Brazil.*

Red-shouldered Tanager *Tachyphonus phoenicius* Tangara Hombrirrojo
16 cm (6.5"). Plate 114. Smaller than widespread White-lined Tanager. Red on male's shoulder is diagnostic if seen. Female is distinctive—dark gray on top and smoky gray below, with blackish head contrasting with white throat. Common and very local in woodlands and savanna in sw Loreto, s San Martín and n Ucayali to 400 m. *S Venezuela and the Guianas to ne Peru and Amazonian Brazil.*

Black-goggled Tanager *Trichothraupis melanops* Tangara de Anteojos
16.5 cm (6.5"). Plate 114. ♪ 797. Male has a diagnostic black mask and a semiconcealed yellow crown patch. Female is similar but lacks "goggles" and crown patch. In flight both sexes show pale underwing patches and white bases to primaries. Uncommon in montane forests on e slope of Andes north to San Martín at 1000-2400 m. *E Brazil to ne Argentina; Andes of Peru and w Bolivia.*

Red-crowned Ant-Tanager *Habia rubica* Tangara-Hormiguera Coronirroja
18 cm (7"). Plate 114. ♪ 797. A tanager of lower story of forest interior. Male with its pale-red throat and crown should not be confused. Browner female is similar to female Silver-beaked Tanager. Common in humid lowland forests e of Andes to 900 m. *Mexico to ne Argentina, w Amazonian and e Brazil.*

Hepatic Tanager *Piranga flava* Piranga Bermeja
18 cm (7"). Plate 114. ♪ 623. Bill is fairly stout, darker above and paler below. Lores are grayish. Dark-red male is darker than adult male Summer Tanager. Female resembles female and immature Summer Tanager, but latter has a uniformly paler, longer bill, and lacks grayish lores. Uncommon in coastal lowlands from La Libertad to Lima, in montane deciduous forests on Pacific slope of Andes, and on e slope generally to 2000 m (sometimes to 3150 m). Peruvian population is part of *lutea* group that is sometimes recognized as a separate species (Highland Hepatic-Tanager). *SW US to n Argentina and Brazil.*

Scarlet Tanager *Piranga olivacea* Piranga Escarlata
18 cm (7"). Plate 114. ♪ 627. Both female and non-breeding male are essentially green with a yellow crissum and dusky (female) or blackish (non-breeding male) wings. Breeding male recalls Vermilion Tanager (black throat). Uncommon northern-winter visitor in humid lowland forests e of Andes to 1500 m. Recently recorded in Tumbes (Pyhälä and Noblecilla). *E Canada and US; winters mainly in upper Amazon basin.*

Summer Tanager *Piranga rubra* Piranga Roja
18 cm (7"). Plate 114. ♪ 626. Bill is fairly long and yellowish. Immature male is similar to female plumage. Cf. Hepatic and Scarlet Tanagers. Uncommon northern-winter visitor in montane forests on Pacific slope, and near base of e slope of Andes to 2000 m. *US and n Mexico; winters to Amazonia and West Indies.*

White-winged Tanager *Piranga leucoptera* Piranga Aliblanca
14 cm (5.5"). Plate 114. ♪ 741CD. The only tanager with such prominent wingbars (both sexes). Fairly common in humid montane forests on e slope of Andes at 1200-2000 m. *Mexico to Venezuela and w Bolivia.*

Red-hooded Tanager *Piranga rubriceps* Piranga Capuchirrojo
18 cm (7"). Plate 114. ♪ EC007T. The only tanager in its range that is all yellow except for a completely red head. Female's red hood is much reduced. Uncommon and local in humid montane forests south to Huánuco at 1700-3000 m. *Andes of Colombia to central Peru.*

Vermilion Tanager *Calochaetes coccineus* Tangara Bermellón
18 cm (7"). Plate 111. The only red tanager with black wings, tail, throat and lores. No known overlap with Masked Crimson Tanager (lower elevation, black band on belly). Rare to uncommon in humid montane forests on e slope of Andes south to Cordillera Vilcabamba at 1100-1900 m. Regularly seen near Abra Divisoria east of Tingo Maria; recorded at La Florida at 2265 m (JFC and TV). *Andes of se Colombia to e Peru.*

***Ramphocelus* Tanagers.** The three Peruvian species all have characteristic metallic-silver bills, and mostly inhabit forest edge.

Masked Crimson Tanager *Ramphocelus nigrogularis* Tangara Enmascarada
18.5 cm (7.2"). Plate 110. ♪ 542. The only red tanager with a black patch on the center of belly and a black mask. Female is similar, but duller, with a brownish patch on belly. Fairly common in lowland *várzea* forests e of Andes to 500 m. *Colombia to n Bolivia and w Amazonian Brazil.*

Huallaga Tanager *Ramphocelus melanogaster* Tangara del Huallaga
18 cm (7"). Plate 111. Similar to widespread Silver-beaked Tanager, but male has a bright red rump and crissum, and is not nearly as dark. Female has red around bill, and is redder than browner Silver-beaked Tanager. Common and local in forest borders and gardens in Río Huallaga Valley (San Martín and Huánuco) at 500-1000 m. *Endemic to Peru.*

Silver-beaked Tanager *Ramphocelus carbo* Tangara de Piquiplateado
18 cm (7"). Plate 110. ♪ 797. Male is unmistakable (but cf. local Huallaga Tanager). Female is uniformly brown with a silvery-gray beak (not nearly as shiny as male's bill). Female resembles female Red-crowned Ant-Tanager. Common in humid lowland forests east of Andes to 1000 m. One of most common tanagers in e lowlands. *S Venezuela and the Guianas to n Bolivia, e Paraguay and Brazil.*

***Thraupis* Tanagers.** Most members of the genus are extremely tolerant of human habitats, making them some of the most familiar birds of the country.

Blue-gray Tanager *Thraupis episcopus* Tangara Azuleja
16.5 cm (6.5"). Plate 110. ♪ 797. Unmistakable in much of its range. Pacific coast race *quaesita* (illustrated) lacks white shoulders of Amazon lowland populations. Immatures of all races have darker crowns (concolor with back) and lack white shoulders. Cf. Sayaca Tanager. Common in lowlands e of Andes and on Pacific slope south to Piura to 1500 m. Introduced in Lima in 1970s and very common. *Mexico to n Bolivia and Amazonian Brazil.*

[Sayaca Tanager] *Thraupis sayaca* Tangara Sayaca
16.5 cm (6.5"). Facing Plate 110. ♪ 797. Nearly identical to immature Blue-gray Tanager and probably cannot be safely separated in the field. Adult of sympatric Blue-gray has conspicuous white shoulders. It has been suggested that the two species are conspecific. Re-examination of specimens from intermontane valleys in Cusco are now believed to be immature Blue-gray Tanagers (pers. comm. TSS). Sight records from Madre de Dios are probably misidentified immature *T. episcopus*. *E Brazil to Bolivia, n Argentina, Uruguay and Paraguay.*

Blue-capped Tanager *Thraupis cyanocephala* Tangara Gorriazul
18 cm (7"). Plate 110. ♪ 797. The only tanager that has a combination of blue cap, olive back, yellow crissum and blue-gray on remaining underparts. Common in humid montane forests and woodlands on e slope of Andes, and on Pacific slope south to Cajamarca at 1800-3000 m. *Venezuela to Andes of Bolivia.*

Blue-and-yellow Tanager *Thraupis bonariensis* Tangara Azulamarillo
18 cm (7"). Plate 110. ♪ 797. Male is unmistakable in its range. Pale-brown female has a gray (sometimes with some blue) head, and resembles females of *Phrygilus* sierra-finches (especially Peruvian and Black-hooded), but note the different-shaped bill. Common in Pacific lowlands, intermontane valleys and Andean slopes to 3600 m. *Andes of Ecuador to n Chile, n Argentina and s Brazil.*

Palm Tanager *Thraupis palmarum* Tangara de Palmeras
18 cm (7"). Plate 110. ♪ 797. No other tanager has a similar wing pattern (blackish rear half of wing and grayish-olive front). Common in lowlands e of Andes (especially in palm groves) to 1200m. *Honduras to n Bolivia and Brazil*

***Buthraupis* Mountain-Tanagers.** Four species of large and boldly patterned tanagers (all with mostly yellow underparts) that inhabit high-elevation forests, generally near timberline.

Hooded Mountain-Tanager *Buthraupis montana* Tangara-de-Montaña Encapuchada
23 cm (9"). Plate 110. ♪ 797. No other tanager in its range has a blue back and nape, a black head and red eyes. Gregarious. Fairly common in humid montane forests on e slope of Andes at 2000-3200 m. *Venezuela to w Bolivia.*

Black-chested Mountain-Tanager *Buthraupis eximia* Tangara-de-Montaña Pechinegro
20 cm (8"). Plate 110. ♪ JM. No other tanager in its limited range has a blue cap, green back, and black face, throat and chest. Uncommon and local in humid montane forests on Cerro Chinguela at 2500 m in Cordillera de Colán. *Andes of sw Venezuela to nw Peru.*

***Golden-backed Mountain-Tanager** Buthraupis aureodorsalis* Tangara-de-Montaña Dorsidorado
22 cm (8.6"). Cover and Plate 111. The golden back of this spectacular tanager makes it virtually unmistakable. Uncommon in elfin forests (especially *Escallonia and Clusia*) near timberline in Andes of San Martín, La Libertad and Huánuco at 3000-3500 m. Best known from Carpish Ridge region (Huánuco), at Quilluacocha at 3325 m and Bosque Unchog at 3600 m. Recently recorded near treeline at Río Abiseo National Park (San Martín) and Mashua at 3200 m. *Endemic to Peru.*

***Masked Mountain-Tanager** Buthraupis wetmorei* Tangara-de-Montaña Enmascarada
20 cm (8"). Plate 110. ♪ JM. Note limited range. Only *Buthraupis* with a black mask, faint yellow superciliary, greenish crown and two blue wingbars. Rare in humid elfin and treeline forests on Cerro Chinguela at 2900 m. *Andes of sw Colombia to nw Peru.*

***Orange-throated Tanager** Wetmorethraupis sterrhopteron* Tangara Gargantinaranja
18 cm (7"). Plate 111. Unmistakable in its limited range. Uncommon and poorly known from humid foothills of Cordillera del Cóndor in drainage of Río Marañón at 600-900 m. Recorded 10 km south of Oracuzar, Amazonas at 450 m; from headwaters of Río Cenepa and hills northeast of Bagua at 600 m; and near Tupac Amaru II along road to Urakuza (Begazo *et al.* 2001). *Extreme se Ecuador in Zamora-Chinchipe and adjacent ne Peru.*

***Anisognathus* Mountain-Tanagers.** Three species of boldly patterned tanagers, generally smaller than *Buthraupis* mountain-tanagers.

Lacrimose Mountain-Tanager *Anisognathus lacrymosus* Tangara-de-Montaña Lacrimosa
18 cm (7"). Plate 110. ♪ EC007T. Widespread nominate ssp. (illustrated) has a single yellow spot below eye. Race *caerulescens* (n of Río Marañón) has an additional yellow spot behind ear coverts. Common in humid montane and elfin forests on e slope of Andes south to Cordillera Vilcabamba at 2500-3600 m. *Mts. of Venezuela to Peru.*

Scarlet-bellied Mountain-Tanager *Anisognathus igniventris* Tangara-de-Montaña Ventriescarlata
18.5 cm (7.2"). Plate 110. ♪ 797. Unlikely to be confused with any other Peruvian tanager. Common in montane and elfin forests near treeline on e slope of Andes at 2500-3500 m. *Andes of Venezuela to w Bolivia.*

Blue-winged Mountain-Tanager *Anisognathus somptuosus* Tangara-de-Montaña Aliazul
18 cm (7"). Plate 110. ♪ 797. An *Anisognathus* with yellow underparts and crown, and a diagnostic wing pattern. Common in humid montane forests on e slope of Andes at 1500-2500 m. *Mts. of Venezuela to Bolivia.*

Yellow-throated Tanager *Iridosornis analis* Tangara Gargantiamarilla
16 cm (6.5"). Plate 111. ♪ 742CD. The only tanager with a bright yellow throat and a tawny belly. Uncommon in humid montane forests on e slope of Andes south to Puno at 1300-2100 m. *Andes of se Ecuador to se Peru.*

Golden-collared Tanager *Iridosornis jelskii* Tangara Collardorado
15 cm (6"). Plate 111. The only tanager in its range with a rufous belly, black mask and yellow neck and crown. Rare to uncommon and local in montane woodlands near treeline north to La Libertad and San Martín at 2500-3500 m. *Andes of e Peru and w Bolivia.*

Golden-crowned Tanager *Iridosornis rufivertex* Tangara Coronidorada
17 cm (6.6"). Plate 118. ♪ LNS. Note limited range. A mostly blue tanager with a bright gold crown. Fairly common in humid montane and elfin forests on Cerro Chinguela (Piura-Cajamarca border) at 2500-3500 m. *Andes of Venezuela to n Peru.*

Yellow-scarfed Tanager *Iridosornis reinhardti* Tangara Bufanda Amarilla
16.5 cm (6.5"). Plate 118. A striking blue tanager with a bright gold scarf on rear crown and sides of neck. Locally common in montane scrub (especially *Chusia*) south and east of Río Marañón from s Amazonas and San Martín to Cordillera Vilcabamba at 2000-3400 m. Commonly recorded near Carpish Pass. *Endemic to Peru.*

Buff-breasted Mountain-Tanager *Dubusia taeniata* Tangara-de-Montaña Pechiantiada
19 cm (7.5"). Plate 110. ♪ LNS. The only tanager with bluish streaks on the crown and nape in race *stictocephala* (illustrated, s of Río Marañón) or a bluish streaked superciliary in nominate race (extreme north). Uncommon in humid montane and elfin forests on e slope of Andes south to Cusco at 2500-3500 m. *Andes of Venezuela to Peru.*

Chestnut-bellied Mountain-Tanager *Delothraupis castaneoventris* Tangara-de-Montaña Ventricastaña
17 cm (6.6"). Plate 111. ♪ 797. If seen well, malar stripe of this species is diagnostic. Smaller Fawn-breasted Tanager lacks malar stripe and is generally paler below. Uncommon in humid montane forests north to e La Libertad at 2200-3600 m. *Andes of e Peru and w Bolivia.*

Fawn-breasted Tanager *Pipraeidea melanonota* Tangara Pechiantiada
14 cm (5.5"). Plate 118. ♪ 797. The only small tanager with bluish upperparts and light buffy underparts. Uncommon in humid woodlands and clearings on e slope of Andes at 1500-2500 m and on Pacific slope south to Lima down to 700 m. *Venezuela to nw Argentina and se Brazil.*

Euphonia **Euphonias.** A genus of small tanagers with short finch-like bills and short tails. Sexually dimorphic. The males are mostly dark purple or dark blue above and yellow or orange below, often with yellow on crown or forehead. Note if throat is dark, and the amount of yellow on crown. Females with their mostly olive-green attire present a real identification challenge. Most of the ten species present in Peru inhabit lowland forest borders.

Plumbeous Euphonia *Euphonia plumbea.* Eufonia Plumbea
9.6 cm (3.75"). Plate 116. Male: upperparts and head are dark gray; remaining underparts yellow (gray scaling on sides) sharply bordered by yellow belly. Color pattern recalls that of Rufous-bellied Euphonia, but latter has blue-black upperparts and rufous belly. Female has a gray head and mantle and greenish-yellow underparts. Recent sight records and tape recordings from Jesus del Monte and near Yurimaguas, San Martín (Begazo *et al.* 2001). Occurrence of this rare euphonia in Peru marks a considerable extension westward from its published range (Ridgely and Tudor 1989). *Guianas, s Venezuela and n Amazonian Brazil.*

Purple-throated Euphonia *Euphonia chlorotica* Eufonia Gargantipurpúrea
10.cm (4"). Plate 116. ♪797. Male has pure yellow underparts and forecrown (that reaches just past eye), a dark throat and white undertail spots. Male Orange-bellied is very similar but has a tinge of ochre on underparts and crown. Female is only female *Euphonia* that is olive above with a small yellow frontlet, yellow flanks and crissum, and mostly white belly. Common in lowland scrub and woodlands along base of Andes north to Cajamarca, and along Amazon River system in Iquitos area to 1200 m. *Colombia to Argentina and Brazil.*

Orange-crowned Euphonia *Euphonia saturata* Eufonia Coroninaranja
10.cm (4"). Plate 116. Note limited range. Male has an orange cap that reaches the rear crown. Lacks white tail spots. Cf. Orange-bellied Euphonia (smaller crown patch, tail spots). Female is like a darker, thinner-billed version of female Thick-billed Euphonia. Rare in deciduous woodlands in Tumbes at 750-1000 m. *Andes of w Colombia to extreme nw Peru.*

Thick-billed Euphonia *Euphonia laniirostris* Eufonia Piquigrueso
11.5 cm (4.5"). Plate 116. ♪797. Note the thick bill in both sexes. Male is only Peruvian euphonia with a yellow throat. Female is nondescript, olive above and greenish-yellow below. Fairly common in humid lowland forests and scrub e of Andes, and south on Pacific slope to Cajamarca to 1200 m. *Costa Rica to n Bolivia and Amazonian Brazil.*

Golden-rumped Euphonia *Euphonia cyanocephala* Eufonia Lomidorado
11.5 cm (4.5"). Plate 116. ♪797. No other euphonia has a blue crown (both sexes). Much duller female recalls female Chestnut-breasted Chlorophonia (lacks rufous forecrown and is greener on throat). Common in humid foothills and montane woodlands on e slope of Andes at 500-2800 m. *Locally in mts. of n and w South America; se Brazil.*

Bronze-green Euphonia *Euphonia mesochrysa* Eufonia Verdibronceada
10.cm (4"). Plate 116. ♪797. Both sexes are nondescript. Male has a yellow forecrown and is similar to female Orange-breasted Euphonia, but has a yellow belly and crissum. Female is duller, has a pale-gray center to belly, and lacks a yellow forecrown. Uncommon in humid montane forests on e slope of Andes at 1000-2200 m. *Andes of Colombia to w Bolivia.*

White-lored Euphonia *Euphonia chrysopasta* Eufonia Loriblanco
11.5 cm (4.5"). Plate 116. ♪797. No other euphonia has a white foreface. Female is duller with grayish underparts, but retains the distinctive white lores and chin. Fairly common in humid lowland forests e of Andes to 900 m. *S Venezuela and the Guianas to Bolivia and Amazonian Brazil.*

White-vented Euphonia *Euphonia minuta* Eufonia Ventriblanco
9.6 cm (3.75"). Plate 116. ♪818CD. The white vent in both sexes is diagnostic. Male is the only euphonia with a yellow forecrown that barely reaches the eye. Female is only euphonia with a white throat and a clear yellow pectoral band. Fairly common in humid *terra firme* and *várzea* forests e of Andes to 1000 m. *Mexico to n Bolivia and Amazonian Brazil.*

Orange-bellied Euphonia *Euphonia xanthogaster* Eufonia Ventrinaranja
11.5 cm (4.5"). Plate 116. ♪797. Four ssp. occur in Peru. Males of all have a forecrown patch that extends past the eye, dark throat and white tail spots. In typical *dilutior* (ne Peru), *brevirostris* (illustrated, most of e Peru) and *quitensis* (nw Peru), underparts and forecrown patch are yellow with a tinge of ochre. Very similar to male Purple-throated Euphonia, but latter's underparts and forecrown are pure lemon-yellow. Race *brunneifrons* (se Peru) has ochre underparts and forecrown. Females of all ssp. have ochre forecrowns and gray rear crowns. Common in humid lowland and foothill forests e of Andes to 2000m, and on Pacific slope south to Lambayeque. Most common euphonia in subtropical forests. *Panama to n Bolivia, Amazonian and se Brazil*

Rufous-bellied Euphonia *Euphonia rufiventris* Eufonia Ventrirrufo
11.5 cm (4.5"). Plate 116. ♪797. Male is only Peruvian euphonia with no yellow/orange on crown. Female has a grayish crown and a yellow forehead (not ochre as in female Orange-bellied), a tawny crissum, grayish belly and olive-yellow flanks (not grayish as in White-lored). Fairly common in humid *terra firme* and *várzea* forests e of Andes to 500 m. *Venezuela to n Bolivia and w Amazonian Brazil.*

Chlorophonia **Chlorophonias.** A pair of small, colorful tanagers. Males in breeding plumage are very colorful; they are outnumbered by females and males in non-breeding plumage (which are similar to females).

Blue-naped Chlorophonia *Chlorophonia cyanea* Clorofonia Nuquiazul
11.5 cm (4.5"). Plate 117. ♪741CD. Male easily recognized. Female is duller, has greenish-yellow belly and greenish back, and a blue rump. Uncommon and local from lowlands to humid montane forests on e slope of Andes at 500-2000 m. *Disjunct in n South America to n Argentina and s Brazil.*

Chestnut-breasted Chlorophonia *Chlorophonia pyrrhophrys* Clorofonia Pechicastaño
11.5 cm (4.5"). Plate 117. ♪EC007T. Male easily recognized. Mostly greenish female has a yellowish belly and blue crown. Female Blue-naped Chlorophonia lacks blue crown; female Golden-rumped Euphonia lacks greenish throat and cheeks. Uncommon in humid montane forests and forest borders on e slope of Andes south to Pasco at 1500-2500m. *Andes of w Venezuela to e Peru*

Orange-eared Tanager *Chlorochrysa calliparaea* Tangara Orejinaranja
12.5 cm (5"). Plate 117. A small, mostly green tanager with an orange rump. Three ssp. occur, differing mostly by male's underparts: race *boucieri* (s to Huánuco, illustrated); nominate race (Pasco to Ayacucho) has deeper blue on belly; and *fulgentissima* (from Cusco south) has extensive violet from throat to mid-belly. Females of all races are duller and more uniform greenish. Fairly common in humid montane forests on e slope of Andes at 1100-1700 m. *Andes of Venezuela to w Bolivia.*

Tangara **Tanagers.** Some of the most colorful birds of the Neotropics belong to this genus. Peru is well-represented with 24 of the 49 members of the genus. Several members of the genus can often be seen together in canopy-feeding flocks in subtropical and montane forests .

Turquoise Tanager *Tangara mexicana* Tangara Turquesa
14 cm (5.5"). Plate 118. ♪797. The only *Tangara* with a dark hood and back, and yellow belly. Fairly common in humid lowland forests (especially *várzea*) e of Andes to 1000 m. *S Venezuela and the Guianas to n Bolivia, Amazonian and se Brazil.*

Paradise Tanager *Tangara chilensis* Tangara del Paraíso
14 cm (5.5"). Plate 117. ♪797. No other *Tangara* has an apple-green head, red rump and blue underparts. Rump and back are red in widespread nominate race, or red back contrasts with yellow rump in *chlorocorys* (upper Huallaga Valley). Common in humid *terra firme* and *várzea* forests e of Andes to 1500 m. *Venezuela to n Bolivia and Amazonian Brazil.*

Green-and-gold Tanager *Tangara schrankii* Tangara Verdidorada
14 cm (5.5"). Plate 117. ♪797. The only green tanager with a yellow belly and rump and streaked mantle. Female has a green crown. Common in humid *terra firme* and *várzea* forests e of Andes to 900m. *Venezuela to n Bolivia, w Amazonian Brazil*

Golden Tanager *Tangara arthus* Tangara Dorada
13.5 cm (5.3"). Plate 117. A golden-yellow *Tangara* with a conspicuous black patch on ear coverts and a streaked back. Fairly common in humid subtropical forests on e slope of Andes at 1000-2500 m. *Mts. of Venezuela to Andes of w Bolivia.*

Golden-eared Tanager *Tangara chrysotis* Tangara Orejidorada
14 cm (5.5"). Plate 117. Similar to Saffron-crowned Tanager, but central crown to nape is black. It has only a black malar (not a black chin). Uncommon in humid montane forests on e slope of Andes at 1100-2300 m. *Andes of Colombia to w Bolivia.*

Saffron-crowned Tanager *Tangara xanthocephala* Tangara Coroniazafrán
13.5 cm (5.3"). Plate 117. ♪EC007T. The only green tanager with a golden head, black chin and tawny belly. Common in humid montane forests on e slope of Andes at 1300-2400 m. *Andes of Venezuela to w Bolivia.*

Flame-faced Tanager *Tangara parzudakii* Tangara Carifluego
14 cm (5.5"). Plate 117. ♪EC007T. Unmistakable. The only black-backed tanager with a black ear-patch and throat (sometimes connected), scarlet forecrown and cheeks. Common in humid montane forests on e slope of Andes s to Cusco at 1500-2500 m. *Andes of Venezuela and Colombia to se Peru.*

Yellow-bellied Tanager *Tangara xanthogastra* Tangara Ventriamarillo
12 cm (4.75"). Plate 117. ♪797. The only small greenish tanager with bluish wings, heavily spotted upperparts and chest, and a yellow belly. Similar Spotted Tanager has whitish face, throat and belly. See local Dotted Tanager. Uncommon in humid *terra firme* and *várzea* forests e of Andes to 900 m. *Venezuela to n Bolivia and Amazonian Brazil.*

Spotted Tanager *Tangara punctata* Tangara Moteada
12.5 cm (5"). Plate 117. Similar to Yellow-bellied Tanager, but throat and belly are whitish, and wings are edged green. Fairly common in humid foothill forests along e base of Andes at 500-1500 m. *S Venezuela and the Guianas to n Bolivia and Amazonian Brazil.*

Dotted Tanager *Tangara varia* Tangara Mancheada
11.5 cm (4.5"). Facing Plate 117. Note limited range. Small, almost entirely grass-green, with bluish wings (greenish in female) and tail. Male has very small black dots on underparts and crown. Both Yellow-bellied and Spotted Tanagers are larger, and heavily spotted on underparts. Rare and local. Recently collected near headwaters of Río Cushabatay (pers. comm. TSS). This is a marked westward extension of previously known range (Ridgely and Tudor 1989). *S Venezuela to the Guianas and n Amazonian Brazil.*

Bay-headed Tanager *Tangara gyrola* Tangara Cabecibaya
14 cm (5.5"). Plate 118. ♪797. Adult is unmistakable. Immature is mostly green with varying amounts of rufous on face. Tumbes race *nupera* lacks yellow nuchal collar. Fairly common in humid lowland and foothill forests e of Andes to 1500 m, and on Pacific slope in Tumbes. *Costa Rica to n Bolivia and Amazonian Brazil.*

Burnished-buff Tanager *Tangara cayana* Tangara Anteado Bruñido
14 cm (5.5"). Plate 118. ♪797. Both sexes have a pale-rufous crown and dark mask. Illustrated male is unmistakable. Female is duller, with a greenish back. Cf. allopatric Green-capped Tanager (green crown). Common and local in arid intermontane valleys in San Martín, and savanna of Pampas del Heath to 1200 m. *S Venezuela and the Guianas to ne Argentina and Amazonian Brazil.*

*Green-capped Tanager *Tangara meyerdeschauenseei* Tangara Gorriverde
14 cm (5.5"). Plate 115. The only tanager in its very limited range with a greenish-straw crown, dull greenish-gray upperparts and grayish-buff underparts. Female is similar, but has a yellower crown. Fairly common and local in semiarid riparian scrub in headwaters of Río Inambari near Sandia, and on w side of Abra de Maruncunca (Puno) at 1750-2200 m. *Endemic to Peru.*

Golden-naped Tanager *Tangara ruficervix* Tangara Nuquidorada
12.5 cm (5"). Plate 118. A blue tanager with a tawny belly. Two ssp. occur in Peru. Illustrated race *inca* (north to Junín) has most of body dark blue, with a rufous nape. Most of body of *amabilis* (south to Huánuco) is lighter blue, nape patch is golden (framed with black), and mantle is spotted. Cf. pale-naped races of Blue-and-black Tanager. Uncommon in humid montane forests on e slope of Andes at 1500-2400 m; rare on Pacific slope in Tumbes. *Andes of Colombia to w Bolivia.*

Metallic-green Tanager *Tangara labradorides* Tangara Verdimetálico
12.5 cm (5"). Plate 117. A dull, bluish-green tanager, with a black cap (contrasting pale forecrown), black scapulars (contrasting bluish-green mantle and shoulders). Uncommon in humid montane forests on e slope of Andes south to San Martín at 1500-2400 m. *Andes of Colombia to ne Peru.*

Blue-browed Tanager *Tangara cyanotis* Tangara Cejiazul
12 cm (4.75"). Plate 118. The only *Tangara* with a mostly black head and back, and a bluish superciliary that reaches nape. Uncommon in humid montane forests on e slope of Andes at 1400-2200 m. *Andes of Colombia to w Bolivia.*

Blue-necked Tanager *Tangara cyanicollis* Tangara Cuelliazul
12.5 cm (5"). Plate 118. Unmistakable. A mostly black tanager with a bright blue hood, and iridescent shoulders and rump. Common in humid montane forests on e slope of Andes at 500-2000 m. *Venezuela to Bolivia and w Amazonian Brazil.*

Masked Tanager *Tangara nigrocincta* Tangara Enmascarada
12.5 cm (5"). Plate 118. ♪797. Pattern similar to Blue-necked Tanager, but has a white belly, blue shoulders and blue rump. Fairly common in humid lowland forests (especially *várzea*) e of Andes to 900 m. *S Venezuela and the Guianas to n Bolivia and w Amazonian Brazil.*

Beryl-spangled Tanager *Tangara nigroviridis* Tangara Lentejuelada
13.5 cm (5.3"). Plate 118. ♪EC007T. Note prominent bluish spangles on underparts. Recalls southern race of Blue-and-black Tanager (darker below, with a smaller black mask that doesn't extend past eye). Common in humid montane forests and forest borders on e slope of Andes at 1500-2500 m. *Mts. of Venezuela to Andes of Bolivia.*

Blue-and-black Tanager *Tangara vassorii* Tangara Azulinegra
12.5 cm (5"). Plate 118. ♪ LNS. Three ssp. occur. Race *atrocaerulea* (illustrated, north to Huánuco) has a pale nape and spotted underparts. Compare Beryl-spangled and Golden-naped Tanagers. Races *branickii* (s of Río Marañón to Huánuco) and *vassorii* (nw Peru) are nearly all blue except for black lores, tail and wings (blue wingbar and lesser coverts). Head is slightly paler and greener in *branickii*. Uncommon in humid montane forests on e slope of Andes and on Pacific slope south to Cajamarca at 2000-3400 m. *Andes of Venezuela to Bolivia.*

Sira Tanager *Tangara phillipsi* Tangara del Sira
12.5 cm (5"). Plate 115. Note limited range. Male is a bluish tanager with a black hood, blue throat and blue ear coverts. Female has green back, bluish throat and ear coverts, bordered below by gray breast. Uncommon in humid montane and cloud forests on Cerros del Sira at 1300-1570 m. *Endemic to Peru.*

Silver-backed Tanager *Tangara viridicollis* Tangara Dorsiplateado
12.5 cm (5"). Plate 115. A dark tanager with orange-rufous throat and ear coverts, and silvery-gray mantle. Female is olive with a brownish head, and orange-brown throat and ear coverts. Fairly common and local in humid montane forests on e slope of Andes at 1000-2200 m. Regular near train station at Machu Picchu. *Andes of s Ecuador and e Peru.*

Straw-backed Tanager *Tangara argyrofenges* Tangara Dorsipaja
12.5 cm (5"). Plate 115. Pattern resembles Silver-backed Tanager, but back is straw-yellow and throat is bluish-green. Female has yellow mantle, rump and sides, greenish wings and tail, bluish-green throat and ear coverts. Rare and local in humid subtropical Andean forests in w San Martín, s Amazonas and Junín at 1300-1700 m. Recorded at Abra Patricia at 1890 m (JFC and TV). *Andes of Peru and w Bolivia.*

Opal-rumped Tanager *Tangara velia* Tangara Lomiopalina
14 cm (5.5"). Plate 118. ♪ 677. The only bluish tanager in its range with a chestnut belly and crissum, and a pale-yellowish rump. Uncommon in humid *terra firme* and *várzea* forests e of Andes to 500 m. *S Venezuela and the Guianas to n Bolivia and Brazil.*

Opal-crowned Tanager *Tangara callophrys* Tangara Coroniopalina
14.5 cm (5.75"). Plate 118. ♪ 542. Recalls Opal-rumped Tanager, but has yellowish superciliary and forehead, and blue belly and crissum. Uncommon in humid *terra firme* and *várzea* forests e of Andes south to Puno to 1000 m. *Colombia to n Bolivia and w Amazonian Brazil.*

Golden-collared Honeycreeper *Iridophanes pulcherrima* Tangara Mielero
12 cm (4.75"). Plate 118. Bill is fairly long and narrow, and eyes are reddish. Male is distinctive (black head, whitish underparts and rump). Female has a rufous collar, olive-brown upperparts, and paler dingy underparts. Uncommon in humid montane forests on e slope of Andes south to Cusco at 900-1900 m. *Andes of Colombia to e Peru.*

Dacnis **Dacnises.** Four species of small tanagers with pointed bills, that display marked sexual dimorphism. Males are mostly blue and black, and females are brownish-olive to vivid green.

White-bellied Dacnis *Dacnis albiventris* Dacnis Ventriblanco
11.5 cm (4.5"). Plate 116. ♪ 797. Male is similar to Black-faced Dacnis, but darker blue (not bright turquoise), and black mask does not extend to nape and mantle. Female is dingy, greenish above and yellowish below. Rare in humid *terra firme* and *várzea* forests e of Andes in Loreto to 400 m. Recently recorded at Manu Lodge (John Arvin). *Venezuela to ne Peru and Amazonian Brazil.*

Black-faced Dacnis *Dacnis lineata* Dacnis Carinegra
11.5 cm (4.5"). Plate 116. Male is distinctive with its turquoise body, black face mask and mantle, and yellow eyes. Female is fairly uniform olive, paler below, with yellow eyes. Common in humid *terra firme* and *várzea* forests e of Andes to 1300 m. *S Venezuela and the Guianas to n Bolivia and Amazonian Brazil.*

Yellow-bellied Dacnis *Dacnis flaviventer* Dacnis Ventriamarillo
12.5 cm (5"). Plate 116. ♪ 677. Male is distinctive (bold black-and-yellow pattern and red eyes). Female is similar to female Black-faced Dacnis, but has red eyes. Uncommon in humid lowland *várzea* forests e of Andes to 500 m. *Venezuela to n Bolivia and w Amazonian Brazil.*

Blue Dacnis *Dacnis cayana* Dacnis Azul
12.5 cm (5"). Plate 116. ♪ 797. Male is distinctive (turquoise body, black chin and red eyes). Female is green-bodied with bluish head. Cf. female Green Honeycreeper (decurved yellowish bill and green head). Common in humid *terra firme* and *várzea* forests e of Andes to 1000 m. *Honduras to ne Argentina and s Brazil.*

Green Honeycreeper *Chlorophanes spiza* Mielero Verde
14 cm (5.5"). Plate 116. ♪ 797. Both sexes have a yellow bill with a black culmen. Male has a black head and red eyes. Two ssp. occur. Male of race *caerulescens* (e Peru) has a more greenish-blue body than illustrated race *exsul* (nw Peru). Female is only nondescript, small green bird with a slightly decurved bill. Common in humid *terra firme* and *várzea* forests e of Andes, and on Pacific slope in open woodlands in Tumbes to 1500 m. *Mexico to Bolivia and Amazonian Brazil.*

***Cyanerpes* Honeycreepers.** A trio of small, short-tailed, nectar-feeding birds with slender, decurved bills. Males are violet-blue and black; females are greenish with streaked underparts.

Short-billed Honeycreeper *Cyanerpes nitidus* Mielero Piquicorto
9.6 cm (3.75"). Plate 116. Shorter-billed than other *Cyanerpes*. Male is similar to Purple Honeycreeper, but legs are reddish (not yellow). Female is similar to female Purple Honeycreeper, but Short-billed has pink legs and lacks buff on ear coverts. Rare in humid *terra firme* and *várzea* forests e of Andes south to Junín and Ucayali to 400 m. *Venezuela to e Peru and w Amazonian Brazil.*

Purple Honeycreeper *Cyanerpes caeruleus* Mielero Púrpura
11.5 cm (4.5"). Plate 116. The male is the only *Cyanerpes* with bright-yellow legs. Female is green above, streaked with green below, and has a blue malar stripe, buffy streaks on ear coverts, and greenish-yellow legs. Common in humid *terra firme* and *várzea* forests e of Andes to 1200 m. *E Panama to n Bolivia and Amazonian Brazil.*

Red-legged Honeycreeper *Cyanerpes cyaneus* Mielero Patirroja
11.5 cm (4.5"). Plate 116. ♪ 797. Both sexes have longer tails than other *Cyanerpes*. Male in breeding plumage is distinctive with its bright red legs and black mantle. In flight shows bright-yellow underwings. Female and non-breeding male are olive above and pale yellowish below, with dusky streaks and reddish legs. Uncommon in humid *terra firme* and *várzea* forests e of Andes to 1000 m. *Mexico to Amazonian Brazil; Cuba.*

Tit-like Dacnis *Xenodacnis parina* Azulito Altoandino
12.5 cm (5"). Plate 115. ♪ LNS. Three ssp. occur. Male of races *petersi* (illustrated, Cordillera Blanca) and *bella* (Amazonas) are larger and more lightly streaked than fairly uniform and duller nominate race (Junín s to Arequipa). Female has rufous-brown underparts with a blue cap (nominate), or blue forecrown (*petersi* and *bella*). Uncommon to common but local in montane scrub and *Gynoxys-Polylepis* forests from Amazonas south to Cusco and Arequipa at 3000-4600 m. *Andes of s Ecuador and Peru.*

Swallow-Tanager *Tersina viridis* Azulejo Golondrina
15 cm (6"). Plate 118. ♪797. Male resembles a blue cotinga in coloration, but has a conspicuous white belly. Often perches on exposed bare branches. Female is greenish with a yellowish belly and greenish barring on flanks. Fairly common but erratic in humid lowland forests e of Andes to 1500 m. *Panama to ne Argentina and Brazil.*

Plush-capped Finch (Plushcap) *Catamblyrhynchus diadema* Gorriafelpado
14 cm (5.5"). Plate 124. ♪797. A distinctive finch-like tanager with a bright yellow forecrown and rufous underparts. Fairly common in humid montane and elfin forests (especially *Chusquea* bamboo) on e slope of Andes, and on Pacific slope south to Lambayeque at 2300-3500 m. *Mts. of n Venezuela to nw Argentina.*

Pardusco *Nephelornis oneilli* Pardusco
12.5 cm (5"). Plate 115. Within its limited range the only brownish bird with a small tit-like bill. Common and local in elfin forest near timberline in San Martín, La Libertad and Huánuco at 3000-3800 m. Best known from Carpish Ridge region of Huánuco. Recently recorded at Kuelap, Amazonas (MP). *Endemic to Peru.*

Emberizidae (Buntings and Sparrows; Semilleros y Espigueros). Species: World 327; Peru 95
Another large family of mostly seed-eating passerines, and a catch-all that includes five main groups—the buntings, brush-finches and the New World finches, seedeaters and sparrows. They are a predominately New World family, but the *Emberiza* buntings are mainly confined to the cooler parts of the Palearctic region. The New World species range from the Arctic tundra to the southern tip of South America. The ubiquitous Rufous-collared Sparrow (*Zonotrichia capensis*) can be found at sea level along the coast of Peru to over 5,000 meters (16,000 feet) on the altiplano. The Yellow-bridled Finch (*Melanodera xanthogramma*) has the distinction of being the southernmost-breeding passerine in the world, inhabiting Chile's bleak Cape Horn Archipelago at 56° S latitude. Recent studies include the nectar-eating flowerpiercers in this faminly.

*****Black-masked Finch** *Coryphaspiza melanotis* Pinzón Enmascarado
13.5 cm (5.3"). Plate 124. ♪797. Note limited range. Both sexes have broad white tips to pointed undertail feathers. Male has a bold head pattern. Female is duller and has "shadow" of male's head pattern. Fairly common in savanna grasslands in Pampas del Heath. *E Brazil to ne Argentina, se Paraguay and extreme se Peru.*

Red-crested (Red-pileated) Finch *Coryphospingus cucullatus* Pinzón Crestirroja
13.5 cm (5.3"). Plate 124. ♪797. Male is the only red finch with a bright red median crown stripe, borered by a black lateral stripe, and a narrow white eye-ring. Duller female lacks male's crown stripes, but retains white eye-ring and pinkish underparts and rump. Common in arid intermontane valleys north to Marañón Valley to 1500 m. *Chaco of Brazil to Argentina, Paraguay and Bolivia.*

Crimson-breasted Finch *Rhodospingus cruentus* Pinzón Carmesí
11.5 cm (4.5"). Plate 122. Male is unmistakable. Drab female has a longer bill than any *Sporophila*, and lacks the yellow wingbar of a siskin. (Sometimes called Crimson Finch, but this conflicts with long-standing English name of *Neochmia phaeton* of Australia and New Guinea). Locally common along Pacific slope in arid scrub south to Piura (rarely Lambayeque) to 300 m. *W Ecuador and extreme nw Peru.*

Phrygilus **Sierra-Finches.** True to their name, the seven species of sierra-finches are all high-Andean species. Some are boldly patterned, while others are dull-plumaged.

Black-hooded Sierra-Finch *Phrygilus atriceps* Fringilo Capuchinegro
15 cm (6"). Plate 124. ♪ 797. Male has a black hood and chestnut mantle. Female has dark-slate hood and rufous-brown mantle. Shows greater sexual dimorphism than Peruvian Sierra-Finch (where both sexes have dark-gray hood and ochre-olive mantle). Common in montane scrub and *Polylepis* woodlands in Arequipa and Tacna at 2400-4000 m. Rare straggler (possibly breeding) at Pampa Galeras. *Andes of s Peru to n Chile and nw Argentina.*

Peruvian Sierra-Finch *Phrygilus punensis* Fringilo Peruano
15 cm (6"). Plate 122. ♪ 797. Over most of its range the only dark-hooded sierra-finch. Sexes are similar (female is duller). In Puno overlaps with Black-hooded Sierra-Finch, but latter's mantle is rufous to chestnut. Fairly common in montane scrub and rocky areas from Cajamarca south to Arequipa and Puno at 2000-4000 m. *Andes of Peru and w Bolivia*

Mourning Sierra-Finch *Phrygilus fruticeti* Fringilo Pechinegro
18 cm (7"). Plate 124. ♪ 797. The largest sierra-finch. Male has a yellow bill, and much of the throat and breast are black. The female is the largest streaky-brown finch in its range, and has two white wingbars and rufous-brown cheeks. Common in arid montane scrub north to Cajamarca at 2000-4000 m. *Andes of Peru to Tierra del Fuego.*

Plumbeous Sierra-Finch *Phrygilus unicolor* Fringilo Plomizo
15 cm (6"). Plate 124. ♪ 797. An all lead-gray sierra-finch. Juvenile is brownish and heavily streaked; females are gray with dark, bold streaks. Ash-breasted Sierra-Finch is smaller and paler. Fairly common in *puna* and *páramo* grasslands at 3000-4500 m. *Andes of Venezuela to Tierra del Fuego.*

White-throated Sierra-Finch *Phrygilus erythronotus* Fringilo Gargantiblanca
18 cm (7"). Plate 122. The only sierra-finch that has a gray mantle with a broad gray breast-band, contrasting with a white throat. Female is similar but has brown mantle. Cf. White-winged Diuca-Finch. Uncommon in high-altitude *puna* grasslands and rocky slopes in Arequipa, Moquegua and Tacna at 3650-4750 m. *Andes of s Peru, w Bolivia and n Chile.*

Band-tailed Sierra-Finch *Phrygilus alaudinus* Fringilo Colifajeado
15 cm (6"). Plate 124. ♪ 797. The only sierra-finch that shows a white band close to the base of the tail (easily visible in flight). Band-tailed Seedeater has a similar tail-band, but is smaller, has a shorter bill, and a chestnut to rusty vent. Female Band-tailed Sierra-Finch is gray with bold streaks on chest. Some males (molting?) are much grayer than illustrated. Fairly common on arid coastal slopes and rocky montane slopes to 3500 m. *Andes of Ecuador to nw Argentina and central Chile.*

Ash-breasted Sierra-Finch *Phrygilus plebejus* Fringilo Pechicenizo
12.5 cm (5"). Plate 124. ♪ 797. A plain-looking sparrow-like sierra-finch. Look for an ash breast and brownish, faintly streaked back. Female and immature are like immature Plumbeous Sierra-Finch, but latter's streaks are bolder and darker. Common in *puna* and *páramo* grasslands and montane scrub at 2500-4500 m. Isolated population near coast in Tumbes and Piura. *Andes of Ecuador to n Chile and nw Argentina.*

White-winged Diuca-Finch *Diuca speculifera* Diuca Aliblanca
19 cm (7.5"). Plate 124. ♪ 797. No other finch in its range has similar markings on wings, throat and below the eye. Common in high-altitude *puna* grasslands north to Ancash and Lima at 4500-5350 m. *Andes of Peru to nw Chile and nw Argentina.*

Short-tailed Finch *Idiopsar brachyurus* Fringilo Colicorta
18.5 cm (7.2"). Plate 122. ♪ 797. Note limited range. Recalls male Plumbeous Sierra-Finch, but is larger with a longer and heavier bill. Rare in boulder-scattered *puna* grasslands in Puno at 3300-4500 m. *S Peru to nw Argentina.*

Cinereous Finch *Piezorhina cinerea* Fringilo Cinéreo
16.5 cm (6.5"). Plate 122. ♪ 797. Note limited range. The only gray finch in its range with a heavy yellow bill. Common in coastal desert plains with scattered shrubs from Tumbes to La Libertad to 300 m. *Endemic to Peru (vagrant to extreme s Ecuador).*

*Slender-billed Finch *Xenospingus concolor* Fringilo Apizarrado
15 cm (6"). Plate 122. The only uniformly gray finch in its range with a slender, bright-yellow bill. Juvenile has an olive back and dark bill. Rare and local and declining along Pacific slope north to Lima to 600 m (occasionally to 1800 m). Best known from El Fiscal (where Pan-American Highway crosses Río Tambo), in riparian thickets at Lagunas de Mejía, Ocucaje, Ica, and olive groves in Yauca Valley (Arequipa). *Coastal w Peru and n Chile.*

Incaspiza **Inca-Finches.** A genus of arid-slope finches endemic to Peru. The five species share the common characteristics of a yellow bill, some black at the base of bill, and white outer tail feathers.

Great Inca-Finch *Incaspiza pulchra* Fringilo-Inca Grande
16.5 cm (6.5"). Plate 119. An inca-finch with a brown mantle and much rufous on wings. Similar to Rufous-backed Inca-Finch (limited overlap), but latter has a rufous mantle. Note also differences in distribution of black on face: Great Inca-Finch has a black bib and lores (gray malar area); Rufous-backed has black surrounding base of bill. Cf. Band-tailed Sierra-Finch. Uncommon and local on xerophytic and cactus-covered mountain slopes on Pacific slope in Ancash and Lima at 1000-2750 m. Regularly reported on upper parts of Santa Eulalia road. *Endemic to Peru.*

Rufous-backed Inca-Finch *Incaspiza personata* Fringilo-Inca Dorsirrufo
16.5 cm (6.5"). Plate 119. Similar to Great Inch-Finch, but entire rufous back recalls Buff-bridled Inca-Finch. Uncommon in dry montane scrub (especially *Puya raimondii*) in upper Río Marañón Valley drainage from s Cajamarca to w Huánuco at 1800-4000 m. Best known from area between Huariaca (Pisco) and Ambo (Huánuco) on Central Highway. *Endemic to Peru.*

*Gray-winged Inca-Finch *Incaspiza ortizi* Fringilo-Inca Aligris
16.5 cm (6.5"). Plate 119. The only inca-finch that lacks any rufous on back or wings. Shy. Uncommon and local on dry cactus-covered hillsides in Piura and Cajamarca at 1800-2300 m. Known from three sites: Hacienda Limón east of Celendín (Cajamarca); La Esperanza, 5 km ne of Santa Cruz (central Cajamarca); and 2 km ne of Huancabamba (Piura). *Endemic to Peru.*

Buff-bridled Inca-Finch *Incaspiza laeta* Fringilo-Inca Frenillo Anteado
14.5 cm (5.75"). Plate 119. The only inca-finch with a buff malar stripe. Shy. Fairly common in xerophytic scrub and *Bombax* woodlands in Marañón Valley from se Cajamarca and extreme s Amazonas to La Libertad and n Ancash at 1500-2750 m. Regularly recorded around 2000 m along Celendín-Balsas-Leimebamba road, and at Huancabamba at 2125 m. *Endemic to Peru.*

Little Inca-Finch *Incaspiza watkinsi* Fringilo-Inca Chico
12.5 cm (5"). Plate 119. The smallest inca-finch, and the only one in its limited-elevation range. Uncommon and poorly known from desert scrub of middle Río Marañón drainage in n Cajamarca and adjacent Amazonas at 700-900 m. Most often recorded in arid scrub near Bagua Grande (Amazonas). *Endemic to Peru.*

Poospiza **Warbling-Finches and Mountain-Finches.** Four species of finches which are mostly well marked and generally inhabit arid montane scrub.

*Plain-tailed Warbling-Finch *Poospiza alticola* Monterita Colisimple
16 cm (6.5"). Plate 119. Unmistakable in its range. Rare to uncommon in *Polylepis-Gynoxys* woodlands in s Cajamarca, w La Libertad and e Ancash at 3500-4300 m, rarely down to 2900 m. Locally fairly common at a few sites in Huascarán National Park. *Endemic to Peru.*

*Rufous-breasted Warbling-Finch *Poospiza rubecula*   Monterita Pechirufo
16.5 cm (6.5"). Plate 117. Unlikely to be confused in its range. Very rare in montane composite shrub (especially *Eupatorium*) on both slopes of w Andes from extreme s Cajamarca to Lima (Ica?) at 2350-3700 m. Only documented breeding is in its stronghold at Bosque Zárate (Lima). Elsewhere recorded from 2790 m between Celendín and Balsas, Cajabamba at 2750 m, La Caldera at 3500 m, and along Santa Eulalia road at elevations ranging from 2400-3650 m. *Endemic to Peru.*

Chestnut-breasted Mountain-Finch *Poospiza caesar*   Monterita Pechicastaño
18.5 cm (7.2"). Plate 119. Unmistakable in its limited range. Fairly common in arid montane scrub in Apurímac, Cusco and Puno at 2600-3900 m. *Endemic to Peru.*

Collared Warbling-Finch *Poospiza hispaniolensis*   Monterita Acollarada
13.5 cm (5.3"). Plate 119. The boldly patterned male is easily identified. Female is duller and browner, and has shadow of male's pattern (cheeks are browner, and collar is replaced by dusky streaking). Uncommon on arid Pacific slope of Andes south to Arequipa to 1500 m, occasionally to 2500 m. *SW Ecuador and w Peru.*

Blue-black Grassquit *Volatinia jacarina*   Semillerito Negriazulado
10.cm (4"). Plate 124. ♪ 797. Male is easily recognized by its glossy, blue-black plumage. Female is a drab brown, pale dusky below, with streaks on the breast and flanks. Male repeatedly jumps up and down from its perch when singing. Common and widespread along Pacific slope, and in lowlands e of Andes to 1000 m. *Mexico to s Argentina and Chile.*

Sporophila **Seedeaters.** Small, sexually dimorphic finches with short, stubby bills. Found mostly in grasses and scrub. Males are often gray or black, occasionally chestnut. Females are difficult to distinguish, and are best identified in presence of males.

Slate-colored Seedeater *Sporophila schistacea*   Espiguero Pizarroso
11.5 cm (4.5"). Plate 122. ♪ 797. Within its limited range. male is the only gray seedeater with a yellow bill. Note small white wingbar, whitish belly and whitish undertail coverts. Female is uniformly brownish above and buffy below. Uncommon in humid lowlands e of Andes in Huánuco and Madre de Dios to 1500 m. *Mexico to n Bolivia and n Brazil.*

Plumbeous Seedeater *Sporophila plumbea*   Espiguero Plomizo
11.5 cm (4.5"). Plate 122. ♪ 797. Note limited range and habitat. Male is the only seedeater with pale-gray upperparts, whitish underparts and a dark bill. Female is nearly identical to female Slate-colored Seedeater, but Plumbeous is a savanna species. Rare in tropical savanna in Pampas del Heath. *S Venezuela and the Guianas to ne Argentina and Amazonian Brazil.*

Caqueta Seedeater *Sporophila murallae*   Espiguero de Caqueta
11.5 cm (4.5"). Plate 109. ♪ 542. Male is black and white with two weak wingbars, whitish rump, black pectoral band (sometimes incomplete or reduced), and a partial nuchal collar. Female is similar to Plumbeous Seedeater, but overall coloration is a warmer brown. Common in lowlands e of Andes south to Cusco and Madre de Dios to 1200 m. *SE Colombia to e Brazil, e Ecuador and e Peru.*

Variable Seedeater *Sporophila corvina*   Espiguero Variable
11.5 cm (4.5"). Plate 109. ♪ 542. Like Caqueta Seedeater (no overlap), but lacks wingbars. Underparts are clean white with a well-defined pectoral band. Females are alike. Formerly considered conspecific with Caqueta Seedeater. Common in agricultural and shrubby areas along Pacific slope south to La Libertad at 1000 m. *Mexico to nw Peru.*

Lesson's Seedeater *Sporophila bouvronides* Espiguero de Lesson
11.5 cm (4.5"). Plate 122. The only seedeater mostly black above and white below, that has an entirely black crown and a prominent white malar stripe. Lined Seedeater has a white crown stripe. The female is buffy-brown above, pale buffy below, and has a horn-yellow bill. Common northern-winter visitor in humid lowlands e of Andes to 800 m. *N South America; winters to n Peru and w Amazonian Brazil.*

Lined Seedeater *Sporophila lineola* Espiguero Lineado
11.5 cm (4.5"). Plate 109. ♪ 797. Similar to Lesson's Seedeater, but has a white median crown stripe. Female is probably inseparable in the field. Common austral-winter migrant in humid lowlands e of Andes to 1200 m. *N Argentina, Paraguay and se Brazil; winters in n South America.*

Black-and-white Seedeater *Sporophila luctuosa* Espiguero Negriblanco
11.5 cm (4.5"). Plate 109. ♪ JM. Male is the only seedeater that has all black upperparts (note small white spot on the wing), with a black throat and white belly. Female is brown above, buffy below and has a dark billl. Cannot be safely separated in the field from female Yellow-bellied Seedeater. Common in montane grasslands on e slope of Andes at 1200-2500 m. *Andes of Venezuela to Bolivia.*

Yellow-bellied Seedeater *Sporophila nigricollis* Espiguero Ventriamarillo
11.5 cm (4.5"). Plate 109. ♪ JM. Male is the only seedeater with a black face and chest, yellowish underparts and olive-green upperparts. Female is like female Black-and-white Seedeater. Common in grassy and agricultural areas on Pacific slope south to Lambayeque and Cajamarca, and in lowlands e of Andes to 2000 m. *Costa Rica to ne Argentina and Brazil.*

Double-collared Seedeater *Sporophila caerulescens* Espiguero Dobleacollarado
11.5 cm (4.5"). Plate 109. ♪ 797. Male is easily recognized by its pale-yellow bill, head pattern and chest band. Brownish female has a whitish belly and yellowish bill. Common austral-winter migrant in lowlands e of Andes to 1000 m. *Brazil to n Argentina, adjacent Bolivia and Paraguay.*

Drab Seedeater *Sporophila simplex* Espiguero Simple
11.5 cm (4.5"). Plate 122. A dull brownish seedeater with a dusky yellowish bill, and two whitish wingbars. Cf. Dull-colored Grassquit and female Parrot-billed Seedeater. Fairly common on lower Andean slopes from La Libertad to Ica and in upper Río Marañón drainage to 1500 m. *Disjunct in arid s Ecuador and w Peru.*

White-bellied Seedeater *Sporophila leucoptera* Espiguero Ventriblanco
12 cm (4.75"). Plate 122. ♪ 797. Accidental. Somewhat similar to Slate-colored Seedeater, but underparts are whiter, giving it a bicolored appearance. Single record from Tambopata. *Suriname and Brazil to ne Argentina, e Bolivia and Paraguay.*

Parrot-billed Seedeater *Sporophila peruviana* Espiguero Pico de Loro
11.5 cm (4.5"). Plate 122. No other seedeater has such a heavy bill with a curved culmen. Female recalls Drab Seedeater. Uncommon and local along arid Pacific littoral south to Ica (occasionally to Arequipa) to 800 m. *SW Ecuador and w Peru.*

Tawny-bellied Seedeater *Sporophila hypoxantha* Espiguero Ventrileonado
10.cm (4"). Plate 122. Accidental. Tawny on entire underparts and tawny rump, pale-gray back and crown. Chestnut-bellied Seedeater has slate-gray rump and gray sides. Recent sight records from Pampas del Heath (Schulenberg *in litt.*). *Savanna of Brazil, Bolivia, Paraguay and n Argentina.*

Dark-throated Seedeater *Sporophila ruficollis* Espiguero Gargantioscura
11 cm (4.25"). 122. Accidental. No other seedeater has a combination of black throat, rufous belly, rufous rump and gray crown. Recent sight records from Pampas del Heath (Schulenberg *in litt.*). *Chaco of s Brazil to n Bolivia, Paraguay and Argentina.*

Chestnut-bellied Seedeater *Sporophila castaneiventris* Espiguero Ventricastaño
10.cm (4"). Plate 109. ♪677. The only primarily slate-gray seedeater with chestnut median underparts. Common in humid lowlands e of Andes to 500 m. Generally the most common seedeater in its range. *S Venezuela and the Guianas to n Bolivia and Amazonian Brazil.*

Chestnut-throated Seedeater *Sporophila telasco* Espiguero Garganticastaña
10.cm (4"). Plate 109. Male is easily recognized by its small chestnut upper throat, a white band on rump and streaking on back. Female is pale-brownish, with dusky streaking above and whitish below, has a horn-colored bill, and a small white patch on the base of the primaries. Common along Pacific littoral and in upper Río Marañón Valley to 1000 m. *Colombia to extreme n Chile.*

Oryzoborus **Seed-Finches.** A trio of finches with enormous bills that exhibit marked sexual dimorphism. Males are mostly black or black and chestnut. Females are tawny and may be confused only with the female Blue-black Grosbeak. The genus poses a great taxonomic headache. We follow the treatment suggested by Sibley 1996.

Large-billed Seed-Finch *Oryzoborus crassirostris* Semillero Piquigrande
14 cm (5.5"). Plate 109. ♪652. Male is mostly black with a white speculum and a huge white bill. Tawny female has a black bill. Uncommon and local in humid lowlands e of Andes from Loreto to Huánuco to 700 m. *Colombia to sw Ecuador, n Peru, Venezuela,the Guianas and n Brazil.*

Black-billed Seed-Finch *Oryzoborus atrirostris* Semillero Piquinegro
15 cm (6"). Plate 122. Similar to Large-billed Seed-Finch, but bill is black. Females cannot be safely separated in the field. Sometimes regarded as a ssp. of Great-billed Seed-Finch (*O. maximilliani*). Rare and local in humid lowlands e of Andes to 1100 m. *E Ecuador, e Peru and n Bolivia.*

Chestnut-bellied (Lesser) Seed-Finch *Oryzoborus angolensis* Semillero Menor
12.5 cm (5"). Plate 109. ♪797. Male: no other finch has the combination of thick bill, black head and chestnut belly. Bròwnish female is similar to other *Oryzoborus* females, but smaller with a smaller bill. Fairly common in humid lowland forests and woodlands e of Andes to 1500 m. *S Colombia to the Guianas, Brazil and ne Argentina.*

Blue Seedeater *Amaurospiza concolor* Semillero Azul
12.5 cm (5"). Plate 113. Accidental? Male is uniformly dark blue-black with a stubby bill. Blueblack Grassquit and Slaty Finch are similar, but both have more pointed bills. Female is uniformly brown. Three specimens recently collected from *Chusquea* bamboo stands in Bosque de Monteseco (Cajamarca) at 2000 m, with possible sight records from Piura (Salinas *et al.* 1998). *Rare and local in mts. of s Mexico to s Ecuador.*

Catemenia **Seedeaters.** A trio of primarily high-elevation grass and shrub seedeaters. Males have chestnut vents and richly colored pink or yellow bills.

Band-tailed Seedeater *Catamenia analis* Semillero Colifajeado
12 cm (4.75"). Plate 109. ♪797. Both sexes have yellow bills and a conspicuous broad white band on tail. Band-tailed Sierra-Finch lacks chestnut vent and has a longer bill. Common in montane grasslands and scrub at 1000-3000 m, down to 300 m on Pacific slope. *Andes of Colombia to n Chile and nw Argentina.*

Plain-colored Seedeater *Catamenia inornata* Semillero Simple
14 cm (5.5"). Plate 109. ♪797. Similar to Páramo Seedeater, but paler, and bill has more reddish tones. Female is similar to female Páramo Seedeater, but is darker (especially on underparts), and crissum is buff. Plain-colored favors drier grassland and scrub; Páramo Seedeater favors edge of cloud forest. Fairly common in montane *puna* and *páramo* grasslands at 2500-3500 m. *Andes of Venezuela to nw Argentina.*

Páramo Seedeater *Catamenia homochroa* Semillero Paramero
13.5 cm (5.3").Plate 122. ♪ 797. A dark seedeater of higher-elevation cloud forests, with a pinkish (or yellow) bill. Similar to Plain-colored Seedeater, but darker, especially around face and breast, and tail feathers are more pointed. Female is dark brown above with streaking, lighter below, with a chestnut crissum and gray cheeks. Rare in humid montane and elfin forests at 2500-3500 m. *Mts. of Venezuela to w Bolivia.*

Dull-colored Grassquit *Tiaris obscura* Semillero Pardo
11.5 cm (4.5"). Plate 122. ♪ 797. Sexes alike. A dull brownish-gray seedeater with paler underparts and a bicolored bill (grayish above and yellowish below). It resembles many female seedeaters, but generally does not associate with them. Watch for pairs or small groups of similar-looking dull seedeaters. Uncommon in woodland borders and clearings on Pacific slope south to Arequipa, and on lower montane slopes of Andes at 500-2000 m. *Venezuela to nw Argentina.*

Slaty Finch *Haplospiza rustica* Fringilo Pizarroso
13 cm (5.2"). Plate 113. ♪ JM. Associated with bamboo. Uniformly slaty, with a conical, very pointed bill. Female is olivaceous above and whitish below. with dark streaks on throat and breast. Blue Seedeater has a thicker bill. Uncommon in humid montane and elfin forests on e slope of Andes, and on Pacific slope south to Lambayeque at 1500-2500 m. *Mexico to w Bolivia.*

Diglossa **Flowerpiercers.** Nine species of warbler-like birds with uniquely shaped, specialized bills used to pierce the base of flowers. The upper mandible ends with a hook, while the lower is upturned. They range mostly in montane forests, occasionally reaching treeline.

Rusty Flowerpiercer *Diglossa sittoides* Pinchaflor Pechicanelo
12 cm (4.75"). Plate 113. ♪ JM. Male is the only flowerpiercer with bluish-slate upperparts and cinnamon underparts. No bird with a similar color pattern has a similar bill. Female is olive-brown with paler underparts. Uncommon on Pacific slope south to Lima, and in humid montane forests on e slope of Andes at 1500-3000 m. *Mts. of Venezuela to nw Argentina.*

White-sided Flowerpiercer *Diglossa albilatera* Pinchaflor Flanquiblanco
13 cm (5.2"). Plate 113. ♪ EC007T. A dark slate-gray flowerpiercer with a partially concealed white tuft at base of wings and underwing coverts (noticeable in flight). Female is olive-brown above, paler below, with less prominent white tufts than male. Common in humid montane forests on e slope of Andes south to Cordillera Vilcabamba at 1800-2800 m. *Mts. of n Venezuela to Andes of Peru.*

Glossy Flowerpiercer *Diglossa lafresnayii* Pinchaflor Satinado
14.5 cm (5.75"). Plate 113. ♪ JM. Within its elevation range generally the only all black flowerpiercer. Usually shows a bluish shoulder patch, and lacks white on underwing. Slightly larger than nearly identical Black Flowerpiercer (latter lacks shoulder patch and usually found at lower elevations). Common in montane forests and shrubby clearings near treeline in Cajamarca at 2700-3700 m. *Andes of Venezuela to n Peru.*

Moustached Flowerpiercer *Diglossa mystacalis* Pinchaflor Mostachoso
14.5 cm (5.75"). Plate 113, 115. ♪ 797. Three ssp. occur in Peru. A large flowerpiercer with a buffy-white malar stripe (*albilinea*, Cusco and Puno) or a malar stripe and pectoral band in races *pectoralis* (Huánuco to Junín), and *unicincta* (Amazonas to c Huánuco). Pectoral band is rufous in *pectoralis* or white with cinnamon upper half of band in *unicincta*. Immature is blackish with mottled underparts and a whitish malar stripe. Uncommon to common in elfin forest and humid *páramo* scrub on e slope of Andes north to Amazonas at 2500-4000 m. *Andes of Peru and w Bolivia.*

Black Flowerpiercer *Diglossa humeralis* Pinchaflor Negro
14 cm (5.5"). Plate 113. ♪ JM. Similar to Glossy Flowerpiercer (limited overlap) but slightly smaller and with a finer bill. Always lacks pale shoulders. Cf. White-sided Flowerpiercer. Common in montane scrub and gardens north and west of Río Marañón (Piura and Cajamarca) at 800-2000 m, occasionally to 3000 m. *Andes of Venezuela to nw Peru.*

Black-throated Flowerpiercer *Diglossa brunneiventris* Pinchaflor Gargantinegra
14 cm (5.5"). Plate 115. ♪ 797. Note rufous underparts with gray flanks, black median throat, rufous malar stripe, black upperparts and gray rump. Immature is similar to immature Moustached Flowerpiercer, but malar stripe is indistinct and underparts are buffier. Fairly common in arid and humid montane forests and *Polylepis* woodlands north to Amazonas and s Cajamarca at 2500-4000 m, occasionally lower. *Andes of n Colombia; Peru to n Chile.*

Deep-blue Flowerpiercer *Diglossopis glauca* Pinchaflor Azul Intenso
12 cm (4.75"). Plate 113. ♪ 797. The only dark blue flowerpiercer with bright yellow eyes. Fairly common in humid montane forests on e slope of Andes at 1100-2300 m. *Andes of Colombia to w Bolivia.*

Bluish Flowerpiercer *Diglossopis caerulescens* Pinchaflor Azulado
13.5 cm (5.3"). Plate 113. ♪ EC007T. A dull bluish flowerpiercer with paler blue upperparts and the only one without a markedly upturned bill. Fairly common in humid montane forests on e slope of Andes at 1600-2700 m. *Mts. of Venezuela to Andes of w Bolivia.*

Masked Flowerpiercer *Diglossopis cyanea* Pinchaflor Enmascarado
15 cm (6"). Plate 113. ♪ 797. The only flowerpiercer that is deep blue with a black mask and red eyes. Common in humid montane and elfin forests on e slope of Andes, and on Pacific slope south to Cajamarca at 2000-3500 m. *Mts. of Venezuela to Andes of w Bolivia.*

Sicalis **Yellow-Finches.** Nine species of large, grain-feeding finches that reach their greatest diversity in the high Andes. They inhabit grasslands and feed on the ground, often in large flocks. Identification is somewhat difficult—note especially location, extent and amounts of yellow, gray, and any streaking (or lack thereof).

Puna Yellow-Finch *Sicalis lutea* Chirigüe de la Puna
13 cm (5.2"). Plate 124. ♪ 797. The brightest unstreaked yellow-finch. Sexes much alike. No other yellow-finch shows as much yellow on upperparts. Greenish Yellow-Finch has a darker, olive-green back. Common in high *puna* grasslands north to Cusco and Arequipa at 3500-4300 m. *S Peru, w Bolivia and nw Argentina.*

Saffron Finch *Sicalis flaveola* Chirigüe Azafranado
14 cm (5.5"). Plate 124. ♪ 797. Male is the only nearly all yellow finch with a conspicuous orange crown. Immature has a unique yellow pectoral band. Common in agricultural and arid scrub along Pacific slope south to Ancash to 1000 m. *Venezuela and Guianas to central Argentina and Brazil.*

Grassland Yellow-Finch *Sicalis luteola* Chirigüe Común
12.5 cm (5"). Plate 123. ♪ 797. A yellow-finch with a streaked back and crown. Best identified by characteristic facial markings—yellow lores and yellow around eye (especially under the eye). Raimondi's is grayer, especially on flanks, and lacks yellow facial markings. Female is duller; immature is browner and heavily streaked. Uncommon along coastal lowlands, and in tall montane grasslands to 3000 m. *Mexico to Chile and s Argentina.*

Stripe-tailed Yellow-Finch *Sicalis citrina* Chirigüe Colilistada
12 cm (4.75"). Plate 123. ♪ 797. Note limited range. If seen, the white stripes on tail are diagnostic. Otherwise, look for a plain-faced, streak-backed yellow-finch with an unstreaked crown and a yellow-orange forecrown. Grassland Yellow-Finch has stronger facial markings and streaked crown. Female Stripe-tailed Yellow-Finch has brownish streaks on yellowish underparts. Rare and local in montane grasslands in Puno at ca. 3000 m. *Venezuela to n Argentina and s Brazil.*

Bright-rumped Yellow-Finch *Sicalis uropygialis* Chirigüe Rabadilla Dorsibrillante
14 cm (5.5"). Plate 124. ♪ 797. Note that yellow rump contrasts with darker back. Male is the only yellow-finch of higher elevations that has gray cheeks and back. Males of races *connectens* (illustrated, Huancavelica to s Cusco) and nominate (Puno) have gray flanks; race *sharpei* (Cajamarca to Junín) is darker on back, has a shorter bill, olive crown, and lacks gray sides. Females are like males but duller, with less defined markings. Common in high *puna* grasslands north to Cajamarca at 4000-4800 m. *Andes of Peru to nw Argentina and n Chile.*

Greenish Yellow-Finch *Sicalis olivascens* Chirigüe Verdoso
14 cm (5.5"). Plate 124. ♪ 797. Male is similar to Puna Yellow-Finch, but has olive-green upperparts and yellow-olive tone to underparts. Female has a brownish-olive back with indistinct streaks. Puna Yellow-Finch favors puna grasslands; Greenish favors cultivated areas and scrub. Common in montane shrubbery on Pacific slope north to Ancash, and in Andes north to La Libertad at 2500-3800 m. *Andes of Peru to n Chile and nw Argentina.*

Orange-fronted Yellow-Finch *Sicalis columbiana* Chirigüe Frentinaranja
11.5 cm (4.5"). Plate 123. Accidental. Similar to Saffron Finch, but smaller. Male shows orange only on forecrown and has gray lores. One old record from the Río Ucayali (Loreto) ca 300 m. *Amazonian Brazil and adjacent Orinoco River basin.*

Raimondi's Yellow-Finch *Sicalis raimondii* Chirigüe de Raimondi
11.5 cm (4.5"). Plate 123. Male in fresh plumage has an unstreaked gray back, flanks, sides and cheeks. Molting male has streaked olive back and crown, and much reduced gray on flanks. Female is plain, drab brownish-gray with dingy underparts. Cf. Grassland Yellow-Finch. Locally fairly common but erratic on arid xerophytic slopes and fog vegetation on Pacific slope from Cajamarca to Arequipa at 500-2000 m (occasionally descends to sea level and recorded as high as 3450 m). Flock of 300 recorded in Quebrada de Burros (Tacna) at 30 m (GE). *Endemic to Peru.*

Sulphur-throated Finch *Sicalis taczanowskii* Chirigüe Gargantiazufrada
12 cm (4.75"). Plate 123. No other finch has such a thick bill and a yellow chin. May be confused only with female Parrot-billed Seedeater, which is more uniform and lacks yellow chin. Often seen in very large flocks. Common but erratic along arid Pacific littoral south to La Libertad to 200 m. *SW Ecuador and nw Peru.*

Wedge-tailed Grass-Finch *Emberizoides herbicola* Sabanero Colicuña
18 cm (7"). Plate 122. ♪ 797. Note limited range. Distinctive with its long pointed tail, heavily streaked upperparts and yellow bill. Common in tall grasslands in Pampas del Heath. *Costa Rica to ne Argentina and Brazil.*

Red-capped Cardinal *Paroaria gularis* Cardenal Gorrirrojo
16.5 cm (6.5"). Plate 121. ♪ 542. Unmistakable and conspicuous. Common along lowland lakes, rivers and streams e of Andes to 400 m. *S Venezuela and Guianas to n Bolivia and Amaz. Brazil.*

Olive Finch *Lysurus castaneiceps* Pinzón Oliváceo
15 cm (6"). Plate 122. ♪ 741CD. A dark finch with olive body, gray face and rufous crown. Rare and local in humid montane forests on e slope of Andes from Piura to Amazonas and Pasco to Cusco at 700-2200 m. *Colombia to e Peru.*

Atlapetes **Brush-Finches.** A large genus of finches, well represented in Peru in mostly montane scrub and forest edge. They often travel in family groups. Head patterns are often diagnostic. The species accounts presented here vary significantly from that in Ridgely and Tudor (1989) and Fjeldså and Krabbe (1990). We follow a recent revision of the genus by Garcia-Moreno and Fjeldså (1999).

Pale-naped Brush-Finch *Atlapetes pallidinucha* Matorralero Nuquipálida
18 cm (7"). Facing Plate 120. ♪ JM. Note limited range. Similar to sympatric race *latinuchus* of Cloud-forest Brush-Finch, but breast is yellow-olive, and crown stripe is cinnamon on forecrown, fading rapidly to whitish rear crown. Lacks wing speculum. Common in montane forests on Cerro Chinguela on Piura-Cajamarca border at 2800-3600 m. *Venezuela to nw Peru.*

Tricolored Brush-Finch *Atlapetes tricolor* Matorralero Tricolor
18 cm (7"). Plate 120. ♪ 742CD. The only *Atlapetes* with a golden-yellow crown stripe and yellow underparts. Sympatric *Atlapetes* have a mostly rufous crown stripe. Uncommon and local in montane forests and scrub on e slope of Andes from San Martín to Puno at 1500-2650 m. *Pacific slope of Colombia and Ecuador and e Andean slope of Peru.*

Cloud-forest Brush-Finch *Atlapetes latinuchus* Matorralero Nuquirrufa
17 cm (6.6"). Plate 120. ♪ 797. Four ssp. occur in Peru. Told from any sympatric brush-finch by solid rufous crown stripe and clear yellow breast. All congeners share rufous crown, black sides to face and yellow underparts. Nominate *latinuchus* (e slope s to Amazonas) has a white speculum on wing (other ssp. lack it); *comptus* (Pacific slope s to Piura) and *baroni* (s Cajamarca to Ancash) have a noticeable yellow supraloral (in other ssp. concolor to crown); *baroni* and *chugurensis* (Pacific slope of Cajamarca) have pale napes (in other ssp. concolor with crown). Common in montane forest borders and shrubs on Pacific slope south to La Libertad at 1500 to 3000 m. *Andes of Colombia to n Peru.*

Rufous-eared Brush-Finch *Atlapetes rufigenis* Matorralero Orejirrufa
19 cm (7.5"). Plate 120. The only gray, rufous-headed *Atlapetes* in its range. Lacks black around the eye or black lores. Locally fairly common in montane scrub and *Polylepis* woodlands in headwaters of Río Marañón in western Andes, generally at 3000-4300 m. *Endemic to Peru.*

Apurímac Brush-Finch *Atlapetes forbesi* Matorralero de Apurímac
19 cm (7.5"). Plate 120. The only gray, rufous-headed *Atlapetes* in its range. Note the black lores and white supraloral spot. Locally fairly common in montane scrub from Apurímac to sw Cusco at 2750-4000 m. Recorded once near Limbani (Puno), and regularly recorded at Bosque de Ampay. *Endemic to Peru.*

Slaty Brush-Finch *Atlapetes schistaceus* Matorralero Pizarroso
18 cm (7"). Facing Plate 120. ♪ JM. A gray brush-finch with a rufous crown, white throat, black malar stripe and white supraloral spot. Race *schistaceus* (Cerro Chinguela) has white wing speculum; race *taczanowskii* (Huánuco to Junín) lacks it. Cf. White-winged Brush-Finch (paler nape). Bay-crowned Brush-Finch is similar, but has a darker crown and is found primarily w of Andes. Fairly common in humid montane forests on Cerro Chinguela on Piura-Cajamarca border, and on e slope of Andes from Huánuco to Junín at 2500-3500 m. *Venezuela to central Peru.*

*Black-spectacled Brush-Finch *Atlapetes melanops* Matorralero de Anteojos
19 cm (7.5"). Plate 120. Note limited range. The only gray, rufous-headed *Atlapetes* in its range. The large black eye-patch is diagnostic. Uncommon and local in montane scrub on both sides of gap where Río Mantaro intersects Cordillera Central (Huancavelica-Ayacucho border) at 2600-3500 m. *Endemic to Peru.*

Vilcabamba Brush-Finch *Atlapetes terborghi* Matorralero de Vilcabamba
17 cm (6.6"). Facing Plate 120. Note limited range. The only *Atlapetes* in its range with combination of greenish-yellow underparts, black forecrown, and rufous on remainder of crown. Sides of head black. Allopatric with Dark-faced Brush-Finch. Uncommon in humid montane forest and shrubs on Cordillera Vilcabamba (Cusco) at 2500-3550 m. *Endemic to Peru.*

Cusco Brush-Finch *Atlapetes canigenis* Matorralero de Cusco
18 cm (7"). Plate 120. The only gray *Atlapetes* in its limited range. Mostly gray with a rufous crown. Fairly common in humid montane forest and scrub in Cusco at 2500-3500 m. *Endemic to Peru.*

Dark-faced Brush-Finch *Atlapetes melanolaemus* Matorralero Boliviano.
17 cm (6.6"). Facing Plate 120. The only *Atlapetes* in its range that has the combination of yellow underparts with black streaks, black forecrown and rufous on remainder of crown. Sides of head black. Fairly common in humid montane forest and shrubs from Cusco to Puno at 2000-3000 m. *SE Peru and nw Bolivia.*

Bay-crowned Brush-Finch *Atlapetes seebohmi* Matorralero Coronibayo
17 cm (6.6"). Plate 120. A gray *Atlapetes* with a dark chestnut crown (slightly paler in race *simonsi* in Piura and Lambayeque), black malar stripe and whitish supraloral spot. Sympatric with White-winged Brush-Finch, but latter has a white speculum and pale-rufous crown. Similar to Slaty Brush-Finch (no overlap) but latter's crown is brighter rufous. Locally fairly common in dry scrub and woodlands on Pacific slope of Andes south to Ancash at 1200-2500 m. *S Ecuador to nw Peru.*

Rusty-bellied Brush-Finch *Atlapetes nationi* Matorralero Ventrirrojizo
17 cm (6.6"). Plate 120. Similar to Bay-crowned Brush-Finch (no overlap), but has rusty vent and belly and a dark crown. Fairly common in dry brushy montane slopes and *Polylepis* woodlands from Lima to Arequipa at 2000-4000 m. *Endemic to Peru.*

White-winged Brush-Finch *Atlapetes leucopterus* Matorralero Aliblanca
15 cm (6"). Plate 120. ♪ JM. A small gray *Atlapetes* with a white wing speculum, pale-rufous crown and a white supraloral. Pacific slope population *dresseri* has varying amounts of white on face. Race *paynteri* (humid scrub from ne Piura to n Cajamarca border region) has paler nape and darker cheeks and may represent a separate species. Fairly common in dry woodlands south to Lambayeque and Cajamarca at 750-2500 m. *W Ecuador to nw Peru.*

White-headed Brush-Finch *Atlapetes albiceps* Matorralero Cabeciblanca
15 cm (6"). Plate 120. An unmistakable gray *Atlapetes* with a white face, black crown and white wing speculum. Locally common in xeric and semiarid woodlands south to Lambayeque at 400-1200 m. *Extreme s Ecuador and nw Peru.*

Chestnut-capped Brush-Finch *Buarremon brunneinucha* Matorralero Gorricastaño
19 cm (7.5"). Plate 121. ♪ 613. An olive-backed brush-finch with a rufous crown and black pectoral band. Cf. Stripe-headed Brush-Finch. Fairly common in humid submontane forests on e slope of Andes south to Puno at 1000-2500 m. *Mexico to se Peru.*

Stripe-headed Brush-Finch *Buarremon torquatus* Matorralero Cabecilistada
19 cm (7.5"). Plate 121. ♪ 797. The only brush-finch with a striped crown. Central and se Peru race *poliophrys* (illustrated) has a black pectoral band, but *assimilis* and *nigrifrons* (both nw Peru) lack pectoral band. Fairly common in humid montane forests on Pacific slope south to La Libertad, and on e slope from Huánuco to Cusco at 1800-3650 m. *Venezuela to nw Argentina*

Arremon **Sparrows.** A trio of forest-floor species, all with bold patterns of black-and-white stripes on head, and a black pectoral band.

Orange-billed Sparrow *Arremon aurantiirostris* Gorrión Piquinaranja
15 cm (6"). Plate 121. ♪613. Distinguished from any other *Arremon* by its bright-orange bill. Uncommon in humid lowland forests e of Andes south to Huánuco, and on Pacific slope in Tumbes to 1200 m. *Mexico to e Peru.*

Pectoral Sparrow *Arremon taciturnus* Gorrión Pectoral
15 cm (6"). Plate 121. ♪797. The only *Arremon* in its Peruvian range. Uncommon in humid lowland forests e of Andes in Cusco, Madre de Dios and Puno to 1000 m. *S Venezuela and the Guianas to n Bolivia and Amazonian Brazil.*

Black-capped Sparrow *Arremon abeillei* Gorrión Gorrinegro
15 cm (6"). Plate 122. Easily told from Orange-billed sparrow by its black bill. Nominate race (w Peru s to Cajamarca) differs from *nigriceps* (upper Marañón Valley) by having a gray mantle and shorter superciliary that begins above the eye. Fairly common in deciduous forests and woodlands on Pacific slope south to Cajamarca, and in Marañón Valley to 900 m. Race *nigriceps* may represent a separate species (Marañón Sparrow). *SW Ecuador and nw Peru.*

Black-striped Sparrow *Arremonops conirostris* Gorrión Negrilistado
17 cm (6.6"). Plate 122. ♪565. Accidental. A sparrow with an olive back, and a gray head with black lateral crown stripes and eye-line. Single record by TAP at Cotrina (Tumbes) at 650 m. *Honduras to Venezuela, w Ecuador and extreme n Brazil.*

Tumbes Sparrow *Aimophila stolzmanni* Gorrión de Tumbes
14.5 cm (5.75"). Plate 122. Unmistakable in its limited range and habitat. Note striped crown and rufous shoulder. Fairly common in arid scrub south to sw Cajamarca and n La Libertad, from sea level to 1400 m. *SW Ecuador and nw Peru.*

Ammodramus **Sparrows.** A pair of brownish sparrows, with varied amounts of yellow on the face, that inhabits grassy areas east of Andes.

Grassland Sparrow *Ammodramus humeralis* Gorrión de Pajonal
12.5 cm (5"). Plate 109. ♪797. Note limited range. Similar to widespread Yellow-browed Sparrow, but inhabits taller grass, and yellow is confined to a supraloral spot. Common in grassy savanna in Pampas del Heath. *Venezuela and the Guianas to Argentina and Brazil.*

Yellow-browed Sparrow *Ammodramus aurifrons* Gorrión Cejiamarilla
13.5 cm (5.3"). Plate 109. ♪797. Similar to previous species, but yellow encompasses much of face (extends to eyebrows, cheeks and malar). Common in grassy and agricultural areas in lowlands along e base of Andes to 1000 m. *S Venezuela to n Bolivia and w Amazonian Brazil.*

Rufous-collared Sparrow *Zonotrichia capensis* Gorrión Cuellirrufo
15 cm (6"). Plate 109. ♪797. One of the most widespread birds in the country. Adult is unmistakable. Streaky juvenile is darker overall than most other similarly streaked birds (finches, etc.), and is often accompanied by adults. Common to abundant throughout montane areas and down to sea level. Absent from Amazonia. *Mexico to Tierra del Fuego.*

Cardinalidae (Saltators, Grosbeaks and Allies; Saltadores y Picogruesos)
Species: World 43; Peru 12

A poorly defined, loose assemblage of passerines, often (and probably better) included in the Emberizidae. This heterogeneous collection includes grosbeaks, cardinals, saltators, some buntings and some finches. Most are seedeaters, and supplement their diets with protein when available.

Saltator **Saltators.** A group of medium-sized arboreal finches that inhabit mostly forest edges.

Streaked Saltator *Saltator striatipectus* Saltador Listado
20 cm (8"). Plate 121. Three ssp. occur in Peru. All have a dark, yellow-tipped bill. Race *immaculatus* (Lambayeque to Ica, illustrated) and *flavicollis* (s to Lambayeque) are similar in having unstreaked underparts and a broad whitish superciliary; *flavicollis* is slightly yellower below and more olive above, and immatures are sometimes streaked below. Race *peruvianus* (upper Marañón Valley) has profusely streaked underparts, dark olive-brown upperparts, and a thin, short white superciliary that only reaches the rear of the eye. Common on arid Pacific slope south to Ica and in upper Río Marañón Valley to 1500 m. *Costa Rica to w Peru.*

Grayish Saltator *Saltator coerulescens* Saltador Grisáceo
20 cm (8"). Plate 121. ♪ 797. The only gray-backed saltator in its range. Common in humid lowland forests and second growth e of Andes to 1000 m. *Mexico to n Argentina and Brazil.*

Buff-throated Saltator *Saltator maximus* Saltador Gargantianteada
20 cm (8"). Plate 121. ♪ 797. The only saltator with an olive-green back and wings, a white chin, and buff throat. Fairly common in humid lowland *várzea* forests and woodlands e of Andes, and on Pacific slope in Tumbes to 1200 m. *Mexico to n Bolivia, Paraguay and s Brazil.*

Slate-colored Grosbeak *Saltator grossus* Picogrueso Piquirrojo
19.5 cm (7.75"). Plate 121. ♪ 797. A distinctive slate-gray grosbeak with a white throat and red bill. Fairly common in humid lowland *terra firme* and *várzea* forests e of Andes to 1200 m. *Honduras to n Bolivia and Amazonian Brazil.*

Black-cowled Saltator *Saltator nigriceps* Saltador Capuchinegro
22 cm (8.6"). Plate 125. Note limited range. The only gray saltator with a black head and a salmon-red bill. Female is duller, with a duller bill. Uncommon in humid montane forests and scrub in Piura and Lambayeque at 1000-2000 m. *S Ecuador and nw Peru.*

Golden-billed Saltator *Saltator aurantiirostris* Saltador Piquidorado
20 cm (8"). Plate 121. ♪ 797. A saltator with a conspicuous postocular stripe, and a black mask that extends into a pectoral band. White throat is conspicuous in illustrated *albociliaris* (north to Ancash and Huánuco) but reduced in *interatus* (Cajamarca to Ancash). Bill is bright orange (male) or dusky-yellow (female and immature). Common in dry montane scrub north to Cajamarca and Amazonas to 3000 m. *Andes of Peru to central Argentina, Paraguay and s Brazil.*

Masked Saltator *Saltator cinctus* Saltador Enmascarado
22 cm (8.6"). Plate 125. ♪ JM. Unlikely to be confused with any other species. The pectoral band, white undertail spots, red bill and black mask are diagnostic. Rare, local and extremely shy in *Chusquea* bamboo thickets on e slope of Andes, mainly at 2150-2950 m. Recorded from Cerro Chinguela, Cordillera de Colán and Carpish Mts. Bird recorded at Playón 2.0 km south of Carmen at 1670 m is lowest altitude reported for the species (J. W. Eley). *Andes of Colombia to ne Peru.*

Yellow-shouldered Grosbeak *Parkerthraustes humeralis* Picogrueso Hombriamarillo
16 cm (6.25"). Plate 121. ♪ 797. The only grosbeak with a gray head, black mask, a white malar stripe and black sub-malar stripe. Recorded at Manu Wildlife Center. Rare in humid lowland forests e of Andes at 200-1000 m. *Colombia to n Bolivia and sw Amazonian Brazil.*

Pheucticus **Grosbeaks.** Three species of medium-size finches with heavy, thick bills. One is a northern-winter visitor. The two resident species are mostly yellow and black.

Golden-bellied Grosbeak *Pheucticus chrysogaster* Picogrueso Ventridorado
21.5 cm (8.4"). Plate 119. ♪ 623. Adult male has a clean yellow head. Female and immature are duller and have dirty yellow heads (yellow with irregular olive mottling). Fairly common in coastal lowlands and montane slopes south to Arequipa and Puno to 3000 m. *Mts. of n Venezuela to Andes of s Peru.*

Black-backed Grosbeak *Pheucticus aureoventris* Picogrueso Dorsinegro
21.5 cm (8.4"). Plate 121. ♪ 797. Adult male has a black head. Female and immature are duller and have dirty brownish heads (dark brown with irregular mottling). Rare and local in lower montane forests on e slope of Andes to 3380 m. *Venezuela to nw Argentina.*

Rose-breasted Grosbeak *Pheucticus ludovicianus* Picogrueso Pechirrosado
18.5 cm (7.2"). Plate 121. ♪ 626. Even non-breeding male shows much pink on the breast. Female is the only grosbeak with crown stripes and streaks on the breast. Rare northern-winter visitor to upper tropical and subtropical forests south to Cusco and Madre de Dios to 2000 m. *E Canada and US; winters w Cuba and Mexico to Peru.*

Blue-black Grosbeak *Cyanocompsa cyanoides* Picogrueso Negriazulado
16 cm (6.25"). Plate 121. ♪ 797. The male is the only grosbeak that is glossy blue-black. Rufescent-brown female is a warmer brown than similar seed-finches. Shyer than other grosbeaks. Uncommon in humid lowland forests e of Andes, and w of Andes in Tumbes to 1000 m. *Mexico to n Bolivia and Amazonian Brazil.*

Icteridae (New World Blackbirds; Vaqueros y Oropendolas) Species: World 99; Peru 34
A diverse New World family, notable for its remarkable adaptive radiation, which includes the cowbirds, oropendolas, caciques, grackles, American orioles, American blackbirds, meadowlarks and Bobolink. Most of the northern migratory species show marked sexual dimorphism, both in color and size. They are best represented in the Neotropics, where they range from sea level to over 4000 meters on the altiplano. The long-distance champion among icterids is the Bobolink, which migrates over 8000 kilometers from southern Canada to its wintering grounds in Argentina.

Bobolink *Dolichonyx oryzivorus* Tordo Arrocero
18 cm (7"). Plate 127. ♪ 626. Note the fairly short, conical bill and pointed tail feathers. Non-breeding birds have streaked mantle, a broad buff superciliary and a crown stripe. Cf. female plumage *Sturnella* (rounded tail, usually reddish tones to underparts). Breeding male is mostly black with a buff nape, white scapulars and rump. Rare migrant and northern-winter visitor along Pacific coast and in lowlands e of Andes. *North America; winters s South America.*

Agelaius **Blackbirds.** Three species of medium-sized blackbirds that favor marsh vegetation, often gathering in large flocks.

Yellow-winged Blackbird *Agelaius thilius* Tordo Aliamarilla
18 cm (7"). Plate 127. ♪ 797. The only blackbird in its range. Female and immature are dark and streaked, but show a trace of yellow on shoulder. Common in reedbeds and marshes on altiplano of Cusco and Puno to 4000 m. *S Peru to central Argentina, Chile and se Brazil.*

Pale-eyed Blackbird *Agelaius xanthophthalmus* Tordo Ojipálido
20 cm (7.8"). Plate 125. No other blackbird in its range and habitat is all black with a black bill and yellow eyes. Giant Cowbird is almost double the size. Uncommon and very local along edges of oxbow lakes e of Andes to 650 m. Regularly recorded at Amazonia Lodge, Manu Lodge, Manu Wildlife Center and Tambopata Candamo Reserve. *E Ecuador and e Peru.*

Yellow-hooded Blackbird *Agelaius icterocephalus* Tordo Capuchiamarillo
18 cm (7"). Plate 127. ♪ 622. Note limited range. An unmistakable black icterid with a yellow hood. Female is duller, but has similar color pattern. Uncommon in lowland marshes and *caña brava* habitats in Loreto. A small colony established from escaped birds existed for many years in marshes at Pantanos de Villa (Lima). *S Venezuela and the Guianas to ne Peru and Amazonian Brazil.*

Red-breasted Blackbird *Sturnella militaris* Pastorero Pechirrojo
18 cm (7"). Plate 127. Accidental. Male in breeding plumage is solid black with a bright-red throat and breast. Female cannot be safely separated from female White-browed Blackbird. Single record from Jeberos on lower Río Huallaga (Loreto). *Costa Rica to n Bolivia and Amazonian Brazil.*

White-browed Blackbird *Sturnella superciliaris* Pastorero Cejiblanca
18 cm (7"). Plate 127. Male is distinctive with its red breast and white postocular stripe. Streaked female has a strong buff superciliary. Rare in humid lowland grasslands and pastures in Madre de Dios and Puno. *SE Peru to n Argentina and Brazil.*

Peruvian Meadowlark *Sturnella bellicosa* Pastorero Peruano
20 cm (7.8"). Plate 127. ♪ JM. Male is unmistakable. Brown female has streaky underparts tinged with red on breast. Common along coast and arid intermontane valley grasslands south to Huánuco to 2500 m. *Ecuador to extreme n Chile.*

Scrub Blackbird *Dives warszewiczi* Tordo de Matorral
25 cm (9.8"). Plate 125. ♪ JFC. Two ssp. occur in Peru, and may represent separate species. Both are somewhat glossy blackbirds with long bills. The legs appear decidedly longer than those of any sympatric blackbird. Nominate (south to La Libertad) is smaller and slighter shorter-billed than *kalinowskii* (illustrated, north to La Libertad). Very glossy Shiny Cowbird has a shorter bill and longer, more pointed wings (Scrub Blackbird has relatively shorter, more rounded wings). Common in agricultural areas along Pacific coast south to Ica, and inland locally to middle Río Marañón Valley. Generally below 1500 m but occasionally to 3000 m. *W Ecuador and w Peru.*

Great-tailed Grackle *Quiscalus mexicanus* Clarinero Coligrande
43 cm (17"). Plate 127. ♪ 623. Note limited range. Male has a diagnostic long keel-shaped tail. Females and immatures are long-tailed and brown, with yellow eyes and pale-brown superciliary. Juveniles have streaked underparts. Fairly common along coastal mangroves and lowlands in Tumbes. *SW US to extreme n Peru.*

Shiny Cowbird *Molothrus bonariensis* Tordo Brilloso
20 cm (7.8"). Plate 127. ♪ 797. Bill is fairly short and conical. Male plumage is highly glossed dark violet, especially on back and chest. Cf. Chopi Blackbird (blacker, less glossy, gloss restricted to nape) and Scrub Blackbird. Female is uniformly brown with paler belly (coastal *occidentalis*) or paler throat (Amazonian *riparius*). Common in agricultural lands along Pacific coast south to Tacna to 2000 m; rare in lowlands e of Andes. *S US and West Indies; Panama to Brazil, Argentina and Chile.*

Giant Cowbird *Scaphidura oryzivora* Tordo Gigante
38 cm (15"). Plate 127. ♪ 797. A heavy, large black icterid, nearly double the size of most other "blackbirds." The male has a prominent neck ruff. Female is somewhat smaller and less iridescent. Eye color varies from yellow to dark. Common in humid lowlands e of Andes, and on Pacific coast in Tumbes to 1000 m. *Mexico to n Argentina and Brazil.*

Icterus **Orioles.** Five species of medium-sized icterids found in lowlands on both sides of Andes.

Moriche Oriole *Icterus chrysocephalus* Bolsero Moriche
20 cm (7.8"). Plate 127. ♪ 652. Within its range the only black icterid with a yellow crown, shoulders, rump and thighs. Uncommon in lowland *Mauritia* palm forests north of the Amazon, and west of the lower Río Ucayali to 500 m. *Venezuela and the Guianas to ne Peru and n Brazil.*

Epaulet Oriole *Icterus cayanensis* Bolsero de Cobijas Canela
20 cm (7.8"). Plate 127. ♪ 797. The only nearly all black oriole in its range with yellow shoulders. Common in lowland forests south of the Amazon and east of the lower Río Ucayali to 900 m. *Tropical South America e of Andes.*

Yellow-tailed Oriole *Icterus mesomelas* Bolsero Coliamarilla
21.5 cm (8.4"). Plate 127. ♪ 623. The only Peruvian oriole with yellow outer tail feathers. Sympatric White-edged Oriole is similar, but has a prominent white wedge on wing and an all black tail. Uncommon in coastal lowlands south to Lambayeque and in upper Marañón Valley south to La Libertad to 500 m. *Mexico to nw Peru.*

White-edged Oriole *Icterus graceannae* Bolsero Filiblanco
20 cm (7.8"). Plate 125. Within its limited range the only oriole with a white wedge (bases of secondaries) on wing. Common in deciduous woodlands and scrub on Pacific slope south to La Libertad to 300 m. *W Ecuador and nw Peru.*

Troupial *Icterus icterus* Bolsero Turpial
23 cm (9"). Plate 127. ♪ 797. The only orange-and-black oriole in its range. Note the white wedge-shaped patch on base of secondaries, and blue orbital skin. Fairly common in lowland forests e of Andes to 500 m. *Venezuela and Guyana to n Argentina and Amazonian Brazil.*

Cacicus **Caciques.** Primarily black icterids with long, dagger-like bills, often with a bright yellow or red rump. Most have pale-yellow bills, with pale-yellow or blue eyes. Caciques contain some of the best-known Neotropical birds (Yellow-billed Cacique) and one of the least known (Selva Cacique).

Yellow-billed Cacique *Amblycercus holosericeus* Cacique Piquiamarillo
23 cm (9"). Plate 126. ♪ 797. A black cacique of the undergrowth, with yellow eyes and pale-yellow bill. Pacific lowlands *flavirostris* is slightly larger than illustrated *australis* 'Chapman's Cacique' (e of Andes). Fairly common in lowlands and foothills in Tumbes, and in lowlands e of Andes from San Martín to Puno to 2000 m. *Mexico to w Bolivia.*

Yellow-rumped Cacique *Cacicus cela* Cacique Lomiamarillo
27 cm (10.5"). Plate 126. ♪ 797. Instantly recognized by its yellow rump, crissum, base of tail and wing-patch. Common in woodlands and *várzea* forests e of Andes to 900 m, and on Pacific slope in Tumbes. *Panama to n Bolivia and Amazonian Brazil.*

Red-rumped Cacique *Cacicus haemorrhous* Cacique Lomirrojo
27 cm (10.5"). Plate 126. ♪ 797. Like Subtropical Cacique (no overlap), but red extends to lower back and rump. Rare and local in humid lowland *terra firme* forests e of Andes to 1000 m. Recorded at Lago Sándoval (PC). *S Venezuela and the Guianas to ne Argentina and Amazonian Brazil.*

Subtropical (Scarlet-rumped) Cacique *Cacicus uropygialis* Cacique Lomiescarlata
27 cm (10.5"). Plate 126. ♪ 613. The only black cacique in its range with a red rump. Uncommon in humid montane forests on e slope of Andes south to Cusco at 1300-2300 m. *Andes of Colombia to Peru.*

Selva Cacique *Cacicus koepckeae* Cacique de Koepcke
23 cm (9"). Plate 125. ♪ 818CD. Note limited range. A small black cacique with a yellow rump, bluish-gray bill and bluish eyes. Sympatric Yellow-rumped Cacique shows considerably more yellow on rump, crissum, tail and wings. Known from two specimens from lowlands near Balta on Río Curanja (se Ucayali) at 300 m. Recently rediscovered and tape recorded along small tributaries of upper Río Urubamba and upper Río Manu. *Endemic to Peru.*

Mountain Cacique *Cacicus chrysonotus* Cacique Montano
30 cm (11.7"). Plate 126. ♪ 797. The only black cacique in its range with a yellow rump. Two ssp. occur. Race *leucoramphus* (n of Junín) has yellow on inner wing coverts; race *chrysonotus* (illustrated, s of Junín) has some or no yellow on the wing. The two races are sometimes considered separate species. Fairly common in humid montane forests on e slope of Andes at 1800-3000 m. *Andes of w Venezuela to w Bolivia.*

Ecuadorian Cacique *Cacicus sclateri* Cacique Ecuatoriano
23 cm (9"). Plate 125. The only black cacique with a bluish-gray bill and blue eyes. Note that immature has dark eyes, but size and shape can aid in identification. Uncommon in humid lowland forests at Huampami, mouth of Río Curaray (n Loreto), and common along Río Samiria in Pacaya Samiria Reserve at 200-600 m. *E Ecuador and extreme n Peru.*

Solitary Cacique *Cacicus solitarius* Cacique Solitario
26 cm (10.1"). Plate 126. ♪ 797. A large black cacique with dark eyes. All other black caciques are smaller, and have pale eyes. Uncommon in humid lowland forests e of Andes to 500 m, occasionally to 800 m. *Venezuela to central Argentina and Amazonian Brazil.*

Psarocolius **Oropendolas.** Most members of the genus are communal nesters, and their pendant nests are among the most memorable sights in the Amazon basin. Nests are usually located on isolated trees to prevent raids by marauding monkeys.

Casqued Oropendola *Psarocolius oseryi* Oropéndola de Casquete
38 cm (15"). Plate 126. ♪ 818CD. The only brown oropendola with a yellow-olive breast and prominent casqued bill. Flight feathers are edged yellow. Fairly common in humid *terra firme* and *várzea* forests e of Andes to 750 m. *E Ecuador and e Peru.*

Crested Oropendola *Psarocolius decumanus* Oropéndola Crestada
45 cm (17.5"). Plate 126. ♪ 797. A dark, mostly black oropendola with a dark chestnut rump and vent, and an ivory bill. Much larger than Band-tailed Oropendola, and has completely yellow outer tail feathers. Common in humid lowland forests and woodlands e of Andes to 1200 m. *Panama to n Argentina and Brazil.*

Green Oropendola *Psarocolius viridis* Oropéndola Verde
48 cm (19"). Plate 126. ♪ 652. The only green oropendola that has a pale-green bill tipped with red, and olive-green wings. Rump and crissum are dark brown. Uncommon in humid lowland *terra firme* forests in Loreto to 500 m. *S Venezuela and the Guianas to ne Peru and Amazonian Brazil.*

Dusky-green Oropendola *Psarocolius atrovirens* Oropéndola Verdioscuro
40 cm (15.5"). Plate 125. ♪ 797. A fairly uniformly colored oropendola. Sympatric with, and similar to, race *alfredi* of Russet-backed Oropendola, but latter is larger, has a brower back, and head is paler than body. Fairly common in humid montane forests on e slope of Andes from Huánuco to Puno at 800-2400 m. *Andes of se Peru and w Bolivia.*

Russet-backed Oropendola *Psarocolius angustifrons* Oropéndola Dorsibermejo
45 cm (17.5"). Plate 126. ♪ 797. Two distinctly different ssp. occur in Peru, and may represent separate species. In northeast *angustifrons* is the only uniformly dark olive-brown oropendola with a dark bill. Race *alfredi* (most of e Peru) has a pale-headed appearance, and has a yellow forehead. Cf. Dusky-green Oropendola. Common in humid lowland and lower montane forests e of Andes to 2000 m. *Mts. of n Venezuela to n Bolivia and w Amazonian Brazil.*

Band-tailed Oropendola *Ocyalus latirostris* Oropéndola Colifajeada
33 cm (13"). Plate 126. ♪ JFC. A small black oropendola with chestnut nape and a unique black terminal tail band. Fairly common in humid *várzea* and river island forests from Loreto south to Pucallpa (Ucayali) to 300 m. *Colombia to ne Peru and extreme w Brazil.*

Amazonian (Olive) Oropendola *Gymnostinops bifasciatus* Oropéndola Amazónica
48 cm (19"). Plate 126. ♪ 797. The only oropendola with a prominent pink facial patch. Note two-toned effect with dark rear end and light green front. The black bill is tipped with red. Peruvian birds sometimes treated as Olive Oropendola (*G. yuracares*), but here considered conspecific with *G. bifasciatus* (Para Oropendola). Common in lowland *terra firme* forests e of Andes to 500 m. *Venezuela to n Bolivia and Amazonian Brazil.*

Oriole Blackbird *Gymnomystax mexicanus* Tordo Oriol
30 cm (11.7"). Plate 127. ♪ 652. A large, distinctive yellow icterid with a black back, wings and tail. Short malar streak and bare ocular area also black. Uncommon in lowland woodlands and marshes e of Andes from Loreto and San Martín south to Pucallpa region (Ucayali) to 600 m. *Venezuela and the Guianas to ne Peru and Amazonian Brazil.*

Chopi Blackbird *Gnorimopsar chopi* Tordo Chopi
23 cm (9"). Plate 127. ♪ 797. Note limited range. A black icterid with a medium-sized bill and a faint blue gloss on the nape. Sexes similar. Shiny Cowbird is glossier overall. Uncommon in savanna and agricultural areas in Pampas del Heath. *SE Peru to n Argentina, e and se Brazil.*

Velvet-fronted Grackle *Lampropsar tanagrinus* Clarinero Frentiatercipelada
23 cm (9"). Plate 127. ♪ 797. A glossy blackbird of the wet lowlands. Similar to Shiny Cowbird, but Velvet-fronted's bill is slimmer and appears more pointed. Also note longer, fan-shaped tail. Sexes similar. Uncommon in lowland *várzea* forests and marshes south to n Ucayali to 400 m. *S Venezuela and the Guianas to n Bolivia and w Amazonian Brazil.*

Endemic Birds of Peru

Taczanowski's Tinamou *Nothoprocta taczanowskii*
Kalinowski's Tinamou *Nothoprocta kalinowskii*
Junin Grebe *Podiceps taczanowskii*
White-winged Guan *Penelope albipennis*
Junin Rail *Laterallus tuerosi*
Yellow-faced Parrotlet *Forpus xanthops*
Cloud-forest Screech Owl *Otus marshalli*
Long-whiskered Owlet *Xenoglaux loweryi*
Koepcke's Hermit *Phaethornis koepckeae*
Spot-throated Hummingbird *Leucippus taczanowskii*
"Ampay" Hummingbird *Leucippus sp.*
Green-and-white Hummingbird *Amazilia viridicauda*
Peruvian Piedtail *Phlogophilus harterti*
Rufous-webbed Brilliant *Heliodoxa branickii*
Black-breasted Hillstar *Oreotrochilus melanogaster*
White-tufted Sunbeam *Aglaeactis castelnaudii*
Purple-backed Sunbeam *Aglaeactis aliciae*
Royal Sunangel *Heliangelus regalis*
Coppery-naped Puffleg *Eriocnemis sapphiropygia*
Bronze-tailed Comet *Polyonymus caroli*
Coppery Metaltail *Metallura theresiae*
Fire-throated Metaltail *Metallura eupogon*
Black Metaltail *Metallura phoebe*
Gray-bellied Comet *Taphrolesbia griseiventris*
Bearded Mountaineer *Oreonympha nobilis*
Marvelous Spatuletail *Loddigesia mirabilis*
Scarlet-banded Barbet *Capito wallacei*
Yellow-browed Toucanet *Aulacorhynchus huallagae*
Speckle-chested Piculet *Picumnus steindachneri*
Fine-barred Piculet *Picumnus subtilis*
Black-necked Woodpecker *Colaptes atricollis*
Coastal Miner *Geositta peruviana*
Dark-winged Miner *Geositta saxicolina*
Thick-billed Miner *Geositta crassirostris*
Striated Earthcreeper *Upucerthia serrana*
Peruvian Seaside Cinclodes *Cinclodes taczanowskii*
White-bellied Cinclodes *Cinclodes palliatus*
Rusty-crowned Tit-Spinetail *Leptasthenura pileata*
White-browed Tit-Spinetail *Leptasthenura xenothorax*
Eye-ringed Thistletail *Schizoeaca palpebralis*
Vilcabamba Thistletail *Schizoeaca vilcabambae*
Puna Thistletail *Schizoeaca helleri*
Apurimac Spinetail *Synallaxis courseni*
Russet-bellied Spinetail *Synallaxis zimmeri*
Chinchipe Spinetail *Synallaxis chinchipensis*
Great Spinetail *Siptornopsis hypochondriacus*
Baron's Spinetail *Cranioleuca baroni*
Marcapata Spinetail *Cranioleuca marcapatae*
Creamy-crested Spinetail *Cranioleuca albicapilla*
Canyon Canastero *Asthenes pudibunda*
Rusty-fronted Canastero *Asthenes ottonis*

Cactus Canastero *Asthenes cactorum*
Pale-tailed Canastero *Asthenes huancavelicae*
Junin Canastero *Asthenes virgata*
Chestnut-backed Thornbird *Phacellodomus dorsalis*
Russet-mantled Softtail *Phacellodomus berlepschi*
Ash-throated Antwren *Herpsilochmus parkeri*
Creamy-bellied Antwren *Herpsilochmus motacilloides*
Black-tailed Antbird *Myrmoborus melanurus*
White-masked Antbird *Pithys castanea*
Pale-billed Antpitta *Grallaria carrikeri*
Rusty-tinged Antpitta *Grallaria przewalskii*
Bay Antpitta *Grallaria capitalis*
Red-and-white Antpitta *Grallaria erythroleuca*
Chestnut Antpitta *Grallaria blakei*
Ochre-fronted Antpitta *Grallaricula ochraceifrons*
Unicolored Tapaculo *Scytalopus unicolor*
Large-footed Tapaculo *Scytalopus macropus*
Rufous-vented Tapaculo *Scytalopus femoralis*
Vilcabamba Tapaculo *Scytalopus urubambae*
Neblina Tapaculo *Scytalopus altirostris*
Ancash Tapaculo *Scytalopus affinis*
Tschudi's Tapaculo *Scytalopus acutirostris*
Peruvian Plantcutter *Phytotoma raimondii*
Bay-vented Cotinga *Doliornis sclateri*
White-cheeked Cotinga *Zaratornis stresemanni*
Masked Fruiteater *Pipreola pulchra*
Cerulean-capped Manakin *Pipra coeruleocapilla*
Inca Flycatcher *Leptopogon taczanowskii*
Lulu's Tody-Tyrant *Poecilotriccus luluae*
White-cheeked Tody-Tyrant *Poecilotriccus albifacies*
Black-backed Tody-Flycatcher *Todirostrum pulchellum*
Mishana Tyrannulet *Zimmerius villarejoi*
Peruvian Tyrannulet *Zimmerius viridiflavus*
Unstreaked Tit-Tyrant *Uromyias agraphia*
Piura Chat-Tyrant *Ochthoeca piurae*
Tumbes Tyrant *Ochthoeca salvini*
Rufous Flycatcher *Myiarchus semirufus*
Peruvian Wren *Cinnycerthia peruana*
Inca Wren *Thryothorus eisenmanni*
Golden-bellied Warbler *Basileuterus chrysogaster*
Parodi's Hemispingus *Hemispingus parodii*
Rufous-browed Hemispingus *Hemispingus rufosuperciliaris*
Brown-flanked Tanager *Thlypopsis pectoralis*
Buff-bellied Tanager *Thlypopsis inornata*
Huallaga Tanager *Ramphocelus melanogaster*
Golden-backed Mountain-Tanager *Buthraupis aureodorsalis*
Yellow-scarfed Tanager *Iridosornis reinhardti*
Green-capped Tanager *Tangara meyerdeschauenseei*
Sira Tanager *Tangara phillipsi*
Pardusco *Nephelornis oneilli*
Cinereous Finch *Piezorhina cinerea*
Great Inca-Finch *Incaspiza pulchra*
Rufous-backed Inca-Finch *Incaspiza personata*

Gray-winged Inca-Finch *Incaspiza ortizi*
Buff-bridled Inca-Finch *Incaspiza laeta*
Little Inca-Finch *Incaspiza watkinsi*
Plain-tailed Warbling-Finch *Poospiza alticola*
Rufous-breasted Warbling-Finch *Poospiza rubecula*
Chestnut-breasted Mountain-Finch *Poospiza caesar*
Raimondi's Yellow-Finch *Sicalis raimondii*
Rusty-bellied Brush-Finch *Atlapetes nationi*
Rufous-eared Brush-Finch *Atlapetes rufigenis*
Cuzco Brush-Finch *Atlapetes canigenis*
Vilcabamba Brush-Finch *Atlapetes terborghi*
Apurímac Brush-Finch *Atlapetes forbesi*
Black-spectacled Brush-Finch *Atlapetes melanops*
Selva Cacique *Cacicus koepckeae*

Several species formerly only known from Peru have recently been discovered in extreme southern Ecuador on the border with Podocarpus National Park. These include Peruvian Pigeon, Marañón Spinetail, Cinnamon-breasted Tody-Tyrant and Marañón Thrush. Tumbes Swallow has been recorded in adjacent coastal southwest Ecuador. The Rufous-fronted Antthrush and Black-faced Cotinga, formerly known only from Madre de Dios, have recently been discovered in adjacent Bolivia and Brazil.

Location	Elevation	Coordinates
Abancay, *Apurímac*	2360m	3 40S 72 47W
Abancay, *Apurímac*	2360m	13 40S 72 47W
Abra Acjanaco, *Cusco*	3536m	13 11S 71 37W
Abra Aricoma, *Puno*	4815m	14 17S 69 47W
Abra Apacheta, *Huancavelica*	4550m	13 10S 74 45W
Abra de Maruncunca, *Puno*	2000m	14 14S 69 17W
Abra de Porculla, *Piura*	2145m	05 51S 79 31W
Abra la Divisoria, *Ucayali*	1613m	09 01S 75 45W
Abra La Raya, *Cusco/Puno*	4315m	14 29S 71 05W
Abra Málaga, *Cusco*	4250m	13 08S 72 19W
Abra Patricia, *San Martín*	1892 m	05 46S 77 41W
ACEER, *Loreto*	120m	03 50S 72 45W
Amazonia Lodge, *Madre de Dios*	605m	12 52S 71 22W
Ampay, *Apurímac*	2800m	13 35S 72 53W
Andahuaylas, *Apurímac*	2835m	13 39S 73 23W
Apacheta Pass, *Ayacucho*	4550m	14 85S 74 09W
Arequipa, *Arequipa*	2286m	16 24S 71 33W
Aricapampa, *San Martín*	3000m	07 45S 77 46W
Atalaya, *Cusco*	655m	12 53S 71 21W
Atuén, *Amazonas*	3350m	06 45S 77 52W
Ayabaca, *Piura*	2715m	04 38S 79 34W
Ayacucho, *Ayacucho*	2750m	13 07S 74 13W
Aypate, *Piura*	2800-3100m	04 42S 79 35W
Azalay, *Puno*	1750m	14 14S 69 17W
Bagua Grande, *Amazonas*	520m	05 35S 78 22W
Bahuaja-Sonene, *Madre de Dios/Puno*	200m	13 00S 69 00W
Balsapuerto trail, *San Martín*	1350m	06 03S 76 44W
Balsas, *Amazonas*	850m	06 50S 79 01W
Balta, *Ucayali*	300m	10 08S 71 13W
Batán Grande, *Lambayeque*	300m	06 25S 79 47W
Bellavista, *Amazonas*	500m	05 37S 78 39W
Biabo Cordillera Azul, *Loreto/Ucayali*	350-2000m	08 30S 76 00W
Boca de Manu, *Madre de Dios*	445m	11 50S 71 20W
Bosque de Ampay, *Apurímac*	2855-4000m	13 38S 72 57W
Bosque de Cuyas, *Piura*	2200-3100m	04 36S 79 44W
Bosque de Naupallagta, *Apurímac*	650m	14 23S 73 09W
Bosque de Noquo, *Ancash*	2850m	10 02S 77 39W
Bosque San Damián, *Ancash*	1800-2400m	09 51S 77 47W
Bosque Unchog, *Huánuco*	3600m	09 42S 76 07W
Bosque Zapatogocha, *Huánuco*	2600-3000m	09 40S 76 03W
Bosque Zárate, *Lima*	2700-3300m	11 53S 76 27W
Cajabamba, *Cajamarca*	2655m	07 37S 78 03W
Cajamarca, *Cajamarca*	2250m	07 10S 78 31W
Calientes, *Tacna*	1300m	17 53S 70 09W
Calipuy, Reserva Nacional, *La Libertad*	2500-3000m	08 32S 78 20W
Campo Verde, *Tumbes*	772m	03 50S 80 10W
Canchaillo, *Cusco*	3500m	13 08S 72 19W
Caño Pichana, *Loreto*	100m	03 20S 71 49W
Carpish Mountains, *Huánuco*	3000m	09 43S 75 54W
Celendín, *Cajamarca*	2350 m	06 52S 78 10W
Cerro Chinguela, *Piura*	±2800m	05 07S 79 23W

Cerro Huansala, *Ancash*	3700m	09 51S	76 59W
Cerro Runtacocha, *Apurímac*	4300m	13 40S	72 46W
Cerros de Amotape, *Tumbes/Piura*	130-975m	04 00S	80 40W
Cerros de Pantiacolla, *Madre de Dios*	600-1400m	12 35S	71 15W
Cerros de Sira, *Huánuco*	1200-2500m	09 21S	74 43W
Cerros del Távara, *Madre de Dios*	300-900m	13 30S	69 41W
Chaccan, *Ancash*	2800m	09 30S	77 47W
Chachapoyas, *Amazonas*	2334m	06 10S	77 50W
Chancay, *Lima*	Sea Level	11 57S	77 25W
Chiclayo, *Lambayeque*	22m	06 46S	79 50W
Chiguata, *Arequipa*	3000 m	16 23S	71 23W
Chinancocha, Laguna, *Ancash*	3250m	09 26S	77 38W
Chinchao, *Huánuco*	2000m	09 40S	76 03W
Chivay, *Arequipa*	3605m	15 30S	71 35W
Cocha Cashu, *Madre de Dios*	150m	11 51S	71 19W
Cock-of-the-rock Rodge, *Cusco*	1400 m	13 20S	71 40W
Colca Lodge, *Arequipa*	3260m	15 39S	71 40W
Contamana, *Loreto*	±1400m	07 05S	75 39W
Cordillera Apolobamba, *Puno*	±1800-2575m	14 30S	69 30W
Cordillera de Carabaya, *Puno*	±3000-4500m	14 0S	70 00W
Cordillera de Colán, *Amazonas*	±1500-2650m	05 40S	78 31W
Cordillera de Lagunillas, *Cajamarca*	3100-3650m	04 47S	79 24W
Cordillera del Cóndor, *Amazonas*	1600-2000m	04 00S	78 30W
Cordillera Urubamba, *Cusco*		13 0S	72 20W
Cordillera Vilcabamba, *Cusco*		13 0S	73 00W
Cordillera Vilcanota, *Cusco*		14 0S	71 00W
Cordillera Yanachaga, *Pasco*		10 33S	75 41W
Corral Quemado, *Amazonas*	500m	05 44S	78 40W
Cotrina, *Tumbes*	600-750m	03 81S	80 12W
Cruz Conga, *Cajamarca*	2700m	07 00S	78 12W
Cruz del Condor, *Arequipa*	3710m	15 36S	71 53W
Cullcui, *Huánuco*	3200m	09 23S	76 42W
Cumpang, *La Libertad*	2400m	08 12S	77 09W
Cushabatay, Río watershed, *Loreto*	±1600m	07 05S	75 39W
Cutervo, *Cajamarca*	2450m	06 10S	78 45W
Cusco, *Cusco*	3248m	13 32S	71 56W
Cusco Amazonico Reserve, *Madre de Dios*	210m	12 32S	69 03W
EcoAmazonia Lodge, *Madre de Dios*	205m	12 31S	68 55W
El Caucho, *Tumbes*	400m	03 50S	80 16W
El Fiscal, *Arequipa*	Sea level	17 03S	71 43W
El Mirador, *Cusco*	1825m	13 04S	71 33W
El Molino, *La Libertad*	±3000m	07 23S	79 47W
El Tocto, *Lambayeque*	270m	05 47S	79 42W
El Toldo, *Piura*	2600m	04 40S	79 31W
ExplorNapo Lodge, *Loreto*	120m	03 26S	72 48W
Hacienda Boca Chica, *Lambayeque*	300m	05 42S	79 48W
Hacienda Buenavista, *La Libertad*	200m	08 29S	78 38W
Hacienda del Solar, *Lambayeque*	180 m	05 59S	79 46W
Hacienda Limón, *Cajamarca*	1800m	06 50S	78 05W
Hacienda Recalí, *Lambayeque*	±500m	05 51S	79 41W
Hacienda Tulpo, *La Libertad*	3000m	08 08S	78 01W
Hacienda Villacarmen, *Cusco*	600m	12 50S	71 15W
Heath River Lodge, *Madre de Dios*	198m	12 40S	68 49W

Location	Elevation	Latitude	Longitude
Hortigal, *Lima*	3800-4350m	12 47S	75 44W
Huampami, *Amazonas*	210m	04 35S	78 12W
Huancarani, *Cusco*	3780m	13 30S	71 38W
Huaráz, *Ancash*	3053m	09 32S	77 32W
Huascarán National Park, *Ancash*	3700-4400m	09 45S	77 28W
Huayllay, *Pasco*	4000m	10 55S	76 20W
Huaytará, *Huancavelica*	2695m	13 26S	75 21W
Ica, *Ica*	406m	14 04S	75 42W
Inca Mine, *Puno*	1690m	13 51S	69 41W
Iquitos, *Loreto*	106m	03 45S	73 10W
Jaén, *Cajamarca*	500m	05 42S	78 47W
Jerillo, *San Martín*	1450m	06 03S	76 44W
Jesús del Monte, *San Martín*	1450m	06 03S	76 48W
Juan Guerra, *Amazonas*	350m	06 35S	76 21W
Junín, Lago de, *Junín*	4080m	11 02S	76 11W
Kusú, *Amazonas*	400m	04 27S	78 12W
La Caldera, *La Libertad*	3500m	08 12S	77 14W
La Esperanza, *Cajamarca*	1800m	06 36S	78 54W
La Florida, *Amazonas*	2265m	05 51S	77 59W
La Oroya, *Junín*	4100m	11 32S	75 54W
La Peca Nueva trail, *Amazonas*	2530m	05 34S	78 17W
La Unión, *Cusco*	1680m	13 03S	71 33W
Lachay Nature Reserve, *Lima*	433 m	11 30S	77 59W
Lagarto, *Ucayali*	300m	05 86S	74 62W
Laguna Chica, *Ica*	Sea level	13 90S	76 31W
Laguna Chinancocha, *Ancash*	3250 m	09 03S	77 37W
Laguna Huacarpay, *Cusco*	3060m	13 38S	71 45W
Laguna Marcapomacocha, *Junín*	4415m	11 26S	76 21W
Laguna Pachuca, *Apurímac*	3090m	13 36S	73 18W
Lagunas de Mejía, *Arequipa*	Sea level	17 08S	71 51W
Lagunas, *Lambayeque*	Sea level	07 05S	79 42W
Lampa, *Puno*	3992m	15 33S	70 35W
Leimebamba, *Amazonas*	3050m	06 41S	77 47 W
Lima, *Lima*	Sea level-100m	12 00S	77 00W
Limbani, *Puno*	3350m	14 12S	69 70W
Lluy, *Amazonas*	3050m	06 45S	77 49W
Lobos de Tierra, Isla, *Piura*	Sea level	06 42S	80 84W
Machu Picchu, *Cusco*	2360m	13 13S	72 35W
Manglares de Tumbes, *Tumbes*	Sea level	03 25S	80 16W
Manu Cloud Forest Lodge, *Madre de Dios*	1680m	13 03S	71 33W
Manu National Park, *Madre de Dios*	200-4000m	12 00S	71 30W
Manu Wildlife Center, *Madre de Dios*	410m	12 57S	70 23W
Marcapomacocha, *Junín*	4415m	11 26S	76 21W
Mashua, *La Libertad*	3350m	08 12S	77 14W
Mocupé, *Lambayeque*	Sea level	07 00S	79 38W
Molino, *Cajamarca*	3000m	07 45S	77 46W
Moquegua, *Moquegua*	1410m	17 10S	70 56W
Moyobamba, *San Martín*	860m	06 01S	77 00W
Mutca, *Apurímac*	2600m	14 17S	73 15W
Nazca, *Ica*	600m	14 50S	74 57W
Nevada Chaiñapuerto, *Cusco*	3800-4500m	13 13S	72 07W
Nevado Chachani, *Arequipa*	3900m	16 12S	71 33W
Ollantaytambo, *Cusco*	2810m	13 02S	72 15W

Location	Elevation	Latitude	Longitude
Olmos, *Lambayeque*	180m	05 59S	79 46W
Ondores, *Junín*	4100m	11 12S	76 00W
Orellana, *Loreto*	400m	06 90S	75 16W
Orosa, *Loreto*	100m	03 26S	72 20W
Pacasmayo, *La Libertad*	Sea level	07 20S	79 35W
Pacaya Samiria Reserve, *Loreto*	±300m	05 30S	75 30W
Pakitza, *Madre de Dios*	350m	11 56S	71 17W
Palambla, *Piura*	1200m	05 23S	79 37W
Pampa del Sacramento, *Loreto*	200m	06 90S	75 16W
Pampa Galeras, *Ayacucho*	3900m	14 40S	74 23W
Pampa Pucacocha, *Junín/Lima*	4400m	11 33S	76 16W
Pampas del Heath, *Madre de Dios*	190m	12 30S	68 40W
Pantanos de Villa, *Lima*	5m	12 11S	77 01W
Pantoja, *Loreto*	150m	00 55S	75 10W
Paracas Peninsula, *Ica*	Sea level	13 53S	76 20W
Paramonga, *Lima*	Sea level	10 40S	77 45W
Paucartambo, *Cusco*	2845m	13 17 S	71 36 W
Pebas, *Loreto*	100m	03 20S	71 84W
Pedro Ruiz, *Amazonas*	1375m	06 10S	77 54W
Peñas ruins, *Cusco*	3505m	13 10S	72 17W
Perico, *Cajamarca*	200m	05 15S	78 45W
Pillahuata, *Cusco*	2590m	13 10S	71 35W
Pisco, *Ica*	Sea Level	03 42S	76 13W
Pisqui, Río, *Loreto*	400m	08 24S	75 42W
Pozo del Pato, *Tumbes*	840m	03 50S	80 12W
Pucallpa, *Ucayali*	154m	08 25S	74 30W
Pucusana, *Lima*	Sea level	12 30S	76 40W
Pueblo Quichas, *Lima*	3980-4200m	10 34S	76 45W
Puerto Maldonado, *Madre de Dios*	200m	12 36S	69 13W
Puerto Pardo, *Madre de Dios*	200m	12 30S	68 39W
Punta Foca, *Tumbes*	Sea level	04 19S	81 23W
Pui Pui, *Junín*		11 20S	74 30W
Puno, *Puno*	3808m	15 60S	70 43W
Putumayo, *Loreto*	200m	00 65S	74 41W
Puquio, *Ayacucho*	3230m	14 41S	74 07W
Quebrada Caballito, *Lambayeque*	770m	05 48S	79 40W
Quebrada Cerro Negro, *Tumbes*	975m	04 00S	80 00W
Quebrada de Llanganuco, *Ancash*	3600-4000m	09 05S	77 39W
Quebrada Faical, *Tumbes*	450-550m	03 49S	80 16W
Quebrada Grande, *Tumbes*	660m	04 11S	80 42W
Quebrada Limón, *Lambayeque*	650m	05 75S	79 05W
Quebrada Tutapac, *Ancash*	3660m	08 39S	77 50W
Quebrada Ucumares, *Tumbes*	30m	03 53S	80 30W
Quilluacocha, *Huánuco*	3325m	09 42S	76 07W
Quincemil, *Cusco*	900m	13 22S	70 62W
Rafán, *Lambayeque*	Sea level	07 03S	79 63W
Reque, *Lambayeque*	Sea level	06 86S	79 81W
Río Abiseo National Park, *San Martín*	±2500m	07 32S	77 20W
Río Cushabatay, *Loreto*	±300m	07 30S	75 51W
Río Huallaga, *Loreto/San Martín*	±300m	05 15S	75 30W
Río Mayobamba, *Ayacucho*	±2700m	14 14S	52 57W
Río Pampas, *Apurímac*	2110m	13 30S	73 48W
Río Pariahuanca, *Huancavelica*	±3000m	12 00S	74 33W

Location	Elevation	Latitude	Longitude
Salinas y Aguada Blanca, *Arequipa*	Sea level	16 00S	71 40W
San Cristóbal, *Amazonas*	3000-5821m	05 50S	78 13W
San Damián, *Ancash*	2200m	09 51S	77 47W
Sándoval, Lago, *Madre de Dios*	210m	12 36S	68 85W
San Gallán, Isla, *Ica*	Sea level	13 50S	76 28W
San Ignacio, *Cajamarca*	800m	05 08S	78 57W
San José de Lourdes, *Cajamarca*	800m	05 02S	78 51W
San Marcos, *Cajamarca*	2300m	07 20S	78 10 W
San Pedro, *Cusco*	1400m	14 18S	71 34W
Sandia, *Puno*	2180m	14 17S	69 26W
Santa Cruz, *Loreto*	300m	05 32S	75 50W
Santa Eulalia Valley, *Lima*	2400-4200m	11 35S	76 22W
Santa María del Valle, *Huánuco*	2000m	09 51S	76 08W
Sariapunta, *Huánuco*	3000m	09 43S	75 54W
Seques, *Lambayeque*	1500m	06 54S	79 18W
Shintuya, *Madre de Dios*	400m	12 66 S	71 24 W
Soquián, *La Libertad*	±1000-2000m	07 51S	77 40W
Succha, *La Libertad*	3000m	07 51S	77 40W
Sunchubamba, *Cajamarca*	2400-3000m	07 25S	78 25W
Tabaconas Namballe, *Cajamarca*	1650m	05 08S	79 15W
Tacna, *Tacna*	562m	18 01S	70 15W
Tahuayo Lodge, *Loreto*	370m	04 18S	73 14W
Talara, *Piura*	Sea level	04 57S	81 27W
Tambopata Candamo, *Madre de Dios*	500-2800m	12 40S	69 40W
Tamborapa, *Cajamarca*	600m	05 24S	78 46W
Tarapoto, *San Martín*	700m	06 49S	76 40W
Tarata, *Moquegua*	4050m	17 28S	70 02W
Taulís, *Cajamarca*	2700m	06 54S	79 03W
Tingo Maria, *Huánuco*	1600m	09 25S	76 00W
Titicaca, Lago de, *Puno*	3808m	15 30S	69 30W
Tocto, *Lambayeque*	450m	05 81S	79 72W
Tulpo, Hacienda, *La Libertad*	3000m	08 08S	78 01W
Tumbes, *Tumbes*	Sea Level	03 30S	80 25W
Unión, *Cusco*	1680m	13 03S	71 33W
Urakuza, *Amazonas*	600m	04 42S	78 03W
Uripa, *Apurímac*	3210m	13 31S	73 40W
Urubamba, *Cusco*	3800m	13 17S	72 05W
Valcón, *Puno*	3000m	14 26S	69 24W
Villa, Pantanos de, *Lima*	5m	12 11S	77 01W
Yanac, *Ancash*	2860m	08 39S	77 50W
Yanachaga Chemillén, *Pasco*	300-4800m	10 20S	75 25W
Yanacocha lakes, *Cusco*	3700m	13 17S	71 59W
Yanuc Coral, *Ancash*	3722m	09 03S	77 37W
Yarinacocha, Lago, *Ucayali*	100m	08 15S	74 43W
Yaulí, *Huancavelica*	3400m	12 47S	74 49W
Yurac Corral, *Ancash*	4285m	09 03S	77 03W
Yuracmarca, *Ancash*	1400m	08 41S	77 53W
Yurimaguas, *Loreto*	700 m	05 88S	76 12W
Zona Reservada de Tumbes, *Tumbes*	450-772m	03 50S	80 13W

Bibliography

Alvarez, José A. 2000. The breeding system of the Orange-crowned Manakin. *Condor* 102: 181-186

Alvarez, José A. and Bret M. Whitney. 2001. A new *Zimmerius* tyrannulet (Aves: Tyrannidae) from white sand forests of northern Amazonian Brazil. *Wilson Bull.* 113 (1): 1-8

American Ornithologists Union. 2000. Forty-second Supplement to the American Ornithologists' Union Checklist of North American Birds. *The Auk* 117 (3): 847-858

Ascanio, David. 1998. Red-billed Ground-Cuckoo *Neomorphus pucheranii* at Pixiana, near Pavas. *Cotinga* 11:102

Bailey, Liberty Hyde and Ethel Zoe Bailey. 1976. *Hortus Third*. New York: Macmillan Pub. Co.

Barnes, Roger, Stuart Butchart, Charles Davies, Mirko Fernández and Nathalie Seddon. 1997. New distributional information on eight bird species from northern Peru. *Bull. B. O. C.* 117 (1): 69-74

Begazo, Alfredo J. and Thomas H. Valqui. 1998. Birds of Pacaya-Samiria National Reserve with a new population (*Myrmotherula longicauda*) and new record for Peru (*Hylophilus semicinereus*). *Bull. B. O. C.* 118 (3): 159-166

Begazo, Alfredo J., Thomas Valqui, Mark Sokol and Elaine Langlois. 2001. Notes on some birds from central and northern Peru. *Cotinga* 15: 81-87

Best, Brinley J., Christopher T. Clark, Matthew Checker, Amanda L. Broom, Richard M. Thewlis, Will Duckworth and Angus McNab. 1993. Distributional records, natural history notes and conservation of some poorly known birds from southwest Ecuador and northwestern Peru. *Bull. B. O. C.* 113: 108-119; 234-255

Best, Brinley J. and Michael Kessler. 1995. *Biodiversity and Conservation in Tumbesian Ecuador and Peru*. Cambridge, U.K.: BirdLife International

BirdLife International. 2000. *Threatened Birds of the World*. Barcelona and Cambridge, UK: Lynx Edicions and BirdLife International

Blake, Emmet R. 1957. A new species of ant-thrush from Peru. *Fieldiana* (*Zoology*) 39: 51-53. Chicago: Field Museum of Natural History

Blake, Emmet R. and Peter Hocking. 1974. Two new species of tanager from Peru. *Wilson Bull.* 86 (4): 321-324

Brack, J. A. 1969-1972. *Catálogo de las aves del Perú*. Lima: Biota 8, 9

Brown, R. G. 1981. Seabirds in northern Peruvian waters, November-December 1977. *In* Investigación cooperativa de la anchoveta y su ecosistema (L. M. Dicki and Jorge E. Valdivia G., Editors) *Bol. Inst. Mar Perú* (Callao), Vol. extraordinario: 34-42

Brumfield, Robb and J. V. Remsen, Jr. 1996. Geographic variation and species limits in *Cinnycerthia* wrens of the Andes. *Wilson Bull.* 108 (2): 205-227

Budney, Gregory F. and Robert W. Grotke. 1997. Techniques for audio recording vocalizations of tropical birds. *Ornithological Monographs* Vol. 48:147-163. American Ornithologists' Union

Capparella, A. P., Gary H. Rosenberg and Steven W. Cardiff. 1997. A new subspecies of *Percnostola rufifrons* (Formicariidae) from northeastern Amazonian Peru, with a revision of the *rufifrons* complex. *Ornithological Monographs* Vol. 48: 165-170. American Ornithologists' Union

Capurro, Víctor Pulido. 1998. *Vocabulario de los Nombres Comunes de la Fauna Silvestre del Perú*. Lima: Víctor Pulido Capurro

Chantler, Phil and Gerald Driessens. 1995. *Swifts: A Guide to the Swifts and Treeswifts of the World*. Sussex: Pica Press

Chapman, F. M. 1926. *The distribution of bird life in Ecuador*. Bulletin American Museum of Natural History. 55: 1-784

Clement, Peter. *Thrushes*. 2000. Princeton University Press

Clements, James F. 1994. *Report on a Natural History Trip to Manu Biosphere Reserve, Peru*. Vista, CA: Ibis Publishing Co.

—1995. *Report on a Trip to the High Andes of Peru*. Vista, CA: Ibis Publishing Company

—1996. On the Trail of Pava Aliblanca. *Wild Bird*, Vol. 11, No. 5
—1997. *Report on a Birding Trip to Iquitos region, Peru.* Vista, CA: Ibis Publishing Co.
—1998. *Report on a Birding Trip to the Southern Andes of Peru.* Vista, CA: Ibis Publishing Co.
—1999. Hummingbird Paradise: Bosque de Ampay. *Wild Bird*, Vol. 13, No. 3
—2000. *Birds of the World: A Checklist.* Fifth Edition. Vista, CA: Ibis Publishing Co.
Cleere, Nigel. 1998. *Nightjars: A Guide to the Nightjars, Nighthawks and Their Relatives.* Sussex: Pica Press
Collar, Nigel, L. P Gonzaga, N. Krabbe, A. Madroño Nieto, L. G. Naranjo, T. A. Parker III and D. C. Wege. 1992. *Threatened Birds of the Americas.* Cambridge: International Council for Bird Preservation
Coopmans, Paul and Niels Krabbe. 2000. A New Species of Flycatcher (Tyrannidae: *Myiopagis*) from Eastern Ecuador and Eastern Peru. *Wilson Bulletin* 112 (3): 305-312
Davis, Tristan J. 1986. Distribution and Natural History of Some Birds from the Departments of San Martín and Amazonas, Northern Peru. *Condor* 88:50-56
Davis, Tristan J. and John P. O'Neill. 1986. A new species of antwren (Formicariidae: *Herpsilochmus*) from Peru, with comments on the systematics of other members of the genus. *Wilson Bull.* 98 (3): 337-352
del Hoyo, Josep, A. Elliot and J. Sargatal, eds. 1992. *Handbook of the Birds of the World.* Volume 1. Ostrich to Ducks. Barcelona: Lynx Edicions
—1994. *Handbook of the Birds of the World.* Volume 2. New World Vultures to Guineafowl. Barcelona: Lynx Edicions
—1996. *Handbook of the Birds of the World.* Volume 3. Hoatzin to Auk. Barcelona: Lynx Edicions
—1997. *Handbook of the Birds of the World.* Volume 4. Sandgrouse to Cuckoos. Barcelona: Lynx Edicions
—1999. *Handbook of the Birds of the World.* Volume 5. Barn Owls to Hummingbirds. Barcelona: Lynx Edicions
Diamond, Jared. 1998. Eat Dirt! In the competition between parrots and fruit trees, it's the winners who bite the dust. *Discover.* February 1998: 70-75
Donahue, P. K. and W. R. Petersen. First record of Snowy-crowned Tern (*Sterna trudeaui*) from Peru. *American Birds* 34: 213
Dourojeanni, Marc J. and Carlos F. Ponce. 1978. *Los Parques Nacionales del Peru.* Madrid: Instituto de la Caza Fotográfica y Ciencias de la Naturaleza
Elton, Catherine. 2000. The Plight of the Flightless Grebes. *Audubon* March-April 2000: 732-79
Elwonger, Mark. 1995. *Avian Adventures visits Marcapomacocha and Manu.* Unpublished ms.
Engblom, Gunnar and J. Nordin. 1999. First record of Golden-winged Warbler in Peru. *Cotinga* 11:103
Farquhar, C. Craig. 1998. *Buteo polyosoma* and *B. poecilochrous*, the "Red-backed Buzzards" of South America, are conspecific. *Condor* 100 (1): 27-43
Fitzpatrick, John W. and John P. O'Neill. 1979. A new tody-tyrant from northern Peru. *The Auk* 96: 443-447
—1986. *Otus petersoni*, a new screech-owl from the Eastern Andes, with systematic notes on *O. colombianus* and *O. ingens*. *Wilson Bull.* 98 (1): 1-14
Fitzpatrick, John W. and Douglas F. Stotz. 1997. A new species of tyrannulet (*Phylloscartes*) from the Andean foothills of Peru and Bolivia. *Ornithological Monographs* Vol. 48: 37-44. American Ornithologists' Union
Fitzpatrick, John W., John Terborgh and David Willard. 1977. A new species of wood-wren from Peru. *The Auk* 94: 195-201
Fitzpatrick, John W., D. E. Willard and J. W. Terborgh. 1980. A new species of hummingbird from Peru. *Wilson Bull.* 91:177-186
Fitzpatrick, John W., and David E. Willard. 1990. *Cercomacra manu*, a new species of antbird from southwestern Amazonia. *The Auk.* 107 (2) 239-245
Fjeldså, Jon and Niels Krabbe. 1990. *Birds of the High Andes.* Svendborg, Denmark: Apollo

Flanagan, J. N. M. and W. P. Vellinga. 2000. *Tres bosques de neblina de Ayabaca: su avifauna y conservación*. Piura: ProAvesPerú

Forshaw, Joseph and W. T. Cooper. 1973. *Parrots of the World*. New York: Doubleday

Garcia-Moreno, Jaime and Jon Fjeldså. 1999. Re-evaluation of species limits in the genus *Atlapetes* based on mtDNA sequence data. *Ibis* 141: 199-207

Garcia-Moreno, Jaime, Peter Arctander and Jon Fjeldså. 1998. Pre-Pleistocene Differentiation Among Chat-Tyrants. *Condor* 100:629-640

Gardner, Nick J. 1986. *A Birder's Guide to Travel in Peru*. Surrey, UK: Nick J. Gardner

Garrigues, Richard L. 2001. First nests of Grey-bellied Comet *Taphrolesbia griseiventris*. *Cotinga* 15: 79-80

Gibbs, David, Estace Barnes and John Cox. 2001. *Pigeons and Doves*. Yale University Press

Gochfield, Mike, Start Keith and P. Donahue. 1980. Records of rare or previously unrecorded birds from Colombia. *Bull. B. O. C.* 100: 196-201

González, Oscar. 2001. First records of Purple Martin *Progne subis* in coastal Peru. *Cotinga* 15: 65-66

González, Oscar and Tor Egil Høgsås. 1998. The immature plumages of the Slender-billed Finch *Xenospingus concolor*. *Cotinga* 10: 43-44

González, Oscar, Alejandro Tello y Luis Torres. 1999. El Yanavico *Plegadis ridgwayi*, de migratorio Andino a residente de la costa Peruana. *Cotinga* 11:64-66

Graham, Gary L., Gary R. Graves, Thomas S. Schulenberg and John P. O'Neill. 1980. Seventeen bird species new to Peru from the Pampas de Heath. *The Auk* 97: 366-370

Graves, Gary. 1980. A new species of metaltail hummingbird from northern Peru. *Wilson Bull*. 92 (1): 1-7

—1982. First record of Brown Wood Rail (*Aramides wolfi*) for Peru. *Gerfaut* 72: 327-338

—1987. A cryptic new species of antpitta (Formicariidae: *Grallaria*) from the Peruvian Andes. *Wilson Bull*. 99 (3): 313-321

Graves, Gary, John P. O'Neill and Theodore A. Parker III. 1983. *Grallaricula ochraceifrons*, a new species of antpitta from northern Peru. *Wilson Bull*. 95 (1): 1-6

Graves, Gary and John S. Weske. 1987. *Tangara phillipsi*, a new species of tanager from the Cerros del Sira, eastern Peru. *Wilson. Bull*. 99 (1):1-5

Haase, B. J. M. 1993. Sight Record of Black-legged Kittiwake in Peru. *American Birds*, Fall 1993

Haffer, Jürgen. 1997. Contact zones between birds of southern Amazonia. *Ornithological Monographs* Vol. 48:291. American Ornithologists' Union

Hardy, John W. and Theodore A. Parker III. The nature and probable function of vocal copying in Lawrence's Thrush, *Turdus lawrencii*. 1997. *Ornithological Monographs* Vol. 48: 307-320. American Ornithologists' Union

Harrison, Peter. 1983. *Seabirds: An Identification Guide*. Boston: Houghton Mifflin Co.

Hayman, Peter, John Marchant and Tony Prater. 1986. *Shorebirds: An Identification Guide*. Boston: Houghton Mifflin Co.

Helme, N. A. 1996. New department records for Dpto. La Paz, Bolivia from the Pampas del Heath. *Bull. B. O. C.* 116: 175-177

Hilty, Steven L. and William L. Brown. 1986. *A Guide to the Birds of Colombia*. Princeton University Press

Høgsås, Tor Egil. 1999. An observation of Red-tailed Tropicbird *Phaethon rubricauda* in Tacna, Peru. *Cotinga* 12: 75

Høgsås, Tor Egil, Ernesto Malaga-Arenas and Carlos Collado Valencia. 1999. Tordo Parasitico *Molothrus bonariensis* avanzadzo en el sur del Perú. *Cotinga* 12: 76

Høgsås, Tor Egil, Ernesto Malaga-Arenas and José Pizarro Neyra. 2001. *Noteworthy bird records from southwest Peru*. Unpublished ms.

Hornbuckle, J. 1999. The birds of Abra Patricia and the upper Río Mayo, San Martín, north Peru. *Cotinga* 12: 11-28

Hornbuckle, J. 2000. Comments on the identification of two species of *Mionectes* flycatchers. *Cotinga* 13: 82

Howell, Steve N. G. and Sophie Webb. 1995. *A Guide to the Birds of Mexico and northern Central America.* Oxford University Press

Howell, Steve N. G. and A. Whittaker. 1995. Field identification of Orange-breasted and Bat Falcons. *Cotinga* 4: 36-43

Howell, Steve N. G. 1996. Thick-billed Siskin: *Carduelis crassirostris*. *Cotinga* 5: 92

Hu, Da-Shih, L. Joseph and D. Agro. 2000. Distribution, variation and taxonomy of *Topaza* hummingbirds (Aves: Trochilidae). *Orn. Neotrop.* 11:123-142

Hughes, R. A. 1970. Notes on the birds of the Mollendo district, southwestern Peru. *Ibis* 112: 229-241

Hughes, R. A. 1982. Broad-billed Prion at Mollendo, Peru: first record for the Pacific coast of South America. *Condor* 84:130

—1988. Nearctic migrants in southwest Peru. *Bull. B. O. C.* 108 (1): 29-43.

Isler, Morton L. and Phyllis R. Isler. 1987. *The Tanagers: Natural History, Distribution and Identification.* Washington: Smithsonian Institution Press

Isler, Morton, Phyllis R. Isler, Bret M. Whitney and Barry Walker. 2001. Species limits in antbirds: the *Thamnophilus punctatus* complex continued. *Condor* 103: 278-286

Jahncke, J. 1993. Report on the first known Markham's Storm-Petrel breeding area. *Pacific Seabird Group Bullletin* 20 (1): 58

Jahncke, J. 1998. Abundancia relativa y distribution de aves marinas frente a la costa Peruana. Crucero BIC Humboldt 9808-09, de Piura a Lima. *Bol. Inst. Mar Perú* (Callao) 141: 85-95

Johnsgard, Paul A. 1988. *The Quails, Partridges, and Francolins of the World.* Oxford: Oxford University Press

—1981. *The Plovers, Sandpipers and Snipes of the World.* University of Nebraska Press

—2000. *Trogons and Quetzals of the World.* Washington: Smithsonian Institution Press

Johnson, N. K. and R. E. Jones. 1990. Geographic differentiation and distribution of the Peruvian Screech-Owl. *Wilson Bull.* 102: 199-212

—2001. A new species of tody-tyrant (Tyrannidae: *Poecilotriccus*) from northern Peru. *The Auk* 118 (2): 334-341

Juniper, Tony and Mike Parr. 1998. *Parrots: A Guide to Parrots of the World:* New Haven: Yale University Press

Koepcke, Maria. 1970. *The Birds of the Department of Lima, Peru.* Newton Square, PA: Harrowood Books

—1970. Birds of the western slope of the Andes. *American Museum Novitates* 1028

König, Claus, Friedhelm Weick and Jan-Hendrik Becking. 1999. *Owls: A Guide to the Owls of the World.* Sussex: Pica Press

Krabbe, Niels, Morton L. Isler, Phyllis R. Isler, Bret M. Whitney, José Alvarez and Paul Greenfield. 1999. A new species in the *Myrmotherula haematonota* superspecies (Aves: Thamnophilidae) from the western Amazonian lowlands of Ecuador and Peru. *Wilson Bull.* 111 (2): 157-165

Krabbe, Niels and Thomas S. Schulenberg. 1997. Species limits and natural history of *Scytalopus* tapaculos (Rhinocryptidae), with descriptions of the Ecuadorian taxa, including three new species. *Ornithological Monographs* Vol. 48: 47-88. American Ornithologists' Union

Krabbe, Niels, S. James and B. Walker. 2001. An observation of Herring Gull *Larus argentatus* on the Peruvian coast. *Cotinga* 15: 66

Kratter, A. 1997. Birding on the Río Tambopata, Peru: macaws and bamboo specialists. *Birding* 29 (5): 402-409

Lanyon, Wesley. 1975. Behavior and generic status of the Rufous Flycatcher of Peru. *Wilson Bull.* 87 (4): 441-454

Lloyd, Huw. 2000. Population densities of the Black-faced Cotinga *Conioptilon mcilhennyi* in south-east Peru. *Bird Conservation International* 10: 277-285

Lowery, George H., Jr. and John P. O'Neill. 1964. A new genus and species of tanager from Peru. *The Auk* 81: 125-131

—1965. A new species of *Cacicus* (Aves: Icteridae) from Peru. *Occasional Papers Museum of Zoology Louisiana State University* 33: 1-5

—1966. A new genus and species of cotinga from eastern Peru. *The Auk* 83: 1-9

—1969. A new species of antpitta from Peru and a revision of the subfamily Grallariinae. *The Auk* 86: 1-12

Lowery, George H., Jr. and Dan A. Tallman. 1976. A new genus and species of nine-primaried oscine of uncertain affinities from Peru. *The Auk* 93: 415-428

Mackiernan, Gail, Peter Lonsdale, Noam Shany, Barry Cooper and Peter Ginsburg. 2001. Observations of seabirds in Peruvian and Chilean waters during the 1998 El Niño. *Cotinga* 15: 88-94

Marantz, Curtis A. 1997. Geographic variation of plumage patterns in the woodcreeper genus *Dendrocolaptes* (Dendrocolaptidae). *Ornithological Monographs* Vol. 48: 399-429

Meeth, P. and K. Meeth. 1977. Blue Petrels off Peru. *Ardea* 65: 90-91

Meyer de Schauensee, Rodolphe. 1982. *A Guide to the Birds of South America.* Pan American Section: International Council for Bird Preservation

Meyer de Schauensee, Rodolphe and William H. Phelps. 1978. *A Guide to the Birds of Venezuela.* Princeton University Press.

Morrison, A. 1940. Notas sobre las aves del lago de Junín. Lima: *Boletín del Museo de Historia Natural 'Javier Prado'* 4 (12): 84-92

—1940. Las aves de Huancavelica. *Boletín del Museo de Historia Natural 'Javier Prado'* 4 (13): 242-246

Munn, Charles and John W. Terborgh. 1979. Multi-species territoriality in Neotropical foraging flocks. *Condor* 81: 338-47

Ochoa, Julio, W. Galliano and Alfredo Tupayachi. 1996. *Interaccion Flores-Trochilidos en la Foracion Estival del Santuario Nacional de Ampay-Apurímac.* Cuzco: UNSAAC

O'Neill, J. P. 1969. Distributional notes on the birds of Peru, including twelve species previously unreported from the republic. *Occasional Papers Museum of Zoology Louisiana State University* 37: 1-11

—1992. A general overview of the montane avifauna of Peru. *Mem. Mus. Hist. Nat. 'Javier Prado'* 21: 47-55

O'Neill, John and Gary Graves. 1977. A new genus and species of owl from Peru. *The Auk* 94: 409-416

O'Neill, John P., Daniel F. Lane, Andrew W. Kratter, Angelo P. Capparella and Cecilia Fox Joo. 2000. A Striking New Species of Barbet (Capitoninae: *Capito*) from the Eastern Andes of Peru. *The Auk* 117 (3):569-577.

O'Neill, John P. and Theodore A. Parker III. 1997. New subspecies of *Myrmoborus leucophrys* (Formicariidae) and *Phrygilus alaudinus* (Emberizidae) from the upper Huallaga Valley, Peru. *Ornithological Monographs* Vol. 48: 485-491. Washington: American Ornithologists' Union

O'Neill John and D. L. Pearson. 1974. Un estudio preliminar de las aves de Yarinacocha, Dpto. Loreto, Peru. *Publicaciones del Museo Natural 'Javier Prado'* Series A: 25: 1-13

O'Neill, John and Thomas Schulenberg. 1979. Notes on the Masked Saltator, *Saltator cinctus*, in Peru. *The Auk* 96: 610-613

Orlans, Gordon. 1985. *Blackbirds of the Americas.* University of Washington Press

Ortiz, Fernando, Paul Greenfield and Juan Carlos Matheus. 1990. *Aves del Ecuador.* Quito: Feprotur

Parker, Theodore A. 1976. The Marvelous Spatuletail. *Birding* May 1976: 175

—1982. Observations of some unusual rainforest and marsh birds in southeastern Peru. *Wilson Bull* 94 (4): 477-493

Parker, Theodore A. and John P. O'Neill. 1976. An introduction to bird finding in Peru. Part I. The Paracas Peninsula and Central Highway (Lima to Huánuco City). *Birding* (2) 140-143

—1976. Introduction to bird-finding in Peru: Part II. The Carpish Pass Region of the Eastern Andes along the Central Highway. *Birding* (3) 205-216

—1980. Notes on little known birds of the upper Urubamba valley, southern Peru. *The Auk* 97: 167-176

Parker, Theodore A. III, Susan Allen Parker and Manuel A. Plenge. 1982. *An Annotated Checklist of Peruvian Birds*. Vermillion, South Dakota: Buteo Books

Parker, Theodore A. III, Thomas S. Schulenberg, G. R. Graves and M. J. Braun. 1985. The avifauna of the Huancabamba region, northern Peru. In: *Neotropical Ornithology*, eds. P. A. Buckley, M. S. Foster, E. S. Morton, R. S. Ridgely and F. G. Buckley. pp. 169-197. *Ornithological Monograph* 36. American Ornithologists' Union

Parker, Theodore A. III, Thomas S. Schulenberg, Michael Kessler and Walter H. Wust. 1995. Natural history and conservation of the endemic avifauna in north-west Peru. *Bird Conservation International* 5: 201-231

Pearson, David L. 1975. Range extensions and new records for bird species in Ecuador, Peru and Bolivia. *Condor* 77: 96-99

Pearson, David L. and Manuel A. Plenge. 1974. Puna bird species on the coast of Peru. *The Auk* 91: 626-631

Petersen, R. W. 1981. First record of Dunlin (*Calidris alpina*) for Peru and continental South America. *American Birds* 35: 342-343

Pierson, Jan. 2000. Fresh from the Field. *Field Guides News* March 2000.

Pitman, Robert L. 1986. *Atlas of Seabird Distribution and Relative Abundance in the Eastern Tropical Pacific*. Washington: National Oceanic and Atmospheric Administration

Pittman, Robert L. and Joseph R. Jehl, Jr. 1998. Geographic variation and reassessment of species limits in the "masked" boobies of eastern Pacific Ocean. *Wilson Bull.* 110 (4): 155-170

Plenge, Manuel A. 1974. Notes on some birds in west-central Peru. *Condor* 76: 326-330

Prum, Richard O. 2001. A new genus for the Andean Green Pihas (Cotingidae). *Ibis* 143: 307-309

Pulido, Victor. 1991. *El Libro Rojo de la Fauna Silvestre del Peru*. Lima: Instituto Nacional de Investigacion Agraria y Agroindustrial

Pyhälä, Mikko. 1999. *Informe Ornitológico de una Visita al Norte del Perú (Tumbes, Lambayeque) Dec. 29 1998 to Jan. 3, 1999*. Unpublished ms.

Pyhälä, Mikko and Donald Brightsmith. 1999. *Informe Ornitológico de una Visita a La Virgen, Piura, August 1, 1999*. Unpublished ms.

Pyhälä, Mikko and Hugo Noblecilla P. 2000. *Informe Ornitológico de una Visita al Bosque Nacional de Tumbes Feb. 28-29, 2000*. Unpublished ms..

Remsen, J. V., Jr. 1984. Geographic variation, zoogeography, and possible rapid evolution in some *Cranioleuca* spinetails (Furnariidae) of the Andes. *Wilson Bull.* 96 (4): 515-523.

—1993. Zoogeography and geographic variation of *Atlapetes rufinucha* (Aves: Emberizinae), including a distinctive new subspecies, in southern Peru and Bolivia. *Proc. Biol. Soc. Wash.* 106 (3): 429-435

—1997. A new genus for the Yellow-shouldered Grosbeak. *Ornithological Monographs* Vol. 48: 89-90. Washington: American Ornithologists' Union

Remsen, J. V., Jr. and W. S. Graves IV. 1995a. Distribution patterns and zoogeography of *Atlapetes* brush finches (Emberizinae) of the Andes. *Auk* 112: 210-224

—1995b. Distribution patterns of *Buarremon* brush-finches (Emberizinae) and interspecific competition in Andes birds. *Auk* 112: 225-236

Ridgely, Robert, Paul J. Greenfield and Mauricio Guerrero G. 1998. *An Annotated List of the Birds of Mainland Ecuador*. Quito: Fundación Ornitológico del Ecuador, CECIA

Ridgely, Robert and Guy Tudor. 1989. *The Birds of South America. Volume I: The Oscine Passerines*. Austin: University of Texas Press

—1994. *The Birds of South America. Volume II: The Suboscine Passerines.* Austin: University of Texas Press

Ridgely, Robert and Paul Greenfield. 2001a. *The Birds of Ecuador: Status, Distribution and Taxonomy.* Ithaca, NY: Comstock Publishing Associates

—2001b. *The Birds of Ecuador: Field Guide.* Ithaca, NY: Comstock Publishing Associates

Ripley, S. Dillon. 1977. *Rails of the World.* Boston: David Godine

Robbins, Mark B. and Steve N. G. Howell. 1995. A new species of pygmy-owl (Strigidae: *Glaucidium*) from the Eastern Andes. *Wilson Bull.* 107 (1): 1-6

Robbins, Mark, Gary H. Rosenberg, Francisco Sornoza Molina and Marco A. Jácome. 1997. Taxonomy and Nest Description of the Tumbes Swallow (*Tachycineta* [*albilinea*] *stolzmanni*). *Ornithological Monographs* 48: 609-612

Robbins, Mark and Gary Stiles. 1999. A new species of pygmy-owl (Strigidae: *Glaucidium*) from the Pacific slope of the northern Andes. *The Auk* 116:305-315

Roberson, Don. 1996. A range extension of Oche-faced Tody-Flycatcher *Todirostrum plumbeiceps* in Peru. *Cotinga* 6: 30-31

Rosenberg, Gary. 1990. Habitat specialization and foraging behavior by birds of Amazonian river islands in northeastern Peru. *Condor* 62: 427-443

Salinas, Letty, Irma Franke, Maria Samame and Jon Fjeldså. 1998. Primer registro de *Amaurospiza concolor* (Emberizidae: Passeriformes) para el Peru. *VII Reunion Científica ICBAR*

Schulenberg, Thomas S. 1983. Foraging behavior, eco-morphology, and systematics of some antshrikes (Formicariidae: *Thamnomanes*). *Wilson Bull.* 95 (4): 505-521

Schulenberg, T. S., S. E. Allen, D. F. Stotz and D. A. Widenfeld. 1984. Distributional records from the Cordillera Yanachaga, central Peru. *Gerfault* 74: 59-68

Schulenberg, Thomas S. and Laurence C. Binford. 1985. A new species of tanager (Emberizidae: Thraupinae, *Tangara*) from southern Peru. *Wilson Bull.* 97 (4): 413-420

Schulenberg. Thomas S. and Theodore A. Parker III. 1997. Notes on the Yellow-browed Toucanet *Aulacorhynchus huallagae*. *Ornithological Monographs* 48: 717-720. American Ornithologists' Union

Schulenberg. Thomas S. and Theodore A. Parker III. 1997. A new species of tyrant-flycatcher (Tyrannidae: *Tolmomyias*) from the western Amazon Basin. *Ornithological Monographs* 48: 723-731. American Ornithologists' Union

Schulenberg, Thomas S. and Morris D. Williams. 1982. A new species of antpitta (*Grallaria*) from northern Peru. *Wilson Bull.* 94 (2): 105-113

Schulenberg, Thomas S. and Walter Wust. 1997. Birds of the upper Río Comainas, Cordillera del Cóndor. In The Cordillera del Cóndor region of Ecuador and Peru: a biological assessment (Schulenberg, T. S. and Kim Awbrey, eds). Conservation International, *RAP Working Papers* 7: 66-88; 180-187

Seddon, N., R. Barnes, S. H. M. Buchart, C. W. N. Davies and M. Fernandez. 1995. Recent observations and notes on the ecology of the Royal Sunangel (*Heliangelus regalis*). *Bull. B. O. C.* 116 (1): 46-49

Servat, G. and D. L. Pearson. 1991. Natural history notes and records for seven poorly known bird species from Amazonian Peru. *Bull. B. O. C.* 111 (2): 79-80

Short, Lester L. 1969. A new species of blackbird (*Agelaius*) from Peru. *Occasional Papers Museum of Zoology Louisiana State University* 36: 1-8

—1970a. Notes on the habits of some Argentine and Peruvian woodpeckers (Aves: Picidae). *Amer. Museum Novitates* 2413: 15-16

—1982. *Woodpeckers of the World.* Delaware Museum of Natural History

Sibley, Charles. 1996. *Birds of the World*, version 2. Cincinnati, Ohio: Thayer Birding Software

Simon, E. 1921. *Histoire Naturelle des Trochilidae (Synopsis et Catalogue)* pp. i-vi, 1-416. Encyclopedia Roret. Paris: L. Mulo

Snow, David. 1982. *The Cotingas.* Ithaca: Cornell University Press

Soukop, Jaraslov. 1979. *Vocabulario de los nombres vulgares de la flora Peruana y catálogo de los gereros.* Lima: Editorial Salesiana

Stattersfield, Alison, Michael Crosby, Adrian Long and David Wege. 1997. *Endemic Bird Areas of The World.* Cambridge: BirdLife International

Stotz, Douglas F., John W. Fitzpatrick, Theodore A. Parker III and Debra K. Moskovits. 1996. *Neotropical Birds: Ecology and Conservation.* University of Chicago Press

Taczanowski, M. L. 1884-1886. *Ornithologie du Péru* (3 vol.). Berlin: Friedlander & Sons

Taylor, Barry. 1998. *A Guide to the Rails, Crakes, Gallinules and Coots of the World.* Yale University Press

Terborgh, John. W. 1971. Distribution on environmental gradients: theory and a preliminary interpretation of distributional patterns in the avifauna of the Cordillera Vilcabamba, Peru. *Ecology* 52 (1): 23-40

Terborgh, John W., John W. Fitzpatrick and Louise Emmons. 1984. Annotated Checklist of Bird and Mammal Species of Cocha Cashu Biological Station, Manu National Park, Peru. *Fieldiana (Zoology)* 21: 1-29. Chicago: Field Museum of Natural History

Todd, Frank. 1986. *Natural History of the Waterfowl.* Vista, CA: Ibis Publishing Company

Toyne, E. P. and Flanagan, J. N. M. 1996. The first nest record of Red-faced Parrot *Hapalopsittaca pyrrhops. Cotinga* 5: 43-45

Trevis, Barry. 1994. Andean Potoo *Nyctibius maculosus. Cotinga* 1: 35

Tubaro, Pablo Luis and Bettina Mahler. 1998. Acoustic frequencies and body mass in New World doves. *Condor* 100: 54-61

Turner, Angela and Chris Rose. 1989. *Swallows and Martins: An Identification Guide.* Boston: Houghton Mifflin Company

Valqui, Thomas. 1994. The extinction of the Junín Flightless Grebe? *Cotinga* 1: 42-44

Valqui, Thomas and Jon Fjeldså. 1999. New brush-finch *Atlapetes* from Peru. *Ibis* 141: 194-198

Van der Gaast, J. 1997. Canyon canastero *Asthenes pudibunda* in northern Chile. *Cotinga* 5: 24-27

Vaurie, C. 1972. An ornithological gazetteer of Perú (based on information compiled by J. T. Zimmer. *American Museum Novitates* 2491

—1980. *Taxonomy and geographical distribution of the Furnariidae.* American Museum of Natural History Volume 166, article 1

Wege, David C. and Adrian J. Long. 1995. *Key Areas for Threatened Birds in the Neotropics.* Cambridge: BirdLife International

Weske, John S. and John W. Terborgh. 1974. *Hemispingus parodii,* a new species of tanager from Peru. *Wilson Bull.* 86 (2): 97-103

—1977. *Phaethornis koepckeae,* a new species of hummingbird from Peru. *Condor* 79: 143-147

—1981. *Otus marshalli,* a new species of screech-owl from Peru. *The Auk* 98 (1): 1-7

Wheatley, Nigel. 1994. *Where to watch birds in South America.* London: Christopher Helm

Whiffen, Mark and Lisa Sadgrove. 2000. *Expedición Tumbes 2000—Reporte Preliminar.* Piura: ProAvesPerú

Whitney, Bret M. 1996. Flight behavior and other field characteristics of the genera of Neoptropical parrots. *Cotinga* 5: 32-42

Whitney, Bret M. and José Alvarez Alonso. 1998. A new *Herpsilochmus* antwren (Aves: Thamnophilidae) from northern Amazonian Peru and adjacent Ecuador: The role of edaphic heterogeneity of terra firme forest. *The Auk* 115 (3): 559-576

Whittaker, Andrew and David C. Oren. 1999. Important ornithological records from the Rio Jurúa, western Amazonia, including twelve additions to the Brazilian avifauna. *Bulletin B. O. C.* 119 (4): 235-260

Whittingham, M. J. and R. S. R. Williams. 2000. Notes on morphogical differences exhibited by Royal Flycatcher *Onychorhynchus coronatus* taxa. *Cotinga* 13: 14-16

Wust, Walter H., Alfredo Begazo and Thomas Valqui. 1990. Las Aves de Rupac. Lima: *Boletin de Lima* 71: 19-22

Wust, Walter, Anthony Luscombe and Thomas Valqui. 1994. *Las Aves de los Pantanos de Villa y Alrededores.* Lima: Asociation de Ecologia y Conservation

Zimmer, Kevin. 1997. Species limits in *Cranioleuca vulpina. Ornithological Monographs* Vol. 48: 849-864

Index of Scientific Names

abeillei, Arremon 231
aburri, Aburria 33
Aburria 33
Accipiter 25-26
accipitrinus, Deroptyus 61
Acropternis 146
Actites 44
acutipennis, Chordeiles 69
    Pseudocolopteryx 163
acutirostris, Scytalopus 146
Adelomyia 81
aedon, Troglodytes 191
aegithaloides, Leptasthenura 107
Aegolius 67
aenea, Chloroceryle 91
aeneocauda, Metallura 86
aequatorialis, Momotus 92
aequinoctialis, Geothlypis 202
    Procellaria 9
Aeronautes 73
aethereus, Nyctibius 68
    Phaethon 12
aethiops, Thamnophilus 125
affinis, Scytalopus 146
    Veniliornis 101
agami, Agamia 16
Agamia 16
Agelaius 233-234
agilis, Oporornis 201
Aglaeactis 82
Aglaiocercus 88
agraphia, Uromyias 162
Agriornis 175
Agyrtria 80
Aimophila 231
Ajaia 19
ajaja, Ajaia 19
alaudinus, Phrygilus 221
alba, Ardea 15
    Calidris 44
    Tyto 63
albescens, Synallaxis 108
albicapilla, Cranioleuca 110
albicaudatus, Buteo 28
albiceps, Atlapetes 230
    Cranioleuca 110
    Elaenia 156
albicollis, Leucopternis 26
    Nyctidromus 70
    Porzana 37
    Turdus 195
albifacies, Poecilotriccus 164
albifrons, Conirostrum 205
    Muscisaxicola 176
    Pithys 137
albigula, Buteo 28
    Grallaria 141
    Upucerthia 105
albigularis, Sclerurus 119
    Synallaxis 108

albilatera, Diglossa 226
albilora, Muscisaxicola 176
albipennis, Penelope 33
albirostris, Galbula 92
albitarsus, Ciccaba 66
albiventer, Fluvicola 178
    Tachycineta 186
albiventris, Dacnis 218
    Myiornis 163
albocristata, Sericossypha 205
albogriseus, Pachyramphus 183
albogularis, Brachygalba 92
    Otus 65
    Tyrannus 182
albolineatus, Lepidocolaptes 123
albonotatus, Buteo 29
albus, Eudocimus 18
alexandrinus, Charadrius 41
aliciae, Aglaeactis 82
alinae, Eriocnemis 84
alnorum, Empidonax 172
alpina, Calidris 45
    Muscisaxicola 176
alpinus, Anairetes 162
alticola, Charadrius 42
    Poospiza 222
altiloquus, Vireo 198
altirostris, Scytalopus 145
amaurocephalus,
    Leptopogon 158
amaurochalinus, Turdus 195
Amaurolimnas 37
Amaurospiza 225
Amazilia 80
amazilia, Amazilia 80
Amazona 61
amazona, Chloroceryle 91
amazonica, Amazona 61
amazonicus, Thamnophilus 126
ambiguus, Ramphastos 99
Amblycercus 235
americana, Chloroceryle 91
    Mycteria 17
americanus, Coccyzus 62
    Daptrius 30
amethysticollis, Heliangelus 84
amethystina, Calliphlox 89
Ammodramus 231
Ampelioides 148
Ampelion 147
Anabacerthia 115
anabatinus, Thamnistes 127
Anairetes 162-163
analis, Catamenia 225
    Formicarius 139
    Iridosornis 213
Anas 21-22
Ancistrops 117
andecola, Stelgidopteryx 187
andecolus, Aeronautes 73

andicola, Agriornis 175
    Grallaria 140
    Leptasthenura 106
Andigena 98
andina, Gallinago 42
    Recurvirostra 40
andinus, Phoenicopterus 19
angolensis, Oryzoborus 225
angustifrons, Psarocolius 237
Anhima 19
Anhinga 14
anhinga, Anhinga 14
ani, Crotophaga 62
Anisognathus 213
anthonyi, Caprimulgus 71
Anthracothorax 77
Anthus 188
antillarum, Sterna 51
antisianus, Pharomachrus 90
antisiensis, Cranioleuca 110
Anurolimnas 35-36
Aphriza 44
Aptenodytes 5
aquila, Eutoxeres 74
Ara 56
aradus, Cyphorhinus 192
Aramides 37
Aramus 35
ararauna, Ara 56
Aratinga 56-57
arcuata, Pipreola 148
Ardea 15
ardesiaca, Conopophaga 143
    Fulica 38
ardesiacus, Thamnomanes 128
Arenaria 44
arequipae, Asthenes 112
argentatus, Larus 49
argyrofenges, Tangara 218
aricomae, Cinclodes 106
armata, Merganetta 20
aroyae, Thamnophilus 125
Arremon 231
Arremonops 231
arthus, Tangara 216
Arundinicola 178
Asio 67-68
assimilis, Haplophaedia 85
    Myrmotherula 131
    Puffinus 10
    Tolmomyias 167
Asthenes 112-113
Asturina 27
atacamensis, Cinclodes 106
ater, Haematopus 39
    Ibycter 30
aterrimus, Knipolegus 177
Athene 67
Atlapetes 229-230
atrata, Carduelis 200

Index of Scientific Names

atratus, Coragyps 22
   Scytalopus 145
atricapillus, Donacobius 189
atricaudus, Myiobius 170
atriceps, Phrygilus 221
atricilla, Larus 49
atricollis, Colaptes 102
atrimentalis, Phaethornis 75
atrinucha, Thamnophilus 126
atrirostris, Oryzoborus 225
atrocapillus, Crypturellus 3
atronitens, Xenopipo 153
atropileus, Hemispingus 206
atrothorax, Myrmeciza 137
atrovirens, Psarocolius 236
Attagis 47
Atticora 187
Attila 178-179
Augastes 88
Aulacorhynchus 97
aura, Cathartes 22
aurantiacus, Metopothrix 114
aurantiirostris, Arremon 231
   Saltator 232
aurantiivertex, Heterocercus 153
aurantioatrocristatus,
   Griseotyrannus 182
auratus, Capito 96
aurea, Aratinga 57
   Jacamerops 93
aureodorsalis, Buthraupis 212
aureoventris, Pheucticus 233
aurescens, Heliodoxa 81
auriceps, Pharomachrus 90
auriculata, Zenaida 53
aurifrons, Ammodramus 231
   Psilopsiagon 58
   Picumnus 99
aurita, Conopophaga 143
   Heliothryx 88
aurovirens, Capito 96
Automolus 118-119
autumnalis, Dendrocygna 20
axillaris, Aramides 37
   Herpsilochmus 132
   Myrmotherula 130
aymara, Metriopelia 54
azara, Pteroglossus 98
azarae, Synallaxis 108

baeri, Leucippus 79
bahamensis, Anas 21
bairdii, Calidris 45
   Myiodynastes 181
balliviani, Odontophorus 34
bambla, Microcerculus 191
barbata, Penelope 32
barbatus, Myiobius 170
baroni, Cranioleuca 110
barrabandi, Pionopsitta 60

bartletti, Crypturellus 3
Bartramia 43
Baryphthengus 92
Basileuterus 202-203
beauharnaesii, Pteroglossus 98
belcheri, Larus 48
   Pachyptila 9
bellicosa, Sturnella 234
benjamini, Urosticte 85
berlepschi, Hylopezus 142
   Phacellodomus 114
Berlepschia 116
bernardi, Sakesphorus 124
bicolor, Accipiter 26
   Conirostrum 204
   Dendrocygna 20
   Tachycineta 186
bidentatus, Harpagus 24
bifasciatus, Gymnostinops 237
bivittatus, Basileuterus 202
blakei, Grallaria 142
bogotensis, Anthus 188
Boissonneaua 82
boissonneautii,
   Pseudocolaptes 115
Bolborhynchus 58
boliviana, Chiroxiphia 151
bolivianum, Glaucidium 66
bolivianus, Attila 178
   Scytalopus 145
   Zimmerius 160
bombus, Chaetocercus 89
bonapartei, Nothocercus 2
bonariensis, Molothrus 234
   Thraupis 212
Botaurus 17
bougainvillii, Phalacrocorax 14
bougueri, Urochroa 82
bourcieri, Phaethornis 75
bourcierii, Eubucco 96
bouvronides, Sporophila 224
Brachygalba 92
brachyura, Chaetura 73
   Myrmotherula 128
   Synallaxis 108
brachyurus, Buteo 28
   Graydidascalus 60
   Idiopsar 221
bracteatus, Nyctibius 69
branickii, Heliodoxa 82
   Leptosittaca 57
   Odontorchilus 189
   Theristicus 18
brasilianum, Glaucidium 67
brasilianus, Phalacrocorax 14
brevicauda, Muscigralla 176
Brotogeris 58-59
brunnea, Nonnula 95
brunneinucha, Buarremon 230
brunneiventris, Diglossa 227

brunnescens, Premnoplex 115
Buarremon 230
Bubo 65
Bubulcus 16
Bucco 94
buckleyi, Columbina 53
   Micrastur 31
buffoni, Circus 25
buffonii, Chalybura 81
bulleri, Thalassarche 7
   Puffinus 10
Burhinus 40
burrovianus, Cathartes 23
Busarellus 27
Buteo 28-29
Buteogallus 27
Buthraupis 212
Butorides 16

cabanisi, Synallaxis 108
cachinnans, Herpetotheres 31
Cacicus 235-236
cactorum, Asthenes 113
   Melanerpes 100
caerulea, Egretta 16
   Halobaena 9
caerulescens, Diglossopis 227
   Geranospiza 26
   Sporophila 224
   Thamnophilus 126
   Theristicus 18
caeruleus, Cyanerpes 219
caesar, Poospiza 223
caesius, Thamnomanes 128
Cairina 20
cajanea, Aramides 37
Calidris 44-46
callinota, Terenura 133
calliparaea, Chlorochrysa 215
Calliphlox 89
callonotus, Veniliornis 101
callophrys, Tangara 218
Calochaetes 211
calophrys, Hemispingus 206
calopterum, Todirostrum 166
calopterus, Aramides 37
   Mecocerculus 162
campanisona, Chamaeza 139
   Myrmothera 142
Campephilus 103
Camptostoma 154
Campylopterus 76
Campylorhamphus 123
Campylorhynchus 189
canadensis, Sakesphorus 124
   Wilsonia 202
candidus, Melanerpes 100
caniceps, Myiopagis 155
canigenis, Atlapetes 230
canigularis, Chlorospingus 206

Index of Scientific Names

cantator, Hypocnemis 135
canus, Scytalopus 146
canutus, Calidris 44
capense, Daption 7
capensis, Bucco 94
    Zonotrichia 231
capistrata, Muscisaxicola 175
capitalis, Grallaria 141
    Poecilotriccus 164
Capito 96
Caprimulgus 70-71
Capsiempis 154
Caracara 30
carbo, Ramphocelus 211
Carduelis 199-200
caripensis, Steatornis 68
carmioli, Chlorothraupis 208
caroli, Polyonymus 86
carneipes, Puffinus 10
carolina, Porzana 37
carrikeri, Grallaria 141
Casiornis 179
castanea, Hapaloptila 95
    Pithys 137
castaneiceps, Anurolimnas 35
    Conopophaga 143
    Lysurus 228
castaneiventris, Sporophila 225
    Delothraupis 213
castaneus, Pachyramphus 183
castanotis, Pteroglossus 98
castelnau, Picumnus 100
castelnaudii, Aglaeactis 82
castro, Oceanodroma 11
Catamblyrhynchus 220
Catamenia 225-226
Catharacta see Stercorarius
Cathartes 22-23
Catharus 193
Catoptrophorus 44
caudacutus, Sclerurus 119
caudata, Drymophila 133
cauta, Thalassarche 7
cayana, Cotinga 150
    Dacnis 219
    Piaya 62
    Tangara 217
    Tityra 184
cayanensis, Icterus 235
    Leptodon 24
    Myiozetetes 180
cayanus, Vanellus 40
cayennensis, Columba 53
    Mesembrinibis 18
    Panyptila 73
ceciliae, Metriopelia 54
cela, Cacicus 235
Celeus 102-103
Cephalopterus 150
cephalotes, Myiarchus 180

Cercomacra 133-134
certhia, Dendrocolaptes 121
Certhiaxis 111
cerulea, Dendroica 201
Ceryle 91
chacuru, Nystalus 94
Chaetocercus 89
Chaetura 72-73
chalcopterus, Pionus 60
Chalcostigma 87
chalcothorax, Galbula 93
chalybea, Progne 185
chalybeus, Lophornis 77
Chalybura 81
Chamaepetes 33
Chamaeza 139
chapmani, Chaetura 73
Charadrius 41-42
Chauna 19
Chelidoptera 96
cheriway, Caracara 30
cherriei, Myrmotherula 129
    Synallaxis 109
chiguanco, Turdus 194
chihi, Plegadis 18
chilensis, Phoenicopterus 19
    Stercorarius 47
    Tangara 216
    Vanellus 40
chimachima, Milvago 30
chinchipensis, Synallaxis 109
chionogaster, Leucippus 79
chiriquensis, Elaenia 156
Chiroxiphia 151
Chlidonias 51
Chloephaga 20
chloris, Piprites 153
chlorocercus, Leucippus 79
Chloroceryle 91
Chlorochrysa 215
chlorolepidota, Pipreola 148
chloromeros, Pipra 152
Chlorophanes 219
Chlorophonia 215
Chloropipo 151
chloroptera, Ara 56
chloropus, Gallinula 38
Chlorornis 205
Chlorospingus 206
Chlorostilbon 78
Chlorothraupis 208
chlorotica, Euphonia 214
choliba, Otus 64
Chondrohierax 24
chopi, Gnorimopsar 237
Chordeiles 69
chrosocephalum, Neopelma 153
chrysocephalus, Icterus 235
    Myiodynastes 181
chrysochloros, Piculus 102

chrysocrotaphum,
    Todirostrum 166
chrysogaster, Basileuterus 202
    Pheucticus 233
chrysonotus, Cacicus 236
chrysopasta, Euphonia 214
chrysops, Zimmerius 161
chrysoptera, Vermivora 200
chrysopterus, Masius 152
Chrysoptilus 102
chrysostoma, Thalassarche 7
chrysotis, Tangara 216
Chrysuronia 79
Ciccaba 65-66
Cichlopsis 193
Ciconia 18
cinchoneti, Conopias 181
Cinclodes 105-106
Cinclus 189
cincta, Dichrozona 131
cinctus, Saltator 232
cinerascens, Cercomacra 133
cinerea, Muscisaxicola 176
    Piezorhina 222
    Procellaria 9
    Serpophaga 157
    Xolmis 174
cinereicapillus, Zimmerius 160
cinereiceps, Phyllomyias 160
cinereiventris, Chaetura 72
    Microbates 196
cinereum, Conirostrum 204
    Todirostrum 166
cinereus, Circus 25
    Coccyzus 61
    Contopus 172
    Crypturellus 2
cinnamomea, Certhiaxis 111
    Neopipo 171
    Pyrrhomyias 171
cinnamomeipectus,
    Hemitriccus 165
cinnamomeiventris,
    Ochthoeca 173
cinnamomeus, Attila 178
Cinnycerthia 189-190
Circus 25
cirrocephalus, Larus 49
Cissopis 205
Cistothorus 191
citrina, Sicalis 228
citriniventris, Attila 178
clamator, Asio 67
Claravis 54
climacocerca, Hydropsalis 71
Cnemarchus 174
Cnemoscopus 206
Cnemotriccus 171
Cnipodectes 166
coccineus, Calochaetes 211

Index of Scientific Names

Coccyzus 61-62
Cochlearius 16
cochlearius, Cochlearius 16
cocoi, Ardea 15
coelestis, Forpus 58
Coeligena 83
coeligena, Coeligena 83
Coereba 204
coeruleicinctis,
    Aulacorhynchus 97
coeruleocapilla, Pipra 152
coerulescens, Saltator 232
Colaptes 102
Colibri 76-77
collaris, Accipiter 25
    Charadrius 41
    Microbates 196
    Trogon 90
colma, Formicarius 139
Colonia 178
colonus, Colonia 178
Columba 52-53
columbarius, Falco 32
columbiana, Sicalis 228
Columbina 53-54
concolor, Amaurolimnas 37
    Amaurospiza 225
    Xenospingus 222
condamini, Eutoxeres 74
Conioptilon 150
conirostris, Arremonops 231
Conirostrum 204-205
Conopias 181
Conopophaga 143
Conothraupis 205
Contopus 171-172
cookii, Pterodroma 8
cooperi, Contopus 171
cora, Thaumastura 88
Coragyps 22
coraya, Thryothorus 190
cornuta, Anhima 19
coronata, Pipra 152
coronatus, Basileuterus 203
    Onychorhynchus 169
    Platyrinchus 168
correndera, Anthus 188
corvina, Sporophila 223
coruscans, Colibri 77
Coryphaspiza 220
Coryphospingus 220
Corythopis 166
Cotinga 149-150
cotinga, Cotinga 149
couloni, Propyrrhura 56
courseni, Synallaxis 108
Cranioleuca 110-111
crassirostris, Carduelis 199
    Geositta 104
    Oryzoborus 225

Crax 34
Creagrus 50
creatopus, Puffinus 10
crepitans, Psophia 35
Creurgops 209
crinitus, Myiarchus 180
cristata, Elaenia 156
    Lophostrix 66
cristatus, Oxyruncus 185
    Tachyphonus 209
Crotophaga 62-63
cruentatus, Melanerpes 100
cruentus, Rhodospingus 220
cruziana, Columbina 54
cryptoleucus, Thamnophilus 125
cryptolophus, Snowornis 149
cryptoxanthus, Myiophobus 170
Crypturellus 2-3
cryptus, Cypseloides 72
cucullata, Andigena 98
cucullatus, Coryphospingus 220
culminatus, Ramphastos 99
cumanensis, Pipile 33
cunicularia, Geositta 104
    Athene 67
cupripennis, Aglaeactis 82
curtata, Cranioleuca 111
curucui, Trogon 90
curvirostris, Nothoprocta 4
cuvieri, Ramphastos 99
cyanea, Chlorophonia 214
    Diglossopis 227
Cyanerpes 219
cyanescens, Galbula 93
cyaneus, Cyanerpes 219
cyanicollis, Galbula 92
    Tangara 217
cyanocephala, Euphonia 214
    Thraupis 212
Cyanocompsa 233
Cyanocorax 196-197
cyanoides, Cyanocompsa 233
cyanoleuca, Pygochelidon 186
Cyanolyca 197
cyanomelas, Cyanocorax 197
cyanoptera, Anas 21
cyanoptera, Brotogeris 59
cyanopterus, Pterophanes 83
cyanotis, Tangara 217
cyanus, Hylocharis 79
Cyclarhis 199
Cymbilaimus 124
Cyphorhinus 192
Cypseloides 72

dachilleae, Nannopsittaca 59
Dacnis 218-219
dactylatra, Sula 13
Damophila 78
Daption 7

Daptrius 30
darwinii, Nothura 4
dea, Galbula 93
Deconychura 120
decumanus, Psarocolius 236
decurtatus, Hylophilus 199
defilippiana, Pterodroma 8
deiroleucus, Falco 32
delattrei, Lophornis 77
Delothraupis 213
delphinae, Colibri 76
Dendrexetastes 121
Dendrocincla 120
Dendrocolaptes 121
Dendrocygna 20
Dendroica 201
dentata, Creurgops 209
derbianus, Aulacorhynchus 97
desolata, Pachyptila 9
devillei, Drymophila 132
diadema, Catamblyrhynchus 220
    Ochthoeca 173
Dichrozona 131
Diglossa 226-227
Diglossopis 227
dignissima, Grallaria 140
dignus, Veniliornis 101
Diomedea 6
Diopsittaca 56
discors, Anas 21
Discosura 78
Diuca 221
Dives 234
doliatus, Thamnophilus 124
Dolichonyx 233
Doliornis 147
domesticus, Passer 197
dominica, Oxyura 22
    Pluvialis 41
dominicanus, Larus 48
dominicensis, Progne 185
dominicus, Tachybaptus 5
Donacobius 189
dorbygnianus, Picumnus 100
dorsalis, Automolus 118
    Phacellodomus 114
Doryfera 76
Dromococcyx 63
dryas, Catharus 193
Drymophila 131-132
Dryocopus 103
Dubusia 213
dugandi, Herpsilochmus 132
dumetaria, Upucerthia 105
Dysithamnus 127

ecaudatus, Myiornis 163
egregia, Chaetura 73
Egretta 16
eisenmanni, Thryothorus 190

Index of Scientific Names

Elaenia 155-157
Elanoides 24
Elanus 24
elatus, Tyrannulus 154
Electron 92
elegans, Celeus 103
   Laniisoma 147
   Melanopareia 144
   Progne 186
   Sterna 50
   Xiphorhynchus 122
eludens, Grallaria 140
Emberizoides 228
Empidonax 172
Empidonomus 182
Ensifera 83
ensifera, Ensifera 83
Entomodestes 193
episcopus, Thraupis 211
epomophora, Diomedea 6
Eriocnemis 84
erythrocephala, Pipra 152
erythrocephalus, Hylocryptus 119
erythrocercus, Philydor 117
erythrogenys, Aratinga 57
erythroleuca, Grallaria 141
erythronotus, Phrygilus 221
erythrops, Neocrex 37
erythroptera, Ortalis 32
   Phlegopsis 138
erythropterus, Philydor 117
erythrophthalma, Netta 22
erythropthalmus, Coccyzus 62
erythropygius, Cnemarchus 174
   Pteroglossus 98
erythrura, Myrmotherula 130
erythrurus, Terenotriccus 170
estella, Oreotrochilus 82
Eubucco 96-97
Eucometis 208
Eudocimus 18
euleri, Lathrotriccus 171
eulophotes, Lophotriccus 164
euophrys, Thryothorus 190
Euphonia 214-215
eupogon, Metallura 86
euryptera, Opisthoprora 87
Eurypyga 39
Euscarthmus 163
Eutoxeres 74
exilis, Ixobrychus 17
   Laterallus 36
eximia, Buthraupis 212
externa, Pterodroma 8
exulans, Diomedea 6

Falco 31-32
falklandicus, Charadrius 41
fanny, Myrtis 89
fannyi, Thalurania 78

farinosa, Amazona 61
fasciata, Atticora 187
   Columba 53
fasciatum, Tigrisoma 17
fasciatus, Anurolimnas 36
   Campylorhynchus 189
   Myiophobus 170
fasciicauda, Pipra 151
fedoa, Limosa 43
femoralis, Falco 32
   Scytalopus 145
ferox, Myiarchus 180
ferruginea, Calidris 46
   Hirundinea 171
   Oxyura 22
ferrugineipectus,
   Grallaricula 142
ferrugineiventre, Conirostrum 205
festiva, Amazona 61
filicauda, Pipra 151
fimbriata, Polyerata 80
fjeldsaai, Myrmotherula 129
flammeus, Asio 68
flammulata, Asthenes 113
flammulatus, Hemitriccus 164
   Thripadectes 116
flava, Piranga 210
flaveola, Capsiempis 154
   Coereba 204
   Sicalis 227
flavicans, Myiophobus 169
flavicollis, Hemithraupis 208
flavigula, Piculus 101
flavigularis, Chlorospingus 206
   Platyrinchus 168
flavinucha, Muscisaxicola 176
flavipes, Notiochelidon 187
   Tringa 43
flavirostris, Anairetes 163
   Anas 21
   Grallaricula 142
   Monasa 95
   Porphyrula 38
flaviventer, Dacnis 219
flaviventris, Tolmomyias 168
flavivertex, Myiopagis 155
flavogaster, Elaenia 156
flavoviridis, Vireo 198
flavus, Celeus 103
Florisuga 76
fluviatilis, Muscisaxicola 175
Fluvicola 178
foetidus, Gymnoderus 150
forbesi, Atlapetes 229
forficatus, Elanoides 24
Formicarius 139
Formicivora 132
Forpus 58
fortis, Myrmeciza 137
franciae, Agyrtria 80

fraseri, Basileuterus 202
   Oreomanes 205
Frederickena 124
Fregata 15
Fregetta 11
frenata, Geotrygon 55
frontalis, Hemispingus 207
   Muscisaxicola 176
   Ochthoeca 172
   Pipreola 148
fruticeti, Phrygilus 221
fucata, Stelgidopteryx 187
Fulica 38
fulica, Heliornis 39
fulicaria, Phalaropus 46
fuliginosa, Dendrocincla 120
   Schizoeaca 111
Fulmarus 7
   Cinnycerthia 190
fulvicauda, Basileuterus 203
fulvipectus, Rhynchocyclus 167
fulviventris, Hylopezus 142
   Turdus 194
fulvogularis, Malacoptila 94
fulvus, Lanio 209
fumicolor, Ochthoeca 174
fumigatus, Contopus 171
   Myiotheretes 174
   Veniliornis 101
furcata, Thalurania 78
furcatus, Anthus 188
   Creagrus 50
Furnarius 106
fusca, Dendroica 201
   Malacoptila 94
fuscata, Sterna 51
fuscater, Catharus 193
   Turdus 194
fuscatus, Cnemotriccus 171
fuscescens, Catharus 193
fuscicauda, Ramphotrigon 167
fusciceps, Phacellodomus 114
fuscicollis, Calidris 45
fuscocinereus, Lipaugus 149
fuscorufus, Myiotheretes 174
fuscus, Cinclodes 105

gaimardi, Phalacrocorax 14
gaimardii, Myiopagis 154
Galbalcyrhynchus 92
Galbula 92-93
galeatus, Lophotriccus 164
Gallinago 42-43
gallinago, Gallinago 42
Gallinula 38
Gampsonyx 24
garnotii, Pelecanoides 12
gayaquilensis, Campephilus 103
gayi, Attagis 47
genibarbis, Thryothorus 190

Index of Scientific Names

gentryi, Herpsilochmus 132
geoffroyi, Neomorphus 63
   Augastes 88
georgica, Anas 21
Geositta 104-105
Geothlypis 202
Geotrygon 55
Geranoaetus 27
Geranospiza 26
gigantea, Fulica 38
giganteus, Macronectes 7
gigas, Elaenia 156
   Patagona 84
gilvicollis, Micrastur 31
glacialoides, Fulmarus 7
glauca, Diglossopis 227
Glaucidium 66-67
Glaucis 74
globulosa, Crax 34
Glyphorynchus 121
Gnorimopsar 237
goeldii, Myrmeciza 136
goudotii, Chamaepetes 33
graceannae, Icterus 235
gracilipes, Zimmerius 161
gracilis, Oceanites 11
Grallaria 140-142
grallaria, Fregetta 11
Grallaricula 142-143
grammicus, Celeus 102
granadensis, Hemitriccus 165
   Myiozetetes 181
grandis, Nyctibius 68
granti, Sula 13
Graydidascalus 60
griseicapillus, Sittasomus 120
griseiceps, Myrmeciza 137
   Phyllomyias 160
griseipectus, Lathrotriccus 171
griseiventris, Taphrolesbia 87
griseogularis, Phaethornis 75
griseomurina, Schizoeaca 111
Griseotyrannus 182
griseus, Limnodromus 43
   Nyctibius 68
   Puffinus 10
grossus, Saltator 232
gryphus, Vultur 23
guainumbi, Polytmus 79
gualaquizae, Phylloscartes 159
guarauna, Aramus 35
guatimalensis, Grallaria 140
guianensis, Morphnus 29
guimeti, Klais 77
guira, Hemithraupis 208
gujanensis, Cyclarhis 199
   Odontophorus 34
   Synallaxis 109
gularis, Heliodoxa 81
   Hellmayrea 110

Paroaria 228
guttata, Ortalis 32
guttatus Tinamus 1
   Xiphorhynchus 122
guttuligera, Premnornis 114
gutturata, Cranioleuca 111
guy, Phaethornis 74
Gymnoderus 150
Gymnomystax 237
Gymnopithys 137-138
Gymnostinops 237
gyrola, Tangara 217

Habia 210
haemastica, Limosa 43
haematogaster, Campephilus 103
haematonota, Myrmotherula 130
Haematopus 39
haemorrhous, Cacicus 235
haliaetus, Pandion 23
Halobaena 9
hamatus, Rostrhamus 24
Hapalopsittaca 60
Hapaloptila 95
haplonota, Grallaria 140
Haplophaedia 85
Haplospiza 226
hardyi, Glaucidium 67
Harpagus 24
Harpia 29
Harpyaliaetus 27
harpyja, Harpia 29
harrisii, Aegolius 67
harterti, Phlogophilus 81
hauxwelli, Myrmotherula 129
   Turdus 195
Heliangelus 84
helias, Eurypyga 39
Heliodoxa 81-82
Heliomaster 88
Heliornis 39
Heliothryx 88
helleri, Schizoeaca 112
Hellmayrea 110
hellmayri, Anthus 188
   Mecocerculus 162
hemileucurus, Phlogophilus 81
hemileucus, Myrmochanes 135
hemimelaena, Myrmeciza 136
Hemispingus 206-207
Hemithraupis 208
Hemitriccus 164-165
Henicorhina 191
herbicola, Emberizoides 228
herodias, Ardea 15
Herpetotheres 31
Herpsilochmus 131-132
herrani, Chalcostigma 87
Heterocercus 153
Heteroscelus 44

Himantopus 40
himantopus, Calidris 45
hirsuta, Glaucis 74
hirundinacea, Sterna 50
Hirundinea 171
Hirundo 188
hirundo, Sterna 51
hispaniolensis, Poospiza 223
hispidus, Phaethornis 74
hoazin, Opisthocomus 35
holochlora, Chloropipo 151
holosericeus, Amblycercus 235
holostictus, Thripadectes 116
homochroa, Catamenia 226
homochrous, Pachyramphus 184
hornbyi, Oceanodroma 12
huallagae, Aulacorhynchus 97
huancavelicae, Asthenes 112
hudsoni, Knipolegus 177
huetii, Touit 59
huhula, Ciccaba 66
humboldti, Spheniscus 5
humeralis, Ammodramus 231
   Parkerthraustes 232
   Diglossa 227
humeralis, Terenura 133
humilis, Asthenes 113
Hydropsalis 71
Hylexetastes 121
Hylocharis 78-79
Hylocryptus 119
Hyloctistes 117
Hylopezus 142
Hylophilus 198-199
Hylophylax 138
Hymenops 178
hyperythra, Myrmeciza 136
Hypocnemis 135
Hypocnemoides 135
hypochondriacus,
   Siptornopsis 110
hypoglauca, Andigena 98
hypoleuca, Grallaria 141
   Serpophaga 157
hypopyrra, Laniocera 147
hypospodia, Synallaxis 108
hypostictus, Leucippus 80
hypoxantha, Hypocnemis 135
hypoxanthus, Hylophilus 198

ibis, Bubulcus 16
Ibycter 30
icterocephalus, Agelaius 234
icterophrys, Satrapa 178
Icterus 235
icterus, Icterus 235
Ictinia 25
Idiopsar 221
igniventris, Anisognathus 212
ignobilis, Turdus 195

Index of Scientific Names

iheringi, Myrmotherula 131
imperialis, Gallinago 43
inca, Coeligena 83
    Larosterna 52
incanus, Heteroscelus 44
Incaspiza 222
inda, Chloroceryle 91
inerme, Ornithion 154
Inezia 162
infuscatus, Automolus 118
ingens, Otus 64
inornata, Catamenia 225
    Inezia 162
    Thlypopsis 208
inornatus, Myiophobus 169
inquisitor, Tityra 184
inscriptus, Pteroglossus 98
intermedia, Pipreola 148
interpres, Arenaria 44
involucris, Ixobrychus 17
Iodopleura 149
iohannis, Hemitriccus 165
Iridophanes 218
Iridosornis 213
iris, Coeligena 83
irrorata, Phoebastria 6
isabellae, Iodopleura 149
isidorei, Pipra 152
isidori, Oroaetus 30
Ixobrychus 17

Jabiru 18
Jacamerops 93
Jacana 39
jacana, Jacana 39
jacarina, Volatinia 223
jacquacu, Penelope 33
jamaicensis, Laterallus 36
jamesi, Phoenicopterus 19
jamesoni, Gallinago 43
jardinii, Glaucidium 66
jelskii, Iridosornis 213
    Ochthoeca 173
    Upucerthia 105
johannae, Doryfera 76
jubata, Neochen 20
julie, Damophila 78
julius, Nothocercus 2
juninensis, Muscisaxicola 176

kalinowskii, Nothoprocta 4
kingi, Aglaiocercus 88
kirkii, Veniliornis 101
Klais 77
Knipolegus 177
koepckeae, Cacicus 236
    Otus 64
    Phaethornis 75
kuhli, Leucopternis 26

labradorides, Tangara 217
lacrymiger, Lepidocolaptes 123
lacrymosus, Anisognathus 213
lactea, Polyerata 80
laeta, Incaspiza 222
Lafresnaya 83
lafresnayi, Lafresnaya 83
    Picumnus 99
lafresnayii, Diglossa 226
Lampropsar 237
Lamprospiza 205
lanceolata, Micromonacha 95
langsdorffi, Discosura 78
laniirostris, Euphonia 214
Laniisoma 147
Lanio 209
Laniocera 147
lansbergi, Coccyzus 62
largipennis, Campylopterus 76
Larosterna 52
Larus 48-49
Laterallus 36
Lathrotriccus 171
latinuchus, Atlapetes 229
latirostre, Todirostrum 166
latirostris, Ocyalus 237
latrans, Scytalopus 144
lawrencii, Turdus 195
leadbeateri, Heliodoxa 81
Legatus 182
Leistes see Sturnella
lemosi, Cypseloides 72
Lepidocolaptes 123
Leptasthenura 106-107
Leptodon 24
Leptopogon 157-158
Leptosittaca 57
Leptotila 55
Lesbia 85
Lessonia 177
leucaspis, Gymnopithys 137
Leucippus 79-80
leucocephala, Arundinicola 178
leucocephalus, Cinclus 189
leucogaster, Pionites 59
    Sula 14
    Thamnophilus 126
leucogenys, Cichlopsis 193
leucolaemus, Piculus 101
leucomelas, Turdus 195
leuconota, Pyriglena 134
leucophaius, Legatus 182
leucophrys, Henicorhina 191
    Mecocerculus 161
    Myrmoborus 134
    Ochthoeca 174
    Vireo 197
leucophthalma, Myrmotherula 129
leucophthalmus, Aratinga 57
leucops, Platycichla 193

leucoptera, Henicorhina 191
    Piranga 210
    Psophia 35
    Sporophila 224
Leucopternis 26
leucopterus, Atlapetes 230
    Nyctibius 69
leucopus, Furnarius 106
leucopyga, Nyctiprogne 70
leucorhoa, Oceanodroma 12
leucorrhoa, Tachycineta 186
leucorrhous, Buteo 28
leucospodia, Pseudelaenia 155
leucosticta, Henicorhina 191
leucostictus, Dysithamnus 127
leucostigma, Percnostola 136
leucotis, Entomodestes 193
    Galbalcyrhynchus 92
    Thryothorus 190
    Vireolanius 199
leucurus, Elanus 24
    Threnetes
leveriana, Cissopis 205
lherminieri, Puffinus 10
lictor, Philohydor 180
limicola, Rallus 36
Limnodromus 43
Limosa 43
lineata, Dacnis 219
lineatum, Tigrisoma 17
lineatus, Cymbilaimus 124
    Dryocopus 103
lineola, Bolborhynchus 58
    Sporophila 224
linteatus, Heterocercus 153
lintoni, Myiophobus 169
Liosceles 144
Lipaugus 149
littoralis, Ochthornis 174
livia, Columba 52
lobatus, Phalaropus 46
Lochmias 119
Loddigesia 88
longicauda, Bartramia 43
    Deconychura 120
    Myrmotherula 129
longicaudatus, Mimus 192
longicaudus, Stercorarius 48
longipennis, Myrmotherula 131
longirostris, Caprimulgus 70
    Heliomaster 88
    Nasica 121
    Phaethornis 74
    Pterodroma 9
    Rallus 36
Lophornis 77
Lophostrix 66
lophotes, Percnostola 136
Lophotriccus 164
lorata, Sterna 51

Index of Scientific Names

loweryi, Xenoglaux 67
lubomirskii, Pipreola 148
luctuosa, Sporophila 224
luctuosus, Tachyphonus 209
ludovicae, Doryfera 76
ludovicianus, Pheucticus 233
lugubris, Brachygalba 92
    Myrmoborus 134
lululae, Poecilotriccus 164
lunulata, Gymnopithys 137
Lurocalis 69
lutea, Sicalis 227
luteiventris, Myiodynastes 182
    Myiozetetes 181
luteola, Sicalis 227
luteoviridis, Basileuterus 203
lutescens, Anthus 188
lutetiae, Coeligena 83
lyra, Uropsalis 71
Lysurus 228

macao, Ara 56
macconnelli, Mionectes 157
maccormicki, Stercorarius 47
Machaeropterus 152
macloviana, Muscisaxicola 175
macrodactylus, Bucco 94
Macronectes 7
macropus, Scytalopus 145
macrorhynchos, Notharchus 93
macrourus, Campylopterus 76
macularia, Actitis 44
macularius, Hylopezus 142
maculatum, Todirostrum 166
maculatus, Myiodynastes 181
    Pardirallus 37
maculicauda, Asthenes 113
    Hypocnemoides 135
maculicaudus, Caprimulgus 70
maculipennis, Larus 49
maculirostris, Muscisaxicola 175
    Turdus 195
maculosa, Columba 52
maculosus, Nyctibius 68
magellanica, Carduelis 199
magellanicus, Otus 65
magnificens, Fregata 15
magnirostris, Buteo 28
maguari, Ciconia 18
major, Crotophaga 62
    Podiceps 5
    Schiffornis 183
    Taraba 124
    Tinamus 1
Malacoptila 94-95
malaris, Phaethornis 75
Manacus 151
manacus, Manacus 151
manilata, Orthopsittaca 56
manu, Cercomacra 134

maranonica, Melanopareia 144
    Synallaxis 109
maranonicus, Turdus 194
marcapatae, Cranioleuca 110
margaritaceiventer,
    Hemitriccus 165
margaritae, Conirostrum 204
margaritatus, Megastictus 127
Margarornis 115
marginatus, Microcerculus 191
    Pachyramphus 184
mariae, Pteroglossus 98
marina, Pelagodroma 11
maritima, Geositta 104
markhami, Oceanodroma 12
marshalli, Otus 65
martii, Baryphthengus 92
martinica, Porphyrula 38
Masius 152
matthewsii, Boissonneaua 82
mauri, Calidris 45
maxima, Sterna 50
maximus, Saltator 232
maynana, Cotinga 149
mcilhennyi, Conioptilon 150
Mecocerculus 161-162
megacephala,
    Ramphotrigon 167
megalopterus, Phalcoboenus 30
Megarhynchus 180
Megastictus 127
melacoryphus, Coccyzus 62
melambrotus, Cathartes 23
melancholicus, Tyrannus 182
Melanerpes 100
melania, Oceanodroma 12
melanocephala, Pionites 59
melanocephalus, Myioborus 202
melanoceps, Myrmeciza 136
melanogaster,
    Oreotrochilus 82
    Piaya 62
    Ramphocelus 211
melanogenys, Adelomyia 81
melanolaemus, Atlapetes 230
melanoleuca, Lamprospiza 205
    Tringa 43
melanoleucos, Campephilus 103
melanoleucus, Geranoaetus 27
    Spizastur 29
melanonota, Pipraeidea 213
Melanopareia 144
melanopezus, Automolus 118
melanophaius, Laterallus 36
melanophris, Thalassarche 6
melanopis, Schistochlamys 205
    Theristicus 18
melanopogon,
    Hypocnemoides 135
melanops, Gallinula 38

Leucopternis 26
Phleocryptes 107
Trichothraupis 210
melanoptera, Chloephaga 20
    Metriopelia 54
melanorhynchus, Thripadectes 116
melanosticta,
    Rhegmatorhina 138
melanota, Pulsatrix 66
melanotis, Coryphaspiza 220
    Hapalopsittaca 60
    Hemispingus 207
melanotos, Calidris 45
    Sarkidiornis 20
melanura, Pyrrhura 57
melanurus, Himantopus 40
    Myrmoborus 135
    Ramphocaenus 196
    Trogon 90
mellisugus, Chlorostilbon 78
mellivora, Florisuga 76
meloda, Zenaida 53
meloryphus, Euscarthmus 163
menetriesii, Myrmotherula 131
menstruus, Pionus 60
mentalis, Dysithamnus 127
mercenaria, Amazona 61
Merganetta 20
meridionalis, Buteogallus 27
merula, Dendrocincla 120
Mesembrinibis 18
mesochrysa, Euphonia 214
mesomelas, Icterus 235
Metallura 86-87
Metopothrix 114
Metriopelia 54
mexicana, Tangara 215
mexicanum, Tigrisoma 17
mexicanus, Gymnomystax 237
    Himantopus 40
    Quiscalus 234
    Sclerurus 119
meyeni, Tachycineta 186
meyerdeschauenseei,
    Tangara 217
Micrastur 31
micrastur, Heliangelus 84
Microbates 196
Microcerculus 191
Micromonacha 95
microptera, Agriornis 175
    Rollandia 5
micropterus, Scytalopus 145
Micropygia 35
Microrhopias 132
microrhynchum,
    Ramphomicron 86
microsoma, Oceanodroma 11
micrura, Myrmia 89
militaris, Ara 56

Index of Scientific Names

Sturnella 234
milleri, Xenops 115
Milvago 30
Mimus 192
miniatus, Myioborus 202
minimus, Catharus 193
   Hemitriccus 165
minor, Chordeiles 69
   Fregata 15
   Furnarius 106
   Mecocerculus 162
   Pachyramphus 184
   Percnostola 136
minuta, Columbina 53
   Euphonia 215
   Piaya 62
minutilla, Calidris 45
minutus, Xenops 115
Mionectes 157
mirabilis, Loddigesia 88
mirandollei, Micrastur 31
mississippiensis, Ictinia 25
mitchellii, Phegornis 42
mitrata, Aratinga 56
Mitrephanes 171
Mitu 33-34
Mniotilta 201
modesta, Asthenes 112
modestus, Charadrius 42
modestus, Larus 48
   Sublegatus 161
moesta, Synallaxis 109
mollissima, Chamaeza 139
Molothrus 234
momota, Momotus 91
Momotus 91-92
Monasa 95
mondetoura, Claravis 54
montagnii, Penelope 33
montana, Agriornis 175
   Buthraupis 212
   Geotrygon 55
montivagus, Aeronautes 73
Morphnus 29
morphoeus, Monasa 95
moschata, Cairina 20
motacilloides,
   Herpsilochmus 132
mulsant, Chaetocercus 89
multostriata, Myrmotherula 129
murallae, Sporophila 223
murina, Notiochelidon 187
   Phaeomyias 154
murinus, Thamnophilus 125
murphyi, Progne 186
Muscigralla 176
Muscisaxicola 175-176
mustelina, Certhiaxis 111
Myadestes 192
Mycteria 17

mycteria, Jabiru 18
Myiarchus 179-180
Myiobius 170
Myioborus 202
Myiodynastes 181-182
Myiopagis 154-155
Myiophobus 169-170
Myiornis 163
Myiotheretes 174
Myiotriccus 169
Myiozetetes 180-181
myotherinus, Myrmoborus 134
Myrmeciza 136-137
Myrmia 89
Myrmoborus 134-135
Myrmochanes 135
Myrmornis 138
Myrmothera 142
Myrmotherula 128-131
Myrtis 89
mystacalis, Cyanocorax 197
   Diglossa 226
mystaceus, Platyrinchus 168

nacunda, Podager 70
naevia, Hylophylax 138
   Sclateria 135
   Tapera 63
nana, Grallaricula 143
Nannopsittaca 59
napensis, Stigmatura 162
Nasica 121
nationi, Atlapetes 230
nebouxii, Sula 13
necopinus, Xiphorhynchus 122
neglecta, Pterodroma 8
nematura, Lochmias 119
Nemosia 209
nengeta, Fluvicola 178
Neochelidon 187
Neochen 20
Neocrex 37
Neoctantes 127
Neomorphus 63
Neopelma 153
Neopipo 171
Nephelornis 220
Netta 22
niger, Chlidonias 51
   Neoctantes 127
   Rynchops 52
   Threnetes 74
nigrescens, Caprimulgus 71
   Cercomacra 133
   Contopus 172
nigricans, Pardirallus 37
   Sayornis 172
nigriceps, Saltator 232
   Turdus 194

Veniliornis 101
nigricollis, Anthracothorax 77
   Busarellus 27
   Phoenicircus 147
   Sporophila 224
nigrifrons, Monasa 95
nigripennis, Pterodroma 8
nigrirostris, Andigena 98
   Cyclarhis 199
nigrocapillus, Nothocercus 2
   Phyllomyias 160
nigrocincta, Tangara 217
nigrocristatus, Anairetes 162
   Basileuterus 203
nigrogularis, Ramphocelus 211
nigrolineata, Ciccaba 65
nigromaculata, Phlegopsis 138
nigroviridis, Tangara 217
nilotica, Sterna 50
nitida, Asturina 27
nitidus, Cyanerpes 219
niveigularis, Tyrannus 182
nobilis, Chamaeza 139
   Diopsittaca 56
   Gallinago 42
   Oreonympha 86
Nonnula 95
notatus, Chlorostilbon 78
Notharchus 93-94
Nothocercus 2
Nothocrax 33
Nothoprocta 4
Nothura 4
Notiochelidon 187
noveboracensis, Seiurus 201
nuchalis, Grallaria 141
Numenius 43
nuna, Lesbia 85
Nyctanassa 16
Nyctibius 68-69
Nycticorax 16
nycticorax, Nycticorax 16
Nyctidromus 70
Nyctiphrynus 70
Nyctiprogne 70
Nystalus 94

obsoletus, Turdus 195
obscura, Elaenia 157
   Myrmotherula 128
   Tiaris 226
obscurior, Sublegatus 161
obsoletum, Camptostoma 154
obsoletus, Crypturellus 2
   Xiphorhynchus 122
occidentalis, Leucopternis 26
   Onychorhynchus 169
   Pelecanus 13
occipitalis, Podiceps 6
oceanicus, Oceanites 11

Index of Scientific Names

Oceanites 11
Oceanodroma 11-12
ocellatus, Nyctiphrynus 70
    Xiphorhynchus 122
ochraceiceps, Hylophilus 199
ochraceifrons, Grallaricula 143
ochraceiventris, Leptotila 55
    Myiophobus 170
ochrocephala, Amazona 61
ochrolaemus, Automolus 118
Ochthoeca 172-174
Ochthornis 174
Ocreatus 85
Ocyalus 237
ocypetes, Chaetura 73
odomae, Metallura 87
Odontophorus 34
Odontorchilus 189
oenanthoides, Ochthoeca 173
oenone, Chrysuronia 79
oenops, Columba 53
olallai, Myiopagis 154
oleagineus, Mionectes 157
olivacea, Carduelis 200
    Piranga 210
olivaceum, Chalcostigma 87
olivaceus, Hylophilus 198
    Mionectes 157
    Mitrephanes 171
    Picumnus 100
    Rhynchocyclus 167
    Vireo 198
olivascens, Cinnycerthia 189
    Sicalis 227
oneilli, Nephelornis 220
    Platyrinchus 168-169
ophthalmicus,
    Chlorospingus 206
    Phylloscartes 158
Opisthocomus 35
Opisthoprora 87
Oporornis 201
orbignyianus, Thinocorus 47
orbitalis, Phylloscartes 158
orbygnesius, Bolborhynchus 58
ordii, Notharcus 93
oreas, Lessonia 177
orenocensis, Knipolegus 177
Oreomanes 205
Oreonympha 86
Oreopholus 42
Oreotrochilus 82
ornata, Myrmotherula 130
    Nothoprocta 4
    Thlypopsis 208
ornatus, Cephalopterus 150
    Myiotriccus 169
    Spizaetus 29
Ornithion 154
Oroaetus 30

Ortalis 32
orthonyx, Acropternis 146
Orthopsittaca 56
ortizi, Incaspiza 222
oryzivora, Scaphidura 234
oryzivorus, Dolichonyx 233
Oryzoborus 225
oseryi, Psarocolius 236
osgoodi, Tinamus 1
ottonis, Asthenes 112
Otus 64-65
Oxyruncus 185
Oxyura 22

Pachyptila 9
Pachyramphus 183-184
pallatangae, Elaenia 157
palliatus, Cinclodes 106
    Haematopus 39
    Thamnophilus 125
pallidinucha, Atlapetes 229
palmarum, Thraupis 212
palpebralis, Schizoeaca 111
palpebrata, Phoebetria 7
Pandion 23
Panyptila 73
papa, Sarcoramphus 23
Parabuteo 27
paradisaea, Sterna 51
paraguaiae, Gallinago 42
parasiticus, Stercorarius 48
Pardirallus 37-38
pareola, Chiroxiphia 151
parina, Xenodacnis 219
parkeri, Glaucidium 67
    Herpsilochmus 131
    Phylloscartes 159
    Scytalopus 147
Parkerthraustes 232
parkinsoni, Procellaria 10
Paroaria 228
parodii, Hemispingus 206
Parula 200
parulus, Anairetes 163
parva, Conopias 181
parvirostris, Chlorospingus 206
    Crypturellus 3
    Elaenia 156
    Scytalopus 145
parvulus, Caprimulgus 71
parzudakii, Tangara 216
Passer 197
passerinus, Veniliornis 101
pastazae, Galbula 93
Patagona 84
patagonicus, Aptenodytes 5
Pauxi 34
pavoninus, Dromococcyx 63
    Pharomachrus 91
pectoralis, Thlypopsis 208

pelagica, Chaetura 73
Pelagodroma 11
Pelecanoides 12
Pelecanus 13
pelzelni, Elaenia 156
    Pseudotriccus 158
Penelope 32-33
penicillata, Eucometis 208
pennata, Rhea 1
pentlandii, Nothoprocta 4
    Tinamotis 4
peposaca, Netta 22
Percnostola 136
peregrinus, Falco 32
personata, Incaspiza 222
personatus, Trogon 90
perspicillata, Pulsatrix 66
perspicillatus, Hymenops 178
peruana, Cinnycerthia 190
peruanum, Glaucidium 67
peruviana, Conopophaga 143
    Geositta 104
    Grallaricula 143
    Rupicola 150
    Sporophila 224
petechia, Dendroica 201
petersoni, Otus 64
Petrochelidon 187
Phacellodomus 114
phaeocephalus, Myiarchus 180
Phaeomyias 154
phaeopus, Numenius 43
Phaeoprogne 185
phaeopygia, Pterodroma 8
Phaethon 12-13
Phaethornis 74-75
Phaetusa 52
Phalacrocorax 14
Phalaropus 46
Phalcoboenus 30
Pharomachrus 90-91
phasianellus, Dromococcyx 63
Phegornis 42
Pheucticus 233
philippii, Phaethornis 75
phillipsi, Tangara 218
Philohydor 180
Philomachus 46
Philydor 117-118
Phlegopsis 138
Phleocryptes 107
Phlogophilus 81
Phoebastria 6
phoebe, Metallura 87
Phoebetria 7
Phoenicircus 147
phoenicius, Tachyphonus 210
phoenicomitra, Myiophobus 169
Phoenicopterus 19
Phrygilus 221

Index of Scientific Names

Phyllomyias 159-160
Phylloscartes 158-159
Phytotoma 147
Piaya 62
picta, Pyrrhura 57
picui, Columbina 54
Piculus 101-102
Picumnus 99-100
picumnus, Dendrocolaptes 121
picus, Xiphorhynchus 122
Piezorhina 222
pileata, Leptasthenura 107
    Nemosia 209
pileatus, Lophotriccus 164
    Pilherodius 15
Pilherodius 15
pinnatus, Botaurus 17
Pionites 59
Pionopsitta 60
Pionus 60
Pipile 33
pipixcan, Larus 49
Pipra 151-152
pipra, Pipra 151
Pipraeidea 213
Pipreola 148
Piprites 153
Piranga 210
pitangua, Megarynchus 180
Pitangus 180
Pithys 137
pitiayumi, Parula 200
Pitylus see Saltator
piurae, Ochthoeca 173
plancus, Caracara 30
platalea, Anas 22
platensis, Cistothorus 191
Platycichla 193
platypterus, Buteo 28
platyrhynchos, Anas 21
platyrhynchos, Platyrinchus 168
platyrhynchum, Electron 92
Platyrinchus 168
plebejus, Phrygilus 221
Plegadis 18
plumbea, Columba 53
    Euphonia 214
    Ictinia 25
    Leucopternis 26
    Polioptila 196
    Sporophila 223
plumbeiceps, Phyllomyias 160
    Todirostrum 166
pluricinctus, Pteroglossus 98
Pluvialis 41
Podager 70
Podiceps 6
podiceps, Podilymbus 5
Podilymbus 5
poecilocercus, Knipolegus 177

Mecocerculus 161
poecilochrous, Buteo 29
poecilonota, Hylophylax 138
poecilotis, Phylloscartes 159
Poecilotriccus 164
poecilurus, Knipolegus 177
poliocephalus, Tolmomyias 168
poliogaster, Accipiter 25
Polioptila 196
Polioxolmis 175
pollens, Campephilus 103
polychopterus,
    Pachyramphus 183
Polyerata 80
Polyonymus 86
polyosoma, Buteo 29
Polytmus 79
pomarinus, Stercorarius 48
poortmani, Chlorostilbon 78
Poospiza 222-223
popelairii, Discosura 78
Porphyrolaema 149
porphyrolaema,
    Porphyrolaema 149
Porphyrula 38
Porzana 37
prasinus, Aulacorhynchus 97
Premnoplex 115
Premnornis 114
pretiosa, Claravis 54
prevostii, Anthracothorax 77
princeps, Leucopternis 26
Procellaria 9-10
procurvoides,
    Campylorhamphus 123
Progne 185-186
promeropirhynchus,
    Xiphocolaptes 121
propinqua, Synallaxis 109
Propyrrhura 56
przewalskii, Grallaria 141
psaltria, Carduelis 200
Psarocolius 236-237
Pseudelaenia 155
Pseudocolaptes 115
Pseudocolopteryx 163
Pseudotriccus 158
Psilopsiagon 58
Psophia 35
Pterodroma 8-9
Pteroglossus 98
Pterophanes 83
pucherani,
    Campylorhamphus 123
pucheranii, Neomorphus 63
pudibunda, Asthenes 112
Puffinus 10
pugnax, Philomachus 46
pulchella, Ochthoeca 173
    Silvicultrix

pulchellum, Todirostrum 166
pulcher, Myiophobus 169
pulcherrima, Iridophanes 218
pulchra, Incaspiza 222
    Pipreola 148
Pulsatrix 66
puna, Anas 21
punctata, Tangara 216
punctigula, Colaptes 102
punctulata, Hylophylax 138
punensis, Geositta 104
    Phrygilus 221
punicea, Xipholena 150
purpurascens, Penelope 33
purpurata, Querula 150
    Touit 59
purusianus, Galbalcyrhynchus 92
pusilla, Calidris 45
pusillus, Campylorhamphus 123
Pygiptila 126
Pygochelidon 186
pyra, Topaza 77
Pyriglena 134
Pyrocephalus 172
pyrocephalus,
    Machaeropterus 152
Pyroderus 150
pyrrhodes, Philydor 118
Pyrrhomyias 171
pyrrhonota, Petrochelidon 187
pyrrhophrys, Chlorophonia 215
pyrrhops, Hapalopsittaca 60
pyrrhopterus, Brotogeris 59
Pyrrhura 57

Querula 150
Quiscalus 234
quitensis, Grallaria 142
quixensis, Microrhopias 132

raimondii, Phytotoma 146
    Sicalis 228
ralloides, Myadestes 192
Rallus 36
Ramphastos 99
Ramphocaenus 196
Ramphocelus 211
Ramphomicron 86
Ramphotrigon 167
Recurvirostra 40
reevei, Turdus 194
regalis, Heliangelus 84
reguloides, Anairetes 163
regulus, Machaeropterus 152
reinhardti, Iridosornis 213
reinwardtii, Selenidera 99
remseni, Doliornis 147
resplendens, Vanellus 40
Rhea 1
Rhegmatorhina 138

Index of Scientific Names

Rhodopis 88
Rhodospingus 220
Rhynchocyclus 167
Rhynchotus 3
Rhytipterna 179
richardsoni, Eubucco 96
ridgwayi, Plegadis 18
riefferii, Chlorornis 205
    Pipreola 148
rikeri, Berlepschia 116
Riparia 187
riparia, Riparia 187
Rissa 50
rivolii, Piculus 102
roboratus, Otus 64
rolland, Rollandia 5
Rollandia 5
roraimae, Myiophobus 169
Rostrhamus 24
rothschildi, Cypseloides 72
rubecula, Nonnula 95
    Poospiza 223
ruber, Phaethornis 75
rubica, Habia 210
rubiginosus, Automolus 119
    Piculus 102
rubinoides, Heliodoxa 81
rubinus, Pyrocephalus 172
rubra, Piranga 210
rubricauda, Phaethon 13
rubriceps, Piranga 211
rubricollis, Campephilus 103
rubrigastra, Tachuris 163
rubrirostris, Cnemoscopus 206
rubrocapilla, Pipra 152
rubrocristata, Ampelion 147
rufa, Casiornis 179
    Formicivora 132
    Malacoptila 95
rufaxilla, Ampelion 147
    Leptotila 55
rufescens, Rhynchotus 3
ruficapilla, Grallaria 140
    Nonnula 95
ruficapillus, Thamnophilus 126
ruficauda, Ramphotrigon 167
    Upucerthia 105
ruficaudatus, Philydor 117
ruficeps, Chalcostigma 87
    Poecilotriccus 164
    Pseudotriccus 158
    Thlypopsis 208
ruficervix, Tangara 217
ruficollis, Calidris 45
    Micrastur 31
    Oreopholus 42
    Stelgidopteryx 187
    Syndactyla 116
ruficrissa, Urosticte 85
rufifrons, Formicarius 139

Fulica 38
Phacellodomus 114
rufigenis, Atlapetes 229
rufigula, Dendrexetastes 121
rufigularis, Falco 32
    Hemitriccus 165
    Sclerurus 119
rufimarginatus,
    Herpsilochmus 132
rufipectoralis, Ochthoeca 173
rufipectus, Formicarius 139
    Leptopogon 157
rufipennis, Polioxolmis 175
rufipileatus, Automolus 118
rufiventer, Tachyphonus 209
rufiventris, Euphonia 215
    Lurocalis 69
    Picumnus 100
rufivertex, Iridosornis 213
    Muscisaxicola 176
rufocollaris, Petrochelidon 187
rufosuperciliaris,
    Hemispingus 207
rufosuperciliata, Syndactyla 116
rufula, Grallaria 141
rufus, Caprimulgus 70
    Pachyramphus 184
    Philydor 118
    Tachyphonus 210
    Trogon 90
rumicivorus, Thinocorus 47
rupestris, Chordeiles 69
Rupicola 150
rupicola, Colaptes 102
Pyrrhura 57
rustica, Haplospiza 226
    Hirundo 188
ruticilla, Setophaga 201
rutila, Streptoprocne 72
rutilans, Synallaxis 109
    Xenops 115
Rynchops 52

sabini, Xema 49
Sakesphorus 124
Saltator 232
salvini, Gymnopithys 138
    Mitu 33
    Tumbezia 174
sanctaemariae, Cymbilaimus 124
sanctithomae, Brotogeris 59
sandvicensis, Sterna 50
sanguinolentus, Pardirallus 38
saphirina, Geotrygon 55
sapphirina, Hylocharis 78
sapphiropygia, Eriocnemis 84
Sappho 85
Sarcoramphus 23
Sarkidiornis 20
Satrapa 178

saturata, Euphonia 214
saturatus, Platyrinchus 168
saturninus, Thamnomanes 127
savana, Tyrannus 183
saxicolina, Geositta 104
sayaca, Thraupis 211
Sayornis 172
Scaphidura 234
Schiffornis 183
schistacea, Leucopternis 26
    Percnostola 136
    Sporophila 223
schistaceus, Atlapetes 229
    Thamnophilus 125
schisticolor, Myrmotherula 130
Schistochlamys 205
schistogynus,
    Thamnomanes 128
Schizoeaca 111-112
schomburgkii, Micropygia 35
schrankii, Tangara 216
schreibersii, Heliodoxa 81
schulenbergi, Scytalopus 146
sclateri, Asthenes 113
    Cacicus 236
    Doliornis 147
    Forpus 58
    Myrmotherula 129
    Nonnula 95
    Phyllomyias 159
    Picumnus 99
    Thryothorus 190
Sclateria 135
Sclerurus 119
scrutator, Thripadectes 116
scutatus, Pyroderus 150
Scytalopus 144-146
seebohmi, Atlapetes 230
segmentata, Uropsalis 71
Seiurus 201
Selenidera 99
semibrunneus, Hylophilus 198
semicincta, Malacoptila 94
semicinereus, Hylophilus 198
semifasciata, Tityra 184
semipalmatus, Catoptrophorus 44
    Charadrius 41
semiplumbeus, Rallus 36
semirufus, Myiarchus 179
semitorquatus, Lurocalis 69
    Micrastur 31
senilis, Myornis 144
sericocaudatus, Caprimulgus 70
serrana, Upucerthia 105
serranus, Larus 49
Serpophaga 157
Turdus 194
Sericossypha 205
Serpophaga
serva, Cercomacra 134

Index of Scientific Names

Setophaga 201
severa, Ara 56
sharpei, Terenura 133
sibilator, Sirystes 179
sibilatrix, Anas 21
Sicalis 227-228
siemiradzkii, Carduelis 200
signatus, Basileuterus 203
    Knipolegus 177
similis, Myiozetetes 181
simonsi, Scytalopus 145
Simoxenops 117
simplex, Phaetusa 52
    Pseudotriccus 158
    Rhytipterna 179
    Sporophila 224
singularis, Xenerpestes 114
Siptornis 114
Siptornopsis 110
Sirystes 179
Sittasomus 120
sitticolor, Conirostrum 205
sittoides, Diglossa 226
Snowornis 149
sociabilis, Rostrhamus 24
solitaria, Tringa 44
solitarius, Cacicus 236
    Harpyaliaetus 27
solstitialis, Troglodytes 191
somptuosus, Anisognathus 213
sordida, Thlypopsis 208
sordidulus, Contopus 172
sordidus, Pionus 60
soui, Crypturellus 2
souleyetii, Lepidocolaptes 123
spadiceus, Attila 179
sparganura, Sappho 85
sparverius, Falco 31
speciosa, Columba 52
speciosum, Conirostrum 204
speciosus, Odontophorus 34
spectabilis, Celeus 103
    Elaenia 155
specularioides, Anas 21
speculifera, Diuca 221
speculigera, Conothraupis 205
Spheniscus 5
spirurus, Glyphorynchus 121
spixii, Xiphorhynchus 122
spiza, Chlorophanes 219
Spizaetus 29
Spizastur 29
spodionota, Myrmotherula 130
    Ochthoeca 173
spodioptila, Terenura 133
spodiurus, Pachyramphus 184
Sporophila 223-225
squamata, Tachornis 73
squamiger, Margarornis 115
squamigera, Grallaria 140

squatarola, Pluvialis 41
stanleyi, Chalcostigma 87
Steatornis 68
steindachneri, Picumnus 100
Stelgidopteryx 187
stellaris, Pygiptila 126
stellatus, Odontophorus 34
Stercorarius 47-48
Sterna 50-51
sterrhopteron,
    Wetmorethraupis 212
stictolaema, Deconychura 120
stictolophus, Lophornis 77
stictoptera, Touit 59
stictopterus, Mecocerculus 162
stictothorax, Synallaxis 109
sticturus, Herpsilochmus
Stigmatura 162
stolzmanni, Aimophila 231
    Oreotrochilus 82
    Tachycineta 186
    Tyranneutes 153
strepera, Elaenia 156
Streptoprocne 72
stresemanni, Hylexetastes 121
    Zaratornis 147
striata, Dendroica 201
    Leptasthenura 107
striaticeps, Phacellodomus 114
striaticollis, Anabacerthia 115
    Hemitriccus 165
    Mionectes 157
    Myiotheretes 174
    Siptornis 114
striatipectus, Saltator 232
striatus, Butorides 16
strigilatus, Ancistrops 117
strigulosus, Crypturellus 3
striolatus, Nystalus 94
stuarti, Phaethornis 75
Sturnella 234
stygius, Asio 67
subalaris, Snowornis 149
    Syndactyla 116
subbrunneus, Cnipodectes 166
subis, Progne 185
Sublegatus 161
subplacens, Myiopagis 155
subruficollis, Tryngites 45
subtilis, Buteogallus 27
    Picumnus 100
subulatus, Hyloctistes 117
subvinacea, Columba 53
Sula 13-14
sula, Sula 14
sulcirostris, Crotophaga 63
sulphuratus, Pitangus 180
sulphurea, Tyrannopsis 182
sulphureiventer, Neopelma 153
sulphurescens, Tolmomyias 167

sunensis, Myrmotherula 130
superciliaris, Burhinus 40
    Hemispingus 297
    Leptopogon 158
    Phylloscartes 159
    Sterna 51
    Sturnella 234
    Thryothorus 191
superciliosus, Accipiter 25
surinamus, Tachyphonus 209
swainsoni, Buteo 28
    Myiarchus 179
swainsonii, Gampsonyx 24
Synallaxis 107-109
Syndactyla 116
syrmatophorus, Phaethornis 75

Tachornis 73
Tachuris 163
Tachybaptus 5
Tachycineta 186
Tachyphonus 209-210
taciturnus, Arremon 231
taczanowskii, Cinclodes 105
    Leptopogon 158
    Leucippus 79
    Nothoprocta 4
    Podiceps 6
    Sicalis 228
taeniata, Dubusia 213
talpacoti, Columbina 54
tamarugense, Conirostrum 204
tamatia, Bucco 94
tanagrinus, Lampropsar 237
Tangara 215-218
tao, Tinamus 1
Tapera 63
tapera, Phaeoprogne 185
Taphrolesbia 87
Taphrospilus
Taraba 124
tataupa, Crypturellus 3
tectus, Notharchus 94
telasco, Sporophila 225
tenebrosa, Chelidoptera 96
tenuepunctatus, Thamnophilus 125
tenuirostris, Geositta 105
    Xenops 115
terborghi, Atlapetes 230
Terenotriccus 170
Terenura 133
Tersina 220
tethys, Oceanodroma 11
thagus, Pelecanus 13
Thalassarche 6-7
thalassinus, Colibri 76
Thalurania 78
Thamnistes 127
Thamnomanes 127-128
Thamnophilus 124-126

Index of Scientific Names

Thaumastura 88
theresiae, Metallura 86
   Polytmus 79
Theristicus 18
thilius, Agelaius 233
Thinocorus 47
Thlypopsis 208
thoracica, Ochthoeca 173
thoracicus, Cyphorhinus 192
   Hylophilus 198
   Liosceles 144
Thraupis 211-212
Threnetes 74
Thripadectes 116
Thryothorus 190-191
thula, Egretta 16
Tiaris 226
tibialis, Neochelidon 187
Tigrisoma 17
Tinamotis 4
Tinamus 1
tithys, Synallaxis 109
Tityra 184
toco, Ramphastos 99
Todirostrum 166
Tolmomyias 167-168
tombacea, Galbula 93
Topaza 77
torquata, Ceryle 91
   Chauna 19
   Coeligena 83
   Corythopis 166
   Hydropsalis 71
   Myrmornis 138
torquatus, Buarremon 230
   Celeus 103
torridus, Attila 178
   Furnarius 106
Touit 59
transfasciatus, Crypturellus 3
traylori, Tolmomyias 168
triangularis, Xiphorhynchus 122
Trichothraupis 210
tricolor, Atlapetes 229
   Egretta 16
   Phalaropus 46
tridactyla, Rissa 50
trifasciatus, Basileuterus 203
   Crypturellus 3
   Hemispingus 207
Tringa 43-44
tristriatus, Basileuterus 203
trivirgata, Conopias 181
trochilirostris,
   Campylorhamphus 123
Troglodytes 191
Trogon 89-90
tropica, Fregetta 11
trudeaui, Sterna 51
Tryngites 46

tschudii, Ampelioides 148
tuberculifer, Myiarchus 179
tuberosa, Mitu 34
tucinkae, Eubucco 97
tuerosi, Laterallus 36
Tumbezia 174
tumultuosus, Pionus 60
turcosa, Cyanolyca 197
turdinus, Campylorhynchus 189
   Schiffornis 183
Turdus 194-195
turtur, Pachyptila 9
Tyranneutes 153
tyrannina, Dendrocincla 120
Tyrannopsis 182
Tyrannulus 154
tyrannulus, Myiarchus 180
Tyrannus 182-183
tyrannus, Spizaetus 29
Tyrannus 182
tyrianthina, Metallura 86
Tryngites
Tyto 63

ucayalae, Simoxenops 117
ultima, Pterodroma 8
uncinatus, Chondrohierax 24
underwoodii, Ocreatus 85
undulatus, Crypturellus 2
   Zebrilus 17
unduligera, Frederickena 124
unicinctus, Parabuteo 27
unicolor, Chloropipo 151
   Phrygilus 221
   Scytalopus 144
   Thamnophilus 125
unicornis, Pauxi 34
unirufa, Cinnycerthia 189
   Synallaxis 108
Upucerthia 105
Urochroa 82
Uromyias 162
Uropsalis 71
uropygialis, Cacicus 235
   Carduelis 200
   Lipaugus 149
   Phyllomyias 160
   Sicalis 228
Urosticte 85
urubambae, Scytalopus 145
urubambensis, Asthenes 113
urubitinga, Buteogallus 27
urumutum, Nothocrax 33
ustulatus, Catharus 193

validus, Pachyramphus 184
Vanellus 40
varia, Grallaria 140
   Mniotilta 201
   Tangara 216

variegata, Sula 13
variegatus, Crypturellus 3
varius, Empidonomus 182
vassorii, Tangara 218
velia, Tangara 218
Veniliornis 101
ventralis, Accipiter 25
   Phylloscartes 159
vermiculatus, Otus 65
verreauxi, Leptotila 55
versicolor, Eubucco 97
   Lanio 209
   Pachyramphus 183
versicolurus, Brotogeris 58
verticalis, Creurgops 209
   Hemispingus 207
vesper, Rhodopis 88
vestitus, Eriocnemis 84
victoriae, Lesbia 85
viduata, Dendrocygna 20
vilcabambae, Schizoeaca 112
villarejoi, Zimmerius 161
villaviscensio, Campylopterus 76
villosus, Myiobius 170
viola, Heliangelus 84
violacea, Geotrygon 55
   Nyctanassa 16
violaceus, Cyanocorax 197
   Trogon 90
violifer, Coeligena 83
virens, Contopus 172
Vireo 197-198
Vireolanius 199
virgata, Aphriza 44
   Asthenes 113
   Ciccaba 65
virginianus, Bubo 65
viridicata, Myiopagis 155
viridicauda, Leucippus 80
viridicollis, Tangara 218
viridicyana, Cyanolyca 197
viridiflavus, Zimmerius 161
viridis, Anurolimnas 36
   Psarocolius 236
   Tersina 220
   Trogon 89
vitiosus, Lophotriccus 164
vittata, Pachyptila 9
vociferans, Lipaugus 149
vociferus, Charadrius 41
Volatinia 223
vulpecula, Cranioleuca 111
Vultur 23

wagleri, Aratinga 56
wallacei, Capito 96
warszewiczi, Dives 234
watkinsi, Grallaria 140
   Incaspiza 222
watsonii, Otus 65

Index of Scientific Names

weddellii, Aratinga 57
westlandica, Procellaria 10
wetmorei, Buthraupis 212
Wetmorethraupis 212
Wilsonia 202
wilsonia, Charadrius 41
wolfi, Aramides 37
wyatti, Asthenes 113

xanthocephala, Tangara 216
xanthogaster, Euphonia 215
xanthogastra, Carduelis 200
    Tangara 216
xanthogenys, Pachyramphus 183
xanthophthalmus, Agelaius 233
    Hemispingus 207
xanthops, Forpus 58
xanthopterygius, Forpus 58
Xema 49
Xenerpestes 114
Xenodacnis 219
Xenoglaux 67
Xenopipo 153
Xenops 115
Xenospingus 222
xenothorax, Leptasthenura 107
Xiphocolaptes 121
Xipholena 150
Xiphorhynchus 122
Xolmis 174

yanacensis, Leptasthenura 107
yarrellii, Myrtis 89
yncas, Cyanocorax 197

Zaratornis 147
zarumae, Thamnophilus 124
Zebrilus 17
zeledoni, Phyllomyias 160
Zenaida 53
zimmeri, Synallaxis 107
Zimmerius 160-161
zonaris, Streptoprocne 72
Zonotrichia 231
zosterops, Hemitriccus 165

Index of English Names

Albatross, Black-browed **3**, 6
  Buller's **3**, 7
  Gray-headed **3**, 7
  Light-mantled 7
  Royal **3**, 6
  Shy **3**, 7
  Wandering **3**, 6
  Waved **3**, 6
  White-capped see Shy
Anhinga **9**, 14
Ani, Greater **30**, 62
  Groove-billed **30**, 63
  Smooth-billed **30**, 62
Antbird, Amazonian **69**, 136
  Ash-breasted **76**, 134
  Band-tailed **74**, 135
  Banded **76**, 131
  Bicolored **76**, 137
  Black **75**, 134
  Black-and-white **74**, 135
  Black-chinned **74**, 135
  Black-faced **76**, 134
  Blackish **75**, 133
  Black-tailed **71**, 135
  Black-throated **75**, 137
  Chestnut-tailed **75**, 136
  Dot-backed **76**, 138
  Goeldi's **69**, **75**, 136
  Gray **75**, 133
  Gray-headed **71**, 137
  Hairy-crested **69**, 138
  Long-tailed **74**, 133
  Lunulated **69**, 137
  Manu **69**, 134
  Plumbeous **75**, 136
  Scale-backed **76**, 138
  Silvered **76**, 135
  Slate-colored **74**, 136
  Sooty **75**, 137
  Spot-backed **76**, 138
  Spot-winged **74**, 136
  Striated **69**, 132
  Warbling **74**, 135
  White-browed **76**, 134
  White-lined **69**, **75**, 136
  White-masked **77**, 137
  White-plumed **77**, 137
  White-shouldered **75**, 136
  White-throated **76**, 138
  Wing-banded **77**, 138
  Yellow-browed **74**, 135
Antpipit, Ringed **86**, 166
Antpitta, Amazonian **79**, 142
  Bay **79**, 141
  Chestnut **79**, 142
  Chestnut-crowned **78**, 140
  Chestnut-naped **78**, 141
  Elusive **79**, 140
  Jocotoco **78**, 141
  Ochre-breasted **79**, 142

  Ochre-fronted **79**, 143
  Ochre-striped **78**, 140
  Pale-billed **79**, 141
  Peruvian **79**, 143
  Plain-backed 140
  Red-and-white **79**, 141
  Rufous **79**, 141
  Rusty-breasted **79**, 142
  Rusty-tinged **79**, 141
  Scaled **78**, 140
  Scrub see Watkin's
  Slate-crowned **78**, 143
  Spotted **78**, 142
  Stripe-headed **79**, 140
  Tawny **78**, 142
  Thrush-like **78**, 142
  Undulated **78**, 140
  Variegated **78**, 140
  Watkins' **79**, 140
  White-bellied **78**, 141
  White-lored **78**, 142
  White-throated **78**, 141
Antshrike, Amazonian **70**, 126
  Bamboo **69**, 124
  Barred **68**, 124
  Black-crested **68**, 124
  Bluish-slate **70**, **71**, 128
  Castelnau's **71**, 125
  Chapman's **71**, 124
  Chestnut-backed **71**, 125
  Cinereous **70**, 128
  Collared **71**, 124
  Dusky-throated **70**, 128
  Fasciated **68**, 124
  Great **68**, 124
  Lined **68**, 125
  Mouse-colored **70**, 125
  Pearly **68**, 127
  Plain-winged **70**, 125
  Rufous-capped **68**, **69**, 126
  Russet **68**, 127
  Saturnine **70**, 127
  Spot-winged **70**, 126
  Undulated **68**, 124
  Uniform **70**, 125
  Upland **71**, 125
  Variable **70**, 126
  White-shouldered **70**, 125
Ant-Tanager
  Red-crowned **114**, 210
Antthrush, Barred **77**, 139
  Black-faced **77**, 139
  Noble see Striated
  Rufous-breasted **77**, 139
  Rufous-capped **77**, 139
  Rufous-fronted **69**, **77**, 139
  Short-tailed **77**, 139
  Striated **71**, 139
Antvireo, Plain **72**, 127
  White-streaked **72**, 127

Antwren, Ancient **73**, 132
  Ash-throated **73**, 131
  Ash-winged 133
  Banded see Banded Antbird
  Brown-backed **73**, 129
  Cherrie's **72**, 129
  Chestnut-shouldered **74**, 133
  Creamy-bellied **73**, 132
  Dot-winged **69**, 132
  Dugand's **73**, 132
  Foothill **73**, 130
  Gray **72**, 131
  Ihering's **73**, 131
  Leaden **72**, 131
  Long-winged **72**, 131
  Ornate **73**, 130
  Plain-throated **72**, 129
  Pygmy **72**, 128
  Rio Suno **73**, 130
  Rufous-rumped **74**, 133
  Rufous-tailed **72**, 130
  Rufous-winged **73**, 132
  Rusty-backed **74**, 132
  Salvadori's 131
  Sclater's **73**, 129
  Short-billed **72**, 128
  Slaty **72**, 130
  Stipple-throated **73**, 130
  Streaked
  Stripe-chested **72**, 129
  White-eyed **72**, **73**, 129
  White-flanked **72**, 130
  Yasuni see Brown-backed
  Yellow-breasted **74**, 132
  Yellow-rumped **73**, 133
Aracari, Brown-mandibled **53**, 98
  Chestnut-eared **53**, 98
  Curl-crested **53**, 98
  Ivory-billed **53**, 98
  Lettered **53**, 98
  Many-banded **53**, 98
  Pale-mandibled **53**, 98
Attila, Cinnamon **99**, 178
  Citron-bellied **88**, 178
  Dull-capped see White-eyed
  Ochraceous **95**, 178
  White-eyed **99**, 178
Avocet, Andean **20**, 40
Avocetbill, Mountain **40**, 87

Bamboo-Tyrant
  Flammulated **89**, 164
Bananaquit **109**, 204
Barbet, Gilded **49**, 96
  Lemon-throated **49**, 96
  Red-headed **49**, 96
  Scarlet-banded **52**, 96
  Scarlet-crowned **49**, 96
  Scarlet-hooded **52**, 97
  Versicolored **52**, 97

Index of English Names

Barbtail, Rusty-winged **63**, 114
  Spotted **63**, 115
Barbthroat, Pale-tailed **37**, 74
Bare-eye, Black-spotted **77**, 138
  Reddish-winged **77**, 138
Barred-Woodcreeper
  Amazonian **66**, 121
Beardless-Tyrannulet
  Southern **86**, 154
Becard, Barred **99**, 183
  Black-and-white **99**, 183
  Black-capped **99**, 184
  Chestnut-crowned **99**, 183
  Cinereous **99**, 184
  Crested **99**, 184
  One-colored **99**, 184
  Pink-throated **99**, 184
  Slaty **95**, 184
  White-winged **99**, 183
  Yellow-cheeked **99**, 183
Bittern, Least **7**, 17
  Pinnated **7**, 17
  Stripe-backed **7**, 17
Blackbird, Chopi **127**, 237
  Oriole **127**, 237
  Pale-eyed **125**, 233
  Red-breasted **127**, 234
  Scrub **125**, 234
  White-browed **127**, 234
  Yellow-hooded **127**, 234
  Yellow-winged **127**, 233
Black-Hawk, Great **13**, **16**, 27
  Mangrove **13**, 27
Black-Tyrant, Amazonian **97**, 177
  Hudson's **97**, 177
  White-winged **97**, 177
Bobolink **127**, 233
Booby, Blue-footed **10**, 13
  Brown **10**, 14
  Masked **10**, 13
  Nazca **10**, 13
  Peruvian **6**, 13
  Red-footed **10**, 14
Brilliant, Black-throated **42**, 81
  Fawn-breasted **43**, 81
  Pink-throated **42**, **43**, 81
  Rufous-webbed **42**, 82
  Violet-fronted **43**, 81
Bristle-Tyrant
  Marble-faced **87**, 158
  Spectacled **88**, 158
  Variegated **87**, 159
Brush-Finch, Apurímac **120**, 229
  Bay-crowned **120**, 230
  Black-spectacled **120**, 229
  Chestnut-capped **121**, 230
  Cloud-forest **120**, 229
  Cusco **120**, 230
  Dark-faced **120**, 230
  Pale-naped **120**, 229

Rufous-eared **120**, 229
Rusty-bellied **120**, 230
Slaty **120**, 229
Stripe-headed **121**, 230
Tricolored **120**, 229
Vilcabamba **120**, 230
White-headed **120**, 230
White-winged **120**, 230
Bushbird, Black **68**, 127
Bush-Tanager
  Ashy-throated **112**, 206
  Common **112**, 206
  Gray-hooded **112**, 206
  Short-billed see
    Yellow-whiskered
  Yellow-throated **112**, 206
  Yellow-whiskered **112**, 206
Bush-Tyrant, Red-rumped **92**, 174
  Rufous-bellied **93**, 174
  Smoky **92**, 174
  Streak-throated **92**, 174
Buzzard-Eagle
  Black-chested **14**, **16**, 27

Cacique, Ecuadorian **125**, 236
  Mountain **126**, 236
  Red-rumped **126**, 235
  Scarlet-rumped see Subtropical
  Selva **125**, 236
  Solitary **126**, 236
  Subtropical **126**, 235
  Yellow-billed **126**, 235
  Yellow-rumped **126**, 235
Canastero, Cactus **59**, 113
  Canyon **59**, 112
  Cordilleran **58**, 112
  Dark-winged **59**, 112
  Junín **59**, 113
  Line-fronted **59**, 113
  Many-striped **58**, 113
  Pale-tailed **59**, 112
  Puna **58**, 113
  Rusty-fronted **59**, 112
  Scribble-tailed **59**, 113
  Streak-backed **58**, 113
  Streak-throated **59**, 113
Caracara, Black **14**, 30
  Crested **16**, 30
  Mountain **14**, **16**, 30
  Red-throated **14**, 30
  Southern **14**, 30
  Yellow-headed **14**, **16**, 30
Cardinal, Red-capped **121**, 228
Casiornis, Rufous **99**, 179
Chachalaca
  Rufous-headed **17**, 32
  Speckled **17**, 32
Chat-Tyrant
  Brown-backed **91**, 174
  Crowned **92**, 172

D'Orbigny's **91**, 173
Golden-browed **91**, 173
Jelski's **91**, 173
Maroon-chested **91**, 173
Peruvian **91**, 173
Piura **91**, 173
Rufous-breasted **92**, 173
Slaty-backed **92**, 173
White-browed **91**, 174
Yellow-bellied **92**, 173
Chlorophonia
  Blue-naped **117**, 215
  Chestnut-breasted **117**, 215
Cinclodes, Bar-winged **58**, 105
  Peruvian Seaside **57**, 105
  Royal **57**, 106
  White-bellied **57**, 106
  White-winged **58**, 106
Cock-of-the-rock, Andean **83**, 150
Comet, Bronze-tailed **42**, 86
  Gray-bellied **45**, 87
  Red-tailed **44**, 85
Condor, Andean **11**, 23
Conebill, Bicolored **109**, 204
  Blue-backed **109**, 205
  Capped **109**, 205
  Chestnut-vented **109**, 204
  Cinereous **109**, 204
  Giant **115**, 205
  Pearly-breasted **115**, 204
  Tamarugo **115**, 204
  White-browed **115**, 205
Coot, Andean **6**, 38
  Giant **18**, 38
  Red-fronted **18**, 38
  Slate-colored see Andean
Coquette, Festive **39**, 77
  Rufous-crested **39**, 77
  Spangled **39**, 77
Cormorant, Guanay **6**, 14
  Neotropic **5**, 14
  Red-legged **6**, 14
Coronet
  Chestnut-breasted **43**, 82
Cotinga, Bay-vented **82**, 147
  Black-faced **82**, 150
  Black-necked Red **83**, 147
  Chestnut-bellied **82**, 147
  Chestnut-crested **82**, 147
  Plum-throated **82**, 149
  Pompadour **82**, 150
  Purple-breasted **82**, 149
  Purple-throated **82**, 149
  Red-crested **82**, 147
  Shrike-like **81**, 147
  Spangled **82**, 150
  White-cheeked **82**, 147
Cowbird, Giant **127**, 234
  Shiny **127**, 234

Index of English Names

Crake, Ash-throated **19**, 37
  Black-banded **19**, 36
  Chestnut-headed **19**, 35
  Gray-breasted **19**, 36
  Ocellated **19**, 35
  Paint-billed **19**, 37
  Rufous-sided **19**, 36
  Russet-crowned **19**, 36
  Uniform **19**, 37
Crescentchest, Elegant **80**, 144
  Marañon **70**, 144
Cuckoo, Ash-colored **30**, 61
  Black-bellied **30**, 62
  Black-billed **30**, 62
  Dark-billed **30**, 62
  Gray-capped **30**, 62
  Little **30**, 62
  Pavonine **30**, 63
  Pheasant **30**, 63
  Squirrel **30**, 62
  Striped **30**, 63
  Yellow-billed **30**, 62
Curassow, Horned **17**, 34
  Nocturnal **17**, 33
  Razor-billed **17**, 34
  Salvin's **17**, 33
  Wattled **17**, 34

Dacnis, Black-faced **116**, 219
  Blue **116**, 219
  Tit-like **115**, 219
  White-bellied **116**, 218
  Yellow-bellied **116**, 219
Dipper, White-capped **106**, 189
Diuca-Finch
  White-winged **124**, 221
Diving-Petrel, Peruvian **6**, 12
Donacobius
  Black-capped **104**, 189
Doradito, Subtropical **90**, 163
Dotterel, Rufous-chested **20**, 42
  Tawny-throated **20**, 42
Dove, Eared **24**, 53
  Gray-fronted **25**, 55
  Ochre-bellied **26**, 55
  Pacific **24**, 53
  Rock **24**, 52
  White-tipped **25**, 55
Dowitcher, Short-billed **22**, 43
Duck, Andean **10**, 22
  Comb **10**, 20
  Crested **9**, 21
  Masked **9**, 22
  Muscovy **9**, 20
  Torrent **9**, 20
Dunlin **21**, 46

Eagle
  Black-and-chestnut **15**, 30
  Crested **15**, 29
  Harpy **14**, **16**, 29
  Solitary **15**, 27
Earthcreeper
  Plain-breasted **58**, 105
  Scale-throated **58**, 105
  Straight-billed **58**, 105
  Striated **57**, 105
  White-throated **57**, 105
Egret, Cattle **8**, 16
  Great **7**, 15
  Snowy **7**, 16
Elaenia, Brownish **93**, 156
  Foothill **86**, 154
  Forest **86**, 154
  Gray **86**, 155
  Greenish **86**, 155
  Highland **93**, 157
  Large **93**, 155
  Lesser **93**, 156
  Mottle-backed **86**, 156
  Pacific **95**, 155
  Plain-crested **86**, 156
  Sierran **93**, 157
  Slaty **93**, 156
  Small-billed **93**, 156
  White-crested **86**, **93**, 156
  Yellow-bellied **93**, 156
  Yellow-crowned **88**, 155
Emerald, Andean **41**, 80
  Blue-tailed **39**, 78
  Glittering-throated **41**, 80
  Sapphire-spangled **40**, 80
  Short-tailed 78
  Versicolored 80
Euphonia, Bronze-green **116**, 214
  Golden-rumped **116**, 214
  Orange-bellied **116**, 215
  Orange-crowned **116**, 214
  Plumbeous **116**, 214
  Purple-throated **116**, 214
  Rufous-bellied **116**, 215
  Thick-billed **116**, 214
  White-lored **116**, 214
  White-vented **116**, 215

Fairy, Black-eared **46**, 88
Falcon, Aplomado **14**, **16**, 32
  Bat **14**, 32
  Laughing **14**, 31
  Orange-breasted **14**, 32
  Peregrine **14**, 32
Field-Tyrant, Short-tailed **95**, 176
Finch, Black-masked **124**, 220
  Cinereous **122**, 222
  Crimson-breasted **122**, 220
  Olive **122**, 228
  Plush-capped **124**, 220
  Red-crested **124**, 220
  Saffron **124**, 227
  Short-tailed **122**, 221
  Slaty **113**, 22
  Slender-billed **122**, 222
  Sulphur-throated **123**, 228
Fire-eye, White-backed **75**, 134
Flamingo, Andean **8**, 19
  Chilean **6**, **8**, 19
  James' see Puna
  Puna **8**, 19
Flatbill, Dusky-tailed **88**, 167
  Fulvous-breasted **86**, 167
  Large-headed **88**, 167
  Olivaceous **86**, 167
  Rufous-tailed **86**, 167
Flicker, Andean **56**, 102
Flowerpiercer, Black **113**, 227
  Black-throated **115**, 227
  Bluish **113**, 227
  Deep-blue **113**, 227
  Glossy **113**, 226
  Masked **113**, 227
  Moustached **113**, **115**, 226
  Rusty **113**, 226
  White-sided **113**, 226
Flycatcher, Alder **97**, 172
  Baird's **95**, 181
  Black-tailed **92**, 170
  Boat-billed **98**, 180
  Bran-colored **92**, **95**, 170
  Brown-crested **97**, 180
  Brownish **86**, 166
  Cinnamon **92**, 171
  Cliff **92**, 171
  Dusky-capped **97**, 179
  Dusky-chested **98**, 181
  Euler's **88**, 171
  Flavescent **94**, 169
  Fork-tailed **98**, 183
  Fuscous **92**, 171
  Golden-crowned **98**, 181
  Gray-breasted **95**, 171
  Gray-capped **98**, 181
  Gray-crowned **86**, 168
  Great-crested 180
  Handsome **94**, 169
  Inca **94**, 158
  Lemon-browed **98**, 181
  McConnell's **88**, 157
  Ochraceous-breasted **94**, 170
  Ochre-bellied **87**, 157
  Olive see Olive-tufted
  Olive-chested **94**, 170
  Olive-sided **97**, 171
  Olive-striped **87**, 157
  Olive-tufted **94**, 171
  Orange-banded **94**, 169
  Orange-crested **94**, 169
  Orange-eyed **88**, 168
  Ornate **92**, 169
  Royal see Royal-Flycatcher
  Pale-edged **97**, 180

273

Index of English Names

Piratic **98**, 182
Roraiman **94**, 169
Ruddy-tailed **92**, 170
Rufous **95**, 179
Rufous-breasted **87**, 157
Rusty-margined **98**, 180
Sepia-capped **87**, 158
Short-crested **97**, 180
Slaty-capped **87**, 158
Social **98**, 181
Sooty-crowned **95**, 180
Streaked **98**, 181
Streak-necked **87**, 157
Sulphur-bellied **98**, 182
Sulphury **98**, 182
Swainson's **97**, 179
Tawny-breasted **92**, 170
Three-striped **98**, 181
Unadorned **94**, 169
Variegated **98**, 182
Vermilion **92**, **95**, 172
Whiskered **92**, 170
Yellow-breasted **86**, 168
Yellow-margined **86**, 167
Yellow-olive **86**, 167
Yellow-throated **98**, 181
Foliage-gleaner
  Brown-rumped **64**, 118
  Buff-browed **64**, 116
  Buff-fronted **64**, 118
  Buff-throated **64**, 118
  Chestnut-crowned **64**, 118
  Chestnut-winged **64**, 117
  Cinnamon-rumped **64**, 118
  Crested see Dusky-cheeked
  Dusky-cheeked **64**, 118
  Henna-hooded **65**, 119
  Lineated **64**, 116
  Montane **64**, 115
  Olive-backed **64**, 118
  Ruddy **64**, 119
  Rufous-necked **65**, 116
  Rufous-rumped **64**, 117
  Rufous-tailed **64**, 117
Forest-Falcon, Barred **12**, 31
  Buckley's **12**, 31
  Collared **12**, **16**, 31
  Lined **12**, 31
  Slaty-backed **12**, 31
Frigatebird, Great **10**, 15
  Magnificent **10**, 15
Fruitcrow, Bare-necked **83**, 150
  Purple-throated **83**, 150
  Red-ruffed **83**, 150
Fruiteater, Band-tailed **81**, 148
  Barred **81**, 148
  Black-chested **81**, 148
  Fiery-throated **81**, 148
  Green-and-black **81**, 148
  Masked **81**, 148

Scaled **81**, 148
Scarlet-breasted **81**, 148
Fulmar, Southern **4**, 7

Gallinule, Azure **19**, 38
  Purple **19**, 38
  Spot-flanked **19**, 38
Gnatcatcher, Tropical **108**, 196
Gnateater, Ash-throated **80**, 143
  Chestnut-belted **80**, 143
  Chestnut-crowned **80**, 143
  Slaty **69**, 143
Gnatwren, Collared **104**, 196
  Long-billed **104**, 196
  Tawny-faced **104**, 196
Godwit, Hudsonian **22**, 43
  Marbled **22**, 43
Golden-Plover, American **22**, 41
Goldenthroat, Green-tailed **41**, 79
  White-tailed **41**, 79
Goldfinch, Lesser **123**, 200
Goose, Andean **9**, 20
  Orinoco **9**, 20
Goshawk, Gray-bellied **15**, 25
Grackle, Great-tailed **127**, 234
  Velvet-fronted **127**, 237
Grass-Finch
  Wedge-tailed **122**, 228
Grassquit, Blue-black **124**, 223
  Dull-colored **122**, 226
Graytail, Equatorial **61**, 114
Grebe, Great **5**, 6
  Junín **5**, 6
  Least **5**, 5
  Pied-billed **5**, 5
  Short-winged **5**, 5
  Silvery **5**, 6
  Titicaca Flightless see
    Short-winged
  White-tufted **5**, 5
Greenlet, Ashy-headed **107**, 198
  Dusky-capped **107**, 198
  Gray-chested **107**, 198
  Lemon-chested **107**, 198
  Lesser **107**, 199
  Olivaceous **107**, 198
  Rufous-naped **107**, 198
  Tawny-crowned **107**, 199
Grosbeak, Black-backed **121**, 233
  Blue-black **121**, 233
  Golden-bellied **121**, 233
  Rose-breasted **121**, 233
  Slate-colored **121**, 232
  Yellow-shouldered **121**, 232
Ground-Cuckoo
  Red-billed **30**, 63
  Rufous-vented **30**, 63
Ground-Dove, Bare-faced **24**, 54
  Black-winged **24**, 54
  Blue **25**, 54

Croaking **25**, 54
Ecuadorian **25**, 53
Golden-spotted **24**, 54
Maroon-chested **25**, 54
Picui **25**, 54
Plain-breasted **25**, 53
Ruddy **25**, 54
Ground-Tyrant
  Black-fronted **96**, 176
  Cinereous **96**, 176
  Cinnamon-bellied **96**, 175
  Dark-faced **96**, 175
  Little **92**, 175
  Ochre-naped **96**, 176
  Plain-capped **96**, 176
  Puna **96**, 176
  Rufous-naped **96**, 176
  Spot-billed **96**, 175
  White-browed **96**, 176
  White-fronted **96**, 176
Guan, Andean **17**, 33
  Bearded **17**, 32
  Crested 33
  Sickle-winged **17**, 33
  Spix's **17**, 33
  Wattled **17**, 33
  White-winged **17**, 33
Gull, Andean **23**, 49
  Band-tailed **23**, 48
  Belcher's see Band-tailed
  Brown-hooded, 49
  Franklin's **23**, 49
  Gray **6**, 48
  Gray-headed **23**, 49
  Herring **23**, 49
  Kelp **6**, 48
  Laughing **23**, 49
  Sabine's **23**, 49
  Swallow-tailed **23**, 50

Harrier, Cinereous **13**, **16**, 25
  Long-winged **15**, 25
Hawk, Barred **15**, 26
  Bay-winged see Harris'
  Bicolored **13**, **16**, 26
  Black-collared **14**, 27
  Black-faced **15**, 26
  Broad-winged **15**, 28
  Crane **12**, **16**, 26
  Gray-backed **13**, 26
  Gray **15**, 27
  Gray-lined see Gray
  Harris' **13**, **16**, 27
  Plain-breasted **13**, 25
  Plumbeous **15**, 26
  Puna see Variable
  Red-backed see Variable
  Roadside **13**, **16**, 28
  Savanna **13**, 27
  Semicollared **13**, 25

Index of English Names

Hawk, Short-tailed **15**, 28
  Slate-colored **12**, 26
  Swainson's **15**, 28
  Tiny **13**, 25
  Variable **13**, **16**, 29
  White **15**, 26
  White-browed **13**, 26
  White-rumped **15**, 28
  White-tailed **15**, 28
  White-throated **15**, 28
  Zone-tailed **11**, **15**, 29
Hawk-Eagle, Black **15**, 29
  Black-and-white **15**, 29
  Ornate **15**, 29
Hemispingus
  Black-capped **112**, 206
  Black-eared **112**, 207
  Black-headed **112**, 207
  Drab **113**, 207
  Oleaginous **112**, 207
  Orange-browed **113**, 206
  Parodi's **113**, 206
  Rufous-browed **113**, 207
  Superciliaried **112**, 207
  Three-striped **113**, 207
Hermit, Black-throated **37**, 75
  Gray-chinned **37**, 75
  Great-billed **37**, 75
  Green **37**, 74
  Koepcke's **38**, 75
  Needle-billed **38**, 75
  Reddish **37**, 75
  Rufous-breasted **37**, 74
  Straight-billed **37**, 75
  Tawny-bellied **37**, 75
  Western Long-tailed **37**, 74
  White-bearded **37**, 74
  White-browed **38**, 75
Heron, Agami **8**, 16
  Boat-billed **8**, 16
  Capped **8**, 15
  Cocoi **8**, 15
  Great Blue 15
  Little Blue **7**, 16
  Striated **7**, 16
  Tricolored **7**, 16
  Zigzag **8**, 17
Hillstar, Andean **40**, 82
  Black-breasted **43**, **45**, 82
  Green-headed **43**, 82
  White-tailed **43**, 82
Hoatzin **8**, 35
Honeycreeper
  Golden-collared **118**, 218
  Green **116**, 219
  Purple **116**, 219
  Red-legged **116**, 219
  Short-billed **116**, 219
Hookbill, Chestnut-winged **64**, 117
Hornero, Bay **65**, 106

Lesser **58**, 106
Pale-legged **58**, 106
Hummingbird, Amazilia **38**, 80
  "Ampay" **41**, 80
  Giant **40**, 84
  Green-and-white **38**, 80
  Many-spotted **38**, 80
  Oasis **45**, **46**, 88
  Olive-spotted **38**, 79
  Speckled **39**, 81
  Spot-throated **38**, 79
  Swallow-tailed **40**, 76
  Sword-billed **40**, 83
  Tumbes **38**, 79
  Violet-bellied **39**, 78
  Violet-headed **39**, 77
  Wedge-billed **46**, 88
  White-bellied **38**, **40**, 79

Ibis, Andean **11**, 18
  Black-faced **11**, 18
  Green **11**, 18
  Plumbeous 18
  Puna **11**, 18
  White **11**, 18
  White-faced **11**, 18
Inca, Bronzy **43**, 83
  Collared **40**, 83
  Gould's **43**, 83
Inca-Finch
  Buff-bridled **119**, 222
  Gray-winged **119**, 222
  Great **119**, 222
  Little **119**, 222
  Rufous-backed **119**, 222

Jabiru **11**, 18
Jacamar, Blue-cheeked **49**, 92
  Bluish-fronted **51**, 93
  Brown **49**, 92
  Chestnut see Purus
  Coppery-chested **49**, 93
  Great **49**, 93
  Paradise **49**, 93
  Purplish **49**, 93
  Purus **51**, 92
  White-chinned **49**, 93
  White-eared **49**, 92
  White-throated **51**, 92
  Yellow-billed **49**, 92
Jacana, Wattled **19**, 39
Jacobin, White-necked **40**, 76
Jaeger, Long-tailed **22**, 48
  Parasitic **22**, 48
  Pomarine **22**, 48
Jay, Green **100**, 196
  Purplish **100**, 197
  Turquoise **100**, 197
  Violaceous **100**, 197
  White-collared **100**, 197

White-tailed **100**, 197
Jewelfront, Gould's **42**, 81

Kestrel, American **14**, 31
Killdeer **20**, 41
Kingbird, Eastern **98**, 182
  Snowy-throated **95**, 182
  Tropical **98**, 182
  White-throated **98**, 182
Kingfisher, Amazon **48**, 91
  American Pygmy **48**, 91
  Green **48**, 91
  Green-and-rufous **48**, 91
  Ringed **48**, 91
Kiskadee, Great **98**, 180
  Lesser **98**, 180
Kite, Double-toothed **12**, **16**, 24
  Gray-headed **12**, **16**, 24
  Hook-billed **12**, **16**, 24
  Mississippi **12**, 25
  Pearl **12**, 24
  Plumbeous **13**, **16**, 25
  Slender-billed **12**, 24
  Snail **12**, **13**, 24
  Swallow-tailed **12**, 24
  White-tailed 24
Kittiwake, Black-legged **21**, 50
Knot, Red **21**, 44

Lancebill, Blue-fronted **37**, 76
  Green-fronted **37**, 76
Lapwing, Andean **20**, 40
  Pied **20**, 40
  Southern **20**, 40
Leaftosser, Black-tailed **63**, 119
  Gray-throated **63**, 119
  Short-billed **63**, 119
  Tawny-throated **63**, 119
Limpkin **9**, 35

Macaw, Blue-and-yellow **27**, 56
  Blue-headed **26**, 56
  Chestnut-fronted **27**, 56
  Military **27**, 56
  Red-and-green **27**, 56
  Red-bellied **27**, 56
  Red-shouldered **27**, 56
  Scarlet **27**, 56
Mallard 21
Manakin, Band-tailed **84**, **85**, 151
  Black **85**, 153
  Blue-backed **84**, **85**, 151
  Blue-crowned **84**, **85**, 152
  Blue-rumped **84**, 152
  Cerulean-capped **84**, 152
  Fiery-capped **84**, 152
  Flame-crested **85**, 153
  Golden-headed **85**, 152
  Golden-winged **85**, 152
  Green **85**, 151

Index of English Names

Jet **84**, 151
Orange-crested **84**, 153
Red-headed **84**, 152
Round-tailed **84, 85**, 152
Striped **85**, 152
White-bearded **85**, 151
White-crowned **85**, 151
Wing-barred see Piprites
Wire-tailed **85**, 151
Yungas **84**, 151
Mango, Black-throated **41**, 77
 Green-breasted **41**, 77
Marsh-Tyrant
 White-headed **97**, 178
Martin, Brown-chested **102**, 185
 Caribbean **102**, 185
 Gray-breasted **102**, 185
 Peruvian **101**, 186
 Purple **102**, 185
 Sand see Bank Swallow
 Southern **102**, 186
Meadowlark, Peruvian **127**, 234
Merlin **14**, 32
Metaltail, Black **45**, 87
 Coppery **45**, 86
 Fire-throated **45**, 86
 Neblina **45**, 87
 Scaled **45**, 86
 Tyrian **46**, 86
Miner, Coastal **57**, 104
 Common **57, 58**, 104
 Dark-winged **57**, 104
 Grayish **57**, 104
 Puna **58**, 104
 Slender-billed **58**, 105
 Thick-billed **57**, 104
Mockingbird, Long-tailed **105**, 192
Monjita, Gray **92**, 174
Monklet, Lanceolated **50**, 95
Moorhen, Common **19**, 38
Motmot, Blue-crowned **48**, 91
 Broad-billed **48**, 92
 Highland **48**, 92
 Rufous **48**, 92
Mountaineer, Bearded **42**, 86
Mountain-Finch
 Chestnut-breasted **119**, 223
Mountain-Tanager
 Black-chested **110**, 212
 Blue-winged **110**, 213
 Buff-breasted **110**, 213
 Chestnut-bellied **111**, 213
 Golden-backed **111**, 212
 Hooded **110**, 212
 Lacrimose **110**, 213
 Masked **110**, 212
 Scarlet-bellied **110**, 213
Mountain-Toucan
 Black-billed **54**, 98
 Gray-breasted **54**, 98

Hooded **54**, 98
Mourner, Cinereous **83**, 147
 Grayish **83**, 179

Negrito, Andean **91**, 177
Nighthawk, Band-tailed **34**, 70
 Common **34**, 69
 Lesser **34**, 69
 Nacunda **34**, 70
 Rufous-bellied **34**, 69
 Sand-colored **34**, 69
 Semicollared see Short-tailed
 Short-tailed **34**, 69
Night-Heron
 Black-crowned **7**, 16
 Yellow-crowned **7**, 16
Nightingale-Thrush
 Slaty-backed **106**, 193
 Spotted **106**, 193
Nightjar, Anthony's (see Scrub)
 Band-winged **35**, 70
 Blackish **35**, 71
 Ladder-tailed **34**, 71
 Little **34**, 71
 Lyre-tailed **35**, 71
 Rufous **35**, 70
 Scissor-tailed **34**, 71
 Scrub **34**, 71
 Silky-tailed **35**, 70
 Spot-tailed **35**, 70
 Swallow-tailed **35**, 71
Nothura, Darwin's **1**, 4
Nunbird, Black-fronted **50**, 95
 White-faced **50**, 95
 White-fronted **50**, 95
 Yellow-billed **50**, 95
Nunlet, Brown **50**, 95
 Fulvous-chinned **50**, 95
 Gray-cheeked see
  Rufous-capped
 Rufous-capped **51**, 95
 Rusty-breasted **50**, 95

Oilbird **31**, 68
Oriole, Epaulet **127**, 235
 Moriche **127**, 235
 White-edged **125**, 235
 Yellow-tailed **127**, 235
Oropendola, Amazonian **126**, 237
 Band-tailed **126**, 237
 Casqued **126**, 236
 Crested **126**, 236
 Dusky-green **125**, 236
 Green **126**, 236
 Russet-backed **126**, 237
Osprey **13**, **16**, 23
Owl, Band-bellied **31**, 66
 Barn **31**, 63
 Black-and-white **33**, 65
 Black-banded **33**, 66

Buff-fronted **33**, 67
Burrowing **31**, 67
Crested **33**, 66
Great Horned **33**, 65
Magellanic Horned **31**, 65
Mottled **31**, 65
Rufous-banded **31**, 66
Short-eared **33**, 68
Spectacled **31**, 66
Striped **33**, 67
Stygian **33**, 67
Owlet, Long-whiskered **32**, 67
Oystercatcher, American **22**, 39
 Blackish **6**, 39

Palmcreeper, Point-tailed **63**, 116
Palm-Swift, Fork-tailed **36**, 73
Parakeet, Andean **26**, 58
 Barred **28**, 58
 Black-capped **28**, 57
 Canary-winged **28**, 58
 Cobalt-winged **28**, 58
 Dusky-headed **27**, 57
 Golden-plumed **26**, 57
 Gray-cheeked **26**, 59
 Maroon-tailed **28**, 57
 Mitred **27**, 56
 Mountain **28**, 58
 Painted **28**, 57
 Peach-fronted **27**, 57
 Red-masked **26**, 57
 Rock see Black-capped
 Scarlet-fronted **27**, 56
 Tui **28**, 59
 White-eyed **27**, 57
Pardusco **115**, 220
Parrot, Black-headed **29**, 59
 Black-winged **26**, 60
 Blue-headed **29**, 60
 Bronze-winged **29**, 60
 Festive **29**, 61
 Mealy **29**, 61
 Orange-cheeked **29**, 60
 Orange-winged **29**, 61
 Red-billed **29**, 60
 Red-faced **26**, 60
 Red-fan **29**, 61
 Scaly-naped **29**, 61
 Short-tailed **29**, 60
 Speckle-faced **26**, 60
 White-bellied **29**, 59
 Yellow-crowned **29**, 61
Parrotlet, Amazonian **26**, 59
 Blue-winged **28**, 58
 Dusky-billed **28**, 58
 Pacific **26**, 58
 Sapphire-rumped **28**, 59
 Scarlet-shouldered **28**, 59
 Spot-winged **29**, 59
 Yellow-faced **26**, 58

Index of English Names

Parula, Tropical **107**, 200
Pauraque **35**, 70
Pelican, Brown **5**, 13
  Peruvian **5, 6**, 13
Penguin, Humboldt **6**, 5
  King **5**
Peppershrike, Black-billed 199
  Rufous-browed **107**, 199
Petrel, Antarctic Giant **3**, 7
  Black-winged **4**, 8
  Blue **4**, 9
  Cape **4**, 7
  Cook's **4**, 8
  Dark-rumped **4**, 8
  Defilippe's **4**, 8
  Gray **4**, 9
  Juan Fernández **4**, 8
  Kermadec **4**, 8
  Murphy's **4**, 8
  Parkinson's **4**, 10
  Stejneger's **4**, 9
  Westland **4**, 10
  White-chinned **4**, 9
Pewee, Blackish **97**, 172
  Smoke-colored **97**, 171
  Tropical **97**, 172
Phalarope, Red **21**, 46
  Red-necked **21**, 46
  Wilson's **20**, 46
Phoebe, Black **97**, 172
Piculet, Bar-breasted **52**, 99
  Ecuadorian **52**, 99
  Fine-barred **52**, 100
  Lafresnaye's **52**, 99
  Ocellated **52**, 100
  Olivaceous **52**, 100
  Plain-breasted **52**, 100
  Rufous-breasted **52**, 100
  Speckle-chested **52**, 100
Piedtail, Ecuadorian **38**, 81
  Peruvian **38**, 81
Pigeon, Band-tailed **24**, 53
  Pale-vented **24**, 53
  Peruvian **26**, 53
  Plumbeous **24**, 53
  Ruddy **24**, 53
  Scaled **24**, 52
  Spot-winged **24**, 52
Piha, Dusky **83**, 149
  Gray-tailed **83**, 149
  Olivaceous **83**, 149
  Scimitar-winged **83**, 149
  Screaming **83**, 149
Pintail, White-cheeked **6**, 21
  Yellow-billed **10**, 21
Piping-Guan, Blue-throated **17**, 33
Pipit, Correndera **102**, 188
  Hellmayr's **102**, 188
  Páramo **102**, 188

Short-billed **102**, 188
Yellowish **102**, 188
Piprites, Wing-barred **85**, 153
Plantcutter, Peruvian **82**, 146
Plover, Black-bellied **22**, 41
  Collared **20**, 41
  Gray see Black-bellied
  Kentish see Snowy
  Puna **20**, 42
  Semipalmated **20**, 41
  Snowy **20**, 41
  Two-banded 41
  Wilson's **20**, 41
Plumeleteer, White-vented **41**, 81
Plushcap see Plush-capped Finch
Plushcrown
  Orange-fronted **63**, 114
Pochard, Rosy-billed **10**, 22
  Southern **10**, 22
Poorwill, Ocellated **35**, 70
Potoo, Andean **33**, 68
  Common **33**, 68
  Great **33**, 68
  Long-tailed **33**, 68
  Rufous **33**, 69
  White-winged **33**, 69
Prickletail, Spectacled **63**, 114
Prion, Antarctic **4**, 9
  Broad-billed **4**, 9
  Fairy **4**, 9
  Slender-billed **4**, 9
Puffbird, Black-streaked **50**, 94
  Brown-banded **50**, 93
  Chestnut-capped **50**, 94
  Collared **50**, 94
  Pied **50**, 94
  Rufous-necked **50**, 95
  Semicollared **51**, 94
  Spotted **50**, 94
  Striolated **51**, 94
  White-chested **50**, 94
  White-eared **50**, 94
  White-necked **50**, 93
Puffleg, Buff-thighed **44**, 85
  Coppery-naped **44**, 84
  Emerald-bellied **44**, 84
  Glowing **44**, 84
Purpletuft, White-browed **81**, 149
Pygmy-Owl, Amazonian **32**, 67
  Andean **31**, 66
  Ferruginous **31**, 67
  Peruvian **32**, 67
  Subtropical **32**, 67
  Yungas **32**, 66
Pygmy-Tyrant
  Bronze-olive **90**, 158
  Double-banded **90**, 164
  Hazel-fronted **89**, 158
  Helmeted **90**, 164
  Long-crested **89**, 164

Rufous-headed **87**, 158
Scale-crested **90**, 164
Short-tailed **90**, 163
Tawny-crowned **95**, 163
White-bellied **89**, 163

Quail-Dove, Ruddy **25**, 55
  Sapphire **25**, 55
  Violaceous **25**, 55
  White-throated **25**, 55
Quetzal, Crested **47**, 90
  Golden-headed **47**, 90
  Pavonine **47**, 91

Racket-tail, Booted **44**, 85
Rail, Black **19**, 36
  Blackish **19**, 37
  Bogotá **19**, 36
  Clapper **19**, 36
  Junín **19**, 36
  Plumbeous **19**, 38
  Spotted **19**, 37
  Virginia **19**, 36
Recurvebill, Peruvian **65**, 117
Redstart, American **107**, 201
  Slate-throated **107**, 202
  Spectacled **107**, 202
Reeve 46
Rhea, Lesser **1**, 1
Royal-Flycatcher
  Amazonian **86**, 168
  Pacific **86**, 169
Ruff **21**, 46
Rushbird, Wren-like **63**, 107
Rush-Tyrant
  Many-colored **90**, 163

Sabrewing, Gray-breasted **37**, 76
  Napo **38**, 76
Saltator, Black-cowled **125**, 232
  Buff-throated **121**, 232
  Golden-billed **121**, 232
  Grayish **121**, 232
  Masked **125**, 232
  Streaked **121**, 232
Sanderling **21**, 44
Sandpiper, Baird's **21**, 45
  Buff-breasted **21**, 46
  Curlew **21**, 46
  Least **21**, 45
  Pectoral **21**, 45
  Semipalmated **21**, 45
  Solitary **22**, 44
  Spotted **21**, 44
  Stilt **21**, 46
  Upland **22**, 43
  Western **21**, 45
  White-rumped **21**, 45
Sandpiper-Plover
  Diademed **20**, 42

Index of English Names

Sapphire, Blue-chinned **39**, 78
  Golden-tailed **39**, 79
  Rufous-throated **39**, 78
  White-chinned **39**, 79
Sapphirewing, Great **40**, 83
Schiffornis, Greater **99**, 183
  Thrush-like **99**, 183
  Várzea see Greater
Screamer, Horned **9**, 19
  Southern **9**, 19
Screech-Owl, Cinnamon **32**, 64
  Cloud-forest **32**, 65
  Koepcke's **32**, 64
  Peruvian **32**, 64
  Rufescent **31**, 64
  Tawny-bellied **31**, 65
  Tropical **31**, 64
  Vermiculated **33**, 65
  White-throated **31**, 65
Scrub-Flycatcher
  Amazonian **87**, 161
  Southern **87**, 161
Scythebill, Brown-billed **67**, 123
  Curve-billed **67**, 123
  Greater **65**, 123
  Red-billed **67**, 123
Seedeater, Band-tailed **109**, 225
  Black-and-white **109**, 224
  Blue **113**, 225
  Caqueta **109**, 223
  Chestnut-bellied **109**, 225
  Chestnut-throated **109**, 225
  Dark-throated **122**, 224
  Double-collared **109**, 224
  Drab **122**, 224
  Lesson's **122**, 224
  Lined **109**, 224
  Páramo **122**, 226
  Parrot-billed **122**, 224
  Plain-colored **109**, 225
  Plumbeous **122**, 223
  Slate-colored **122**, 223
  Tawny-bellied **122**, 224
  Variable **109**, 223
  White-bellied **122**, 224
  Yellow-bellied **109**, 224
Seed-Finch
  Black-billed **122**, 225
  Chestnut-bellied **109**, 225
  Large-billed **109**, 225
  Lesser see Chestnut-bellied
Seedsnipe, Gray-breasted **20**, 47
  Least **20**, 47
  Rufous-bellied **20**, 47
Sharpbill **99**, 185
Sheartail, Peruvian **45**, 46, 88
Shearwater, Audubon's **4**, 10
  Buller's **4**, 10
  Flesh-footed **4**, 10
  Little **4**, 10

Pink-footed **4**, 10
Sooty **4**, 10
Shoveler, Red **9**, 22
Shrike-Tanager, Fulvous **114**, 209
  White-winged **114**, 209
Shrike-Tyrant
  Black-billed **93**, 175
  Gray-bellied **93**, 175
  White-tailed **93**, 175
Shrike-Vireo
  Slaty-capped **107**, 199
Sicklebill, Buff-tailed **40**, 74
  White-tipped **37**, 74
Sierra-Finch
  Ash-breasted **124**, 221
  Band-tailed **124**, 221
  Black-hooded **124**, 221
  Mourning **124**, 221
  Peruvian **122**, 221
  Plumbeous **124**, 221
  White-throated **122**, 221
Sirystes **99**, 179
Siskin, Black **123**, 200
  Hooded **123**, 199
  Olivaceous **123**, 200
  Saffron **123**, 200
  Thick-billed **123**, 199
  Yellow-bellied **123**, 200
  Yellow-rumped **123**, 200
Skimmer, Black **6**, 52
Skua, Chilean **22**, 47
  South Polar **22**, 47
Slaty-Antshrike, Marañón **71**, 126
  Western **70**, 126
Slaty-Flycatcher, Crowned **98**, 182
Slaty-Thrush, Andean **105**, 194
Snipe, Andean **18**, 43
  Commom 42
  Imperial **18**, 43
  Noble **18**, 42
  Puna **18**, 42
  South American, 42
Softtail, Plain **58**, 114
  Russet-mantled **65**, 114
Solitaire, Andean **106**, 192
  Rufous-brown **105**, 193
  White-eared **105**, 193
Sora **19**, 37
Spadebill
  Cinnamon-crested **90**, 168
  Golden-crowned **90**, 168
  White-crested **90**, 168
  White-throated **90**, 168
  Yellow-throated **90**, 168
Sparrow, Black-capped **122**, 231
  Black-striped **122**, 231
  Grassland **109**, 231
  House **123**, 197
  Orange-billed **121**, 232
  Pectoral **121**, 231

Rufous-collared **109**, 231
Tumbes **122**, 231
Yellow-browed **109**, 231
Spatuletail, Marvelous **45**, 88
Spinetail, Apurímac **60**, 108
  Ash-browed **61**, 111
  Azara's **61**, 108
  Baron's **61**, 110
  Black-faced see
    Blackish-headed
  Blackish-headed **58**, 109
  Cabanis' **60**, 108
  Chestnut-throated **61**, 109
  Chinchipe **60**, 109
  Cinereous-breasted **61**, 108
  Creamy-crested **60**, 110
  Dark-breasted **61**, 108
  Dusky **61**, 109
  Great **60**, 110
  Light-crowned **60**, 110
  Line-cheeked **60**, 110
  Marañón **60**, 109
  Marcapata **60**, 110
  Necklaced **60**, 109
  Pale-breasted **61**, 108
  Parker's **61**, 111
  Plain-crowned **61**, 109
  Red-and-white **61**, 111
  Ruddy **61**, 109
  Rufous **61**, 108
  Russet-bellied **60**, 107
  Slaty **61**, 108
  Speckled **61**, 111
  White-bellied **61**, 109
  White-breasted see Parker's
  White-browed **61**, 110
  Yellow-chinned **61**, 111
Spoonbill, Roseate **11**, 19
Starfrontlet, Buff-winged **43**, 83
  Rainbow **42**, **43**, 83
  Violet-throated **42**, **43**, 83
Starthroat, Long-billed **44**, 88
Stilt, Black-necked **20**, 40
  White-backed **20**, 40
Stint, Red-necked **21**, 45
Stork, Maguari **11**, 18
  Wood **11**, 17
Storm-Petrel, Band-rumped **3**, 11
  Black **3**, 12
  Black-bellied **3**, 11
  Elliot's see White-vented
  Galápagos 11
  Harcourt's see Band Rumped
  Hornby's see Ringed
  Leach's **3**, 12
  Least **3**, 11
  Madeiran see Band-rumped
  Markham's **3**, 12

Index of English Names

Storm-Petrel, Ringed **3**, 12
  Wedge-rumped **3, 4,** 11
  White-bellied **3**, 11
  White-faced **3**, 11
  White-vented **3**, 11
  Wilson's **3, 6,** 11
Streaked-Antwren
  Amazonian **72**, 129
Streamcreeper
  Sharp-tailed **63**, 119
Sunangel
  Amethyst-throated **44**, 84
  Little **44**, 84
  Purple-throated **42**, 84
  Royal **42**, 84
Sunbeam, Purple-backed **42**, 82
  Shining **40**, 82
  White-tufted **42**, 82
Sunbittern **8**, 39
Sungrebe **86**, 38
Surfbird **21**, 44
Swallow, Andean **101**, 187
  Bank **102**, 187
  Barn **102**, 188
  Blue-and-white **101**, 186
  Brown-bellied **102**, 187
  Chestnut-collared **101**, 187
  Chilean **101**, 186
  Cliff **102**, 187
  Pale-footed **101**, 187
  Southern Rough-winged **101**, 187
  Tawny-headed **102**, 187
  Tree 186
  Tumbes **101**, 186
  White-banded **101**, 187
  White-rumped **101**, 186
  White-thighed **102**, 187
  White-winged **101**, 186
Swallow-Tanager **118**, 220
Swallow-wing **50**, 96
Swift, Andean **36**, 73
  Chapman's **36**, 73
  Chestnut-collared **36**, 72
  Chimney **36**, 73
  Gray-rumped **36**, 72
  Lesser Swallow-tailed **36**, 73
  Pale-rumped **36**, 73
  Rothschild's **36**, 72
  Short-tailed **36**, 73
  Tumbes **36**, 73
  White-chested **36**, 72
  White-chinned **36**, 72
  White-collared **36**, 72
  White-tipped **36**, 73
Sylph, Long-tailed **46**, 88

Tanager, Bay-headed **118**, 217
  Beryl-spangled **118**, 217
  Black-and-white **111**, 205
  Black-faced **110**, 205
  Black-goggled **114**, 210
  Blue-and-black **118**, 218
  Blue-and-yellow **110**, 212
  Blue-browed **118**, 217
  Blue-capped **110**, 212
  Blue-gray **110**, 211
  Blue-necked **118**, 217
  Brown-flanked **115**, 208
  Buff-bellied **115**, 208
  Burnished-buff **118**, 217
  Carmiol's see Olive
  Dotted **117**, 216
  Fawn-breasted **118**, 213
  Flame-crested **114**, 209
  Flame-faced **117**, 216
  Fulvous-crested **114**, 209
  Golden **117**, 216
  Golden-collared **111**, 213
  Golden-crowned **118**, 213
  Golden-eared **117**, 216
  Golden-naped **118**, 217
  Grass-green **117**, 205
  Gray-headed **114**, 208
  Green-and-gold **117**, 216
  Green-capped **115**, 217
  Guira **112**, 208
  Hepatic **114**, 210
  Hooded **112**, 208
  Huallaga **111**, 211
  Magpie **110**, 205
  Masked **118**, 217
  Masked Crimson **110**, 211
  Metallic-green **117**, 217
  Olive **114**, 208
  Opal-crowned **118**, 218
  Opal-rumped **118**, 218
  Orange-eared **117**, 215
  Orange-headed **112**, 208
  Orange-throated **111**, 212
  Palm **110**, 212
  Paradise **117**, 216
  Red-billed Pied **110**, 205
  Red-hooded **114**, 211
  Red-shouldered **114**, 210
  Rufous-chested **112**, 208
  Rufous-crested **114**, 209
  Rust-and-yellow **112**, 208
  Saffron-crowned **117**, 216
  Sayaca **110**, 211
  Scarlet **114**, 210
  Silver-backed **115**, 218
  Silver-beaked **110**, 211
  Sira **115**, 218
  Slaty **114**, 209
  Spotted **117**, 216
  Straw-backed **115**, 218
  Summer **114**, 210
  Turquoise **118**, 215
  Vermilion **111**, 211
  White-capped **111**, 205
  White-lined **114**, 210
  White-shouldered **114**, 209
  White-winged **114**, 210
  Yellow-backed **114**, 208
  Yellow-bellied **117**, 216
  Yellow-crested **111**, 209
  Yellow-scarfed **118**, 213
  Yellow-throated **111**, 213
Tapaculo, Ancash **80**, 146
  Ash-colored **80**, 144
  Blackish 144
  Bolivian 145
  Chusquea 146
  Diademed **80**, 146
  Large-footed **80**, 145
  Long-tailed 145
  Neblina 145
  Ocellated **80**, 146
  Páramo 146
  Puna 145
  Rufous-vented **80**, 145
  Rusty-belted **80**, 144
  Trilling 145
  Tschidi's **80**, 146
  Unicolored **80**, 144
  Vilcabamba **80**, 145
  White-crowned **80**, 145
Tattler, Wandering **21**, 44
Teal, Blue-winged **10**, 21
  Cinnamon **6**, 21
  Puna **9**, 21
  Speckled **10**, 21
Tern, Arctic **23**, 51
  Black **23**, 51
  Common **23**, 51
  Elegant **23**, 50
  Gull-billed **23**, 50
  Inca **6**, 52
  Large-billed **9**, 52
  Least **23**, 51
  Peruvian **6**, 51
  Royal **23**, 50
  Sandwich **23**, 50
  Snowy-crowned **23**, 51
  Sooty **23**, 51
  South American **23**, 50
  Yellow-billed **9**, 51
Thick-knee, Peruvian **20**, 40
Thistletail, Eye-ringed **62**, 111
  Mouse-colored **62**, 111
  Puna **62**, 112
  Vilcabamba **62**, 112
  White-chinned **62**, 111
Thornbill
  Blue-mantled **42**, 87
  Olivaceous **42**, 87
  Purple-backed **46**, 86
  Rainbow-bearded **46**, 87
  Rufous-capped **40**, 87

Index of English Names

Thornbird
  Chestnut-backed **65**, 114
  Common **58**, 114
  Streak-fronted **58**, 114
Thorntail, Black-bellied **39**, 78
  Wire-crested **38**, 78
Thrush, Black-billed **105**, 195
  Chestnut-bellied **106**, 194
  Chiguanco **105**, 194
  Creamy-bellied **105**, 195
  Ecuadorian **105**, 195
  Glossy-black **106**, 194
  Gray-cheeked **106**, 193
  Great **105**, 194
  Hauxwell's **105**, 195
  Lawrence's **105**, 195
  Marañón **105**, 194
  Pale-breasted **106**, 195
  Pale-eyed **106**, 193
  Pale-vented 195
  Plumbeous-backed **105**, 194
  Swainson's **106**, 193
  White-necked **106**, 195
Tiger-Heron, Bare-throated **7**, 17
  Fasciated **8**, 17
  Rufescent **8**, 17
Tinamou, Andean **1**, 4
  Bartlett's **2**, 3
  Black **1**, 1
  Black-capped **2**, 3
  Brazilian **2**, 3
  Brown **2**, 2
  Cinereous **2**, 2
  Curve-billed **1**, 4
  Gray **2**, 1
  Great **2**, 1
  Highland **2**, 2
  Hooded **1**, 2
  Kalinowski's **1**, 4
  Little **2**, 2
  Ornate **1**, 4
  Pale-browed **2**, 3
  Puna **1**, 2
  Red-winged **2**, 3
  Rusty 3
  Small-billed **2**, 3
  Taczanowski's **1**, 4
  Tataupa **2**, 3
  Tawny-breasted **2**, 2
  Undulated **2**, 2
  Variegated **2**, 3
  White-throated **2**, 1
Tit-Spinetail, Andean **62**, 106
  Plain-mantled **61**, 107
  Rusty-crowned **62**, 107
  Streaked **62**, 107
  Tawny **62**, 107
  White-browed **62**, 107
Tit-Tyrant, Ash-breasted **91**, 162
  Black-crested **91**, 162

Pied-crested **91**, 163
Tufted **90**, 163
Unstreaked **91**, 162
Yellow-billed **90**, 163
Tityra
  Black-crowned **100**, 184
  Black-tailed **100**, 184
  Masked **100**, 184
Tody-Flycatcher
  Black-backed **89**, 166
  Common **90**, 166
  Golden-winged **89**, 166
  Ochre-faced **89**, 166
  Rusty-fronted **90**, 166
  Spotted **90**, 166
  Yellow-browed **90**, 166
Tody-Tyrant
  Black-and-white **89**, 164
  Black-throated **90**, 165
  Buff-throated **89**, 165
  Cinnamon-breasted **89**, 165
  Johannes' **89**, 165
  Lulu's **89**, 164
  Pearly-vented **90**, 165
  Rufous-crowned **89**, 164
  Stripe-necked **90**, 165
  White-cheeked **89**, 164
  White-eyed **90**, 165
  Zimmer's **90**, 165
Topaz, Fiery **41**, 77
Toucan, Black-mandibled **54**, 99
  Cuvier's **54**, 99
  Toco **54**, 99
  Yellow-ridged **54**, 99
Toucanet, Blue-banded **53**, 97
  Chestnut-tipped **53**, 97
  Emerald **53**, 97
  Golden-collared **53**, 99
  Yellow-browed **53**, 97
Trainbearer, Black-tailed **44**, 85
  Green-tailed **40**, 85
Treehunter, Black-billed **64**, 116
  Buff-throated **65**, 116
  Flammulated **64**, 116
  Peruvian see Buff-throated
  Striped **64**, 116
Treerunner, Pearled **63**, 115
Trogon, Black-tailed **47**, 90
  Black-throated **47**, 90
  Blue-crowned **47**, 90
  Collared **47**, 90
  Masked **47**, 90
  Violaceous **47**, 90
  White-tailed **47**, 89
Tropicbird, Red-billed **10**, 12
  Red-tailed **10**, 13
Troupial **127**, 235
Trumpeter, Gray-winged **18**, 35
  Pale-winged **18**, 35
Tuftedcheek, Streaked **63**, 115

Turnstone, Ruddy **21**, 44
Twistwing, Flycatcher see Brownish Flycatcher
Tyrannulet, Ashy-headed **87**, 160
  Black-capped **87**, 160
  Bolivian **94**, 160
  Buff-banded **88**, 162
  Cinnamon-faced **92**, 159
  Ecuadorian **88**, 159
  Golden-faced **87**, 161
  Gray-and-white **95**, 155
  Mishana **87**, 161
  Mottle-cheeked **88**, 159
  Mouse-colored **86**, **95**, 154
  Peruvian **94**, 161
  Plain **88**, 162
  Plumbeous-crowned **87**, 160
  Red-billed **94**, 160
  River **88**, 157
  Rufous-browed **88**, 159
  Rufous-winged **87**, 162
  Sclater's **88**, 159
  Slender-footed **87**, 161
  Sooty-headed **87**, 160
  Sulphur-bellied **87**, 162
  Tawny-rumped **87**, 160
  Torrent **86**, 157
  White-banded **87**, 162
  White-fronted **88**, 159
  White-lored **86**, 154
  White-tailed **87**, 161
  White-throated **87**, 161
  Yellow **86**, 154
  Yellow-crowned **86**, 154
Tyrant, Andean **91**, 177
  Cinnamon **92**, 171
  Long-tailed **97**, 178
  Plumbeous see Andean
  Riverside **97**, 177
  Rufous-tailed **97**, 177
  Rufous-webbed **93**, 175
  Spectacled **97**, 178
  Tumbes **95**, 174
  Yellow-browed **97**, 178
Tyrant-Manakin, Dwarf **85**, 153
  Saffron-crested **85**, 153
  Sulphur-bellied **84**, 153

Umbrellabird
  Amazonian **83**, 150

Veery **106**, 193
Velvetbreast, Mountain **43**, 83
Violetear, Brown **41**, 76
  Green **41**, 76
  Sparkling **41**, 77
Vireo, Black-whiskered **107**, 198
  Brown-capped **107**, 197
  Red-eyed **107**, 198
  Yellow-green **107**, 198

Index of English Names

Vulture, Black **11**, 22
  Greater Yellow-headed **11**, 23
  King **11**, 23
  Lesser Yellow-headed **11**, 23
  Turkey **11**, 22

Wagtail-Tyrant, Lesser **90**, 162
Warbler
  Black-and-white **107**, 201
  Blackburnian **107**, 201
  Black-crested **108**, 203
  Blackpoll **107**, 201
  Buff-rumped **108**, 203
  Canada **107**, 202
  Cerulean **107**, 201
  Citrine **108**, 203
  Connecticut **107**, 201
  Golden-bellied **108**, 202
  Golden-winged **107**, 200
  Gray-and-gold **108**, 202
  Pale-legged **108**, 203
  Russet-crowned **108**, 203
  Three-banded **108**, 203
  Three-striped **108**, 203
  Two-banded **108**, 202
  Yellow **107**, 201
Warbling-Finch
  Collared **119**, 223
  Plain-tailed **119**, 222
  Rufous-breasted **119**, 223
Waterthrush, Northern **107**, 201
Water-Tyrant
  Black-backed **97**, 178
  Drab **92**, 174
  Masked **95**, 178
Whimbrel **22**, 43
Whistling-Duck
  Black-bellied **10**, 20
  Fulvous **10**, 20
  White-faced **10**, 20
Whitetip, Purple-bibbed **44**, 85
  Rufous-vented **44**, 85
Wigeon, Chiloe **10**, 21
Willet **22**, 44
Woodcreeper, Bar-bellied **66**, 121
  Black-banded **66**, 121
  Buff-throated **66**, 122
  Cinnamon-throated **67**, 121
  Elegant **66**, 122
  Lineated **67**, 123
  Long-billed **67**, 121
  Long-tailed **66**, 120
  Montane **67**, 123
  Ocellated **66**, 122
  Olivaceous **67**, 120
  Olive-backed **67**, 122
  Plain-brown **67**, 120
  Spix's see Elegant
  Spot-crowned
  Spot-throated **66**, 120

Straight-billed **66**, 122
Streak-headed **67**, 123
Striped **66**, 122
Strong-billed **66**, 121
Tyrannine **65**, 120
Wedge-billed **67**, 121
White-chinned **67**, 120
Zimmer's **66**, 122
Woodhaunter, Striped **64**, 117
Woodnymph, Fork-tailed **39**, 78
  Green-crowned **39**, 78
Woodpecker, Bar-bellied **55**, 101
  Black-necked **51**, 102
  Chestnut **56**, 103
  Cream-colored **56**, 103
  Crimson-bellied **56**, 103
  Crimson-crested **56**, 103
  Crimson-mantled **55**, 102
  Golden-green **55**, 102
  Golden-olive **55**, 102
  Guayaquil **56**, 103
  Lineated **56**, 103
  Little **55**, 101
  Powerful **56**, 103
  Red-necked **56**, 103
  Red-rumped **55**, 101
  Red-stained **55**, 101
  Ringed **56**, 103
  Rufous-headed **51**, 103
  Scaly-breasted **56**, 102
  Scarlet-backed **51**, 101
  Smoky-brown **55**, 101
  Spot-breasted **55**, 102
  White **55**, 100
  White-fronted **55**, 100
  White-throated **55**, 101
  Yellow-throated **55**, 101
  Yellow-tufted **55**, 100
  Yellow-vented **55**, 101
Wood-Pewee, Eastern **97**, 172
  Western **97**, 172
Wood-Quail, Marbled **18**, 34
  Rufous-breasted **18**, 34
  Starred **18**, 34
  Stripe-faced **18**, 34
Wood-Rail, Brown **19**, 37
  Gray-necked **19**, 37
  Red-winged **18**, 37
  Rufous-necked **18**, 37
Woodstar, Amethyst **46**, 89
  Chilean **45**, 89
  Little **45**, 89
  Purple-collared **45**, **46**, 89
  Short-tailed **45**, 89
  White-bellied **40**, **46**, 89
Wood-Wren, Bar-winged **103**, 191
  Gray-breasted **104**, 191
  White-breasted **104**, 191
Wren, Buff-breasted **104**, 190
  Chestnut-breasted **103**, 192

Coraya **104**, 190
Fasciated **103**, 189
Fulvous **103**, 190
Gray-mantled **104**, 189
House **104**, 191
Inca **103**, 190
Mountain **104**, 191
Moustached **104**, 190
Musician **104**, 192
Peruvian **103**, 190
Plain-tailed **103**, 190
Rufous **103**, 189
Scaly-breasted **104**, 191
Sedge **104**, 191
Sharpe's **103**, 189
Speckle-breasted **103**, 190
Superciliated **103**, 191
Thrush-like **104**, 189
Wing-banded **104**, 191

Xenops, Plain **63**, 115
  Rufous-tailed **63**, 115
  Slender-billed **63**, 115
  Streaked **63**, 115

Yellow-Finch
  Bright-rumped **124**, 228
  Grassland **123**, 227
  Greenish **124**, 228
  Orange-fronted **123**, 228
  Puna **124**, 227
  Raimondi's **123**, 228
  Stripe-tailed **123**, 228
Yellowlegs, Greater **22**, 43
  Lesser **22**, 43
Yellowthroat, Masked **108**, 202

Protected Area	#	Department	Hectares	Acres
Aledaño Bocatoma C. N. I.	43	Lima	18	44
Alexander von humboldt	42	Ucayali/Huánuco	469,744	1,160,267
Algarrobal El Moro	33	La Libertad	320	790
Alto Mayo	47	San Martín	182,000	449,540
Ampay	20	Apurímac	3,635	8,978
Apurímac	28	Junín/Cusco	1,669,200	4,122,924
Aymara-Lupaca	35	Puno	300,000	741,000
Bahuaja-Sonene	8	Madre de Dios/Puno	537,053	1,326,520
Batán Grande	31	Lambayeque	13,400	33,098
Biabo Cordillera Azul	41	Loreto/Ucayali/San Martin	2,084,500	5,148,715
Calipuy	15	La Libertad	64,000	158,080
Calipuy	18	La Libertad	4,500	11,115
Cerros de Amotope	5	Tumbes/Piura	91,300	225,511
Chacramarca	23	Junín	2,500	6,175
Chancaybaños	34	Cajamarca	2,600	6,422
Cutervo	1	Cajamarca	2,500	6,175
El Angolo	37	Piura	65,000	160,550
Huascarán	4	Ancash	340,000	839,800
Huallay	17	Pasco	6,815	16,833
Junín	10	Junín/Pasco	53,000	130,910
Lachay	12	Lima	5,070	12,522
Lagunas de mejia	19	Arequipa	690	1,704
Laquipampa	27	Lambayeque	11,346	28,024
Machu Picchu	25	Cusco	32,592	80.502
Manglares de Tumbes	21	Tumbes	2,972	7,340
Manu	3	Cusco/Madre de Dios	1,532,806	3,786,030
Manu	26	Madre de Dios	257,000	634,790
Mariscal Cáceres	40	Madre de Dios	337,000	832,390
Pacaya Samiria	13	Loreto	2,080,000	5,137,600
Pagaibamba	48	Cajamarca	2,078	5,132
Pampa Galeras	9	Ayacucho	6,500	16,055
Pampas de Ayacucho	24	Ayacucho	300	741
Pantanos de Villa	29	Lima	396	978
Paracas	11	Ica	335,000	827,450
Pastaza-Morena-Marañon	39	Loreto	375,000	926,250
Pui Pui	45	Junín	60,000	148,200
Puqio Santa Rosa	44	La Libertad	72	177
Río Abiseo	6	San Martin	274,520	678,064
Salinas y Aguada Blanca	14	Arequipa/Moquegua	366,936	906,331
San Matiás, San Carlos	46	Pasco	145,818	360,770
Sunchubamba	36	Cajamarca	59,735	147,545
Tabaconas Namballe	22	Cajamarca	29,500	72,865
Tambopata Candamo	30	Madre de Dios/Puno	1,043,998	2,578,675
Tingo Maria	2	Huánuco	18,000	44,460
Titicaca	16	Puno	36,180	89,364
Tumbes	32	Tumbes	75,102	185,501
Yanachaga Chemillén	7	Pasco	122,000	301,340
Yanesha	38	Pasco	34,774	85,891
		Total	**13,137,470**	**32,450,138**

Major Protected Areas in Peru

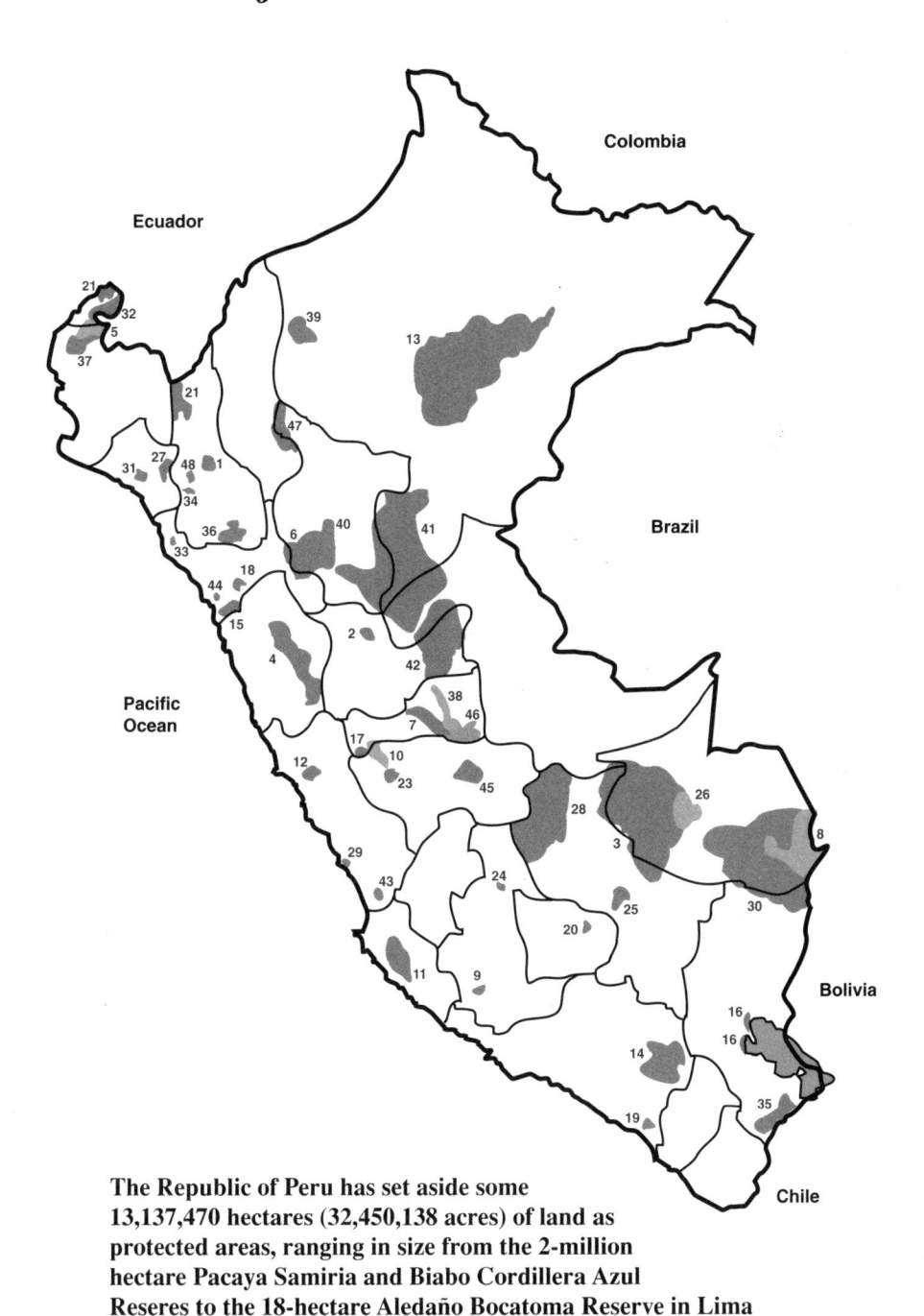

Colombia

Ecuador

Brazil

Pacific Ocean

Bolivia

Chile

The Republic of Peru has set aside some 13,137,470 hectares (32,450,138 acres) of land as protected areas, ranging in size from the 2-million hectare Pacaya Samiria and Biabo Cordillera Azul Reseres to the 18-hectare Aledaño Bocatoma Reserve in Lima